BEYOND
INTEGRITY

BEYOND INTEGRITY

A Judeo-Christian
Approach to Business Ethics

SCOTT B. RAE AND KENMAN L. WONG

ZondervanPublishingHouse
Grand Rapids, Michigan

A Division of HarperCollinsPublishers

Beyond Integrity
Copyright © 1996 by Scott B. Rae and Kenman L. Wong

Requests for information should be addressed to:

 ZondervanPublishingHouse
Grand Rapids, Michigan 49530

Library of Congress Cataloging-in-Publication Data

Beyond integrity : a Judeo-Christian approach to business ethics / [edited by] Scott B. Rae and
  Kenman L. Wong.
     p. cm.
    Includes bibliographical references and index.
    ISBN 0-310-20173-X (hardcover)
    1. Business ethics. 2. Business—Religious aspects—Christianity. 3. Business—Religious
aspects—Judaism. I. Rae, Scott B. II. Wong, Kenman L., 1964– .
    HF5387.B49 1996
    174'.4–dc20
                                 95-52888
                                    CIP

All Scripture quotations in the authors' original material, unless otherwise indicated, are taken
from the *Holy Bible: New International Version*®. NIV© 1973, 1978, 1984 by International
Bible Society. Used by permission of Zondervan Publishing House. All rights reserved.

For permission to use copyrighted material, grateful acknowledgment is made to the copyright
holders on pages 651–55, which are hereby made part of this copyright page.

Supervising editor: James E. Ruark
Copy editor: Gerard H. Terpstra
Interior designer and compositor: Sherri L. Hoffman

Printed in the United States of America

01 02❖ DC/ 10 9 8 7 6

This edition printed on acid-free paper and meets the American National Standards Institute
Z39.48 standard.

Contents in Brief

Contents

Part II: Capitalism and Christian Values

Part III: Business and Society

Part IV: Ethics and Individuals

ACKNOWLEDGMENTS

Many of our colleagues, friends, and family members have played an important role in the completion of this work. We would like to express our gratitude here to just a few of them in particular:

To Deans Larry Strand and Dennis Dirks and a number of faculty colleagues at the School of Business and Talbot School of Theology, Biola University.

To Professors Glenn Dill and Paul Buegler from the School of Business, who have been consistent sources of wisdom and encouragement. To Professors Walt Russell, Paul Cox, J. P. Moreland, Doug Geivett, and Klaus Issler from Talbot School of Theology, who have offered much encouragement.

To Administrative Assistants Carolyn Crawford and especially Kathliene Pedrick, who went way beyond our expectations in managing the administrative aspects of this project. We could not have completed this work without Kathliene's exceptional organizational skills.

To Research Assistant Chad Williams, who spent long hours in libraries insightfully tracking down and screening valuable resources so that we could devote ourselves to editing and writing.

To many former students who have played a significant role in this work. Although there are too many to be named here, they have sharpened us by providing insightful comments and challenges to our thoughts and ideas. Their wise questions and observations are woven throughout these pages. We are especially grateful to them, since this book is the result of a very satisfying five-year team-teaching relationship.

To our editors and the staff at Zondervan: Ed van der Maas, for seeing the possibilities and championing this project from a simple proposal to the finished product; Jim Ruark and his team, who turned an enormous project into a book with which we are very pleased.

Scott wishes to express thanks to the Fieldstead Foundation, which provided the funding for a semester at half teaching load to allow concentration on writing the book. Further, to his colleagues in the Christianity and Economics Faculty Development Seminar, who gave valuable feedback for some of the chapters in the book.

Kenman wishes to thank his grandfather, Ben S. Wong, at whose knee an indelible impression about right and wrong was made early in life.

Finally, we would like to thank our families, who keep us balanced and remind us what a good life is all about: Marika A. Wong, Sally A. Rae, and Taylor, Cameron, and Austin Rae.

INTRODUCTION

I already have the guilty conscience, I may as well have the money too!

Legendary U.S. Marshal Wyatt Earp in the movie *Tombstone*,
on his decision to leave law enforcement and enter business

INTRODUCTION

Once mentioned only in the context of comedic oxymorons, issues in business ethics have become the stuff of popular lore. A plethora of Hollywood movie releases in the last decade has forever lodged scenarios in which profit competes with morality into the consciousness of contemporary culture. Films such as *Wall Street, The Firm, Quiz Show, The Pelican Brief,* and *Tucker* portray key decision makers within corporations as scheming characters who will stop at nothing—not even murder in some cases—to line their pockets. Even action-film star Steven Seagal has gotten into the act. The recent film *On Deadly Ground* pits Seagal against the financial interests of a seedy oil company in a violent battle of good versus evil. While it has yet to eclipse the CIA (a.k.a. "The Company") as the most often portrayed omnipresent evil force behind all social ills, the business world is increasingly characterized in movies as a dark, lurking shadow whose pursuit of profit is inherently at odds with society's well-being.

Since the film industry is itself a big business whose profits depend upon entertainment value rather than truthfulness, one must ask whether these story lines aren't a case of the pot calling the kettle black. In fact, Hollywood is merely picking up on themes that have historically been discussed in churches, academia, and political circles. The pursuit of wealth and its influence on society have long been subjects for cautionary sermons, literature, and philosophical debate. Thus, it should come as no surprise that ethical issues in business are receiving prominent attention in other popular media forums. After the revelations of criminal wrongdoings on Wall Street in the late 1980s, frequent television and newspaper stories have appeared to describe the latest scandals in business. In one week alone recently, three of the one-hour news format shows on the major networks broadcast investigative reports relating to business ethics. ABC's *20/20* ran a story on the sales tactics of used-car dealers while its *Prime Time Live* investigated an in-home health-care company alleged to have paid large kickbacks to doctors for prescribing over-priced services to unwitting patients. NBC's *Dateline* revealed allegations of deceptive practices in the airline industry with respect to prices in ticket advertisements. Major newspapers run similar stories at least several times a week.

The moral climate of the world of business is so often called into question in the popular culture that it is not uncommon to observe Christian business people taking an apologetic stance for engaging in "worldly" rather than "spiritual" career pursuits.

Fortunately, these popular portrayals only show one side of the story. There are many corporations and proprietorships whose stated missions and actions resemble those of the most praiseworthy citizens. For example, a recent event that made national headlines involved the moral heroism of Aaron Feuerstein, the owner of a textile mill in New England that manufactures Polartec, a lightweight fabric used to provide warmth in winter clothing. Two weeks before Christmas 1995, the people of the town of Methuen, Massachusetts, watched Malden Mills—one of the last remaining large-scale textile mills in the region and the town's employment and economic lifeline—burn to the ground on a windy night. The fire injured 24 people, left 1,400 workers unemployed, and confirmed fears that the town would be destroyed economically—the plight suffered by many New England towns as other mills were shut down and relocated in search of lower wage scales.

Taking everyone by surprise, the seventy-year-old Feuerstein, who could have simply retired on the insurance money, immediately announced plans to rebuild, with the goal of having his workers back in the mill within a few months. Furthermore, Feuerstein gave every employee a Christmas bonus of $275 and a coupon for food worth $20 at a local supermarket. Amid cheers from his employees, he then announced that for at least the next thirty days he would pay every worker's salary in full and continue their health insurance for the next ninety days. Citing his faith and his belief that difficult circumstances provide the real test of moral convictions, Feuerstein stated that collecting the insurance money and retiring was never a thought that crossed his mind. "My commitment is to Massachusetts and New England. It's where I live, where I play, where I worship. Malden Mills will rebuild right here," he said.[1]

A well-publicized decision by a leading pharmaceutical company, Merck & Co., offers an equally outstanding example of a publicly held (shareholder-owned) corporation's going against the common image of corporations as "profit at all costs" entities. A number of years ago, a

[1]David Lamb, "Massachusetts Mill Town Gets Angel for Christmas," *Los Angeles Times*, 19 December 1995, A24.

Merck scientist discovered that an adaptation of one of the company's drugs could be used to kill the parasite that causes a disease called river blindness. The disease starts with a seemingly innocuous insect bite that allows the parasites to lay the larvae of worms—which eventually grow to two feet in length—in the body. Over time, these worms produce thousands of microscopic worms. Victims can experience suffering so severe that some elect suicide rather than endure the pain. A common result of the disease is a scarring of the eye that produces blindness.

While the discovery of the cure was cause for celebration, Merck soon found itself in a dilemma: none of the "customers" who needed the drug could afford to pay for it. The disease afflicts mainly people in the Third World, particularly parts of Africa and Central and South America. Merck tried in vain to obtain financial support to help offset the costs of developing the drug and getting it where it was needed.

In the end, Merck stayed true to a key element of its company philosophy: "We try never to forget that medicine is for the people. It is not for the profits. The profits follow, and if we remember that, they have never failed to appear. The better we have remembered it, the larger they have been." Merck promised to give the drug away and pay to transport it (at a cost of $20 million per year) to any country that requested it, forever.[2]

Even though the actions of Aaron Feuerstein and Merck & Co. undoubtedly exceed the norm in the world of commerce, business as a system has to rely on sound ethics for its very success. Contrary to the popular image, only a small fraction of the millions of business transactions that occur daily are of the scheming variety reported in the media. Although capitalism is cast as a system that relies on greed, the free market would fall apart if it were not for traditional moral virtues such as trust, honesty, and cooperation. Despite the traditional interpretations of his work, Adam Smith wrote *The Wealth of Nations* within a context of his moral philosophy as developed in his *Theory of Moral Sentiments*. Thus, even the so-called father of what many regard today as economic evils believed that capitalism would work only if tempered by the moral restraints of a British gentleman.[3]

To be sure, though, many subtle and troubling ethical dilemmas arise when the pursuit of profit and the self-interest of fallen human nature converge. Although they may not be of the sensational variety portrayed by the entertainment industry, business professionals are often confronted with choices having moral ramifications. For example, routine situations such as deciding how much to reveal in sales transactions and advertising or negotiating in international settings have ethical dimensions to them.

[2]The Business Enterprise Trust, "Merck & Co. (Part A&B)," cited in Andrew Wicks, "Albert Schweitzer or Ivan Boesky? Why We Should Reject the Dichotomy Between Medicine and Business," *Journal of Business Ethics* 14, no. 5 (May 1995): 339–51.

[3]Patricia H. Werhane, *Adam Smith and His Legacy for Modern Capitalism* (New York: Oxford University Press, 1991).

"Is That All There Is?"

Ironically, at the same time that issues in business ethics are receiving much attention in the popular media, they often seem to be strangely absent from church pulpits and other religious institutions. People looking for answers are apt to encounter few sophisticated treatments of these issues. Much that comes from the pulpit or can be found on the shelves of religious bookstores consigns business ethics to matters of personal integrity. The people are typically reminded with biblical chapter and verse to come to work on time, avoid calling in sick falsely, and not steal from the supply room—as if that were all there is to a Christian perspective on workplace conduct.

In doing the research for his book *God and Mammon in America*, Princeton sociologist Robert Wuthnow found that for many people with religious faith, ethics in the workplace is reduced to a simple matter of honesty.[4] While honesty and personal integrity are essential character traits, they are not enough by themselves to resolve some of the thornier dilemmas that business people face. Moreover, reducing ethics to simple honesty apart from its context significantly reduces the scope to which ethics applies. Wuthnow argues that with such a limited view, "one's behavior may contribute to the burning of rain forests and the perpetuation of world hunger and yet, as long as one tells the truth, ethics is not a problem."[5]

We have probably all experienced the spirit of Wuthnow's point while viewing a movie in which the portrayal of "honor among thieves" is a central theme in the plot. One recent example is the film *Heat*, which pits Neal MacCauley (played by Robert De Niro), an eerily calm leader of a gang that pulls off precision heists, against edgy detective Vincent Hanna (portrayed by Al Pacino). MacCauley elicits sympathy from the audience for his portrayal of a man of strong character possessing incredible skill, honor, and discipline. He shows no limits to the loyalty and commitment he gives to the well-being of his partners and love interest. He is considerate to patrons during a bank robbery and stays true to the "discipline" of his profession by being ready to drop everything in an instant "if he feels the heat is around the corner." In an expression of mutual respect, MacCauley and Detective Hanna eventually sit down in a face-to-face exchange about their "professions." In one sentence, MacCauley morally neutralizes the fact that he robs for a living and almost christens his work a calling with the words, "Like you, I gotta do what I do best." Through the remainder of the film, audiences seem torn in their allegiance, but many in the crowd eventually pull for MacCauley. They cheer when he eludes the authorities and groan when he is about to be caught, all the while

[4] Robert Wuthnow, *God and Mammon in America* (New York: Free Press, 1994).

[5] Ibid., 84.

seemingly missing the fact that he steals, with machine gun in hand, to enrich himself.

Undoubtedly, MacCauley displays in the film what many would consider admirable character traits. However, what is glaringly missing from his life is direction in the form of a moral compass to guide his "virtues" by considering the larger context of his actions. The very idea of a "virtuous bank robber" seems dubious, yet because no attention is given to the broader context, the crowd cheers him on. It is not difficult to see that this situation offers many parallels to legitimate employment settings.

What if evangelism and simple matters of integrity such as not padding an expense account or getting to work on time were the only moral issues for Christians in the workplace? If this were so, it would seem that as long as they followed these simple admonitions and led a weekly Bible study on the premises, they could be loyal to a company engaged in deceitful sales practices or that used sex gratuitously in its advertisements and still be considered ethical. In spite of these blind spots, it appears that there is little guidance on these matters coming from churches. A true Christian approach to business ethics requires much more than a simple appeal to personal integrity. A consideration of the larger context of one's actions is critical if Christian moral principles are to be upheld in the workplace.

Filling a Critical Gap

It is with this need in mind that we present *Beyond Integrity*. Our aim is to offer a sophisticated treatment of issues facing people in business and in other kinds of enterprise from within a Judeo-Christian perspective. While we believe that ethics begins with a rightly ordered soul and with character traits that empower self-restraint and the ability to do the things we ought to do, we believe it is critical that we as Christians progress well beyond simple admonitions to integrity. We must also use our reason to help set our moral compasses and to give direction to our character, lest we become guilty of the blind loyalty just described.

Unfortunately, voices that speak from within a Judeo-Christian framework are often missing from the mainstream debate on issues in business ethics. Yet most Christians spend the bulk of their day employed in secular organizational settings where business dimensions pertain. Furthermore, a large percentage of the public regularly indicates in surveys that they attend church and believe in Christian moral standards.[6] If these numbers are accurate, the absence of a Christian voice is a curious one indeed. It may indicate that many—perhaps even

[6]See Gallup surveys on religious practices.

most—Christians have not examined their work or work-related behavior in light of their faith commitments.

Some of the factors involved in this dearth of a Christian perspective can be arguably explained as a bias towards religion by secular minds. However, Wuthnow suggests that this absence results from churches having had, in recent history, very little to say about these matters. With his survey data in mind, Wuthnow concludes that religion functions as a kind of "therapy," providing comfort to decisions already made but having little influence as a challenging force to workplace thinking and behavior. Thus, it seems that Christians largely approach work with secular market-based criteria rather than Judeo-Christian criteria for thinking and acting. If Wuthnow is correct, then the notable absence of intelligent inquiry and debate on workplace morality from a distinctly Christian perspective may be one of our own doing. Perhaps Christians have too easily bought into secular ways of thinking about work and business practices without stopping to ask whether these practices are really consistent with the morals of their tradition.

Many books from Christian authors express a single, simple viewpoint without interaction with conflicting opinions. By contrast, the most popular texts in secular classrooms typically offer articles with conflicting viewpoints and then simply wish the reader *bon voyage* to wander aimlessly without a means of adjudicating the various truth claims. We contend that works of this kind risk insidiously and unintentionally leading readers to the relativistic conclusion that since there are "valid" points on both sides, it is safer (and better) not to commit to any viewpoint.

The simplicity of Christian resources on the one hand and the relativism inherent in secular perspectives on the other have left a critical gap that we hope to fill through this text. In the chapters that follow, we will introduce many of the current ethical issues in the world of business. Included is an outstanding anthology of readings by both secular and Christian thinkers in the field. For further discussion and application, case studies will follow these readings, most of them based on actual events. Finally, we will offer our comments on the various issues and the perspectives of the authors who address them.

Some readers will undoubtedly wonder why secular perspectives have been included in a book that carries the subtitle "A Judeo-Christian Approach to Business Ethics." These essays have been included because we believe it is of the utmost importance that Christians enter into an ongoing dialogue with the secular community that has largely set the terms of discussion. Many of the articles represent the "classics" in the rapidly developing field of business ethics. More importantly, they express widely held viewpoints in the "real world" of business. Rather than trying to assist readers in "preaching to the choir," we intend to help Christians learn to carry on dialogue more intelligently with the world around them. To do so, it is important that Christians thoroughly understand the broad range of perspectives that exist and the arguments that are commonly employed by the people they live among and work with.

In the commentary sections at the end of each chapter, we do not claim to have the final word or a God's-eye view on these issues. We recognize that in some cases "suspended judgment" is the correct expression of intellectual honesty and humility. Consistent with the approach we have used in the classroom over the years, we welcome disagreement with our thoughts and perspectives. Our goal is not to have the closing arguments, but rather to stimulate discussion and contribute a Christian voice to the ongoing dialogue about current moral issues in the operations of business and the economy.

OVERVIEW AND STRUCTURE OF THE BOOK

This book is divided into several key sections. Part I, "Christians, Markets, and Postmodern Morality" (chaps. 1–3), examines some of the conflicts between Christian moral obligations and dominant business values. One often hears that unless we are willing to leave our personal morals at the door and abide by the "rules of the game," we will not be successful in the business world. How, then, are Christians to respond? Can we adhere to a Judeo-Christian moral framework and still experience success in business? Can Christians succeed simply because good ethics really are good business in a financial sense? These critical questions are addressed in chapter 1.

Another attitude common today is that success depends on compartmentalizing our values because the globalization of business and postmodern notions of morality promote cultural relativism and personal subjectivism as modes of moral reflection and decision making. This leads one to question the place of Christian ethics in public discussions about morality in a pluralistic world. How are Christians to respond to this rapidly changing world without lapsing into relativism? Yet, how can we succeed in business abroad or in our own changing society without following the rules of the surrounding culture? On what basis can Christians have meaningful dialogue with those who reject the Bible out of hand as their authority on moral matters? These questions will be addressed in chapters 2 and 3, the latter having a focus on the development of a philosophical and theological foundation for Christian ethics in business.

Part II, "Capitalism and Christian Values" (chaps. 4–5), critiques the very foundations and moral assumptions of the free-market system from a Christian worldview. While socialism has collapsed in many parts of the world, the debate over the morality of capitalism shows no signs of ebbing in many circles, particularly the religious and academic. It is critical to examine this debate in detail because it is the foundation for business and the free-enterprise system under which Americans live and after which many developing nations are currently modeling themselves. While economics as a discipline has traditionally been concerned with efficiency, costs, and trade-offs, it has an important moral dimension. Many current public debates and referenda center on important questions involving ethics and the economy.

Part III, "Business and Society" (chaps. 6–13), examines the role of the corporation in society. To some, corporations have a primary duty to maximize shareholder wealth within the boundaries of the law, and this is therefore the one and only "social responsibility" of business. However, this position is increasingly coming under attack from people who believe that business organizations have more responsibilities to their surrounding communities than just earning profits. Many argue that they should also contribute to the common good through more direct means. As you read this book, you may note that most of the issues in business ethics come down to how one resolves this critical question. Thus, it is important that we develop a self-conscious view of the moral role of corporations in our society.

Chapters 10–13 deal with many of the hottest topics of current debate involving conflicts over the obligations of corporations to their employees and to the general public. In particular, questions over employee rights and privacy in the workplace, affirmative action, advertising content, and insider trading, to name a few, will be addressed. These issues receive widespread attention in the press and have important ramifications for corporations and the people in them. It is extremely crucial that Christians understand the nuances involved in these issues and how to approach them from the moral values of their tradition.

Finally, Part IV, "Ethics and Individuals" (chaps. 14–16), gives attention to the people who make up contemporary organizations. Since many business decisions are made in the context of the organizations, it is important to understand the influence of these organizations on the decision making of individuals; here we observe the dynamics that can lead to a climate that allows scandals to occur. The text then examines some very insightful works that offer practical suggestions on how to improve the organizational climate for ethical behavior in the workplace. Finally, a model is presented that serves as a guide to ethical decision making.

Before we begin exploring specific issues in business ethics, we should examine the most common ways by which people approach moral problems. This will lay a foundation and provide a framework with which to view the readings and case examples in the chapters that follow. Readers with a sufficient background in the philosophical study of ethics can skip directly to the last section of this introduction, "A Judeo-Christian Approach to Business Ethics."

AN INTRODUCTION TO ETHICAL REASONING

In our contemporary culture, people use many methods of moral reasoning. They employ different ethical systems at different times as they wrestle with what is right or wrong, or what is one's moral obligation in a specific instance. One place to see these various modes of moral reasoning is in the way that the debate over various social issues is conducted. In fact, one reason that so many of these debates seem unresolvable is that their participants are using drastically different methods of arriving at their conceptions of right and wrong. Take, for example, the following scenario:[7]

[7]Adapted from "Where Do You Draw the Line?"—a case written by William W. May of the University of Southern California.

Imagine that you are an executive for a company that depends largely on government contracts for business. You have prepared a proposal for a project that could amount to a $50 million contract for your firm over the next five years. You are now flying to meet with government officials to bid on the project. You cannot help but notice that two executives from a competing firm are sitting in front of you. You know who they are, but are sure they don't know who you are. They are talking about a program on which they are bidding—the same contract that you are hoping to secure for your firm. Now, where could you justify drawing the line with regard to the following possibilities? Try to answer yes or no and give a rationale for your decision.

- Is it okay for you to actively listen with a view toward picking up information that may be useful to you?
- Their conversation continues with a lot of numbers being mentioned. Is it okay for you to take a few notes?
- The material is coming faster than you can write. Would it be okay to turn on your dictation machine to record their conversation?

- As your competitors leave the plane, you see that they have left some materials in the seat-back pocket that are not marked confidential. Is it okay to take them and to use the information?
- The materials *are* marked confidential—so is it okay to take them?
- When you arrive at your hotel, you see the two competitors at the check-in desk. Is it okay to linger in the hotel lounge to see if you can pick up more loose conversation?
- You find to your surprise that the competitors are in the room next to you. Is it okay to turn down your television set to try to hear what they are saying?
- Even with the TV turned off, their voices are muffled. Is it okay to put your ear to the wall to hear better?
- If the voices are still unclear, is it okay to put a drinking glass to the wall to enhance the sound?

After quickly appraising the situation, your conscience interrupts your impulse and you stop yourself from getting out your dictation machine. After submitting the bid, you are troubled on the flight home that you may not have done the right thing. After all, not only is your career in jeopardy if you fail to win the contract, but hundreds of jobs are also at stake for your company. Upon returning home, you are still bothered as you await word about the contract, so you bring the situation up for discussion at the next meeting of the local chamber of commerce. Many of your closest friends and associates are among the participants. However, they seem only to add to your confusion since each one approaches moral problems with a different methodology. Each of the participants (with their respective approaches in parentheses) responds to you in the following way:

Participant #1: The President of a Community Business (Ethical Egoist)

Why is this a moral discussion at all? I would have no problem doing anything that you have just stated. You see, for me it all boils down to the fact that I have a business to run and the only thing that matters is if I can make a profit provided I stay within the bounds of the law. In fact, the only business ethic worth its weight is "do unto others before they do unto you." There is no doubt that my competitors would do this to me. Hey, if they're dumb enough to be so careless, they deserve to lose. It's their responsibility to protect the information—if they don't want it heard, they shouldn't say it in public—it's that simple! It's not my job to look out for every sucker out there. After all, if my own job is dependent on this contract, what's my family going to do? Starve, so that I can feel good about myself? Forget it! Besides, how do I know that the two competitors were not planted there to mislead me? Maybe the competition is smarter than we think! Aside from all of this, isn't capitalism based upon self-interest anyway? You guys are so naive—I mean, it's a rough-and-tumble world; if I don't look out for my needs, who will? A book that you should all read is *Looking Out for Number One*. It says it all!

Participant #2: The Head of the Local Chamber of Commerce (a Utilitarian)

Wow, what a scenario! I admit, taking their materials and listening through the wall would bother me a bit. But if I were you, I think I could justify my actions based upon the good that it will do for my employees and for the local community. Just think, without this contract, hundreds of jobs are at stake. That could devastate our local economy. But if we were to secure the deal, we could create jobs, expand our tax base, and go forward with those badly needed community improvement projects. I know that the competing company would be hurt, but their business just doesn't depend upon government contracts to the degree that yours does. You see, I believe that it is not necessarily principles that determine right and wrong, but the consequences produced by the actions in question. If a particular course of action or decision produces the best set of consequences, then it seems to me that it should be allowed. To put it another way, the action that produces the greatest balance of benefits over harms is the one that is the most moral. So in this case, what is important to determine is whether or not taking the information would produce the greatest good for the greatest number of people.

As I just pointed out, this could produce a lot of good for the people in your company, and on balance your competitor is in a much better position to absorb the loss than you are. Now, there may be situations in which a similar action may produce, on balance, more negative than positive consequences. In those cases, it should not be allowed. We should be careful of setting hard-and-fast rules that don't take the consequences into account.

Participant #3: The President of the Area Christian Business Woman's Chapter (Deontologist, or Believer in Principle-Based Ethics)

Hey, wait a minute! Doesn't this simply come down to stealing? Now, I might listen to the conversation because I'm not proactively trying to take advantage of the situation. However, most of the other actions constitute theft, to which my moral authority—the Bible—and common morality are clearly opposed. Thus, it doesn't matter to me how many people would lose their jobs or what our community would gain from the contract. It equally doesn't matter if I might lose my job. Stealing is wrong, period. If torn between loyalty to my employer and loyalty to God, there's no question as to whom I will honor first. Likewise, you should instead trust that God will provide if you honor his principles first.

Participant #4: Local Television Talk Show Host (Emotivist)

I hate to throw a monkey wrench into this whole discussion, but in my view, all of the participants so far are trying to do the impossible. Each person so far has attempted to make some kind of determination of what is right or wrong in this case. I don't think that's possible. They are really using the language of right and wrong to mask their personal preferences. What I mean is, anytime a person says that something is right or wrong, all they are saying—and can say—about it is that they either like or dislike the action or position under consideration. We should be honest and admit that we're only talking about our preferences and just using moral language to give greater persuasive power to our argument. In this specific case, you should ask yourself about how you feel about it. Feelings are more important than any reasoning you could do. In my own view, my feelings would not be bothered by any of this, so I think I'm okay.

Participant #5: An Atheist Philosophy Professor (Relativist)

I clearly reject what my friend from the Christian business woman's society says, because the Bible is not my moral authority! Now, I'm not prepared to say that there is no such thing as genuine right and wrong, but I do think that there is no universal, absolute standard of right and wrong. What is moral depends on the situation and on what the cultural consensus of right and wrong is at that time. For example, if the culture has reached a consensus that euthanasia should be allowed, then I see no reason why it should not be allowed.

Conversely, if the culture is opposed to the practice, I see no good reason why euthanasia should be forced on them in this case. I know that in some parts of Southeast Asia, corporate espionage is just a part of the game. Some corporations there assume the responsibility of regularly searching for bugs and other data-interception devices when they hold meetings or use their computers.

Even though it seems terrible to us, who are we to judge what is right for them? We should simply respect their norms. But in the state of Utah where there are so many religious Mormons, or in the Bible Belt where there are so many conservative Christians, the culture will undoubtedly be against such practices and that too should be respected. So, the operative question that we should be asking is whether or not this is an acceptable part of the business culture as opposed to the morality of other parts of life. You know, what is the right thing to do while in Rome?

Participant #6: A Minister (Virtue Theorist)

I'd like to put a slightly different slant on this issue. You see, I believe that there's more to morality than simply arguing about correct decisions when a person is faced with a moral dilemma. There is more to the moral life than simply *doing* the right thing and making the correct decision. *Being* the right type of person is more important. Thus, we cannot neglect the place of an individual's character, or virtue, when considering ethical questions. Simply debating issues is powerless if we continue to ignore the character traits that give people the ability to actually do the right thing. After all, most of the recent business ethics scandals in the headlines involved participants who were educated at the nation's elite universities. So it couldn't have been just a matter of knowing right from wrong.

You see, it was plainly a matter of character. As such, I believe that there are more important questions that need to be asked in this situation. For example, what does a person's attitude toward fair competition tell us about his or her character? What does support for taking the information, or opposition to it, say about our society? Does it say that as a society we no longer value fair competition upon the merits of the product or the service? Besides, as I mentioned earlier, what good is only debating about ethics when our schools and communities no longer agree about or seek to equip our children with the character necessary to carry out what they know to be right? These are very important questions that cannot be ignored in any discussion of ethics in business.

A bit confusing, isn't it? No wonder we have so many disagreements about morality in society. Each person in this discussion has argued using a distinctive style of moral reasoning, from a specific ethical system. Each represents one of the predominant modes of moral reasoning that are used in the debate today over current moral issues. We can frequently observe examples of these different styles in the media. You will very likely find most of these systems employed regularly if you are careful to watch for them.

One notable exception, however, is the approach taken by the last participant—the virtue or character approach. Though it has made somewhat of a resurgence in recent years, this view is still largely absent from public debate. Yet it is an approach that we believe is essential to the very functioning and survival of the free-market system. We will say more about this in the last part of this chapter. In what follows, we will analyze each of the ethical systems used by the participants in this panel (with the exception of the viewpoint of participant #4—relativism, which we will address in chapter 2), spelling out the positive elements of each system as well as offering a critique of each system.

Ethical Egoism

Ethical egoism is the theory that the morality of an act is determined by one's self-interest. Those actions that advance self-interest are moral and those that do not are not moral. To say that one is an ethical egoist is not to say that he or she is egotistical. This is a common confusion. The label "ethical egoist" simply identifies self-interest as the method of making moral decisions and does not necessarily suggest that the person is narcissistic in character. Participant #1 is a clear example of an ethical egoist, because he was basing his moral decision strictly on self-interest. We could cite other contemporary examples of ethical egoism at work. Take, for example, physicians in medical practice who may make decisions with the overriding concern to cover themselves to prevent their being sued. There is certainly nothing wrong in most cases with the desire to avoid ending up in a lawsuit, but the point here is that this desire is a clear example of ethical egoism. According to egoism, the right thing for physicians to do is what will protect them from being sued, or what is in their self-interest.

Ethical egoism is also used in the Bible as a way of motivating people to be obedient to God. For example, the covenant blessing and curses set forth in Deuteronomy 27–30 promise Old Testament Israel agricultural prosperity and military peace as consequences of obedience, and threaten the opposite should the nation turn to idolatry and disobey God. What is in Israel's national self-interest is clearly a motivation for doing the right thing. Another example is accepting Christ and inheriting eternal life as a result (something that is clearly in a person's self-interest) and doing altruistic acts because of the way it makes us feel good about ourselves.

Some have even suggested that the Bible is entirely egoistic and simply changes the categories of what constitutes a person's self-interest. That is probably too strong a statement, but it is true that the Bible never condemns self-interest, but only requires that it be balanced by concern for others (Philippians 2:4). It is one thing to occasionally employ appeal to self-interest as the Bible does, but quite another to claim, as consistent ethical egoists do, that egoism is a sufficient ethical system. This latter claim is the one we will examine in this section.

According to ethical egoism, our only moral duty is to our own self-interest. This is not to say that we should avoid actions that help others, since our interests and the interests of others can coincide. It may be that helping others may be a means to the end of our self-interest. It is also not to say that our short-term interests are primary. We may forego short-term advantage to ensure long term interests. This is what the original ethical egoist, Thomas Hobbes, suggested by saying that to keep the pursuit of self-interest from destroying society, people voluntarily give up some freedom to pursue their interests so that each one's long-term interests might be protected.[8]

[8]For further discussion of Hobbes's system of ethical egoism, see his *Leviathan*.

Although egoism has its appeal in the comtemporary culture, there are problems with it as an all-encompassing ethical system. First, egoism does not provide any way to umpire conflicting interests without appeal to some other system. What happens when my self-interest conflicts with yours? All the egoist can do to resolve that conflict is to reassert his basic premise of self-interest. The system has no resources to solve conflicts of interest between individuals and groups. It is naive to think that interests never conflict. Yet this assumption seems to be necessary if ethical egoism is to be a workable system.

A second difficulty is that ethical egoism ultimately collapses into anarchy. For example, Hobbes (1588–1679) realized that to make ethical egoism work required an absolute monarch (whom he called "the Leviathan," the title of his work that explains this concept) to keep self-interest from disintegrating into anarchy. Yet there were no guarantees that the monarch would not also pursue his own self-interest.

[9]Adam Smith, in his defense of capitalism of an economic system, employed ethical egoism to some degree in his justification of it. He argued that there was an "invisible hand" that coordinated each person's pursuit of self-interest and made it work for the common good. It should be recognized that Smith held to an *enlightened* self-interest, presumably self-interest regulated by Christian morality as the key to making capitalism work. See his classic work *The Wealth of Nations* for further discussion of this.

It takes great faith to believe that some kind of "invisible hand" mysteriously works all things out.[9] Again, for the system to work, it requires resources outside of it. If one must assume some sort of natural law to keep egoism in check, then the underlying premise known as psychological egoism—that people are incapable of acting except in their own self-interest—is much less credible. The Bible teaches that human depravity gives us our bent toward self-interest and that the image of God and common grace balance this out even for the unbeliever. For the believer, the resources also include the indwelling Holy Spirit to balance depravity.

A third problem with ethical egoism as a sufficient system of ethics is that the Scripture calls believers and unbelievers both to a balance of self-interest and altruism. We are called to care about the needs of others because they are comparable to our own and because a significant part of being a disciple of Christ entails following his altruistic example. Believers are called to be servants, and that invariably involves periodically putting another's need ahead of our own. It does not, however, obligate believers to neglect legitimate self-interest. The Bible does not call believers to the kind of extreme altruism that ethical egoists claim it does. One should remember that, at times, even Jesus walked away from the crowds in order to have time alone with his heavenly Father. Thus there is a place for legitimate self-interest, to which the Bible periodically appeals, but it is balanced by a compassionate concern for the interests of others.

Utilitarianism

Utilitarianism is what is known as a teleological system (taken from the Greek word *telos*, meaning "end"), in which the end produced is what determines the morality of an act. In fact, sometimes the terms *utilitarianism* and *teleological ethics* are used interchangeably. The most common form of utilitarianism today is the idea that the act that produces the greatest good for the greatest number is the moral thing to do. That is, the course of action that produces the greatest balance of good consequences over harmful ones is correct. This type of moral reasoning is also called *consequentialism* because of its overriding emphasis on the consequences of actions.

The Ford Motor Company used this line of reasoning in perhaps the most (in)famous episode in business ethics, the case of the Ford Pinto. In that situation, Ford was under intense pressure in the early 1970s to release a compact car to compete with the Japanese models. Knowing full well that the current design of the gas tank would lead to explosions and human casualties upon impact at a relatively low level of speed, company executives decided to use a cost-benefit analysis in deciding whether to make the necessary safety changes or to release the car in its then unsafe condition. Weighing the benefits of saved human lives (which they priced at $200,000 each) against the cost of the changes ($11 per car), Ford decided to release the Pinto into the market because their calculated costs exceeded the benefits. The rest is business ethics history: numerous death and burn injuries, litigation and financial liability, and the demise and end to production of this type of car.

Utilitarianism has its roots in the philosophies of Jeremy Bentham and John Stuart Mill. Bentham (1748–1832) held to a hedonistic utilitarianism, that is, the idea that the most moral acts were those that maximized pleasure and minimized pain. Mill (1806–1873) refined this notion away from hedonism toward a more general concept of maximizing the general happiness, or the greatest good for the greatest number. Utilitarianism was a radical theory when it was proposed, since it divorced morality from divine revelation and from any view of nature. Thus moral behavior became separated from faithfulness to divine ordinances and rigid rules.

Utilitarian modes of moral reasoning are widely applied today. Most public policy in the United States and Western Europe is still decided on overwhelmingly utilitarian grounds. As was evident from Participant #2, a good deal of the discussion about morals in business is conducted on utilitarian grounds, where the principles take a back seat to consideration of the consequences. If, on balance, the action provides more beneficial consequences for more people, then it is considered the most moral course of action. Utilitarianism also comes into play when companies consider closing plants or laying off workers to maintain their competitive position in the marketplace. Often a firm's executives will justify these measures by acknowledging that they are producing harm for some, but on balance are safeguarding the jobs of the rest of the employees by keeping the company in business, thus producing a greater balance of benefits over harms.

There are two primary schools of utilitarianism, known as *act utilitarianism* and *rule utilitarianism*. Act utilitarianism uses the consequences of any given course of action to determine its morality. In doing so, act utilitarians treat each moral decision separately and weigh the consequences of each isolated act. Rule utilitarians, however, have formulated moral rules to guide behavior that do not depend on a separate calculation of beneficial and harmful consequences each time one needs to make a moral decision. Rather, rule utilitarians use the "track record" of actions in producing a consistent set of consequences and thus formulate the rules based on the tendency of certain actions to produce a predictable set of consequences. For example, there would be a moral rule against rape, not based on some principle, but because in the great majority of cases, on balance, rape produces more harmful than beneficial consequences. The same could be said about many other actions such as truth-telling, promise keeping, rules against murder and other violent crimes, and rules against fraud and deceit in business.

Though utilitarianism has its appeal, especially in a secular society, it also has its shortcomings. The most common charge against utilitarianism is that it cannot protect the rights of minorities and sometimes can justify obvious injustices because the "greater good" is served. For example, slavery in the South in the era preceding the Civil War was clearly justifiable from a utilitarian point of view. It provided cheap labor that made the South very prosperous, and so it benefited more people than it harmed. But no one today would justify slavery on any grounds, let alone utilitarianism. The good consequences that it produced appear not only irrelevant, but also callous toward the suffering that so many slaves endured. The reason that slavery was immoral has little to do with the balance of consequences. Rather, it has to do with a universal principle that directs us to safeguard the basic rights and dignity of each individual, ultimately because humans are made in the image of God.

Even though utilitarianism has wide popular appeal and is the basis for much public policy, there are other problems that remain for this system. First, not only are the consequences of actions difficult to predict and measure, but the notions of benefit and harm are not value-neutral. What may be a benefit to one person may not be to another. It is not entirely accurate to say that the utilitarian uses nonmoral criteria to evaluate the morality of an action; in many cases, one must appeal to principles to give substance to the idea of a benefit or to arbitrate competing claims about a benefit. There is as much diversity and pluralism about what constitutes a benefit and a harm as there is about the definition of the good.

Second, utilitarianism offers no criteria to direct the *distribution* of benefits in a group. It tends to be an aggregate theory in that what counts is the overall amount of benefit—that is, the greatest good for the greatest number. The distribution of benefits is just as important, if not more so, as the overall amount of benefit accorded to the aggregate group.

Third, utilitarianism allows no place for the notion of individual deserts and merit. The reason it is deemed right that a person gets a promotion over a sluggard or that a person gets to keep what he or she has earned is not that it serves the general utility—it is that the person has earned it. We recognize merit as a reason for treating people in different ways, without being guilty of discrimination, because we treat people as autonomous responsible human beings, irrespective of the consequences produced by treating people that way.

Given the problems with utilitarianism, it is important to take the consequences of actions and decisions seriously, since there may be times when appeal to principles does not resolve a dilemma. And it may be that at times, consequences may force us to admit that there are periodic exceptions to our deontological principles.

Emotivism

Emotivism is an approach to morality that has made a significant resurgence in recent decades. Listening to callers and guests of popular radio and television talk shows, one could easily conclude that this is one of the dominant methods for addressing ethical questions today.[10] Participant #4 represents this approach. According to emotivism, personal feelings are the most important determinant of right and wrong. Since feelings differ from person to person, however, morality quickly breaks down to a matter of personal preference and, thus, to subjectivism.

In one sense, subjectivism is the extension of relativism (see chap. 2) to apply to the beliefs that are developed in our own culture. Subjectivists hold that morality is dependent on how we feel about an action. Subjectivists will say that a statement that "X is wrong" is simply saying that one disapproves of X. He holds that "morality (not beauty) is in the eye of the beholder." Many of the same criticisms of ethical relativism also apply to ethical subjectivism.

Emotivism goes beyond subjectivism and is a theory about the language of morality. The emotivist holds that the judgments expressed by moral language simply communicate a person's emotions about a subject, and thus nothing anyone says in moral language can be true or false. Ethical statements are considered by an emotivist as attitudes masquerading as facts.

The essential difference between the subjectivist and the emotivist is that for the subjectivist, moral judgments are facts in that they are *reports of a person's attitude* about morality, and for the emotivist, moral judgments are *expressions of an attitude* about an action or person. The subjectivist who says that "stealing is wrong" means "I disapprove of stealing"; the emotivist saying the same thing means "stealing, boo!" or "stealing, yeech!" For the subjectivist, moral judgments are statements of fact about the attitude of the person who says them. For the emotivist, moral judgments are not facts at all, but emotional expressions about the subject at hand. Emotivism is thus a more

[10]For futher commentary on this, see Thomas Sowell, "The Mushing of America," *Forbes* (18 July 1994): 69.

sophisticated theory than subjectivism. Both have in common the notions that moral judgments are not normative statements and there is no such thing as an objective moral fact.

One of the primary criticisms of emotivism is that it cannot account for the place of reason in ethics. Emotivism sets up a false dichotomy that is as follows:

(1) Either there are moral facts, as there are facts about the sciences, or

(2) Values are nothing more than expressions of our subjective feelings.

But there is another critical possibility: that moral truths are truths of reason, or a moral judgment is true if it is backed up by better reasons than the alternatives. We would also say as Christians that moral truths are also truths of revelation and that there is a strong connection between the facts of creation and the facts of morality. Good reasons usually resolve moral disagreements, but for the emotivist, giving good reasons and manipulation would amount to much the same thing. There is no good reason to assume that moral language is not also factual language and that moral judgments are cognitive statements, not just expressions of emotion or preference. It should not be surprising that ethical statements are not empirically verifiable, since right and wrong are not empirically observable qualities. But neither are they simply emotive expressions.

To be sure, Scripture talks about the importance of obeying your conscience and following your heart. However, this differs from emotivism. In the biblical tradition, one's conscience is more of an inner voice in need of accountability to a community or wise counsel rather than a mere feeling. Today's expressions of emotivism seem only to seek what is pleasurable in terms of feelings.

Deontological Systems

In contrast to teleological forms of moral reasoning, deontological moral systems are based on principles. The term *deontological* is derived form the Greek term *dei*, meaning "it is necessary." From this comes the notion of moral obligations that are inherently necessary and not contingent on the ends or consequences they produce. Deontological obligations are moral duties because they are inherently the right thing to do. The deontologist would say, for example, that theft is wrong, period, irrespective of who benefits from it. The consequences of actions are not that relevant for determining right and wrong, since moral obligations come from principles, not ends. Participant #3 takes this approach.

There are various types of deontological systems, both from religious perspectives and from more secular views of the world. In fact, most religious traditions that are centered around a book, such as Judaism, Christianity, and Islam, are strongly deontological in their ethical outlook, since the principles come from either the words or the ideas (or both) of the sacred book. This is usually called the "divine command theory" of ethics, wherein the divine commands recorded in the inspired literature form the primary source of moral guidance for the religion's followers.

A second form of deontological morality is employed by Roman Catholics in their use of natural law. Natural law refers at the least to universal moral principles that are evident from the world around us. These principles derive from nature, empirical observation, and reason. They are usually broad, general, universally accepted principles such as prohibitions against murder and the affirmation of truth-telling, covenant keeping, trust, mercy, and compassion toward the vulnerable. Principles derived from natural law help form a bridge between religious perspectives and a secular world in matters of ethics. In fact, adherence to natural law is critical if Christians in business are to communicate a specifically Christian ethic to colleagues and others in business who may not share a Christian view of the world. Because of this, we have devoted an entire chapter (chap. 3) to natural law and its implications for business ethics.

A third form of deontological reasoning is based on reason alone. This is most commonly identified with the moral philosophy of Immanuel Kant, who sought to construct a system in which one could formulate moral absolutes without any recourse to religious authority but only to human reason. His use of what he called the "categorical imperative" is a process for arriving at moral principles that are inherently right and good. Kant (1724–1804) strongly believed that the consequences of actions or how one felt about actions were irrelevant to the morality of the action. It was the principle behind the action, derived by reason, that counted.

Actually, the principles that determine morality may come from a wide variety of sources. For example, in public policy in the United States, the Constitution provides many of the basic principles that govern social ethics for the broader society. The right to privacy, the right to free expression of one's ideas, and the right to due process of law are considered fundamental moral principles on which our society is built. They come not specifically from any religious documents, but from the Constitution, though the framers of that document were clearly influenced by the Judeo-Christian tradition.

Adherence to deontological principles puts one at the more absolutist end of the spectrum (with relativism at the other end). However, it does not necessarily follow that just because one is committed to a deontological view of morality, he or she is an absolutist, admitting no exceptions to the principles. Rather, commitment to principles makes one at least a prima facie absolutist—that is, an absolutist on the surface, but able to make periodic exceptions to general principles when the circumstances warrant this. For example, truth-telling is a clear deontological principle. But if someone came to you with a gun and asked where your best friend went, we would hope you would not tell that person the truth, so as to save the life of your friend. But in most cases, truth-telling is a moral obligation that must be upheld.

Because of a commitment to the authority of the Bible, adherents of a Judeo-Christian ethic will usually be predominantly deontological in their view of morality. Given the emphasis on God's commands and natural-law moral principles, the Judeo-Christian ethicist will lean toward deontological ethical systems. However, this does not justify simplistic proof-texting, which is often done out of context, to address complex ethical problems in business. Rather, we go to the Scripture primarily to discover broad principles that we can then apply to specific situations encountered in business. It is true that Scripture has a good deal to say about wealth and materialism. But that has more to do with what people do with their wealth and their attitude toward it than some of the specific issues in the practice of business today. However, we should realize that when Scripture speaks on a subject, it is authoritative even though its application may be debated and controversial. Given the Judeo-Christian commitment to the commands of God, it should not be surprising that its ethical outlook is predominantly, though not exclusively, deontological.[11]

A second criticism of deontology is that sometimes the principles conflict. For example, during World War II, when Corrie Ten Boom gave sanctuary to Jews in her native country of the Netherlands, she was often asked by the authorities if she was hiding Jews in her home. If she told the truth, the Jews would have been taken to extermination camps. But if she lied, they would have been saved. Here she was faced with a genuine moral dilemma, or a conflict of commands. She had a moral duty to tell the truth, but she was also responsible for preventing harm when it was in her power to do so, especially when it involved saving life. What was she morally obligated to do?

Or consider the example in Joshua 2, where Rahab the prostitute was commended for her faith in sheltering the Israelite spies sent out on a reconnaissance mission to the Promised Land. She was directly

[11]For example, the wisdom literature—particularly the Proverbs—also uses a form of utilitarianism because it has a more universal audience to which it is appealing. Many of the sentence Proverbs are constructed around a consideration of consequences that guide right behavior. (For specific examples, see Proverbs 10:1, 4; 11:2; 26:27.)

asked by the authorities if she knew the whereabouts of any Israelite spies, and she not only told them she did not, but also sent the authorities "after them" in the wrong direction. She was actually hiding the spies in her attic. Rahab is included in God's Hall of Faith in Hebrews 11, and though she is never directly commended for her lie, she is praised for her act of faith in providing a safe refuge for the spies. Clearly, part of providing that refuge was her deceiving the authorities who were after the spies.

One way to resolve dilemmas like this one is to recognize that God's laws are absolute, yet there are higher and lower laws, or a hierarchy within God's laws.[12] For example, the apostles were instructed to obey God's commands to preach the gospel over his command to be in submission to the state (Acts 4:13–20). Jesus makes reference to the "weightier matters of the law" (Matthew 23:23–24 KJV), a reference to the greater importance of justice, mercy, and compassion over the law of tithing. This hierarchical view attempts to combine the nature of God's commands, the reality of life in a fallen world, and a proper understanding of moral accountability. Thus, according this view, Corrie Ten Boom would have been morally justified in lying to protect the lives of the Jews she was protecting.

Not only do principles conflict at times, but in some cases, the principles—particularly those from a religious source—do not address the specific issue at hand. For example, even though the Bible has much to say about wealth and possessions, it is silent on many of the issues of business ethics debated today. In fact, it is unreasonable to expect that the Bible would directly address complex issues such as insider trading, mergers and acquisitions, and consumer safety, since these are relatively new issues, far removed from the sociological world of biblical times. When faced with an issue that the Scripture does not address or at least does not address as clearly as we would like, we must appeal to other considerations—such as consequences—to resolve the issue. Although the principles undergirding most deontological morality cover a good bit of ground, there are times when they do not apply or they are so general that good people disagree on how they should be applied to the issue under discussion.

Virtue Theory

As we previously noted, virtue approaches to ethics have been strangely absent from today's public discussion over moral issues. However, the consideration of character in ethics has made a resurgence of late. There has been a host of academic publications on the topic, and best-selling books such as *Seven Habits of Highly Effective*

[12]For further discussion of this, see Norman L. Geisler, *Christian Ethics* (Grand Rapids: Baker, 1989), 86–110.

People and *Principle Centered Leadership* by Steven R. Covey and *The Book of Virtues* by William J. Bennett are evidence that the approach is making a comeback in popular circles as well. As the comments offered by Participant #6 indicate, the virtue approach greatly differs from the other methods.

All of the normative theories examined to this point are action-oriented ethical systems. Every participant in the chamber of commerce discussion with the exception of the last participant uses one of these methods. Most ethical theories in modern times have focused on doing the right action, or making the right decision, when confronted by a moral dilemma. Many of the major debates in ethics have revolved around the basis for determining what is the right action, whether consequences or principles provide that basis and whether the right action is universal or relative. The proponent of virtue theory (also called *aretaic ethics*, from the Greek term for virtue, *arete*) holds that there is more to morality than simply doing the right thing. The foundational moral claims made by the virtue theorist concern the character of the moral agent (the person doing the action) rather than an exclusive focus on the act that the agent performs.

The tradition of virtue theory is a long one, going back to Plato and Aristotle, and includes the Gospels, the Stoics and Epicureans, and Thomas Aquinas. One of the unfortunate casualties of the collapse of the medieval worldview during the Renaissance and Enlightenment was Thomas's emphasis on Aristotelian virtue theory.

Some virtue theorists hold that virtue theory can stand alone as an adequate system of ethics. Others hold that virtues and moral rules, or principles, need each other, although how exactly they fit together is a point of debate. For the Christian with both natural law and divine commands, it is hard to see how one could not embrace some sort of deontological ethics. But it is equally hard to see how the Christian could ignore virtue ethics in favor of act-based ethics, given the high place in the New Testament to our developing the character of Christ, which would seem to be prior to doing the right thing. It may be that virtues are logically prior to principles in that the virtues emerge from God's character and that moral rules and principles then are those that are consistent with the outworking of God's virtue.

Some of the main differences between virtue ethics and standard act-oriented ethics include an emphasis on being over doing, an emphasis on who a person should become over what a person should do, the importance of following exemplary people over following moral rules, an emphasis on a person's motive and attitude over action, and a stress on developing character over obeying rules. Virtue theory is an ethics of character, not duty. These emphases are certainly consistent with the biblical emphasis on sanctification as being growth in Christlikeness, or emulating the character of Christ, and avoidance of dry legalism, wherein a person is simply going through the motions spiritually without much growth in Christlikeness. There is more consensus that act-oriented systems are not adequate to produce moral people—not to mention spiritually mature people—and that they need to be supplemented by at least some component of virtue theory. Given the biblical emphasis, it would appear that action-oriented ethics by itself gives a person an overly narrow view of the moral life.

Most of these ethical systems are still widely in use in the contemporary culture. As you read and hear different pressing moral issues being debated in public, be sure to watch for which of these styles of moral reasoning are used.

A JUDEO-CHRISTIAN APPROACH TO BUSINESS ETHICS

With such a wide variety of approaches, it is easy to see why there continues to be much disagreement over ethical issues in our contemporary culture. Amid such confusion, relativism can easily become an attractive option. Consequently, here in the last section of this introduction we will broach a Judeo-Christian framework with which to evaluate moral issues in general, with specific application to ethical issues involving business and the economy.

The shortcomings of each of the systems discussed above (with the exception of virtue theory) illustrate the need for moral reasoning based on a word from God, either general revelation or natural law, or special revelation in the Scriptures. The Bible does employ different types of moral reasoning from time to time, but nowhere does it suggest that any of the systems mentioned in this chapter are all-sufficient. The biblical emphasis seems to be strongly deontological (a blend of divine commands, natural law, and virtues), with periodic use of egoism and utilitarianism when appropriate. Furthermore, as mentioned earlier, Scripture also places a strong emphasis on moral character. Thus, the Bible seems to support a total approach to ethics that is based on moral principles that are guided by character traits such as prudence and courage in their application.

Solid moral character is essential to business ethics for several reasons that are highlighted by the fact that many of the most egregious scandals in recent years have involved participants who graduated from some of the country's elite schools and who certainly knew right from wrong. For example, whether one wants to call his character flaw greed or pride, Michael Milken was earning more than $350 million a year before he was tried and convicted of cheating through insider trading. There is no question of Milken's intelligence—he was a financial genius who graduated from a top Ivy League school and went on to become the country's most powerful investment banker. Milken was also certainly aware that his actions were wrong as he engaged in numerous actions to cover up his transgressions. This proves that ethics, then, is not just a matter of knowing right from wrong through moral reason, but also involves the effects of one's character on one's actions.

By contrast, profiles of the life of Aaron Feuerstein, the man whom we cited earlier for his moral heroism in his decision to rebuild Malden Mills, indicate that this was no isolated episode of generosity, nor was it done for public relations purposes. Many of Feuerstein's employees testified in newspaper accounts that kindness has long been a part of his persona. Like a well-trained and disciplined athlete responding to physical action on the field, it seems right that for Aaron Feuerstein, praiseworthy actions on the moral plane are a natural outflow of his character. Popular author Steven R. Covey likens this natural outflow to the physical laws that govern a farm: Just as we cannot expect to harvest crops after neglecting plowing, planting, and watering, we cannot expect to respond correctly to situations if they have not formed correct habits of character through discipline and training.[13]

Capitalism is a system that requires, in addition to character for producing good actions, virtues such as trust, honesty, and cooperation for its very functioning. Consequently, the foundations of capitalism may be doomed without the character necessary to exercise self-restraint on the part of the participants. Indeed, the founders of the United States believed that the democratic experiment would work only if there was virtue in the citizens. Contrary to popular belief, total liberty was never the founding fathers' intent. Rather, their vision was one of "ordered" or "restrained" liberty—that is, freedom tempered by morals and character.[14]

The alarming direction of many recent trends and their impact on society reveals the truthfulness of what the founding fathers envisioned. Because business in a free-enterprise system is a cornerstone of democracy, we should all be worried about the future of the free-market economy if virtue isn't once again taken seriously in the public dialogue about morality.

However, as we discussed earlier, simple admonitions to virtues such as integrity without the use of reason can lead to some uneasy scenarios of a blind obedience. It has been said that "reason without

[13]Steven R. Covey. *Principle Centered Leadership* (New York: Simon & Schuster, 1990). For more detailed discussions of character development and Christian living, see Dallas Willard, *The Spirit of the Disciplines* (San Francisco: HarperCollins, 1988), and Richard J. Foster, *The Challenge of the Disciplined Life* (San Francisco: Harper & Row, 1985).

[14]See Michael Novak, *This Hemisphere of Liberty* (Washington, D.C.: AEI Press, 1992), chap. 2, for a more detailed discussion about the role of "ordered liberty" in the economy.

virtue is powerless, while virtue without reason is blind."[15] Thus, there is clearly a need for *both* reason and virtue in a comprehensive approach to ethics.

[15]Adapted from William Frankena, *Ethics*, 2d ed. (New York: Prentice-Hall, 1973), 65.

Career or Calling?

Besides an emphasis on reason and character, the Judeo-Christian tradition has also uniquely relied on the concept of "calling" with which to view one's work. Contrary to contemporary uses of the term, it is not only ministers and missionaries who are called to their professions. As the Protestant Reformers envisioned it, all Christians have a calling, even those who are led to embrace "secular" positions. In fact, the Reformers made clear that many have a calling to serve God in "mundane," or worldly, professions because all of creation, not just what we have falsely segregated into the "spiritual realm," plays a central role in God's ongoing drama of redemption.

The concept of a calling has serious implications for the motives with which we as Christians are to approach our work and has direct application to many of the issues that we will discuss in this book. In *Habits of the Heart*, Robert Bellah offers a useful and important distinction between calling and career. Whereas the concept of "career" focuses more on external rewards and measurements of success such as advancement, prestige, and social standing, "calling" is radically different. Bellah writes:

> In the strongest sense of a "calling," work constitutes a practical ideal of activity and character that makes a person's work morally inseparable from his or her life. . . . activity has meaning in itself, not just the output or profit that results from it. . . . A calling links a person to a larger community, a whole in which the calling is a contribution to the good of all. . . . When the trajectory of a career flattens out, and it becomes clear that one will not, after all, make it to the top, then making it loses its meaning—as opposed to continuing in a calling and practicing law, carpentry, or scholarship as best one can, even if one cannot be the best.[16]

[16]Robert Bellah, *Habits of the Heart* (Berkeley: University of California Press, 1985), 66–69. See also Alisdair MacIntyre, *After Virtue* (South Bend, Ind.: University of Notre Dame Press, 1991), chap. 10.

As we can see, an approach to work as a calling is quite different from our contemporary fixation on the concept of a career. The distinction is critical to the Christian life, yet it goes alarmingly unrecognized or unpracticed, even among those whose work is exclusively—and wrongfully—viewed as a calling: ministers of the gospel. One insightful student remarked that if ministers truly approach their work as a calling and not a career, why are they almost always "called" to higher positions or to minister to larger congregations? Indeed, even the clergy often give in to the external measures of success that are central to a *career*-oriented approach to work. And who can blame them? From the time we are children, we are inundated by inquiries from our parents, relatives, and teachers about our future *career* plans. Moreover, the educational system has career centers that conduct career workshops and offer career counseling.

In contrast to a career-oriented approach, people who view their work as a calling will focus more on the intrinsic nature of the work as a means to glorify God rather than to reap external rewards. Rather than defining success as climbing a corporate ladder or accumulating material things, they will measure it by how true they stay to the story to which God has called them. As Bellah has stated, since calling implies service rather than material gain or prestige, work will still have tremendous meaning even if we cannot be the best at our tasks.

The critical distinction between calling and career has many direct points of relevance for business ethics. For one, it will directly affect one's profession. A career in the Mafia or a job pulling off ingenious heists is clearly ruled out. And since calling implies service to God and the community that he has created, it demands that we approach our work with the motive of directly contributing to God's kingdom. While those called to serve in business can glorify God through earning money and using it wisely or through evangelism in the workplace, they must approach their work tasks with the primary goal of service to God's kingdom in mind. Thus, rather than focusing solely on maxmizing profits, Christian business people—especially leaders—should see their work as a means to contribute to quality workplaces and improve their surrounding communities.

The service inherent in one's calling further implies that value should be added to each business transaction. It is hard to see how service results from zero-sum situations in which there is a clear loser in the transaction. If we gain in a transaction, it should be because we have added value and each party has clearly benefited. Moreover, our work must add true value and not dubious social value, as there are many ingenious ways to earn money that contribute nothing at all worthwhile to society. Many examples of such practices will be discussed in this book.

Moreover, the idea of calling does not merely contribute another angle to an approach to ethics that emphasizes both reason and character. Indeed, it undergirds them on a broader level. Approaching work as a calling adds unique obligations to Christians in the workplace because this attitude entails that the principle of service is foundational to all that is done. In addition, it speaks to one's character because service must be accomplished with the right motives. As you read through the various essays and cases in this book, attempt to place yourself in the situations that are described; then, taking into account the various methods of ethical reasoning we have described, ask yourself whether certain courses of action can be consistent with one's calling. The answers to these questions provide the "oughts" by which we should act and think in the world of commerce, and they provide the direction toward which we should develop our character in cooperation with the miraculous work of grace.

FOR FURTHER READING

Frankena, William. *Ethics*. 2d ed. New York: Prentice-Hall, 1973.

Holmes, Arthur. *Ethics: Approaching Moral Decisions*. Downers Grove, Ill.: Intervarsity Press, 1984.

Pojman, Louis P. *Ethics: Discovering Right and Wrong*. Belmont, Calif.: Wadsworth, 1990.

Rachels, James. *The Elements of Moral Philosophy*. Phildelphia, Pa.: Temple University Press, 1986.

Rae, Scott. B., *Moral Choices: An Introduction to Ethics*. Grand Rapids: Zondervan, 1995.

Part I

Christians, Markets, and Postmodern Morality

ONE

The Ethics of Business Culture

A sudden submission to Christian ethics by businessmen would bring about the greatest economic upheaval in history!

A chief executive officer, quoted in "Is Business Bluffing Ethical?"
by Albert Z. Carr

Integrity pays! You don't have to cheat to win!

Kenneth Blanchard and Norman Vincent Peale,
The Power of Ethical Management

INTRODUCTION

Several scandals that have recently surfaced portray the business world as a murky realm with a unique set of moral rules that often differ from the standards that govern other arenas of life. For example, Teledyne, Inc., recently acknowledged guilt and subsequently paid millions of dollars in fines for its role in selling weapons technology to Iran despite a government prohibition against supplying defense secrets to a potentially hostile enemy. What is notable about this case is that there is no probable reason to doubt that the Teledyne employees involved in these transgressions are anything less than loyal citizens in their "private lives." Yet when a profit of millions of dollars was at stake, they were willing to compartmentalize their values and engage in behavior that most would consider grossly immoral.

It indeed appears that many business people live with two conflicting sets of rules: one for business and one for their individual lives. In fact, when many alleged wrongdoings in the corporate world are brought to light, a common defense on the part of the perpetrators is explaining that they were simply playing by the unspoken rules of the game, rules that all interested parties were aware of and to which they readily and freely adhered.

More troubling, however, is the further claim made by some that unless one is willing to deliberately leave private morals at the door and play by the rules of the game, one will not be very successful in business. This notion is particularly problematic for those who adhere to a belief system that holds that a unified set of values should be applicable to life in its totality. Many are disturbed by the idea that the very virtues that govern their lives outside of work could be the ones that jeopardize their ability to succeed within it. Moreover, if the above claim is true, we are led to the inevitable conclusion that all who have achieved success in business from a financial standpoint have somehow compromised their moral standards on the path to success. On the surface, at least, it seems that in many instances when morality and the potential for profit meet, there is an uneasy tension between Christian standards of conduct and the norms of business behavior.

In response to this uneasiness, commentators such as Kenneth Blanchard and Norman Vincent Peale have popularized the notion that good ethics *is* good business in the sense of long-term profits.[1] After all, it is claimed, a reputation for honesty and fairness will only enhance a business because it will attract customers through word of mouth. Thus ethics and profits do not clash at all. It is only the prospect of short-term profits that may have to be sacrificed at the altar of morality.

In this chapter we will examine the scope and nature of this conflict and how Christians have attempted to reconcile it. In particular, we will be asking if one can adhere to traditional virtues such as honesty, trustworthiness, and honor and still participate successfully in business or if one has to jettison his or her moral ideals in order to do so. We will also inquire into the truthfulness of the recently popularized notion that honesty makes for good business from a financial perspective. Through the years, numerous authors have addressed these questions by contributing some provocative insights into the morals of the culture of business. Several of these works are included in this chapter. The cases that are included present this dilemma in real-world situations.

Albert Z. Carr's classic article "Is Business Bluffing Ethical?" takes the posture that having two sets of morals, one for business and one for private life, is an inescapable reality of working in our economy. Using the game of poker as an analogy to business, Carr argues that business should be judged by its own set of morals and not by "the ethical principles preached in churches." Since all who sit at a poker table are aware that bluffing is a part of the game, bluffing ceases to be deception and thus should be judged in its own context. Likewise,

[1] Kenneth Blanchard and Norman Vincent Peale, *The Power of Ethical Management* (New York: Wm. Morrow, 1988).

he argues, business is a game that also operates with rules of its own. Consequently, it too should not be held to the moral standards that govern other parts of life. In fact, Carr concludes that those who try to apply their private morals at the workplace will likely fail to attain much success at all.

Norman Bowie's "Does It Pay to Bluff in Business?" offers insightful criticism into some of Carr's key assumptions. He agrees that "bluffing" is frequently practiced in business and that it does not always constitute deception. In some well-defined instances, such as car sales and labor negotiations, all of the reasonable participants are aware of the operative rules. Thus one does not need to compromise on the principle of truthfulness in order to participate. However, in sharp disagreement with Carr, he asserts that business is not analogous to poker because there are clear examples of practices in which some people get hurt because they are not (and cannot reasonably be expected to be) privy to the unspoken norms of conduct.

Amar Bhide and Howard H. Stevenson address the popular notion that good ethics is good business in their article entitled "Why Be Honest If Honesty Doesn't Pay?" They argue that people are trustworthy in the business world because they want to be, not because it pays. While it has been popular to equate ethics with good business, Bhide and Stevenson argue that while the notion that "honesty is the best policy for economic gain" makes intuitive sense, it is an unsubstantiated claim. In their research, they have found that in many cases breaking one's word is actually handsomely rewarded or at the very least seldom punished. Even so, they argue that the trust necessary for business relationships is alive and well because for many business people, honesty is a matter of conscience and morality rather than strategy.

Louke van Wensveen Siker offers an insightful typology of how Christians have attempted to reconcile the moral demands of their faith with business in *Christ and Business: A Typology for Christian Business Ethics.* Corollary to the varying perspectives taken by the other authors in this chapter, van Wensveen Siker illustrates how Christian thinkers have also approached the problem from a continuum of viewpoints. This has ranged from the rejection of the total enterprise of business to a belief that there is no fundamental contradiction between the demands of their faith and those of business. As you read this essay, you may find it helpful to try to place the other authors in this chapter in van Wensveen Siker's typology.

READINGS

Christ and Business: A Typology for Christian Business Ethics

Louke van Wensveen Siker

Journal of Business Ethics 8 (1989): 883–88. Copyright © 1989 Kluwer Academic Publishers.

Introduction

As the field of business ethics is becoming more defined, the sub-discipline of Christian business ethics is taking on a multi-faceted shape. In this paper I shall take stock of the variety of ways in which Christian business ethicists currently conceive of ethical change in business. In order to do so, one needs an appropriate set of organizing categories. Simply adopting the traditional categories used by applied philosophers to organize the field—utilitarian, Kantian, etc.—will not do, for Christian ethicists rarely structure their work along these lines. Rather, I shall show that traditional theological categories can go a long way in helping one appreciate the scope and variety of Christian business ethics as a relatively new area of inquiry. The categories I have chosen are inspired by the typology set forth in H. Richard Niebuhr's classic study, *Christ and Culture.*[1]

The Typology

Before I proceed, let me briefly call to mind the main features of Niebuhr's typology. The book *Christ and Culture* explores how Christians over the centuries have dealt with what Niebuhr calls "the enduring problem of the relation between the authorities of Christ and culture."[2] Niebuhr discerns a pattern of recurring answers to this problem, which he proceeds to organize in the form of five types. First he presents the most extreme answers. Here one finds the views of radical Christians, who stress the presence of evil in culture to such a degree that they can see Christ only in opposition to it ("Christ Against Culture").

At the opposite end of the spectrum one finds the position of cultural Christians, who see no basic contradiction between the demands of culture and the demands of Christ ("The Christ of Culture"). Between these extremes, Niebuhr locates three other typical positions. So-called synthesist Christians tend to establish a hierarchy in which the authority of culture is affirmed, yet also superseded by the authority of Christ ("Christ Above Culture"). Dualist Christians struggle with the ambivalence created by seeing culture as both fallen and preserved by God ("Christ and Culture in Paradox"). Finally, conversionist Christians tend to affirm culture insofar as it is the arena of Christ's transforming work ("Christ the Transformer of Culture").

Niebuhr's typology is well suited to serve as a heuristic device for understanding the rich variety inherent in the work of Christian business ethicists. Its focus, the relation between the authorities of Christ and culture, must naturally also be a main theme in an area of inquiry characterized as both Christian and concerned with business. In fact, for the purposes of this study, Niebuhr's five types can simply be narrowed down into the following subset: Christ Against Business, the Christ of Business, Christ Above Business, Christ and Business in Paradox, and Christ the Transformer of Business. In each case, "Business" refers to the prevailing capitalist business culture. These categories will provide a uniquely theological way of identifying various approaches in Christian business ethics. While the categories used by applied philosophers reflect different foundations of moral authority, an adaptation of Niebuhr's typology will show various ways in which *one* ultimate moral authority, Christ, is thought to relate to an area of life that also claims human loyalty, business. In other words, these categories will highlight a range of beliefs about the ramifications of Christ's work and being for the possibility and dynamics of ethical change in business.

As we shall see, each of Niebuhr's five types is indeed clearly represented among Christians reflecting on ethics in business. This is not to say, however, that any one approach exactly fits a particular type. As Niebuhr observes, "when one returns from the hypothetical scheme to the rich complexity of individual events, it is evident at once that no person or group ever conforms completely to a type."[3] Yet to the extent that the typology can provide a rough background against which various approaches may be grouped (and exceptions noted!), it will serve a useful purpose. Given this qualification, I will now proceed to show what a Niebuhrian typology of Christian business ethics might look like.

Type I: Christ Against Business—Pietism

At some point in time, every Christian business ethicist is likely to encounter the skepticism or even opposition of those among the faithful who assume that the business world can never be salvaged from its corruption. The arguments sound familiar, all variations on the theme, "Business ethics, isn't that an oxymoron?" Niebuhr himself points to an early proponent of this attitude, the church father Tertullian, who argued that trade "is scarcely 'adapted for a servant of God,' for apart from covetousness, which is a species of idolatry, there is no real motive for acquiring."[4]

The skepticism of the radical Christian about ethical change in business seems to be a permanent motif among the various ways of relating Christ and business, akin to the attitude Niebuhr has described with his "Christ Against Culture" type. Theologically speaking, such skepticism is rooted in the assumption that the current business culture must be marked off as a realm of evil and idolatry, a realm that must be destroyed, rather than changed. As a Christian, one must dissociate oneself as much as possible from the corruption of

the business world, while focusing on the new order established by Christ. A modern example of such radical skepticism about ethical change in business can be found in the writings of Franz Hinkelammert, a Marxist theologian who has been working in Costa Rica. Hinkelammert describes a capitalist business world marked by idolatry, where commodities and corporations are treated as independent agents, requiring the total subjection of all business people. He concludes that Christians confessing faith in God clearly have no choice but to repudiate this realm of idolatry.[5]

Overall, it is fair to say that the "Christ Against Business" type forms the anti-type of any method in Christian business ethics. It denies the validity of the discipline, because it denies the legitimacy of anything resembling the prevailing form of business enterprise.

Type II: The Christ of Business—Christ Subsumed by Business

In a scene from *The Power of Ethical Management* by Kenneth Blanchard and Norman Vincent Peale, a minister says to a bewildered businessman, "When you have patience, you realize that if you do what is right—even if it costs you in the short run—it will pay off in the long run."[6] The minister also explains that having patience means trusting in the timing of a higher power, which could be called God. If you do that, things will always work out. This scene epitomizes the assumption that God's aims and the aims of business are essentially in harmony. While the business world may still contain a fair share of corruption, the argument goes, in essence it bears the stamp of goodness. Overcoming the corruption is not only possible, but also relatively easy. After all, most business people have good intentions and basically know right from wrong. They only need some guidance in making concrete moral decisions. Business ethicists, in the role of consultants, can provide such guidance and thus facilitate ethical change. This familiar approach to business ethics can be classified as the "Christ of Business" type.

Niebuhr's observations regarding cultural Christians help to highlight further the features of the "Christ of Business" type. Niebuhr notes, for example, that "the cultural Christians tend to address themselves to the leading groups in a society."[7] Similarly, the "Christ of Business" approach involves targeting mainly top-level managers as the agents of ethical change. Niebuhr notes also that cultural Christians use the language of these sophisticated circles. Similarly, Christian business ethicists often swap theological categories for a mixture of generally accepted ethical terms and the straight business talk of the corporations they consult. A most notable example of this kind of adaptation is the catch phrase "good ethics means good business." Finally, Niebuhr notes that, in their zeal to recommend Christ to the cultured, cultural Christians "want to make discipleship easy."[8] Similarly, the "Christ of Business" approach makes ethics look simple and attractive, a matter of positive thinking, a message that sells at a two-day management retreat. All in all, Niebuhr's "Christ of Culture" type helps us to understand how the specific features of this widely practiced approach to business ethics flow from the basic assumption that Christ and business are essentially aligned.

Type III: Christ Above Business—Christ Subsumes Business

Niebuhr's third type, "Christ Above Culture," helps us gain perspective on a somewhat less optimistic, yet even more widespread Christian approach to business ethics. The so-called synthetic type is based on the largely Thomistic assumption that ethical change resembles step-for-step elevation to a higher level of existence, a process guided by the rational discernment and application of natural law and, ultimately, divine law. In Christian business ethics, this assumption finds expression in the method of applying general norms to specific situations by means of careful, deductive reasoning. The general norms, such as human dignity, justice, and co-creation, are thought to have universal moral authority. They provide the unequivocal basis for the field of business ethics. The main task of the discipline is to guide the transformation of business according to these ultimate foundations, usually by means of rationally developed medial norms, such as subsidiarity and proportionality. A

perfect example of this approach can be found in an essay by Theodore V. Purcell, S.J., entitled "Management Development: A Practical Ethical Method and a Case."[9]

In sum, unlike the radical Christians, synthesist business ethicists do not assume that the modern business world needs to be destroyed. After all, it is still part of the created order. Nor, on the other hand, do they follow the cultural Christians in believing that business already carries the full potential of goodness within its own laws. Rather, they assume that business life needs to be elevated by means of authoritative, external guidelines. This may not be an easy task. For example, as Thomas McMahon has asked, how does one apply the justice-based concept of a family living wage in a business world guided by the notion of compensation based on comparable worth?[10] Yet despite such difficulties, adherents of the synthesist view of transformation believe that with thorough and imaginative reasoning, it is possible to find authoritative direction.

Type IV: Christ the Transformer of Business

Niebuhr's fifth type, the conversionist approach to the problem of Christ and culture, is marked by nuances rather than tensions. It expresses awareness of the perversion of culture, combined with affirmation of culture as the arena of God's transforming work. Conversionists see transformation as a process which begins with a conversion of the human spirit, and ends in action and social change. Given these inner-worldly possibilities of change, they believe, it is appropriate for Christians to focus more on positive practice than on negative action toward sin.

Conversionist business ethicists will combine awareness of serious evil in the business world with hope for actual, historical transformation of business life. In their attempts to seek out this transformation, they will try to work *with* business, rather than always *against* it. Also, they will take a holistic approach, paying attention to the spiritual as well as the material, the individual as well as the communal. Notions such as character, embodiment, and story may well appear in their work.

A good example of a conversionist approach can be found in Max Stackhouse's book *Public Theology and Political Economy*.[11] In chapter 7, entitled "Spirituality and the Corporation," Stackhouse argues:

> the ideal of social democracy borne by the ecumenical church ... must, without extensive political [sic], economic, or technological power, develop a new spirituality, based on a public theology, to transform the materialist and reductionist preoccupation of all present economic forms and ideologies. This is possible because already within the modern corporation are residual ecclesiological elements wherein spiritual matters are intrinsically related to social ones, and therefore are potentially related to new patterns of material and organizational embodiment.[12]

This brief passage captures the main features of the conversionist type in almost a textbook manner, showing both concern for economic distortions and hope for a spirit-based, yet fully historical transformation.

Type V: Christ and Business in Paradox

"Christ and culture stand in a relation of paradox," observes Robert S. Bachelder, a congregational pastor. As a result,

> executives should expect that their general and personal callings will exist in tension. But this tension need not create defeatism and cynicism. It can give rise to alertness and moral imagination. What executives must do is accept the moral ambiguities of their companies and yet fully participate in them, trusting all the while in God to open the way to new moral possibilities.[13]

Niebuhr's "Christ and Culture in Paradox" type could not have been more adequately expressed in relation to a business context. And, as we shall see, Bachelder is not the only one to perceive ethical change in business as a matter of tension and paradox. Once again, we are dealing with a distinctive motif in Christian business ethics.

In describing the paradox type, Niebuhr observes that dualist Christians are highly sensitive to the fallenness of culture. Yet at the same time they feel called to participate in culture. After all, God continues to sustain the world in its sin, so to escape it would mean to counter God's plan. Living with this tension between judgment and participation, dualist Christians tend to have only limited expectations of social transformation. The sins of this world can be kept in check through laws and countervailing force, yet the Kingdom of God is not of this world. Meanwhile, God's grace does work transformation in individuals. Yet even forgiven sinners are left to juggle the imperfect options of social life, being always forced again to "sin boldly" with no positive rules to guide their actions.

In a business context, one finds this type expressed in various ways. One manifestation, at a social level, is the activist attempt to channel the power of big business by means of external pressure, such as strikes, boycotts, shareholder resolutions, publicity, and legislation. I am thinking, for example, of the work of the Interfaith Council on Corporate Responsibility under the direction of Tim Smith. At a personal level, one recognizes the type when business ethicists, like Robert Bachelder, stress the necessity to live with compromise and ambiguity, and the need to use one's best personal judgment in the absence of clear-cut rules. My favorite example along these lines comes actually not from a business ethicist, but from Dietrich Bonhoeffer, who observes in his *Ethics* that in extreme situations, one may sometimes have to opt for "the destruction of human livelihoods in the interest of the necessities of business."[14]

All in all, dualist business ethicists are likely to speak the realistic language of power struggles and necessary compromises. Yet with all the stress on freedom of judgment and the absence of fixed rules, this realism can just as easily express itself in liberal as in conservative recommendations (witness the examples mentioned above!). Thus dualist business ethicists are not likely to excel in predictability. But then, of course, their strength lies in providing a witness to the courage and freedom found in a living faith.

Evaluation

...Now let me turn to the pay-off for Christian business ethics. Most obviously, Niebuhr's typology could assist Christian business ethicists in their efforts at maintaining methodological self-awareness in a new area of inquiry. Taken one step further, Niebuhr's typology could also provide fresh opportunities for approaching the work of colleagues in the field. After all, the nuances of the various types prevent the kind of black-and-white vision that does not do justice to the work of another. For example, one is less liable to lump together dualists with the radical approach, or conversionists with the cultural approach, to mention some common errors. On that basis, the typology may even become the occasion for an open discussion on the relative adequacy of each approach....

This leads to my final observation. Niebuhr's typology may ultimately challenge Christian business ethicists to investigate how their methods may be complementary. Niebuhr himself carefully avoided designating any one of his types as the most authoritative answer to the enduring problem of the relation between Christ and culture.[15] He advocated what we might nowadays call a reflective equilibrium approach, arguing that each type contributes something indispensable and yet insufficient in itself. Thus the radical Christian reminds one of the force of Christ's authority, the cultural Christian shows how the gospel can be brought to leading groups in society, the synthesist reminds one that salvation affirms creation, the dualist adds a healthy dose of suspicion and realism, and the conversionist calls one to positive, confessional action. In a similar vein, the various theological approaches to seeking ethical change in business may well complement each other in unexpected ways. In that case, we should be listening carefully to Norman Vincent Peale as well as to Tim Smith!

Notes

[1]H. Richard Niebuhr, *Christ and Culture* (Harper & Row, New York, 1951).

[2]*Christ and Culture*, 11. Niebuhr's statement of the problem can be criticized for implying that Christ and human life may potentially be conceived of apart from culture. Yet, as Charles Scriven argues in his recent study, *The Transformation of Culture* (Herald Press, Scotsdale, PA, 1988), Niebuhr generally seems to refer to the authority of the *prevailing* culture. Given this understanding, statements concerning Christ's opposition to culture, or Christian withdrawal from culture, make more sense.

[3]*Christ and Culture*, 43–44.

[4]*Ibid.*, 54. Citation from Tertullian, *On Idolatry*, xi.

[5]Franz Hinkelammert, "The Economic Roots of Idolatry: Entrepreneurial Metaphysics," in *The Idols of Death and the God of Life: A Theology*, ed., Pablo Richard et al. (Orbis Books, Maryknoll, NY, 1983), 165–93.

[6]Kenneth Blanchard and Norman Vincent Peale, *The Power of Ethical Management* (William Morrow, New York, 1988), 60.

[7]*Christ and Culture*, 104.

[8]*Ibid.*, 126.

[9]Theodore V. Purcell, S.J., "Management Development: A Practical Ethical Method and a Case," in *Doing Ethics in Business*, ed. Donald G. Jones (Oelgeschlager, Gunn & Hain, Cambridge, MA, 1982), 187–202.

[10]Thomas F. McMahon, "The Contributions of Religious Traditions to Business Ethics," *Journal of Business Ethics* 4 (1985): 344.

[11]Max L. Stackhouse, *Public Theology and Political Economy: Christian Stewardship in Modern Society* (Eerdmans, Grand Rapids, 1987).

[12]*Ibid.*, 131. In this passage Stackhouse uses dialectical language to throw a different light on an earlier developed argument. Overall, his argument does not depend on a dialectical reading of history.

[13]Robert S. Bachelder, "Ministry to Managers," *The Christian Ministry* 15 (September 1984): 14.

[14]Dietrich Bonhoeffer, *Ethics* (Macmillan, New York, 1955), 239.

[15]Yet, personally Niebuhr seems to prefer the conversionist type. See, for example, Paul Ramsey, *Nine Modern Moralists* (Prentice-Hall, Englewood Cliffs, N.J., 1962), 149–79.

Is Business Bluffing Ethical?

Albert Z. Carr

Harvard Business Review (January–February 1968). Copyright © 1967.

The ethics of business are not those of society, but rather those of the poker game.

Foreword

"When the law as written gives a man a wide-open chance to make a killing, he'd be a fool not to take advantage of it. If he doesn't, somebody else will," remarked a friend of the author. Mr. Carr likens such behavior to the bluffing of the poker player who seizes every opportunity to win, as long as it does not involve outright cheating. "No one thinks any the worse of you on that account," says the author. "And no one would think any the worse of the game of business because its standards of right and wrong differ from the prevailing traditions of morality in our society."

Mr. Carr became interested in this subject when he was a member of a New York firm of consultants to large corporations in many fields. The confidences of many stress-ridden executives made him aware of the extent to which tensions can arise from conflicts between an individual's ethical sense and the realities of business. He was struck also by the similarity of the special ethical attitude shown by many successful and stress-free businessmen in their work to that of good poker players.

Mr. Carr was Assistant to the Chairman of the War Production Board during World War II and later served on the White House staff and as a Special Consultant to President Truman. He is now writing full-time. Among his books is *John D. Rockefeller's Secret Weapon*, a study of corporate development. This article is adapted from a chapter in his newest book, *Business As a Game*, to be published by New American Library in March 1968.

A respected businessman with whom I discussed the theme of this article remarked with some heat, "You mean to say you're going to encourage men to bluff? Why, bluffing is nothing more than a form of lying! You're advising them to lie!"

I agreed that the basis of private morality is respect for truth and that the closer a businessman comes to the truth, the more he deserves respect. At the same time, I suggested that most bluffing in business might be regarded simply a game strategy—much like bluffing in poker, which does not reflect on the morality of the bluffer.

I quoted Henry Taylor, the British statesman who pointed out that "falsehood ceases to be falsehood when it is understood on all sides that the truth is not expected to be spoken"—an exact description of bluffing in poker, diplomacy, and business. I cited the analogy of the criminal court, where the criminal is not expected to tell the truth when he pleads "not guilty." Everyone from the judge down takes it for granted that the job of the defendant's attorney is to get his client off, not to reveal the truth; and this is considered ethical practice. I mentioned Representative Omar Burleson, the Democrat from Texas, who was quoted as saying, in regard to the ethics of Congress, "Ethics is a barrel of worms"[1]—a pungent summing up of the problem of deciding who is ethical in politics.

I reminded my friend that millions of businessmen feel constrained every day to say *yes* to their bosses when they secretly believe *no* and that this is generally accepted as permissible strategy when the alternative might be the loss of a job. The essential point, I said, is that the ethics of business are game ethics, different from the ethics of religion.

He remained unconvinced. Referring to the company of which he is president, he declared: "Maybe that's good enough for some businessmen, but I can tell you that we pride ourselves on our ethics. In 30 years not one customer has ever questioned my word or asked to check our figures. We're loyal to our customers and fair to our suppliers. I regard my handshake on a deal as a contract. I've never entered into price-fixing schemes with my competitors. I've never allowed my salesmen to spread injurious rumors about other companies. Our union contract is the best in our industry. And, if I do say so myself, our ethical standards are of the highest!"

He really was saying, without realizing it, that he was living up to the ethical standards of the business game—which are a far cry from those of private life. Like a gentlemanly poker player, he did not play in cahoots with others at the table, try to smear their reputations, or hold back chips he owed them.

But this same fine man, at that very time, was allowing one of his products to be advertised in a way that made it sound a great deal better than it actually was. Another item in his product line was notorious among dealers for its "built-in obsolescence." He was holding back from the market a much-improved product because he did not want it to interfere with sales of the inferior item it would have replaced. He had joined with certain of his competitors in hiring a lobbyist to push a state legislature, by methods that he preferred not to know to much about, into amending a bill then being enacted.

In his view these things had nothing to do with ethics; they were merely normal business practice. He himself undoubtedly avoided outright falsehoods—never lied in so many words. But the entire organization that he ruled was deeply involved in numerous strategies of deception.

Pressure to Deceive

Most executives from time to time are almost compelled, in the interests of their companies or themselves, to practice some form of deception when negotiating with customers, dealers, labor unions, government officials, or even other departments of their companies. By conscious misstatements, concealment of pertinent facts, or exaggeration—in short, by bluffing—they seek to persuade others to agree with them. I think it is

fair to say that if the individual executive refuses to bluff from time to time—if he feels obligated to tell the truth, the whole truth, and nothing but the truth—he is ignoring opportunities permitted under the rules and is at a heavy disadvantage in his business dealings.

But here and there a businessman is unable to reconcile himself to the bluff in which he plays a part. His conscience, perhaps spurred by religious idealism, troubles him. He feels guilty; he may develop an ulcer or a nervous tic. Before any executive can make profitable use of the strategy of the bluff, he needs to make sure that in bluffing he will not lose self-respect or become emotionally disturbed. If he is to reconcile personal integrity and high standards of honesty with the practical requirements of business, he must feel that his bluffs are ethically justified. The justification rests on the fact that business, as practiced by individuals as well as by corporations, has the impersonal character of a game—a game that demands both special strategy and an understanding of its special ethics.

The game is played at all levels of corporate life, from the highest to the lowest. At the very instant that a man decides to enter business, he may be forced into a game situation, as is shown by the recent experience of a Cornell honor graduate who applied for a job with a large company:

This applicant was given a psychological test which included the statement, "Of the following magazines, check any that you have read either regularly or from time to time, and double-check those which interest you most. *Reader's Digest, Time, Fortune, Saturday Evening Post, The New Republic, Life, Look, Ramparts, Newsweek, Business Week, U.S. News & World Report, The Nation, Playboy, Esquire, Harper's Sports Illustrated.*"

His tastes in reading were broad, and at one time or another he had read almost all of these magazines. He was a subscriber to *The New Republic*, an enthusiast for *Ramparts*, and an avid student of the pictures in *Playboy*. He was not sure whether his interest in *Playboy* would be held against him, but he had a shrewd suspicion that if he confessed to an interest in *Ramparts* and *The New Republic*, he would be thought a liberal, a radical, or at least an intellectual, and his chances of getting the job, which he needed, would greatly diminish. He therefore checked some of the more conservative magazines. Apparently it was a sound decision, for he got the job.

He had made a game player's decision, consistent with business ethics.

A similar case is that of a magazine space salesman who, owing to a merger, suddenly found himself out of a job:

This man was 58, and, in spite of a good record, his chance of getting a job elsewhere in business where youth is favored in hiring practice was not good. He was a vigorous, healthy man, and only a considerable amount of gray to his hair suggested his age. Before beginning this job search he touched up his hair with a black dye to confine the gray to his temples. He knew that the truth about his age might well come out in time, but he calculated that he could deal with that situation when it arose. He and his wife decided that he could easily pass for 45, and he so stated his age on his résumé.

This was a lie; yet within the accepted rules of the business game, no moral culpability attaches to it.

The Poker Analogy

We can learn a good deal about the nature of business by comparing it with poker. While both have a large element of chance, in the long run the winner is the man who plays with steady skill. In both games ultimate victory requires intimate knowledge of the rules, insight into the psychology of the other players, a bold front, a considerable amount of self-discipline, and the ability to respond swiftly and effectively to opportunities provided by chance.

No one expects poker to be played on the ethical principles preached in churches. In poker it is right and proper to bluff a friend out of the rewards of being dealt a good hand. A player feels no more than a slight twinge of sympathy, if that, when—with nothing better than a single ace in his hand—he strips a heavy loser, who holds a pair, of the rest of his chips. It was up to the other

fellow to protect himself. In the words of an excellent poker player, former President Harry Truman, "If you can't stand the heat, stay out of the kitchen." If one shows mercy to a loser in poker, it is a personal gesture, divorced from the rules of the game.

Poker has its special ethics, and here I am not referring to rules against cheating. The man who keeps an ace up his sleeve or who marks the cards is more than unethical; he is a crook, and can be punished as such—kicked out of the game or, in the Old West, shot.

In contrast to the cheat, the unethical poker player is one who, while abiding by the letter of the rules, finds ways to put the other players at an unfair disadvantage. Perhaps he unnerves them with loud talk. Or he tries to get them drunk. Or he plays in cahoots with someone else at the table. Ethical poker players frown on such tactics.

Poker's own brand of ethics is different from the ethical ideals of civilized human relationships. The game calls for distrust of the other fellow. It ignores the claim of friendship. Cunning deception and concealment of one's strength and intentions, not kindness and open-heartedness, are vital in poker. No one thinks any the worse of poker on that account. And no one should think any the worse of the game of business because its standards of right and wrong differ from the prevailing traditions of morality in our society.

Discard the Golden Rule

This view of business is especially worrisome to people without much business experience. A minister of my acquaintance once protested that business cannot possibly function in our society unless it is based on the Judeo-Christian system of ethics. He told me:

I know some businessmen have supplied call girls to customers, but there are always a few rotten apples in every barrel. That doesn't mean the rest of the fruit isn't sound. Surely the vast majority of businessmen are ethical. I myself am acquainted with many who adhere to strict codes of ethics based fundamentally on religious teachings. They contribute to good causes. They participate in community activities. They cooperate with other companies to improve working conditions in their industries. Certainly they are not indifferent to ethics.

That most businessmen are not indifferent to ethics in their private lives, everyone will agree. My point is that in their office lives they cease to be private citizens; they become game players who must be guided by a somewhat different set of ethical standards.

The point was forcefully made to me by a Midwestern executive who has given a good deal of thought to the question:

"So long as a businessman complies with the laws of the land and avoids telling malicious lies, he's ethical. If the law as written gives a man a wide-open chance to make a killing, he'd be a fool not to take advantage of it. If he doesn't, somebody else will. There's no obligation on him to stop and consider who is going to get hurt. If the law says he can do it, that's all the justification he needs. There's nothing unethical about that. It's just plain business sense."

This executive (call him Robbins) took the stand that even industrial espionage, which is frowned on by some businessmen, ought not to be considered unethical. He recalled a recent meeting of the National Industrial Conference Board where an authority on marketing made a speech in which he deplored the employment of spies by business organizations. More and more companies, he pointed out, find it cheaper to penetrate the secrets of competitors with concealed cameras and microphones or by bribing employees than to set up costly research and design departments of their own. A whole branch of the electronics industry has grown up with this trend, he continued, providing equipment to make industrial espionage easier.

Disturbing? The marketing expert found it so. But when it came to a remedy, he could only appeal to "respect for the golden rule." Robbins thought this a confession of defeat, believing that the golden rule, for all its value as an ideal for soci-ety, is simply not feasible as a guide for business. A good part of the time the businessman is trying to do unto others as he hopes others will *not* do unto him.[2] Robbins continued:

"Espionage of one kind or another has become so common in business that it's like taking a drink during Prohibition—it's not considered sinful. And we don't even have Prohibition where espionage is concerned; the law is very tolerant in this area. There's no more shame for a business that uses secret agents than there is for a nation. Bear in mind that there already is at least one large corporation—you can buy its stock over the counter—that makes millions by providing counterespionage service to industrial firms. Espionage in business is not an ethical problem; it's an established technique of business competition."

"We Don't Make the Laws"

Wherever we turn in business, we can perceive the sharp distinction between its ethical standards and those of the churches. Newspapers abound with sensational stories growing out of these distinctions:

- We read one day that Senator Philip A. Hart of Michigan has attacked food processors for deceptive packaging of numerous products.[3]
- The next day there is a Congressional to-do over Ralph Nader's book, *Unsafe at Any Speed*, which demonstrates that automobile companies for years have neglected the safety of car-owning families.[4]
- Then another Senator, Lee Metcalf of Montana, and journalist Vic Reinemer show in their book, *Overcharge*, the methods by which utility companies elude regulating government bodies to extract unduly large payments from users of electricity.[5]

These are merely dramatic instances of a prevailing condition; there is hardly a major industry at which a similar attack could not be aimed. Critics of business regard such behavior as unethical, but the companies concerned know that they are merely playing the business game.

Among the most respected of our business institutions are the insurance companies. A group of insurance executives meeting recently in New England was startled when their guest speaker, social critic Daniel Patrick Moynihan, roundly berated them for "unethical" practices. They had been guilty, Moynihan alleged, of using outdated actuarial tables to obtain unfairly high premiums. They habitually delayed the hearings of lawsuits against them in order to tire out the plaintiffs and win cheap settlements. In their employment policies they used ingenious devices to discriminate against certain minority groups.[6]

It was difficult for the audience to deny the validity of these charges. But these men were business game players. Their reaction to Moynihan's attack was much the same as that of the automobile manufacturers to Nader, of the utilities to Senator Metcalf, and of the food processors to Senator Hart. If the laws governing their businesses change, or if public opinion becomes clamorous, they will make the necessary adjustments. But morally they have in their view done nothing wrong. As long as they comply with the letter of the law, they are within their rights to operate their businesses as they see fit.

The small business is in the same position as the great corporation in this respect. For example:

- In 1967 a key manufacturer was accused of providing master keys for automobiles to mail-order customers, although it was obvious that some of the purchasers might be automobile thieves. His defense was plain and straightforward. If there was nothing in the law to prevent him from selling his keys to anyone who ordered them, it was not up to him to inquire as to his customers' motives. Why was it any worse, he insisted, for him to sell car keys by mail, than for mail-order houses to sell guns that might be used for murder? Until the law was changed, the key manufacturer could regard himself as being just as ethical as any other businessman by the rules of the business game.[7]

Violations of the ethical ideals of society are common in business, but they are not necessarily violations of business principles. Each year the Federal Trade Commission orders hundreds of companies, many of them of the first magnitude, to "cease and desist" from practices which, judged by ordinary standards, are of questionable morality but which are stoutly defended by the companies concerned.

In one case, a firm manufacturing a well-known mouthwash was accused of using a cheap form of alcohol possibly deleterious to health. The company's chief executive, after testifying in Washington, made this comment privately:

"We broke no law. We're in a highly competitive industry. If we're going to stay in business, we have to look for profit wherever the law permits. We don't make the laws. We obey them. Then why do we have to put up with this 'holier than thou' talk about ethics? It's sheer hypocrisy. We're not in business to promote ethics. Look at the cigarette companies, for God's sake! If the ethics aren't embodied in the laws by the men who made them, you can't expect businessmen to fill the lack. Why, a sudden submission to Christian ethics by businessmen would bring about the greatest economic upheaval in history."

It may be noted that the government failed to prove its case against him.

Cast Illusions Aside

Talk about ethics by businessmen is often a thin decorative coating over the hard realities of the game:

Once I listened to a speech by a young executive who pointed to a new industry code as proof that his company and its competitors were deeply aware of their responsibilities to society. It was a code of ethics, he said. The industry was going to police itself, to dissuade constituent companies from wrongdoing. His eyes shone with conviction and enthusiasm.

The same day there was a meeting in a hotel room where the industry's top executives met with the "czar" who was to administer the new code, a man of high repute. No one who was present could doubt their common attitude. In their eyes the code was designed primarily to forestall a move by the federal government to impose stern restrictions on the industry. They felt that the code would hamper them a good deal less than new federal laws would. It was, in other words, conceived as a protection for the industry, not for the public.

The young executive accepted the surface explanation of the code; these leaders, all experienced game players, did not deceive themselves for a moment about its purpose.

The illusion that business can afford to be guided by ethics as conceived in private life is often fostered by speeches and articles containing such phrases as, "It pays to be ethical," or, "Sound ethics is good business." Actually this is not an ethical position at all; it is a self-serving calculation in disguise. The speaker is really saying that in the long run a company can make more money if it does not antagonize competitors, suppliers, employees, and customers by squeezing them too hard. He is saying that oversharp policies reduce ultimate gains. That is true, but it has nothing to do with ethics. The underlying attitude is much like that in the familiar story of the shopkeeper who finds an extra $20 bill in the cash register, debates with himself the ethical problem—should he tell his partner?—and finally decides to share the money because the gesture will give him an edge over the s.o.b. the next time they quarrel.

I think it is fair to sum up the prevailing attitude of businessmen on ethics as follows:

We live in what is probably the most competitive of the world's civilized societies. Our customs encourage a high degree of aggression as the individual's striving for success. Business is our main area of competition, and it has been ritualized into a game of strategy. The basic rules of the game have been set by the government, which attempts to detect and punish business frauds. But as long as a company does not transgress the rules of the game set by law, it has the legal right to shape its strategy without reference to anything but its profits. If it sets a long-term view of its profits, it will preserve amicable relations, so far as possible, with those with whom it deals. A wise businessman will not seek advantage to the point where he generates dangerous hostility among employees, competitors, customers, government, or the public at large. But decisions in this area are, in the final test, decisions of strategy, not of ethics.

The Individual and the Game

An individual within a company often finds it difficult to adjust to the requirements of the business game. He tries to preserve his private ethical standards in situations that call for time strategy. When he is obliged to carry out company policies that challenge his conception of himself as an ethical man, he suffers.

It disturbs him when he is ordered, for instance, to deny a raise to a man who deserves it, or fire an employee of long standing, to prepare advertising that he believes to be misleading, or conceal facts that he feels customers are entitled to know, to cheapen the quality of materials used in the manufacture of an established product, to sell as new a product that he knows to be rebuilt, to exaggerate the curative powers of a medicinal preparation, or to coerce dealers. There are some fortunate executives who, by the nature of their work and circumstances, never have to face problems of this kind. But in one form or another the ethical dilemma is felt sooner or later by most businessmen. Possibly the dilemma is most painful not when the company forces the action on the executive but when he originates it himself—that is, when he has taken or is contemplating a step which is of his own interest but which runs counter to his early moral conditioning. To illustrate:

- The manager of an export department, eager to show rising sales, is pressed by a big customer to provide invoices which, while containing no overt falsehood that would violate a U.S. law, are so worded that the customer may be able to evade certain taxes in his homeland.
- A company president finds that an aging executive, within a few years of retirement and his pension, is not as productive as formerly. Should he be kept on?
- The produce manager of a supermarket debates with himself whether to get rid of a lot of half-rotten tomatoes by including one, with its good side exposed, in every tomato six-pack.
- An accountant discovers that he has taken an improper deduction on his company's tax

return and fears the consequences if he calls the matter to the president's attention, though he himself has done nothing illegal. Perhaps if he says nothing, no one will notice the error.

- A chief executive officer is asked by his directors to comment on a rumor that he owns stock in another company with which he has placed large orders. He could deny it, for the stock is in the name of his son-in-law and he has earlier formally instructed his son-in-law to sell the holding.

Temptations of this kind constantly arise in business. If an executive allows himself to be torn between a decision based on business considerations and one based on his private ethical code, he exposes himself to a grave psychological strain.

This is not to say that sound business strategy necessarily runs counter to ethical ideals. They may frequently coincide; and when they do, everyone is gratified. But the major tests of every move in business, as in all games of strategy, are legality and profit. A man who intends to be a winner in the business game must have a game player's attitude.

The business strategist's decisions must be as impersonal as those of a surgeon performing an operation—concentrating on objective and technique, and subordinating personal feelings. If the chief executive admits that his son-in-law owns the stock, it is because he stands to lose more if the fact comes out later than if he states it boldly and at once. If the supermarket manager orders the rotten tomatoes to be discarded, he does so to avoid an increase in consumer complaints and a loss of goodwill. The company president decides not to fire the elderly executive in the belief that the negative reaction of other employees would in the long run cost the company more than it would lose in keeping him and paying his pension.

All sensible businessmen prefer to be truthful, but they seldom feel inclined to tell the *whole* truth. In the business game truth-telling usually has to be kept within narrow limits if trouble is to be avoided. The point was neatly made a long time ago (in 1888) by one of John D. Rockefeller's associates, Paul Babcock, to Standard Oil Company executives who were about to testify before a government investigating committee: "Parry every question with answers which, while perfectly truthful, are evasive of *bottom* facts."[8] This was, is, and probably always will be regarded as wise and permissible business strategy.

For Office Use Only

An executive's family life can easily be dislocated if he fails to make a sharp distinction between the ethical systems of the home and the office—or if his wife does not grasp that distinction. Many a businessman who has remarked to his wife, "I had to let Jones go today" or "I had to admit to the boss that Jim has been goofing off lately," has been met with an indignant protest. "How could you do a thing like that? You know Jones is over 50 and will have a lot of trouble getting another job." Or, "You did that to Jim? With his wife ill and all the worry she's been having with the kids?"

If the executive insists that he had no choice because the profits of the company and his own security were involved, he may see a certain cool and ominous reappraisal in his wife's eyes. Many wives are not prepared to accept the fact that business operates with a special code of ethics. An illuminating illustration of this comes from a Southern sales executive who related a conversation he had had with his wife at a time when a hotly contested political campaign was being waged in their state:

"I made the mistake of telling her that I had had lunch with Colby, who gives me about half my business. Colby mentioned that his company had a stake in the election. Then he said, 'By the way, I'm treasurer of the citizens' committee for Lang. I'm collecting contributions. Can I count on you for a hundred dollars?'

"Well, there I was. I was opposed to Lang, but I knew Colby. If he withdrew his business I could be in a bad spot. So I just smiled and wrote out a check then and there. He thanks me, and we started to talk about this next order. Maybe he thought I shared his political views. If so, I wasn't going to lose any sleep over it.

"I should have had sense enough not to tell Mary about it. She hit the ceiling. She said she was disappointed in me. She said I hadn't acted like a man, that I should have stood up to Colby.

"I said, 'Look, it was an either-or situation. I had to do it or risk losing the business.

"She came back at me with, 'I don't believe it. You could have been honest with him. You could have said that you didn't feel you ought to contribute to a campaign for a man you weren't going to vote for. I'm sure he would have understood.'

"I said, 'Mary, you're a wonderful woman but you're way off the track. Do you know what would have happened if I had said that? Colby would have smiled and said, "Oh, I didn't realize. Forget it." But in his eyes from that moment I would be an oddball, maybe a bit of a radical. He would have listened to me talk about his order and would have promised to give it consideration. After that I wouldn't hear from him for a week. Then I would telephone and learn from his secretary that he wasn't yet ready to place the order. And in about a month I would hear through the grapevine that he was giving his business to another company. A month after that I'd be out of a job.'

"She was silent for a while. Then she said, 'Tom, something is wrong with business when a man is forced to choose between his family's security and his moral obligation to himself. It's easy for me to say you should have stood up to him—but if you had, you might have felt you were betraying me and the kids. I'm sorry that you did it, Tom, but I can't blame you. Something is wrong with business!'"

This wife saw the problem in terms of man's obligation as conceived in private life; her husband saw it as a matter of game strategy. As a player in a weak position, he felt that he could not afford to indulge an ethical sentiment that might have cost him his seat at the table.

Playing to Win

Some men might challenge the Colbys of business—might accept serious setbacks to their business careers rather than risk a feeling of moral cowardice. They merit our respect—but as private individuals, not businessmen. When the skillful player of the business game is compelled to submit to unfair pressure, he does not investigate himself for moral weakness. Instead, he strives to put himself into a strong position where he can defend himself against such pressures in the future without loss.

If a man plans to take a seat in the business game, he owes it to himself to master the principles by which the game is played, including a special ethical outlook. He can then hardly fail to recognize that an occasional bluff may well be justified in terms of the game's ethics and warranted in terms of economic necessity. Once he clears his mind on this point, he is in a good position to match his strategy against that of the other players. He can then determine objectively whether a bluff in a given situation has a good chance of succeeding and can decide when and how to bluff, without a feeling of ethical transgression.

To be a winner, a man must play to win. This does not mean that he must be ruthless, cruel, harsh, or treacherous. On the contrary, the better his reputation for integrity, honesty, and decency, the better his chances of victory will be in the long run. But from time to time every businessman, like every poker player, is offered a choice between certain loss or bluffing within the legal rules of the game. If he is not resigned to losing, if he wants to rise in his company and industry, then in such a crisis he will bluff—and bluff hard.

Every now and then one meets a successful businessman who has conveniently forgotten the small or large deceptions that he practiced on his way to fortune. "God gave me my money," old John D. Rockefeller once piously told a Sunday school class. It would be a rare tycoon in our time who would risk the horse laugh with which such a remark would be greeted.

In the last third of the twentieth century even children are aware that if a man has become prosperous in business, he has sometimes departed from the strict truth in order to overcome obstacles or has practiced the more subtle deceptions of the half-truth or the misleading omission. Whatever the form of the bluff, it is an integral part of the game, and the executive who does not master its techniques is not likely to accumulate much money or power.

Notes

[1]*The New York Times*, March 9, 1967.
[2]See Bruce D. Henderson, "Brinkmanship in Business," HBR March-April 1967, 49.
[3]*The New York Times*, November 21, 1966.
[4]New York, Grossman Publishers, Inc., 1965.
[5]New York, David McKay Company, Inc., 1967.

[6]*The New York Times*, January 17, 1967.
[7]Cited by Ralph Nader in "Business Crime," *The New Republic*, July 1, 1967, p. 7.
[8]Babcock in a memorandum to Rockefeller (Rockefeller Archives).

The Ethics of Bluffing in Business

Norman E. Bowie

Business Ethics, 2d ed. (Englewood Cliffs, N.J.: Prentice-Hall, 1982): 338–47.
Copyright © 1982 Prentice-Hall.

One of the classic expressions of [the] point of view [that business practice is analogous to poker, and hence a considerable amount of deception is not only common but could be universalized without undermining business practice] is Albert Z. Carr's "Is Business Bluffing Ethical?" In that article, Carr maintains that the proper analogy for understanding business ethics is that of poker. . . .

Carr raises several important challenges to anyone discussing business ethics. Among the challenges that he raises are the following: (1) that the most appropriate analogy for understanding business is the game of poker, (2) that competition and negotiation require a form of deception that includes conscious misstatement and the concealment of pertinent facts, and (3) that a successful businessperson must "do unto others as he hopes others will not do unto him.". . .

Before responding to Carr's challenges, it seems important to indicate that Carr is not saying that business can ignore all moral rules. If it did, I think that Carr would agree with Kant that such a position would be self-defeating. However, Carr does

think that business practice can and does require a great deal of deception: "conscious misstatements, concealment of pertinent facts, and exaggeration."

Moreover, one does not need extensive experience in business to know that there are many types of deception, like bluffing, that are both widely practiced and widely accepted. A few examples suffice. It is common knowledge that auto dealers do not expect people to pay the sticker price for automobiles. A certain amount of bargaining is taken for granted. The same is true for real estate prices. The asking price for a house is seldom the selling price. At the initial bargaining session, labor leaders also overstate wage demands, and management also understates the wage increases it is willing to grant. In all these instances, the final price or wage contract is arrived at through a process that does resemble the poker game Carr uses as an analogy. The price or wage contract does depend in part on the strength of one's hand and on one's bluffing ability. In the late 1970's, one did need to pay the sticker price for small foreign cars with good gas mileage.

Surely the auto dealers and sellers of homes cannot be accused of immoral behavior when they post prices above those that they are willing to accept. Surely the labor leader is not behaving immorally when he overstates the wage increases that his union expects to receive.

But equally surely there are limits. Let us return to the real estate example. Suppose that I am willing to sell my home for $60,000 if that is the best price I can get. I ask $70,000. A potential buyer's initial offer is $60,000. I turn it down and tell him that $65,000 is my rock bottom price. He purchases the home for $65,000.[1]

Many people would characterize my behavior as shrewd bluffing rather than as an immoral lie. Most people would think more of me rather than less. However, suppose that I had manufactured the claim that someone else had promised me that they were in the process of writing up a contract for $65,000 for the house but that I would sell it to him since we were both members of Rotary International. In this case most people would agree that I had told an immoral lie. By the way, it would not improve the moral character of my action to have my brother pretend to make me an offer so that the prospective buyer would be pressured to actually buy. That would be a case of an immoral lie as well.

Sometimes how the vast majority of people feels about whether an action is a lie or merely bluffing cannot be determined. Consider the following examples from collective bargaining negotiations:

1. Management negotiators saying, "We can't afford this agreement," when it would not put the firm out of business but only reduce profits from somewhat above to somewhat below the industry average.
2. Union negotiators saying, "The union membership is adamant on this issue," when they know that, while one half of the membership is adamant, the other half couldn't care less.
3. Union negotiators saying, "If you include this provision, we'll get membership approval of the contract," when they know that they'll

have an uphill battle for approval even with the provision.[2]

Perhaps the debate on the line between harmless exaggeration and immoral deception is most intense in the discussion of advertising ethics. Horror stories concerning deceptive advertising abound. Language changes its meaning in many ads. "Noncancellable" and "guaranteed renewable" have technical meanings not at all what one would expect. Often age stipulations are thrown in. The physical world is subject to optical illusions that the advertiser can exploit as well. Marketing research has shown that, if housewives are given the choice between two boxes of cereal, one short and squat and the other tall and narrow, they will almost invariably choose the tall and narrow box, even if it contains less and costs more. Boxes and bottles are often much larger than needed for the quantity of material contained therein. Testimonials, until recently, were also under attack. And so it goes. To many, these practices indicate that advertising is an inherently deceptive industry.

Yet others would argue that much of what critics call "deceptive advertising" is nothing more than harmless bluffing. They argue that the purpose of advertising is to sell a product. To sell a product, you must put a product in its best light, you must emphasize its good points, you must exaggerate a bit. So long as this commercial context is understood, exaggeration, puffery, and hyperbole are not deceptive. The claim that one's product is the best or the use of other such superlatives should not cause anyone problems. . . .

Almost all of us try to sell ourselves. Whether searching for a job or searching for a mate, we engage in exaggeration, puffery, and hyperbole about ourselves. And we expect others to do the same. . . . Perhaps the world would be a better place if human beings could avoid hyperbole or puffery. . . .

With these thoughts in mind, we need some criteria to distinguish the relatively harmless cases of puffery from the immoral lies and deceptions. A lie might be defined as a false statement uttered with the intention to mislead. The addition of the intentionality condition is extremely important. It allows many false statements not to be lies. Fortunately, mistaken utterances, although false, are not lies; otherwise, most of us would be frequent, if not habitual, liars. It also exempts poets. "He has the heart of a lion" is not a lie, although it is surely false. Sometimes advertisements are akin to poetry. "Esso puts a tiger in your tank" is false, but surely it is not a lie.

The intentionality condition is useful in areas beyond poetry. The Supreme Court decided in favor of a Federal Trade Commission (FTC) ruling that determined the Colgate-Palmolive's ad that Rapid Shave could soften even the toughness of sandpaper that had been generously lathered with Rapid Shave. Now the FTC admitted that Rapid Shave could soften sandpaper so that it could be shaved. However, the sandpaper needed to soak in Rapid Shave for approximately eighty minutes before it could be shaved. On the basis of this, the FTC declared the ad deceptive because the television viewer was deceived into believing that the actual experiment was being shown; the viewer was not informed about the eighty-minute wait.

Colgate-Palmolive disagreed that there was any deception. It compared its "experiment" with the use of mashed potatoes instead of ice cream in all television ice cream ads. Just as the television lights made the use of ice cream impossible, so the working time made an actual experiment impossible. The court turned down the analogy on the grounds that the mashed potatoes prop was not being used for additional proof of the quality of the product while the Rapid Shave commercial certainly was trying to provide additional proof. Perhaps the Rapid Shave decision could be generalized to make the following point: Within that pecuniary context, any deception or false statement that is not related to the cost, amount, or quality of the product is not an example of immoral deception in advertising. Such a principle would enable us to focus on the context in which advertising takes place.

Yet another criterion could be stated as follows: Any exaggeration that would not deceive the rational person is not inappropriate. No rational person will believe that the foam of Old Froshingslosh beer will really be on the bottom. (Whether such deception would be immoral within some other context is not a matter for discussion here.) Deception in advertising involves the use of false statements or inaccurate depictions of a product that are material to the consumer's decision to purchase and that are undertaken intentionally to mislead rational consumers. On that account, most advertising is not deceptive. However, equally on that account some advertising is deceptive and, more important, some advertising or marketing practices are deceptive. Packaging techniques are surely one example of a practice that deceives in terms of amount.

But what counts as a rational consumer? The federal agency that has confronted this question head on is the Federal Trade Commission. The commission has drawn a distinction between the rational consumer and the ignorant consumer. The ignorant consumer takes everything literally. He or she really does believe that, when Old Froshingslosh beer advertises that the foam will be on the bottom, it really will be on the bottom. The ignorant consumer does not show any common sense. It is generally agreed that, to require business practice to be so open and literal that even the ignorant consumer would not be deceived would stifle business and seriously affect productivity. On that point, the conventional wisdom seems correct. However, the definition of the "rational consumer" is fairly amorphous. Sometimes "rational consumer" is just a synonym for "average consumer." Advertisements, like television programs, would have to be aimed at those with the reading ability of a twelve-year-old. At other times "rational consumer" is given a more normative definition. It is equated with what a consumer should know. Perhaps the normative definition puts more responsibility on the consumer than does the definition that appeals to the average consumer.

Another way to handle this debate over where to draw the line between misstatement and fraud is to appeal to a criterion of public openness. A business practice is not deceptive when that business acknowledges the rules it is playing under. The ads for the auto dealers and for real estate make it perfectly clear that the "asking price" is not the "real price." An ad for a home that says "Asking $120,000" virtually announces that the homeowner is in a mood to deal. Auto ads for individual dealers stress the fact that they will match any other deal in town. They explicitly acknowledge the bargaining aspect of auto sales. Grocery store ads by and large contain none of this bargaining language. The price of oranges is not a function of an individual bargain worked out between the individual purchaser and the supermarket.

Deception enters when a businessperson announces that he or she is playing by one set of rules when in fact he or she is playing by another. Of course immorality also enters when one partner to a contract breaks his or her end. But, so long as the rules of the game are known, then most people will accept consequences of business practice that they might not accept in other circumstances. Consider the following case:

The Leaking Valve[3]

The Hawley Corporation, which ranks among the nation's one hundred largest manufacturing firms, had a persistent problem with a leaking valve assembly on the hydraulic presses it makes and distributes. Unable to remedy the defect on its own, Hawley engineers called in several vendors of this type of assembly and described the problem to them. The Hawley group explained that it hoped that the vendors would be willing to find a solution to the problem but that corporate policy did not permit paying for this sort of developmental work done outside the company.

Only one of the vendor firms, Allbright, Inc., decided to proceed on this basis with developing something that could answer Hawley's difficulty. Allbright reasoned that if it produced the remedy it would be in an excellent position to get the contract for supplying Hawley with the improved assembly.

The engineering department of the two firms worked together, and after a fairly lengthy effort a modification of the Hawley assembly was perfected that eliminated the leaking.

The Hawley purchasing department then sent our requests for bids on the new assembly to a number of vendors, Allbright included. Reston Corporation underbid Allbright and was awarded the order by Hawley.

Most of my students who analyze this case agree that Allbright had no right to the contract. Their argument is almost always the same: The rules were known and hence Allbright knew it was taking a risk when it agreed to assist Hawley.

One should compare this case with another:

A Big Break for Fenwick Creations

Fenwick Creations, a manufacturer of men's and women's sportswear, had come up with an exceptionally well-designed new line of clothes for tennis, jogging, and cycling. Initial response from buyers was so favorable that Fenwick's sales managers thought they had a good chance of finally attaining one of their goals: to get their merchandise into the locally prestigious Wilton-Cool and Company department store.

Wilton-Cool was known in the trade for acceptance of new lines. It was also known for making acceptance contingent upon special incentives from suppliers.

Fenwick's sales office offered to guarantee the resale of Wilton-Cool's total order, within a period of time agreeable to the department store. Fenwick offered further to take Wilton-Cool's statement about sales without a check of inventories by Fenwick.

Wilton-Cool accepted the proposition and ordered 500 articles of sportswear from Fenwick. After the previously arranged termination date, the department store claimed to have sold 325 of the items. In fact, 450 had been sold; but Fenwick abided by the guarantee. It was understood on both sides—though never stated—that what had occurred was standard practice and that prices charged by the supplier took these costs into account.

In this case, most of my students do not accept the morality of the practice. Even though the two businesses, Fenwick and Wilton-Cool, were aware of the rules, other relevant parties were not. The consumers were particularly adversely affected. Consumers believe that, in a competitive market economy, purchase decisions among businesses are made on the basis of quality and price. Those are the operative rules of the game. But clearly these rules are being violated in this case.

We now have a much better handle on what we mean by deceptive advertising. Deceptive advertising is advertising that is intentionally designed to mislead the rational consumer who knows the rules of the game about the cost, amount, or quality of a product....

Let us take Carr's analogy seriously. Should the stockholders applaud a chief executive officer whose operating procedure is analogous to the operating procedure of a poker player? In Carr's view, "A good part of the time the businessman is trying to do unto others as he hopes others will not do unto him." But surely such a practice is very risky. The danger of discovery is great, and our experience of the past several years indicates that many corporations that have played the game of business like the game of poker have suffered badly. Moreover, if business practice consisted essentially of these conscious misstatements, exaggerations, and the concealment of pertinent facts, it seems clear that business practice would be inherently unstable. Contemporary business practice presupposes such stability, and business can only be stable if the chief executive officer has a set of moral standards higher than those that govern the game of poker.

This philosophical point, that deception must be very limited if society is to be stable, has been enriched by the appearance of Dr. Sissela Bok's book, *Lying: Moral Choice in Public and Private Life*, which reaffirms the centrality of the moral rule, "Do not lie." One of the points Dr. Bok most emphatically makes is that the existence of soci-ety itself depends upon the acceptance by the members of society of the rule "Do not lie."

Trust in some degree of veracity functions as a foundation of relations among human beings; when this trust shatters or wears away, institutions collapse.... A society, then, whose members were unable to distinguish truthful messages from deceptive ones, would collapse. But even before such a general collapse, individual choice and survival would be imperiled. The search for food and shelter could depend on no expectations from others. A warning that a well was poisoned or a plea for help in an accident would come to be ignored unless independent confirmation could be found.[4]

Dr. Bok's point can be restated so that it applies specifically to business.

Central to the philosophy of most businesspersons is the view that government should not intrude extensively into business. With respect to business, *laissez-faire* is the dominant view. However, even those with libertarian philosophies allow one important function to government. Government is to be the police officer that enforces the rules of business activity. Most important, government is to uphold the sanctity of contracts. This view is expressed clearly in the classical treatment of the merits of capitalism.

However, if business activity is to thrive, most people most of the time must uphold voluntarily the sanctity of contracts. No government can serve as an omnipresent police officer. Indeed, even within the competitive marketplace, the basic moral nature of persons must be assumed. Usually, people will keep to their contracts even when it does not work out to their advantage to do so. If this were not true, law enforcement would soon become impossibly burdensome. Indeed, we assume that even with limited cheating at least the police are honest. The uncovering of a dishonest cop is always a great shock. Commerce requires a basically honest society and honest police.

A cause of growing concern is the increased cheating on the part of an increasing number of citizens. Internal revenue spokespersons fear that, as American citizens face higher taxes through inflation and as they hear of cheating by others, they will tend to cheat on their own taxes. Internal revenue officials concede that enforcement agents could not deal with widespread cheating and that such a situation would undermine the income tax system. One need not wait for the collapse of the income tax to observe breakdowns in the market that result from breakdowns in the obligation to the sanctity of contracts.

Shoplifting has approached epidemic proportions. Since shoplifters are difficult to apprehend and even more difficult to convict, a partial "solution" is to figure into the retail price of a good a certain markup to cover the cost of shoplifting. The result is an increase on the price of goods. Of course as prices rise, one would expect shoplifting to increase. This is especially true when people realize that a portion of the price of their goods is set aside to cover shoplifting. Why shouldn't they shoplift, too, if they are already paying the cost of the shoplifters who shoplift with impunity?

If such a view becomes widespread, the market system will break down just the way a rationing scheme does when cheating is both widely known about and goes unpunished. Suppose that there is a ban on watering the lawn that is not enforced. Sam, who has followed the ban but who sees all his neighbors water the lawn, will be silly if he continues to refrain from watering his lawn. As a result, the rationing system breaks down.

All of this is fairly obvious. Bok's most significant point is that rather minor acts of deception like white lies, puffery, and exaggeration all contribute to a general instability. In other words, Carr underestimates the undesirable effects of such practices. If I were to summarize Bok's book in one sentence, I would say, "Even white lies, flattery, and deceptive practices that are *publicly known and accepted* undermine social institutions." Bok's critique of "white lies" and the use of placebos applies equally well to deception in business:

> Triviality surely does set limits to when moral inquiry is reasonable. But when we look more closely at practices such as placebo-giving, it becomes clear that all lies

defended as "white" cannot be so easily dismissed. In the first place, the harmlessness of lies is notoriously disputable. What the liar perceives as harmless or even beneficial may not be so in the eyes of the deceived. Second, the failure to look at an entire practice rather than at their own isolated case often blinds liars to cumulative harm and expanding deceptive activities. Those who begin with white lies can come to resort to more frequent and more serious ones. Where some tell a few white lies, others may tell more. Because lines are so hard to draw, the indiscriminate use of such lies can lead to other deceptive practices. The aggregate harm from a large number of marginally harmful instances may, therefore, be highly undesirable in the end—for liars, those deceived, and honesty and trust more generally.[5]

In Bok's view even the bluffing that goes on in real estate and auto sales has its dangers. So does the hyperbole that accompanies advertising and the excessive demands that are characteristic of the early stages of collective bargaining negotiations. Those of us in academic life can see Bok's point when we consider what has happened as the result of grade inflation and the inflating of letters of recommendation. The professional and graduate schools are suspicious of high grades. Hardly anyone takes letters of recommendation seriously anymore.

In the area of business, a number of parents, like myself, have simply taught our children to regard all advertising as deceptive. Often, that type of teaching is not difficult. After eating three boxes of cereal so that one can send three box tops and 50 cents for a marvelous Star Wars toy, the toy almost never seems worth it. Children learn the lesson early. Jokes about used car salesmen are so ingrained in the public that honest used car ads just aren't taken seriously.

The growth of the large firm, the complexity of business decisions, the need for planning and stability, and the undesirable effects of puffery, exaggeration, and deception all count against

Carr's view that the ethics of business should be the ethics of a poker game. Just how much puffery and exaggeration business practice can permit without serious undesirable consequences is a matter for further empirical investigation.

But how much deception, exaggeration, and puffery should business practice permit?. . . One condition that seemed to distinguish legitimate from illegitimate bluffing in our earlier examples was whether or not all parties knew that bluffing was taking place. The bluffing that goes on in used-car lots is legitimate because everyone knows that asking prices are just that. This open-ness condition, as I chose to call it, is often the basis for legislation as well. People should be free to speculate in stocks, but if an accountant, lawyer, or other person obtains inside information, that person is not free to buy or sell the stock of that company or the stock of any other company that would be significantly affected if the inside information were publicly known. In a context in which bluffing and exaggeration are permitted, open access to all relevant information is a moral necessity. Otherwise, the rules of the bluffing game are unfair. Poker is unfair when some of the players do not know the rules that are being used.

Notes

[1]These examples are adopted from Thomas L. Carson and Richard E. Wokutch, "Ethical Perspectives on Lying, Deception and Bluffing in Business," unpublished manuscript, 1–2.

[2]Ibid., 3–4.

[3]This case and the subsequent case, "A Big Break for Fenwick Creations," was prepared by the Committee for Education in Business Ethics under a grant from the National Endowment for the Humanities.

[4]Sissela Bok, *Lying: Moral Choice in Public and Private Life* (New York: Pantheon Books, 1978), 19, 31.

[5]Ibid., 60.

Why Be Honest If Honesty Doesn't Pay?

Amar Bhide and Howard H. Stevenson

Harvard Business Review (September–October 1990): 121–29. Copyright © 1990.

Business men and women keep their word because they want to, not because honesty pays.

We bet on the rational case for trust. Economists, ethicists, and business sages had persuaded us that honesty is the best policy, but their evidence seemed weak. Through extensive interviews we hoped to find data that would support their theories and thus, perhaps, encourage higher standards of business behavior.

To our surprise, our pet theories failed to stand up. Treachery, we found, can pay. There is no compelling economic reason to tell the truth or keep one's word—punishment for the treacherous in the real world is neither swift nor sure.

Honesty is, in fact, primarily a moral choice. Businesspeople do tell themselves that, in the long run, they will do well by doing good. But there is little factual or logical basis for this conviction. Without values, without a basic preference for right over wrong, trust based on such self-delusion would crumble in the face of temptation.

Most of us choose virtue because we want to believe in ourselves and have others respect and believe in us. When push comes to shove, hard-headed businessfolk usually ignore (or fudge) their dollars-and-cents calculations in order to keep their word.

And for this, we should be happy. We can be proud of a system in which people are honest because they want to be, not because they have to be. Materially, too, trust based on morality provides great advantages. It allows us to join in great and exciting enterprises that we could never undertake if we relied on economic incentives alone.

Economists and game theorists tell us that trust is enforced in the marketplace through retaliation and reputation. If you violate a trust, your victim is apt to seek revenge and others are likely to stop doing business with you, at least under favorable terms. A man or woman with a reputation for fair dealing will prosper. Therefore, profit maximizers are honest.

This sounds plausible enough until you look for concrete examples. Cases that apparently demonstrate the awful consequences of abusing trust turn out to be few and weak, while evidence that treachery can pay seems compelling.

The moralists' standard tale recounts how E. F. Hutton was brought down by its check-kiting fraud.[1] Hutton, once the second largest broker in the nation, never recovered from the blow to its reputation and finances and was forced to sell out to Shearson.

Exxon's Valdez disaster is another celebrated example. Exxon and seven other oil companies persuaded the town of Valdez to accept a tanker terminal by claiming that a major spill was "highly unlikely." Their 1,800-page contingency plan ensured that any spill would be controlled within hours. In fact, when Exxon's supertanker spewed forth over 240,000 barrels of oil, the equipment promised in the cleanup plan was not available. The cost? According to recent (and still rising) estimates, Exxon's costs could exceed $2 billion, and the industry faces severe restrictions on its operations in Alaska.

But what do these fables prove? Check-kiting was only one manifestation of the widespread mismanagement that plagued Hutton and ultimately caused its demise. Incompetently run companies going under is not news. Exxon's underpreparedness was expensive, but many decisions turn out badly. Considering the low probability of a spill, was skimping on the promised cleanup equipment really a bad business decision at the time it was taken?

More damaging to the moralists' position is the wealth of evidence against trust. Compared with the few ambiguous tales of treachery punished, we can find numerous stories in which deceit was unquestionably rewarded.

Philippe Kahn, in an interview with *Inc.* magazine, described with apparent relish how his company, Borland International, got its start by deceiving an ad salesman for *BYTE* magazine.

Inc.: The story goes that Borland was launched by a single ad, without which he wouldn't be sitting here talking about the company. How much of that is apocryphal?

Kahn: It's true: one full-page ad in the November 1983 issue of *BYTE* magazine got the company running. If it had failed, I would have had nowhere else to go.

Inc.: If you were so broke, how did you pay for the ad?

Kahn: Let's put it that we convinced the salesman to give us terms. We wanted to appear only in *BYTE*—not any of the other microcomputer magazines—because *BYTE* is for programmers, and that's who we wanted to reach. But we couldn't afford it. We figured the only way was somehow to convince them to extend us credit terms.

Inc.: And they did?

Kahn: Well, they didn't *offer*. What we did was, before the ad salesman came in—we existed in two small rooms, but I had hired extra people so we would look like a busy, venture-packed company—we prepared a chart with what we pretended was our media plan for the computer magazines. On the chart we had *BYTE* crossed out. When the salesman arrived, we made sure the phones were ringing and the extras were scurrying around. Here was this chart he thought he wasn't supposed to see, so I pushed it out of the way. He said, "Hold on, can we get you in *BYTE*?"

I said, "We don't really want to be in your book, it's not the right audience for us."

"You've got to try," he pleaded. I said, "Frankly, our media plan is done, and we can't afford it." So he offered good terms, if only we'd let him run it just once. We expected we'd sell maybe $20,000 worth of software and at least pay for the ad. We sold $150,000 worth. Looking back now, it's a funny story; then it was a big risk.[2]

Further evidence comes from professional sports. In our study, one respondent cited the case of Rick Pitino, who had recently announced his decision to leave as coach of the New York Knicks basketball team with over three years left on his contract. Patino left, the respondent wrote, "to coach the University of Kentucky (a school of higher learning, that like many others, is a party in breaking contracts)." Pitino was quoted in the *New York Times* the week before as saying that he never broke a contract. But he's 32 years old and has had five jobs. What he neglected to say is that he's never completed a contract. The schools always let him run out, as they don't want an unhappy coach.

"The same thing is done by professional athletes every year. They sign a long-term contract and after one good year, they threaten to quit unless the contract's renegotiated. The stupidity of it all is that they get their way."

Compared with the ambiguity of the Hutton and Exxon cases, the clear causality in the Kahn and Pitino cases is striking. Deceiving the *BYTE* salesman was crucial to Kahn's success. Without subterfuge, Borland International would almost certainly have folded. And there is a hard dollar number (with lots of zeros in it) that professional athletes and coaches gain when they shed a contract.

What of the long term? Does treachery eventually get punished? Nothing in the record suggests it does. Many of today's blue chip companies were put together at the turn of the century under circumstances approaching securities fraud. The robber barons who promoted them enjoyed great material rewards at the time—and their fortunes survived several generations. The Industrial Revolution did not make entirely obsolete Machiavelli's observation, "Men seldom rise from low condition to high rank without employing either force or fraud."[2]

Power can be an effective substitute for trust. In theory, Kahn and Coach Pitino should suffer the consequences of their deceits and incomplete contracts: scorned by its victims and a just society, Borland shouldn't be able to blow a whistle. But they continue to prosper. Why do reputation and retaliation fail as mechanisms for enforcing trust?

Power can be an effective substitute for trust.

Power—the ability to do others great harm or great good—can induce widespread amnesia, it appears. Borland International's large ad budget commands due respect. Its early deceit is remembered, if at all, as an amusing prank. Pitino's record for winning basketball games wipes out his record for abandoning teams in midstream.

Prestigious New York department stores, several of our respondents told us, cavalierly break promises to suppliers:

"You send the department store an invoice for $55,000 and they send you $38,000. If you question it they say, 'Here is an $11,000 penalty for being two days late; here is the transportation tax and a dockage fee. . . . You didn't follow our shipping instructions, Clause 42, Section 3C. You used the wrong carrier.' And half the time they call the order in and send the 600-page confirming document later, and they say you didn't follow our order."

"Department stores are horrible! Financial types have taken control, the merchants are out. The guy who keeps beating you down goes to his boss at the end of the year and says 'Look at the kind of rebates I got on freight reduction—$482,000. I delayed payments an average of 22 days from my predecessor at this kind of amount, and this is what I saved.'"

Nevertheless, suppliers still court their tormentors' orders.

"Don't tell me that department stores will go out of business because they treat their suppliers like that! I don't believe that at all. They have too much power—they screw one guy, and guys are waiting in line to take a shot at them again."

Heroic resistance to an oppressive power is the province of the students at Tiananmen Square, not the businessfolk in the capitalist societies the students risk their lives to emulate. Businesspeople do not stand on principle when it comes to dealing with abusers of power and trust. You have to adjust, we were told. If we dealt only with customers who share our ethical values, we would be out of business.

A real estate developer we interviewed was blunt:

> People are really whores. They will do business with someone they know they can't trust if it suits their convenience. They may tell their lawyers: "Be careful, he's dishonest; he's not reliable and he will try to get out of the contract if something happens." But those two do business with each other.... I've done transactions with people knowing that they were horrible and knowing that I'd never talk to them. But the deal was so good, I just accepted it, did the best I could, and had the lawyers make triply sure that everything was covered.

Sometimes the powerful leave others no choice. The auto parts supplier has to play ball with the Big Three, no matter how badly he or she has been treated in the past or expects to be treated in the future. Suppliers of fashion goods believe they absolutely have to take a chance on abusive department stores. Power here totally replaces trust.

Usually, though, power isn't quite that absolute, and some degree of trust is a necessary ingredient in business relationships. Pitino has demonstrated remarkable abilities in turning around basketball programs, but he isn't the only coach available for hire. Borland International's business is nice to have, but it can't make or break a computer magazine. Nevertheless, even those with limited power can live down a poor record of trustworthiness. Cognitive inertia—the tendency to search for data that confirm one's beliefs and to avoid facts that might refute them—is one reason why.

To illustrate, consider the angry letters the mail fraud unit of the U.S. Post Office gets every year from the victims of the fake charities it exposes. Apparently donors are annoyed that they can't keep sending contributions to a cause they believed in. They want to avoid information that says they have trusted a fraud.

When the expected reward is substantial and avoidance becomes really strong, reference checking goes out the window. In the eyes of people blinded by greed, the most tarnished reputations shine brightly.

Many a commodity broker's yacht has been financed by cleaning out one customer after another. Each new doctor or dentist who is promised the moon is unaware of and uninterested in his or her predecessor's fate. Such investors want to believe in the fabulous returns the broker has promised. They don't want references or other reality checks that would disturb the dreams they have built on sand. Thus can the retail commodity brokerage business flourish, even though knowledgeable sources maintain that it wipes out the capital of 70% of its customers every year.

The search for data that confirm wishful thinking is not restricted to naive medical practitioners dabbling in pork bellies. The *Wall Street Journal* recently detailed how a 32-year-old conglomerateur perpetrated a gigantic fraud on sophisticated financial institutions such as Citibank, the Bank of New England, and a host of Wall Street firms. A Salomon Brothers team that conducted due diligence on the wunderkind pronounced him highly moral and ethical. A few months later—

Even with a fully disclosed public record of bad faith, hard-nosed businesspeople will still try to find reasons to trust. Like the proverbial "other woman," they'll reason, "It's not his fault." And so it comes to pass that Oscar Wyatt's Coastal Corporation can walk away from its gas-supply contracts;[3] then, with the consequent lawsuits not yet settled, issue billions of dollars of junk bonds. Lured by high yields, junk bond investors choose to believe that their relationship will be different: Wyatt *had* to break his contracts when energy prices rose; and a junk bond is so much more, well, *binding* than a mere supply contract.

Similarly, we can imagine, every new Pitino employer believes the last has done Pitino wrong. Their relationship will last forever.

Ambiguity and complexity can also take the edge off reputational enforcement. When we trust others to keep their word, we simultaneously rely on their integrity, native ability, and favorable external circumstances. So when a trust appears to be breached, there can be so much ambiguity that even the aggrieved parties cannot apprehend what happened. Was the breach due to bad faith, incompetence, or circumstances that made it impossible to perform as promised? No one knows. Yet without such knowledge, we cannot determine in what respect someone has proved untrustworthy: basic integrity, susceptibility to temptation, or realism in making promises.

The following example, in which we hear the buyer of a company who was taken in by the seller's representations, is instructive:

"The seller said: 'We have a technology that is going to be here for a long time. We own the market.' We liked this guy so much, it was funny. He's in the local area, he knew my father. He's a great guy to talk to, with all sorts of stories.

"He managed to fool us, our banks, and a mezzanine lender, and he ended up doing quite well on the deal. Then the company went on the skids. The funny thing is, afterwards he bought the business back from us, put a substantial amount of his own capital in, and still has not turned it around. I'm just not sure what was going on.

"I guess he believed his own story and believed it so much that he bought the business back. He was independently wealthy from another sale anyway, and I think he wanted to prove that he was a great businessman and that we just screwed the business up. If he was a charlatan, why would he have cared?"

Where even victims have difficulty assessing whether and to what extent someone has broken a trust, it is not surprising that it can be practically impossible for a third party to judge.

That difficulty is compounded by the ambiguity of communication. Aggrieved parties may underplay or hide past unpleasantness out of embarrassment or fear of lawsuits. Or they may exaggerate others' villainies and their own blamelessness. So unless the victims themselves can be trusted to be utterly honest and objective, judgments based on their experiences become unreliable and the accuracy of the alleged transgressor's reputation unknowable.

Businesspeople learn not to get hung up about other people's pasts.

A final factor protecting the treacherous from their reputations is that it usually pays to take people at face value. Businesspeople learn over time that "innocent until proven guilty" is a good working rule and that it is really not worth getting hung up about other people's pasts.

Assuming that others are trustworthy, at least in their initial intentions, *is* a sensible policy. The average borrower does not plan million-dollar scams, most coaches do try to complete their contracts, and most buyers don't "forget" about their suppliers' bills or make up reasons for imposing penalties.

Even our cynical real estate developer told us:

"By and large, most people are intrinsically honest. It's just the tails, the ends of the bell-shaped curve, that are dishonest in any industry, in any area. So it's just a question of tolerating them."

Another respondent concurred:

"I tend to take people at face value until proven otherwise, and more often than not, that works. It doesn't work with a blackguard and a scoundrel, but how many total blackguards and scoundrels are there?"

Mistrust can be a self-fulfilling prophecy. People aren't exclusively saints or sinners; few adhere to an absolute moral code. Most respond to circumstances, and their integrity and trustworthiness can depend as much on how they are treated as on their basic character. Initiating a relationship assuming that the other party is going to try to get you may induce him or her to do exactly that.

Overlooking past lapses can make good business sense too. People and companies do change. It is more than likely that once Borland International got off the ground, Kahn never pulled a fast one on an ad salesman again. Today's model citizen may be yesterday's sharp trader or robber baron.

Trust breakers are not only unhindered by bad reputations, they are also usually spared retaliation by parties they injure. Many of the same factors apply. Power, for example: attacking a more powerful transgressor is considered foolhardy.

"It depends on the scale of the pecking order," we were told. "If you are a seller and your customer breaks promises, by and large you don't retaliate. And if you are an employee and your employer breaks promises, you usually don't retaliate either."

Where power doesn't protect against retaliation, convenience and cognitive inertia often do. Getting even can be expensive; even thinking about broken trusts can be debilitating. "Forget and move on" seems to be the motto of the business world.

Businesspeople consider retaliation a wasteful distraction because they have a lot of projects in hand and constantly expect to find new opportunities to pursue. The loss suffered through any individual breach of trust is therefore relatively small, and revenge is regarded as a distraction from other, more promising activities.

Retaliation is a luxury you can't afford, respondents told us.

"You can't get obsessed with getting even. It will take away from everything else. You will take it out on the kids at home, and you will take it out on your wife. You will do lousy business."

"It's a realization that comes with age: retaliation is a double loss. First you lose your money; now you're losing time."

"Bite me once, it is your fault; bite me twice, my fault. . . . But bite me twice, and I won't have anything to do with you, and I'm not going to bite back because I have better things to do with my life. I'm not going to litigate just for the pleasure of getting even with you."

Only those who have their best years behind them and see their life's work threatened actively seek to retaliate. In general, our interviews suggested, businesspeople would rather switch than fight. An employee caught cheating on expenses is quietly let go. Customers who are always cutting corners on payments are, if practicable, dropped. No fuss, no muss.

Our interviewees also seemed remarkably willing to forget injuries and to repair broken relationships. A supplier is dropped, an employee or sales rep is let go. Then months or years later the parties try again, invoking some real or imaginary change of circumstances or heart. "The employee was under great personal strain." "The company's salesman exceeded his brief." "The company is under new management." Convenience and cognitive inertia seem to foster many second chances.

"Retaliation is a double loss. First you lose your money; then you lose your time."

What about the supposed benefits of retaliation? Game theorists argue that retaliation sends a signal that you are not to be toyed with. This signal, we believe, has some value when harm is suffered outside a trusting relationship: in cases of patent infringement or software piracy, for example. But when a close trusting relationship exists, as it does, say, with an employee, the inevitable ambiguity about who was at fault often distorts the signal retaliation sends. Without convincing proof of one-sided fault, the retaliator may get a reputation for vindictiveness and scare even honorable men and women away from establishing close relationships.

Even the cathartic satisfaction of getting even seems limited. Avenging lost honor is passé, at least in business dealings. Unlike Shakespeare's Venetian merchant, the modern businessperson isn't interested in exacting revenge for its own sake and, in fact, considers thirsting for retribution unprofessional and irresponsible.

"There is such a complete identification in my mind between my company's best interests and what I want to do that I am not going to permit anything official out of spite. If I can't rationalize [retaliation] and run it through my computer brain, it will be relegated to my diary and won't be a company action."

We would be guilty of gross exaggeration if we claimed that honesty has no value or that treachery is never punished. Trustworthy behavior does provide protection against the loss of power and against invisible sniping. But these protections are intangible, and their dollars-and-cents value does not make a compelling case for trustworthiness.

A good track record can protect against the loss of power. What if you stop being a winning coach or your software doesn't sell anymore? Long-suppressed memories of past abuses may then come to the fore, past victims may gang up to get you.

A deal maker cited the fate of an investment bank that was once the only source of financing for certain kinds of transactions.

"They always had a reputation for being people who would outline the terms of the deal and then change them when it got down to the closing. The industry knew that this is what you had to expect; our people had no choice. Now that the bank has run into legal problems and there are other sources of funds, people are flocking elsewhere. At the first opportunity to desert, people did—and with a certain amount of glee. They are getting no goodwill benefit from their client base because when they were holding all the cards they screwed everybody."

Another entrepreneur ascribed his longevity to his reputation for trustworthiness:

"The most important reason for our success is the quality of my [product] line. But we wouldn't have survived without my integrity because our lines weren't always very successful. There are parabola curves in all businesses, and people still supported me, even though we had a low, because they believed in me."

Trustworthiness may also provide immediate protection against invisible sniping. When the abuse of power banishes trust, the victims often try to get their own back in ways that are not visible to the abuser: "I'm not in business just to make a profit. If a client tries to jerk me around, I mark up my fees." "The way to get even with a large company is to sell more to them."

On occasion, sniping can threaten the power it rebels against. The high-handedness of department stores, for example, has created a new class of competitors, the deep discounter of designer apparel.

"Ordinarily, manufacturers don't like to sell their goods at throwaway prices to people like us," says one such discounter. "But our business has thrived because the department stores have been systematically screwing their suppliers, especially after all those leveraged buyouts. At the same time, the manufacturers have learned that we treat them right. We scrupulously keep our promises. We pay when we say we'll pay. If they ask us not to advertise a certain item in a certain area, we don't. If they make an honest mistake in a shipment, we won't penalize them.

"The department stores have tried to start subsidiaries to compete with us, but they don't understand the discount business. Anyone can set up an outlet. What really matters is the trust of the suppliers."

How can you quantify the financial repercussions when suppliers you have abused ship hot items to your competitors first?

Neither of these benefits can be factored easily into a rational business analysis of whether to lie or keep a promise. Sniping is invisible; the sniper will only take shots that you cannot measure or see. How could you possibly quantify the financial repercussions when suppliers you have abused refuse your telephone orders or ship hot items to your competitors first?

Assessing the value of protection against the loss of power is even more incalculable. It is almost as difficult to anticipate the nature of divine retribution as it is to assess the possibility that at some unknown time in the future your fortunes *may* turn, whereupon others *may* seek to cause you some unspecified harm. With all these unknowns and unknowables, surely the murky future costs don't stand a chance against the certain and immediate financial benefits from breaking an inconvenient promise. The net present values, at any reasonable discount rate, must work against honoring obligations.

Given all this, we might expect breaches of trust to be rampant. In fact, although most businesspeople are not so principled as to boycott powerful trust breakers, they do try to keep their own word most of the time. Even allowing for convenient forgetfulness, we cannot help being swayed by comments like this:

"I've been in this business for 40 years. I've sold two companies; I've gone public myself and have done all kinds of dealings, so I'm not a babe in the woods, OK? But I can't think of one situation where people took advantage of me. I think that when I was young and naive about many things, I may have been underpaid for what my work was, but that was a learning experience."

One reason treachery doesn't swamp us is that people rationalize constancy by exaggerating its economic value.

"Costs have been going up, and it will cost me a million dollars to complete this job. But if I don't, my name will be mud and no one will do business with me again."

"If I sell this chemical at an extortionate price when there is a shortage, I will make a killing. But if I charge my customers the list price, they will do the right thing by me when there is a glut."

Just as those who trust find reasons for the risks they want to run, those who are called on to keep a difficult promise cast around for justification even when the hard numbers point the other way. Trustworthiness has attained the status of "strategic focus" and "sustainable competitive advantage" in business folklore—a plausible (if undocumented) touchstone of long-term economic value.

But why has it taken root? Why do business men and women want to believe that trustworthiness pays, disregarding considerable evidence to the contrary? The answer lies firmly in the realm of social and moral behavior, not in finance.

The businesspeople we interviewed set great store on the regard of their family, friends, and the community at large. They valued their reputations, not for some nebulous financial gain but because they took pride in their good names. Even more important, since outsiders cannot easily judge trustworthiness, businesspeople seem guided by their inner voices, by their consciences. When we cited examples to our interviewees in which treachery had apparently paid, we heard responses like:

"It doesn't matter how much money they made. Right is right and wrong is wrong."

"Is that important? They may be rich in dollars and very poor in their own sense of values and what life is about. I cannot judge anybody by the dollars; I judge them by their deeds and how they react."

"I can only really speak for myself, and to me, my word is the most important thing in my life and my credibility as an individual is paramount. All the other success we have had is secondary."

The importance of moral and social motives in business cannot be overemphasized. A selective memory, a careful screening of the facts may help sustain the fiction of profitable virtue, but the fundamental basis of trust is moral. We keep promises because we believe it is right to do so, not because it is good business. Cynics may dismiss the sentiments we heard as posturing, and it is true that performance often falls short of aspiration. But we can find no other way than conscience to explain why trust is the basis for so many relationships.

At first, these findings distressed us. A world in which treachery pays because the average businessperson won't fight abusive power and tolerates dishonesty? Surely that wasn't right or efficient, and the system needed to be fixed! On further reflection, however, we concluded that this system was fine, both from a moral and a material point of view.

The moral advantages are simple. Concepts of trust and, more broadly, of virtue would be empty if bad faith and wickedness were not financially rewarding. If wealth naturally followed straight dealing, we would only need to speak about conflicts between the long term and the short, stupidity and wisdom, high discount rates and low. We would worry only about others' good sense, not about their integrity. It is the very absence of predictable financial reward that makes honesty a moral quality we hold dear.

Trust based on morality rather than self-interest also provides a great economic benefit. Consider the alternative, where trust is maintained by fear.

A world in which the untrustworthy face uncertain retribution is a small world where everyone knows (and keeps a close eye on!) everyone else. A village, really, deeply suspicious not only of commodities brokers but also of all strangers, immigrants, and innovators.

No shades or ambiguities exist here. The inhabitants trust each other only in transactions in which responsibilities are fully specified—"deliver the diamonds to Point A, bring back cash"—and breaches of trust are clear. They do not take chances on schemes that might fail through the tangled strands of bad faith, incompetence, overoptimism, or plain bad luck.

A dark pessimism pervades this world. Opportunities look scarce and setbacks final. "You can't afford to be taken in even once" is the operating principle. "So when in doubt, don't."

In this world, there are no second chances either. A convicted felon like Thomas Watson, Sr. would never be permitted to create an IBM. A Federal Express would never again be extended credit after an early default on its loan agreements. The rules are clear: an eye for an eye and a tooth for a tooth. Kill or be killed.

Fortunately, our world is full of trusting optimists—a Steve Jobs with no track record to speak of can start an Apple.

Little, closed, tit-for-tat worlds do exist. Trust is self-reinforcing because punishment for broken promises is swift—in price-fixing rings, loan-sharking operations, legislative log rolling, and the mutually assured destruction of nuclear deterrence. Exceed your quota and suffer a price war. Don't pay on time and your arm gets broken. Block my pork barrel project and I'll kill yours. Attack our cities and we'll obliterate yours.

At best such a world is stable and predictable. Contracts are honored and a man's word really does become his bond. In outcome, if not intent, moral standards are high, since no one enters into relationships of convenience with the untrustworthy. On the other hand, such a world resists all change, new ideas, and innovations. It is utterly inimical to entrepreneurship.

Fortunately, the larger world in which we live is less rigid. It is populated with trusting optimists who readily do business with strangers and innovators. A 26-year-old Steve Jobs with no track record to speak of or a 52-year-old Ray Kroc with nearly ten failures behind him can get support to start an Apple or a McDonald's. People are allowed to move from Maine to Montana or from plastics to baked goods without a lot of whys and wherefores.

Projects that require the integrity and ability of a large team and are subject to many market and technological risks can nonetheless attract enthusiastic support. Optimists focus more on the pot of gold at the end of the rainbow than on their ability to find and punish the guilty in case a failure occurs.

Our tolerance for broken promises encourages risk taking. Absent the fear of debtors' prison and the stigma of bankruptcy, entrepreneurs readily borrow the funds they need to grow.

Tolerance also allows resources to move out of enterprises that have outlived their functions. When the buggy whip manufacturer is forced out of business, we understand that some promises will have to be broken—promises that perhaps ought not to have been made. But adjustments to the automobile age are more easily accomplished if we don't demand full retribution for every breach of implicit and explicit contract.

Even unreconstructed scoundrels are tolerated in our world as long as they have something else to offer. The genius inventors, the visionary organizers, and the intrepid pioneers are not cast away merely because they cannot be trusted on all dimensions. We "adjust"—and allow great talent to offset moral frailty—because we know deep down that knaves and blackguards have contributed much to our progress. And this, perhaps unprincipled, tolerance facilitates a dynamic entrepreneurial economy.

Since ancient times, philosophers have contrasted a barbaric "state of nature" with a perfect, well-ordered society that has somehow tamed humankind's propensity toward force and fraud. Fortunately, we have created something that is neither Beirut nor Bucharest. We don't require honesty, but we honor and celebrate it. Like a kaleidoscope, we have order and change. We make beautiful, well-fitting relationships that we break and reform at every turn.

We should remember, however, that this third way works only as long as most of us live by an honorable moral compass. Since our trust isn't grounded in self-interest, it is fragile. And, indeed, we all know of organizations, industries, and even whole societies in which trust has given way either to a destructive free-for-all or to inflexible rules and bureaucracy. Only our individual wills, our determination to do what is right, whether or not it is profitable, save us from choosing between chaos and stagnation.

Notes

[1]The HBR Collection *Ethics in Practice* has six citations (Boston: Harvard Business School Press, 1989).

[2]"Management by Necessity," *Inc.*, March 1989, p. 33. Reprinted with permission. Copyright © 1989 by Goldhirsh Group, Inc., 38 Commercial Wharf, Boston, Mass. 02310.

[3]*The Discourses*, Chapter XIII, Book 2, Modern Library Edition, 1950.

[4]"In the early 1970s," reports *Forbes* (Toni Mack, "Profitable If Not Popular," May 30, 1988, 34), "Wyatt found himself squeezed between rising natural gas prices and low-priced contracts to supply gas to cities like San Antonio and Austin. His solution? Renege. He simply refused to honor the contract."

CASES

Case 1.1: Borland's Brave Beginnings

Philippe Kahn*, the colorful former CEO and current chairman of Borland International, built a powerful software company from the ground up with a series of brilliant business moves including the 1991 acquisition of Ashton-Tate, one of the software industry's biggest companies, for $440 million. Until very recently, the company was extremely successful, culminating in the building of a palatial headquarters complex costing nearly $100 million. At one point, Kahn even entertained thoughts of challenging Microsoft as the world's top software manufacturer.[2] Although the company has recently fallen on hard times, its beginning is one that some would consider morally questionable, while others would say it was nothing more than "smart moves within the game of business."

In an interview with *Inc.* magazine in 1989, Kahn told the story of Borland's humble beginnings. Operating out of two small rooms and strapped for cash, he couldn't afford to place an ad in *Byte* magazine, the best forum to reach his target market. In order to convince the ad salesman to extend credit terms, Kahn hired "extra people" to scurry around and made sure the phones were ringing in order to look busy. He prepared a media plan on a chart in which *Byte* was crossed out but made sure the salesman "accidentally" saw the chart. When the salesman asked if they wanted to advertise in *Byte*, Kahn replied that it was not the right audience and that they couldn't afford it. The salesman pleaded and eventually gave good terms of credit. The ad ran once and sold $150,000 worth of software, launching the upstart venture on the path to succcess.[3]

*See the reading "Why Be Honest If Honesty Doesn't Pay?," esp. p. 71.

[2] Julie Pitta, "The Barbarian Steps Down," *Los Angeles Times*, 12 January 1995, D1+.

[3] See "Managing by Necessity," *Inc.* (March 1989): 33+.

Questions for Discussion:

1. Are Kahn's actions unethical in any way? Is this deception or just shrewd business sense at work? How would Carr and Bowie respond?
2. One could argue that it was the salesman's responsibility to check Kahn's financial documents, so it was his fault for being lured into lending credit. Do you agree? What would be the reasonable responsibilities of the salesman, according to the "rules of the game"?

3. Many would argue that everyone benefited and no one was hurt, thus the action was moral. Do you agree? Why or why not?

Case 1.2: Sales Tactics at MetLife

In late 1993, the insurance industry was rocked by allegations that some offices of the Metropolitan Life Insurance Company (MetLife) were engaged in deceptive sales practices. MetLife is the company that uses the characters of the Peanuts gang in its advertisements. Its agents were accused of misleading people around the country into buying life insurance policies by telling them that these policies were high-interest retirement savings plans. In particular, nurses were targeted by agents who called themselves "nursing specialists," and the word "deposit" was substituted for the term "premiums" to describe the payments.[4] Other agents call themselves "financial advisers" instead of "insurance agents" for public relations purposes.[5] The nurses' program is just a derivative of a popular insurance marketing program called private pension plans, which are insurance products that carry both a death and an investment benefit. Glenn Daily, a New York insurance consultant says of such practices, "it's just a hook, it's marketing puffery."[6] Life insurance can be an appropriate form of savings; however, it is most beneficial for its death benefit. A clear beneficiary in the sale of a life insurance policy is the agent. A first-year agent can receive a first-year commission of up to 55% or $550 on a $1,000 whole-life policy. In comparison, selling an annuity nets about 2% or $20 on the same investment.[7] While most agents disclose the fact that they are selling insurance and MetLife was the only company investigated, some experts report that the practice is widespread in the industry.[8]

[4]Greg Steinmetz, "MetLife Probed in Several States for Sales Tactics," *Wall Street Journal* (Eastern ed.), 6 October 1993, A3+.

[5]Greg Steinmetz, "MetLife Got Caught; Others Sent Same Letter," *Wall Street Journal* (Eastern ed.), 6 January 1994, B1+.

[6]Ibid.

[7]Suzanne Woolley and Gail DeGeorge, "Policies of Deception?" *Business Week* (17 January 1994): 24–25.

[8]Ibid.

Questions for Discussion:

1. How much should a salesperson be expected to reveal to customers? Is not engaging in full disclosure really just another form of lying or just harmless puffery? How might Carr respond?

2. At a car dealership, most people know that the stated price isn't the real price; thus consumers who pay full price are labeled foolish. Can one legitimately argue that it is the consumers' responsibility to know the rules of the game in this situation as well? What might be the critical difference between the two scenarios?

COMMENTARY

Despite Max Weber's enduring yet controversial thesis on the contribution of Protestant beliefs to the progress of capitalism (see p. 195), many persons of the Christian faith still feel an uneasy tension between the moral values that seem to permeate commerce and the behavioral standards they believe should govern all of their affairs. For many, the most troubling aspect of participation in business is the perception that there must be a significant compromise of moral ideals in order to gain material success. Indeed, it often seems that the distinction between outright dishonesty and shrewd business decisions is a blurred one. The Borland case included in this chapter is a case in point. It poignantly portrays the dilemma between truth-telling and smart business strategy.

Like the Borland case, many situations in business involve a clear conflict of values. However, we are firmly convinced that one can achieve success without compromise in many commercial practices. In fact, as Bhide and Stevenson assert, contrary to popular belief, trust and honesty are probably more the norms of business practice than the rare exceptions. As such, we believe that Christian businesspeople can live with a unified set of ethical guidelines that can govern their lives in totality though at times it may carry a direct financial cost. One can indeed simultaneously fully honor God and participate in most of the affairs of business.

With this in mind, let us examine the classic essays that are included in this chapter. Albert Z. Carr argues that there are indeed two operative sets of ethics for participants in business, one for private life and one for commercial transactions. He offers a provocative defense of the morality of business by arguing that it is analogous to the rules that govern the game of poker. He is right that bluffing is an ethical aspect of the game of poker because all who sit at the table are aware of the rules in operation. However, what we must ask ourselves is whether or not the same can be said for business. Should business be in fact judged by its own special moral rules because it is like a poker game? Does this mean, then, that participants must live with two operative sets of values?

Norman Bowie offers some very insightful comments in response to these questions. In contrast to Carr, Bowie argues that there are clearly situations in which the game analogy does not fit, because, unlike poker players, not all of the participants or those who are affected by their decisions are at the table by choice. Take, for example, consumers who are not members of the business community yet who are affected by dangerous products or who are swindled out of their retirement money.

Furthermore, not all of the "players" are aware of, nor could they be reasonably expected to be aware of, the operative rules. The case of former Borland CEO Philippe Kahn and his company's beginnings is an excellent example of a situation that clearly renders the poker analogy inadequate. As a side note, there is at least one company of which we are aware whose business is that of renting office space, equipment, and employees on a *very* short-term basis. Thus Borland's start is probably not an isolated episode of puffery.

To some, this is a cute story of success and Kahn's actions are simply regarded as smart business moves. To others, however, his actions constitute outright deception and if it were not for the successful outcome, Kahn's deception of the *Byte* salesman could even be regarded as fraud.

While Borland's start is a nice story, Kahn's actions are morally unacceptable. If the story had turned out differently and Borland could not pay for the space, there would be nothing endearing about the tale at all. *Byte* would have lost $20,000, and the salesman would possibly have been fired from his position. While these are arguably small losses, it is the principle (not principal) that is at stake.

Some will undoubtedly still argue that the salesman should not have been so naive as to have been persuaded into extending credit without a thorough check of Borland's financial documents. However, a reasonable and competent salesperson does not anticipate being misled in such a manner. Nor are salespersons typically expected to review financial documents.

Some will still be unconvinced that any wrong was done by Kahn. However, two parallel examples should serve to reinforce our point. The first involves former L.A. Kings hockey team and Toronto Argonauts football franchise owner Bruce McNall, who had amassed a fortune in the antique coin business before entering the lucrative world of sports franchise ownership. He is probably best known for bringing hockey star Wayne Gretzky to the Los Angeles Kings. Recently McNall's reputation began to quickly crumble along with his financial empire, culminating in a declaration of bankruptcy in 1994. With the loss of his wealth came accusations of fraud. In late 1994 McNall pleaded guilty of defrauding several banks out of more than $236 million. His crime was that he falsified financial documents and transactions in order to inflate the extent and worth of the coin collection he pledged as collateral for loans.[9]

The second case involves the quick fall of wonder boy Barry Minkow's carpet cleaning company, ZZZZBest, in the late 1980s. By age eighteen, Minkow had achieved millionaire status and was heralded as a genius for the overnight success of his company. Just as quickly as the company soared, however, came its demise. Minkow was recently

[9]"Sports Executive Enters Guilty Plea," *New York Times* (late N.Y. ed.), 15 December 1994, D7.

released from prison for his role in defrauding investors and lenders out of more than $100 million. One of his transgressions was that he tricked investors by inflating the sales and profitability figures of his company. On several occasions, Minkow fooled an independent auditor into believing that he had multimillion-dollar building restoration contracts in Sacramento and San Diego. Minkow and several employees set up "quick offices" in both cities, and a warehouse near San Diego was filled with carpets to make the operations look credible. Then they set up ZZZZBest signs and phony contractors' permits in the high-rise buildings and brought the auditor in on a weekend when they knew the buildings would be empty.[10] In reality, the structures were not ZZZZBest accounts at all, just scenes of a sneaky and well-acted scam.

One wonders if there is any difference between the actions of McNall and Minkow and those of Philippe Kahn. The only real differences are matters of degree and outcome. However, as we mentioned in the book's introduction, consequences are an inadequate measure for morality, since they are usually not in our control.

The MetLife case is another instance in which Carr's poker analogy seems faulty. Clearly the average consumer does not know that they are buying life insurance when they are being told otherwise. While one could argue that perhaps it is the consumers' responsibility to be more sophisticated in these situations, insurance agents are placed in positions of trust as experts much the way doctors, lawyers, and accountants are. As professionals in positions of trust, they should have fiduciary-type responsibilities to look out for the best interests of their clients rather than their own. MetLife was investigated by Florida regulators and ended up agreeing to pay a $20 million fine to settle the accusations. The company also pledged up to $76 million to refund premiums to about 60,000 policyholders who may have been misled from 1990 to 1993. Several executives and agents were fired, and sales of individual policies plunged amid the allegations.[11] These are clear examples of deception in which one cannot participate without a definite compromise of moral integrity.

In other instances, however, Carr's poker analogy seems correct. Some business dealings have the element of a game in which the application of the standard for truthfulness deviates from other dimensions of life. Consider a situation to which we can all readily relate, the process of searching for work. It is an understood part of the "game" that job seekers dress their best and include only the highlights from their past experiences on their résumés. Potential employers are aware that applicants are merely putting their best foot forward. They also generally take it upon themselves to ask appropriate questions during the interview process and bear the responsibility of checking the

[10]Daniel Akst, "How Barry Minkow Fooled the Auditors," *Forbes* (2 October 1989): 126–32; Kevin Kelly, "Rich, Young and Sleazy: An 80's Morality Tale," *Business Week* (26 February 1990): 22–23.

[11]Leslie Scism, "MetLife's Sales of Individual Policies Plunge Amid Allegations of Sales Tactics," *Wall Street Journal* (Eastern ed.), 18 May 1994, A4.

references that are provided. Moreover, employers themselves are also playing by the understood rules. Most often, they reveal only the most positive aspects of their companies in order to attract the best possible employees.

Imagine what the employment process would be like if the same standards for forthrightness applied to other parts of life were expected to apply here. Some may be forced to write self-descriptive statements in cover letters such as "difficult, often late, nonself-starter seeks non-challenging, high-paying position with a long lunch break and a push-over for a supervisor." Likewise, some companies would have to advertise their openings by stating "struggling company with low morale seeks strong candidate willing to work long hours for a nasty boss in exchange for an average benefits package and low wages."

Consider further most car- and home-sales transactions in which the stated price and "final offers" are not actually true because bartering is the known and expected norm. These are morally acceptable practices because in these situations all reasonable participants are indeed aware of what the operative rules are. However, Carr and Bowie are correct in saying that there are still ethical principles to be followed in these situations as there are in poker. In car sales, rolling back odometers is not acceptable within the rules. In the employment process, lying and falsifying credentials is clearly outside of the normal standards of conduct. However, in some very specific situations "bluffing" is justifiable. Because everyone has access to the rules, no reasonable participant is being deceived. As such, participants should not be considered unethical, as they have not deviated from the principle of truthfulness. In these well-defined and specific instances there is no real conflict of morals at all.

Some, however, claim not only that there is no conflict between solid moral values and profits but also that good ethics is actually good for long-term business. There are at least several recent books with titles that proclaim the truthfulness of this assertion. Moreover, many businesses seem to believe that at least the perception of ethical conduct is rewarding, as consumers are constantly inundated with slogans from companies that claim to value ethics in their dealings.

Bhide and Stevenson argue that although the idea makes intuitive sense, there is no empirical evidence to back the claim that honesty will actually pay. In most cases, they assert, violations of honesty go unpunished because many victims refuse to acknowledge that they have been duped, or they choose to simply move on with their lives rather than be tied up in costly litigation. Furthermore, they cite several examples in which transgressors of truth actually have been handsomely rewarded for their efforts because of inequities in power. Bhide and Stevenson come to the conclusion that honesty must be, and in most instances is, adhered to as a value for purposes of morality rather than for the sake of profits.

Although the Bible has plenty to say about business practice, Christian ethics and profitability are not synonymous. Morality is not a magical blueprint for a successful business in the material sense. While numerous businesses have indeed been built upon reputations for honesty and fairness, there is no perfect correlation between good ethics and good business. If there were, there would be no need for books or courses on business ethics, as nearly everyone would practice solid moral behavior because of the prospect of financial reward. The only topic left for debate would be a matter of short-term versus long-term strategy. Although sound moral behavior may be honored in the life to come, good ethical practices do not necessarily amount to material success in this one. Business professionals must be ethical because it is right and because truly virtuous acts are those that are also done for the right reasons.

As van Wensveen Siker reminds us, perhaps we can learn from all of these differing approaches to the conflicts between Christian ethics and business practice. Carr may be accurate from a *descriptive* viewpoint that ethical dilemmas will be experienced, as there are times when the two sets of values are in conflict. However, Bowie and Bhide and Stevenson are correct from a *normative* viewpoint, that is how we *ought* to view this issue, in arguing that compartmentalization is not the answer. In addition to their insightful comments, we further question the viability of Carr's suggestion that one must function as a dualist. We wonder whether someone can consistently act with one set of values in the business world and then come home to treat family and neighbors with another. In conclusion, while many standard business behaviors are fully compatible with Christian ethics, it is clear that it is the demands of business that must give way to the moral imperatives of Christ when the two are in conflict, not the other way around.

The cases in this chapter clearly illustrate that business certainly presents situations in which there is a clear conflict between Christian ethics and what some would call smart financial maneuvering. In many other cases, though, there is no real conflict at all in terms of underlying principles. "Bluffing" in some well-defined instances in which all of the reasonable players are abiding by the same rules does not compromise a commitment to the ideal of truthfulness. One can indeed successfully participate in business while maintaining a unified set of moral beliefs. However, there are clearly situations in which adhering to one's morals will entail a direct financial cost. Thus the claim that good ethics is good business may be true in some instances, but while it makes intuitive sense, the relationship may not be a consistent one.

TWO

Ethics in a Global Economy

Only in special circumstances is it right to do in Rome as the Romans do.

Norman E. Bowie, "Business Ethics and Cultural Relativism"

If we wanted our product to have a chance to win on its own merits, we had to follow the functioning system.

Former Lockheed CEO Carl Kotchian on his decision to pay bribes
to Japanese officials in order to sell a large contract

INTRODUCTION

With the rapid globalization of the economy come increasing tensions over the moral norms that govern business practices throughout the world. Imagine yourself as a business executive responsible for expanding your firm's markets into different international arenas. As a result of different ethical standards of doing business, you will be faced with the temptation to offer bribes to high government officials in order to secure access to the market for your product. Such bribes will be expected as a normal part of doing business in that part of the world, though they are considered immoral and illegal in much of the West. What will you do? Will you adhere to what you consider a universal standard that does not permit bribery? Or will you adopt the philosophy that "when in Rome, [you may feel free to] do as the Romans do," and justify offering the bribes because that is acceptable in that culture?

Or imagine that you are a project manager for a large construction company that is expanding its business into the Third World, where safety and environmental standards are significantly lower than in the United States. By adopting lower safety standards, your company can save a great deal of money, but at what risk to the people living in the community? Do you uphold the higher safety standards or play by the rules in the country in which you are building the projects, justifying lower standards by doing business like the Romans when in Rome?

Conflicts over differences in morals in situations like these can indeed cause a tremendous amount of confusion over what set of norms should be followed when one is working abroad. Like the issues addressed in chapter 1, this is particularly problematic for those who believe that Judeo-Christian morals are absolute and should govern their lives in totality.

Traditionally, there have been two ways to address the problem. The first is to follow the edict that one should "act like the Romans, when in Rome" and abide by the standards of the "host" country. Relying on arguments that all morals are culturally rather than transcendentally defined, one may convince himself that to abide by the standards of one's own country is to engage in an unacceptable form of ethnocentrism. This appeal to what is known as "cultural relativism" asserts that moral standards are relative from culture to culture. As such, no one can say with certainty that the standards of one culture are superior to those of another.

For example, in a well-publicized case in the 1970s that involved bribery, Lockheed CEO Carl Kotchian testified before Congress that he had paid millions of dollars in bribes to Japanese officials in order to secure a multi-million-dollar contract for his firm.[1] He reasoned that since these types of payments were common practice in Japan, his actions were morally acceptable though the practice is disapproved of in the U.S. Moreover, he argued, if he would have adhered to American beliefs about bribery, his company would have lost the contract and, with it, thousands of jobs here in the U.S.

In disdain of the relativism in the do-as-the-Romans-do approach, others have chosen to resolve the tension by simply abiding by the standards of their home country. A well-known case involving Italian tax practices provides a classic illustration. It is an excellent example of the effect that such a stance can have on one's ability to successfully do business in a foreign land. Unlike corporations operating in America under American tax laws, corporations operating in Italy are not expected to report the "true" amount of taxes due the government on their tax forms. Instead, the initial amount stated is viewed by the Italian government as the opening position for negotiation. Government officials will in turn counter the figure and eventually the amount owed will be worked out. Believing it was tantamount to cheating, one young American bank executive refused to abide by these standards and filed in the American manner. In reward for his "honesty" his company was stuck with a tax bill several times the amount stated on their forms.[2]

[1] Carl Kotchian, "The Payoff: Lockheed's 70-Day Mission to Tokyo," *Saturday Review* (9 July 1977): 7–12; cited in Thomas Donaldson and Patricia Werhane, *Ethical Issues in Business: A Philosophical Approach*, 2d ed. (Englewood Cliffs, N.J.: Prentice-Hall, 1983), 25–33.

[2] Arthur L. Kelley, "Italian Tax Mores," in Donaldson and Werhane, *Ethical Issues in Business: A Philosophical Approach*, 84–86.

On the surface, these examples illustrate the tensions that can occur when an individual is working abroad. For those who hold that values are absolute and should govern one wherever he engages in economic transactions, adapting to the ethics of different countries can lead to some unacceptable compromises of values. Conversely, it seems that maintaining the values of the home country in a simplistic manner can, at the least, appear culturally insensitive, and at worst even jeopardize the ability to succeed in a foreign land. Thus a troubling question that arises is whether or not one can succeed in international business while abiding by Judeo-Christian ethics. Should one strictly adhere to Western standards of conduct even if it means the loss of ability to engage in business? Or are ethics really culturally determined, so that one can in good conscience do as the Romans do?

While these questions are indeed difficult to resolve, the articles that are included in this chapter have some important insights to contribute to the issue. Norman Bowie offers a profound critique of cultural relativism in his article "Business Ethics and Cultural Relativism." He rejects cultural relativism on philosophical grounds, arguing that many apparent moral disagreements may really be over facts and not underlying ethical principles. Moreover, he argues, cultural relativism is inconsistent with our use of moral language and provides no defense for a lapse into individual relativism. He concludes that the nuances of the ethics in international business are more complex than they first appear. Thus the notion "when in Rome do as the Romans do" is inadequate as a consistent standard to guide business behavior in a foreign land.

Thomas Donaldson offers a practical model to guide moral decision making in the context of multi-national corporations. Specifically, he addresses those instances in which the ethical norms of the host country appear to be of a lower standard than those of the home country. In order to resolve these dilemmas, he constructs an ethical algorithm based on morally minimal duties as a guide to decision making that seems to avoid both the pitfalls of total relativism and cultural imperialism.

READINGS

Business Ethics and Cultural Relativism

Norman E. Bowie

Multinational Ethics (Englewood Cliffs, N. J.: Prentice-Hall, 1989), 366–82. Copyright © 1989 by Norman E. Bowie.

Introduction

Business people doing business abroad know full well that ethical practices, including ethical practices in business, differ among cultures. You can't rely on what is ethical in the U.S. when you do business abroad. How should American companies practice business in other countries? A popular way of raising this issue is to ask whether U.S. multinationals should follow the advice "When in Rome, do as the Romans do."

In discussing this issue, a distinction must be made between home and host countries. The home country is where the corporation has its charter of incorporation. Usually the multinational has major facilities in the home country and has had a long history of business practice there. The host country is any other country where the multinational does business. If European and Japanese companies build manufacturing plants in the U.S., the United States is the host country.... Foreign firms face their own version of the U.S. multinational question: When in America, should you do as the Americans do?...

When two cultures have different moral traditions and a corporation does business in both, how should the company behave? The first option is that the company follow the moral practices of its own country. Most Americans would find this option unacceptable and would not, for example, want foreign companies to treat American women the way women allegedly are treated in certain other countries.

Another alternative is for the company to follow the moral practices of the host country. Most Americans would find that option unacceptable as well. If that option were required; American corporations would have to treat women in foreign countries where they do business as women are treated in those countries. In many cases Americans would object, just as they would object if American corporate officials treated black South Africans the way South Africa does.

The principle "When in Rome do as the Romans do" might seem like a reasonable and tolerant position to adopt, and many officers and managers of multinationals often speak as if this is the position they have adopted. Who are we, they argue, to impose our moral standards on the rest of the world? For example, the Foreign Corrupt Practices Act, which prohibits the payment of unrecorded bribes to foreign governments or officials, has come under intense attack. After all, if the payment of bribes is morally acceptable in country *x*, why should we impose our moral views about bribery on that country? Besides, if American multinationals don't bribe, German and Japanese multinationals will—or so the argument goes. Former President Jimmy Carter's attempt to include a country's record on violating or not violating fundamental human rights when making foreign policy decisions came under the same kind of criticism.

Philosophers have given a name to the when-in-Rome-do-as-the-Romans-do position. Cultural relativism is the doctrine that what is right or wrong, good or bad, depends on one's culture. If the Irish consider abortion to be morally wrong, abortion *is* morally wrong in Ireland. If the

Swedes do not consider abortion to be morally wrong, then abortion *is not* morally wrong in Sweden. There is no universal principle to which the Swedes and the Irish can appeal that determines whether abortion really is wrong or not.

Philosophers have given a name to the when-in-Rome-do-as-the-Romans-do position: cultural relativism.

This relativistic way of thinking has always been prominent in the thinking of many social scientists. After all, the discoveries by anthropologists, sociologists, and psychologists documented the diversity of moral beliefs and punctured some of the pseudo-justifications that had been given for the superiority of white Western male ways of thinking. Philosophers, by and large, welcomed the corrections to prejudicial moral thinking but nonetheless found the doctrine of cultural relativism to be seriously flawed. That people and cultures disagree as to what is right or wrong, good or bad, and behave accordingly can be accepted as a fact. But what implications does this fact have for ethical decision making? Some have argued that the diversity of "moral" behavior shows that the theory of moral relativism is true. How do relativists establish their position? Many relativists have pointed to the fact that different individuals and cultures hold different views about what constitutes moral behavior as evidence for the truth of their position. Philosophers are virtually unanimous in the opinion that this is an invalid argument.

First, many philosophers claim that the "facts" aren't really what they seem. Several writers refer to the fact that in some cultures, after a certain age parents are put to death. In our culture such behavior would be murder. We take care of our parents. Does this difference in behavior prove that the two cultures disagree about matters of ethics? No, it does not. Suppose the other culture believes that people exist in the afterlife in the same condition that they leave their present life. It would be very cruel to have one's parents exist

eternally in an unhealthy state. By killing them when they are relatively active and vigorous, you insure their happiness for all eternity. The underlying ethical principle of this culture is that children have duties to their parents, including the duty to be concerned with their parents' happiness as they approach old age. This ethical principle is identical with our own. What looked like a difference in ethics between our culture and another turned out, upon close examination, to be a difference based on factual evidence alone.

Here is another example that shows how the "facts" really aren't what they seem. Cultures differ in physical setting, in economic development, in the state of their science and technology, in their literacy rate, and in many other ways. Even if there were universal moral principles, they would have to be applied in these different cultural contexts. Given the different situations in which cultures exist, it would come as no surprise to find universal principles applied in different ways. Hence the differences in so-called ethical behavior among cultures would be superficial differences only. The cultures would agree on fundamental universal moral principles. One commonly held general principle appeals to the public good; it says that social institutions and individual behavior should be ordered so that they lead to the greatest good for the greatest number. Many different forms of social organization and individual behavior are consistent with this principle. The point of these two arguments is that superficial differences among cultures on so-called ethical behavior may not reflect genuine disagreement about ethics. Unless the relativist can establish basic differences about matters of ethics, the case for relativism cannot be made.

This discussion is important because it shows that ethical judgments are bound up in some complicated way with the facts. The existence of simple, safe birth-control methods has implications for sexual morality. The existence of sophisticated mechanical techniques for prolonging human life has implications for medical ethics. Since our ethical judgments depend in part upon what the facts are, the first step in resolving disputes about ethics should be to determine whether or not the disputants are disagreeing over the facts. If the disagreement is factual, it will need to be resolved before tackling any ethical disagreement. If the factual disagreement is resolved, the ethical disagreement often dissolves.

Some philosophers have made the strong claim that ultimately all the disagreement between cultures is either about the facts or about nothing more than the attempt to apply universal moral principles to specific situations. These philosophers claim that the apparent diversity in behavior among cultures is only apparent, and that ultimately cultures do agree on certain fundamental ethical standards. A discussion of this claim would take us beyond philosophy to anthropology, history, theology, and a host of other disciplines. The analysis thus far, though, should have established the early contention that you can't claim that cultural relativism is true just because cultures have different moral standards.

> ### If cultural relativism were true, there would be no place for the concept of a moral reformer.

Another common strategy for criticizing relativism is to show that the consequences of taking the perspective of ethical relativism lead to some rather bizarre results. One of the bizarre results is that if relativism is true, then agreement on morals is, in principle, impossible. Of course, in this context *agreement* means agreement on the basis of reasons. There can be agreement by force. That's equivalent to "Worship my God or I'll cut off your head." Why there can be no rational agreement is obvious when an examination is made of the definition of relativism. Cultural relativism is the view that what is right or wrong is determined by culture. So if one culture says that abortion is right and another says it is wrong, that has to be the end of the matter. Abortion *is* morally permissible in some cultures and morally wrong in others.

But suppose a person from one culture moves to another and tries to persuade the other culture to change its view. Suppose someone moves from a culture where slavery is immoral to one where slavery is morally permitted. Normally, if a person were to try to convince the culture where slavery was permitted that slavery was morally wrong, we would refer to such a person as a moral reformer. But if cultural relativism were true, there would be no place for the concept of a moral reformer. Slavery is right in those cultures that say it is right and wrong in those cultures that say it is wrong. If the reformer fails to persuade a slave-holding country to change its mind, the reformer's antislavery position was never right. If the reformer is successful in persuading a country to change its mind, the reformer's antislavery views would be wrong—until the country did, in fact, change its view. Then the reformer's antislavery view was right. Now that's a bizarre result.

Underlying these two objections is the broader objection that relativism is inconsistent with our use of moral language. When Russia and the United States argue about the moral rights of human beings, they seem to be genuinely disagreeing about a matter of ethics. How unfortunate it would be if that dispute had to be resolved by nonrational means, since rational agreement is in principle impossible. People do marshal arguments in behalf of ethical views. If relativism is true, such arguments are doomed to failure or are a mere subterfuge to creating agreement. Similarly, we do have a place in our language for the concept of a moral reformer. Is this use of language really deviant, as it would have to be if relativism were true?

By virtue of the arguments developed so far, we see that you can't move from the facts of diversity in so-called ethical behavior and disagreement in ethics to moral relativism. The facts really don't establish ethical relativism, and the facts about our use of moral language are inconsistent with a relativist theory.

Although these arguments are powerful ones, they do not deliver a knockout blow to cultural relativism. A cultural relativist might admit that cultural relativism doesn't follow from the fact of cultural diversity. However, in the absence of universal moral principles, cultural relativists could argue that cultural relativism is the only theory available to help make sense of moral phenomena. Some cultural practices might be shown to be based on common moral principles, but the relativists doubt that all can.

Similarly, the cultural relativist might argue that our language does reflect a commitment to universal moral principles but that since we are mistaken about the existence of such principles, our language should be reformed. We should talk differently. At one time people used to talk and act as if the world were flat. Now they don't. Surely we can change our ethical language in the same way. Future historians could note that people used to talk as if there were universal moral principles, but of course we don't talk that way anymore. The cultural relativist insists that the only knockout blow against cultural relativism is to establish the truth or correctness of at least one universal moral principle that applies to all cultures.

Such confidence by the cultural relativist might not be warranted. Consider this argument against cultural relativism:[1] A spectrum of moral positions is laid out in Figure 1.

FIGURE I

Individual Relativism	Cultural Relativism	Universalism

Individual relativism is the view that what is right or wrong, good or bad, depends on the feelings or attitudes of the individual. If an individual believes abortion is wrong, then abortion is wrong for that individual. If another individual believes abortion is not wrong, then abortion is not wrong for *that* individual. There is no valid cultural norm that will tell us which individual is objectively right.

The strategy is to show that any argument the cultural relativist uses against universalism can also be used by the individual relativist against cultural relativism. Similarly, any argument the cultural relativist uses against the individual relativist can be used by the universalist against the cultural relativist. The cultural relativist is constantly fighting a war on two fronts.

For example, against an individual relativist, a cultural relativist would often argue that if individual relativism were the prevailing view, a stable society would be impossible. Arguments from Thomas Hobbes or decision theory would prove the point. If individual relativism were the prevailing norm, life would be "nasty, brutish, and short" in the words of Hobbes' *Leviathan* (1650).

But in the world of today, any arguments that appeal to social stability will have to be applied universally. In the atomic age and in an age where terrorism is in some societies an acceptable form of political activity, the stability problems that affect individual relativism equally afflict cultural relativism. If the necessity for social stability is a good argument for a cultural relativist to use against an individual relativist, it is an equally good argument for a universalist to use against a cultural relativist.

Multinational CEOs are likely to accept the argument thus far, however, because multinationals need a stable international environment if they are to make a profit in the long run. As any adviser for any multinational will tell you, one of the chief factors affecting an investment decision in a foreign country is the political stability of both that individual country and of the region surrounding it. An unstable country or region is highly inimical to the conduct of international business.

On the other hand, if the cultural relativist argues that there is no objective basis for asserting a universal moral principle, an individual relativist could make the same charge against the cultural relativist. What justification can a culture give for saying that the moral principles of some people are right but that the moral values of others, e.g., the reformer or prophet, are wrong? My hypothesis is that the types of argument available for the cultural relativist against the individual relativist are also available to the universalist against the cultural relativist. The real battle in ethics is not between the cultural relativist and the universalist but between the individual relativist and the universalist.

Even if this argument succeeds, the international business person has not been helped very much. She still doesn't know what her company should do when behaving abroad, and executives with other companies don't know what to do when they practice business in the United States. Despite appearances to the contrary, a great deal of morality has already been internationalized, either explicitly, by treaty or by belonging to the U.N.; or implicitly, through language and conduct.

> **Despite appearances to the contrary, a great deal of morality has already been internationalized, either explicitly or implicitly.**

For example, American business leaders engaged in business abroad often complain that the Foreign Corrupt Practices Act puts American business at a competitive disadvantage in doing business abroad. They argue that bribery is standard business practice abroad and that our laws against bribery put American firms at a disadvantage. You get the impression from reading the press that the U.S. is fairly unique in making bribery illegal and that bribery is a common practice in many parts of the world.

Such an impression is seriously mistaken, however. As Michael Bogdan, Professor of International Law at the University of Jund, Sweden, has pointed out, bribery—at least of public officials—is prohibited by the laws of practically every nation.[2] Member countries of the OECD have adopted guidelines, albeit voluntary ones, against bribery. Both the International Chamber of Commerce and the Permanent Council of the Organization of American States have called on states to pass antibribery legislation outlawing the bribery of officials in host countries. Sweden has enacted such a law. Finally the General Assembly of the United Nations adopted Resolution 3514, condemning bribery among other practices. Research has also shown that U.S. multinationals were involved in Middle East scandals nearly twice as often as multinational corporations of other nationalities.[3] Moreover, for those scandals involving non-U.S. multinationals, the host countries in the Mideast generally originated the investigation. The notion

that bribery is generally permitted and practiced abroad does not stand up to empirical scrutiny.

Whereas the explicit acceptance of a universal morality has often been commented upon, the implicit acceptance of universal standards has not. Note the following: The words *democracy* and *democratic* have become honorific terms. Nearly all national states claim they are democracies—people's democracies, worker democracies, but democracies nonetheless. The August 4, 1986, issue of *Newsweek* carried a story about repression and the denial of civil rights in Chile. The president of Chile responded to his critics by calling his dictatorship "a democratic government with authority." I have yet to come across a state that brags that it is not a democracy and has no intention of being one. (Some nations do indicate they don't want to be a democracy like the U.S.)

A notion of shared values can be of assistance here as well. There is a whole range of behavior—e.g., torture, murder of the innocent, racism—that nearly all agree is wrong. A government accused of torture does not respond by saying that a condemnation of torture is just a matter of subjective morality. It doesn't respond by saying, "We think torture is right but you don't." Rather, the standard response is to deny that any torture took place. If the evidence of torture is too strong, a finger will be pointed either at the victim or at the morally outraged country: "They do it too." In this case the guilt is spread to all. Even the Nazis denied that genocide took place. What is important to note is that *no* state replies that there is nothing wrong with genocide or torture.

This conceptual argument is buttressed by another. Suppose an anthropologist discovers a large populated South Pacific island. How many tribes are on the island? Part of the answer to that question will be determined by seeing if such things as killing and murder are permitted, and if so, against whom? If they are not permitted, that counts as evidence that there is only one tribe. If people on the northern half of the island permit stealing directed against southerners but do not permit northerners to steal from one another, that provides evidence that there are at least two tribes. What often distinguishes one society from another is the fact that society *A* does not permit murder, lying, and stealing against members of *A*—society *A* couldn't permit that and still be a society, but society *A* does permit that kind of behavior against society *B*. What this strategy shows is that one of the criteria for having a society is that there be a shared morality among the individuals that comprise it.

What follows from this is that there are certain basic rules that must be followed in each society; e.g., don't lie, don't commit murder. There is a moral minimum in the sense that if these specific moral rules aren't generally followed, then there won't be a society at all. These moral rules are universal, but they are not practiced universally. That is, members of society *A* agree that they should not lie to each other, but they think it is permissible to lie to the members of other societies. Such moral rules are not relative; they simply are not practiced universally.

However, multinational corporations are obligated to follow these moral rules. Since the multinational is practicing business in the society, and since these moral norms are necessary for the existence of the society, the multinational has an obligation to support those norms. Otherwise multinationals would be in the position of benefiting from doing business with the society while at the same time engaging in activity that would undermine the society. Such conduct would be unjust.

Since the norms constituting a moral minimum are likely to be few in number it can be said that the argument thus far has achieved something—i.e., multinationals are obligated to follow the moral norms required for there to be a society at all—but it hasn't achieved very much, and most issues surrounding multinationals do not involve alleged violations of these norms. Perhaps a stronger argument can be found by making explicit the morality of the marketplace. That there is an implicit morality in the market is a point that is often ignored by most economists and many business people.

Although economists and business people assume that individuals are basically self-interested, they must also assume that people involved

in business transactions will honor their contracts. In most economic exchanges the transfer of product for money is not simultaneous. You deliver and I pay, or vice versa. . . .

Multinationals are obligated to follow the moral norms of the market. Contrary behavior is inconsistent and ultimately self-defeating.

This point can be illustrated by considering whether a business person should keep her contract when it is to her advantage not to. The contract device is extremely useful in business. The hiring of employees, the use of credit, the ordering and supplying of goods, and the notion of warranty, to name but a few, all make use of the contract device. Indeed, the contract is such an important part of business operation that it is often overlooked. I maintain that if contract breaking were universalized, then business practice would be impossible. If a participant in business were to universally advocate violating contracts, such advocacy would be self-defeating, just as the universal advocacy of lying and cheating are self-defeating in a given society. . . .

The implications of this analysis for multinationals are broad and important. If activities that are permitted in other countries violate the morality of the marketplace, e.g., undermine contracts or involve free-loading on the rules of the market, they are nonetheless morally prohibited to multinationals that operate there. Such multinationals are obligated to follow the moral norms of the market. Contrary behavior is inconsistent and ultimately self-defeating.

. . . If the moral norms of a host country are in violation of the moral norms of the marketplace, then the multinational is obligated to follow the norms of the marketplace. Systematic violation of marketplace norms would be self-defeating. Moreover, whenever a multinational establishes businesses in a number of different countries, the multinational provides something approaching a universal morality—the morality of the marketplace itself. If Romans are to do business with the Japanese, then whether in Rome or Tokyo, there is a morality to which members of the business community in both Rome and Tokyo must subscribe—even if the Japanese and Romans differ on other issues of morality. As we have seen from our analysis of lying, contract breaking, theft, fraud, kickbacks, and bribery, these activities, prohibited by norms of the market, are quite extensive.

However, many would point out that the norms of the market are not extensive enough. They have nothing to say about how companies should behave in countries where human rights are violated, e.g., should companies behave in South Africa as the law requires them to? Violating the rights of a minority class allegedly is not a violation of market morality. Does that mean that when in South Africa a company should do as the South African government does?

It seems that the answer to this last question should be no, but some arguments for a negative answer are needed. First, an argument can be made that the morality of the market does require that the rights of economic agents in the country be recognized and respected. Business activity on the market model assumes that contracts are made voluntarily. An involuntary contract is usually not considered to be a valid contract. Market morality explicitly requires that market transactions be voluntary and hence implicitly recognizes the right to liberty of participants in business. What justifies the voluntariness requirement? The right to liberty.

But what about the right to liberty in the political realm? What arguments can be given for civil and political liberty? A common argument is to appeal to a general right to liberty. Think of the argument in the Declaration of Independence. If economic, political, and civil liberties are *all* justified by the human right to liberty, then a recognition of the right to liberty brings with it a recognition of the other rights that are justified by it as well. You have to take the whole package. Thus it would be wrong for business to behave in South Africa as the South African government does.

Does that mean that American companies shouldn't do business in South Africa? That depends on whether or not international business can serve as a catalyst for democratic reform and the promotion of human rights. If business actively promotes democracy and human rights, despite laws against such activity on the part of business, then a moral argument can be made to justify business activity there. The multinational is serving the moral end of making the government less repressive. By the way, this is precisely the argument that many have used to justify business practice in South Africa. Indeed the South African situation can serve as an interesting case study. The point of the Sullivan principles, a set of ten criteria for ethical corporate behavior offered by Rev. Leon Sullivan, is to provide moral guidelines so that a company may be morally justified in having plants in South Africa without becoming part of the system of exploitation. The Sullivan principles also prevent profit-seeking corporations from morally justifying immoral behavior. No company can passively do as the South Africans do and then claim that their presence will bring about a more democratic, less racist regime. After all, if it is plausible to argue that capitalism can help create a democracy, it seems equally plausible to argue that a totalitarian regime may corrupt capitalism. The Sullivan principles help keep multinationals with South African facilities morally honest.

Moreover, the morality of the Sullivan principles depends on an empirical claim that profit-seeking corporations behaving in accordance with marketplace morality and acknowledging universally recognized human rights will in fact help transform totalitarian or repressive regimes into more democratic, more human regimes. If that transformation does not take place within a reasonable amount of time, the moral justification for having facilities in that country disappears. Leon Sullivan recognized that point when he set May 31, 1987, as the deadline for reform of the South African government. When the deadline passed, he insisted that American companies suspend operations in South Africa. . . .

Part of what it means to be a democracy is that respect be shown for fundamental human rights. The only justification for a multinational doing business with a regime that violates human rights is the claim that in so doing, the country's human-rights record will improve. Again, business activity under that justification will have to be judged on results.

Hence, only in special circumstances is it right to do in Rome as the Romans do. Similarly it is only right in certain circumstances for the Japanese to do in New York as the Japanese do in Tokyo. What set-tles this question are moral principles that either have been accepted by all parties—as in U.N. treaties and other multinational agreements—or the principles of morality required by the practice of business itself. Since the practice of business requires an underlying business ethic, the international practice of business brings with it an international ethic that must be practiced everywhere. . . .

Notes

[1] This is an adaptation of an argument against prudential-ism by Derek Parfit, *Reasons and Persons* (New York: Oxford University Press, 1986), 126–27.

[2] Michael Bogdan, "International Trade and the New Swedish Provisions on Corruption," *American Journal of Comparative Law*, Vol. 29, #4 (Fall 1979), 665.

[3] Kate Gillespie, "Middle East Response to the U.S. Foreign Corrupt Practices Act," *California Management Review*, Vol. XXIX, Number 4 (Summer 1987), 21–22.

Multinational Decision-Making: Reconciling International Norms

Thomas Donaldson

Journal of Business Ethics 4 (1985): 357–66. Copyright © 1985 by Thomas Donaldson.

Jurisprudence theorists are often puzzled when, having thoroughly analyzed an issue within the boundaries of a legal system, they must confront it again outside those boundaries. For international issues, trusted axioms often fail as the secure grounds of legal tradition and national consensus erode. Much the same happens when one moves from viewing a problem of corporate ethics against a backdrop of national moral consensus to the morally inconsistent backdrop of international opinion. Is the worker who appeals to extra-national opinion while complaining about a corporate practice accepted within his or her country, the same as an ordinary whistle-blower? Is a factory worker in Mexico justified in complaining about being paid three dollars an hour for the same work a U.S. factory worker, employed by the same company, is paid eight dollars?[1] Is he justified when in Mexico the practice of paying workers three dollars an hour—and even much less—is widely accepted? Is an asbestos worker in India justified in drawing world attention to the lower standards of in-plant asbestos pollution maintained by an English multinational relative to standards in England, when the standards in question fall within Indian government guidelines and, indeed, are stricter than the standards maintained by other Indian asbestos manufacturers?

What distinguishes these issues from standard ones about corporate practices is that they involve reference to a conflict of norms, either moral or legal, between home and host country. This paper examines the subclass of conflicts in which host country norms appear substandard from the perspective of home country, and evaluates the claim often made by multinational executives that the prevalence of seemingly lower standards in a host country warrants the adoption by multinationals of the lower standards. It is concerned with cases of the following form: A multinational company (C) adopts a corporate practice (P) which is morally and/or legally permitted in C's host country (B), but not in C's home country (A). The paper argues that the presence of lower standards in B justifies C's adopting the lower standards only in certain, well-defined contexts. It proposes a conceptual test, or ethical algorithm, for multinationals to use in distinguishing justified from unjustified applications of standards. This algorithm ensures that multinational practice will remain faithful at least to the enlightened standards of home country morality.

If C is a non-national, that is to say a multinational corporation, then one may wonder why home country opinion should be a factor in C's decision-making. One reason is that although global companies are multinational in doing business in more than one country, they are uninational in composition and character. They are chartered in a single country, typically have over ninety-five percent of their stock owned by citizens of their home country, and have managements dominated by citizens of their home country. Thus, in an important sense the term "multinational" is a misnomer. For our purposes it is crucial to acknowledge that the moral foundation of a multinational, i.e., the underlying assumptions of its managers infusing corporate policies with a basic sense of right and wrong, is inextricably linked to the laws and mores of the home country.

Modern textbooks dealing with international business consider cultural relativity to be a powerful factor in executive decision-making. Indeed they often use it to justify practices abroad which, although enhancing corporate profits, would be questionable in the multinational's home country. One prominent text, for example, remarks that "In situations where patterns of dominance-subordination are socially determined, and not a function of demonstrated ability, management should be cautioned about promoting those of inferior social status to positions in which they are expected to supervise those of higher social status."[2] Later, referring to multiracial societies such as South Africa, the same text offers managers some practical advice: ". . . the problem of the multiracial society manifests itself particularly in reference to promotion and pay. And equal pay for equal work policy may not be acceptable to the politically dominant but racial minority group. . . ."[3]

Consider two actual instances of the problem at issue:

———

Charles Pettis. In 1966 Charles Pettis, employee of Brown and Root Overseas, Inc., an American multinational, became resident engineer for one of his company's projects in Peru: a 146 mile, $46 million project to build a highway across the Andes. Pettis soon discovered that Peruvian safety standards were far below those in the United States. The highway design called for cutting channels through mountains in areas where rock formations were unstable. Unless special precautions were taken, slides could occur. Pettis blew the whistle, complaining first to Peruvian government officials and later to U.S. officials. No special precautions were taken, with the result that thirty-one men were killed by slides during the construction of the road. Pettis was fired for his trouble by Brown and Root and had difficulty finding a job with another company.[4]

American bank in Italy. A new American bank in Italy was advised by its Italian attorneys to file a tax return that misstated income and expenses and consequently grossly underestimated actual taxes due. The bank learned, however, that most other Italian companies regarded the practice as standard operating procedure and merely the first move in a complex negotiating process with the

Italian Internal Revenue Service. The bank initially refused to file a fallacious return on moral grounds and submitted an "American style" return instead. But because the resulting tax bill was many times higher than what comparable Italian companies were asked to pay, the bank changed policy in later years to agree with "Italian style."[5]

A. The Moral Point of View

One may well decide that home country standards were mandatory in one of the above cases, but not in the other. One may decide that despite conforming to Peruvian standards, Peruvian safety precautions were unacceptable, while at the same time acknowledging that however inequitable and inefficient Italian tax mores may be, a decision to file "Italian style" is permissible.

Despite claims to the contrary, one must reject the simple dictum that whenever P violates a moral standard of country A, it is impermissible for C. Arnold Berleant has argued that the principle of equal treatment endorsed by most U.S. citizens requires that U.S. corporations pay workers in less developed countries exactly the same wages paid to U.S. workers in comparable jobs (after appropriate adjustments are made for cost of living levels in the relevant areas).[6] But most observers, including those from the less developed countries, believe this stretches the doctrine of equality too far in a way detrimental to host countries. By arbitrarily establishing U.S. wage levels as the benchmark for fairness one eliminates the role of the international market in establishing salary levels, and this in turn eliminates the incentive U.S. corporations have to hire foreign workers. If U.S. companies felt morally bound to pay Korean workers exactly the wages U.S. workers receive for comparable work, they would not locate in Korea. Perhaps U.S. firms should exceed market rate for foreign labor as a matter of moral principle, but to pay strictly equal rates would freeze less developed countries out of the international labor market. Lacking, then, a simple formula of the sort, "P is wrong when P violates A's norms," one seems driven to undertake a more complex analysis of the types and degrees of responsibilities multinationals possess. . . .

For purposes of discussing multinationals, it is best to distinguish between "minimal" and "enlightened" duties, where a minimal duty is one the persistent failure of which to observe would deprive the corporation of its moral right to exist, i.e., a strictly mandatory duty, and an enlightened duty is one whose fulfillment would be praiseworthy but not mandatory in any sense. In the present context, it is the determination of minimal duties that has priority since in attempting to answer whether P is permissible for C in B, the notion of permissibility must eventually be cashed in terms of minimal standards. Thus P is not impermissible for C simply because C fails to achieve an ideal vision of corporate conduct; and C's failure to contribute generously to the United Nations is a permissible, if regrettable, act.

Because minimal duties are our target, it is appropriate next to invoke the language of rights, for rights are entitlements that impose minimum demands on the behavior of others.

B. The Appeal to Rights

Theorists commonly analyze the obligations of developed to less developed countries in terms of rights. James Sterba argues that "distant peoples" (e.g., persons in Third World countries) enjoy welfare rights that members of the developed countries are obliged to respect.[7] Welfare rights are defined as rights to whatever is necessary to satisfy "basic needs," and "basic needs," in turn, as needs "which must be satisfied in order not to seriously endanger a person's health and sanity."[8] It follows that multinationals are obliged to avoid workplace hazards that seriously endanger workers' health.

A similar notion is advanced by Henry Shue in his book, *Basic Rights*. The substance of a basic right for Shue is "something the deprivation of which is one standard threat to rights generally."[9] He considers it a "minimal demand" that "no individuals or institutions, including corporations, may ignore the universal duty to avoid depriving persons of their basic rights."[10] Since one's physical security, including safety from exposure to harmful chemicals or pollution, is a condition for one's enjoyment of rights generally, it follows that the right to physical security is a basic right that imposes specific obligations on corporations.

Equally important for our purposes is Shue's application elsewhere of the "no harm" principle to the actions of U.S. multinationals abroad.[11] Associated with Mill and traditional liberalism, the "no harm" principle reflects a rights based approach emphasizing the individual's right to liberty, allowing maximal liberty to each so long as each inflicts no avoidable harm on others. Shue criticizes as a violation of the no-harm principle a plan by a Colorado based company to export millions of tons of hazardous chemical waste from the U.S. for processing and disposal in the West African nation of Sierra Leone.[12] Using the same principle, he is able to criticize any U.S. asbestos manufacturing corporation which, in order to escape expensive regulations at home, moves its plant to a foreign country with lower standards.

Thus the Shue-Sterba rights based approach recommends itself as a candidate for evaluating multinational conduct. It is irrelevant whether the standards of B comply or fail to comply with home country standards; what is relevant is whether they meet a universal, objective minimum. In the present context, the principal advantage of a rights based approach is to establish a firm limit to appeals made in the name of host country laws and morals—at least when the issue is a clear threat to workers' safety. Clear threats such as in-plant asbestos pollution exceeding levels recommended by independent scientific bodies, are incompatible with employees' rights, especially their right not to be harmed. It is no excuse to cite lenient host country regulations or ill-informed host country public opinion.

But even as a rights oriented approach clarifies a moral bottom line for extreme threats to workers' safety, it leaves obscure not only the issue of less extreme threats, but of harms other than physical injury. The language of rights and harm is sufficiently vague so as to leave shrouded in uncertainty a formidable list of issues crucial to multinationals.

When refined by the traditions of a national legal system, the language of rights achieves great precision. But left to wander among the concepts of general moral theory, the language proves less exact. Granted, the celebrated dangers of asbestos call for recognizing the right to workers' safety no matter how broadly the language of rights is framed. But what are we to say of a less toxic pollutant? Is the level of sulfur-dioxide air pollution we should demand in a struggling nation, say, one with only a few fertilizer plants working overtime to help feed its malnourished population, the same we should demand in Portland, Oregon? Or taking a more obvious case, should the maximal level of thermal pollution generated by a poor nation's electric power plants be the same as West Germany's? Since thermal pollution raises the temperature of a given body of water, it lowers the capacity of the water to hold oxygen and in turn the number of "higher" fish species, e.g., Salmon and Trout. But whereas the tradeoff between more Trout and higher output is rationally made by the West German in favor of the Trout, the situation is reversed for the citizen of Chad, Africa. This should not surprise us. It has long been recognized that many rights, e.g., the right to medical care, are dependent for their specification on the level of economic development of the country in question.

Nor it is clear how a general appeal to rights will resolve issues that turn on the interpretation of broad social practices. For example, in the Italian tax case mentioned earlier, the propriety of submitting an "Italian" vs. "American" style tax return hinges more on the appraisal of the value of honesty in a complex economic and social system, than on an appeal to inalienable rights.

C. An Ethical Algorithm

What is needed, then, is a test for evaluating P more comprehensive than a simple appeal to rights. In the end nothing short of a general moral theory working in tandem with an analysis of the foundations of corporate existence is needed. That is, ultimately there is no escape for the multinational executive from merging the ordinary canons of economic decision-making, of profit maximization and market share, with the principles of basic moral theory. But this formidable task, essential as it is, does not preclude the possibility of discovering lower-order moral concepts to clarify the moral intuitions already in use by multinational decision-makers. Apart from the need for general theories of multinational conduct there is need for pragmatic aids to multinational decision-making that bring into relief the ethical implications of views already held. This suggests, then, the possibility of generating an interpretive mechanism, or algorithm, that managers of multinationals could use in determining the implications of their own moral views about cases of the form, "Is *P* permissible for *C* when *P* is acceptable in *B* but not in *A*?"

The first step in generating such an ethical algorithm is to isolate distinct senses in which *B*'s norms may conflict with the norms of *A*. Now, if *P* is morally and/or legally permitted in *B*, but not in *A* then either:

(1) The moral reasons underlying *B*'s view that *P* is permissible refer to *B*'s relative level of economic development; or

(2) The moral reasons underlying *B*'s view that *P* is permissible are independent of *B*'s relative level of economic development.

Let us call the conflict of norms described in (1) a "type #1" conflict. In such a conflict, an African country that permits slightly higher levels of thermal pollution from electric power generating plants, or a lower minimum wage, than those prescribed in European countries would do so not because higher standards would be undesirable *per se*, but because its level of economic development requires an ordering of priorities. In the future when it succeeds in matching European economic achievements, it may well implement the higher standards.

Let us call the conflict of norms described in (2) a "type #2" conflict. In such cases levels of economic development play no role. For example, low level institutional nepotism, common in many underdeveloped countries, is justified not on economic grounds, but on the basis of clan and family loyalty. Presumably the same loyalties should be operative even after the country has risen to economic success—as the nepotism prevalent is Saudi Arabia would indicate. The Italian tax case also reflects an Italian cultural style with a penchant for personal negotiation and an unwilling-

ness to formalize transactions, more than a strategy based on level of economical development.

When the conflicts of norms occurs for reasons other than relative economic development (type #2), then the possibility is increased that there exists what Richard Brandt has called as "ultimate ethical disagreement." An ultimate disagreement occurs when two cultures are able to consider the same set of facts surrounding a moral issue while disagreeing on the moral issue itself. An ultimate disagreement is less likely in a type #1 case since after suitable reflection about priorities imposed by differing economic circumstance, the members of *A* may come to agree that *given* that facts of *B*'s level of economic development, *P* is permissible. On the other hand, a type #2 dispute about what Westerners call "nepotism" will continue even after economic variables are discounted.[13]

The status of the conflict of norms between *A* and *B*, i.e., whether it is of type #1 or #2, does not fix the truth value of *B*'s claim that *P* is permissible. *P* may or may not be permissible whether the conflict is of type #1 or #2. This, however, is not to say that the truth value of *B*'s claim is independent of the conflict's type status, for a different test will be required to determine whether *P* is permissible when the conflict is of type #1 than type #2. In a type #1 dispute, the following formula is appropriate:

> *P* is permissible if and only if the members of *A* would, under conditions of economic development relevantly similar to those of *B*, regard *P* as permissible.

Under this test, excessive levels of asbestos pollution would almost certainly not be tolerated by the members of *A* under relevantly similar economic conditions, whereas higher levels of thermal pollution would be. The test, happily, explains and confirms our initial moral intuitions.

Yet, when as in type #2 conflicts the dispute between *A* and *B* depends upon a fundamental difference of perspective, the step to equalize hypothetically the levels of economic development is useless. A different test is needed. In type #2 conflicts the opposing evils of ethnocentrism and ethical relativism must be avoided. A multinational must forego the temptation to remake all societies in the image of its home society, while at the same time rejecting a relativism that conveniently forgets ethics when the payoff is sufficient. Thus the task is to tolerate cultural diversity while drawing the line at moral recklessness.

Since in type #2 cases P is in conflict with an embedded norm of A, one should first ask whether P is necessary to do business in B, for if not, the solution clearly is to adopt some other practice that is permissible from the standpoint of A. If petty bribery of public officials is unnecessary for the business of the Cummins Engine Company in India, then the company is obliged to abandon such bribery. If, on the other hand, P proves necessary for business, one must next ask whether P constitutes a direct violation of a basic human right. Here the notion of a right, specifying a minimum below which corporate conduct should not fall, has special application. If Polaroid, an American company, confronts South African laws that mandate systematic discrimination against non-whites, then Polaroid must refuse to comply with the laws. Thus in type #2 cases, P would be permissible if and only if the answer to both of the following questions is "no."

(a) It is possible to conduct business successfully in B without undertaking P?

(b) Is P a clear violation of a basic human right?

What sorts of practice might pass both conditions a and b? Consider the practice of low-level bribery of public officials in some under-developed nations. In some South American countries, for example, it is impossible for any company, foreign or national, to move goods through customs without paying low-level officials a few dollars. Indeed, the salaries of such officials are sufficiently low that one suspects they are set with the prevalence of the practice in mind. The payments are relatively small, uniformly assessed, and accepted as standard practice by the surrounding culture. Here, the practice of petty bribery would pass the type #2 test and, barring other moral factors, would be permissible.

A further condition, however, should be placed on multinationals undertaking P in type #2 con-

texts. The companies should be willing to speak out against, and be willing to work for change of P. Even if petty bribery or low-level nepotism passes the preceding tests, it may conflict with an embedded norm of country A, and as a representative of A's culture, the company is obliged to take a stand. This would be true even for issues related exclusively to financial practice, such as the Italian tax case. If the practice of underestimating taxes due is (1) accepted in B, (2) necessary for successful business, and (3) does not violate any basic human rights, then it satisfies the necessary conditions of permissibility. Yet insofar as it violates a norm accepted by A, C should make its disapproval of the practice known.

To sum up, then, two complementary tests have been proposed for determining the ultimate permissibility of P. If P occurs in a type #1 context, then P is not permissible if:

> The members of A would not, under conditions of economic development relevantly similar to those of B, regard P as permissible.

If P occurs in a type #2 context, then P is not permissible if either:

(1) It is possible to conduct business successfully in B without undertaking P or

(2) P is a direct violation of a basic human right.

. . . .

D. Some Practical Considerations and Objections

The algorithm does not obviate the need for multinational managers to appeal to moral concepts both more general and specific than the algorithm itself. It is not intended as a substitute for a general theory of morality or even an interpretation of the basic responsibilities of multinationals. Its power lies in its ability to tease out implications of the moral presuppositions of a manager's acceptance of "home" morality and in this sense to serve as a clarifying device for multinational decision-making. But insofar as the context of a given conflict of norms categorizes it as a type #1 rather than type #2 conflict, the algorithm makes no appeal to a universal concept of morality (as the appeal to basic human rights does in type #2 cases) save for the purported universality of the ethics endorsed by culture *A*. This means that the force of the algorithm is relativized slightly in the direction of a single society. When *A*'s morality is wrong or confused, the algorithm can reflect this ethnocentricity, leading either to a mild paternalism or to the imposition of parochial standards. For example, *A*'s oversensitivity to aesthetic features of the environment may lead it to reject a given level of thermal pollution even under hypothetically lowered economic circumstances, thus yielding a paternalistic refusal to allow such levels in *B*, despite *B*'s acceptance of the higher levels and *B*'s belief that tolerating such levels is necessary for stimulating economic development. Or, *A*'s mistaken belief that the practice of hiring twelve-year-olds for full-time, permanent work, although happily unnecessary at its relatively high level of economic development, would be acceptable and economically necessary at a level of economic development relevantly similar to *B*'s, might lead it both to tolerate and undertake the practice in *B*.

Nor is the algorithm a substitute for more specific guides to conduct such as the numerous codes of ethics now appearing on the international scene. A need exists for topic-specific and industry-specific codes that embody detailed safeguards against self-serving interpretations. Consider the Sullivan Standards, designed by the black American minister, Leon Sullivan, drafted for the purpose of ensuring non-racist practices by U.S. multinationals operating in South Africa. As a result of a lengthy lobbying campaign by U.S. activists, the Sullivan principles are now endorsed and followed by almost one third of all American multinationals with South African subsidiaries. Among other things, companies complying with the Sullivan principles must:

Remove all race designation signs.

Support the elimination of discrimination against the right of Blacks to form or belong to government registered unions.

Determine whether upgrading of personnel and/or jobs in the lower echelons is needed (and take appropriate steps).[14]

. . . Despite these limitations, the algorithm has important application in countering the well documented tendency of multinationals to mask immoral practices in the rhetoric of "tolerance" and "cultural relativity." Utilizing it, no multinational manager can naively suggest that asbestos standards in Chile are permissible because they are accepted there. Nor can he infer that the standards are acceptable on the grounds that the Chilean economy is, relative to his home country, underdeveloped. A surprising amount of moral blindness occurs not because people's fundamental moral views are confused, but because their cognitive application of those views to novel situations is misguided.

What guarantees that either multinationals or prospective whistle-blowers possess the knowledge or objectivity to apply the algorithm fairly? As Richard Barnet quips, "On the 56th floor of a Manhattan skyscraper, the level of self-protective ignorance about what the company may be doing in Colombia or Mexico is high."[15] Can Exxon or Johns Manville be trusted to have a sufficiently sophisticated sense of "human rights," or to weigh dispassionately the hypothetical attitudes of their fellow countrymen under conditions of "relevantly similar economic development?" My answer to this is "probably not," at least given the present character of the decision-making procedures in most global corporations. I would add, however, that this problem is a contingent and practical one. It is not a theoretical flaw of the proposed algorithm that it may be conveniently misunderstood by a given multinational. . . .

What would need to change in order for multinationals to make use of the algorithm? At a minimum they would need to enhance the sophistication of their decision-making mechanisms. They would need to alter established patterns of information flow and collection in order to accommodate moral information. The already complex parameters of corporate decision-making would become more so. They would need to introduce alongside analyses of the bottom line analyses of historical tendencies, nutrition, rights, and demography. And they would need to introduce a new class of employee to provide expertise in these areas. However unlikely such changes are, I believe they are within the realm of possibility. Multinationals, the organizations capable of colonizing our international future, are also capable of looking beyond their national borders and applying—at a minimum—the same moral principles they accept at home.

Notes

[1]An example of disparity in wages between Mexican and U.S. workers is documented in the case-study "Twin-Plants and Corporate Responsibilities" by John H. Haddox, in *Profits and Responsibility*, ed. Patricia Verhane and Kendall D'Andrade (New York: Random House, 1985)

[2]Richard D. Robinson, *International Business Management: A Guide to Decision Making*, 2d ed. (Hinsdale, Ill.: The Dryden Press, 1978), 241.

[3]Robinson, 241.

[4]Charles Peters and Taylor Branch, *Blowing the Whistle: Dissent in the Public Interest* (New York: Praeger Publishers, 1972), 182–85.

[5]Arthur Kelly, "Italian Bank Mores," in *Case-Studies in Business Ethics*, ed. T. Donaldson (Englewood Cliffs: Prentice-Hall, Inc., 1984).

[6]Arnold Berleant, "Multinationals and the Problem of Ethical Consistency," *Journal of Business Ethics* 3 (August 1982): 185–95.

[7]James Sterba, "The Welfare Rights of Distant Peoples and Future Generations: Moral Side Constraints on Social Policy," in *Social Theory and Practice* 7 (Spring, 1981), 110.

[8]Sterba, "Hazards," 111.

[9]Henry Shue, *Basic Rights, Subsistence, Affluence, and U.S. Foreign Policy* (Princeton, N.J.: Princeton University Press, 1981), 34.

[10]Shue, *Basic Rights*, 170.

[11]Henry Shue, "Exporting Hazards," *Ethics* 91 (July 1981): 579–606.

[12]Shue, "Hazards," 579–80.

[13]Richard Brandt, "Cultural Relativism," in *Ethical Issues in Business*, 2d ed., ed. T. Donaldson and P. Werhane (Englewood Cliffs: Prentice-Hall, 1983).

[14]See "Dresser Industries and South Africa," by Patricia Mintz and Kirk O. Hanson, in *Case Studies in Business Ethics*, ed. Thomas Donaldson (Englewood Cliffs: Prentice-Hall, Inc. 1984).

[15]Richard J. Barnet and Ronald Muller, *Global Reach: The Power of Multinational Corporations* (New York: Simon and Schuster, 1974), 185.

CASES

Case 2.1: The Maquiladoras

Throughout the last two decades, many U.S. companies have turned to other countries as sources of cheap labor in order to reduce costs in the production process. In the name of long-term competitiveness, many firms have shut down facilities in the U.S. and moved their plants to countries where they are not subject to the same wage scales or environmental or employee-relations standards, all of which increase costs.

Mexico is a case in point, where a host of American companies, including RCA, General Electric, and General Motors, have taken advantage of an agreement that allows them to set up operations there virtually free from all tariffs and trade restrictions. In a typical situation, an American company ships parts to Mexico for final assembly in the Maquiladoras plants and then exports the finished products back to the United States.

Even though the wages paid to the workers in the plants may be high by Mexican standards, critics of these operations claim that the pay is so low when compared with U.S. wages that it amounts to exploitation. A typical Mexican worker receives between $30 to $50 per week in exchange for approximately a fifty-hour work week compared with American labor rates of around $15 per hour for similar work. Critics also claim that the working conditions are nothing more than modern-day sweatshops with troubling labor practices that do little to protect employee rights. Turnover in some factories is as high as 100 percent per year. Living conditions around the factories consist of shanty towns, with open sewage and other types of air and water pollution a common sight, since Mexico has less stringent environmental standards than the U.S.

Supporters of the American companies argue that they have a right to pay what the market will bear and that they must lower labor costs to ensure international competitiveness. Furthermore, they claim that the companies are doing a tremendous amount of good, witnessed by the fact that they are providing jobs to more than a half-million workers who willingly migrate to the area near the U.S. border in order to take positions in the plants.[3]

[3]See further in James W. Russell, "Sweatshops Across the Rio Grande," *The Progressive*, L984; cited in Peter Madsen and Jay M. Shafritz, *Essentials of Business Ethics* (College Park, Md.: Meridian Books, l990), 400–407.

Questions for Discussion:

1. Is there anything morally wrong with U.S. companies taking advantage of the cost savings available through lower wages and relaxed environmental and employee relations standards in Mexico? Is it okay for them to act like the Romans while in Rome and take advantage of the laws of Mexico?

2. What responsibilities might the Mexican government have to protect its own citizens? In the absence of governmental intervention, what moral responsibilities do the U.S. companies have to these employees and the communities that surround the factories they operate?

Case 2.2: Unocal in Myanmar

Undeterred by prospects of public protest and a consumer boycott, Unocal Corporation recently signed a contract giving it a significant role in a $1 billion oil pipeline project across Myanmar (formerly known as Burma). Critics of the deal say that the pipeline project will enrich the brutal regime known as the State Law and Order Restoration Council (SLORC). The leaders of this regime are accused of slaughtering thousands of prodemocracy demonstrators in 1988 and using terror against their political opponents ever since. Furthermore, opponents of the deal say that the regime is displacing ethnic groups living along the pipeline route and using forced labor to work on the project, charges that Unocal denies. Finally, critics say that the pipeline will destroy one of the country's largest remaining rain forests. Several well-known companies including Levi Strauss and Eddie Bauer have already withdrawn from operating in Myanmar.

Unocal President John F. Imle believes that the economic development resulting from the project will benefit Myanmar's 43 million people and provide a healthy return for company shareholders. He also maintains that the regime is sensitive to human rights issues and that monitoring during construction will ensure that no abuses will occur. Imle further maintains that he welcomes the scrutiny because it will put pressure on foreign governments to create better business climates.

The issue facing Unocal is a vexing one for corporations and democratic governments. It has long been debated whether the carrot or the stick is the better approach to improving international human rights and drawing attention to environmental issues. It is indeed a difficult question whether it is worth the cost of enriching a brutal regime in order to establish a platform from which to press for more democratic conditions or to simply withdraw until such governments clean up their act. This case is even more troubling because many governments do not recognize human rights as universal moral obligations.[4]

[4]See further in Evelyn Iritani, "Feeling the Heat: Unocal Defends Myanmar Pipeline Deal," *Los Angeles Times*, 20 February 1995, D1+.

Questions for Discussion:

1. If the allegations about the project are true, what do you think would be a responsible moral action on the part of Unocal? Would the damage be worth the possibility of helping the people of Myanmar in the long term?
2. Could the company viably argue that since human rights are not recognized the way they are in the U.S., it is okay "to do as the Romans do"?
3. Apply Donaldson's decision-making model to this case. According to this model, what should Unocal do? Do you agree with the outcome?

Case 2.3: Lockheed Bribes the Japanese

In the late 1970s, Carl Kotchian was attempting to sell roughly $400 million worth of Lockheed's Tri-Star aircraft to a Japanese airline, All Nippon Airlines. He worked through a broker who was representing the company to the Japanese. The broker informed him upon his arrival in Japan that certain "pledges" were necessary to be paid to specific high-ranking government officials in return for their help in securing the contracts which Kotchian was seeking to finalize. There was virtually no doubt where the money was eventually headed, and Kotchian was informed that the amount needed was approximately $1.7 million. To secure the support of other key officials, additional pledges were necessary, Kotchian was informed. Two other payments of $1.7 million (500 million yen, Japanese) were arranged, and Kotchian thought that all the arrangements that were needed had been made. These were all under-the-table demands, made in secrecy, yet Kotchian was led to believe that this was a standard means of doing business with the Japanese. Some time passed, and the contract negotiations stalled. To bring them to completion, Kotchian was informed that other pledges were necessary. He agreed to pay them all, totaling roughly an additional $500,000. Other pledges that were required brought the total payments to the Japanese officials to approximately $12 million.

[5]See further in A. Carl Kotchian, "The Payoff: Lockheed's 70-Day Mission to Tokyo," *Saturday Review* (9 July 1977): 7–12; and James F. Peltz, "Lockheed Agrees to Pay Record Fine," *Los Angeles Times*, 28 January 1995, D1, 8.

Kotchian considered not paying any of the pledges, but that would have jeopardized the contract with the airline, and Lockheed desperately needed this contract to keep people employed and the company in good financial condition. Lockheed's payments to Japanese officials totaled less than 5 percent of the total worth of the contract, a drop in the bucket compared to the revenue they would take in over the course of the contract. At the time he paid the pledges, it was not in violation of American law, though the Foreign Corrupt Practices Act was passed in the aftermath of this deal being made public. Lockheed recently ran afoul of that law and agreed to pay a $24.8 million fine for bribing Egyptian officials in attempts to sell military aircraft to them.[5]

Questions for Discussion:

1. Do you think Kotchian was justified in paying the pledges? What would you have done if you had been in his place?
2. Do you think that American laws now in place that make bribery of foreign officials illegal unfairly limit the ability of American business to be competitive in the global marketplace?
3. Using Donaldson's ethical algorithm, what decision would you make in this case? Would Bowie agree or disagree with your conclusion?

COMMENTARY

A particularly salient moral issue that has arisen with the expansion of business across global boundaries is the existence of conflicting moral norms that seem to vary according to nations and cultures. For those that engage in economic transactions in international settings, a great deal of tension exists over whether or not they should adapt their behaviors to fit in with the dominant practices of a particular culture. While simply "doing as the Romans do" makes sense from a strictly financial standpoint, many are uncomfortable with the notion that engaging in practices that would constitute a compromise of their Christian moral ideals may be necessary in order to operate successfully in a foreign land.

While cultural sensitivity is undoubtedly important and cultural relativism has recently been a popular position to take on this issue, there are many instances in which simply following the popular mores of the land is clearly immoral. However, this does not lead to the conclusion that a Christian cannot be successful while doing business internationally. There are many other situations in which a conflict of ethics is only apparent. As Norman Bowie points out, upon closer examination, many instances that resemble moral conflicts are really arguments over facts and procedures instead of underlying ethical principles. In these latter cases one can participate successfully in international business while consistently abiding by the norms of Christian morality.

Many who hold to the view that people should behave "like the Romans while in Rome" base their position on ethical relativism. Ethical relativism became popular as a result of the observations of cultural anthropologists, who observed that different cultures have widely varying moral codes and concepts of right and wrong. Its key advocates have included primarily anthropologists in the early part of the twentieth century, such as William Graham Sumner, who wrote his classic book *Folkways*, outlining his notion of relativism; Ruth Benedict; Melville Herskovits; and, more recently, philosopher John Ladd.[6] As they studied different cultures, they were struck by the lack of a uniform concept of right and wrong. For example, some cultures practice polygamy, others practice monogamy. Some cultures consider it a moral obligation to give one of their children to an infertile couple. Some cultures, such as certain groups of Eskimos, practice euthanasia and infanticide in ways that seem ghastly and immoral to many in other cultures. Among the Auca Indians of South America, treachery was considered the highest virtue, and missionaries, after they brought the gospel to

[6]Their main works in this area are as follows: William Graham Sumner, *Folkways* (New York: Ginn, 1906); Ruth Benedict, *Patterns of Culture* (New York: New American Library, 1934); Melville Herskovits, *Cultural Relativism* (New York: Random House, 1972); John Ladd, ed., *Ethical Relativism* (Belmont, Calif.: Wadsworth, 1973).

them, were horrified to learn that the hero of the gospel was not Jesus, but Judas. These are just a sample of the great variety in the way morality is conceived and practiced.

As a result of these observations, new conclusions were being drawn about the nature of morality. It was suggested that in view of such moral diversity, belief in universal moral values that applied irrespective of culture could not be maintained. Such moral diversity called into question ethical systems that posited absolute, unchanging moral principles that could be universally applied. The more "enlightened" way of viewing morality was to view it as being relative to the culture in which one found himself or herself. Rather than being derived from universal moral absolutes, morality was seen as relative to the cultural consensus.

To be sure, some anthropologists pointed out the differences between cultures only when it came to moral codes. They held to what is called *cultural relativism*. This is simply a descriptive notion that there are widely differing standards of right and wrong among different cultures in the world. But many went further and espoused a stronger form of relativism, called *ethical relativism*. This strong form of relativism holds that all values are culturally created, and as a result there are no objective, universal moral principles that are binding on all cultures and in all time periods. To be sure, values are shaped by the culture in which they are practiced. The history of ethics shows how sociological conditions strongly influenced the emphases of different thinkers. But the ethical relativist is saying much more than that. He holds that morality is dependent on the cultural context in which one finds himself or herself, and therefore there are no objective, universally binding moral principles for all cultures and in all time periods.

Ethical relativism has become the dominant form of moral theory used in international business today. Many executives will justify decisions to offer bribes or forego worker and product safety standards in the name of cultural relativity.

Despite its philosophical shortcomings, ethical relativism does have appeal, particularly to the popular culture.[7] The first appeal of relativism is based on the important notion that morality does not occur in a sociological vacuum. Some of our values were formed in reaction to or affirmation of the social conditions of our time. Unfortunately, these have been mistaken for absolute standards, whereas in reality, they are little more than the biases of the dominant culture, dressed up in moral language. A good example of this was slavery in the Civil War era. Although it was clearly immoral for human beings to own other human beings, and in many cases, treat them like animals, many in the South attempted to justify slavery as an institution, sometimes

[7]Louis P. Pojman, *Ethics: Discovering Right and Wrong* (Belmont, Calif.: Wadsworth, 1990), 34–36.

using biblical grounds. Slavery, which greatly benefited agricultural interests in the South, was considered moral, and the right to own slaves was regarded as an absolute right. Of course, it was nothing of the sort, and a cultural creation was regarded as an absolute moral right, mistaking the absolute for the sociologically relative.

A second appeal of relativism comes from the way it is presented. Frequently relativism is presented as though it and its polar opposite, absolutism, were the only two valid alternatives. The absolutist holds to absolute moral principles rigidly and does not allow for any exceptions regardless of the circumstances. This is clearly not an attractive or realistic position to hold and if relativism is presented as the only alternative to this kind of absolutism, it is not hard to see why people would prefer relativism. It is better, however, to see morality on a continuum, with absolutism at one extreme and relativism at the other. One can hold to objective moral principles and not be an absolutist; that is, one can be what is called a prima facie absolutist, or an absolutist "on the surface." The prima facie absolutist recognizes the importance of objective moral principles, which do not change according to how one feels about them, but he also allows for periodic exceptions to general principles, depending on the circumstances. On selected issues, most people who hold to the importance of principles would admit exceptions. In the case of abortion, it is widely agreed that in the rare cases in which the mother's life is at imminent risk from continuing a pregnancy, it is justifiable to end the pregnancy. Similarly, if someone comes into your house with a gun ready to shoot and asks where your husband or wife is, you are not obligated to tell him the truth. Thus the relativist's appeal rests on a false dichotomy.

A third appeal of relativism comes from the emphasis in the 1990s on sensitivity to different cultures, called *multiculturalism*. There is great emphasis on tolerance of other cultures' distinctives, including values, which moves one strongly in the direction of being a relativist. Yet most people realize that lines must be drawn somewhere, and that there must be some standards that transcend culture if society is to arbitrate competing cultural values. We will discuss this in further detail in the next chapter.

A fourth appeal of relativism comes from the modern emphasis on scientific objectivity. When applied to morality, this takes the form of value neutrality, presumed by the culture to be a good thing. Yet it is becoming more recognized in scholarly circles that value neutrality is actually a myth, and even if it were possible, it may not even be desirable. But in the popular culture, holding to absolute values that transcend culture is considered the equivalent of imposing one's values on other people and cultures. The person who does this is considered, at best, somewhat unenlightened and, at worst, a narrow, rigid fundamentalist. Given that alternative to relativism, again, it is not surprising that relativism has appeal.

In spite of its appeal and widespread use in the popular culture, relativism has significant philosophical shortcomings. Norman Bowie points out several objections—for example, its reducibility to personal subjectivism and its inconsistency with our language and metaphors. In addition, there are several other critical weaknesses of relativism. First, in terms of the observations of the cultural anthropologists who developed relativism, the degree of moral diversity is overstated and the high degree of moral consensus is understated. There is a good deal more moral consensus among cultures than was first believed. Anthropologist Clyde Kluckhohn has noted the following:

> Every culture has a concept of murder, distinguishing this from execution, killing in war and other justifiable homicides. The notions of incest and other regulations upon sexual behavior, the prohibitions on untruth under defined circumstances, of restitution and reciprocity, of mutual obligations between parents and children—these and many other moral concepts are altogether universal.[8]

[8]Clyde Kluckhohn, "Ethical Relativity: Sic et Non," *Journal of Philosophy* (1955): 52; see also E. O. Wilson, *On Human Nature* (New York: Bantam Books, 1979).

A second shortcoming is related to the first. Many of the observations of moral diversity were differences in moral practices. But diversity in practice does not necessarily equal diversity in underlying values or principles. There is much less moral diversity than many anthropologists think they have observed. A person who holds to the reality of objective moral values can easily account for varieties in practices from the perspective of the underlying principles.

A third weakness of relativism is that ethical relativism cannot be drawn from the observations of the cultural relativist. Ethical relativism as a system does not follow from the empirical data of moral diversity among cultures. Simply because different cultures have different moral standards, even if the degree of moral diversity were not overstated, it does not follow that there is no such thing as absolute values that transcend culture.

For instance, although bribery is supposedly "commonly practiced," very high-level Japanese and Korean government and business officials have been brought down by recent scandals in which bribery was involved. Moreover, if bribery is readily accepted, one wonders why it is always done in secret. And, in fact, no nation that we are aware of defends bribery to the international community. When someone is accused of it, he usually denies that it occurred rather than mounting a defense of the practice itself.

A fourth weakness of relativism is that it provides no way to arbitrate among competing cultural value claims. This is critical as business begins to expand across national boundaries and countries are attempting to create trade agreements. In the absence of transcendent norms, the United States cannot rightfully accuse China of wrongdoing in its alleged failures to crack down on the piracy of intellectual property such as computer software. Furthermore, many countries recognize the high degree of cultural diversity within their own populations. Thus there must be a way to adjudicate the various moral claims that occur as a result of inevitable cultural clashes.

The fifth, and the most serious, charge against relativism is an extension of the fourth weakness. The relativist cannot morally evaluate any clearly oppressive culture or, more specifically, any obvious tyrant. In the absence of absolutes, no one can rightfully claim the existence of international human rights. Cultures that relegate women to the status of second-class citizens cannot be evaluated by the relativist, since morality is dependent on the cultural context. Similarly, the relativist cannot pass judgment on someone like Hitler, who oppressed a minority with the permission, if not approval, of the majority, since there is no moral absolute that transcends culture to which the relativist can appeal as a basis for that judgment.

A final objection to relativism is the charge that its central premise, that there are no moral absolutes, is a self-defeating statement, because that statement is an absolute itself. However, the relativist could respond by saying that that statement is only a formal absolute, not a material one; that is, it is a statement that describes the procedure of relativism, not a moral principle that is absolute. That distinction is valid, but there is still a moral absolute for the relativist that makes the system self-defeating—the absolute of tolerance and respect for the values of other cultures. The relativist could not likely tolerate any culture that had intolerance as one of its central virtues.

While these objections to relativism can seem quite abstract, they are critical when considering particular situations that arise in international business settings. Clearly, some cases of "doing as the Romans do" can violate a transcendent norm for moral behavior. As mentioned above, bribery is a case in point. Although it may be common, all signs lead to a conclusion that it is still universally regarded as immoral. Thus one should not bribe just because it seems to be a common practice.

There are other instances in which appealing to cultural relativism to justify simply abiding by the host country standards is morally wrong. Consider the fact that unlike the industrialized countries, there are many governments who do not even attempt to consider or represent the best interests of their citizens when enacting legislation.

While we take democratic government for granted, it is charitable to call the ruling parties of some countries "governments" at all, since they do little that represents what governing implies. For example, without apparent consideration of the interests of their citizens, some governments will accept toxic chemicals from industrialized countries and unsafely dispose of them in exchange for large sums of money. For a company to "export death" in such a manner is irresponsible and immoral, given the risks involved and the fact that the money is probably for the enrichment of a few government officials.

Even when governments do look out for the interests of their citizens, there can be problems. Certain countries are in no position to insist on high moral standards for their business practices. As Thomas Donaldson points out, some developing countries must accept lower standards for wages and environmental protection in order to give an incentive for foreign investment. In some instances, they have very little bargaining power with other governments and corporations. Often they are forced to choose between accepting these tradeoffs or foregoing economic development.

Since many of the laws of these countries are inadequate to the task of protecting their citizens, it would be clearly immoral for American companies to simply abide by the rules of the land. Consider the actions of Union Carbide in Bhopal, India. This is a certain instance in which an American company adhered to existing laws of the land in terms of safety standards and were undeniably immoral in so doing. In a clear violation of higher moral norms, they knowingly risked the lives of many and paid dearly when thousands died in one of the greatest environmental disasters in history.

If the accusations in the Unocal in Myanmar case have merit, it is another useful example of a conflict of norms. The decison of whether to stay and conduct business or leave a country has been a recurring one in international business. The issue was sharply debated during the tragic rule of apartheid in South Africa as many American firms were under public pressure to withdraw their operations from the country lest they contribute to an immoral government regime. Although staying in a country to improve conditions is a viable approach to the problem, Unocal officials should be certain that they will not be enriching their shareholders at the direct expense of the people of Myanmar. Even though Unocal will be obeying the law of that land as the Myanmar government maintains the legality of their tactics, there are clear moral dilemmas that are raised.

As illustrated in case 2.1, the Maquiladoras industry in Mexico provides another useful example. In the American-owned plants operating there, many workers have no other option than to accept low wages in exchange for their labor, which can take place under miserable conditions. Because of the surplus of labor in Mexico, these employees cannot simply quit and take another position, nor can they unionize without fear of retribution. Thus, to treat them poorly and to pay them the lowest wage possible fits a textbook definition of exploitation, in which a party with all the power forces another to abide by their rules.

Clearly it would be unnecessary to pay these workers the exact amount that American workers receive. The incentive to set up shop would be immediately destroyed. Moreover, wages vary with geographical locations in our own country. The goal should be, however, to provide a wage that provides a decent standard of living. The dual aims of treating employees with dignity and saving on labor costs seem achievable together. A living wage can be paid and companies can still save on labor costs because it would be far short of what companies have had to pay American workers.

With these glaring examples in mind, it would appear that every instance of adapting to the host country norms would constitute a violation of ethics. However, as we earlier stated, one can consistently abide by Judeo-Christian morals and succeed in international business settings. For example, with respect to bribery, there is no empirical evidence that it is even necessary in order to gain success in those parts of the world where it is "commonly" practiced. Research conducted by John Graham shows that American firms were never held at a disadvantage through legislation against bribery.[9]

Moreover, as the second shortcoming of relativism described above notes, many instances in which ethical conflicts appear are really disagreements over application and not underlying moral principles. The Italian tax practices case mentioned in the introduction to this chapter serves as an excellent example. On the surface, this situation seems to pit conflicting standards of truth-telling against each other. However, upon closer examination, this is really a conflict over procedure and not ultimate ethical principles. Contrary to taxation policies in the U.S., the Italian version of the Internal Revenue Service is probably not as concerned with exactness when it comes to taxes owed. The common practice there is to negotiate until an agreeable figure is reached between the company and the government. Thus there is no real conflict over norms for truth-telling at all. The underlying principle that is really at stake here is rendering to Caesar what is Caesar's. Since the Italian government determines the amount owed through the process of bargaining rather than predetermined tax rates rounded to the nearest cent, the real conflict in this situation is one of procedure and not of morality. Thus when such conflicts occur, the

[9]"Bribes Don't Help," *USA Today*, 5 August 1983; "Foreign Corrupt Practices: A Manager's Guide," *Columbia Journal of World Business* (Fall 1983): 89–94.

immediate question that must be asked is whether or not a real conflict of underlying moral principles is taking place.

These are just a few examples of situations that lead to the question of how to act when in a cross-cultural situation. We cannot possibly address every instance that could arise. This is where Thomas Donaldson's ethical algorithm is a useful, though limited, tool to guide decision making in instances of conflicts between sets of norms. Donaldson is correct in his assumptions that when the potential for material gain is in conflict with a moral principle, it is profit that must give way.

In summary, "when in Rome do as the Romans do" is an inadequate guide to moral action while operating in different cultures. Cultural relativism as a theory has some significant shortcomings and simply adapting to the norms of a host country can lead to some serious transgressions of Judeo-Christian morality. However, many other instances are merely apparent and not real conflicts of underlying ethical principles that can be resolved with a closer look at the facts. Thus Christians can indeed be successful in international business while remaining consistent with the long-held moral beliefs of their tradition.

THREE

Christian Business Ethics in a Postmodern World

There are two kinds of injustice: the first is found in those who do an injury, the second in those who fail to protect another from injury when they can.

Cicero

I know that the more difficult decisions come when we have to choose between good and better. The toughest calls of all are those we have to make between bad and worse.

Oliver L. North, quoted in "Moral Relativism? 'You Don't Get It'"
by Neal Gabler

INTRODUCTION

While business can appear to be a world of its own, it is really one part of a host of social agreements and practices. As such, it is greatly affected by the cultural values and the other institutions in its surrounding environment. Educational institutions, media, government, communities, churches, and families do much in the way of preparing future employees and leaders. Moreover, many of the daily economic transactions we take for granted are utterly dependent on the time-honored virtues of honesty, trust, and cooperation.[1] For example, customers trust that when they pay for a purchase in advance, the goods will arrive. Workers believe that they will be paid at the end of the month in exchange for their labor. Employers must rely on competent and honest employees to manage the daily affairs of an enterprise. Without these simple moral virtues, the market economy cannot function.

However, as the previous chapter on ethics in international business has shown, some of these time-honored values are being called into question in today's global environment in which moral norms can

[1]For further discussion of this, see Francis Fukuyama, *Trust: The Social Virtues and the Creation of Prosperity* (New York: Free Press, 1995).

117

seem to vary according to place and time. Further challenging long-held values in contemporary American culture is the movement known as "political correctness," which claims that many traditional moral values are actually damaging for society in that they are oppressive to those who choose not to adopt them.

The "P.C." movement, as it has come to be known, bases many of its arguments against traditional morality on the postmodern rejection of truth claims. Its adherents argue that no one can claim truthfulness, especially when it comes to moral values. Thus, judgment should be withheld and society should simply be "tolerant" of a wide variety of beliefs and behaviors. Moreover, they argue that laws and public policy should be enacted to protect the rights of many who have experienced any form of oppression, including many whose behaviors were once regarded as aberrant.

To some extent, the P.C. movement resembles relativism taken to its extreme of personal subjectivism. From this perspective, ethics are not bound even by culture, but are relative to each *individual*. Thus, it is claimed that no one can judge another person's actions, because right and wrong are defined as each person sees it. A brief episode of channel surfing through our dizzying array of daytime talk shows can attest to the popularity of this viewpoint.

To be clear, political correctness and its accompanying move toward multiculturalism (the view that the different traits of diverse cultures have equal value) have some morally praiseworthy intentions. The emphasis on speech can serve as an important reminder for awareness and sensitivity in addressing others, especially in the workplace. It is certainly helpful to learn about and appreciate other cultural traditions. Moreover, for some groups, degrading terms are more than mere words when they have been accompanied by a history of violence.

However, the editorial "998 Points of Light" shows that though motivated by good intentions, the protection of group rights can go to ridiculous lengths. More importantly, if we are to take the claims of political correctness and multiculturalism seriously, it would appear that we would also have to accommodate a host of apparent differences in morals. For example, one recent case, mentioned in Neal Gabler's insightful essay "Moral Relativism? 'You Don't Get It,'" involves an Arab-American family who had moved from the Middle East to California and was confronted by the adult daughter's desire to choose her own husband—contrary to Middle Eastern practice, in which the parents of the bride and groom arrange the marriage.

The girl's father insisted that her marriage be arranged in the traditional fashion. The girl refused, and when she announced her engagement to a man of her choosing, her father took the appropriate step to discipline his daughter according to his Middle Eastern background: he killed her. He was charged with murder. In his defense, the father's attorney argued that the fact that this action is acceptable in Middle Eastern culture should be taken into account by the jury in deciding his guilt or innocence. In other words, even though he acted in this country, under American laws, his action was a norm according to his culture, and the morality of his action should be determined by his cultural context. Not to consider this would surely be unjust on the part of the jury. An appeal to ethical relativism through multiculturalism was used to attempt to justify an otherwise heinous act.

Rightfully, the jury convicted the man of murder. However, we live in a culture in which claims for tolerance and rights through appeals to both cultural relativism and personal subjectivism are made with increased regularity. In many countries in the West, and particularly the United States, pluralism—or tolerance of practically any view of the world—is considered one of the mainstays of the political system, undergirding the notions of religious, political, and economic freedom. Given the available alternatives, most people would rather live in a pluralistic culture than one in which the state dictates specific religious and philosophical beliefs.

Nevertheless, a diversity of worldviews can be a problem when it comes to morality. When different cultures and subcultures within a society disagree about what is right and wrong, without more universal standards, resolving moral conflicts becomes very difficult. If one only has the standards of the culture—whether that is a national culture or a particular corporate culture—as moral guidelines, it is problematic to work them out without appealing to the exercise of power (in which one side imposes its will and standard on the other) or litigation or some sort of arbitrating principles that can sort out the conflict.

Within this climate, it is reasonable to wonder how the economy, which is so dependent upon traditional moral virtues, can continue to function in an efficient manner. More importantly, many are inquiring as to whether we can function as a society with such differing conceptions of moral norms. In particular, we have heard many Christians wondering out loud whether it is even possible to dialogue about ethical issues in a world that rejects Judeo-Christian morality.

The plurality of voices in the public square unsuccessfully arguing that their viewpoints are the correct ones clearly illustrates the need for moral values that can transcend a specific cultural consensus. Although he does not argue from a distinctly Christian perspective, Neal Gabler clearly recognizes the need for a moral consensus in his essay in this chapter. Yet, other than stating the obvious need, he stops short of offering a legitimate basis upon which to establish this consensus. What should serve as this foundation? This is a difficult question indeed.

In a pluralistic society, appeals to religious revelation or authority, though important, are of little help, since many people do not accept the authority of the religious tradition to which one is appealing. In a culture where many do not accept the authority of the Bible as a source of universal moral principles, there must be some other basis for suggesting that there are universal values that indeed do transcend culture. In this chapter we examine the notion that natural law provides such a basis. In brief, the concept of natural law argues that just as there are laws of nature that govern the physical aspects of the universe, there are also universal laws for morality.

The concept of natural law was systematized by theologians in the Middle Ages. It was part of the Roman Catholic Church's attempt to be a universal church and appeal to as wide an audience as possible by grounding moral views, not in the Bible, but in God's general revelation—his revelation that is accessible to all people through creation, observation, experience, and reason. The concept of natural law has been applied most commonly to questions of reproduction and sexuality, but recently it has been debated by the legal community. Natural law in this context refers to objective moral values that are independent of social consensus.

The question the legal community faces is, on what basis does a society have law and human rights? Are those things based on consensus, or are they based on some connection to universal objective moral principles? Advocates of a natural law judicial philosophy—also known as moral realism—insist that laws are based on moral rights and principles that predate the formation of the law. One such advocate is Michael Moore, a professor of law at the University of Pennsylvania, whose article appears in this chapter. Opponents of such a legal philosophy, known as legal positivists, deny this foundation and suggest that the laws of the land only reflect social consensus.

There has been very little formal discussion of natural law as it applies to business ethics. Yet a flourishing economy in which businesses are successful presumes a commitment to certain moral principles that seem to be independent of a particular social consensus. These include things like fulfillment of contracts (or simply keeping one's promises), fair treatment of employees and customers, a level competitive "playing field," truth-telling in the disclosure of information, and the value of diligent work. These values are necessary for the day-to-day transactions that constitute doing business. Adherents to the Judeo-Christian tradition cannot appeal to the Bible to support these values and expect to persuade people who do not accept its authority. In a pluralistic society, where there is a variety of moral persuasions, it is unrealistic to expect that everyone would accept the Bible as the source of moral authority. Thus, there needs to be some other basis to ground the values necessary to conduct business in a pluralistic culture and a global marketplace. In addition, the person who holds the Judeo-Christian view of the world needs some basis other than the Bible to encourage others in business to conduct it ethically. It is naive to suggest that business needs to conduct itself along the lines of Judeo-Christian ethics and only use the Bible to support that effort.

In "Unnatural Brawl Over Natural Law," Michael Moore argues that natural law has been a long-standing part of the way in which the West has viewed the world and is an essential part of our legal philosophy. His argument is supported by theologian Norman L. Geisler in "Natural Law and Business Ethics," who suggests that the Bible supports the existence of objective moral values outside of it. Geisler gets us started in thinking about how natural law might apply to business ethics. Writing from a Reformed theological perspective, political philosopher James Skillen is skeptical about the claims of natural law and encourages Christians not to dismiss the Bible prematurely as the source for public dialogue with non-Christians. He suggests that there is no such thing as a worldview-neutral moral argument and that the Bible teaches that God's creation order is binding on every human being and provides the basis for public debate and discussion.

READINGS

Moral Relativism? "You Don't Get It"

Neal Gabler

Los Angeles Times, 14 June 1992, M1. Copyright © 1992.

For the last few years, a hot-button cultural debate in this country has been raging over multiculturalism and the competing claims of Afrocentrism and Euro-centrism. But under cover of multiculturalism, something has been smuggled in that could have far greater consequences: The belief that morality itself is culture-bound and therefore, in an increasingly pluralistic society, wholly malleable.

Moral revolutions are usually obstreperous affairs. This time, multiculturalism stealthily slid into moral relativism without anyone paying much attention to the confusion between the anthropological and moral realms. Yet, the new swell of moral relativism challenges the predicates of our moral system. It says any behavior is all right, as long as there is some culture or subculture that permits it. All this converts the popular T-shirt slogan—"It's a——thing. You wouldn't understand"—from a cultural assertion into a new moral standard.

It was on these grounds that Harvard Professor Orlando Patterson excused Justice Clarence Thomas' alleged remarks to Anita F. Hill. He asserted that what Thomas supposedly said "may have been completely out of the cultural frame of his white, upper-middle-class work world, but immediately recognizable to Professor Hill" as a form of "down-home courting." In other words: It's a Southern black thing. you wouldn't understand.

It was on similar grounds that two Palestinian emigres, who had slaughtered their Americanized teen-age daughter, asked for acquittal. As a friend said, "We follow our religion." If the parents hadn't disciplined their wayward daughter, "they'd be embarrassed in front of everybody." In short: It's a Palestinian thing. You wouldn't understand. With Leona Helmsley, it's a rich thing; with the Mob, a Cosa Nostra thing; with crooked politicians, a political thing; with looters, a poverty thing. You wouldn't understand.

Applied to culture, this may be a sensible formulation. We don't always understand other cultures, even other American subcultures, and we often aren't in a position to judge customs, languages, aesthetics, mythologies, even cosmologies. Applied to morality, on the other hand, it can become a license to do anything you like and not feel responsible, since no one's moral coordinates can be imposed on anyone else's actions—certainly not the coordinates of white middle-class morality. The result is not just that people think they can get away with anything, it is that they believe they are entitled to get away with anything.

As fundamental a change as this is, one reason it has received so little attention is that no one really objects to it—at least in his own bailiwick. For years, liberals have offered explanations for what might be regarded as antisocial behavior by the underprivileged and the disenfranchised. These explanations, as one saw vividly after the Los Angeles riots, often sounded remarkably like excuses. If society was at fault for creating a culture of poverty, individuals were not responsible for abiding by the values of that culture. In any case, many liberals have become uncomfortable about judging the poor and minorities by white middle-class standards of moral conduct—as if it were as unfair as using white, middle-class-biased IQ tests to determine their intelligence.

If anything, conservatives found morality even more flexible than liberals, though their blather about traditional values did as much to hide the rise of moral relativism as the liberal insistence on multiculturalism. However, it was only minorities that needed to be lashed with the moral whip. What liberals were excusing because of poverty, conservatives were excusing because of wealth and patriotism. As both Wall Street and Irangate made clear, amorality in the furtherance of the conservative cause is no vice. In this view, Michael Milken and Oliver L. North were both heroes snagged by legal technicalities, not wrongdoers receiving justice.

Perhaps the major casualty of moral relativism has been the notion of guilt. For when there is easy absolution, there is no guilt—at last not moral guilt. To everyone from the drug lords to insider traders, getting caught was the real crime. Recently, former Wall Street sovereign and current convict Milken labeled the six counts of criminal fraud, to which he had pleaded guilty, as "securities violations." For Milken and his advocates, there is no wrong involved. "It's a Wall Street thing. You wouldn't understand."

Similarly, North cannot conceive that he may have done wrong and hence he cannot possibly feel guilt—though he baldly lied. "I know the difference between right and wrong," he wrote, "and I can tell good from bad. But I also know that the more difficult decisions come when we have to choose between good and better. The toughest calls of all are those we have to make between bad and worse." North makes these calls and gets cheered for them, but—it's a conservative thing. You wouldn't understand.

For too many conservatives, guilt is the psychological equivalent of all those government regulations they abhor. Guilt is an encumbrance that keeps one from the untrammeled pursuit of wealth, which is the engine of our welfare.

Meanwhile, the self-help movement may have inadvertently abetted the lack of remorse by targeting guilt as psychologically damaging. We have to learn to love ourselves, forgive ourselves, or so the experts say. Their idea is that there is too much guilt, while the real problem may be that there may be too little—not the unmoored Freudian anxiety that parades as guilt, but the moral variety that tells us when we have transgressed.

Admittedly, when you talk about guilt this way, you are bound to sound like one of those moral troglodytes who assume their own standards are universal and immutable. Indeed, Samuel Johnson may have been wrong—morality, not patriotism, is the last refuge of a scoundrel. Whenever the prevailing social order has been challenged in this country, its defenders have always waved the bloody shirt of morality and condemned the challengers as insufficiently versed in our values—just as Dan Quayle is doing now.

No doubt that is why some people, skeptical that moral rearmament can ever be anything more than the last gasp of the withering genteel Establishment, believe that when we argue morality, we are really arguing politics; that the real issue is *whose* morality? I wouldn't dispute that. Morality is a function of many factors, including culture; from one society to another, one set of moral precepts may indeed be no more valid than another.

But in this country, while we may disagree on which issues are moral ones—prostitution, for example—and while we may be divided over selected moral problems, such as abortion, there has long been a surprising consensus over morality. In arguing against moral relativism, I am not arguing the Judeo-Christian moral consensus is the only one, or even the right one. Nor am I arguing that morality is a rigid thing, impervious to changing times. A consensus, after all, is organic.

It is simply that the old consensus is under siege and we need some consensus—something that enables us to say Milken, the Palestinian parents and the looters were wrong. By declaring instead that there are dozens, hundreds, of separate moral systems within America, all perfectly acceptable, proponents of moral relativism strike at the heart of our social covenant, at the very basis of our society in a way cultural relativism does not.

Without a consensus, we will have not just moral anomie; we will have a society so fragmented that it ceases to exist.

998 Points of Light

Wall Street Journal, 19 September 1990. Copyright © 1990.

Two separate instances in recent days prove what we have always known. Our sentinels of progress and social welfare never sleep. Now, in their endless struggle on behalf of the needy, they have taken on both Mother Teresa and the Salvation Army.

The conflict involving Mother Teresa began when her order, the Missionaries of Charity, undertook to renovate two old buildings in New York City into residences for the homeless. Bearing all the costs of the extensive renovation themselves, the nuns planned to provide food, clothing, shelter and job referrals for more than 60 homeless men.

The trouble began when New York City officials demanded that the nuns install an elevator for disabled tenants, as per the requirement that such housing include facilities for the handicapped. The nuns, unprepared for the additional expenditure of something close to an additional $100,000, assured the city that they stood ready to carry any handicapped resident who could not climb stairs. They asked for a waiver of the elevator requirement, which the city's Buildings Department was prepared to grant. Until, that is, Mayor David Dinkins's Office for People With Disabilities weighed in.

As Director Anne M. Emerman saw it, approving the waiver didn't just have to do with elevators; it had to do with the endorsement of wrong *values*. Explaining why the nuns carrying people upstairs would not do for New York City (also occasionally known as Calcutta on the Hudson), Ms. Emerman noted, "Their attitude in India is, they go out and carry people in off the street. . . . We said no, you don't carry people up and down in our society. That's not acceptable here."

Thanks to this intercession, Mother Teresa's nuns have scuttled their project to house the homeless of New York City. In place of housing for the homeless, the city instead got the Mayor's Office for People With Disabilities providing a ringing reaffirmation of our prevailing societal and cultural standards. That should help keep the homeless warm this winter.

Meanwhile, the Bush administration's Labor Department has gone to war with the Salvation Army, which has for more than a hundred years fed, sheltered and counseled the poor. Those who receive their services of food, board and roughly $20 a week are required, in exchange, to perform a modicum of work for the Army, such as gathering old clothes, unloading trucks or assisting in the kitchen.

The Labor Department has decided that the Salvation Army is an employer guilty of exploiting workers under the terms of the Fair Labor Standards Act and is demanding that the Army's beneficiaries be paid the minimum wage. The Salvation Army argues, unanswerably, that the destitute to whom they assign work, and whom they feed and try to teach discipline, cannot be considered employees in the usual sense of the word. The Labor Department's efforts to force them to pay a wage would, moreover, force their service centers out of business by bankrupting them. Until now, the Salvation Army has been providing 11,000 beds at 117 centers around the country.

We will continue to monitor the efforts of the public welfare bureaucracy to extinguish the 1,000 points of light one by one.

Unnatural Brawl Over Natural Law

Michael Moore

Los Angeles Times, 3 September 1991, B5.

In the current debate about the nomination of Judge Clarence Thomas to the Supreme Court, there has been an increasing focus on his natural-law philosophy. A nominee's judicial philosophy is a proper area of concern for the Senate Judiciary Committee as it considers confirmation, for that philosophy tells us how the nominee conceives of the office for which he is being consid-

ered. Unfortunately most of what has recently been written about a natural-law philosophy either deliberately misstates it, or is ignorant of its nature. Since we must judge Thomas mainly by his judicial philosophy, it is important that we get it right.

Some of the least accurate characterizations of the philosophy have come from someone who should know better, Laurence Tribe, one of America's most respected constitutional scholars. According to Tribe, belief in natural law today is both as rare as belief in ghosts, and about as credible.

Only someone who misunderstands natural law as a judicial philosophy can make such charges. The philosophy has two distinct parts. One is the view that values like equality and liberty are as real as the natural qualities of heat, color or mass. The existence of such values means that it is morally wrong to treat people unequally or to violate their liberty, even in a society in which most people do not think it is morally wrong. The moral truth about such behavior no more consists in what most people think than do scientific truths about planetary motion.

Second, the philosophy conceives of law, including constitutional law, as intrinsically connected to objective moral truth. One might think, for example, that the legal right to equal protection of the laws under our Constitution derives its content from the pre-existing moral right to equal treatment that all persons possessed before the 14th Amendment became the law of the land.

There is nothing about a natural-law view that ties it to praising supposedly "natural" human behavior, functions or capacities. That non-heterosexual relations cannot serve a reproductive function, for example, or that women have a reproductive capacity that men lack, commits a natural lawyer neither to condemn homosexuality nor to consign women to a child-rearing function.

Further, there is nothing intrinsic to a natural-law view that commits it to devaluing the liberal goods of pluralism, tolerance and autonomy. Indeed, a clear-headed natural lawyer should see that because values are objective, any view he holds about them might be in error, so he has reason to tolerate the differing (and potentially correct) moral views of others.

Is this view of law and morality hopelessly old-fashioned or otherwise "troubling"?

According to Tribe, Thomas "is the first Supreme Court nominee in 50 years" to hold these views, and "the last time a Supreme Court majority invoked natural-rights theories [was] some 80 years ago."

This is untrue. Take one well-known example from our very recent past: At the confirmation hearings on Supreme Court nominee Robert Bork several years ago, Senator Joseph Biden (D-Del.) aptly asked Bork whether he did not believe in the existence of a right to privacy, a right, as Biden put it, "that is older than our Bill of Rights." One of the main criticisms of Bork's judicial philosophy was that he did not believe that citizens possessed natural rights such as those to liberty or privacy. For this skepticism, Bork was characterized as being outside the mainstream of American legal theory.

Moreover, the line of U.S. Supreme Court decisions that both liberals and libertarian conservatives applaud are paradigms of natural-law philosophy in action. Griswold vs. Connecticut, upholding a married couple's right to use birth-control devices, and Roe vs. Wade, upholding a woman's right to choose whether to abort her fetus, are decisions grounded in the view that judges must interpret the meaning of legal words like "liberty" in the 14th Amendment via their own best theories of the nature of the moral right to liberty that all persons possess.

> **It is no accident that in our constitutional practices, the natural-law view has predominated.**

It is no accident that in our constitutional practices, the natural-law view has predominated. For on any other judicial philosophy, it is difficult to justify why nine non-elected bureaucrats should have the power to overturn the decisions of the democratic, legislative process.

It is only on the supposition that individuals have rights that even democratic majorities cannot suppress that judicial review makes any sense. If those rights do not have a status and a content independent of social consensus—if they were not natural rights—when would a court ever be justified in overturning the kind of social consensus a statute presumptively represents?

The real reason that liberals oppose Thomas' nomination cannot lie with a judicial philosophy that links law to moral values. Rather, the liberal objection to Thomas is to his values. What values Thomas holds is also a legitimate matter of concern. After all, given the intimate tie of values to law in the natural-law view, we are entitled to know what sort of values we might be empowering by Thomas' confirmation. Assessing these values openly will only be possible if we get rid of the ploy of pretending that Thomas holds some antiquated, suspected judicial philosophy last held by theologians in the Middle Ages.

Natural Law and Business Ethics

Norman L. Geisler

From *Biblical Principles in Business: The Foundations,* ed. Richard Chewning (Colorado Springs: NavPress, 1991), 157–74.

If the Bible is sufficient for believers in matters of faith and practice, then what need is there for natural law? Only believers accept the Bible. But business must be done with unbelievers. Therefore, it is necessary for us to have some common ethical ground on which to engage in commercial transactions with them.

All business presupposes an ethical standard on which it is conducted. But whose ethical system should be used? In a pluralistic culture we cannot expect Muslims to accept the Bible as a basis for doing business with Christians. We cannot expect Christians to accept the Koran as the grounds for engaging in business with Muslims. And, of course, secular humanists will not accept either book. Whose ethical standard, then, shall we use?

We must utilize some moral standard, but no one religious group will accept the divine (scriptural) law of the other. Unless there is a moral law common to all men, regardless of their differing religious authorities, there will be no ethical basis on which to conduct business with nonChristians.

I. The Nature of Natural Law

God has two revelations: one in His world and the other in His Word. The former is called general revelation and the latter special revelation. Divine law is a special revelation to believers. Natural law is a general revelation to all persons.

A. Definition of natural law—Natural law is described in the Bible as that which human beings "do by nature"; it is the law written on the hearts of all men (see Rom. 2:14). Those who disobey it go contrary to nature (see Rom. 1:27). The natural law condemns such things as "wickedness, evil, greed and depravity." The actions opposed to it are "envy, murder, strife, deceit and malice." Those who oppose it are called "gossips, slanderers, God-haters, insolent, arrogant and boastful." They "disobey their parents; they are senseless, faithless, heartless, [and] ruthless" (Rom. 1:29–31). According to Paul, all of these actions are contrary to natural law.

B. History of natural law—Belief in natural law did not begin with Christians. It is found in ancient Hindu, Chinese, and Greek writings. Even before Socrates, the Greek philosopher Heraclitus believed in an unchanging Logos (Reason) behind the changing flux of human experience. Plato held to moral absolutes. The Stoics developed natural law theories well before the time of Christ.

1. St. Augustine on natural law—The concept of natural law has a venerable history among great Christian thinkers. Like others before him, St. Augustine believed that God gave the Gentiles "the law of nature." He referred to it as "the system of nature." This law is "implanted by nature" in all men. Natural law is reflected in the image of God in man. To be sure, Augustine believed this image was marred by sin, but he insisted that "the image of God is not wholly blotted out in these unbelievers." Thus, Augustine held that God was just in punishing unbelievers for not living in accordance with this "law written on their hearts."

2. Thomas Aquinas on natural law—Following Augustine's view on natural law, Thomas Aquinas declared that "natural law is nothing else than the rational creature's participation in eternal law." Law is "an ordinance of reason made for the common good." It is the "rule and measure of acts." Eternal law is the divine reason by which God governs the universe; natural law is simply the human participation in this eternal law. It is the first principle governing human action, as the laws of logic are the first principles governing human thought.

Aquinas distinguishes natural law, which is common to all rational creatures, and divine law, which is imposed only on believers. Natural law is directed toward man's temporal good; divine law is aimed toward his eternal good. Divine law is for the Church; natural law is for society as a whole. The basis for human law is natural law. Since business is conducted in the context of civil laws, it is subject to both human laws and natural law on which they are based.

3. John Calvin on natural law—Just like Augustine and Aquinas before him, John Calvin believed that natural law is ingrained by God in the hearts of all men: "That there exists in the human mind, and indeed by natural instinct, some sense of Deity, we hold to be beyond dispute." He contended that "there is no nation so barbarous, no race so brutish, as not to be imbued with the conviction that there is a God." This "sense of Deity is so naturally engraved on the human heart, in fact, that the very reprobate are forced to acknowledge it."

This innate knowledge of God includes a knowledge of His righteous law. Calvin held that since "the Gentiles have the righteousness of the law naturally engraved on their minds, [so] we certainly cannot say that they are altogether blind as to the rule of life." He calls this moral awareness "natural law," which is "sufficient for their righteous condemnation" but not for salvation. By means of this natural law, "the judgment of conscience" is able to distinguish between "the just and the unjust." God's righteous nature "is engraved in characters so bright, so distinct, and so illustrious, that none, however dull and illiterate, can plead ignorance as their excuse."

Not only is the "natural law" clear; it is also specific. It includes a sense of justice "implanted by nature in the hearts of men." There "is imprinted on their hearts a discrimination and judgment, by which they distinguish between justice and injustice, honesty and dishonesty." According to Calvin, it is what makes them "ashamed of adultery and theft." The natural law even governs "good faith in commercial transactions and contracts." Even the heathen "prove their knowledge . . . that adultery, theft, and murder are evils, and honesty is to be esteemed." Calvin summarizes man's "natural knowledge of the law [as] that which states that one action is good and worthy of being followed, while another is to be shunned with horror."

4. Thomas Jefferson on natural law—The roots of early American natural law views derive from John Locke. He believed that the "laws of Nature" teach us that "being all equal and independent, no one ought to harm another in his life, health, liberty or possessions; for men being all the workmanship of one omnipotent and infinitely wise Maker." This same view was expressed by Thomas Jefferson in the Declaration of Independence (1776) when he wrote, "We hold these truths to be self-evident, that all men are created equal, that they are endowed by their Creator with certain unalienable Rights, that among these are Life, Liberty, and the pursuit of Happiness."

Jefferson believed that these unalienable rights are rooted in the "Laws of Nature," which derive from "Nature's God." On the Jefferson Memorial in Washington, D.C., are inscribed these words he wrote: "God who gave us life gave us liberty. Can the liberties of a nation be secure when we have removed a conviction that these liberties are the gift of God?" Here again it is clear that Jefferson's America was based on the concept of God-given rights grounded in God-given moral rules called "Nature's Laws." So for Jefferson, too, natural law was not a descriptive "is" but a divinely prescriptive "ought."

II. The Need for Natural Law

In their zeal to advertise their commitment to God's infallible and inerrant revelation in Scripture, some evangelical Christians overstate their case. In so doing, they diminish or negate the need for natural law. John W. Montgomery, for example, recently declared that natural laws are, at best, formal, ambiguous, devoid of substantial content, and incapable of independent justification apart from that of Scripture. But if This is the case, God is guilty of sending unbelievers to their eternal doom for not living in accord with purely formal, ambiguous, and vacuous natural revelation (see Rom. 1:20; 2:12). If there is no natural law, God is unjust. . . .

B. The need for natural law in business ethics—Business is conducted within pluralistic societies and among a multiplicity of nations. Within these social groups are various religious groups, and each has its own religious authority, whether the Torah, the Bible, the Koran, the Gita, or the Analects. Since no one group accepts the religious authority of the other groups, there is no way that any single religious book will, by common consent, become the authority for doing business with other countries. Thus, there is a pressing need for some moral standard on which the various religious groups can conduct mutual business.

Business cannot be conducted in a moral vacuum. Commerce depends on common ethical commitments. Parties doing business must assume general moral principles, such as honesty and good faith. They must assume promises will be kept and contracts honored. But since no one of the various religious authorities is acceptable to all the participants in the international community, the only recourse is some kind of moral law common to all men. This is precisely where natural law becomes necessary for business. But is there a natural law common to all men? Where is it found? How is it recognized?

III. Some Manifestations of Natural Law

One of the most commonly heard objections to natural law, as opposed to moral laws revealed in the Bible, is that natural law is not clear. Opponents claim that there is no place one can read these natural laws. It is vague, if not vacuous. Natural law can be easily distorted by depraved minds. On the other hand, they insist that the Bible is clear and contentful. Let us briefly consider these objections.

A. Some objections to natural law—Before we discuss the role of natural law in business ethics, several objections to it need to be addressed. Some object to natural law, in favor of divine law in the Bible. However, there are serious problems with this position. . . .

2. *Is natural revelation unclear?*—In their evangelical zeal to exalt God's special revelation in the Bible, some have overstated their case. Just because the Bible is superior in content to natural revelation does not mean that natural revelation is inadequate for its God-given task. True, sin impairs man's ability to apply natural revelation to his life. But the defect is not in the revelation but in man's refusal to accept it. According to Romans 1, natural revelation "is plain to them, because God has made it plain to them" (v. 19). The problem is that "the man without the Spirit does not accept the things that come from the Spirit of God" (1 Cor. 2:14). The revelation is *perceived* but not received.

3. *Is natural revelation distorted?*—God has clearly revealed Himself in nature and in the conscience. So the problem with unbelievers is that they shun the truth natural revelation discloses to them (see Rom. 1:18). Rejecting the truth is not unique to unbelievers with God's general revelation. Believers do not always live according to the truth of God's special revelation, either.

To claim that general revelation is inadequate because unbelievers have distorted it is to reject special revelation for the same reason. Peter, for example, tells us that "people distort [Paul's writings], as they do the other Scriptures, to their own destruction" (2 Pet. 3:15–16). Everything God has revealed in Scripture has been subjected to similar distortions as those moral truths He has revealed to all men in His natural law. There is no defect with either of God's revelations. The problem is not with God's disclosure but with man's distortion of it.

The existence of hundreds of religious sects and cults, all claiming that the Bible is their revelation, is ample testimony to the fact that even the teachings of supernatural revelation in Scripture are not immune to distortion. In fact, the distortions of the teachings of the natural law among various human cultures is no greater than the distortions of the teachings of supernatural revelation among the various cults. Careful examination of both areas indicates that in spite of the clarity of both revelations, depraved human beings have found a way to deflect, divert, or distort God's commands. So the teachings of the Bible have no edge on natural revelation in the matter of immunity from distortion.

4. Is natural revelation identifiable?—For many, the Bible has an advantage over natural law in moral matters in that the Scriptures have a specifiable content. We know where to go to get a Bible, and we can read what it says. But where does one go to read natural law? The biblical answer to this question is twofold: it is "written on [the] hearts" of all men, and it can be seen in what they "do by nature" (Rom. 2:14–15). The first manifestation is the inner side of the natural law, and the second, the outer side. Let us consider the areas in which natural law is revealed.

(a) Natural law impressed inwardly on the heart—What is written on perishable paper can be erased, but what is written on the heart of an imperishable person is not completely erasable. Virtually all theologians agree, no matter how Calvinistic they are, that the image of God is not completely destroyed in fallen man; it was effaced but not erased. As we have demonstrated, this was true of Augustine and Calvin. And it is also true of Luther.

The Bible is very clear that even fallen men bear God's image. For example, the prohibition against murder is based on the fact that all men, even in their sinful condition, are still in the image of God. Moses wrote, "Whoever sheds the blood of man, by man shall his blood be shed; for in the image of God has God made man" (Gen. 9:6). Likewise, James says not to curse other humans because they "have been made in God's likeness" (James 3:9). If it is morally wrong to kill or curse human beings because the image of God includes some moral likeness to God, then we can understand something of God's moral nature by looking at our own nature made in His image.

The natural law is written in the most readily available place for people—in the heart. It is also written in a way everyone can read—intuitively. No lessons in language are necessary, and no books are needed. Natural law can be seen "instinctively" (Rom. 2:14, NASB). It is known by inclination even before it is known by cognition. We know what is right and wrong by our natural intuitions. Our very nature predisposes us in that direction. Being selfish creatures, we do not always desire to do what is right, but we do nonetheless desire that it be done to us. This is why Jesus summarized the moral law by declaring, "In everything, do to others what you would have them do to you" (Matt. 7:12). Confucius recognized the same truth by general revelation when he said, "Never do to others what you would not like them to do to you."

The natural law is not hard to understand; it is hard to practice. We know what we want others to do to us even if we do not always want to do the same to them. The natural law, then, can be seen better in human reactions than in actions. That is, one's real moral beliefs are manifest not so much in what he does but in what he wants done to him. Some may cheat, but no businesspersons want to be cheated. Others may be dishonest in their dealings, but none of them like to be lied to in any of their deals.

(b) Natural law as expressed in reactions—Our actions are often contrary to our moral inclinations. That explains why our best understanding of the natural law comes not from seeing our actions but from observing our reactions. This is true because we know the moral law instinctively. We do not have to read it in any books; we know it intuitively since it is written on our own hearts. So when we read the natural law, we must be careful to read it from actions truly indicative of it. These are not necessarily the ones we do to others, but those that we desire to be done to us. Paul speaks to this point when he writes of the things we "do by nature" that "show" the moral law "written on [our] hearts" (Rom. 2:14–15).

Our moral inclinations are manifest in our reactions when others violate our rights. We do not see the moral law nearly as clearly when we violate others' rights. Herein is revealed our depravity; our sinfulness is found in our unwillingness to do the moral thing.

The kind of reaction that manifests the natural moral law was brought home forcefully to me when a professor I know graded a student's paper written in defense of moral relativity. After carefully reading the well-researched paper, the professor wrote, "'F.' I do not like blue folders." The student stormed into his office protesting, "That's not fair. That's not just!" The student's reaction to the injustice done to him revealed, contrary to what he wrote, that he truly believed in an objective moral principle of justice. The real measure of his morals was not what he had written in his paper but what God had written on his heart. What he really believed was right manifested itself when he was wronged.

(c) Natural law as expressed in writings—Contrary to popular belief, the great moral writings of the world do not manifest a total diversity of perspectives. There is a striking similarity among them. In fact, the similarity within writings expressing the natural law is just as great as that within writings on the divine law. That is, the great ethicists have read general revelation with as much agreement as theologians have read special revelation. Within both groups there are conservatives and liberals, rightists and leftists, strict constructionists and broad constructionists.

The stark truth is that it matters little whether it is the Bible, general revelation, or the U.S. Constitution; a bad hermeneutic can distort one as well as the other. The problem is not with the divine revelation but with the human interpretation of it. No revelation is immune from distortion by fallible and fallen human beings who wish to make it fit their depraved desires and actions.

In spite of human distortions of God's general revelation, there remains a general agreement among nonChristian writers on the nature of the natural law. C. S. Lewis has provided a noteworthy service in cataloging many of these expressions of the natural moral law. (Of course there is diversity of ethical expression among the great cultures, too, but this diversity no more negates their unanimity than diversity of belief among evangelicals negates their unity on the essential Christian teachings.) This general agreement is manifest in the following quotations:

1) The Law of General Beneficence
"Utter not a word by which anyone could be wounded." (Hindu)
"Never do to others what you would not like them to do to you." (Ancient Chinese)
"Men were brought into existence for the sake of men that they might do one another good." (Roman, Cicero)

2) The Law of Special Beneficence
"Surely proper behavior to parents and elder brothers is the trunk of goodness." (Ancient Chinese)
"Love thy wife studiously. Gladden her heart all thy life long." (Ancient Egyptian)
"Natural affection is a thing right and according to Nature." (Greek)
"The union and fellowship of men will be best preserved if each receives from us the more kindness in proportion as he is more closely connected with us." (Roman, Cicero)

3) Duties to Parents, Elders, Ancestors
"Has he despised Father and Mother?" (Babylonian)
"[There is a duty] to care for parents." (Greek)
"I tended the old man, and I gave him my staff." (Ancient Egyptian)

4) Duties to Children and Posterity
"Nature produces a special love of offspring" and "To live according to Nature is the supreme good." (Roman, Cicero)

"The Master said, Respect the young." (Ancient Chinese)

5) The Law of Justice

"Has he drawn false boundaries?" (Babylonian)

"I have not stolen." (Ancient Egyptian)

"Justice is the settled and permanent intention of rendering to each man his rights." (Roman, Justinian)

"Whoso takes no bribe . . . well pleasing is this to Samas." (Babylonian)

6) The Law of Good Faith and Veracity

"A sacrifice is obliterated by a lie and the merit of alms by an act of fraud." (Hindu, Janet)

"Whose mouth, full of lying, avails not before thee: thou burnest their utterance." (Babylonian)

"The Master said, Be of unwavering good faith." (Ancient Chinese)

"The foundation of justice is good faith." (Roman, Cicero)

7) The Law of Mercy

"I have given bread to the hungry, water to the thirsty, clothes to the naked, a ferry boat to the boatless." (Ancient Egyptian)

"One should never strike a woman; not even with a flower." (Hindu, Janet)

"You will see them take care of . . . widows, orphans, and old men, never reproaching them." (Redskin)

8) The Law of Magnanimity

"There are two kinds of injustice: the first is found in those who do an injury, the second in those who fail to protect another from injury when they can." (Roman, Cicero)

"To take no notice of a violent attack is to strengthen the heart of the enemy. Vigour is valiant, but cowardice is vile." (Ancient Egyptian)

"Nature and Reason command that nothing uncomely, nothing effeminate, nothing lascivious be done or thought." (Roman, Cicero)

B. Manifestation of natural law in business ethics—The moral principles cited above apply to business as well as to any other area of human relations. The natural law teaches honesty, fidelity, and industry. It is opposed to lying, promise breaking, and laziness. Thus, the businessman can consult his own inclinations and expectations. When in doubt, he can ask, "What would I like someone else to do to me?" Through the "spectacles" of this question, he can read the natural law written by God on his own heart. All businesspersons, whether Buddhist, Christian, Jewish, Muslim, or secular humanist, can do this. Good moral principles are not unique to the Bible; they are written on the hearts of all men.

IV. Some Contributions of Natural Law to Business Ethics

. . . The importance of a natural law ethic is that this approach can be taken into the business world without showing favor to any religious group. Without an objective ethical basis for our actions, there is no realistic alternative to antinomianism. But business cannot proceed as usual without an objective ethical standard common to all who engage in the business transactions. Thus, natural law is essential to a viable business ethic in our religiously pluralistic world.

Furthermore, a natural law basis for business ethics helps avoid another problem that arises out of using religious authorities (such as the Bible), which are private to one religious group. We sometimes hear public figures make statements like this: "I personally do not believe that it is right to do such-and-such, but I would not impose my belief on others." This bifurcation of private and public ethic often springs out of the mistaken idea that one's ethic comes out of his own private religious book. And, of course, he does not want to impose his religious beliefs on someone else.

A natural law ethic avoids this private-public split. Regardless of what one's private religious authority tells him, a public moral law binds all persons and institutions. Thus, on a natural law view, there is no difference between a private ethic and a corporate ethic. If it is wrong for a person to intentionally take innocent human lives, then it is also wrong for a corporation to do it. If stealing is wrong for citizens, then it is also wrong for companies. The natural law transcends both individuals and institutions.

The natural law opposes an "end justifies any means" ethic on both a private and a public level. This is particularly applicable in a capitalistic business context in which the profit motive is so dominant. Capitalism based on an antinomian ethic is destructive of society. It feeds on greed, produces poverty, and leads to revolution and war. Universal moral restraints, such as the natural law, are necessary to keep capitalism in check. Otherwise, money becomes the end. Moral principles are sacrificed for monetary profit. Here again a universal moral law that is binding on both national and international business is necessary to avoid antinomianism and its concomitant evils. . . .

Conclusion

Natural law is the indispensable basis for an adequate business ethic. It is common to both believers and unbelievers, but believers are also bound by a higher law (see 1 Cor. 13). So, while the natural law obligates Christians to gain justly, the divine law urges us to give liberally. Paul reminded Timothy of the special duty placed on Christians who profit in business.

Command those who are rich in this present world not to be arrogant nor to put their hope in wealth, which is so uncertain, but to put their hope in God, who richly provides us with everything for our enjoyment. Command them to do good, to be rich in good deeds, and to be generous and willing to share. (1 Tim. 6:17–18)

Common Moral Ground and the Natural Law Argument

James W. Skillen

Introduction

At the most basic level of disagreement about whether there is a rational, moral "natural law," some people reject the idea of any binding standard that does not originate within the individual's own autonomy, while others contend that, despite all protestations to the contrary, some kind of natural law holds all humans accountable. Within the camp of those who believe that nonsubjective principles of some kind bind all humans, there is disagreement about whether those principles are socially shared values, unchanging rational-moral principles, or divinely ordained commands. There is also very little agreement today among natural-law proponents about what kind of social order best comports with the natural law and how its moral obligations should be allocated among families, governments, corporations, schools, churches, and various professional and voluntary associations.

The question with which I begin, therefore, is whether an argument for natural law can ever succeed in demonstrating what the argument takes for granted—namely, the reality of a universal moral ground that is supposedly needed in order for business (and other human activities) to be conducted across religious, philosophical, and cultural divides. One reason why many Christians, for example, have appealed to natural law is to find a common basis for communicating (or doing business or whatever) with non-Christians, since an appeal to the Bible would seem to exclude those who do not accept biblical authority.[1] But what if the people with whom Christians are trying to communicate do not accept the authority of natural law or of natural-law reasoning? Where, then, can people find common ground beneath the disagreement over natural law itself? A Christian (or anyone else) may *believe* that some kind of nonsubjective moral order is available to all rational human beings, but if not everyone shares this conviction, then the natural-law proponent is still left standing on a platform that does not include everyone—a platform that is, therefore, uncommon ground. In that case, what is the practical advantage of a natural-law position that is not universally acknowledged?

A natural-law proponent might, of course, be convinced that those who do not acknowledge the natural law are mistaken and that their mistake can be demonstrated through rational argument. But how does this help two parties reach a business deal if they have not agreed ahead of time on a common moral-philosophical basis and if the dissenting party cannot be persuaded of the "mistake" of rejecting natural law? Furthermore, how does the believer in natural law account for this lack of agreement over the existence and universality of natural law? A natural-law argument seems to end in self-contradiction when it posits a common moral foundation that turns out not to be recognized as common at all.

This is not the place to try to summarize the ways in which various types of natural-law proponents might respond to the challenge sketched above. But I would like to try to move the discussion forward by entering it from a self-professed biblical point of view.

Don't Dismiss the Bible Too Quickly

In the first place, it seems to me that Christian proponents of natural-law who dismiss the Bible as irrelevant for reaching common-terrain moral agreement with non-Christians do so too quickly. The Bible may not be accepted as a binding authority by non-Christians, but, as I have just suggested, neither is natural law accepted as a binding authority by everyone, and the meaning of natural law is much less clear than the Bible. Moreover, the Bible is not a text of secret mysteries, but a public, covenantal witness that, from

beginning to end, sustains the claim that God is the Creator, Judge, and Redeemer of the whole world. Much of the Bible addresses the very questions that concern us here, namely, those about what is common and uncommon among human beings. Many who make natural-law arguments even appeal to Romans 1 and other passages of Scripture to explain what they mean. Consequently, the challenge Christians should accept is not that of trying to figure out how to make moral arguments without appeal to the Bible, but how, from a thoroughly biblical point of view, to engage in arguments with people who may not acknowledge the Bible as their own highest authority.

Natural-Law Arguments Are Not Neutral

Stating the challenge this way—and this is my second point—is to begin to undermine one of the assumptions that many natural-law proponents cherish: the assumption that there is a neutral or universally common way to make a natural-law argument. My contention, to the contrary, is that there is no such thing as a common or neutral moral argument. In fact, this is one reason why not everyone recognizes natural law or agrees on its meaning. I, for example, believe that all humans do in fact share something in common: all have been created in God's image and live in the same universe governed by him. Following the biblical story, I accept this as a "creation-order" viewpoint, loaded with all the baggage of a Christian view of history, of human nature, of divine sovereignty, and much more. Someone else may hold natural-law convictions within an Aristotelian framework or a Stoic framework or a Thomist, Kantian, or Jeffersonian framework. But the fact that all may agree that some kind of moral order is "out there" does not in itself give us common ground for practical moral discourse and decision making.

Part of what I am saying is that the mere reference to natural law does little to establish the ground that many natural-law proponents think can be established on a natural-law foundation. Therefore, rather than try to maintain the myth of the natural law's universality while discarding the Bible as parochial, the better approach for Christians would be to acknowledge at the outset that their biblical view of creation order opens the way to a distinctive approach to the debate over natural law and moral order. Christians, in other words, should mine the biblical texts and the Christian point of view for all they are worth and urge others to make clear their own distinctive assumptions and particular points of departure.

Clarifying Agreements and Disagreements

What this helps us do—and here begins my third point—is to clarify both the agreements and disagreements among people about the moral order of the universe. In my interpretation of human experience, disagreement over moral foundations is to be expected, since, from a biblical point of view, all humans are sinners. It is not just that some people are willful, selfish, immature, irrational, or unenlightened. Those errors and inadequacies at the purely human level might be resolved by better education, better child rearing, and the adequate isolation of truly irrational and irresponsible persons. But from a biblical point of view, the reason people act immaturely, deviantly, and at times with evil intent is that, ultimately, they are rebels against God and against the creation's inescapable moral standards. Consequently, I am not surprised that some of my fellow human beings will disagree that this is God's world, or that to be human is to be the image of God, or that we are all sinners. My own starting point prepares me for disagreement at a very fundamental level, and seeing it deepens my conviction that all humans share both creatureliness and sinfulness.

But even this is not all that I bring to a public conversation, or to a business situation, or to the political debate. I also bring the conviction—whether or not others share it—that by God's providence and grace it is often possible for sinful creatures who start with different basic convictions to reach agreement on some things and, at times, to change their minds and hearts in ways that can lead to deeper agreement. Therefore, while I will always be very cautious and careful in

drawing up contracts and communicating with people who may disagree with me at the foundations, I will also engage them openly, looking for the possibility of real communication and agreement because I believe we are both upheld by God's grace in God's world.

In other words, the strength of the common creation order does not depend on the extent of human agreement about it, but on God's sustaining commitment to the creation. That is, our common human bond in creatureliness and sinfulness is tied up with the additional common bond of God's restraining and enabling grace that upholds the creation order and all of us within it. The common moral order of creation is thus not an independent, neutral frame of reference for all rational people regardless of the differing religious authorities they acknowledge. No, from a biblical point of view, God's creation order, which commonly binds all creatures, is an order that proves itself in the face of disobedience and rejection as well as obedience and acceptance. There is simply no neutral way either to access it or to resist it.

This is how I interpret the apostle Paul's argument in his letter to the Romans (1:18–2:16). Paul is confident that God's creation order holds all humans accountable and without excuse. Even unbelievers may at times "show that the requirements of the law are written on their hearts" (2:14–15). But Paul did not, on this basis, hold out the hope that all humans, in common, can depend on a "natural law" for human society regardless of their deep religious differences. To the contrary, many people neither glorify God nor give thanks. In their sinfulness, their thinking itself becomes futile and their hearts darkened; they exchange the truth of God for a lie and worship created things rather than the Creator (1:18–25). The creation order holds for all, but not everyone recognizes or obeys it.

What is Paul's answer to this predicament? He does not argue that we should give up on the Bible's revelation about the universal embrace of God's law, but rather (as he explains in the remaining chapters of Romans) that in face of human sin and disobedience we should recognize that God upholds the creation order, brings ungodliness to judgment, and, through Christ, draws repentant sinners back to the true path of life. Natural law is not something that can be abstracted from creation, sin, and redemption and used as an independent, rational instrument. "Natural law," properly understood, is God's order for creation.

God and the Creation Order

In keeping with the biblical witness, therefore—and in the fourth place—I would urge fellow Christians to go all the way in developing a full-blown view of creation order. A general appeal to "natural law" will not take us very far. Today many of society's important public moral questions have to do with the nature and limits of institutional responsibility. For example, what part of a "just price" for goods and services should be set by the market and what part set by government regulations? Should environmental protection be the primary obligation of government, or should it be left to manufacturers, farmers, and others who use natural resources and discharge pollutants into the air, soil, and water? Should schools try to teach a common morality to all students, or should they leave moral training to parents and churches? Should government even continue to operate common schools at taxpayer expense if fewer and fewer citizens use them, or should government support the parental choice of diverse schools through vouchers or some other means? Should health care become a matter of greater public responsibility, or should it be left to market mechanisms even if that means an expanding population of poor people without adequate health care? What should and should not be defined as a crime? What is and is not a government's responsibility?

These and countless other questions of a public moral nature demand answers and policy decisions every day. A general appeal to "natural law" does little to help answer questions about the distinguishable, differentiated responsibilities and jurisdictions of diverse institutions. The best and most complete answers to questions like these within a natural-law framework were given by Thomas Aquinas and lesser fathers of the church

in the twelfth-to-fourteenth centuries. But those answers made sense within a social order of a particular kind, led by strong ecclesiastical authority with its international canon law. The late medieval world was socially complex, but it had a kind of hierarchy that depended on only two primary authorities competent to make law—the church and, under the church, various political authorities. Science, art, business and commerce—not to speak of education, family life, and professions—were not independent of ecclesiastical jurisdiction as they are today.

The aim in our day surely cannot be to retrieve the Middle Ages. Instead, it should be to deal with diverse moral questions in a way that helps sort out the various competencies and obligations belonging to different persons and institutions. In a highly differentiated society such as that in the United States, this requires a moral philosophy of considerable depth and range that can sustain an integral argument about multiple interrelated human obligations. In what follows, I will try to hint at some ways that a creation-order philosophy can respond to this challenge, but it can be only a hint.[2] The main point, however, should be clear: there is no universal, rational, agreed-upon natural law that draws everyone into common moral discourse and agreements, and there is certainly not one that is neutral and secular apart from all competing religious (and other) convictions. Thus there is no alternative in our multicultural, multireligious world but for diverse communities of shared conviction to clarify their fundamental commitments and assumptions as they seek to cooperate and communicate with one another, realizing that the very nature of what we hold in common will be disputed.

A Biblical Perspective

The biblical testimony carried forward from Israel to Paul constantly reaffirms divine standards or principles that hold all human creatures accountable. These creation norms, I believe, are indeed universal and do not originate within individual or social subjectivity. At the same time, these standards of love, justice, stewardship, honor, humility, and more come from God as "norms," not as rational "forms" (in a Greek sense). Psalm 119:105 speaks of God's word (standards, precepts, laws, decrees, statutes) as "a lamp to my feet and a light for my path." The point of God's commands is to illuminate real life in this world, to show us how to live meaningfully and wisely as we make decisions and fulfill responsibilities of family life, work, leisure, worship, and civic responsibility before his face.

Furthermore, the Bible speaks of human obligation as something that develops over generations with the unfolding of many kinds of talents and creational potentials—family life, agriculture, science, music, law, and much, much more. From this point of view, reality is an unfolding creation that moves historically from lesser to greater social complexity. This is why we must never identify God's creation-order—the moral law-order for creation—with positive laws or with a particular philosophy of natural law or with a particular kind of social order, whether medieval or contemporary. All human efforts—whether legal, philosophical, or otherwise—have the character of a response to God's standards for creaturely life. The normative principles and precepts always remain out ahead of us, holding us accountable, calling us to account for disobedience, remaining incapable of being confined within our positivizations.

The Dutch Christian statesman and theologian Abraham Kuyper coined a phrase—which in English reads "sphere sovereignty"—to get at some features of the perspective I am hinting at here. One thing he meant by this phrase is that our world is an ordered creation under God's sovereignty and that diverse human responsibilities, each with its own proper place in creation, should be seen as spheres of delegated authority under God. How shall we properly distinguish economic from educational from scientific from political responsibilities? Kuyper said that apart from responding obediently to God in tune with the mandates for a dynamically unfolding creation, there is no way to get those distinctions right. Or to say it positively, the task of fulfilling human moral obligations will require the hard work of clarifying the differences among various kinds of responsibilities we bear as humans—in the workplace, in schools, in laboratories, in churches, in families, and in the market.[3]

Thus, for example, for government truly to do justice, it must give proper recognition in law to the various kinds of nongovernmental responsibilities people hold as parents, teachers, employers, church officials, and so forth. The complex social order cannot be reduced to an omnicompetent political order or, as classical liberalism has tried to achieve, to autonomous individuals who supposedly create all social order (and all obligations) through contracts.

Of course, Christians themselves do not agree about how to distribute moral obligations across society. They do not hold in common a creation-order philosophy. So we should not be surprised that human beings in general do not share this view of life. But the challenge to Christians and to everyone else today is not first of all to win a philosophical argument, but to figure out how to live responsibly together in a complex society. It is ordinary parents, school teachers, business people, and legislators who have to decide every day what they *ought* to do based on some kind of moral reference.

The fact is that people in our society do not share a natural-law approach to decision making. Some are pragmatists, some utilitarians, some Thomists, some personalists, and perhaps most are simply confused or opportunistic. This is the setting in which Christians should be seeking to develop the best and the highest, the most adequate and the most complete approach to business stewardship, sound law making, integral education, and loving families.

A rounded creation-order philosophy should be able to help people answer many questions: Should a large corporation, which increasingly finds that it must reeducate new employees because of poor public schools, push for education reform that will radically reform the governance of education, or should it simply spend its own money for reeducation? Should a responsible manufacturer, realizing that natural resources are limited in supply, support broader environmental regulations? Should citizens disturbed by increasing family breakdowns and poverty ask their local government to require public schools to remain open during noninstructional hours to provide child care, recreation, and other activities, or should they look at a wider range of options that would not further burden the schools?

The answers to these and similarly complex questions depend very much on what we believe to be the proper obligations of governments, families, schools, and business enterprises. It is not enough for us simply to notice that a problem exists (such as pollution or needy children) and then appeal to someone (or to everyone in general) to do something. Without an argument from principle about who is responsible to do what, all moral pleadings amount to little more than opinion mongering and power brokering.

Summary

A creation-order moral argument represents an attempt to deal with the same issues and challenges that other natural-law arguments deal with. But it does so by trying immediately to clarify the entire framework of assumptions and presuppositions that contextualize its appeal to the moral order that binds human beings. A creation-order argument does not hide its presuppositions. It encourages others to disclose their own. It admits to its own nonneutrality even as it seeks to make clear the nature of the universal order that binds all humans. In the face of the lack of consensus about what commonly binds humans, a creation-order viewpoint probes to the roots of disagreements and social conflicts by seeking to show how disobedience to divine standards both accounts for various problems and helps illuminate the continuing validity of God's inescapable norms. And finally, a creation-order approach is continually concerned with how people should act concretely in the different spheres of personal and social accountability. The chief goal is not to win a philosophical argument by proving that this is the best kind of natural-law reasoning. Rather, the goal is to help clarify the nature of actual normative obligations in a differentiated society in God's good but fallen creation.

Notes

[1] This appears to be Norman Geisler's aim in "Natural Law and Business Ethics."

[2] I have developed in greater detail an argument for political and social ethics grounded in a creation-order philosophy in *Recharging the American Experiment: Principled Pluralism for Genuine Civic Community* (Grand Rapids: Baker, 1994). By the use of diverse texts and commentaries on them, Rockne M. McCarthy and I have compared Catholic natural-law philosophy with a creation-order philosophy in *Political Order and the Plural Structure of Society* (Atlanta: Scholars Press, 1991), especially pages 135–417.

[3] An introduction to the work of Abraham Kuyper along with two of his important texts can be found in McCarthy and Skillen, *Political Order and the Plural Structure of Society*, 235–64. See also Kuyper's Princeton "Stone Lectures" (1898) in *Lectures on Calvinism* (Grand Rapids: Eerdmans, 1931), and Kuyper, *The Problem of Poverty*, ed. James Skillen (Grand Rapids: Baker, 1991).

CASES

Case 3.1: Extending Benefits to "Spousal Equivalents"

In the last few years, several major corporations, such as Ben & Jerry's and Lotus Development, and many local governments have responded to employee requests and have established policies that extend medical benefits to partners of homosexual employees. Traditionally, such benefits were only offered to legally married spouses of heterosexual employees. However, because of recent cultural and demographic changes, many employers are adapting their policies to fit these new demographics. Proponents of such changes argue that the traditional nuclear family represents a decreasing percentage of the population and should not be the only definition of family that receives such benefits. Furthermore, homosexual employees argue that since they cannot legally marry, they are being discriminated against in company benefit plans.

These policies are, however, not without their opponents. Some opponents regard employers who take steps to recognize same-sex marriages as immoral. Others argue that since unmarried heterosexual couples do not receive such benefits, neither should homosexuals; in response, many of these employers offer benefits to live-in heterosexual couples as well.[2] Similar measures were rejected in the city of Philadelphia after vigorous protest by religious groups.[3] One was repealed by vote in the city of Austin, Texas, and the neighboring county of Williamson tried to deny Apple Computers tax breaks for similar policies until former Governor Ann Richards pressured county commissioners to reconsider.

[2]See William M. Bulkely, "Lotus Creates Controversy by Extending Benefits to Partners of Gay Employees," *Wall Street Journal*, 25 October 1991, B1, B6; and Max Aguilera Hellweg, "Gay in Corporate America," *Fortune* (16 December 1991).

[3]Randy Frame, "Christians Turn Back City Hall," *Christianity Today* (16 August 1993): 49.

Questions for Discussion:

1. Do you think employers should extend such benefits? If not, is it a legitimate form of discrimination?
2. What role do specifically Christian values have in a pluralistic society? If very limited, whose values should govern?

Case 3.2: Work and Family Policies

As the Vice President of the United States, Dan Quayle was perhaps best known for his criticism of television character "Murphy Brown" when the situation comedy's story line had her bearing a child as a single parent. Quayle lamented the way in which the media elite and much of the popular culture celebrated single parenthood by praising Brown's character for her courage in having the child on her own. Following his remarks, many newspapers and newsmagazines focused on the debate over family values, asking questions like "whose values?" and "whose definition of a family?" This entire episode made family values an issue in the 1992 presidential campaign, with all three of the major candidates competing to see who could be the most consistent advocate of family values.

A few months after the clamor over Quayle's remarks died down, the *Atlantic Monthly* published a cover story with the startling title "Dan Quayle Was Right." The article offered evidence that two-parent families do make a difference in the way children are raised and how they turn out. Many family specialists—particularly conservative Jews, Catholics, and Protestants—pointed out that they have been saying this for some time.

In 1994–95, some of the most direct evidence came to light that links single-parent families with high rates of school dropout, juvenile delinquency, and crime. For example, the best-seller entitled *Fatherless America* by family advocate David Blankenhorn cites numerous studies that indicate the importance of a present, involved father for the emotional and moral health of children. That is not to say that single mothers cannot do a good job of raising children alone when that is their only option. But it is to say that intentionally planning to raise children alone may not be the wisest course for society to follow.

In light of this evidence, many companies are offering paternity leave for men who have just begun families. This is consistent with the Family Leave Act passed in 1993, which mandates that medium-to-large companies offer employees up to twelve weeks of unpaid leave at the birth of a child. Other companies are offering on-site day care where employees can work and have contact with their children at certain times during the workday. Others are enabling employees to telecommute and work at home, giving them more flexibility in their schedules in order to accommodate the needs of their families. Companies argue that such flexibility is necessary to keep good employees, and it also keeps overhead costs down by reducing the amount of office space needed for operations. Others suggest that this is good social policy, that whatever nurtures the family is good for

[4]See Aaron Bernstein, "Family Leave May Not Be That Big a Hardship for Business," *Business Week* (5 June 1991): 28; and Barbara Dafoe Whitehead, "Dan Quayle Was Right," *Atlantic Monthly* (7 April 1993): 43–44.

society as a whole. But these family-sensitive policies are not without their costs.[4]

Questions for Discussion:

1. Do you believe that there is something universal and natural about the structure of the nuclear family? If so, can you defend that idea without recourse to the Bible?

2. If the nuclear family is part of natural law—that is, it is natural because of creation—does it follow that companies should have family-sensitive employment policies in place? Or are these policies simply good business and should be in place only as they enhance a company's profitability? Or is it simply a matter of obeying the law and offering nothing more than what the law requires?

3. In light of your views of the family and natural law, would you also support a company that offered benefits to nonmarried, live-in partners, either heterosexual or homosexual?

Case 3.3: The Business of Pornography

Pornography is a multibillion-dollar industry in the United States and around the world. In the past twenty-five years, feminists have criticized manufacturers of pornography for the way in which women are portrayed as sex objects, useful only to satisfy the lusts and fantasies of men. They hold that such a portrayal of women violates the widely held and—for some—foundational moral principle, the dignity of the individual person. Human dignity is the cornerstone for all other human rights, and feminists and other critics of pornography cite the way that the dignity of the women involved in such films is routinely and often callously ignored for the sake of profit.

The dignity of the person is such a widely held moral principle—valued in virtually every culture and civilization in history—that many people conclude that its acceptance is not an accident. Rather, it is evidence of a transcendent universal principle—what we are calling in this chapter "natural law." One does not have to accept the Bible, or the view that human beings are made in God's image, to hold to the centrality of human dignity to a person's view of the world and the moral life. It is a principle that God has also revealed outside the Bible, through reason and experience.

Defenders of pornography insist that the women who star in their films are not slaves, but are there by their own choice—a choice that in many cases is well compensated monetarily. They argue that these women choose freely and without coercion to play these roles and therefore the pornography is not a violation of their dignity. These defenders hold that the Constitutional principle of freedom of expression protects the rights of porn makers to engage in their craft. That right should only be restricted when the actresses are forced into those roles with no choice, as is often the case with children in "kiddie porn" films.

Feminists respond that, even so, these films still degrade women because they portray them as things for men's use, not people with inherent dignity. Whether or not the actresses freely consent to play those roles is irrelevant, feminists insist.

Questions for Discussion:

1. Do you think that the principle of human dignity is a universal principle of natural law? Or is it a coincidence that so many cultures have human dignity as one of their founding principles?
2. If you hold that human dignity is a universal principle with natural law as its source, how do you explain the numerous and egregious violations of human rights in the twentieth century by the Communist regimes and the Nazis?
3. If the women who star in pornography do so willingly and without coercion, do you nevertheless consider pornography a violation of a woman's dignity?
4. Do you think that the pornography industry should be further restricted by the law because of the way women are portrayed?

COMMENTARY

Attacks on traditional Judeo-Christian ethics by the movements toward political correctness and extreme forms of multiculturalism have further complicated the moral environment in which business is conducted. Some of the very virtues upon which business and the proper functioning of the economy depend are being assailed as destructive for society as a whole and as oppressive to particular members of it.

Similar to the situation with cultural relativism discussed in chapter 2, there are theoretical flaws that underlie the postmodern movement in favor of a no-holds-barred tolerance of a wide variety of views of right and wrong. In particular, political correctness sends a mixed message that indicates a fundamental contradiction with its emphasis on tolerance. On the one hand, it bases many of its beliefs on the postmodern rejection of truth claims. Arguing on behalf of moral relativism, some of its adherents demand that society become tolerant of others, particularly groups that are deemed to have suffered oppression in some way in the past or present. On the other hand, it is argued that since no group can say that its moral beliefs are superior to another's, tolerance should be society's highest virtue. However, this is a logically inconsistent position to take. If all moral values are truly relative, how could there be a norm called "tolerance" for which all should aim? What would the advocate of political correctness do with another culture in which intolerance was considered the highest virtue?

Furthermore, while the movement argues for "tolerance," its actions often resemble crusades of the most extreme forms of intolerance. In fact, this aspect of the movement on college campuses has lead Dinesh D'souza to title his insightful critique of the movement *Illiberal Education.*[5] The movement seems to argue that tolerance only applies to what it considers "oppressed groups." For example, those who hold religious or moral convictions against abortion and homosexuality are often labeled bigots and are often even barred from speaking in forums.

While many of the conflicts cited in headlines have occurred on college campuses, business must also confront the claims of political correctness. For example, because moral values are assumed to be relative, companies are forced to "tolerate" many more behaviors on the part of their employees than in the past. Two California cities have sought to protect the rights of supposed oppressed groups through "anti-looks" or "lookism" ordinances. The cities of Santa Cruz and San Francisco have recently enacted laws that prohibit discrimination based on an employee's looks. The law in Santa Cruz was established

[5]Dinesh D'souza, *Illiberal Education: The Politics of Race and Sex on Campus* (New York: Free Press, 1991).

on the basis of the case of a twenty-year-old hospital worker, Cooper Hazen, who sued his employer for being fired on the basis of looks discrimination. The hospital allegedly dismissed him because at work he had worn a half-inch-long post with tiny metal balls through the center of his tongue.[6]

Undoubtedly, the protection of the rights of minority groups is of the utmost importance in the workplace. However, it is alarming that what started out as equal rights has led to "special rights." In regards to the "lookism" case, there must be some protection for business to freely operate in a profitable manner. While rejecting someone purely on the basis of looks without any business necessity is abhorrent, an employer who reasonably suspects that an employee's altered appearance will negatively affect the business must have the freedom to make certain decisions.

Another illustration of how changing moral norms are affecting businesses is at the heart of Case 3.1, in which companies are engaging in the controversial practice of extending benefits to homosexual couples.

Business executives must be aware of cultural forces, since these forces can interfere with the daily operation of organizations. More importantly, however, business is dependent on the values of the surrounding culture. If basic virtues of self-restraint such as trust, courage, and prudence continue to erode, free-market institutions are in jeopardy.

Apropos to what Neal Gabler has stated with respect to society at large, business also depends on a core of shared values that transcend any one particular culture or ideology. But what is the foundation for this core? Even as political correctness and multiculturalism argue in support of relativism, they, too, implicitly appeal to an absolute moral standard, that of tolerance. Most people, when pressed, would admit that there are some values that are at least prima facie absolute and that are independent of any cultural setting. Norman Geisler, in his article, outlines an impressive catalog of values that are so widely shared that it is reasonable to conclude they are universal. He argues—correctly, in our view—that the foundation of these core values is natural law.

Given the plurality of viewpoints present in our current culture, especially those that attack traditional Christian ethics, it is unclear on what basis, if any, Christians can have dialogue with nonbelievers about moral issues in the workplace. Believers who adhere to a revealed morality cannot depend on the authority of the Bible to attempt to exercise a moral influence in their work setting. Christians who desire to be the "salt of the earth" and the "light of the world" in

[6]Lucy Howard and Ned Zeman, "A Real Tongue Lashing," *Newsweek* (10 February 1992): 8.

their workplace must appeal to something other than Scripture to be persuasive in articulating a Judeo-Christian ethic for business. We suggest that natural law offers one such basis. We agree with James Skillen that one ought not to dismiss the Bible too quickly, but be equipped to take a biblical position and articulate it persuasively to an audience that does not accept biblical authority. Skillen's creation order is natural law properly understood. Since it is rooted in creation, it can be accessible to every person and does not depend on someone's being a member of the Christian community to acknowledge it.

Among all the unusual circumstances in the confirmation hearings of Supreme Court Justice Clarence Thomas in 1992 was his belief in natural law. As soon as he mentioned it in the course of answering a question, many members of the Senate Judiciary Committee expressed immediate concern, and protests went up from numerous special-interest groups—namely, feminist and gay rights groups. Whatever the reasons for people's objections, it is clear that the concept of natural law is still debated today. Professor Moore's point in "Unnatural Brawl Over Natural Law" is a good one—that the uproar created by Clarence Thomas's views has more to do with his specific values than his natural law judicial philosophy, which has historically been the norm in legal circles.

There has been much disagreement within Judeo-Christian circles about the validity of natural law. Like the Catholic and Islamic theologians of the time, many Jewish rabbis in the Middle Ages acknowledged the existence of moral values outside the Torah and their accessibility to people who did not have the Torah. The Reformers and their predecessors were very skeptical of natural law because of their high view of sin, which made it difficult to discover morality apart from the clear revelation of God in Scripture, and because they gave the Bible the central place as the source of moral and spiritual authority. The Reformers held that the Catholic view of natural law undercut both of those crucial doctrines. A second group of critics was the Protestant neo-orthodox theologians (Karl Barth and Emil Brunner, for example) in the twentieth century who argued that natural law undermined the centrality of Christ for the moral life. Yet, even though these groups were critical of the concept, it may be that they all held to some concept of natural law under the heading of common grace or general revelation.

Ultimately, the degree to which we hold to natural law will determine the way we can try to persuade the world to adopt Judeo-Christian ethics. If natural law is not a viable concept, then believers can only talk to the world with the gospel and would likely hold that the social mission of the church is unimportant or that social change can be accomplished only indirectly, by the witness of life together in community.[7] But if natural law is viable, then religious believers can engage in a legitimate social mission and activism on moral issues that can complement the proclamation of the tradition's central message.

Defining Natural Law

Defining natural law can be quite difficult. In general, there are two primary ways in which the term is used today. The first form refers to broad, general, objective, and widely shared moral values that are not specifically tied to the special revelation of Scripture. Justice, fairness, respect for a person's dignity, the obligation not to harm another, truth-telling, and respect for life in prohibitions against killing—these concepts are all examples of virtually universally shared values that had an origin that predated Scripture.[8] Oxford University theologian John Macquarrie has put it this way:

> In fact the very term "natural law" is misleading if it is taken to mean some kind of code. The natural law is not another code of system of laws in addition to all the actual systems, but is simply our rather inaccurate way of referring to those most general moral principles against which particular rules or codes have to be measured.[9]

To call them natural *laws* can be misleading, since they are the principles on which our specific laws are based.

There is a second and more specific form of natural law, used predominantly in Roman Catholic circles, in which specific moral rules are codified. For example, the Catholic view of reproductive ethics, especially contraception and the use of reproductive technologies to alleviate infertility, uses natural law reasoning to reach conclusions about their validity. Here natural law is more narrowly tied to what is natural in creation. For example, in reproduction, since the natural process that God ordained in creation begins with sexual relations and progresses from conception to pregnancy to birth (assuming no complications), anything that interferes, interrupts, or replaces this natural process is morally wrong. That is why Catholic teaching prohibits contraception, abortion, and most reproductive technologies.

This specific form of reasoning should be evaluated on a case-by-case basis. Most Protestants tend to reject this Catholic reasoning when applied to contraception or reproductive technologies, but embrace it when dealing with issues such as genetic engineering, in which medical researchers are cautioned against "playing God" and interfering with his created order. Evangelicals and Roman Catholics

[7] See, for example, the works of John Howard Yoder, *The Politics of Jesus* (Grand Rapids: Eerdmans, 1972) and *The Priestly Kingdom* (Notre Dame, Ind.: University of Notre Dame Press, 1984).

[8] For a catalog of these values traced historically, see the appendix in C. S. Lewis, *The Abolition of Man* (New York: Macmillan, 1947).

[9] John Macquarrie, "Rethinking Natural Law," in Charles E. Curran and Richard A. McCormick, eds., *Readings in Moral Theology, No. 7: Natural Law and Theology* (New York: Paulist Press, 1991), 239.

[10]For example, see Kai Nielsen, "The Myth of Natural Law," in Sidney Hook, ed., *Law and Philosophy* (New York: NYU Press, 1964), 122–43.

in particular use natural law reasoning in voicing opposition to homosexuality. Homosexual sexual relationships are not legitimate, according to these groups, because they are unnatural—that is, they run counter to the created order that God ordained. From these examples we see that, before dismissing this more specific form of natural law, evangelicals in particular should recognize how frequently they invoke it in their arguments on different social issues. Most secular philosophers thoroughly reject this form of natural law.[10]

The Biblical Basis for Natural Law

Perhaps the central passage in the Bible that affirms natural law, at least in its more broad sense, is Romans 2:1–16. After Paul appeals to creation to point out the sin of the nonreligious—and, interestingly, to oppose homosexuality (Romans 1:18–32)—he proves that the moralistic person is also condemned before God because of his sin. The heart of this passage, as it applies to natural law, is in verses 14–15, where Paul states,

> Indeed, when Gentiles, who do not have the law, do by nature things required by the law, they are a law for themselves, even though they do not have the law, since they show that the requirements of the law are written on their hearts, their consciences also bearing witness, and their thoughts now accusing, now even defending them.

God appears to hold those without the law accountable for their sin in the same way that he holds the Jews accountable (Romans 2:17–29). It is difficult to see how this could be just unless those without the law have some way of knowing what is right and wrong. In other words, for God to legitimately hold the world accountable for sin, everyone must have access to God's standard of morality even if they are without special revelation. This standard would be natural law, or general revelation applied to morality. God has revealed these values outside of Scripture and has made them accessible to those without access to Scripture.

[11]For further exegetical study on the biblical basis for natural law, see Alan F. Johnson, "Is There Biblical Warrant for Natural Law Theories?" *Journal of the Evangelical Theological Society* 27 (June 1982):185–99.

Paul's teaching in Romans 2 is parallel to the oracles to the nations (Isaiah 13–27; Jeremiah 46–51; Ezekiel 25–32; Amos 1–2), in which the prophets condemned Israel's pagan neighbors, who did not have the law, for many of the same things God condemned Israel for, who did have the law. Unless the nations have some access to God's law apart from the written law, it is hard to see how God can be just in holding people accountable for something of which they have no knowledge.[11]

In the Old Testament, the concept of wisdom opens the door for at least the more general form of natural law.[12] In the wisdom literature there are two sources of wisdom, natural and revealed—both legitimate and authoritative, though revealed wisdom (God's wisdom in the Scripture) appeals to its being God's word for its authority and the natural wisdom (God's wisdom revealed outside of Scripture) appeals to empirical evidence that it is reliable.

Scripture affirms that there is a fixed order that governs the physical world, the world of nature (Jeremiah 31:35–36; 33:20–21, 25–26). These are also known as the laws of nature and have been discovered by the hard sciences such as physics, astronomy, chemistry, and biology. This concept is reflected in creation psalms, such as Psalm 19, which praise God for the way he has revealed himself in creation. This is God's ordering wisdom embedded in creation. In Proverbs 8:22–31 it is clear that God's wisdom was intimately bound up with creation (see also Proverbs 3:19–20). God's wisdom was "engraved" into the creation from the very beginning. The Hebrew term translated "fixed order" is *huqqah* (to be engraved) and is the same word used in legal literature for "statute" (Leviticus 18:3–4). That is, what is engraved in the cosmos is one source of what is engraved in the commands of God.

God's ordering wisdom is expanded in Proverbs 8:32–36 to include interpersonal and especially moral knowledge. This wisdom is embedded in nature and can be discovered by reason. The writer draws conclusions about one's character and morality based on adherence to God's wisdom embedded in creation, suggesting that this wisdom includes moral knowledge.

The message of the Proverbs is that living in harmony with this order brings peace (*shalom*) and well-being, but to live at odds with this order is folly and brings self-destruction. Proverbs 8:32–36, in which wisdom is personified and presented in the first person, puts it this way:

> Now then, my sons, listen to me; blessed are those who keep my ways. Listen to my instruction and be wise; do not ignore it. Blessed is the man who listens to me, watching daily at my doors, waiting at my doorway. For whoever finds me finds life and receive favor from the LORD. But whoever fails to find me harms himself; all who hate me love death.

Because this passage follows directly after Proverbs 8:22–31, which links God's wisdom and the creation, it is the moral and spiritual conclusion drawn from the reality of God's natural wisdom. Notice that all the references to God's wisdom in creation are prior to

[12]We are indebted to our colleague, Dr. John Coe, Rosemead School of Psychology, Biola University, for his insights in this area.

the existence of any special revelation of Scripture. The concept of wisdom, then, suggests that God has revealed objective moral values outside of Scripture, or through natural law.

Limits on Natural Law

Many of the criticisms of natural law relate, not to its existence, but to how reliably it can be known. The Reformers, for example, with their strong view of sin and depravity, held that natural law was virtually useless since man's capacity to discern it apart from Scripture was so flawed that no moral principles apart from Scripture could be confidently known. It is certainly true that mankind's ability to discover natural law has been corrupted by the Fall, particularly in that sin enables human beings to use morality to mask self-interest.[13] Special revelation in Scripture is needed because it is not always clear if something is natural because of sin or because of creation. In addition, many aspects of the spiritual life require special revelation, such as those that relate to salvation and eternity. Although natural law does help reveal some moral obligations, the proper motive, context, and justification of Christian morality all depend on further insight gained from Scripture. It is true that what some might refer to as natural law can and frequently does conflict with Scripture. In these cases, Scripture is the final umpire. All of natural law or general revelation is consistent with Scripture and some of it may be clarified by Scripture, but not all of it is contained in Scripture.

[13]For more on this, see Reinhold Niebuhr, *Moral Man and Immoral Society* (New York: Scribner's, 1932).

Natural Law and Business Ethics

Natural law has clear implications for business ethics in that it provides the critical foundation for the core of shared values necessary for the successful operation of the economy. Two of the most debated issues in business ethics today are employee rights and consumer safety, which will be explored in more detail in later chapters. They are good illustrations of how natural law can be used in business ethics and how Judeo-Christian ethics can appeal to objective moral values outside the Bible as the foundation for positions on these issues.

Consider employee rights. One of the most widely held universal moral principles is the dignity of the individual and the corresponding duty to respect that dignity. Human dignity is ultimately grounded in the image of God, but one does not need to be a religious believer to hold to genuine human dignity. This principle undergirds much of the American Bill of Rights and also the declarations of human rights made around the world in this century. It is also the fundamental moral principle that obligates employers to provide safe and humane working conditions for employees. Workplaces that carry risk of injury are problematic because this risk signifies a lack of respect for the dignity of the individual worker.

Similarly, the substandard living conditions of the Maquiladoras (Case 2.1 in chapter 2) also violate this principle. Firms employing workers in Third World countries have the responsibility to provide wages and working conditions that are consistent with respect for human dignity. That is not to say that employers overseas must provide conditions similar to those in the United States, but that the conditions must not violate basic norms of human dignity. This principle comes from natural law and is central to the discussion of employee rights.

The need of firms to make a reasonable profit must be considered alongside respect for worker dignity. If workers willingly choose to work in substandard conditions, they are responsible for that choice. But in countries where workers have few employment choices, their vulnerability increases the moral obligation of employers to provide humane working conditions.

A second example of the effect of natural law on ethical decisions in business regards consumer safety. Ultimately, the reason that society requires companies to build safe products is that human dignity is highly valued. It is considered immoral for companies to place consumers at risk with reasonable use of their products; the more vulnerable the consumers—such as children—the more is required of firms to make safe products. In addition, the more risk that reasonable use involves—such as driving a car at freeway speeds—the more incumbent it is on companies to manufacture safe products. To be sure, a firm must balance profit and safety, and chapter 11 will provide some guidelines for achieving that balance. But respect for human dignity is the foundation of society's concern with consumer safety. The principle of respect for dignity comes from natural law.

Respect for human dignity is also at the heart of society's concern over sexual harassment and workplace discrimination. Because both men and women possess fundamental dignity from being made in God's image, they are not to be the objects of sexual harassment. They are not to be treated as objectified sexual beings to be used for pleasure, but are to be respected as persons, significant because they bear God's image. Although there is disagreement over the definition of sexual harassment—whether the emphasis on it has gone too far, and how to protect the rights of the accused—virtually everyone agrees that sexual harassment is immoral because it violates a person's essential dignity. Similarly, discrimination on the basis of race, gender, or disability violates the respect for dignity that demands that people be treated fairly.

Finally, the general principle of fairness underlies the concern over insider trading. Defining it may be difficult, but there is general agreement that profiting from use of insider information—that is, information that is not available to the public, even to the most aggressive and legal seeker—is unfair. This concern is magnified by the fact that there are losers as well as winners with insider trading. The principle of fairness, so crucial here, has its roots in natural law.

Part II

Capitalism and Christian Values

FOUR

The Morality of Capitalism

We are seldom kind. When large sums are at stake, kindness is irrelevant.

James H. Michelman,
"Some Ethical Consequences of Economic Competition"

There is not a necessary opposition between doing well and doing good, between taking care of business and taking care of each other. They may actually need one another.

Richard John Neuhaus, *Doing Well and Doing Good:
The Challenge to the Christian Capitalist*

INTRODUCTION

From the advent of the industrial age, capitalism has had its share of both ardent defenders and militant critics. Its defenders point to its clear successes in creating wealth around the world and the way in which it maximizes freedom for consumers and the opportunity for people to better themselves. Its critics have suggested that work in a capitalist system is inherently alienating and that the predictable business cycles that result in unemployment cause morally intolerable levels of hardship on those victimized by the system. They insist that the capitalist system impacts people negatively both when they are on the job and when they are unemployed. This chapter focuses on the critique of capitalism from the perspective of what participating in it does to individuals. This is more of a secular critique; the religiously based debate over capitalism will be addressed in the following chapter.

In the last few years, a number of private and government organizations have conducted research to determine the level of satisfaction enjoyed by people in their jobs. For example, sociologist Studs Terkel, in his best-selling book *Working*, surveyed hundreds of people

153

in their work environments and found that most people suffered from interminable boredom and a lack of purpose in their work. It was simply a means to the ends of paying their bills and financing their weekends. A cover story in a 1995 issue of *Fortune* highlighted the growing number of young MBA graduates from the most prestigious business schools in the United States who have made conscious decisions not to work in large corporations, choosing instead to launch out in their own businesses. The reason they decided to forego much higher incomes and advancement opportunities was that they did not want to subject themselves to life in major corporations. They saw their peers and friends who had been working for some time in corporate America and they did not want those stories to be repeated in their own lives. They saw the high stress, office politics, backbiting and harmful competition, isolation of their work from the end product of the company, and ways in which lower-level employees were treated, and they said "no thanks." Unfortunately, not everyone has that option, and should their planned ventures fail (as the majority of start-up companies do), they will likely find themselves working in an environment that they had wished to avoid. If the work environment is such a negative aspect of employment to highly educated people, think how that is multiplied for the worker who has less education, skill, and opportunity.

The readings in this chapter introduce you to the debate over some of these moral aspects of capitalism. E. F. Schumacher, in his piece "Buddhist Economics" from the book *Small Is Beautiful: Economics As If People Mattered*, argues that capitalism is more concerned with the production of goods than with the welfare of people and produces a culture more interested in consumption than in creative activity. He advocates smaller-scale economies in which local communities produce for local self-sufficiency. He is very skeptical of the global trade network that, in his view, has developed at the expense of work that gives people the chance to develop their creativity and character.

A. R. Gini and T. Sullivan pick up some of Schumacher's themes on work in their insightful piece "Work: The Process and the Person." They point out the potential damaging effects of work on the individual worker—tragic, since work plays such a key role in a person's self-definition and sense of meaning and fulfillment.

Business executive James Michelman writes his article "Some Ethical Consequences of Economic Competition" out of his personal experience as company president. He insists that the competition inherent in capitalism promotes traits that most people would not want to cultivate in their private life. He calls this the tension between desired moral character and desired business character. This may remind you of Albert Carr's work in chapter 1, "Is Business Bluffing Ethical?" in which he argues that business plays by a different set of moral rules than the rules by which one conducts his or her personal life. But whereas Carr holds that this is morally acceptable, Michelman finds it very troubling. Michelman argues that everyone in the competitive world of business must eventually choose between virtue and financial success. He is not jettisoning capitalism, however, only pointing out some moral tensions in the system.

Roman Catholic theologian Michael Novak presents a very different view. Though not using explicit theological language, he maintains that the idea of virtuous self-interest is not an oxymoron, and that the genius of capitalism is that one can do well financially and do good morally at the same time. He suggests that unchecked greed and cutthroat competition will eventually destroy firms that do not exercise some self-restraint in the pursuit of profit maximization.

Critics of capitalism often charge that though it may create wealth better than any other economic system in the world, it does not distribute it justly. They cite the cases of executive compensation as evidence that capitalism produces an unfair distribution of the goods of society. There is a clear disparity between those who have much and those who do not, and many critique capitalism for such inequalities. Others insist that as long as everyone plays by the rules, inequalities may be unfortunate but they are not unfair. The welfare system has been set up primarily to help those who have been hurt by these inequalities in distribution. Marvin Olasky, in his article "Compassion," argues that the way to genuinely help those who have less is not by government handouts but by personal compassion.

The cases in this chapter address what happens to individuals and communities when corporations make changes they deem necessary to maximize their profit. They show the impact of plant closings and taking jobs overseas where labor is much cheaper to employ. The companies respond to this criticism by insisting, as Michelman does, that if a company does not make every attempt to increase its profit, it will eventually succumb to the harsh world of business competition, throwing more people out of work than were put out of work by the plant closings in the first place.

READINGS

Some Ethical Consequences of Economic Competition

James H. Michelman

Journal of Business Ethics 2 (1983): 79–87.
Copyright © 1983 by D. Reidel Publishing Co.

I would like to discuss some fundamental questions regarding business ethics that stem (for me) from personal observations I have made during twenty-five years of responsible activity in the world of free enterprise.[1]

I

First, I note that a conflict exists between attitudes and actions demonstrated by myself and my associates when related to business, and attitudes and actions shown in more private affairs. I am aware of acts of charity, kindness, and public service performed by my co-workers in their private lives. In their dealings with me, they are truthful and faithful; we share common goals. Yet, in our dealings with customers and suppliers neither our truthfulness nor our fidelity can be assumed. If we are truthful and faithful it is because of (economically) rational or sentimental reasons, not because we are determined by moral law. We excuse ourselves by assuming a similar lack of truthfulness and fidelity in our trading partners. And they too, we believe, assume the same of us. Sometimes we are dealt with openly—all cards on the table. In that case, we assume laziness or sentimentality. These attitudes, actions, and reactions derive from the many years we have spent surviving in competitive markets. They are pragmatic; they are learned from experience.

We are seldom kind. When large sums are at stake, kindness is irrelevant. Nor do we look for kindness. Thus sympathy and compassion are excluded from those attitudes and expectations determining our course. The obligation of mutual aid is irrelevant, too. Suppliers are those you buy cheaply from; customers those to whom you sell as dearly as possible. We view competitors as the enemy and suppose that we are the enemy to them. Our relations with them are formal; our attitudes, dislike and fear. An act dictated by thoughts of beneficence[2] toward any of them by any of us would be considered by the rest of us to be a foolish act at best, and, at worst, an act of betrayal. With respect to competing for orders or resources, our gain is our competitors' loss; and we rejoice at our gain. Thus we are undismayed at their loss to which we have contributed. Again, we suppose like feelings on their part. We take none of these attitudes, dispositions, and actions to be exceptional, but rather expect that they are more or less universal in the business world. They seem to be rational attitudes and actions; and their rightness also seems to be confirmed by the (business) benefits they confer, and the (business) losses which follow when their controlling precepts are ignored. Now I have not observed these statements to be always true, of course. But they hold as to primary tendencies.

Certainly, the reader should not rely only upon my personal observations. My business or industry may be peculiar. It is possible that my views are distorted. If the reader is, or has been, engaged in commerce, he can reflect on his own observations to see how they jibe with mine. In addition there are two more investigations he can make. He can examine the daily press to see if the stories printed about business tend to confirm or contradict my reports. And the reader can construct hypothetical situations and note what he would expect the responses of the actors to be.

The press seems to afford confirmation. As an exercise in preparing this paper I noted in *The New York Times* and *The Wall Street Journal* during the period March 9, 1982–April 2, 1982, many articles either stating directly or strongly implying attitudes and actions on the part of persons engaged in business or the professions, or who were "investors," that we probably would take to be violations of accepted moral rules.[3] Two examples illustrate the point clearly.

(1) *The Wall Street Journal*, March 11, 1982, headlined "Comparative Ads Are Getting More Popular, Harder Hitting." Comparative advertising, of course, directly compares the advertiser's product to that of his competitor(s). The competing products are often disparaged; sometimes it is suggested that they are dangerous. . . . Ultimately, it is not other advertisers and other firms, but rather other *people* that are being attacked and presumably will suffer from the success of the "hard hitting" campaign. The executives, copywriters, and art people of the agency whose campaign is less successful will suffer; they may lose their jobs. The persons responsible for merchandising the product under attack will be damaged in some proportion to the rise in fortunes of the attackers.

(2) *The Wall Street Journal*, April 2, 1982, headlined "The Workout Crew: Bankers Who Step In If Loans Go Bad Reveal Lenders' Other Face" with the taglines "There Isn't Any Smile on It: Teams Tell Ailing Clients to Make Changes or Else" and "We See a Management Void." This long lead article begins by stating that ". . . workout specialists, the bankers who take over when a business loan goes bad" are known as "undertakers, morticians, black hats, or goons." They are dreaded. They force firings. . . . "It's always interesting to watch them walk down that corridor, look at that sign (Institutional Recovery Management) [a euphemism] and watch their faces change as it dawns on them they might be in trouble," chuckles [a senior banking officer]." "Bankers say they have only one concern. . .: getting their money back. "We have the right to get paid and they have an obligation to pay us. . . . The bank didn't cause the company to make bad investments or whatever it was that caused them to lose money." The sense of this article is

fear and humiliation on the part of the executives of the company in difficulty, contempt and rationality by the bankers.

Are there necessary *contradictions between generally accepted moral obligations and the laws and rules that flow from the logic of economic competition?*

Neither of these articles (nor the others) conveys any feeling that the actions and attitudes of the participators are unacceptable or even unexpected. Their activities are interesting and so newsworthy. But they are not subject to moral judgment. Yet the comparative advertisers are engaging in an obviously maleficent[4] enterprise (even if unacknowledged by themselves). The workout crews— as described in the article—are brutal. These attributes—maleficence and brutality—are not, of course, those that we would wish our friends and neighbors to hold and express in their dealings with us. Nor may they be warranted by reasoning from a certain justifying premise of free enterprise—one that holds least-cost efficiency to be a proper end of economic activity. For in the case of the advertisers, maleficent effort has been expended merely to induce purchasers to substitute one consume product for a similar one.[5] With respect to the workout crews, brutality is irrelevant. Yet, until we have reason to think that maleficent persons are attracted to the advertising industry and brutal ones to banks, we must concede that maleficence and brutality are characteristics of the job rather than the person.

To further investigate if there is a tendency for business morality to diverge from private, the reader might consider several scenarios and suppose what his own responses would be.

For example, he might suppose himself a purchasing agent, right now in the midst of buying a large quantity of raw material. Would he inform one of his regular suppliers that all the others raised their prices just this week? Or would he do his best to conceal the news? What if the supplier's salesman put the question to him directly. Would he claim ignorance? And if he answered the question truthfully, would he have occasion to feel that he had not fulfilled his obligation to his firm? If he then switched sides of the desk and became the salesman asking the question of the buyer, what assumptions should he make regarding the buyer's response?

Suppose the reader gives himself a promotion. He becomes president of the firm. What would he want—and expect—of his purchasing agent? Truthfulness, or shrewd dealing, assuming that these were in conflict?

Or the reader might suppose himself removed from the world of commercial negotiation. Rather he is an investor who, betting on a weak economy with high unemployment and falling interest rates, has bought fixed income securities. But the economy strengthens, workers are re-hired, and rates rise. How would he respond. Would he be pleased that the misery of hard times has begun to abate? Or would he grieve at the principal losses of his bonds? Suppose that it was not his own money that he had invested, but that of a charitable foundation of which he was trustee. Would this difference alter his response?

All these examples—my own observations, press reports, and reflections by the reader—at least begin to suggest that viewed from a certain standpoint, business competition simply may be amoral. This possibility raises another question—one that asks if there are *necessary* contradictions between generally accepted moral obligations and the laws and rules that flow from the logic of economic competition?

II

Business competition—free enterprise—is a rational undertaking. Profit maximization is the overriding consideration in the competitive universe, and profit maximization is achieved through rationality. These remarks, commonplace in microeconomic theory, may be justified as follows.

Unless a firm can bid successfully for factors of production it cannot survive. And only if it earns at least an average rate of return on its invested capital, will it be able to stay in the auction. The market validates this premise every day. A firm earning less than its competitors loses its ability to pay its more talented employees that wage which they could get elsewhere, and they will leave. Its credit rating sinks; its cost of funds rises. It may have difficulty borrowing regardless of cost. Thus its access to raw materials becomes restricted, and it is unable to pay for new plant and equipment. As a result its unit cost of production increases. These short examples are not exhaustive. But they illustrate real forces which logically must, and ultimately do, drive that firm to bankruptcy or voluntary liquidation.

One could postulate a universe of firms all initially earning about the same rate of return on invested capital but *not* maximizing income. But this universe would be unstable for unless there were legal constraints on return of capital the very engine of free enterprise—the profit motive—would immediately drive at least some firms to maximize profits. Once these became some small significant fraction, that fraction could, and would, outbid the rest for productive resources. Hence, relative stability occurs only when *all* are running their hardest: that is when *all* are seeking to maximize income. The laggards have already fallen by the wayside; future laggards will suffer the same fate.

To maximize profit the firm is obliged to make the most efficient use of its productive factors among which—often the most important—are persons; to choose products for sale which optimize its revenue; to purchase resources—again including persons—at the lowest possible cost, in short, to operate rationally. Else, it is failing to maximize return on invested capital and, sooner or later, must lose out to its competitors and cease to be a firm.

These simple considerations lead to profound ethical consequences.

First, consider our normal sense of what kind of persons we feel we ought to be. What are the attitudes and actions that we would like to think are part of our own moral makeup and that we would wish others to exhibit in their relationships with us? A non-exhaustive list surely includes courage and intelligence, kindness, compassion, honesty, loyalty, respect for others, adherence to the social duties of mutual aid and non-maleficence, and self-respect. Call this set of characteristics our *desired moral character* or the *human virtues*.

What characteristics would we look for in the managers of a company in which we held an important stake? Whatever this catalog turns out to be, call it the *desired business character*. It also certainly includes intelligence and a certain type of courage. But here we value intelligence and courage only insofar as they aid our managers to maximize the profits of our firm.

Next, if we analyze the role of persons as employees of firms engaged in free enterprise we discover an immediate moral paradox. Note that treating an employee as other than a productive factor stems from a philanthropic judgment rather than a business one. It may be rational for a firm to treat (some of) its employees considerately and reward them well, but only up to that point where finally there is no marginal benefit from doing so. Considerations of kindness and sympathy, for example, are irrelevant. A manager's obligation is to his firm, not its employees; and as we have already seen, he has no real choice in the matter if his firm is to survive. But it is clear that in following this reasoning we are struck at once with a contradiction which can be expressed by asking the question, What is the manager's duty to himself? If the discharge of his corporate responsibilities requires him to run counter to his desired moral character and so to violate his own basic self, must he do so? The necessity of profit maximization provides the answer. If the firm is to survive, the manager's obligation must be to it, not to himself. It follows, then, that free enterprise can require the violation of the individual's most basic duties to himself.

As a firm thrives, so do its responsible employees. But *regardless of their own well-being* their duty is to act so as to further the firm's interests which are to maximize its income, to make more and more money, amass more and more wealth. It is likely that these goals will be severely limited since all the firm's competitors, having the very same goals, prevent any single firm from outdistancing the others. But if the firm's policies—and so those of its responsible employees—are not fixed on the main chance, it is bound to fail. Once the firm enters the competition, it must abide by the rules of that competition. And all these rules are comprehended by the single Rule: Let the maxim of your action be that which advances the profitability of your firm. It seems a fair argument that once a rational being enters into—becomes an employee—of a firm (putting aside of course his motive for doing so) insofar as he acts *as an employee*, the maxim of his action must ignore his own moral interest and regard only his duty to make his firm as profitable as possible.

All these rules are comprehended by the single Rule: Let the maxim of your action be that which advances the profitability of your firm.

Nor is this all. Rationality demands that vendors rationalize their customers (sell at the highest possible price) and users rationalize their suppliers (buy at the lowest possible cost). Rationality demands that competitors seek the same orders, the same resources, the same employees—seek that is, their advantage at the expense of others. Given the set of demands engendered by, and inseparable from, the universe of economic competition, it therefore becomes a clear contradiction for an employee of one firm to act upon the laws generated by competition and will also that his suppliers, his customers, his competitors, act upon, and benefit from, those laws as well. For he then would be willing that they do what they can to negate his will. He would be willing war on himself.[6]

In sum, we find that the responsible firm employee must regard co-workers, vendors, and customers only as means to his firm's advantage; and that he himself is mere means to this end. We may conclude that insofar as he is fulfilling the obligation of his job—doing that for which he draws compensation—a corporate executive (for example) is foreclosed from acting toward his associates (superior, peers, subordinates) out of humane considerations, foreclosed from considering the interests of his suppliers and customers, foreclosed from beneficent acts toward his competitors, or indeed toward anyone with whom he has a commercial relationship. He is also thereby foreclosed from acting in accordance with his own moral character. He may, of course, perform *seeming* acts of beneficence or fidelity toward any of these persons or toward himself, but in that case the acts would be the end of rational calculation. If not seeming, they must be neutral acts or done *in spite of* his duty to his firm.

III

In addition to the general moral consequences of economic competition, we can identify specific consequences. Some of the more apparent are cataloged below.

(1) When any business prize—a sale, a purchase, an order to deliver, a contract to perform—is sought by two or more firms, the duties both of mutual aid and of non-maleficence become contradictory. The contradiction of the duty of mutual aid follows at once from the fact of the competition. The impossibility of non-maleficence follows almost as immediately. For under competition there is a winner (or winners), and there is a loser (or losers). Let us think, for example, of two salesmen competing for a contract. The successful salesman, if his compensation is by commission, has benefited directly. It is possible that his life's prospects have been enhanced. If he is a good salesman, that is, a frequent winner, they will have been. But by winning he has hurt his competitor. The loser may suffer real psychic pain, and through loss of prospective income and damaged expectations, real physical injury as well. But all this is of no matter to the winner. For merely by entering the competition he has willed that his competitors be injured.

(2) The obligation to tell the truth is contradicted by the requirements of commercial negotiation. We see this by noting that if there is to be negotiation, rather than a fixed or coerced price[7] there must be *room* for negotiation—call it a negotiating range. The range is defined by the highest price the buyer will pay and the lowest the seller will accept. Within those limits a deal can be struck. Now one or the other must make a statement, else the negotiation could not begin. The statement, however, must be misleading. If the buyer reveals the highest price he is willing to pay (the top of the range) the deal will be made at that figure. Nor can the seller reveal the lowest price he will take. The *duty* of either is to make his opposite believe that the top (bottom) of the possible range is lower (higher) than it really is. And to mislead someone is, of course, to tell him an untruth or, at the least, let him infer what is not the truth. Truth in commercial negotiation is a casualty of the responsibility of the participants to the business entity for whom they work.

(3) The duty of respect for others is irrelevant in determining product choices. At any time, a firm has a limited product transformation function. It cannot make everything. From those things that it can produce it will select the ones that will maximize its profit. Considerations of social benefit or damage have no place. But ideas of social benefit or damage derive ultimately from the idea of respect for others. Hence respect for others has no place in the free market.

Consider the tobacco industry. Surely this is a paradigm example. There exists substantial respected testimony that blames smoking for significant numbers of deaths from cancer, heart, and other diseases. . . . But the Tobacco Institute fought a proposal for more specific labeling about the dangers from smoking on cigarette packages and in advertising. The "chairman of the institute's executive committee said, that the proposal for five labels . . . was a 'thinly veiled effort further to harass and ultimately eliminate an important American Industry.'" . . .

It simply is impossible to conceive of persons engaging in the production or merchandising of products for smoking and at the same time observing the precepts encompassed by the obligation to respect your fellow. A defense based upon a spurious premise of freedom of choice is, of course, negated by the vigorous advertising and merchandising campaigns conducted by the industry.

IV

To this point we have focused mainly, though not entirely, on actions. When we turn to attitudes the matter becomes more complex. I have already introduced the problem in suggesting that a corporate executive carrying out his responsibilities might have to distort his nature. But this possibility itself has more than one aspect. Suppose that he must ignore what is (or has been) his (more or less) settled disposition to act in accordance with the human virtues—to act kindly, generously, truthfully, etc. Does he then override his nature consciously, or finally become unaware? For under the circumstances of competition we might expect that he would develop habitual attitudes of rationality expressed by hardness, shrewdness, and single-mindedness. These attitudes, or some of them, might begin to determine his actions under private circumstances. Or, on one occasion they may overwhelm, and on another be overwhelmed by, the set of softer dispositions.

Because firms are teams and responsible employees generally team members, attitudes congruent with the business characteristics are reinforced. Consider a purchasing agent. He cannot prudently assume that his supplier is dealing with him truthfully. And he has an obligation to his fellow team members not to let them down, to do his job—which is to purchase materials as cheaply as possible—as best he can. These are powerful motives for him to deal shrewdly with no special considerations for truth. Nor are the motives, given their ground, unreasonable.

But we need not stick to particular cases. Ultimately, all firms are engaged in a single overarching competition for capital and return on capital. . . . As a result of this unremitting, relentless competition, both specific and general, responsible firm members do develop, in greater or lesser amounts, a team morality. It is "us agin them." Consequently, the defeat of the opposition becomes a goal in itself. Consequently also, the business characteristics become justified and in terms of the competition they come to be constituents of a certain higher morality. Though by besting a competitor, whether in a single small event such as

getting an order, or in actually driving him out of business, the winner causes the loser real harm, that moral fact never enters the consciousness of the actors as such. The loser does not feel himself ill-used, and as a business competitor he has no moral grounds for resentment. Feelings of beneficence, even of compassion, are effectually blocked; they have no place in this world.

V

If the analyses set down above are correct in the main, what conclusions can we draw from them? The most apparent, and in a way the least helpful, is that free enterprise, like other social schemes in this imperfect world, is a flawed undertaking. Perhaps examining its flaws in some detail will be more helpful.

First, only in the immediate sense is free enterprise free. For, as I have tried to show, it imposes rigid constraints—all stemming from the a priori of profit maximization—on those who operate in its universe. Within a given industry, one firm, by way of policy, may commence to commit what other citizens could look upon as a series of enormities. But if that firm, because of its policy, say, of dumping untreated wastes into rivers and acid particulates into the atmosphere, reduces its cost of production, the others must follow. The remedy, of course, is legislation and enforcement. But, absent that remedy, the executives of the competing firm are choiceless: they too must pollute. Now, even if it is likely that the business characteristics are a part of their settled attitudes, it does not follow that a propensity to poison the environment is ingrained in their psychologies. In fact there is no reason to assume that such an idea is not repugnant to them as moral individuals. To the reader it certainly is repugnant. So the polluters, seeking to maximize the profits of their firms, are forced to attack themselves as moral beings. Justification from considerations of reciprocity becomes in this case very difficult. It appears, in fact, that justification from considerations of corporate survival is the sole possibility. Hence, I suggest that in this example, and in analogous cases, the participants inflict real damage upon their own self-respect.

They themselves are damaging perhaps the most important constituent of their own lives.

The demand that participants attack their own self-respect is not limited to some set of corporate executives. We can see this by observing that ultimately all production, except for government use and private investment, is for private consumption; and so firms increase sales and presumably profit by taking measures to increase and differentiate consumption (differentiation being that means of getting off a horizontal demand curve where it is impossible to earn an economic profit and onto a downward sloping curve where, at appropriate volumes, profits are made). Thus all individuals in the free enterprise system are subject to constant substantial pressures to buy. All, but for a few who for one reason or another exhibit a peculiar indifference—or moral strength—of character, will respond to a degree. But this response is equivalent to a need for extra income and wealth and these—in the free market scheme—are gained through competition. No one, whether he is an assembly line worker, a chief operating officer, a licensed professional or an "investor," sees himself as a producer of social wealth. Rather we view ourselves, and we must view ourselves, as *competitors* for those true economic (scarce) goods, income and jobs to get income. As such we are subject to the laws of competition, and as such our actions are defined at least as much by the devilish among us as by the angelic. The employee always competes with his employer for money, and typically competes with his co-workers as well. If one is an entrepreneur, he competes with the world. Virtue, being displaced by rationality, has no place in this competition; and the individual is obliged to make a choice between virtue and money. We might sketch an indifference function showing virtue vs. income.

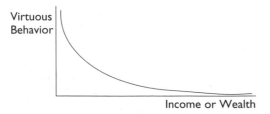

This curve seems reasonable enough. At high levels of virtue, but low income, it assumes the individual will sacrifice a great deal of it (and presumably, his self-respect) in order to gain income. If he already has a large income, he probably will not inflict further damage on his self-respect in order to gain more. In fact, he might cede income in order to gain virtue. But if his (perceived) income is low, and by sacrificing (perceived) virtue he can increase it, he probably will do so. At least to a point. For in order to live other than meanly he must have a decent income. In order to have a decent income he is obliged to compete for it. And if the devilish are willing to sacrifice virtue for income, then so must everyone.

Now those who are obliged to sacrifice their humanity, either in the discharge of corporate duties, or in the pursuit of a decent share of material wealth, cannot call themselves free.

Next, I assume—this journal assumes—that most men would wish to lead lives in which they can express in their work the human virtues. Similarly, they would wish to forego behavior which demonstrates hardness, shrewdness, and single-mindedness. And almost everyone would choose to live in that bright world postulated by John Rawls where it is publicly known that the acceptance of the duty of mutual aid brings "a sense of confidence and trust in other men's good intentions and the knowledge that they are there if we need them."[8] The logic of competition shoves all this aside—an intolerable knowledge which men must deny in order to believe themselves truly human.

Thus the compartmentalization of our souls; the acceptance, but non-acknowledgement of hypocrisy, and so the impossibility of ever achieving a happy society—which can exist nowhere but in the souls of its members. The reader might here object that no one really is forced into the competition, that one *can* live and not compete, or compete minimally. But this objection would be mistaken. If no one competed, society would no longer be competitive—it would be a different society. And if only the ethically indifferent among us competed, ethical indifference would wholly define our economic universe. But most of us, vigorous competitors or not, are not ethically indifferent. Very few of us make always wholly rational competitive judgments, otherwise we would be monsters, not men. It is *that* dichotomy which finally represents the great flawed detail of free enterprise.

Why stress it so? My answer is that otherwise we must fall into a trap which indeed has snared many. The trap is nothing else but the enchantment of the logical beauty of the free market and the seeming freedom it affords. As we have seen, viewed from the standpoint of individual morality, its freedom is largely illusory. Although, as markets approach the conditions of perfect competition, they approach Paretian efficiency, that fact by itself should not stand as sufficient warrant to build an economy on the foundations of free enterprise. The ethical implications, which I have tried to outline here, ought also to be taken into account.

Now all this does not mean that a society necessarily is to reject free enterprise in favor of some other economic scheme. For one thing, the system simply works. And regardless of whether society attempts to solve its economic problems by economic competition or in some other fashion, moral dilemmas will inevitably present themselves. For example, if we would avoid the patent evils of a free-enterprise system, then we must subject ourselves to the patent evils—loss of liberty—of a command system. Nevertheless, I do not think that the immoralities inherent in economic competition can be overemphasized. For to admit the imperfect ability of men and their institutions is not to concede that they cannot be made better. But first we will have to have a clearer understanding of the nature of our current imperfections. If society is to move forward, it better have some collective awareness of what it is about.

Notes

[1] I am grateful to John McMurtry for suggesting this paper and for his valued criticisms. I am also indebted to Barbara Kelly for her wise criticism and her constant encouragement.

[2] Editor's note: "Beneficience" here and elsewhere in the original.

[3] Editor's note: The long list of articles is given with the original article but is not included here.

[4] Editor's note: "Maleficient" here and elsewhere in the original.

[5] The article lists toilet-bowl cleaners, mouthwashes, soft drinks, pizza, and shampoos among others.

[6] It is true that this is a general conclusion which can be drawn from the premises of competition as such, but what we are discussing here is a special kind of competition. It is pervasive, it in large measure defines our lives, and it is impossible to withdraw from it entirely. As we have seen, it forces the competitors to run as fast as they can, without rest. It is well worth focusing on the consequences of *economic* competition, even if some of these may be deduced from the fact of competition itself.

[7] A price set by coercion or bribery would itself be the result of an immoral act.

[8] J. Rawls, *A Theory of Justice* (Harvard University Press, Cambridge, MA, 1971), 338–39.

Virtuous Self-Interest

Michael Novak

From *The Spirit of Democratic Capitalism* (Lanham, Md.: Madison Books/University Press of America, 1991), 92–95.

R. H. Tawney described the age of capitalism as the age of acquisitiveness. Marx described it as the reduction of every human relation to the cash nexus. Pamphleteers for generations have denounced its licensing of greed. Yet simple reflection upon one's own life and the life of others, including the lives of those critics who denounce the system from within, suggests that there are enormous reservoirs of high motivation and moral purpose among citizens in democratic capitalist societies. The history of democratic capitalism is alive with potent movements of reform and idealistic purpose. As the world goes, its people do not in fact seem to be more greedy, grasping, selfish, acquisitive, or anarchic than citizens in traditional or in socialist societies. If democratic capitalism is to be blamed for sins it permits to flourish, the virtues it nourishes also deserve some credit.

In practice, the bone of contention seems most often to be the central concept of self-interest. A system committed to the principle that individuals are best placed to judge their real interests for themselves may be accused of institutionalizing selfishness and greed—but only on the premise that individuals are so depraved that they never make any other choice.

The founders of democratic capitalism did not believe that such depravity is universal. Furthermore, they held that the laws of free economic markets are such that the real interests of individuals are best served in the long run by a systematic refusal to take short-term advantage. Apart from internal restraints, the system itself places restraints upon greed and narrowly construed self-interest. Greed and selfishness, when they occur, are made to have their costs. A firm aware of its long-term fiduciary responsibilities to its shareholders must protect its investments for future generations. It must change with the times.

It must maintain a reputation for reliability, integrity, and fairness. In one large family trucking firm, for example, the last generation of owners kept too much in profits and invested too little in new technologies and new procedures, with the result that their heirs received a battered company unable to compete or to solve its cash-flow problems. Thus a firm committed to greed unleashes social forces that will sooner or later destroy it. Spasms of greed will disturb its won inner disciplines, corrupt its executives, anger its patrons, injure the morale of its workers, antagonize its suppliers and purchasers, embolden its competitors, and attract public retribution. In a free society, such spasms must be expected; they must also be opposed.

The real interests of individuals, furthermore, are seldom merely self-regarding. To most persons, their families mean more than their own interests; they frequently subordinate the latter to the former. Their communities are also important to them. In the human breast, commitments to benevolence, fellow-feeling, and sympathy are strong. Moreover, humans have the capacity to see themselves as others see them, and to hold themselves to standards which transcend their own selfish inclinations. Thus the "self" in self-interest is complex, at once familial and communitarian as well as individual, other-regarding as well as self-regarding, cooperative as well as independent, and self-judging as well as self-loving. Understood too narrowly, self-interest destroys firms as surely as it destroys personal lives. Understood broadly enough, as a set of realistic limits, it is a key to all the virtues, as prudence is.

Like prudence in Aristotelian thought, self-interest in democratic capitalist thought has an inferior reputation among moralists. Thus it is necessary to stress again that a *society* may not work well if all its members act always from benevolent intentions. On the other hand, democratic capitalism as a system deliberately enables many persons to do well by doing good (or even purporting to do good). It offers incentives of power, fame, and money to reformers and moralists.

The economic system of democratic capitalism depends to an extraordinary extent upon the social capacities of the human person. Its system of inheritance respects the familial character of motivation. Its corporate pattern reflects the necessity of shared risks and shared rewards. Its divisions both of labor and of specialization reflect the demands of teamwork and association. Its separated churches and autonomous universities reflect the importance of independent moral communities. The ideology of individualism, too much stressed by some proponents and some opponents alike, disguises the essential communitarian character of its system.

The term "self-interest" includes a view of human liberty that far exceeds self-regard, selfishness, acquisitiveness, and greed.

Regrettably, the theory of democratic capitalism was left too long to economists. While economists are entitled to specialize, theologians also have such rights. A theology of democratic capitalism requires a larger view, of which economists freely concede the legitimacy. Thus, Milton and Rose Friedman in their best-selling *Free to Choose* consciously stress

> ...the broad meaning that must be attached to the concept of "self-interest." Narrow preoccupation with the economic market has led to a narrow interpretation of self-interest as myopic selfishness, as exclusive concern with immediate material rewards. Economics has been berated for allegedly drawing far-reaching conclusions from a wholly unrealistic "economic man" who is little more than a calculating machine, responding only to monetary stimuli. That is a great mistake. Self-interest is not myopic selfishness. It is whatever it is that interests the participants, whatever they value, whatever goals they pursue. The scientist seeking to advance the frontiers of this discipline, the missionary seeking to convert infidels to the true faith, the philanthropist seeking to bring comfort to the needy—all are pursuing their interests, as they see them, as they judge them by their own values.[1]

Under self-interest, then, fall religious and moral interests, artistic and scientific interests, and interests in justice and peace. The interests of the self define the self. In a free society, persons are free to choose their own interests. It is part of the function of a free economy to provide the abundance which breaks the chains of the mere struggle for subsistence, and to permit individual persons to "find themselves," indeed to define themselves through the interests they choose to make central to their lives.

In brief, the term "self-interest" includes a view of human liberty that far exceeds self-regard, selfishness, acquisitiveness, and greed. Adam Smith attempted to suggest this by speaking of *rational* self-interest, by which he meant a specification of human consciousness not only intelligent and judgmental, beyond the sphere of mere desire or self-regard, but also guided by the ideal of objectivity. In *The Theory of Moral Sentiments* (1979), he argued that what is truly rational must be seen to be so not merely from the point of view of the self-interested party but from that of a disinterested rational observer as well. He called the achievement of such realistic judgment "the perfection of human nature." The whole system, as he imagined it, is aimed toward the acquisition of such realism: "We endeavor to examine our own conduct as we imagine any other fair and impartial spectator would examine it." Again: "To feel much for others, and little for ourselves ... to restrain our selfish, and to indulge our benevolent, affections, constitutes the perfection of human nature."[2]

Democratic capitalism, then rests on a complex theory of sin. While recognizing ineradicable sinful tendencies in every human, it does not count humans depraved. While recognizing that no system of political economy can escape the ravages of human sinfulness, it has attempted to set in place a system which renders sinful tendencies as productive of good as possible. While basing itself on something less than perfect virtue, reasoned self-interest, it has attempted to draw from self-interest its most creative potential. It is a system designed for sinners, in the hope of achieving as much moral good as individuals and communities can generate under conditions of ample liberty.

Can human society imitate Providence?

Notes

[1]Milton and Rose Friedman, *Free to Choose* (New York: Harcourt Brace Jovanovich, 1980), 27.

[2]Adam Smith, *Theory of Moral Sentiments* (Indianapolis: Liberty Classics, 1989), 204, 71.

Buddhist Economics

E. F. Schumacher

From *Small Is Beautiful: Economics As If People Mattered* (New York: Harper Perennial, 1973), 56–66.

"Right Livelihood" is one of the requirements of the Buddha's Noble Eightfold Path. It is clear, therefore, that there must be such a thing as Buddhist economics.

Buddhist countries have often stated that they wish to remain faithful to their heritage. So Burma: "The New Burma sees no conflict between religious values and economic progress. Spiritual health and material well-being are not enemies: they are natural allies."[1] Or: "We can blend successfully the religious and spiritual values of our heritage with the benefits of modern technology."[2] Or: "We Burmans have a sacred duty to conform both our dreams and our acts to our faith. This we shall ever do."[3]

All the same, such countries invariably assume that they can model their economic development plans in accordance with modern economics, and they call upon modern economists from so-called advanced countries to advise them, to formulate the policies to be pursued, and to construct the grand design for development, the Five-Year Plan or whatever it may be called. No one seems to think that a Buddhist way of life would call for Buddhist economics, just as the modern materialist way of life has brought forth modern economics.

Economists themselves, like most specialists, normally suffer from a kind of metaphysical blindness, assuming that theirs is a science of absolute and invariable truths, without any presuppositions. Some go as far as to claim that economic laws are as free from "metaphysics" or "values" as the law of gravitation. We need not, however, get involved in arguments of methodology. Instead, let us take some fundamentals and see what they look like when viewed by a modern economist and a Buddhist economist.

There is universal agreement that a fundamental source of wealth is human labour. Now, the modern economist has been brought up to consider "labour" or work as little more than a necessary evil. From the point of view of the employer, it is in any case simply an item of cost, to be reduced to a minimum if it cannot be eliminated altogether, say, by automation. From the point of view of the workman, it is a "disutility"; to work is to make a sacrifice of one's leisure and comfort, and wages are a kind of compensation for the sacrifice. Hence the ideal from the point of view of the employer is to have output without employees, and the ideal from the point of view of the employee is to have income without employment.

The consequences of these attitudes both in theory and in practice are, of course, extremely far-reaching. If the ideal with regard to work is to get rid of it, every method that "reduces the work load" is a good thing. The most potent method, short of automation, is the so-called "division of labour" and the classical example is the pin factory eulogized in Adam Smith's *Wealth of Nations*. Here it is not a matter of ordinary specialization, which mankind has practiced from time immemorial, but of dividing up every complete process of production into minute parts, so that the final product can be produced at great speed without anyone having had to contribute more than a totally insignificant and, in most cases, unskilled movement of his limbs.

The Buddhist point of view takes the function of work to be at least threefold: to give a man a chance to utilize and develop his faculties; to enable him to overcome his ego-centeredness by joining with other people in a common task; and to bring forth the goods and services needed for a becoming existence. Again, the consequences that flow from this view are endless. To organize work in such a manner that it becomes meaningless, boring, stultifying, or nerve-racking for the worker would be little short of criminal; it would indicate a greater concern with goods than with people, an evil lack of compassion and a soul-destroying degree of attachment to the most primitive side of this worldly existence. Equally, to strive for leisure as an alternative to work would be considered a complete misunderstanding of one of the basic truths of human existence, namely that work and leisure are complementary parts of the same living process and cannot be separated without destroying the joy of work and the bliss of leisure.

Work, properly conducted in conditions of human dignity and freedom, blesses those who do it and equally their products.

From the Buddhist point of view, there are therefore two types of mechanization which must be clearly distinguished: one that enhances a man's skill and power and one that turns the work of man over to a mechanical slave, leaving man in a position of having to serve the slave. How to tell the one from the other? "The craftsman himself," says Ananda Coomaraswamy, a man equally competent to talk about the modern West as the ancient East, "can always, if allowed to, draw the delicate distinction between the machine and the tool. The carpet loom is a tool, a contrivance for holding warp threads at a stretch for the pile to be woven round them by the craftsmen's fingers; but the power loom is a machine, and its significance as a destroyer of culture lies in the fact that it does the essentially human part of the work."[4] It is clear, therefore, that Buddhist economics must be very different from the economics of modern materialism, since the Buddhist sees the essence of civilization not in a multiplication of wants but in the purification of human character. Character, at the same time, is formed primarily by a man's work. And work, properly conducted in conditions of human dignity and freedom, blesses those who do it and equally their products. The Indian philosopher and economist J. C. Kumarappa sums the matter up as follows:

> If the nature of the work is properly appreciated and applied, it will stand in the same relation to the higher faculties as food is to

the physical body. It nourishes and enlivens the higher man and urges him to produce the best he is capable of. It directs his free will along the proper course and disciplines the animal in him into progressive channels. It furnishes an excellent background for man to display his scale of values and develop his personality.[5]

If a man has no chance of obtaining work he is in a desperate position, not simply because he lacks an income but because he lacks this nourishing and enlivening factor of disciplined work which nothing can replace. A modern economist may engage in highly sophisticated calculations on whether full employment "pays" or whether it might be more "economic" to run an economy at less than full employment so as to ensure a greater mobility of labour, a better stability of wages, and so forth. His fundamental criterion of success is simply the total quantity of goods produced during a given period of time. "If the marginal urgency of goods is low," says Professor Galbraith in *The Affluent Society*, "then so is the urgency of employing the last man or the last million men in the labour force."[6] And again: "If . . . we can afford some unemployment in the interest of stability—a proposition, incidentally, of impeccably conservative antecedents—then we can afford to give those who are unemployed the goods that enable them to sustain their accustomed standard of living."

From a Buddhist point of view, this is standing the truth on its head by considering goods as more important than people and consumption as more important than creative activity. It means shifting the emphasis from the worker to the product of work, that is, from the human to the subhuman, a surrender to the forces of evil. The very start of Buddhist economic planning would be a planning for full employment, and the primary purpose of this would in fact be employment for everyone who needs an "outside" job: it would not be the maximization of employment nor the maximization of production. Women, on the whole, do not need an "outside" job, and the large-scale employment of women in offices or factories would be

considered a sign of serious economic failure. In particular, to let mothers of young children work in factories while the children run wild would be as uneconomic in the eyes of a Buddhist economist as the employment of a skilled worker as a soldier in the eyes of a modern economist.

While the materialist is mainly interested in goods, the Buddhist is mainly interested in liberation. But Buddhism is "The Middle Way" and therefore in no way antagonistic to physical well-being. It is not wealth that stands in the way of liberation but the attachment to wealth; not the enjoyment of pleasurable things but the craving for them. The keynote of Buddhist economics, therefore, is simplicity and non-violence. From an economist's point of view, the marvel of the Buddhist way of life is the utter rationality of its pattern—amazingly small means leading to extraordinarily satisfactory results.

For the modern economist this is very difficult to understand. He is used to measuring the "standard of living" by the amount of annual consumption, assuming all the time that a man who consumes more is "better off" than a man who consumes less. A Buddhist economist would consider this approach excessively irrational: since consumption is merely a means to human well-being, the aim should be to obtain the maximum of well-being with the minimum of consumption. Thus, if the purpose of clothing is a certain amount of temperature comfort and an attractive appearance, the task is to attain this purpose with the smallest possible effort, that is, with the smallest annual destruction of cloth and with the help of designs that involve the smallest possible input of toil. The less toil there is, the more time and strength is left for artistic creativity. It would be highly uneconomic, for instance, to go in for complicated tailoring like the modern West, when a much more beautiful effect can be achieved by the skillful draping of uncut material. It would be the height of folly to make material so that it should wear out quickly and the height of barbarity to make anything ugly, shabby or mean. What has just been said about clothing applies equally to all other human requirements. The ownership and the consumption of goods is a means to an end, and Buddhist economics is the systematic study of how to attain given ends with the minimum means.

> *Buddhist economics is the systematic study of how to attain given ends with the minimum means. Modern economics considers consumption to be the sole end and purpose of all economic activity.*

Modern economics, on the other hand, considers consumption to be the sole end and purpose of all economic activity, taking the factors of production—land, labour, and capital—as the means. The former, in short, tries to maximize human satisfactions by the optimal pattern of consumption, while the latter tries to maximize consumption by the optimal pattern of productive effort. It is easy to see that the effort needed to sustain a way of life which seeks to attain the optimal pattern of consumption is likely to be much smaller than the effort needed to sustain a drive for maximum consumption. We need not be surprised, therefore, that the pressure and strain of living is very much less in, say, Burma than it is in the United States, in spite of the fact that the amount of labour-saving machinery used in the former country is only a minute fraction of the amount used in the latter. Simplicity and non-violence are obviously closely related. The optimal pattern of consumption, producing a high degree of human satisfaction by means of a relatively low rate of consumption, allows people to live without great pressure and strain and to fulfill the primary injunction of Buddhist teaching: "Cease to do evil; try to do good." As physical resources are everywhere limited, people satisfying their needs by means of a modest use of resources are obviously less likely to be at each other's throats than people depending upon a high rate of use. Equally, people who live in highly self-sufficient local communities are less likely to get involved in large-scale violence than

people whose existence depends on world-wide systems of trade.

From the point of view of Buddhist economics, therefore, production from local resources for local needs is the most rational way of economic life, while dependence on imports from afar and the consequent need to produce for export to unknown and distant peoples is highly uneconomic and justifiable only in exceptional cases and on a small scale. Just as the modern economist would admit that a high rate of consumption of transport services between a man's home and his place of work signifies a misfortune and not a high standard of life, so the Buddhist economist would hold that to satisfy human wants from faraway sources rather than from sources nearby signifies failure rather than success. The former tends to take statistics showing an increase in the number of tons/miles per head of the population carried by a country's transport system as proof of economic progress, while to the latter—the Buddhist economist—the same statistics would indicate a highly undesirable deterioration in the *pattern* of consumption.

Another striking difference between modern economics and Buddhist economics arises over the use of natural resources. Bertrand de Jouvenel, the eminent French political philosopher, has characterized "Western man" in words which may be taken as a fair description of the modern economist:

> He tends to count nothing as an expenditure, other than human effort; he does not seem to mind how much mineral matter he wastes and, far worse, how much living matter he destroys. He does not seem to realize at all that human life is a dependent part of an ecosystem of many different forms of life. As the world is ruled from towns where men are cut off from any form of life other than human, the feeling of belonging to an ecosystem is not revived. This results in a harsh and improvident treatment of things upon which we ultimately depend, such as water and trees.[7]

The teaching of the Buddha, on the other hand, enjoins a reverent and non-violent attitude not only to all sentient beings but also, with great emphasis, to trees. Every follower of the Buddha ought to plant a tree every few years and look after it until it is safely established, and the Buddhist economist can demonstrate without difficulty that the universal observation of this rule would result in a high rate of genuine economic development independent of any foreign aid. Much of the economic decay of southeast Asia (as of many other parts of the world) is undoubtedly due to a heedless and shameful neglect of trees.

Modern economics does not distinguish between renewable and non-renewable materials, as its very method is to equalize and quantify everything by means of a money price. Thus, taking various alternative fuels, like coal, oil, wood, or water-power: the only difference between them recognized by modern economics is relative cost per equivalent unit. The cheapest is automatically the one to be preferred, as to do otherwise would be irrational and "uneconomic." From a Buddhist point of view, of course, this will not do; the essential difference between non-renewable fuels like coal and oil on the one hand and renewable fuels like wood and water-power on the other cannot be simply overlooked. Non-renewable goods must be used only if they are indispensable, and then only with the greatest care and the most meticulous concern for conservation. To use them heedlessly or extravagantly is an act of violence, and while complete non-violence may not be attainable on this earth, there is nonetheless an ineluctable duty on man to aim at the ideal of non-violence in all he does.

Just as a modern European economist would not consider it a great economic achievement if all European art treasures were sold to America at attractive prices, so the Buddhist economist would insist that a population basing its economic life on non-renewable fuels is living parasitically, on capital instead of income. Such a way of life could have no permanence and could therefore be justified only as a purely temporary expedient. As the world's resources of non-renewable fuels—coal, oil and natural gas—are exceedingly unevenly distributed over the globe and undoubtedly limited in quantity, it is clear that their exploitation at an ever-increasing rate is an act of violence against nature which must almost inevitably lead to violence between men.

> *Before we dismiss Buddhist economics as nothing better than a nostalgic dream, we might wish to consider whether the path of economic development outlined by modern economics is likely to lead us to places where we really want to be.*

This fact alone might give food for thought even to those people in Buddhist countries who care nothing for the religious and spiritual values of their heritage and ardently desire to embrace the materialism of modern economics at the fastest possible speed. Before they dismiss Buddhist economics as nothing better than a nostalgic dream, they might wish to consider whether the path of economic development outlined by modern economics is likely to lead them to places where they really want to be. Towards the end of his courageous book *The Challenge of Man's Future*, Professor Harrison Brown of the California Institute of Technology gives the following appraisal:

> Thus we see that, just as industrial society is fundamentally unstable and subject to reversion to agrarian existence, so within it the conditions which offer individual freedom are unstable in their ability to avoid the conditions which impose rigid organization and totalitarian control. Indeed, when we examine all of the foreseeable difficulties which threaten the survival of industrial civilization, it is difficult to see how the achievement of stability and the maintenance of individual liberty can be made compatible.[8]

Even if this were dismissed as a long-term view there is the immediate question of whether "modernization," as currently practiced without regard to religious and spiritual values is actually producing agreeable results. As far as the masses are concerned, the results appear to be disastrous—a collapse of the rural economy, a rising tide of unemployment in town and country, and the growth of a city proletariat without nourishment for either body or soul.

It is in the light of both immediate experience and long-term prospects that the study of Buddhist economics could be recommended even to those who believe that economic growth is more important than any spiritual or religious values. For it is not a question of choosing between "modern growth" and "traditional stagnation." It is a question of finding the right path of development, the Middle Way between materialist heedlessness and traditionalist immobility, in short, of finding "Right Livelihood."

Notes

[1]*The New Burma* (Economic and Social Board, Government of the Union of Burma, 1954).

[2]Ibid.

[3]Ibid.

[4]Ananda K. Gomaraswamy, *Art and Swadeshi* (Madras: Gadesh & Co.).

[5]J. C. Kumarappa, *Economy of Permanence* (Ragghat, Kashi: Sarva Seva Sangh Publications, 1958).

[6]John Kenneth Galbraith, *The Affluent Society* (New York: Penguin Books, 1962).

[7]Cited in Richard B. Gregg, *A Philosophy of Indian Economic Development* (Navajivan Publishing House, Ahnedabad, India, 1958).

[8](New York: The Viking Press, 1954).

Work: The Process and the Person

A. R. Gini and T. Sullivan

Journal of Business Ethics 6 (1987): 649–655. Copyright © 1987 by David Reidel Publishing Company.

For the most of us, working is an entirely non-discretionary activity, an inescapable and irreducible fact of existence. Work is, well, work—an activity required to sustain life. In its very worst light, work is seen as something evil, a punishment, the grindingly inevitable burden of toil laid, along with mortality, upon the human situation.[1] At best, work looms so large and problematic in most of our lives that we either take it for granted and forget about it or we actively suppress its significance on our lives. Work is simply *there*, as illness, death, taxes and mortgage payments are there, something to be endured.[2] *Chicago Tribune* columnist Mike Royko accurately captures the spirit of the "common man's" feelings about work when his alter-ego in the column, Slats, says:

... why do you think the lottery is so popular? Do you think anybody would play if the super payoff was a job on the night shift in a meat packing plant? People play it so if they win they can be rich and idle ...

like I told you years ago—if work is so good, how come they have to pay us to do it?[3]

The common laments against work, however, are not simply based on the fact that most of us are part of the captive work force and hence accept work as inevitable. In well over 100 studies in the last twenty-five years, workers have regularly depicted their jobs as physically exhausting, boring, psychologically diminishing or personally humiliating and unimportant.[4] Over 109 million people constitute the American work force. This vast army of workers labors in 25,000 different full-time occupations, each of which defines its practitioners by income, education, social status, living standard and life style.[5] During the 1970s a great deal of attention was given to "workers' dissatisfaction", (i.e. "white-collar woes" and "blue-collar blues.") Indications are that the problems enumerated in the 1970s will not simply go away in the 1980s and 90s. Indeed, recent surveys indicate increasing job dissatisfaction as well as a direct increase in the commonality of complaints across the spectrum of occupations. The cry of uninteresting, unchallenging, non-stimulating, non-creative work is no longer the exclusive lament of the assembly line, lower status, blue-collar worker. Managers and laborers, office workers and mechanics can now be heard to chorus their disapproval of their occupations. While it is still the case that managers, overall, are more satisfied with their work than are clerical, hourly and piece-work employees, the distinctions and specific issues that once clearly separated management from all other types of employees are becoming blurred.[6]

The results of a 1979 survey published by the University of Michigan indicated that worker dissatisfaction was at its highest point in over a decade. Sixty percent of the workers surveyed wanted new jobs. Thirty-nine percent thought they were under-paid. Thirty-six percent said they had unused skills. Thirty-six percent felt overqualified for their jobs, and fifty-five percent wanted more time off. Unlike their parents' generation, contemporary workers do not see their jobs as a simple contract: A day's work for a day's

pay. Labor-relations analyst John R. Browning has said, "Today's workers want much more. They want nothing less than eight hours of meaningful, skillfully guided, personally satisfying work for eight hours pay and that's not easy for most companies to provide."[7] In 1974, Daniel Yankelovich offered a limited but staggering statistic when he claimed that only one out of every five men (women were not included in the survey) feels that his work fills his psychological as well as economic needs.[8]

The question before us is "Why are so many people so unhappy in their work?" Simply put, the reason people don't like their jobs is that they have bad jobs, or to use E. F. Schumacher's term they have "bad work."

According to Schumacher, bad work is:

Mechanical, artificial, divorced from nature, utilizing only the smallest part of man's potential capabilities; it sentences the great majority of workers to spending their working lives in a way which contains no worthy challenge, no stimulus to self perfection, no chance of development, no element of Beauty, Truth, or Goodness . . .[9]

For Schumacher one of the darkest aspects of contemporary work life is the existence of an appalling number of men and women condemned to work which has no connection with their inner lives, no spiritual meaning for them whatever. Bad work for Schumacher offers no opportunity for the individual to become more than he or she already is, offers no potential for growth, no sense of beauty and delight, no feelings of completeness and no sense of well-being.

> *The distinctions and specific issues that once clearly separated management from all other types of employees are becoming blurred.*

Work for too many is perceived as down-time, something that has to be done, but seldom adding to who we are. Too many workers accurately talk of jobs as having nothing to do with their inner sense of self. Studs Terkel in his now classic *Working* tells us that work for many is a purely alien occupation. One of the people he interviewed remarked, "Unless a guy's a nut, he never thinks about or talks about it. Maybe about baseball or about getting drunk the other night or he got laid or he didn't get laid. I'd say one out of a hundred actually gets excited about work."[10]

To put Schumacher's argument into a more classical perspective, bad work alienates workers both from themselves and from their work. An alienated worker engages in activities that are not intrinsically rewarding, that might be demanding in some respects but permit little or no originality, no latitude and discretion and no sense of fulfillment and completion. Sociologist Robert Kahn suggests that for most workers the only choice is between no work (usually accompanied by severe economic penalties as well as a conspicuous lack of meaningful alternatives) or a job burdened with negative qualities (routine, compulsory scheduling, dependency, etc.) In these circumstances, says Kahn, the individuals have no difficulty with their choice. They choose work as the only real alternative and then pronounce themselves moderately satisfied if not stimulated, enraptured or excited with what they do.[11] Some workers adjust to their tasks by viewing work in purely instrumental terms or as a means to other ends. George Strauss has pointed out that a significant number of workers deliberately take on high paying but boring jobs in order to support their real interests.[12] This is the kind of compromise that many people make. In essence what they say is: "I don't like what I do, but it allows me to do what I like."

These claims of disappointment and distress, however, seem to fly in the face of a study published in the mid-1950s and frequently replicated since then. In 1955 sociologists Nancy Morse and Robert S. Weiss of the University of Michigan's Survey Research Center published the results of a study of more than 400 men. They asked the question, "If by chance you inherited enough money to live comfortably without working, do you think you would work anyway?" The vast majority (80%) of all respondents replied positively even though the percentages were slightly higher for professional and lower white-collar workers (86%) than for the blue-collar workers (76%).[13]

At regular intervals over the next twenty-eight years this survey was expanded (both in numbers surveyed and by the inclusion of women) and repeated by various research organizations. The results of these follow-up surveys essentially reaffirmed the original survey results: the percentage of those choosing to work ranged from 67.4% (1969, University of Michigan), 73% (1974, Yankelovich, *The New Morality)* to 75% (1978, Renwich and Lawler).[14]

The most recent and perhaps the most comprehensive findings on this topic come from a group of researchers at the University of Kentucky in 1983. Of the 7,281 adults polled nationwide, 74% of the men and 64% of the women surveyed said they would continue to work. While married men were more inclined than married women to say they would keep working, single men and women were equally likely to report that they would stick with it. Younger, better educated respondents with more prestigious jobs were more inclined to say that they would stay employed compared with older individuals and less educated respondents. But the majority of all groups still reported that they would stay at work.[15]

The question before us now is "If so many people are so unhappy in their work, why, other than necessity, do people express a desire to work?" A practical response to this question is that one wants to work to occupy time, to have something, anything, to do to avoid the greater burden and stress of deadtime versus downtime. There is certainly the pressure, when answering surveys, to give a socially acceptable answer. The ethic of generations tells us that we *ought* to want to work, that to admit to be willing to retire before one's time is to be somehow weak. Beyond that, however, is a deeper need to be fully occupied, to do good work or, failing that, any work. People want to work because they are intuitively aware that work, be it "bad" or "good" helps to shape them. It gives them a sense of direction and it allows for personal creativity and fulfillment.

The personal meaning of work is as important as its economic and social meaning. Where we live, how well we live, whom we see socially, what and where we consume and purchase, how we educate our children—all of these factors are dominated by the work we do to make a living.[16] While many people don't like their specific jobs, they want to work because they are aware at some level that work plays a crucial and perhaps unparalleled psychological role in the formation of human character. Work is not just a course of livelihood, it is also one of the most significant contributing factors to an inner life. And yet, as Schumacher points out, the question "what the work does to the worker," is seldom asked.[17] It is precisely this question on which I would like to focus attention. I want to examine what work does to and for us no matter what the nature of the product we produce by our labors.

People need to work. People must work to finish, define, and refine their nature; work makes us human because we make something of ourselves through work. Even more than personal survival, mankind creates its own history through his work.[18] Sociologist Peter Berger has said "to be human and to work appear as inextricably intertwined notions."[19] In his earliest philosophical writings in the 1840s, Karl Marx defined the person as a worker. For Marx, persons acquire self-definition through labor. Work is the means by which we become unique individuals; we create ourselves in our work.[20] In Marx we can find full-scale analysis of the meaning of work in human development as well as what he saw as the distortion of this development in capitalistic society.

In the western world, Marx's critique of the work place, and its effect on the individual, gets lost in his overall analysis of capitalism and his attacks on bourgeois society. While many scholars feel that his writings are extremely critical of late 19th century capitalism as a social political system, his real focus and purpose was an examination of the effects of work on the person and how the person affects work. A significant portion of

his doctrine of historical materialism is devoted to his belief that the "material conditions of life" and specifically "the mode of production of the material means of existence" determine much else in human life, consciousness and society. For Marx, the essence of the human being rests upon their work:

> As individuals express their life (sic), so they are. What (individuals) . . . are . . . coincides with their production, both with what they produce and with how they produce. The nature of individuals thus depends on the material conditions determining their production.[21]

As Schumacher has pointed out in Marx's regard, it is a great error to overlook or to underestimate the effects of the "modes of production" upon people's lives. How people work and what they produce necessarily affects what they think and how they perceive their own sense of freedom and independence.[22] In other words, both the process and the product of our work help us to know who and what we are.

A somewhat unexpected but nonetheless important affirmation of Marx's overall thesis on work is Pope John Paul II's 1981 encyclical *Laborem exercens, On Human Work:*

> Man is made to be in the visible universe an image and likeness of God Himself, and he is placed in it on order to subdue the earth. From the beginning he is called to work. . . . Only man is capable of work, and only man works, at the same time by work occupying his existence on earth. Thus work bears a particular mark of man and of humanity, the mark of a person operating within a community of persons.[23]

That by labor or work man "occupies his existence on earth" means that mankind literally creates its own reality by virtue of work. In work, mankind creates and defines the world, and in the process simultaneously becomes more human. According to the encyclical, the human world is not a simple given or a fixed thing. It is rather a "fact" continuously being produced by human labor. Work, the encyclical claims, is a good thing.

It is good in the sense that it is useful or something to enjoy. It is good because it expresses and expands human dignity. Individuals not only transform nature, adopting it to their own needs through work, but they also achieve fulfillment as human beings and, in a sense, become "more a human being."[24] For Pope John Paul II it is through work that people constitute themselves as subjects of their own lives and, collectively, of their common history. He further emphasized that what happens to the "subject of work" at work is more important than what "the work produces." The dignity and honor which work communicates to people is derived not from the "object achieved" but from the individual's "actual engagement" in the process, that is, from the labor of one's hands and mind. In the labor the transformation experienced by the subject is of greater value and importance than the object produces. "The preeminence of the subjective meaning of work over the objective one" is a principle that plays an important part in the reasoning of the entire encyclical. However true it may be that mankind is "destined for work" and "called to work" what must always be kept in clear perspective is that "work is for man and not man for work."[25]

Freud has written that at the very least work gives one "a secure place in the human community."[26] It is also the case that work helps establish the regularity of life, its basic rhythms and cycles of day, week, month and year. Without work, time patterns become confused, days are without pattern.[27] Further, work organized, routinizes and structures our lives. It allows a safe outlet for our competitive strivings and often helps to keep us sane. More than this, as the German philosopher Martin Heidegger stated, "You are your projects."[28] In the vocabulary of metaphysics, Heidegger is implying that through "projects" (work) and the projection and continuation of these "projects" into the future, individuals posit their "being" in the world. Heidegger is suggesting that "You are what you do." Identity is largely a function of concerted action or productive achievement. We are known by others and we know and define ourselves primarily by the projects we devise, by the products we created and by the occupations

which represent these productive pursuits. A person who cannot point to achievements does not and cannot feel like a full person. Subjective experience is simply too diffuse for self-identity. To say "I feel it" is not as definitive as to say "I did it." Nothing else in our lives can give us the sense of objective identity that work can.[29]

When psychiatrists and psychologists talk of "ego boundaries" they mean that a well-balanced people have clear perspectives on the limits and outlines of their own identities. They do not suffer from "boundary diffusion" and possess a clear sense of integrity and continuity. For most of us, the primary source of life's labels and "ego boundaries" is our work. In work we come both to know ourselves and orient ourselves to the external world. Work allows us to establish a "coherent web of expectations" of the rhythm, direction and definition of our lives.[30] Self-definition implies the ability to feel contained within precise outlines. The more descriptive we can be about ourselves the greater our sense of self-definition. Nothing is so uniquely personal, so active a representation of individuals as their skills and works.[31] To use Gregory Baum's handsome phrase, "labor is the axis of human self-making." Work is a necessary attribute of the human personality. Work molds the person and work is the mark of a person. To work is an act of personal freedom, self-assertion, self-fulfillment and self-realization.

In western culture paid employment is, rightly or wrongly, the main activity by which we define and assess ourselves and others.

If there is a congruence between personality and work, then a partial explanation of why people need good work can be found in ways people respond psychologically to the stimuli of work. It is well established that work stress can lead to physical illness, especially heart disease and ulcers—as well as to alcoholism, drug addiction, and a host of psychosomatic ailments. However, the impact of routine or subjectively boring work is less clear and somewhat difficult to measure. A high percentage of people who do objectively routine work report having happy and uncomplicated home lives, but there are enough who do not that statistical studies point to a direct correlation between routine, low skilled work and off-the-job dissatisfaction. These studies imply that at the level of mental health, interesting work is a requirement of adult life. The underlying thesis here is one borrowed from the philosopher Adina Schwartz. According to Schwartz, when persons work for considerable lengths of time at jobs that involve repetitive mechanical activity, they tend to be made less capable of, and less interested in, rationally and independently framing, pursuing and adjusting their own plans during the rest of their non-work time. They thereby lead less autonomous, less interesting and less fulfilling lives.[32]

This thesis is echoed in recent longitudinal studies. In one such study Melvin L. Kohn and Carmi Schooler argue that there is a reciprocal relationship between the substantial complexity of work and intellectual flexibility. Their data indicate that "current job demands affect current thinking processes. . . . If two men of equivalent intellectual flexibility were to start their careers in jobs differing in substantive complexity, the man in the more complex job would be likely to outstrip the other in further intellectual growth."[33] A direct implication of Kohn and Schooler's research is that routine and boring jobs do not simply prevent persons from acting autonomously while at work, but that they also hinder us from developing the intellectual abilities that we must have in order to rationally pursue plans during non-work time. Routine jobs cause persons to be less inclined, in all aspects of their lives, to engage in the purposeful striving that is characteristic of autonomous individuals. Kohn and Schooler conclude that jobs tend to determine personalities more than personalities determine jobs.

Arthur Kornhauser's classic *Mental Health of the Industrial Worker: A Detroit Study*, speaks to this point

> . . . factory employment, especially in routine production tasks, does give evidence of extinguishing workers' ambition, initiative,

and purposeful directions towards life goals. . . . The unsatisfactory mental health of working people consists in no small measure of their dwarfed desires and deadened initiative, reduction of their goals and restriction of their efforts to a point where life is relatively empty and only half meaningful.[34]

Kornhauser's study of the Detroit automobile worker concludes that mental health at work, like job satisfaction, varies according to status. "Mental health is poorer among factory workers as we move from skilled, responsible, varied types of work to jobs lower in those respects."[35] Kornhauser also concluded that mental health was low among those workers who felt that they had no chance to use their abilities.[36] It was suggested that low-grade work caused lowered self-esteem, discouragement, futility, and feelings of failure and inferiority in contrast to a sense of personal growth and self-fulfillment resulting from more varied, responsible, challenging undertakings that afford opportunity to develop and use one's ideas and skills.[37]

The point here is that given what you do, you cannot avoid being who you are. I take it to be the case that each person, having chosen a job, shapes its content. And to a greater or lesser extent the content of the job shapes the person. Not only are we affected by what we do; we tend to become what we do. A person's activities determine self-identity, and in western culture paid employment is, rightly or wrongly, the main activity by which we define and assess ourselves and others.[38]

———

I think it is true that only a statistical minority of the work force is able to find meaning in work beyond the basic reward of the pay check.[39] Nevertheless, satisfaction with life seems to be related to satisfaction on the job.[40] The quality of our lives is dependent on the quality of the work we do—those who are unhappy with their jobs are also likely to be unhappy with life in general. Moreover, to be denied work is to be denied far more than the things that work can buy; it is to be denied the ability to define and respect one's self; and it is to be denied a basic and primary organizing principle in life. As Theodore Roszak quite correctly points out—"the doing is as important as what gets done, the making as valuable as the made."[41]

Good work is the ideal, but clearly good work is hard to find. Perhaps the only realistic compromise available to most of us is to find and embellish whatever good is possible in our work. As individuals we must find work that is good for us, as a society we must create work that is good for individuals. No matter how optimistic the technological forecasts for the future, there is no real possibility that work itself will become obsolete and unnecessary. The challenge will be to make it available and fulfilling.[42] Employment must have meaning beyond the trading of labor for money. If the pursuit of happiness is a good, not to say an inalienable right, then happiness must be sought in the way we spend our days. It quite clearly cannot be attained in the face of eight daily hours of misery and the converse appears more likely to be true; i.e., to be happy in our work is to be happy. The conclusion remains Marx's dictum, "As individuals express their life (sic), so they are."

Notes

[1]"What is the Point of Working?" *Time Magazine*, May 11, 1981, pp. 93, 94.

[2]Lee Braude, *Work and Workers: A Sociological Analysis* (New York: Praeger Publications, 1975), p. 3.

[3]Mike Royko, "Silver Spoon Fits, Why Not Wear It?", *Chicago Tribune*, November 11, 1985, Sect. 1, p. 3.

[4]*Work in America: Report of a Special Task Force to the Secretary of Health, Education and Welfare* (Cambridge Mass.: MIT Press, 1980). p. 13.

[5]Melvin Kranzbert, Joseph Gies, *By the Sweat of Their Brow—Work in the Western World* (New York: G. P. Putnam's, 1975), p. 4.

[6]One of the most important surveys to directly deny this contention is: M. R. Cooper, B. S. Morgan, P. M. Foley, and L. B. Kaplan, 'Changing Employee Values: Deepening Discontent?', *Harvard Business Review*, Jan/Feb. 1979, pp. 117–125.

[7]'New Breed of Workers', *U. S. News and World Report*, September 3, 1979, pp. 35, 36.

[8]Daniel Yankelovich, 'The Meaning of Work', in *The Worker and the Job: Coping with Change*, ed. Jerome M. Rosow (Englewood Cliffs: Prentice Hall, Inc., 1974), pp. 44, 45.

[9]E. F. Schumacher, *Good Work* (New York: Harper Colophoan Books, 1980), p. 27.

[10]Studs Terkel, *Working* (New York: Pantheon Books, 1974), p. xxxiv.

[11]Robert L. Kahn, 'The Meaning of Work: Interpretations and Proposals for Measurement', in *The Human Meaning of Social Change*, ed. Angus Campbell, Philip Converse (New York: Basic Books, 1972).

[12]George Strauss, 'Workers: Attitudes and Adjustment', in *The Worker and the Job: Coping with Change*, ed. Jerome M. Rosow (Englewood Cliffs: Prentice Hall, Inc., 1974), p. 83.

[13]Nancy Morse and Robert Weiss, 'The Function and Meaning of Work', *American Sociological Review* 20, No. 2 (April 1966), pp. 191–198.

[14]Michael Maccoby and Katherine A. Tersi, 'What Happened to the Work Ethic?', *The Work Ethic in Business*, cd. W. Michael Hoffman and Thomas J. Wyly (Cambridge, Mass.: Oelgeschlager, Gunn & Hain Publishers, 1981), p. 33.

[15]Wm. B. Lacy, J. L. Bokemeier, and J. M. Shepard, 'Job Attribute Preferences and Work Commitment of Men and Women in the United States', *Personal Psychology*, 1983, 3, pp. 315–329.

[16]Daniel Yankelovich, 'The Meaning of Work', in *The Worker and the Job: Coping with Change*, p. 19.

[17]E. F. Schumacher, *Good Work*, pp. 2, 3.

[18]Gregory Baum, *The Priority of Labor* (New York: Paulist Press, 1982), p. 9.

[19]Bernard Lefkowitz, *Breaktime* (Hawthorn Books, Inc., 1979), p. 14.

[20]Gregory Baum, *The Priority of Labor*, p. 12.

[21]Karl Marx, 'The German Ideology', ed. Trans. By Loyd Eastern, Kurt Guddat, in *Writings of the Young Marx on Philosophy and Society*, (New York: Doubleday, 1967), p. 409.

[22]E. F. Schumacher, *Good Work*, pp. 41, 42.

[23]*Laborem exercens*, Encyclical Letter of Pope John Paul II, in Gregory Baum, *The Priority of Labor*, p. 95.

[24]*Ibid.*, p. 112.

[25]*Ibid*, pp. 104–106.

[26]Nathan Hale, 'Freud's Reflections of Work and Love', in *Themes of Work and Love and Adulthood*, ed. Neil J. Smelser and Erik A. Erikson (Cambridge, Mass: Harvard University Press, 1980), p. 30.

[27]*Work in America*: HEW Task Force Report, p. 8.

[28]Martin Heidegger, *Being and Time*, trans. By John Macquarrie, Edward Robinson (New York: Harper and Row, 1962), pp. 102–186. Martin Heidegger, *The Basic Problems of Phenomenology*, trans. By Albert Hofstadter (Bloomington, IN: University of Indiana Press, 1982), pp. 168–171.

[29]Erik A. Erikson, 'Themes of Adulthood in the Freud-Jung Correspondence', in *Themes of Work and Love in Adulthood*, pp. 43–74.

[30]Bernard Lefkowitz, *Breaktime*, pp. 16, 17.

[31]Erik A. Erikson, 'Themes of Adulthood in Freud-Jung Correspondence', pp. 55–58.

[32]Adina Schwartz, 'Meaningful Work', *Ethics* 92 (July 1982), pp. 634–646.

[33]Melvin L. Kohn and Carmi Schooler, 'The Reciprocal Effects of the Substantive Complexity of Work and Intellectual Flexibility: A Longitudinal Study', *American Journal of Sociology* 84 (1978): 24–52, pp. 43–48.

[34]Arthur Kornhauser, *Mental Health of the Industrial Worker: A Detroit Study* (New York: John Wiley & Sons, 1964), pp. 252–270.

[35]*Ibid*, p. 262.

[36]For a detailed analysis of the theory that human satisfaction is a function of the perceived fit between what a person has (abilities, resources) and what a person needs and/or wants see:

R. D. Caplan, 'Social Support, Person-Environment Fit', in *Mental Health and the Economy*, ed. By L. A. Ferman and J. P. Gordus (Kalamazoo, Michigan, Upjohn Institute, 1979), pp. 89–137.

'Person-Environment Fit: Past, Present, and Future', in *Stress Research*, ed. By C. L. Cooper (New York: John Wiley and Sons, 1983), pp. 35–77.

R. V. Harrison, 'Person-Environment Fit and Job Stress', in *Stress at Work*, ed. By C. L. Cooper and R. Payne (New York: John Wiley, 1978), pp. 175–205.

'The Person-Environment Fit Model and the Study of Job Stress', in *Human Stress and Cognition in Organizations: An Integrated Perspective*, ed. By T. D. Beehr and R. S. Bhagat (New York: John Wiley), 1982.

For an overview of the topic of *Multiple Discrepancies Theory* also see:

Alex C. Michalos, 'Multiple Discrepancies Theory', *Social Indicators Research* 16 (1985), pp. 347–313.

[37]In recent years, at least five major studies have indicated that job satisfaction increases with a worker's sense of involvement and personal sense of development through work.

T. J. Bergmann, 'Managers and Their Organizations: An Interactive Approach to Multimentional Job Satisfaction', *Journal of Occupational Psychology* 54 (1981), pp. 275–288.

G. J. Groothuis, L. A. Ten Horn, and J. Scheele, 'Attitudes and Work Simplification in a Retail Organization', *Mens en Onderneming* 33 (1979), pp. 501–518.

H. S. Leonard, H. Margolis, and D. J. Keating, 'Silent Factors Influencing Resident Advisor Turnover: An Exploratory Study', *Child Care Quarterly* 10 (1981), pp. 329–333.

D. E. Skodol and J. S. Maxman, 'Role Satisfaction Among Psychiatric Residents', *Comprehensive Psychiatry* 22 (1918), pp. 174–178.

S. Venkataraman and R. N. Anantharaman, 'Need Satisfaction and Need Importance Among Managerial Personnel', *Journal of Psychological Researches* 25 (1981), pp. 15–20.

For a complete review of the literature on job satisfaction and quality of work life issues see:

Alex C. Michalos, 'Job Satisfaction, Marital Satisfaction and the Quality of Life: A Review and a Preview', in *Research and the Quality of Life*, ed. By Frank M. Andres (Ann Arbor, Michigan: University of Michigan Press, 1986), pp. 57–83.

[38]Robert L. Kahn, *Work and Health* (New York: John Wiley & Sons, 1981), p. 11.

[39]Studs Terkel, *Working*, p. xi.

[40]A number of independent studies corroborate the thesis that satisfaction with life as a whole is positively correlated to job satisfaction.

Alex C. Michalos, 'Satisfaction and Happiness', *Social Indicators Research* 8 (1980), pp. 385–422.

C. S. Morgan, 'Female and Male Attitudes Toward Life: Implications for Theories of Mental Health', *Sex Roles* 6 (1980), pp. 367–380.

R. Rose, 'Who Can't Get No Satisfaction?', *New Society* 53 (1980), pp. 265–266.

D. J. Vredenburgh and J. E. Sheridan, 'Individual and Occupational Determinates of Life Satisfaction and Alienation', *Human Relations* 32 (1979), pp. 1023–1038.

T. H. White, 'The Relative Importance of Work as a Factor in Life Satisfaction', *Relations Industrielles* 36 (1981), pp. 179–191.

[41]Theodore Roszak, *Person/Planet* (New York: Doubleday, 1979), p. 227.

[42]Robert Kahn, *Work and Health*, p. 16.

Compassion

Marvin Olasky

From *Religion and Liberty*, newsletter of the Acton Institute (January–February 1992).

At a reunion of Johnson administration officials in Austin, Texas, a quarter century after the War on Poverty fired its cannonades, the mood of reminiscence was akin to Wordsworth's memory of enthusiasm following the French Revolution: "Bliss was it in that dawn to be alive." Sargent Shriver exulted that the Reagan years had not really damaged Great Society programs, most of which were "still in existence, all helping millions of Americans today." *New York Times* columnist Tom Wicker described the sumptuous affair and proposed that it was time to stop moaning and, instead, drink a toast to "vision and aspiration, confidence and compassion." Vision, aspiration, and confidence were all present, but was there compassion? It depends what we mean by the word. When the Speaker of the House, Tip O'Neill, favored more spending on social programs, columnist Mary McGrory wrote that his "compassion was the size of his frame." O'Neill's successor, Jim Wright, also was praised in the *Washington Post* for his billion-dollar compassion for the homeless. Recently Heather Foley, wife of the current speaker [Tom Foley], received a toast in the *Post* when she showed her "compassion" by feeding pizza to ravenous reporters following one late-night legislative vigil. Does compassion merely mean expansion of government (and pizza) transfer programs? Or is it a synonym for leniency, as when lawyers ask a jury to have compassion for an accused murderer by letting him off?

It would be helpful if there were agreement on the nature of compassion among evangelicals who claim to rely on Christian revealed truth. But, while Calvinist poverty-fighter George Grant has correctly charged "centralized government welfare" with "splintering families, crushing incentive, decimating pride, and fouling productivity," a pop-

ular book at many Christian colleges is still Ron Sider's *Rich Christians in an Age of Hunger*, which accepts conventional ideas of poverty-fighting through collective material transfer rather than through individual spiritual challenge. Ironically, ministers influenced by liberation theology and desiring to be quasi-Marxist crusades often find, in the words of the *New York Times*, that inner-city "churchgoers mostly prefer Bible-thumping harangues."

The *Times* may not care for Bible-thumping, but if we open up those Bibles the meaning of "compassion" becomes clear; after all, Hebrew and Greek words commonly translated as "compassion" are used over eighty times in the Bible. Their most frequent use is not as an isolated noun but as the culmination of a process. Repeatedly, in Judges and other books, the Bible shows that when the Israelites had sinned they were to repent and turn away from their sin—only then, as a rule, would God show compassion. Second Chronicles 30:9 states the process precisely: "The Lord your God is gracious and compassionate. He will not turn his face from you if you return to him." Nehemiah 9:27 notes that "when they were oppressed they cried out to you. From heaven you heard them, and in your great compassion you gave them deliverers. . . ."

Americans up to this century regularly read angry biblical descriptions of Israel as "a people without understanding; so their Maker has no compassion on them." They read in Jeremiah of God telling Israel, "You have rejected me . . . I can no longer show compassion." They saw that God did not offer compassion automatically, and they believed it wrong for them to go where angels feared to tread. For example, if a homeless man abandoned his wife and children (perhaps rendering them homeless also), they saw that he did not deserve God's compassion or ours until he turned away from his sinful behavior. They did not want to offer compassion indiscriminately and in that way subsidize sloth and turn neighborhoods into wilderness.

Older anti-poverty programs worked. Up to the past several decades, poor as well as the better-off Americans had the privilege of living in neighborhoods, not wilderness. Even in poor sections of cities—except for those particular blocks handed over for "red light" districts and lands of vice—citizens did not need machetes to make their way along the streets. Only in modern times have the vines and wild forest growths reclaimed the ground of neighborhood. Although some organizations on the left still claim that governments must take the lead in rebuilding neighborhoods, the record of several decades shows that wilderness of the city often was created by officials who claimed they were helping. Now, there is much wringing of hands, because we have rewarded irresponsibility and in that way bought more of it.

As compassion has become indiscriminate, many Americans have become so fed up with waste of money and time that cynicism about "homelessness" is rampant. Yet, some helpless individuals (particularly abandoned mothers with young children) are truly needy. Furthermore, when individuals responsible for their own plight *are* willing to change, Biblical compassion means refusing to settle for the feed-and-forget principle or its equally depersonalizing but harsher opposite, the forget-and-don't-feed standard. It means paying attention to the literal meaning of compassion, as given in the Oxford English Dictionary: "suffering together with another, participation in suffering." The emphasis, as the word itself shows—"com," (with), and "passion," from the Latin *pati* (to suffer)—is on personal involvement with the needy, suffering with them, not just giving to them. "Suffering together" means helping the unemployed-but-willing-to-work, adopting hard-to-place babies, providing shelter to women undergoing crisis pregnancies, tutoring the determined illiterate, and so on.

Our societal problem, however, is that in the twentieth century a second definition of compassion has become common: "The feeling, or emotion, when a person is moved by the suffering or distress of another, and by the desire to relieve it." Currently, in *Webster's Third International Dictionary*, compassion is defined as a "deep feeling for and understanding of misery or suffering and the concomitant desire to promote its alleviation." There is a world of policy difference between "suffering together" and feeling sad: One demands personal action; the other, emotion that can be relieved by sending a check or passing a piece of legislation. Words carry a political charge, as Orwell pointed out so well in his essay, "Politics and the English Language." Words shape our ideas, and the shifting definition of compassion has so shaped our understanding that the *New York Times*, usually a stickler for precise language, prints oxymoronic phrases such as "compassionate observer." The corruption is general: The *Washington Post* refers to "personal compassion" as if compassion does not have to be personal.

The corruption of our language, the related corruption of our thought, and the sadly abundant evidence of the past several decades suggest that the road to effective anti-poverty work in America cannot be paved with more well-intended legislation. Instead, we need to look at ourselves and our society more honestly. We celebrate America as a compassionate, caring society. But most of us are actually stingy—not because we refuse to spend more government money (we're doing quite well there, thank you), but because we no longer offer time and spiritual challenge to the poor. Our willingness to do that shows whether we care for hearts, minds, and souls, and not just bodies. As a society, we fail the test and will continue to do so until we read our Bibles and show love for God and man by doing what God commands.

CASES

Case 4.1: *Roger and Me*—General Motors and Plant Closings

In the mid to late 1980s, General Motors, in an attempt to stay competitive with rival foreign automakers, began closing some of its least productive automobile factories. One of the most well known of these was the Buick plant in Flint, Michigan, which closed in the mid-1980s. GM was downsizing and moving some of those jobs overseas in an effort to cut costs and remain profitable. The film *Roger and Me* was a low-budget documentary designed to show the impact of the plant closing on the community of Flint.

GM argued that it had little responsibility to the community because it had provided jobs and income over the decades for many people there. In addition, they were closing the plant because it was not as efficient as newer ones and the costs of employing the workers was much higher than in other parts of the world. They insisted that they were running a business, not a charity, and that they had every right to close less productive plants because of their obligation to their shareholders to maximize the return on their investment. Further, they held that if they did not downsize they would be overrun by their competitors, jeopardizing the entire company and potentially throwing many more people out of work.

Roger and Me painted a different picture. Once the plant was closed, Flint experienced severe economic problems. Unemployment reached close to 30 percent. Some former plant workers were evicted from their homes. The city responded with some poorly conceived programs to help the displaced workers; these programs actually made the situation worse for the community. For example, they invested millions in a theme park called "Autoworld" designed to attract tourists to Flint. It was a major failure, and many argued that the city could have better spent the money on job training or other assistance for people out of work. With unemployment so high in the community, other subsidiary businesses were also hurt. The impact of the plant closing spread throughout the entire community. To be sure, some people left the city and found jobs in other parts of the country. But they lamented the fact that they had to uproot their families from their communities.[1]

[1] See Joseph B. White, "GM to Accelerate Cost-Cutting Measures, Announce Further Plant Closings Soon," *Wall Street Journal*, 30 April 1992; and Doron P. Levin, "G.M. Is Set to Announce New Wave of Plant Closings," *New York Times*, 3 December 1992.

Questions for Discussion:

1. What responsibility do you think GM had to the community of Flint? Do you think the company was justified in closing the plant, given the impact of the closing on the community?
2. In the 1990s many states and cities have offered companies substantial tax breaks and development projects such as roads and public services to entice them to locate their operations in their cities. In view of this, do you think that companies owe their communities something in return, or is their only obligation to increase the wealth of their shareholders?
3. Who should pay the costs of helping the displaced workers find new jobs and acquire new skills—the individual, GM, or the community? Or should it be a combination of the three? If a combination, who do you think should shoulder the major share of the cost?

Case 4.2: Nike and Cheap Labor

In the early 1990s Nike was a very profitable maker of athletic shoes. Some of the most celebrated athletes in sports such as Michael Jordan endorsed their products, and in most shoe stores such as the Foot Locker chains, scores of Nike brands were selling briskly at high prices. Nike is located in the town of Beaverton, Oregon, a small community in the Pacific Northwest. In the early 1990s, Nike made a decision to move some of its operations to the Philippines, Indonesia, and China, where labor is much cheaper than in the United States. Nike could expect to cut its labor costs at least in half, and they argued that in order to stay competitive in the highly competitive athletic shoe industry, they had to take advantage of every cost-savings opportunity in order not to jeopardize the long-term health of the company.

Opponents of the company's relocation argued that Nike was hardly threatened with bankruptcy when they decided to move some operations overseas. They insist that the company is padding their profit margin at the expense of the community and the people who have faithfully worked for them over the years. They hold that there is a significant difference between a company closing plants in order to survive, and a company closing plants in order to increase their profit margin by a few percentage points.

Nike is hardly alone in this trend of taking jobs overseas because of the costs of labor in the United States. Many companies are taking advantage of global communications and transportation services and drastically cutting their labor costs by taking their operations to parts of the world where people are willing to work for a small fraction of what American workers are paid.[2]

[2]See Richard J. Barnet and John Cavanagh, "Just Undo It: Nike's Exploited Workers," *New York Times*, 13 February 1994.

Questions for Discussion:

1. Do you think there is a moral difference between a company that cuts jobs and transfers operations overseas in order to survive and a company that transfers operations overseas in order to increase its existing profit margin?
2. In the case of Nike, do you think that they are justified in moving operations overseas? Do you think that their obligation to increase their shareholders' wealth should be balanced by a responsibility to their community? Why or why not?

Case 4.3: Executive Compensation

One of the criticisms of capitalism is that it unfairly distributes the goods of society. Nowhere is this more evident than in the annual figures that indicate the compensation packages of CEOs of the Fortune 500 companies. It is not uncommon for some of these CEOs to receive substantial bonuses that are not necessarily tied to the company's performance. Some have received these bonuses during years when their companies lost money or when they underwent significant downsizing to cut costs.

In 1993, for example, Michael Eisner of Disney received a total compensation in excess of $203 million. During 1993 the company's net income fell by over 60 percent, in large part due to the EuroDisney debacle. But since Eisner joined the company as CEO in 1984, the company has done spectacularly well, justifying, in the minds of some, the overall compensation. Others in the top-twenty list of best-paid CEOs include Sanford I. Weill of Travelers ($52 million), Joseph R. Hyde III of Autozone ($32.2 million) and Charles N. Mathewson of International Game Tech ($22.2 million). Add to this the income of the top entertainers and professional athletes, which is in the tens of millions and hundreds of millions for some. When public school teachers are paid less than $50,000 annually, we should have serious questions about what society values.

The 1994 baseball strike epitomized for many the problems with the market system of compensation. Millionaire players were going on strike and were being opposed by millionaire owners who said that their livelihood from baseball was being threatened by the escalating

[3]See Graef S. Crystal, "The Great CEO Pay Sweepstakes," *Fortune* (18 June 1990): 94–102; and Darryl C. Salas, "Are Executives Paid Too Much?" *Business and Society Review* (Summer 1994): 16–19.

players' salaries. One proposal was to cap both player salaries and owner profits and donate all excess revenue to worthy causes such as education.[3]

Questions for Discussion:

1. Do you think that CEOs are generally overpaid? Or do you think that they are entitled to whatever compensation package the market will bear?

2. Do you think that these CEOs are justified in taking their bonuses when the company is not profitable or when it is downsizing significantly to cut costs? Does that reveal a double standard, or should they be compensated for making the hard choices necessary to maintain their firm's competitiveness?

3. Do you have any problem with athletes and entertainers making the amount of money that they do? Would you support a cap on their incomes? Or should they be able to make as much as the market will enable them to?

4. How do you feel about athletes and entertainers making the incomes they do, while public school teachers make much less and are forced often to take pay cuts so that the school system will stay solvent? Does that reflect poorly on the things that society values? Or is that the way it ought to be in the free-market system?

COMMENTARY

The film *Roger and Me* illustrates the impact of corporate decisions to maximize profit on individuals and communities. General Motors' decision to close the Buick plant in Flint, Michigan, in the mid-1980s produced a seriously detrimental effect on the community. Thousands of people were put out of work, affecting the entire economy and causing businesses and banks to fail as unemployment reached close to 30 percent in the town. That scenario has been repeated countless times in the last decade as companies downsize their work force, reduce costs, and position themselves to remain competitive in a global marketplace.

If the workers in the Buick plant had been interviewed before the plant closing, many of them would likely have expressed discontent with their work. Auto manufacturing plants have some of the most specialized assembly lines in the world; workers do the same task repeatedly without seeing any connection to the final product they are helping to produce. It is true, however, that some automobile companies today are trying to change the assembly-line mentality of producing cars. Companies such as Volvo and Saturn are organizing teams of workers together and the entire team is responsible for assembling the entire car. In this way they are not so isolated from the product of their labor.[4] But since the division of labor was widely adopted by business enterprises at the beginning of the Industrial Revolution, capitalism has been criticized for making work something destructive of the human spirit instead of enhancing it. Although it is true that countries in the West, particularly the United States, are moving toward more information economies where there can be more autonomy for workers to control their work and work lives, still an overwhelming number of employees have the gnawing feeling that their work is purposeless and contributes nothing besides a paycheck to their sense of personal fulfillment and well-being. Thus some of the moral charges brought against capitalism are that the high emphasis on competition creates unemployment, which brings hardship to those laid off, and that the nature of work under capitalism causes a worker's sense of alienation from the product and process of work as well as alienation actually from himself or herself.

[4]See the following for more information on these two companies: "Volvo's Radical New Plant: The End of the Assembly Line?" *Business Week* (28 August 1989): 92–93; "Here Comes GM's Saturn," *Business Week* (9 April 1990): 56–62.

How an Economic System Works

Before analyzing these two charges further and commenting on the readings in this chapter, it may be helpful to introduce you to some the basic elements of an economy. Perhaps the best way to do this would be to contrast how a market-oriented economy such as capitalism understands these elements and how more command-oriented economies such as socialism would see them. Keep in mind that these are what are called "ideal types" and neither pure capitalism nor pure socialism exists anywhere in the world. Even in the few remaining socialist countries, there are market incentives that the government uses to motivate producers to produce. There are thriving black-market, or underground, economies in these countries as well, and these economies are probably the closest parallels to pure capitalism anywhere in the world. Most economies are something of a mix of market forces and command forces, though usually it is easy to see which element is the dominant one. Since the collapse of socialism at the end of the 1980s, the debate is not over which economic system is morally superior. Rather, the issue seems to be whether a society's economic problems can be better solved by more government intervention, that is, more command-oriented economics, or by less government intervention, that is, letting the market solve the problems.

In any economy, there are basic questions that the system must address. They concern ownership of property, deciding which goods and services get produced, what price is to be charged for them, what workers' wages will be, how to ensure quality and safety in products, how wealth will be distributed, what level of unemployment is acceptable, and how competition is viewed. In market systems, property, particularly the means of production and businesses, is privately owned. In command systems, most businesses are owned publicly, or more specifically, by the state. In market systems, the forces of supply and demand determine what goods and services will be produced, how much they will cost the consumer, and what workers will be paid. That is, the market determines these elements. In command systems, the state, or whatever authority is responsible for economic central planning, decides what will be produced, the price level, and the wage scale for workers.

In market systems, competition insures product safety and quality, since consumers will not continue to buy from manufacturers who produce shoddy or unsafe products, ultimately driving them out of business if they do not meet the standards of the marketplace. In command systems, the state with its regulatory agencies is responsible for insuring safety. In the United States, which has a predominantly market system, this aspect of insuring safety is highly command oriented. There is relatively little confidence that the market will guarantee consumer safety. Even in market systems where society trusts competition to effect product safety there is an information time lag during

which consumers are unprotected. That is, it ta[...]
pany's reputation for building unsafe products to bec[...]
in the marketplace, during which time consumers are t[...]
buying risky products.

In market systems, wealth is distributed according to meri[...]
measured by the market. As a result wealth tends to be more concentrated in fewer hands in this system. In command-oriented systems, wealth is distributed more equally, often based on need or a
person's social contribution, such as the Olympic athletes' reward in
former Communist countries for outstanding performance. In com-
munistic societies there are fewer incentives for people to take risks
in starting or expanding businesses in what little market segments
the state allows. In market systems, roughly 5 percent unemployment is considered optimal. Should unemployment drop below that
level, that is usually an indication that the economy is growing at too
fast a pace, thereby running the risk of inflation. In fact, the central
bank in many market economies will try to control the money supply in order to keep the economy from becoming inflationary as a
result of growing too rapidly, thus keeping unemployment at a level
where substantial numbers of people will be unemployed at any
given time. In command economies, everyone has a job and there is
0 percent unemployment. However, there is less choice in what job
a person will have, and frequently the work force ends up being
"underemployed." This refers to people doing jobs that are well
beneath their skill level or doing jobs that are simply "make work"
jobs that lack dignity and could be eliminated without any loss or
anyone noticing. For example, this phenomenon can be readily
observed when one travels through countries with strong centrally
planned economies such as China. In some hotels there, a worker has
the sole responsibility of cleaning ashtrays in the lobby areas. With
such menial responsibilities, these employees can be seen rewiping
ashtrays about every fifteen minutes, even if no one has deposited
ashes inside them.

In market systems, competition is viewed as one of the chief positive elements, encouraging quality and innovation, thus giving consumers access to better and cheaper goods and services. Even though
competition can at times be cutthroat and go beyond the bounds of
civility and even beyond the law, the benefits of having an economy
based on competition far outweigh the costs. In command economies,
the people would argue that the costs outweigh the benefits. Some of
the costs would be that (1) some would lose, affecting them negatively
and causing social dislocations, and (2) there would be wasteful duplication of goods and services.

ainst capitalism that come out of these
mpetition undermines virtue (Michel-
st economy produces profound worker
an, Schumacher); that unemployment,
f capitalism, is damaging to individuals and
and that capitalism unfairly distributes the
Novak responds in a general way to some of
helman makes against capitalism.

an, the concept of virtuous self-interest is clearly an
n he contrasts one's desired moral character with
s character, he is setting up two different sets of rules
game of business is played. He argues that there are "nec-
adictions between generally accepted moral obligations
and the /s and rules that flow from the logic of economic competition." As a result, employers are forced to view employees as means
to the firm's advantage of maximizing profit. Here Michelman
assumes the moral philosophy of Immanuel Kant, who held that one
of the primary moral obligations was to treat people as ends in themselves, not means to accomplishing other ends. In other words, we are
to treat people as people with dignity, not as things to be used for our
own interests. Michelman insists that the rules of business competition force people to use people as means to the end of profit, not treating them as individuals worthy of respect and dignity. Surely it is true
that such treatment of employees frequently happens, and the temptation to compromise one's virtue for the sake of profit happens regularly enough to be the subject of this book and others on business
ethics. But whether such compromise is a *necessary* result of economic
competition is debatable.

Michael Novak argues, rightly in our view, that business is built on
a foundation of moral commitments and virtue. Business needs moral
parameters in order to keep acquisitive self-interest from destroying it.
Novak rightly insists that a firm that operates as Michelman suggests
will necessarily anger its customers, damage the morale of its work
force, alienate its suppliers, and likely attract negative public attention,
all of which work against its goal of profit maximization. Most firms
cannot pursue self-interest without restraint, or the kind of competition
that Michelman describes will end up putting the violators out of busi-

ness. For example, firms with a long track record of poor employee relations sooner or later will find it difficult to sustain morale in the work force and continue attracting quality employees. Study after study has shown the importance of workplace morale and satisfaction to the profitability of a firm, and that it is unlikely that a firm could maximize its profit with a work force that is constantly turning over because the work environment is poor.[5] Of course, exceptions to this exist; there are indeed companies that are successful despite a poor ethical track record. Good ethics is not always good business.

Take Michelman's example of firms being forced by competition to become polluters. Although the temptation is undoubtedly there for a company to follow their competition and pollute in the same environmentally damaging way, Michelman fails to point out the risk of the firm's activities being discovered and made public, either by a whistle-blowing employee or some public agency. Should that happen, the public relations damage to the firm would be serious, affecting its long-run ability to maximize its profit as the public turns against it. That risk might motivate the company, in the name of profit, not to pollute. Of course, there are a few companies that are in such powerful positions vis-à-vis customers and employees that they can act with impunity. But those are the exception, not the rule. Even though Michelman's scenario does occur in business, there is hardly a necessary contradiction between business values and personal values. Rather, with Novak, business assumes certain moral parameters in order to function. Business assumes virtues such as telling the truth, keeping promises, and fulfilling contracts, or else it would be difficult to conduct business at all. As Novak rightly insists, restraints on self-interest ultimately enable a company to maximize its profit.

Alienation

A second charge against capitalism is that work in capitalist economies produces alienation. Marx argued that capitalist work produces alienation of the workers from the product they produce, from the process of work itself, and ultimately from the workers themselves. Philosopher Kai Nielsen echoes this criticism when he describes the work of most people as stifling of people's "sensibilities, intellectual capacities, initiative, creativity and autonomy."[6] Schumacher insists that work that does not "nourish and enliven the higher man and urge him to produce the best he is capable," is morally problematic, and his Buddhist economic ethic would encourage work that is stimulating and satisfying. He decries an economic system that puts production ahead of people and consumption ahead of creative activity.

[5]See, for example, the landmark study done by management consultants Tom Peters and Robert Waterman, *In Search of Excellence* (New York: Harper & Row, 1982), in which they portrayed some of the most successful large companies and found them committed to many of the things that Michelman insists cannot take place in firms concerned with profit maximization. See also Peters and Nancy Austin, *A Passion for Excellence* (New York: Random House, 1985), and Waterman, *The Renewal Factor* (New York: Bantam, 1987).

[6]Kai Nielsen, "Alienation and Work," in *Moral Rights in the Workplace*, ed. Gertrude Ezorsky (Albany: State University of New York Press, 1987), 34.

When examined more carefully, this critique of work under capitalism seems to be a bit misplaced. Worker alienation is hardly endemic to capitalism. Rather, it has its roots in the development of the division of labor, one of the key elements necessary for the Industrial Revolution. Every economy, except the most primitive agrarian ones, employs the division of labor. It is more characteristic of industrial and information societies than any one economic system such as capitalism. Prior to 1989, when socialist economies were still widespread in Eastern Europe, one did not have to look hard to notice the profound sense of worker alienation that existed there, particularly with the way in which many people were underemployed. They were alienated from any useful work, simply engaged in make-work for the sake of having something to do during the day. The irony of Marx's criticism of worker alienation is that the socialist economies formed by his successors actually alienated workers far worse than did capitalist systems.

The fact that alienation occurs in both market- and command-oriented systems reflects the biblical perspective on work. God created work and assigned it to Adam and Eve in the garden prior to the entrance of sin into the world (Gen. 1:28; 2:15–16). Their responsibility to take care of the garden into which God had placed them was part of the broader mandate to exercise dominion over the creation. Thus work is inherently good since it was created and endorsed before the fall of mankind into sin. (This may explain the empirical data of Gini and Sullivan that suggest that if people inherited wealth, the majority would continue to work. They rightly point out the power of work to shape a person's life!) However, with the entrance of sin into the world, work, like everything else in creation, was corrupted (3:17–19). It became more arduous and difficult and would not always be pleasurable. Thus work, by its very nature, has the potential to be fulfilling because God ordained it from creation. But it also has the potential to be harsh, demanding, and alienating because it too was affected by sin. Work is both inherently creative and cursed. Thus the alienating aspect of work is not particular to capitalism, but is endemic to work in general. The evidence of work in socialist economies clearly bears this out. Thus the charge that work is alienating cannot be aimed at capitalism alone. It may be that worker dissatisfaction occurs more regularly in some economic arrangements than others. But under capitalism, there are more choices for workers to enter the labor market in areas that they may find fulfilling. Even in the best jobs and in the best companies where worker satisfaction is high, the nature of work as cursed by sin means that some work will be unsatisfying.

Unemployment

The cases in this chapter illustrate the problem of unemployment in capitalist systems. The social costs of business transitions are substantial and include more than simply the financial costs of unemployment compensation and job retraining. They also include the emotional burdens on individuals and families and the costs that communities must bear when large companies close plants and move operations elsewhere. The traditional market explanation for unemployment is that transitions necessarily occur when resources are transferred from unproductive sectors of the economy into more productive ones. In the long run, it does an economy no good for resources to remain in unproductive sectors. But market explanations tend to overlook the human costs of unemployment. To be sure, it is not wise to continue to employ resources in areas where firms cannot profit—that is, in unproductive sectors of the economy. But when a plant closes, there are "transfer costs" to be borne. These include the costs of retraining people for new employment in productive sectors and the costs of supporting people while they are in the process of finding a new job. The government has assumed the major share of these costs through unemployment compensation and job training. If free-market economies can work to guarantee the prospects of long-term employment for those who are willing to relocate and be retrained, this would mitigate suffering and make the system more palatable to some of its critics.

However, the question of who should bear these transfer costs is a pressing one. Some hold that the individual is responsible for them. But to put it entirely on the worker seems unfair since he or she became unemployed through means that are largely out of their control. Of course, it could be argued that they should have foreseen plant closings and layoffs coming, as might be the case with the GM workers at the Flint plant, but in many cases, this is assuming more foresight and information than is reasonable for the average worker. Consider also the experiences of the thousands of laid-off engineers in Southern California who were once employed by the aerospace and defense industries. Undoubtedly, these are well-educated persons who followed market demand when they chose their professions. They cannot reasonably have been expected to forecast the future of their industries since it is largely out of their hands.

Consequently, others suggest that the company that lays off its workers ought to bear some responsibility for transfer costs, and many companies do this, offering generous severance packages and job training and placement programs. Critics argue that the companies should do more, and in some cases that is true. It could probably be argued that GM could have done more for its Flint workers after the plant there was closed. Others suggest that the companies that will eventually hire these workers should bear some of the costs, since they will benefit the most from workers moving between sectors of the economy. However, logistically, it is difficult to see how this could happen, since companies cannot be expected to invest in people prior to hiring them, nor can they be expected to provide the skills their new employees will need for their jobs. Still others suggest that the community should help bear these costs, since it has a great deal at stake if its people remain unemployed. But for many who accept new jobs, it means moving out of the community, and it is hardly just to expect communities to help bear transfer costs for workers who will transfer out of the community to find work. Since unemployment is part of a smoothly functioning capitalist economy, it may be that all who participate in it should bear some of the transfer costs, through publicly financed unemployment benefits and training. In addition, the company that closes its plant surely has some responsibility to the workers put out of work. It is not morally right to close a plant with callous disregard for workers who have served the company well.

However, that does not absolve the community of all responsibility when a plant in it closes. Clearly the community of Flint bears some accountability for becoming so dependent on one industry and not diversifying its economy, leaving it vulnerable to severe economic problems should that industry leave. Many cities previously dependent on the oil industry have learned that lesson and have begun to attract a wider variety of businesses in order to minimize their exposure should economic hard times befall them again. Further, as the film *Roger and Me* depicted Flint, its attempts to diversify were ill-advised, only making a bad situation worse.

It may be that the company has a responsibility also to the community in which it operates. This will be discussed in more detail in chapter 6, which deals with corporate moral responsibility. Many companies are lured to communities with promises of substantial tax breaks and development projects around the area in which they will locate. If a firm leaves an area after being the beneficiary of public benefits, it is reasonable to expect them to pay some of the transfer costs that the community would bear. With more and more businesses being wooed by communities around the world with these kinds of concessions, it seems fair to expect a greater degree of responsibility to the community that is welcoming the company.

Distribution

Executive salaries are a prime indicator of the inequality in income in society. There is little doubt that capitalism is not an egalitarian system when it comes to distributing the goods of society. But the charge that the system is unfair contains certain assumptions about economic justice that need analysis. How you resolve the question of what is called distributive justice has a lot to say about your assessment of capitalism as a system that distributes the goods of society.

Most critics of capitalism assume that the goods of society should be distributed on the basis of need or distributed equally. They have little place for a system that is based on merit. To be sure, some things, such as the basic necessities of life, should be distributed according to need. Some things such as opportunity should be distributed based on equality. But most people hold that workers should get what they earn and that merit, evidenced by hard work and perseverance, should be the primary criterion that determines a person's share of the goods of society. In most Western countries, there is a mixed system—of merit and need-based distribution. There is little doubt that merit-based systems encourage innovation and hard work, which are necessary for productive economies. But there is also a place for need-based distribution of society's goods.

However, Marvin Olasky is certainly correct to question whether one should equate compassion and collective material transfer, or simply transferring from those who have more to those who have less. He rightly insists that this is not genuine compassion and, in many cases, actually rewards irresponsibility with government handouts. Rather, compassion means to "suffer together" with someone in need, one of the purposes of which is to enable that person to become productive and earn an adequate share of society's goods to support himself. The idea of compassion should not have to be qualified with the word "personal." Compassion has historically been personal, and "compassionate observer" is an oxymoron.

The above criticisms of capitalism are legitimately a cause for concern, but echoing Michelman, they are not sufficient to jettison the system. Competition does not necessarily entail widespread moral compromise. Alienation is not endemic to capitalism but is part of work under the curse of sin. While unemployment is a tragic but apparently necessary feature of capitalism, short-term unemployment seems preferable to the lack of dignity created by underemployment. However, it is reasonable and moral for the transfer costs to be shared, not borne entirely by the individual worker. This would mitigate some of the criticism that capitalism receives for being less than ideal.

FIVE

Capitalism and Biblical Values

There can be no question that it [capitalism], rather than socialism, comes closer to matching the demands of the biblical ethic.

Ronald H. Nash, "Does Capitalism Pass the Moral Test?"

The Scriptures are not neutral on questions of economics. The God of the Bible is clearly and emphatically on the side of the poor and the exploited.

Jim Wallis, "The Powerful and the Powerless"

INTRODUCTION

Religious groups throughout the centuries have had a great deal to say about materialism and a person's economic life. For instance, the Bible has more material on wealth and possessions than on the concepts of heaven and hell combined. Other religious traditions have also addressed economics in varying degrees of detail. Until the advent of the Industrial Revolution, religious teaching on economic life was predominantly individualistic, mostly applying to the way the individual gained and/or used his or her wealth. There was very little addressed to the institutional economic system because the economies, for the most part, were simple systems that were agrarian and trade-guild oriented. Well-developed industrial economies had yet to come on the historical scene. With the industrial age came new economic and social arrangements and new challenges that religious groups sought to address.

Sociologist Max Weber, in his classic work *The Protestant Ethic and the Spirit of Capitalism*, defended the idea that Calvinist faith was a key element in the development of capitalist industrial society. Following the publication of this work in the nineteenth century and the growth of the capitalist economic system, scholars and religious

195

authorities have debated the question of whether capitalism is Christian or not. As you read on this subject on your own, you will find an entire spectrum of opinions on the subject. There are those who hold that the Bible condemns capitalism as an inherently immoral system, and they want nothing to do with such a system. On the other extreme are those who insist that capitalism is entirely consistent with biblical values and that virtually any criticism of capitalism is unbiblical. The language of the debate in Christian circles is no less acrimonious than that which occurs in nonreligious arenas. For example, in response to Ronald Sider's *Rich Christians in an Age of Hunger*, David Chilton has written *Productive Christians in an Age of Guilt Manipulators* as a retort.

Of course, there are more moderate positions out there as well. There are those who have more theological reservations about capitalism than others and advocate a greater degree of government intervention to correct some of the abuses they believe are inherent in the free-market system. However, with the end of the Cold War and the collapse of most socialist economies in the past few years, many religious observers have celebrated the victory of capitalism as a moral one, claiming that "God's system" has triumphed. Others have seen that capitalism is the only surviving economic system and take it as a given in the world today. Both those approaches to capitalism tend to soften any criticism of the system.

Until the late nineteenth century, most religious leaders endorsed capitalism with little reservation. Some of the abuses of the industrial age were coming out in England and were the subject of critics like the novelist Charles Dickens, with some churchmen joining in the criticism. But it wasn't until the 1890s with the rise of the social gospel and the advent of Catholic social encyclicals such as *Rerum Novarum*, that Catholic and Protestant leaders began to speak out against the abuses of capitalism. To be sure, capitalism had its defenders, mostly conservative Protestants, but the religious mood at the time was critical of the system, with many critics advocating forms of socialism that nations of Europe were trying.

More recently, in the past thirty years, the debate over capitalism has raged in evangelical Christian circles, echoing many of the themes first raised around the turn of the century. Evangelicals who tend to be more on the political left led the criticism of capitalism in more explicitly biblical terms than the earlier debates. They observed that many of the correctives proposed by the New Deal legislation of the 1930s had not worked, and they concluded that the problems with capitalism were systemic. However, in the current debate, evangelicals on the political right have responded aggressively and defended capitalism as the system most consistent with important biblical values. Some have even observed that Catholic critics of capitalism have softened and recent papal encyclicals such as *Centesimus Annus* have guardedly endorsed the market system. With the economic collapse of socialism in the late 1980s, most of the critics of capitalism no longer have a ready alternative to which they can turn. But they have not embraced capitalism, only admitted that there must be a third way, an alternative to both systems.

The readings in this chapter reflect this more recent aspect of the debate, since recent participants in the debate have restated some of the earlier criticisms and defenses of capitalism. Jim Wallis, the leader of the Sojourners community in Washington, D.C., and probably the most articulate evangelical critic of capitalism, outlines the classic critique of capitalism by the evangelical left in "The Powerful and the Powerless." He insists that the gospel is biased toward the poor and that the concept of private property in which people can justifiably use all their property for self-benefit is not a Christian notion. African economist Safro Kwame, in "Doin' Business in an African Country," argues that the profit motive is not appropriate in certain developing cultures and may actually make economic hardships worse. Fr. Robert Sirico, in his "Entrepreneurial Vocation," defends the business calling as a legitimate end in itself, consistent with the creation mandate to creatively exercise dominion over the creation. Finally, Michael Novak, in his "Theology of the Corporation," expands on this notion by suggesting that the values expressed in capitalism such as freedom, creativity, and productivity tilt the moral balance toward capitalism.

READINGS

Doin' Business in an African Country

Business Ethics and Capitalism in a Poor Country
Safro Kwame

Journal of Business Ethics 2 (1983): 263–68. Copyright © 1983 D. Reidel Publishing Company.

In Africa and other parts of the Third World, it is not uncommon for persons to sell goods far above approved (government controlled) prices,[1] reaping windfall profits in the process. The economic practice of profiteering, often preceded by hoarding, the creation of artificial shortage and overpricing, is better known in the West African country of Ghana as "kalabule."[2] Here in Ghana much of business is taken up by the distribution of goods and services which is largely, though not exclusively, in the hands of women. Business ethics, for Ghanaian businessmen and women, is largely dictated by the maximization of profit. In oversimplified terms, business ethics for "kalabule" businessmen and women states that it is not wrong to maximize profits.

In Ghana, as in other African countries, it is usual for women to queue continually for basic commodities such as soap, sugar, flour and milk while the men are off to work, and resell them to the men and other workers when they (the men) return from work. It is common for "kalabule" businesswomen to buy a cake of soap and a tin of evaporated milk for approximately ¢2[3] each, yet resell them at ¢10 and ¢12 respectively, even though most Ghanaians earn only slightly above the ¢12 minimum wage.

In Sub-Saharan Africa, it is easy to sell basic goods such as soap and sugar at the highest price possible, because most African countries, like their counterparts elsewhere in the Third World, can neither produce nor buy enough of anything to meet national demand. Agricultural production constitutes the main activity of over seventy per-cent of the 300 million people of Sub-Saharan Africa. Sub-Saharan Africa is the region most dependent on agriculture. Yet agricultural production, according to the 1980 World Development Report, continues to be almost uniformly sluggish with food output per person declining in 25 countries (World Bank 1980, p. 86). Being mainly an agricultural production region, the Sub-Saharan depends on the outside world, especially Europe and North America, for both luxuries and basics. Ghana's import program for 1979 was estimated in 1978 to be ¢2,432.6 million with a total of ¢475.00 million being provided for the importation of basic consumer goods. Imports included imputs for textiles, beer, tobacco, soap, milk, beverage, matches and toilet rolls and finished produces such as sugar, meat, canned fish and baby food (G.C.B., 1978, pp. 1 and 2).

Unfortunately, export earnings, which determine the capacity to import, grow (if at all) unsatisfactorily in developing countries due to falling demand and falling prices (World Economic Survey, 1978, p. 32). While Ghana's exports, for example, grew slowly, the *Quarterly Economic Review* of Ghana Commercial Bank indicates that demand for imports grew at a high rate (*op. cit.*, p. 1). Local food production, the Review adds, could not meet growing demand (*ibid.*, p. 1). In the *Quarterly Economic Review* of July–December 1980, the Research Department of the Ghana Commercial Bank writes:

> While the economy was faced with increasingly high cost of crude oil, the price of cocoa, the country's major export, declined

about 14 percent during the year. This seriously curtailed further funds that could have been spent on essential goods and services. The supply of goods and services was, therefore, further worsened despite attempts by the government to improve the flow of goods and check prices.... During the period, therefore, the government sought for a loan of 34.9 cents million to import 73,500 tons of cereals to supplement local production (G.C.B., 1981, p. 1).

Paradoxically, imports into Africa include food. It is noteworthy that Africa imports much of its food requirement. Grain imputs into Sub-Saharan Africa between 1965 and 1975 rose from 1.6 to 2.6 million tons, and it is expected to rise to 4.5 million tones by 1985 (World Bank, 1980, p. 85). According to the Food and Agriculture Organization of the United Nations Organization, "the level of food imports is rising and many developing countries could face grave difficulties in meeting their food deficits over the next decade." (F.A.O., 1979, p. 77). In Africa, the balance of trade has continued to decrease from—1.9 billion dollars in 1974 to 14.7 billion dollars in 1978. In these conditions, it is obvious that most African countries cannot meet even the demand for food and other basic goods. Hence, the business practice of "kalabule" is bound to lead to starvation for most Africans and even death for some.

No wonder half of the population of Sub-Saharan Africa is absolutely poor (World Bank, 1980, p. 86). An absolutely poor person, according to the World Development Report, is one who lives in conditions that fall short of the requirements of any reasonable definition of human decency (*ibid.*, p. 32). Typically, a poor person in Sub-Saharan Africa spends almost his whole income on food which consists of a monotonous diet of gari, yam or cassava. Many of such persons are so malnourished that they are unable to work hard. The physical and mental development of their children is impaired; such children also have low resistance to infection. While most poor persons are sick with malaria, measles or diarrhea, their children are likely to suffer from food-deficiency

diseases such as kwashiorkor and marasmus if they are "lucky" enough to survive the first year of life.

Any system of distribution or marketing that permits businessmen and women to maximize their profits in the sale or distribution of basic goods that are in short supply, is bound to aggravate the situation for an already starving people. I hesitate to describe such a system of distribution which ensures suffering and death for the majority of people in a society as moral. If murder and the unnecessary infliction of pain are bad, so is "kalabule" done with a clear view of the consequences. Murder is the deliberate killing of a human being. To put basic goods out of the economic reach of persons when it is obvious that the lack of such basics leads to starvation and death, is tantamount to murder. So long as rationing could ensure that most persons have these basic goods at (cheaper) government-controlled prices, the practice of "kalabule" could be said to inflict unnecessary suffering on the impoverished peoples of Africa.

Neither Christian nor Akan ethics permits disrespect and unconcern for human beings and their lives.

It is surprising that many of Ghana's "kalabule" businessmen and women are Christians or adherents to Akan Ethics (or both), since neither Christian nor Akan ethics permits disrespect and unconcern for human beings and their lives. An Akan proverb states that it is the human being, not money or clothing, that matters:

Mefre sika sika a, sika nnyeso; mefre natama a, ntama nnye so: Onipa ne asem.

Saint Luke reports Jesus as saying that "it is easier for a camel to go through the eyes of a needle than for a rich man to enter the Kingdom of God" which Christians seek (Luke, 18:25). For it is difficult for rich persons, such as "Kalabule" businesswomen who overprice goods and profiteer in order to maximize profits, to follow Jesus' instruction to give up treasure on earth in favor of treasure in heaven by distributing their wealth to the poor (Luke, 18:22).[3]

It certainly would not surprise Mackie that "kalabule" could be a nation-wide practice in a society such as Ghana in which the major ethnic group is Akan, and Christians form a national majority. Perhaps, Mackie wrote, the truest teachers of moral philosophy are the outlaws and thieves for whom rules of justice and good behaviour are rules of convenience with no pretense of receiving them as innate laws of nature (Mackie, 1977, pp. 10–11). Values, for Mackie, are not part of the fabric of the world to be discovered (*ibid.*, p. 15); they have to be made, tailored to suit our goals and desires:

> The objective values which I am denying would be action-directing absolutely, not contingently upon the agent's desires and inclinations (Mackie, 1977, p. 29).

Hence, if this view is accepted in so far as "kalabule" ethics, we have to make a choice depending on our desires concerning the type of society we wish to build—one that is concerned about the plight of its members or one that is indifferent to the suffering of the majority.

If ethics is discovered rather than invented, we would have to decide, without recourse to our desires, preferences and inclinations, whether it is the Akan-Christian ethics (which might not be entirely compatible with each other) or rather the ethics associated with "kalabule" that is real. I do not see how this can be done so successfully as to eliminate moral skepticism, in the light of diversity and variability in moral values as well as of our conflicting claims to moral knowledge. Certainly if we share with Singer the assumption that suffering and death from lack of food, shelter or medical care are bad (Singer, 1972, p. 231), we ought to abandon "kalabule" ethics in favor of ethics of the Akan-Christian type. But for those who disagree (supposing that some do) and rather believe for example that it is good to die or suffer for lack of food, shelter or medical care through no fault of the victim, it is, as far as I can see, difficult to argue them out of disagreement. I see, however, that the above-given considerations on murder and the unnecessary infliction of pain may go some way in making such disagreers less certain; and, in any case, there are very few, if any, practitioners of "kalabule" who so disagree.

Experience has shown that mass suffering and starvation associated with "kalabule" are precisely what the practice of capitalism, also called free private enterprise, does to people who can neither produce nor buy their needs in sufficient quantities. Samuelson tells us that "the price mechanism, working through supply and demand in competitive markets, operates to answer the three fundamental problems or economic organization in our [American] mixed private enterprise system." (Samuelson, 1976, p. 55). The three problems concern WHAT commodities shall be produced and in what quantities, HOW they shall be produced and FOR WHOM (The rich or the poor, the rich man's dog or the poor man's daughter?). "In a system of free private enterprise," Samuelson remarks, "no individual or organization is *consciously* concerned with the triad of economic problems. WHAT, HOW, and FOR WHOM." (*ibid.*, p. 41). "This fact," he adds, "is really remarkable." (*ibid.*, p. 41).

It surely is remarkable that the profit motive of suppliers (sellers) and the basic and non-basic needs of demanders (buyers) operating in a market should determine the What, How and For Whom rather than any conscious planning on the part of individuals and organizations. In a rich society of abundance, such as the United States of America, one can afford not to be "consciously concerned"; in poor countries such as those of Sub-Saharan Africa, it may be immoral (or cruel) to do so in the face of the mass suffering and starvation we have noted. Galbraith realizes this:

> The poor country has no such easy-going options. It must use its resources for the right things; if it fails to do so—if funds go into fancy housing, a glittering airport or official Cadillacs—the cries of outrage and horror will come first of all from the most rugged American free-enterprisers (Galbraith, 1971, p. 180).

This, in Galbraith's opinion, indicates that free enterprise—which he takes to be the practice of letting the market decide—is a product of well-being (*ibid.*, p. 180). Planning, Galbraith continues, is dictated by poverty (*ibid.*, p. 180). Yet, paradoxically, an unplanned economy is easier and cheaper to run because the distribution and production of even necessities of life are the result of what Samuelson terms "the unconscious automatic price mechanism" (*op. cit.*, p. 43) which lacks central direction and master planning. In other words, an unplanned economy is easier or cheaper to run because, in a sense, it is neither planned nor run. Often it is neither run nor planned because (in a rich society of abundance) there is no need to do so. In the face of acute scarcity, mass suffering and starvation, however, there is a need to do so—as every war-torn capitalist country would confirm. The problem with most of the poor countries of the South is that they are almost permanently in war-torn conditions.

The price mechanism is a product of the market economy, and the problem with it is that it operates beautifully and with entirely good consequences only in the unearthly perfect market.

The price mechanism is a product of the market economy and the problem with it (the price mechanism), as almost every economist would tell you, is that it operates beautifully and with entirely good consequences only in the unearthly perfect market. In the real-life imperfect market filled with psychological egoists, the profit motive of sellers and the inelastic demand of buyers of necessities are, as indicated by the African situation, incapable of preventing "kalabule." With private ownership of the means of production, the price mechanism is incapable of ensuring that what is produced and how it is produced is for those who are badly in need or even those with the greatest contribution. Capitalism, Cairncross points out, embraces both the price mechanism and a particular set of institutions governing the ownership and control of property just referred to above (Cairncross, 1973, p. 181). Both operate on individual profit. An official endorsement of capitalism, thus, stands in danger of raising psycho-

logical egoism to the level of ethical egoism. Such endorsement could be taken as saying that people seek their selfish interests in a market economy and they ought to (be permitted to) do so.

The principle of capitalism rests on the profit motive. The mainspring of the capitalist system, Macpherson wrote, "is that men do act as their calculation of net gain dictates" (Macpherson, 1973, p. 181). "As long as prices still move in response to these calculated decisions, and as long as prices still elicit the production of goods and determine their allocation," Macpherson continued, "we may say that the essential nature of the system has not changed." (*Ibid.*, pp. 181–82). The basic principle of "kalabuleism," we noted, is the maximization of profit. It seems to me that in the Christian countries of the North, such as the United Kingdom and the United States of America, the reason for relative absence of most of the adverse or "unethical" effects of "kalabule" is that the Northern countries are countries of relative abundance (not scarcity).

If the practice of capitalism in conditions of scarcity is likely to lead to the "evil" practices of "kalabule" (assuming that we accept them as evil), it is immoral to recommend capitalism to poor countries such as are found in Africa and other parts of the South. Yet the Friedmans recommend capitalism to poor countries on the grounds that "it is moral and progressive." "Free trade at home and abroad," according to Milton and Rose Friedman, "is the best way that a poor country can promote the well being of its citizens" (Friedman, 1980, p. 31). The Friedmans cite correlations between capitalism and development, against central planning and the authoritarian allocation of goods and services:

Intellectuals everywhere take for granted that free enterprise capitalism and a free market are devices for exploiting the masses, while central economic planning is the wave of the future that will set their countries on the road to rapid economic progress. . . .

The facts themselves are different. Wherever we find any large element of individual freedom, some measure of progress in the material comforts at the disposal of ordinary citizens, and widespread hope of further progress in the future, there we also find that economic activity is organized mainly through the free market. Wherever the state undertakes to control in detail the economic activities of its citizens, wherever, that is, detailed central economic planning reigns, there ordinary citizens are in political fetters, have a low standard of living and have little power to control their own destiny (Friedman, 1980, 46).

To substantiate their argument, Milton and Rose Friedman refer to the contrast between East and West Germany (*ibid.*, 47). They ask:

Which [East or West Germany] has prospered? Which had to erect a wall to pen in its citizens? Which must man it today with armed guards, assisted by fierce dogs, minefields, and similar devices of devilish ingenuity in order to frustrate brave and desperate citizens who are willing to risk their lives to leave their communist paradise for the capitalist hell on the other side of the wall? (Friedman, 1980, 47).

Malaya, Singapore, Korea, Taiwan and Japan—all relying extensively on private markets—, the Friedmans wrote, are thriving (*ibid.*, p. 48). Their peoples, they continued, are full of hope (*ibid.*, p. 48). By contrast, they added, India, Indonesia and Communist China—all relying on central planning—have experienced economic stagnation and political repression (*ibid.*, p. 49).

What the Friedmans forget is that correlation is not causation, and to identify the one with the other is to expose oneself to the fallacy of false cause. Nothing that the Friedmans have "said" indicates that capitalism is the cause of economic progress and the humane treatment of persons. In fact we have cited the Ghanaian experience as a counterexample, since "kalabule" was at its height immediately before and after the 112-day "moral revolution" which sought to do away with "kalabule" in Ghana. In Ghana, the price-control system of the pre-"moral revolution" administration of ex-General Kutu Acheampong did give way to the lais-

sez-faire economic activity of market women, when "kalabule" was at its height. After the uprising of 4th June 1979, a "moral revolution" which sought to use executions to abolish "kalabule" ethics was launched. But the "kalabule" ethics, guided by the maximization of profits operating in a free market system, re-emerged in the 1979–81 Limann administration that was capitalist in all but theory. Hence, the launching of the "holy war" against "kalabuleism" in the wake of the forcible overthrow of the Limann administration on 31st December 1981.

In my opinion, the attempt to fight the business ethics of "kalabule" by the way of indiscriminate violence and terrorism through the use of machine guns, in the name of a moral revolution or a holy war, is misplaced. If suffering and death resulting from business practices that seek to maximize profits are intuitively immoral, so are suffering and death resulting from terrorizing the society by machine guns. Experience has shown that in such conditions of "machine-gun ethics," the supply of even locally produced basics such as food disappear from the markets creating starvation and suffering. The subsequent attempt to use guns to get goods back on the market at controlled prices results in further killing or harming of poor non-"kalabule" persons (among others). Such "moral revolutionaries" and "holy warriors" seem not to appreciate that sanctions are external to morality and that ethics are made or invented not discovered. To invent ethics, we noted, the conditions must be conducive to the creation of the kind of values we are interested in. In a society of scarcity and capitalists, we are unlikely to have the resources with which to invent anything but "kalabule" ethics. If the prevailing conditions are not conducive to making non-"kalabule" ethics, it is futile to force people to embrace any other ethics. The mark of ethical conduct in a society of adult human beings, is that the members of the society can discriminate between good and evil and conduct themselves well by the use of reason, unlike children and subhumans. If ethics is to be discovered, then we need not force people to give up one system of ethics for the other, because there is no evidence that at any point in time all or several societies have discovered exactly the same ethical system. Further, if people ought to be forced in order that they do what they do, what guarantee is there that they do what they do because it is good and not because of fear?

In conclusion, I wish to note the following. That Akans who are Christians could subscribe to "kalabule" which conflicts with Christian and Akan ethics, indicate (though it does not prove) that ethics is man-made or invented from the prevailing conditions rather than God-given or society-given to be discovered whatever the conditions are. If we wish to make or invent Akan-like or Christian-like ethics, we would have to create the conditions conducive to the making of it. I have suggested that the adoption of wholesale capitalism in conditions of acute shortage of basic goods is unconducive to the invention or practice of or belief in Akan and Christian ethics. In consequence, I have recommended central planning only with respect to the necessities of life when supply is greatly inadequate.

I do not for a moment think that central planning (in whatever form) is sufficient for ensuring progress, development or that moral standards are high. I merely note its importance for poor countries. Hence the attack by the Friedmans, if intended to show that central planning does not ensure development, is at best uninteresting. Central planning—in the recommended form of rationing—which is tainted with corruption, would be tantamount to the practice of capitalism. In fact corrupt rationing would lead to "kalabuleism"; since it would replace the equitable system of rationing with inequities in supply to individuals which would permit those with more than what the rationing system would have permitted them to have to sell at whatever price to those who received less than their ration. The problem of "kalabule" and the solution to it are economic. Hence the prevailing African attempt to solve such problems by means of coup d'états and the consequent almost exclusive appeal to force, side-track the issue. To the extent that "moral revolutions" and "holy wars" rely on armed force rather than the reason (logic) of economic considerations associated with ideologies, to that extent would they be counterproductive in the attempt to revolutionize business ethics; especially if the "moral revolutionaries" and "holy warriors" are motivated by the belief that revolutionary ethics are discoverable on earth or in heaven, in our past or future.

References

Caincross, A., *Introduction to Economics*, 5th ed. (Butterworth & Co. Ltd., 1973).

Economic Survey 1978: Current Trends in the World Economy (UN, New York, 1980).

F.A.O., *Fighting World Hunger* (L 8403/E79 Rome).

Friedman, Milton and Rose Friedman, *Free to Choose* (Avon Books, New York, 1980).

Galbraith, J. K., *Economics, Peace and Laughter* (Penguin Books Ltd., Harmondsworth, 1971).

GCB, 1978, *Quarterly Economic Review* (Econ. Research Department of Ghana Commercial Bank, 1978).

GCB, 1981, *Quarterly Economic Review* (Research Department of Ghana Commercial Bank, 1980).

Luke, The Gospel according to, *The Holy Bible*, Revised Standard Version.

Mackie, J. L., *Ethics: Inventing Right and Wrong* (Penguin Books, Harmondsworth, 1977).

Macpherson, C. B., *Democratic Theory* (Oxford Univ. Press, 1973).

Samuelson, Paul, *Economics* (McGraw-Hill Inc., New York, 1976).

Singer, Peter, "Morality, Famine and Affluence," in *Philosophy and Public Affairs* (1973).

World Bank, *World Development Report* (IBRD Washington D.C., 1980).

World Economic Survey 1978: Current Trends in the World Economy (UN, New York, 1980).

Notes

[1] Also called "reasonable prices" in some parts of Africa.
[2] Pronounced as "kaela-'buli" as in "Cala-bully."

[3] Read as "Two Cedis" (Ghanaian currency).

The Powerful and the Powerless

Jim Wallis

Agenda for Biblical People (New York: Harper & Row, 1976), 60–72.

The Church's Identity with the Poor

Issues of wealth, poverty, and economic justice are central in the Bible. The sheer bulk of the biblical teaching about the rich and the poor is overwhelming. The Old Testament is filled with it. Jesus talks more about it than almost any other single issue. The apostles regard the relationship to money and the poor as a primary test of obedience to God. The people of God, in both the Old and New Testaments, are seen as offering an *economic alternative* to the prevailing assumptions of the world that surrounds them.

Contrary to the dominant attitude of our own society, one's economic life and standard of living is not a private matter. It is a critical issue of faith and discipleship. Not only is the Bible's teaching on the rich and the poor striking in its quantity, it is uncomfortably plain and clear in its meaning. The Scriptures are not neutral on questions of economics. The God of the Bible is clearly and emphatically on the side of the poor and the exploited.

Throughout Scripture we find an insistence that a vital relationship to God will evidence itself in an active serving of social and political justice as witness to God's gift of life. The prophets warned that piety, proper religion, and ritual observance are inadequate. They demanded economic and political justice. Isaiah tells us that the fast in which God delights involves breaking the yoke of oppression, sharing our bread with the hungry, and bringing the homeless poor into our homes (58:5–7). Amos claims that worship and praise are not acceptable to God unless justice rolls down like waters and righteousness like an ever-flowing stream (5:21–24).

The coming of Jesus, as we have noted, brings social revolution. The downtrodden were objects of Christ's compassion. When questioned if he was the "one to come" from God, Jesus offered proof of his messiahship by his ministry to the concrete needs of the suffering and afflicted (Matt. 11:5). Later on, Jesus warns those who would call his name that they will be judged by how they respond to the hungry, the poor, the naked, the imprisoned, the sick, and the stranger. The parable of the Good Samaritan demonstrates that our responsibility for our neighbor extends to anyone in need and leaps over the human barriers of race and class at personal cost of time, money, and danger. The apostles repeatedly claim that faith without works that demonstrate obedience is dead, that the quality of our love for God is shown in our practical and sacrificial love for our brothers and sisters.

Nowhere in Scripture are the rights of the rich proclaimed; nowhere is God seen as the Savior and defender of the rich and their wealth; nowhere are the poor exhorted to serve the needs of the rich and be poor for the sake of the wealthy. Throughout Scripture, however, the rights of the poor are proclaimed; God is revealed as their Savior, deliverer, and avenger; and the rich are instructed to serve the poor and relinquish their wealth and power for the sake of the poor. Nowhere in Scripture is wealth praised or admired or the rich upheld and exalted over the poor. In many places in the Bible, however, the poor are blessed and uplifted, and the message of God's Word carries with it the hope of justice and liberation for the poor. Riches are seen in the Bible as, at best, a great spiritual danger and, most often, as a sign of sinful disobedience to God. Just because the rich are rich, it will be harder for them to enter into the kingdom than for a camel to pass through the eye of a needle. The gospel is preached to the poor, and the rich are told to sell what they have and give to the poor for the sake of the kingdom.

The Bible makes clear that money and possessions are deeply spiritual concerns at the core of human experience and, perhaps, reveal more about an individual than any other aspect of a person's life. The danger of riches in the Old Testament is in the misuse of wealth and power in the oppression and exploitation of the poor. The earth and its fullness belong only to God and are given for the life and development of all God's children. The Jewish tradition of Jubilee Year provided for a periodic redistribution of land and wealth that militated against the accumulation of riches. In the thunderings of the prophets, God was powerfully revealed as the God of the poor and dispossessed, pouring out his wrath upon the rich and powerful whose affluence crushed the poor and powerless.

In the New Testament, the teaching on wealth is intensified, and its possession is seen as a great spiritual danger. The possession of wealth twists and distorts people's priorities and values and is a crucial obstacle in their sensitivity to God. The New Testament condemns, not just improper attitudes toward wealth, but also the mere possession of undistributed wealth.

One of the very first tests of discipleship to Jesus Christ is a radical change in one's relationship to money and the possession of wealth. The demands of mammon are completely irreconcilable with a total commitment to God. Jesus says, "You cannot serve God and mammon." Notice that he does not suggest that you should not; he simply says that you cannot. He assumes that the will of God and the demands of mammon directly contradict each other, and loyalty must be given to one or to the other.

If Jesus was so concerned about the danger of money and possessions in a simple agrarian society, how much more do we, living in the most affluent nation the world has ever known, need to break radically with the power and authority of money and possessions in our lives. An affluent church witnesses to its radical dependence upon wealth, not upon God, and has almost nothing to say to the dispossessed majority of the globe.

We need to hear again the words of the New Testament applied with their full force to us.

> Woe to you that are rich, for you have received your consolation. Woe to you that are full now, for you shall hunger.
>
> (Luke 6:24–25)

> So therefore, whoever of you does not renounce all that he has cannot be my disciple.
>
> (Luke 14:33)

> Do not lay up for yourselves treasures on earth, . . . but lay up for yourselves treasures in heaven. . . . For where your treasure is, there will your heart be also.
>
> (Matt. 6:19–21)

> No one can serve two masters. . . . You cannot serve God and mammon.
>
> (Matt. 6:24)

> Lord, when did we see thee hungry or thirsty or a stranger or naked or sick or in prison, and did not minister to thee? . . . Truly, I say to you, as you did it not to one of the least of these, you did it not to me.
>
> (Matt. 25:44, 45)

> Other seed fell among thorns and the thorns grew up and choked it, and it yielded no grain. . . . [T]hey are those who hear the word, but the cares of the world, and the delight in riches, and the desire for other things, enter in and choke the word, and it proves unfruitful.
>
> (Mark 4:7, 18–19)

> Take heed, and beware of all covetousness; for a man's life does not consist in the abundance of his possessions.
>
> (Luke 12:15)

I do not mean that others should be eased and you burdened, but that as a matter of equality your abundance at the present time should supply their want.

(2 Cor. 8:13–14)

Be sure of this, that no immoral or impure man, or one who is covetous (that is, an idolater), has any inheritance in the kingdom of Christ and of God. Let no one deceive you with empty words, for it is because of these things that the wrath of God comes upon the sons of disobedience.

(Eph. 5:5, 6)

If we have food and clothing, with these we shall be content. But those who desire to be rich fall into temptation, into a snare, into many senseless and hurtful desires that plunge men into ruin and destruction. For the love of money is the root of all evils.

(1 Tim. 6:8–10)

What does it profit, my brethren, if a man says he has faith but has not works? Can his faith save him? If a brother or sister is ill-clad and in lack of daily food, and one of you says to them, "Go in peace, be warmed and filled," without giving them the things needed for the body, what does it profit? So faith by itself, if it has no works, is dead.

(James 2:14–17)

It is well to remember that the mark of sacrificial giving in the New Testament is not in how much is given but, rather, in how much is left over after the giving is finished (Luke 21:1–4). We cannot give sacrificially and still remain wealthy. It is critical that we constantly heed the biblical warning against minimizing the cost of a visible, outward break with the power of money and possessions. An affluent church cannot say, "Gold and silver have I none," and neither can it say, "In the name of Jesus of Nazareth, walk!"

The church is the body of Christ. This dramatic biblical metaphor speaks of the powerful way the work of Christ has united us to him and to each other. It means that Christ is alive and present in the community and is head over the body. It means that the church is called to embody the presence of Christ in the world by obeying his words, reflecting his mind, and continuing his mission in the world by following the manner and style of his life, death, and resurrection. Jesus tells us that he came into the world not to be served but to serve, and so it is with us. Our vocation is to serve men and women in his name. We are called, not to be conquerors, but to be a self-giving body whose leader was crucified on a cross and asks his followers to take up that same cross. We are called, not to accumulate wealth and influence or to strive to manipulate power, but to empty ourselves as he did for the sake of others.

The mark of sacrificial giving in the New Testament is not in how much is given but, rather, in how much is left over after the giving is finished.

We are called to give a cup of cold water in his name, which will mean feeding the hungry, meeting the needs of the homeless and the refugees, supporting the imprisoned, befriending the lonely, standing with the poor and the outcasts, loving the unloved. This means confronting with our lives the institutional and root causes of the condition of the oppressed. The life that Christ gives is meant to be spread about and not hoarded and shut up for the private edification of the believers. The compassion of Christ always resulted in action, and so must ours. John, the apostle, exhorts us:

By this we know love, that he laid down his life for us; and we ought to lay down our lives for the brethren. But if any one has the world's goods and sees his brother in need, yet closes his heart against him, how does God's love abide in him? Little children, let us not love in word or speech but in deed and in truth.

By this we shall know that we are of the truth, and reassure our hearts before him.

(1 John 3:16–19)

The cross of Christ is both the symbol of our atonement and the pattern for our discipleship. Today many who name the name of Christ have removed themselves from human hurt and suffering to places of relative comfort and safety. Many have sought to protect themselves and their families from the poor masses for whom Christ showed primary concern. In affluent societies, our approach to social problems is to decrease their visibility. The migration patterns of Christians and their churches have again reflected the dominant social practice. The church's compassionless inactivity stems from being faithful to the biblical mandates. How can we open our hearts and lives to those whom we have hardly ever seen, let alone ever known?

The biblical idea of love carries with it the deliberate extension of ourselves to others. The incarnation, the supreme act of Gods' love, required the intentional plunge of the Lord of Glory into the chaotic, violent, and rebellious human situation at tremendous cost (Phil. 2: 6–11). But this act brought the salvation of the world. We cannot profess the name of Jesus without seeking to incarnate his pattern of self-emptying love and servanthood. Again, this is not only an individual effort but a corporate one undertaken by a body of people who have given themselves over to Christ and his kingdom, to each other, and to serving in the midst of the broken world for which he died.

God entered the human situation as one of the poor and powerless. Thomas Merton speaks of the meaning of the incarnation:

> Into this world, this demented inn, in which there is absolutely no room for Him at all, Christ has come uninvited. But because He cannot be at home in it, because He is out of place in it, His place is with those others for whom there is no room. His place is with those who do not belong, who are rejected by power because they are regarded as weak, those who are discredited, who are denied the status of persons, who are tortured, bombed, and exterminated. With those for whom there is no room, Christ is present in

the world. He is mysteriously present in those for whom there seems to be nothing but the world at its worse. . . . It is in these that He hides Himself, for whom there is no room. (*Raids on the Unspeakable*, quoted in *The Catholic Worker*, December 1973)

The gospel knows nothing of what sociologists call "upward mobility." In fact, the gospel of Jesus Christ calls us to the reverse; the gospel calls us to a downward pilgrimage. Former attachments and securities in the false values of wealth and power are left behind as we are empowered by the Holy Spirit to seek first the kingdom. From an obscure birth in a dirty animal stable to the crucifixion of a poor suffering servant who never had a place to lay his head, the gospel witnesses to God's identification with the poor and powerless. Such a life of identification will bring rejection from the world, and if one becomes too prominent, one might even be crucified. We may measure our obedience to the gospel by the degree of tension and conflict with the world that is present in our lives. If our lives are secure, comfortable, and at home with wealth and power, we belong to the world rather than to Christ.

Our downward pilgrimage will drive us to community and is meant to take place in the context of a common shared life. The life of the early Christian fellowships, as seen in the Book of Acts and elsewhere in Scripture, presents the Christian life as a common life, the life of a people more than the life of individuals. Here were the ones who had known Jesus, had walked with him, talked with him, listened to him, and lived with him for three years. They had seen him live and die and rise again from the dead. They were eyewitnesses to the gospel. They had both followed him and forsaken him. He had set their feet upon a new path, and they gathered in an upper room to wait for the promised coming of the Spirit.

At the day of Pentecost, they were all in one place, waiting, when suddenly there came a sound like "a strong driving wind" and "they were all filled with the Holy Spirit." The consequence of the outpouring of the Spirit was a bold and mighty proclamation of the gospel, repentance on the part of many who saw and heard, and the establishment of a *common life* among the believers.

> And they devoted themselves to the apostles' teaching and fellowship, to the breaking of bread and the prayers.

> And fear came upon every soul; and many wonders and signs were done through the apostles. And all who believed were together and had all things in common; and they sold their possessions and goods and distributed them to all, as any had need. And day by day, attending the temple together and breaking bread in their homes, they partook of food with glad and generous hearts, praising God and having favor with all the people. And the Lord added to their number day by day those who were being saved.
>
> (Acts 2:42–47)

The coming of the Spirit resulted in a common life springing up among the early believers.

> Now the company of those who believed were of one heart and soul, and no one said that any of the things which he possessed was his own, but they had everything in common. And with great power the apostles gave their testimony to the resurrection of the Lord Jesus, and great grace was upon them all. There was not a needy person among them, for as many as were possessors of lands or houses sold them, and brought the proceeds of what was sold and laid it at the apostles' feet; and distribution was made to each as any had need.
>
> (Acts 4:32–35)

The holding of "all things in common" was not merely a futile experiment, nor did this practice end at Jerusalem. Rather, the common life and sharing are shown throughout the New Testament and became the distinguishing mark of the early church. This shared common life contradicts the ordinary social value that the possession of money and property carries the inalienable right to use and dispose of those assets for one's own benefit. The doctrine of private property as the right to use all of one's material and other resources for one's

own purposes is a ruling social axiom. However, this most basic economic assumption is decidedly not Christian. Rather, the descriptions of the Christian fellowships in Acts and elsewhere point to a common use and consumption of resources, assets, and gifts of the body. The key here is the common use according to need rather than a particular form or legal status of common ownership.

The Spirit had shattered the normal assumptions of the economic order, and the early believers realized that the way of Christ militated against the private use and disposition of resources and led to the sharing of all resources as needs arose in the community. Material resources, no less than spiritual gifts, were to be shared and freely given for the good of the body and not for the personal gain and advantage of the one who possessed them. A whole new system of distribution had been created in God's new community with each person in a process of giving and receiving according to ability and need.

The common life and sharing are shown throughout the New Testament and became the distinguishing mark of the early church.

The self-giving of the church, as the history of the early church testifies, happens within the body and also spreads out to any and all who are poor and in need. The people of God will always and everywhere follow the will of their God and the example of their Lord in serving the poor of the earth. In its life as a servant people, the church is guided by the Holy Spirit and energized by the love of Christ that has transformed our lives. Jesus Christ is the leader of the new community. In John 17, he prays for the new community.

> But now I am coming to thee; and these things I speak in the world, that they may have my joy fulfilled in themselves. I have given them thy word; and the world has hated them because they are not of the world, even as I am not of the world. I do not pray that thou shouldst take them out

of the world, but that thou shouldst keep them from the evil one. They are not of the world, even as I am not of the world. Sanctify them in the truth; thy word is truth. As thou did send me into the world, so I have sent them into the world. And for their sake, I consecrate myself, that they may also be consecrated in truth. I do not pray for these only, but also for those who are to believe in me through their word, that they may all be one; even as thou, Father, art in me, and I in thee, that they also may be in us, so that the world may believe that thou hast sent me.

(John 17:13–21)

The Entrepreneurial Vocation

Fr. Robert Sirico

Unpublished paper of the Acton Institute for the Study of Religion and Liberty. Copyright © 1996 Fr. Robert Sirico.

I. The Entrepreneurial Vocation

One may say, without fear of contradiction, that prejudice against minorities is unpopular in modern society. And with good reason: the idea that people are judged merely by the group that they happen to belong to, without any regard for their person and individual qualities, is properly odious to anyone with moral sensibilities.

Yet despite this laudable attitude prevalent throughout the popular culture, there remains one minority group upon which an unofficial open-season has been declared: the entrepreneur! One sees evidence of this prejudice everywhere about us, and one need only look at the popular culture's means of communications to see the prejudice made abundantly clear. Consider the books (say of Dickens or Sinclair Lewis), television programs (like *Dallas* or *Dynasty*), films (*China Syndrome, Wall Street,* or even some versions of *A Christmas Carol*), cartoons strips (like "Doonesbury") and even sermons that you've heard in which the business person is depicted. Meditate on the image that is being projected.[1] Does even one positive image emerge?

Even when opinion makers, especially moral leaders, are not occupied with denouncing the "rapacious appetite" and "obscene and conspicuous consumption" of these capitalists, the best one comes to expect of them is that they might tolerate business merely as a necessary evil which is in need of a broad and complicated network of controls in order to force it to serve human needs. And this is, all too often, the attitude of even capitalism's friends! In this presentation I hope to offer a differing point of view.

> *It is as though business people and those who work for the church employ two different models in their day-to-day operations—and indeed they do.*

My particular concern here is the prevalent bias against capitalism among religious leaders.

Why the negative attitude of entrepreneurs on the part of religious leaders? Not very long ago an article of mine was published in the *Wall Street Journal* in which I criticized the anti-free market sentiments of the Sandinista regime in Nicaragua. I pointed to this bias as the primary reason that the nation was suffering from heart-rending poverty. A very curious thing began to happen the next day. I began to receive phone calls from people all throughout the U.S. The strange thing about this series of phone callers was the similar profile they shared. After some perfunctory remarks about Nicaragua, I found that most of these callers really weren't interested in talking about Latin America at all. Each was a relatively successful business person; each had deep moral and religious convictions; and each of them was utterly astounded that a Catholic priest would explicitly defend the free market as a morally preferable system.

These people represented a variety of Christian traditions and told me that they each felt disenfranchised and alienated from their churches. I recall one man in particular, who described himself as a conservative Catholic, saying that he no longer attended Mass because he refused to sit and be condemned from the pulpit for his business skills.

A recent book by former Ambassador Michael Novak tells of his experience at a conference on economics where a group of Latin American priests were participants. The conference went for several days during which time cogent and fact filled arguments were presented demonstrating the ways in which a free economy can lift the poor from poverty by the production of wealth. The priests said nothing until the final day of the conference. Mr. Novak recounts the experience: "At the last session of what had been a happy seminar, one of the priests arose to say that his colleagues had assembled the night before and asked him to make a statement on their behalf. . . ." "We have," he said, "greatly enjoyed this week. We have learned a great deal. We see very well that capitalism is the most effective means of producing wealth, and even that it distributes wealth more broadly and more evenly than the economic systems we see in Latin America. But we still think that Capitalism is an immoral system."[2]

My guess is that many of you sitting here have heard similar things in your congregations. Why does this state of affairs exist? Why is it that the very best you business people get to hear from a religious leader so often is, "Well, the way to redeem yourself is to give us your money"? Why does there appear to be such ignorance on the part of clergy and religious leaders about the realities of the market and how it operates, and its moral basis?

One very obvious reason is the sheer lack of any course in virtually all the seminaries I am acquainted with, in economics. This, of course, has not deterred religious leaders from pronouncing on economic matters.

In addition to this intellectual gap, there is a practical gap. There seems to be such a gap between religious leaders and business people in their understanding of market operations because the two groups tend to operate out of two very different worlds and proceed from two very different sets of assumptions. It is as though business people and those who work for the church employ two different models in their day-to-day operations—and indeed they do.

It will help to bridge this gap by proving the religious model and the business model briefly. Simply put, people who work in the church operate from a distributivist economic model. By this I mean that on Sunday morning a collection basket is passed. On Monday the bills are paid, acts of charity are attended to, etc. If Sunday collections come up short on a regular basis, making it difficult to pay the bills, most preachers begin to turn up the screws a notch or two and lay on another layer of guilt. Thus, in the minds of many clergy, the economic world they see is like a pie that is in need of being divided up. They view the world of money as static, so in order for one to obtain a larger piece of that pie, it will be necessary for someone else to get a somewhat smaller piece.

Now the business person operates from a very different model. The entrepreneur talks of *making* money, not collecting it. In other words, for the business person, who must consider the needs, wants and desires of the consumer, the way to get money is to offer something of value. The world of money for these people is dynamic. It is this process, which we call the free market that is responsible for the "wealth of nations," a phrase associated in the popular mind with the title of Adam Smith's classic book, but which was first employed in the Book of Isaiah (60:5).

Let me be clear that I am not advocating that religion adopt a bottom line mentality with regard to its mission. There are some matters which simply do not fit within an economic calculus and which cannot be evaluated in terms of "dollar and cents." What I am saying, however, is that before religious leaders choose to pronounce on economic matters, they do well to become informed.

Another factor that plays into the hostility one frequently encounters regarding capitalism in religious circles comes from a noble, if mistaken, source. Many religious leaders spend a great deal of their lives confronting the wretchedness of poverty in close proximity. Anyone here who has traveled in Third World countries knows the cry of the human heart that yells "Stop!" when confronted with such human misery. Unnecessary poverty angers us, and we want to put an end to it. This sentiment is an exactly proper Christian sentiment.

The problem results when this sentiment is combined with the economic ignorance I described previously. When this happens the cry against poverty is easily converted into a rage against wealth, which, while understandable, is ill-informed and even deadly. It is deadly because it fails to see that the amelioration of poverty can only be achieved by the production of wealth. It is deadly because is seeks to kill the goose that will lay the golden egg; indeed, it will kill the goose that will hatch other golden-egg-laying geese!

II. Toward a Positive View of Entrepreneurial Activity

As the lady in the musical once said, let's begin at the very beginning, which is a very good place to start. And, I don't mean our Do Re Mes, I mean the book of Genesis and the creation of the world.

A. The Creation

I am sure that you all know the dramatic account of God making the heavens and the earth, the ocean and the dry land, the stars of the heavens, all of the creeping things of the earth, and finally the apex of his creation: Man and Woman. Do you recall God's reaction after each act of creation? Over six times on the first page of Scripture one refrain is repeated over and over again: "God saw that it was good."

This view of the created order, specifically the goodness of the material world that God made, has not been accepted without controversy, even within the Christian tradition. When we look back into the first centuries of Christianity we see that a movement developed which regarded that material world as fundamentally evil, created by a demi-god. This movement was known as Gnosticism, and the Gnostic impulse has surfaced and resurfaced under many guises throughout Christian history.

B. The Incarnation

Of course, no orthodox Christian can be agnostic, if for no other reason than the fact of the Incarnation of Christ. The Incarnation is the breaking into human history of the Divine. We Christians believe that it is through the Incarnation that God has elected to reconcile the world to Himself.

The implications of this are astounding, and throughout history, believers have been uncomfortable with them. In the fourth century the Arians believed that Jesus was certainly man; so much did they believe that Jesus was man that they could not bring themselves to believe that he was God; in the second century the Docetists believed that Jesus was divine; so much did they believe Jesus was divine that they couldn't bring themselves to believe that he was really man.

In the face of these two errors, what Scripture scholar Raymond Brown calls "the Great Church," pronounced that Jesus was *both* God and man, thus showing that the Incarnation radically accomplishes the creation, enabling the creation to discover its meaning. Jesus is true God and true man; authentic anthropology, then, is Christology; for, to use the words of the Second Vatican Council and the present Pope, it is "Christ the Redeemer" who "fully reveals man to himself."[3]

C. Two Approaches

I have taken us on this rather technical theological excursion because, in a real sense, it is the fundamental goodness of this material dimension of human existence that is at the root of the conflict over the morality of capitalism, the free market and what I call, the entrepreneurial vocation. There are two potential mistakes that can develop with regard to the proper relation of the human person to the material world. Both stem from the Gnostic-inspired view that sees the material world as evil and unrelated to spirituality.

The first view reasons that because all matter is evil, its possession and use is likewise evil. Throughout the centuries this tendency has recurred in various forms; from radical proponents of apostolic poverty like the Spiritual Franciscans of the middle ages to the Marxist inspired Liberation Theologians of today. For these, poverty is the only way to spirituality (unlike other orders that take a vow of poverty who say only that God is calling *them* to poverty, not everyone). The implication here is that wealth is axiomatically sinful, and that the wealthy must be relieved of their money in order to be absolved from their sin.

A second branch from the same root takes an opposite twist. This is seen in what are called the "Prosperity Gospel" people. They say that wealth is a sign of God's blessing, and that poverty is a result of sin. An appreciation of the balanced view of man's relation to the material world held by the majority of Christians throughout the ages can offer a corrective to such imbalances.

D. The Uniqueness of Human Nature

An entrepreneur is a kind of *impressairo*, one who organizes numerous factors, and brings things into connection so as to produce. It is this creative aspect of the entrepreneur that is so akin to God's creative activity as we read it in the book of Genesis. In this sense, I would argue, the entrepreneur participates in that call to productivity that God

gives to the whole human race. It is a distinct call, this entrepreneurial vocation, to be sure, like that of being a parent. But if it is not quite as sublime as, say, Motherhood, the keenness of insight required of the entrepreneur remains sacred.

In order to carry out this creative enterprise, the entrepreneur must have access to the material factors of production; he must be permitted to acquire and trade property. Santayana once said, "to be is to be something in particular," and it is with this focus that we can explore what it is about humans that justifies their having rights, specifically the right to private property. One thing that the human person is "in particular" is a concrete body which puts the human person into some kind of relation with the material order, as noted above. Observe how humans are related to the material way uniquely different than are animals. Animals are bound to things by instinct; humans are related to things by reason, and this is the other thing that humans are in particular: We are self-reflecting, thinking beings who survive by the use of our reason. The mind is the predominant element which makes humans distinctly human. (The fact that some humans have a diminished capacity to reason in no way changes the fact that human nature has this rational component.) Thus, we are generically and essentially distinct from the animal which cannot reason.

The rational relationship between the human person and nature is what gives rise to property. It is our capacity to reason, our rational faculty, which causes us to relate to the material order in a way that is more than immediate and temporary: our relation to the material is, rather, general and permanent. Stability and permanency are the expression in time of the universality of the relationship of humans to things. Nor is ours merely a relationship of consumption, but possession and production.

Property is the foundation and context of this relationship. By the relationship of the human person to nature, we leave the imprint of our individuality upon nature by means of the time, effort, and ability we extend which in turn produces wealth and property. Wealth and property do not exist in a state of nature, where Hobbes said, "life is brutish, mean, nasty and short; red in claw and tooth." They come into existence only when people place value on things. This is seen in that black, sticky, smelly, unpleasant substance that was mostly an annoyance until a way was found to process and refine it in such a way that petroleum was produced.

When seen in this light, property rights are really an expression and a safeguard to personal rights. The defense of the right to property, then, ought not be seen as the defense of detached material objects in themselves, but of the dignity, liberty and very nature of the human person who, to allude to John Locke, has mixed his labor with nature to produce property. The right to property, then, is an extension and exercise of human rights.

Perhaps the greatest economist of this century, Lugwig von Mises, drew the connection between economic and personal liberty very clearly when he said, "Choosing determines all human decisions. In making his choice man chooses not only between various material things and services. All human values are offered for option."

Another writer put it this way: "Choice is fundamental to economics because it is fundamental to the moral nature of man. It is crucial to recall that before becoming what some have called "the first economist," Adam Smith was a moral philosopher. Although he authored the famous *Wealth of Nations*, which I mentioned earlier, few people realize that its companion work is entitled *Theory of Moral Sentiments*.

III. The Sanctity of the Entrepreneurial Vocation

The total dynamism of the Christian life of necessity encompasses the material order— including the world of business and finance—by virtue of the Creation and the Incarnation, as outlined above. There are two popular but mistaken views of the role of the laity in the Christian vocation of the apostolate. One view implies that if you can't be a full-time minister or priest you have to settle for second best; the second view says that if you can't be a full-time minister or priest your call is to pay the bills, which your business will enable you to do.

I remember when I was a seminarian assigned to work one summer in Austin, Texas I met a lady who asked why I wanted to become a priest (never an easy question to answer). As we drove along the freeway with the top down she appeared to be in a nostalgic mood and said, "My husband had a vocation once, and then he met me."

This view seems to assume that lay people don't really have vocations, but that they do the best they can under the circumstances. Or, if they do have vocations, this view tends to think that it is less than, and inferior to that of the full-time missionary.

A second view that firmly believes that business people have a defined and God-appointed vocation, I believe is equally problematic. Simply put, this view sees the task of the business person as paying the bills that the clergy run up. These views are superficial, as are my descriptions of them, yet they both have some truth to them, even while they essentially lack depth.

Of course the vocation of the business person is different than that of the ordained ministers, in much the same way that the vocation of being a mother is distinct from being a father. Likewise, it *is* the responsibility of lay people to make possible the practical dimensions of the apostolate, even as it is the responsibility for the clergy to do the same. The manner in which each fulfills that vocation will depend upon the concrete circumstances of the individuals involved.

To hear some people speak you would get the impression that the vocation of the entrepreneur is somehow prompted by the shortage of priests, or ministers, or missionaries, which would mean, of course, that if there were no shortage, the laity would have nothing to do with the Church's apostolate. I am reminded here of a conversation that my spiritual mentor Cardinal Newman had with Bishop Ullathorne over 100 years ago. The bishop is reported as having bemoaned, somewhat haughtily, "The laity, the laity. What are the laity?" To which Newman replied, "Without them, my lord, the hierarchy would look rather foolish."

You see, the vocation of the business person, the vocation of those who have the talent to produce wealth, to use their abilities to build the kingdom of God in conjunction with their leaders, is nothing new. The vocation of the laity, Yves Congar reminds us in his classic work *Lay People in the Church*, "existed from the beginning of the Church, and today it takes new forms, better adapted to the present era."[4] We must find new ways to present, Isaac Hecker (founder of the Paulist Fathers) once said, "Old truths in new forms"—ways to reproduce, consecrate and give new qualification to the apostolic already incumbent upon the faithful by virtue of the sacrament of initiation: Baptism and confirmation.

The challenge, then, is not so much to bring Christ with us into our work, but to discover his presence already there, precisely through the natural order that he created in the first instance, because, of course, God is no stranger to the world he made. The task of the lay person, the special challenge of the entrepreneur, is to allow grace to "build upon nature," as Aquinas tells us.

The task is less one of "Christianizing" as much as it is to "Christofinalize." We are called to bring our fullest potential to all that God has gifted us with. The great philosopher Etienne Gilson said it much better than I ever could. Permit me to quote him at length:

> If one wants to practice science for God's sake, the first condition is to practice it for its own sake, or as if for its own sake, because that it is the only way to learn it. . . . It is the same with an art: one must have it before one can put it to God's service. We are told that faith built the medieval cathedrals: no doubt, but faith would not have built anything had there been no architects and craftsmen. If it be true that the west front of Notre Dame is a raising of the soul to God, that does not prevent its being a geometrical composition as well: to build a front that will be an act of charity, one must first understand geometry. We . . . who acclaim the high worth of nature because it is God's work, should show our respect for it by taking as our first rule of action *that piety is never a substitute for technique;* for technique is that without which the most

fervent piety is powerless to make use of nature for God's sake. Nothing and nobody obliges a Christian to occupy himself with science, art or philosophy, for there is no lack of other ways of serving God; but *if he has chosen this way of serving him*, the end he puts before himself obliges him to excel; the very intention that guides him compels him to be a good scholar, a good philosopher, a good artist: it is the only way he can become a good servant.[5]

"By themselves brilliant ideas do not serve humankind; to be brought into service to man, they must be transformed through complex processes of design and production."

What does this call mean to those of you in the vocation of enterprise? It will mean that you must strive to be more fully what you are, to display more fully the virtue of inventiveness; to act more boldly with the virtue of creativity; to continue to be other-regarding as you anticipate market demands, as you develop in yourselves and school others in the virtue of thrift; not to merely share your wealth with those in need, but to tutor others, by your example and your mentorship, how to become independent and to produce wealth themselves.

Your entrepreneurial vocation will require of you that you continue to be watchful practitioners in the art of discovery, for by it you will create employment opportunities for those who would otherwise go without. In a reflection on the faith dimensions of the American economy, a group of leading lay people penned these lines: "By themselves brilliant ideas do not serve humankind; to be brought into service to man, they must be transformed through complex processes of design and production. The talent to perform this transformation is as rare and as humanly precious as talent in any other field."[6]

In the pursuit of your vocation you will be tempted in many ways. You may be tempted to give up and think that the sometimes mundane world of finances, business and materialism has no spiritual dimension or meaning. Or perhaps you will be tempted in the opposite direction: to think that all that matters is the bottom line, and that no other values can have any bearing.

In those moments, this priest prays that you will remember the Incarnation, and the cost that was paid by the Son of God in that freely chosen action to enter the material world and to sanctify it. In those moments, when you are buffeted, when you are judged and condemned, and when even those you'd hoped would offer understanding, guidance and support seek to intervene into your creative endeavor, I urge you to remember the Parable of the Talents and be refreshed.

Know that it is God who has entrusted you with His talents, and that he expects you to be industrious with them; to be productive with them; to be creative with them.

If you will be faithful to this sacred call, then He shall say to you, on that Great Day when all wrongs will be made right, what He said to those servants in Matthew's Gospel: "Well done, good and faithful servant; you have shown yourself faithful in small ways . . . come and join your master's happiness" (chapter 25).

Notes

[1]For a fuller description of how the businessman has been depicted in literature see Michael McTague, *The Businessman in Literature: Dante to Melville* (New York: Philosophical Library, 1979).

[2]Michael Novak, *This Hemisphere of Liberty* (Washington, D.C.: The AEI Press, 1990), 38.

[3]Vatican Council II: Pastoral Constitution on the Church in the Modern World *Guardium et Spes*, 22: AAS 58 (1966), 1042–43; as quoted by John Paul II in *Redemptor Hominis*, #10.

[4]Yves Congar, O. P., *Lay People in the Church* (Westminster, MD: Newman Press, 1965).

[5]Etienne Gilson, "L'Intelligence au service du Christ-Roi," in *Christianisme et Philosophie* (Paris, 1936), 155–56, cited in Congar, Op. Cit., 388.

[6]*Toward the Future—Catholic Social Thought and the U.S. Economy* (New York: American Catholic Committee, 1984), 28.

A Theology of the Corporation

Michael Novak

The Corporation: A Theological Inquiry (Washington, D.C.: American Enterprise Institute for Public Policy Research, 1981), 203–24. Copyright © 1981 American Enterprise Institute for Public Policy Research.

Our task is to set forth some steps toward a theology of the corporation. We need such a theology so that the ministers who serve businessmen and workers might be able to preach more illuminating and practical sermons and so that critics might have at their disposal a theologically sound standard of behavior for corporations. . . .

Theological Beginnings

In thinking about the corporation in history and its theological significance, I begin with a general theological principle. George Bernanos once put it this way: "Grace is everywhere."[1] Wherever we look in the world, there are signs of God's presence: in the mountains, in a grain of sand, in a human person, in the poor and the hungry. "The earth is charged with the grandeur of God." So is human history.

If we look for signs of grace in the corporation, we may discern seven of them—a suitably sacramental number.

1. Creativity

The Creator locked great riches in nature, riches to be discovered only gradually through human effort. John Locke observed that the yield of the most favored field in Britain could be increased a hundredfold if human ingenuity and human agricultural science were applied to its productivity.[2] Nature *alone* is not as fecund as nature *under intelligent cultivation*. The world, then, is immeasurably rich as it comes from the Creator, but only potentially so. This potential was hidden for thousands of years until human discovery began to release portions of it for human benefit. Yet even today we have not yet begun to imagine all the possibilities of wealth in the world the Creator designed. The limits of our present intelligence restrict the human race to the relative poverty in which it still lives.

During 1979 Atlantic Richfield ran an advertisement based on a theme first enunciated, as far as I can tell, by Father Hesburgh of Notre Dame; namely, that 40 percent of the world's energy is used by the 6 percent of the world's population residing in the United States.[3] This way of putting the facts is an example of the cultivation of guilt. A moment's thought shows that it is a preposterous formulation.

What the entire human race meant by energy until the discovery of the United States and the inventions promoted by its political economy were the natural forces of sun, wind, moving water, animals, and human muscle. Thomas Aquinas traveled on foot or by burro from Rome to Paris and back seven times in his life. The first pope to be able to make that voyage by train did so six centuries later, in the mid-nineteenth century. Until then, people traveled exactly as they had done since the time of Christ and before—by horse and carriage, by donkey, or by foot. History for a very long time seemed relatively static. The social order did not promote inventions and new technologies, at least to the degree lately reached. The *method* of scientific discovery had not been invented.

In 1809 an American outside Philadelphia figured out how to ignite anthracite coal. The ability to use anthracite, which burned hotter and more steadily than bituminous coal, made practical the seagoing steamship and the locomotive.

In 1859 the first oil well was dug outside Titusville, Pennsylvania. Oil was known in Biblical times but used only for products like perfume and ink. Arabia would have been as rich then as now, if anybody had known what to do with the black stuff.

The invention of the piston engine and the discovery of how to drill for oil were also achieved in the United States. The first electric light bulb was illuminated in 1879 in Edison, New Jersey.

After World War II the U.S. government dragooned the utilities into experimenting with nuclear energy. They knew nothing about it. They did not need it; they did not want it. Oil and coal were cheap. The government, however, promoted the peaceful uses of the atom.

Thus 100 percent of what the modern world means by energy was invented by 6 percent of the world's population. More than 60 percent of that energy had been distributed to the rest of the world. Though the United States can, of course, do better than that, we need not feel guilty for inventing forms of energy as useful to the human race as the fire brought to earth by Prometheus.

The agency through which inventions and discoveries are made productive for the human race is the corporation. Its creativity makes available to mass markets the riches long hidden in creation. Its creativity mirrors God's. That is the standard by which its deeds and misdeeds are properly judged.

2. Liberty

The corporation mirrors God's presence also in its liberty, by which I mean independence from the state. That independence was the greatest achievement of the much-despised but creative 6 percent of the world's population. Advancing the works of their forebears, they invented the concept and framed the laws that for the first time in history set boundaries on the state, ruling certain activities off-limits to its interference. Rights of person and home, free speech in public, a free press, and other liberties came to be protected both by constitutional law and by powerful interests actively empowered to defend themselves under that law. Legal autonomy was such that even the king could not forcibly enter the home of a peasant; a peasant's home was as protected as a duke's castle—rights which the colonists in America demanded for themselves. Private business corporations were permitted to become agents of experimentation, of trial and error, and for good reason: to unleash economic activism. The state

retained rights and obligations of regulation, and undertook the indirect promotion of industry and commerce. The state alone was prohibited from becoming the sole economic agent. A sphere of economic liberty was created.

The purpose of this liberty was to unlock greater riches than the world had ever known. Liberty was to be an experiment, for which Adam Smith and others argued, that might (or might not) prove to be in accordance with nature and with the laws of human society. Pleading for room to experiment, their practical, empirical arguments flew in the face of entrenched ideological opposition. The case for liberty prevailed.

The foundational concept of democratic capitalism, then, is not, as Marx thought, private property. It is limited government. Private property, of course, is one limitation on government.[4] What is interesting about private property is not that *I* own something, that *I* possess; its heart is not "possessive individualism," in C. B. Macpherson's phrase.[5] Quite the opposite. The key is that the *state* is limited by being forbidden to control all rights and all goods. It cannot infringe on the privacy of one's home or on one's right to the fruit of one's labors and risks. Herbert Stein has a useful definition of capitalism: "The idea of a capitalist system has nothing to do with capital and has everything to do with freedom. I think of capitalism as a system in which ability to obtain and use income independently of other persons or organizations, including government, is widely distributed among the individuals of the population."[6]

This is the distinctively American way of thinking about private property. In this framework, property is important less for its material reality than for the legal rights its ownership and use represent and for the limits it imposes on the power of the state. Such liberty was indispensable if private business corporations were to come into existence. Such corporations give liberty economic substance over and against the state.

3. Birth and Mortality

In coming into being with a technological breakthrough, and then perishing when some new technology causes it to be replaced, a typical corporation mirrors the cycle of birth and mortality. New corporations arise every day; dead ones litter history. Examining the *Fortune* 500 at ten-year intervals shows that even large corporations are subject to the cycle: new ones keep appearing and many that were once prominent disappear. Of the original *Fortune* 500, first listed in 1954, only 285 remained in 1974. Of the missing 215, 159 had merged, 50 had become too small to be listed or had gone out of business, and 6 were reclassified or had unavailable data.[7] Recently, Chrysler has been number 10. Will it by 1990 be gone from the list? Will Ford be gone from the list? It is entirely possible. As products of human liberty, corporations rise and fall, live and die. One does not have in them a lasting home—or even an immortal enemy.

4. Social Motive

Corporations, as the very word suggests, are not individualistic in their conception, in their operations, or in their purposes. Adam Smith entitled his book *An Inquiry into the Nature and Causes of the Wealth of Nations*. Its social scope went beyond individuals and beyond Great Britain to include all nations. The fundamental intention of the system from the beginning has been the wealth of all humanity.

The invention of democratic capitalism, the invention of the corporation, and the liberation of the corporations from total control by state bureaucracies (although some control always, and properly, remains) was *intended* to be multinational. Smith foresaw an interdependent world, for the first time able to overcome immemorial famine, poverty, and misery. He imagined people of every race, every culture, and every religion adopting the new knowledge about the causes of wealth. One does not need to be Christian or Jewish, or to share the Judeo-Christian worldview, to understand the religious and economic potency of the free economy. Smith did not exactly foresee Toyota and Sony. But he certainly would have been delighted to add a chapter to his immense study showing how the Japanese demonstrated the truth of his hypothesis.

5. Social Character

The corporation is inherently and in its essence corporate. The very word suggests communal, nonindividual, many acting together. Those who describe capitalism by stressing the individual entrepreneur miss the central point. Buying and selling by individual entrepreneurs occurred in Biblical times. What is interesting and novel—at least what struck Max Weber as interesting and novel—is the communal focus of the new ethos: the rise of communal risk taking, the pooling of resources, the sense of communal religious vocation in economic activism. To be sure, certain developments in law and in techniques of accounting had to occur before corporations could be institutionalized in their modern form. In this sense, too, they are social creations.

Corporations depend on the emergence of an infrastructure in intellectual life that makes possible new forms of communal collaboration. They depend on ideas that are powerful and clear enough to organize thousands of persons around common tasks. Moreover, these ideas must be strong enough to endure for years, so that individuals who commit themselves to them can expect to spend thirty to forty years working out their vocation. For many millions of religious persons the daily milieu in which they work out their salvation is the communal, corporate world of the workplace. For many, the workplace is a kind of second family. Even those who hate their work often like their co-workers. This is often true in factories; it is also true in offices. Comradeship is natural to humans. Labor unions properly build on it.

6. Insight

The primary capital of any corporation is insight, invention, finding a better way. Insight is of many kinds and plays many roles: it is central to invention; it lies at the heart of organization; it is the vital force in strategies for innovation, production, and marketing. Corporate management works hard at communal insight. Constantly, teams of persons meet to brainstorm and work out common strategies. Insight is the chief resource of any corporation, and there cannot be too much of it. Its scarcity is called stupidity.

Karl Marx erred in thinking that capital has to do primarily with machinery, money, and other tangible instruments of production. He overlooked the extent to which the primary form of capital is an idea.[8] The right to patent industrial ideas is an extremely important constitutional liberty. It is indispensable to the life of corporations, as indispensable as the copyright is to writers. Money without ideas is not yet capital. Machinery is only as good as the idea it embodies. The very word "capital," from the Latin *caput*, "head," points to the human spirit as the primary form of wealth. The miser sitting on this gold is not a capitalist. The investor with an idea is a capitalist. Insight makes the difference. . . .

7. The Risk of Liberty and Election

A corporation faces liberty and election; it is part of its romance to do so. Tremendous mistakes in strategy can cripple even the largest companies. Easy Washing Machines of Syracuse once made an excellent washing machine, but Maytag's discovery of a new technology took away part of Easy's market. Easy had all its assets sunk in a plant that it could not redo quickly enough to incorporate the new technology, and the company collapsed. Thus a sudden technological breakthrough, even a relatively minor one, can cripple a company or an industry. A simple strategic mistake by a team of corporate executives about where to apply the company's energies over a year or two can end up dimming the company's outlook for many years. A failure to modernize can bring about bankruptcy. The corporation operates in a world of no scientific certainty, in which corporate leaders must constantly make judgments about reality when not all evidence about reality is in. Such leaders argue among themselves about strategic alternatives, each perhaps saying to himself, "We will see who is right about this," or "The next year or two will tell." But a judgment must be made and the investment committed *before* the telling is completed. Thus decision makers often experience the risks inherent in their decisions. At the very least they always face the risk of doing con-

siderably less well than they think they are going to do.

In these seven ways, corporations offer metaphors for grace, a kind of insight into God's ways in history. Yet corporations are of this world. They sin. They are *semper reformanda*—always in need of reform. . . .

Three Systems—Three Fields of Responsibility

The most original *social* invention of democratic capitalism, in sum, is the private corporation founded for economic purposes. The *motivation* for this invention was also *social*: to increase "the wealth of nations," to generate (for the first time in human history) sustained economic development. This effect was, in fact, achieved. However, the corporation—as a type of voluntary association—is not merely an economic institution. It is also a moral institution and a political institution. It depends upon and generates new political forms. In two short centuries, it has brought about an immense social revolution. It has moved the center of economic activity from the land to industry and commerce. No revolution is without social costs and sufferings, which must be entered on the ledger against benefits won. Universally, however, the idea of economic development has now captured the imagination of the human race. This new possibility of development has awakened the world from its economic slumbers.

Beyond its economic effects, the corporation changes the ethos and the cultural forms of society. To some extent, it has undercut ancient ways of human relating, with some good effects and some bad. After the emergence of corporations, religion has had to work upon new psychological realities. The religion of peasants has given way to the religion of new forms of life: first that of an urban proletariat, then that of a predominantly service and white-collar society. The productivity of the new economics has freed much human time for questions other than those of mere subsistence and survival. The workday has shrunk and "weekends" have been invented. After work, millions now take part in voluntary activities that fill, in effect, another forty-hour week (meetings, associations, sports, travel, politics, religion, and the like). Personal and social mobility has increased. Schooling has become not only common but mandatory. Teenagerhood has been invented. The "stages of human life" have drawn attention as room has been created for the emergence of the private self.

But the corporation is not only an economic institution and a moral-cultural institution. It also provides a new base for politics. Only a free political system permits the voluntary formation of private corporations. Thus, those who value private economic corporations have a strong interest in resisting both statism and socialism. It would be naive and wrong to believe that persons involved in corporations are (or should be) utterly neutral about political systems. An economic system within which private corporations play a role, in turn, alters the political horizon. It lifts the poor, creates a broad middle class, and undermines aristocracies of birth. Sources of power are created independent of the power of the state, in competition with the powers of the state, and sometimes in consort with the powers of the state. A corporation with plants and factories in, say, 120 congressional districts represents a great many employees and stockholders. On some matters, at least, these are likely to be well-organized to express their special political concerns. Political jurisdictions often compete to attract corporations, but their arrival also creates political problems.

Corporations err morally, then, in many ways. They may through their advertising appeal to hedonism and escape, in ways which undercut the restraint and self-discipline required by a responsible democracy and which discourage that deferral of present satisfaction on which savings and investment for the future depend. They may incorporate methods of governance that injure dignity, cooperation, inventiveness, and personal development. They may seek their own immediate interests at the expense of the common good. They may become improperly involved in the exercise of political power. They may injure the conscience of their managers or workers. They are as capable of sins as individuals are and, in the fashion of all institutions, of grave institutional sins as well. Thus, it is a perfectly proper task of all

involved within corporations and in society at large to hold them to the highest moral standards, to accuse them when they fail, and to be vigilant about every form of abuse. Corporations are human institutions designed to stimulate economic activism and thus to provide the economic base for a democratic policy committed to high moral-cultural ideals. When they fall short of these purposes, their failure injures all.

Private corporations are *social* organisms. Neither the ideology of laissez faire nor the ideology of rugged individualism suits their actual practice or their inherent ideals. For corporations *socialize* risk, invention, investment, production, distribution, and services. They were conceived and designed to break the immemorial grip of mercantilist and clerical systems upon economic activity. On the other hand, they cannot come into existence, and certainly cannot function, except within political systems designed to establish and to promote the conditions of their flourishing. Among these are a sound currency, a system of laws, the regulation of competitive practices, the construction of infrastructures like roads, harbors, airports, certain welfare functions, and the like. The state, then, plays an indispensable role in democratic capitalism. The ideals of democratic capitalism are not those of laissez faire. The relations between a democratic state and a social market economy built around private corporations are profound, interdependent, and complex.

The ideals of democratic capitalism are not purely individualist, either, for the corporation draws upon and requires highly developed social skills like mutual trust, teamwork, compromise, cooperation, creativity, originality and inventiveness, and agreeable management and personnel relations. The rugged individualist of an earlier mythology may be, if anything, an endangered species.

Great moral responsibility, then, is inherent in the existence of corporations. They may fail economically. They may fail morally and culturally. They may fail politically. Frequently enough, they err in one or all of these areas. They are properly subjected to constant criticism and reform, but types of criticism may be distinguished. Some critics accept the ideals inherent in the system of private business corporations, and simply demand that corporations be faithful to these ideals. Some critics are opposed to the system *qua* system. Among these, some wish to restrain, regulate, and guide the business system through the power of the state and through moral and cultural forces like public opinion, shame, ridicule, boycotts, and moral persuasion ("do not invest in South Africa," and the like). In the theory of "mixed systems," the ideal of democratic capitalism shades off into the ideal of democratic socialism—one leaning more to the private sector, the other leaning more to the public sector. Still other critics wish to make the business system directly *subject* to the state. These last may be, according to their own ideals, corporate statists or socialists. They may be state socialists or local participatory politics socialists. Criticism from any of these quarters may be useful to the development and progress of democratic capitalism, even from those who would wish to destroy it.

There is plenty of room—and plenty of evidence—for citing specific deficiencies of corporations: economic, political, and moral-cultural. To be sure, there is a difference between accusations and demonstrated error. Like individuals, corporations are innocent until proven guilty. A passionate hostility toward bigness (or even toward economic liberty), like a passionate commitment to statism, may be socially useful by providing a searching critique from the viewpoint of hostile critics. But unless it gets down to cases and sticks to a reasoned presentation of evidence, it must be recognized for what it is: an argument less against specifics than against the radical ideal of democratic capitalism and the private corporation. It is useful to distinguish these two types of criticism, and helpful when critics are self-conscious and honest about which ideals actually move them. To criticize corporations in the light of their *own* ideals, the ideals of democratic capitalism, is quite different from criticizing them in the name of statist or socialist ideals incompatible with their existence. Clarity about ideals is as necessary as clarity about cases.

Theologians, in particular, are likely to inherit either a precapitalist or a frankly socialist set of ideals about political economy. They are especially likely to criticize corporations from a set of ideals foreign to those of democratic capitalism. To those who do accept democratic capitalist ideals, then, their criticisms are likely to have a scent of unreality and inappropriateness. Wisdom would suggest joining argument at the appropriate level of discourse: whether the argument concerns general economic concepts, whether it concerns the rival ideals of democratic capitalism and socialism, or whether it concerns concrete cases and specific matters of fact. Each of these levels has its place. Wisdom's principal task is *distinguer*.

> ### *Theologians, in particular, are likely to inherit either a precapitalist or a frankly socialist set of ideals about political economy.*

Managing a free society aimed at preserving the integrity of the trinitarian system—the economic system, the political system, and the moral-cultural system—is no easy task. An important standard set by Edmund Burke is cited as the epigraph of a masterly work by Wilhelm T. Roepke, *A Humane Economy*:

> To make a government requires no great prudence. Settle the seat of power; teach obedience: and the work is done. To give freedom is still more easy. It is not necessary to guide; it only requires to let go the rein. But to form a free *government*; that is, to temper together these opposite elements of liberty and restraint in one consistent work, requires much thought, deep reflection, a sagacious, powerful and combining mind.[9]

To govern a free *economy* is yet more difficult than to form a free government. It is hard enough to govern a government. It is difficulty squared to govern a free economy—to establish the conditions for prosperity, to keep a sound currency, to promote competition, to establish general rules and standards binding upon all, to keep markets free, to provide education to all citizens in order to give them opportunity, to care for public needs, and to provide succor to the unfortunate. To have the virtue to do all these things wisely, persistently, judiciously, aptly is surely of some rather remarkable theological significance. It may even represent—given the inherent difficulties—a certain amazing grace. To fall short is to be liable to judgment.

Christians have not, historically, lived under only one economic system; nor are they bound in conscience to support only one. Any real or, indeed, any imaginable economic system is necessarily part of history, part of this world. None is the Kingdom of Heaven—not democratic socialism, not democratic capitalism. A theology of the corporation should not make the corporation seem to be an ultimate; it is only a means, an instrument, a worldly agency. Such a theology should attempt to show how corporations may be instruments of redemption, of humane purposes and values, of God's grace; it should also attempt to show their characteristic and occasional faults in every sphere. Like everything else in the world, corporations may be seen as both obstacles to salvation and bearers of God's grace. The waters of the sea are blessed, as are airplanes and ploughshares and even troops making ready for just combat. A city in Texas may be named Corpus Christi, and a city in California Sacramento. Christianity, like Judaism, attempts to sanctify the real world as it is, in all its ambiguity, so as to reject the evil in it and bring the good in it to its highest possible fruition.

Most Christians do not now work for major industrial corporations. Instead, they work for the state (even in state universities), for smaller corporations, restaurants, barbershops, and other businesses, and in other occupations. Still, a Christian social theology that lacks a theology of the large corporation will have no effective means of inspiring those Christians who do work within large corporations to meet the highest practicable Christian standards. It will also have no means of criticizing with realism and practicality those features of corporate life that deserve to be changed. Whether to treat big corporations as potential vessels of Christian vocation or to criticize them for their inevitable sins, Christian theology must advance much further than it has in understanding exactly and fairly every aspect of corporate life. The chief executive officer of General Electric needs such a theology. So do those critics of the corporation at the Interfaith Center for Corporate Responsibility. If we are to do better than clash like ignorant armies in the night, we must imitate Yahweh at Creation when he said, "Let there be light." We have not yet done all we should in casting such light.

Notes

[1]George Bernanos, *Diary of a Country Priest*, trans. Pamela Morris (New York: Macmillan Col., 1962), 233.

[2]John Locke, *Second Treatise of Civil Government* (New York: Macmillan Co., 1947), 20.

[3]Theodore Hesburgh, *The Humane Imperative: A Challenge for the Year 2000* (New Haven: Yale University Press, 1974), 101.

[4]See Paul Johnson, "Is There a Moral Basis for Capitalism?" *Democracy and Mediating Structures: A Theological Inquiry*, ed. Michael Novak (Washington, D.C.: American Enterprise Institute, 1980), 49–58.

[5]C. B. Macpherson, *The Political Theory of Possessive Individualism: Hobbes to Locke* (New York: Oxford University Press, 1962), 263.

[6]Herbert Stein, *Capitalism—If You Can Keep It* (Washington, D.C.: American Enterprise Institute, 1980), 6.

[7]Linda Grant Martin, "The 500: A Report on Two Decades," *Fortune*, May 1975, 238.

[8]Stephen B. Roman and Eugene Loebl write: "Economy is essentially the transformation of natural forces and natural goods into forces and goods that serve humanity. It is an order created by thinking people, and one that has developed as a result of people's intellectual and spiritual growth. Further, it should be clear that when we regard economy as the creation of thinking human beings, economic wealth becomes nothing more than the transformation of natural wealth. There is no material wealth except that of nature and that created by humans from nature." *The Responsible Society* (New York: Regina Ryan Books/Two Continents, 1977), 22–23.

[9]See Wilhelm T. Roepke, *The Humane Economy: The Social Framework of a Free Society* (Chicago: Henry Regnery, 1960), facing p. 1; the quotation is from Edmund Burke, *Reflections on the Revolution in France* (1790).

CASES

Case 5.1: Third World Capitalism: Does It Work?

In some Third World countries, especially in Africa, the practice of profit maximization is viewed as not particularly helpful to the overall economy. For example, in Ghana and other parts of sub-Saharan Africa, it is not unusual for people to hoard and resell basic commodities such as soap, sugar, flour, and milk. The reason for this is that prices are controlled by the government and are artificially low. Demand for basic necessities exceeds the available supply because many of these countries can neither produce nor import sufficient quantities to meet the demands of the people. Thus a thriving black market exists and people can make a profit by charging as much for a bar of soap as the minimum daily wage earned by the majority of people there. The practice of hoarding and reselling products is known as "kalabule," the Western equivalent of maximizing profit. Yet this will lead to starvation, as the higher prices eat up so much of a person's wages and the available supply of products rapidly sells out at the government's artificially low price. Ghana is in a difficult position because the government could not let prices float to reflect the market since the people could hardly afford any necessities at market prices. The practice of capitalism seems to contradict the experience of other developing countries that are very poor in natural resources, such as Japan, Singapore, Taiwan, and South Korea. This raises the question of whether or not capitalism can work in lifting some Third World countries out of poverty, or whether it actually makes the problem worse.[1]

[1] See Safro Kwame, "Doin' Business in an African Country: Business Ethics and Capitalism in a Poor Country," *Journal of Business Ethics* 2 (1983): 263–68.

Questions for Discussion:

1. Do you think that the practice of "kalabule" is consistent with Christian ethics and helpful to the countries that are trying to develop a market economy?
2. Do you think that if the government lifted price controls that more people would be without basic necessities, or would there be incentives for producers to increase supply and bring more goods to the market?
3. Do you think that capitalism is the best solution for lifting poor countries out of poverty? Or is a more command-style economy better for some countries based on their cultural distinctives?

Case 5.2: The Christian Call to a Simple Lifestyle

The Bible has a great deal to say about wealth and materialism. "The love of money is a root of all kinds of evil" (1 Tim. 6:10) and "No one can serve two masters. . . . You cannot serve both God and Money" (Matt. 6:24) are for many the sine qua non of the biblical teaching on the pursuit of wealth and possessions. When Christans, especially from the West, which is widely regarded around the world as the headquarters for materialism as a way of life, go to poorer parts of the world, their comparatively great wealth is a cause of offense to the local people. This is especially acute when they go to serve as missionaries and end up being the wealthiest people by far when compared with those to whom they are coming to minister. Some suggest that the prime evidence of Christian materialism is the church parking lot every Sunday morning. In many churches in North America the parking lot is filled with expensive cars that cost more than the annual income of many people in the church, not to mention many people around the world.

In response to the biblical teaching, some have proposed that the Christian calling is to live as simple a lifestyle as possible. This would mean different things for different people and would be dependent on the cost of living in the region in which one lives. But at its core, it means that an individual or family would live as simply as they can and either give up the pursuit of wealth or if God's calling for them is in business, give away as much as possible to causes that genuinely advance God's kingdom. One specific proposal is that a family set a goal to live on roughly $20,000 per year and give the rest away. The specific dollar amount is not really important. What counts is that the number reflects an annual income that would provide for a family's needs and allow them to give away as much as they could. Another proposal is to structure one's giving in the same way the government has structured the tax system—progressively. That is, you give a higher percentage of your income away as you make more money. This is called a graduated tithe. A family might give 10 percent of the first $30,000 of income and give 20 percent of the next $20,000 and 30 percent of the next $20,000. Again the numbers are not the important thing—if one gets the principle. Advocates of this kind of simple lifestyle suggest that limiting one's consumption avoids the materialism that is so prevalent in Western societies and enables a person to walk faithfully with Christ.

Questions for Discussion:

1. Do you think that the Scripture condemns the accumulation of wealth? Or does it condemn only the wrong attitude toward it and the wrong use of it? Support your position with passages from the Bible.
2. Do you believe that a simple lifestyle is required of people who genuinely desire to be faithful to Christ? If so, would you be willing to try setting an income ceiling or using a graduated tithe such as advocates of a simple lifestyle suggest?
3. If you could afford it with money you earned, do you think you could justify buying a car such as a Rolls Royce that costs roughly $150,000–$200,000? What if the car were a Mercedes that cost in the area of $60,000? Why or why not?

COMMENTARY

Since Max Weber's controversial thesis in *The Protestant Ethic and the Spirit of Capitalism* was published, people have paid a great deal of attention to the intersection of religion and economics. Weber argued that Calvinism provided the ideological engine for the growth of capitalism in three primary ways. First, Calvin adopted and expanded Martin Luther's view of worldly callings, that is, a person can have a legitimate calling from God to work in industry and commerce, not just in the formal ministry. This is in sharp contrast to the dominant beliefs held from Medieval times until the Reformation, when only the religious had callings and the rest of the population simply had jobs. Luther, and Calvin after him, argued that since God was sovereign over all, the whole world was the theater of his glory. Thus all occupations, even politics, were capable of demonstrating his majesty, and should be pursued. Second, the habits of discipline, namely hard work and thrift, that Calvinism encouraged were essential to a changing concept of work. People were encouraged to work for more than simply providing for their subsistence needs. Third, and perhaps most important, Calvinism, according to Weber, encouraged its adherents to "prove their election/salvation" by achieving success and prosperity in the world. This was seen as a sign of God's blessing on them and evidence that their election to salvation was secure. Although there were other factors, such as the division of labor that also contributed to the rise of capitalism, the Calvinist ethos was a part of it. Assumed in the Calvinist view of the world were also the virtues necessary to restrain self-interest and a concern for the common good, both necessary to keep the engine of capitalism under control. Adam Smith assumed both of these elements in his classic work *The Wealth of Nations*. For him the capitalist was also the gentleman, who was bound by Judeo-Christian moral restraints on self-interest and an interest in business and commerce serving the community in which it was conducted. Few people remember that Adam Smith was not an economist but a moral philosopher, and the capitalism that Smith advocated was not at all like its modern media portrayal in films like *Wall Street*. It is important to keep this in mind as we consider the various critiques of capitalism, that the capitalism being criticized is the current practice, not the original idea proposed by Adam Smith.

The central questions addressed by these readings are these: Given that no economic system is perfect, do you believe that capitalism is essentially consistent with or contradictory to biblical principles? Or do you believe that the Bible is neutral when it comes to evaluating different economic systems? To put the question a bit differently, does the Bible essentially condemn or condone capitalism? Even though capitalism is essentially unchallenged today by other economic systems, that does not exempt it from biblical and theological assessment. This does not mean that one must take it as a given in today's world apart from criticism of some of its alleged weaknesses.

The most common critique of capitalism concerns its foundational motive—greed. It is alleged that capitalism is a system based on greed, or what Adam Smith called the invisible hand of self-interest. Capitalism is run by individuals seeking their self-interest, or maximizing their profit, and the assumption is that to succeed they must make a useful product or perform a useful service and in so doing contribute to the common good. Yet the critics observe that individual acquisitive self-interest (greed) has not contributed to the common good, but has undermined it. It has, for example, created enormous disparities in the distribution of income and concentrated wealth in the hands of a relative few at the expense of the majority of the poor of the world. Certainly Wall Street, both in reality and in its media portrayals, has reinforced the notion that capitalism is based on greed. The prevailing ethos there is that "greed is good" as exemplified by corporate raider Gordon Gekko in the film *Wall Street*, and by his real-life counterpart, Ivan Boesky. Critics of capitalism insist that a system fueled by a trait that Scripture clearly identifies as a vice cannot possibly be Christian. Although not stated explicitly, this criticism underlies most of Wallis's critique of capitalism. Expanding American profit and power, the rise of the consumer society, and our overconsumption all assume that greed fuels the economic system.

A second critique is that capitalism leads to an unjust concentration of wealth and global inequalities in resource use. For example, the United States has roughly 5 percent of the world's population, yet uses over 50 percent of the world's resources. In the Third World, the situation is the reverse, with far more people and far fewer of the world's goods at their disposal. Wallis cites the growing concentration of economic and thus political power in the hands of a few around the world. This power is concentrated in the handful of multinational corporations that control a disproportionate amount of wealth and power and exercise it unjustly to maintain their "empires" often at the expense of the poor.

This leads to a third major criticism of capitalism, that first-world capitalism is responsible for Third World poverty. The concentration of economic power in the West enables the West to dictate economic terms to the Third World and continue to exploit its people in order to increase its own wealth and power. The statement is startling to some but commonplace to critics of capitalism, namely, that the poor around the world and in this country are poor because we in the First World are rich. The critics argue that the poverty of the world is maintained by capitalism, not alleviated by it. They think that it is preposterous to suggest that capitalism might be the solution to the problem of poverty, since they hold that it is clearly the cause.

A fourth criticism is that capitalism leads to overconsumption. Goods that appear to have no socially redeeming value are produced and consumed simply because in the capitalist system, supply follows demand. If there is a market for a certain good, someone will make it, regardless of its social value. The only value of a product that counts is its economic value, as measured by the market. Products like pornography, a billion-dollar business annually in the United States, and cigarettes, which (disputed only by tobacco companies) kill thousands of people each year and cost billions in medical care, are examples of products that society would undoubtedly be better off without, yet they are produced in mass quantities simply because the market demands it. Moreover, producers are accused of undermining autonomy through "creating" demand in the minds of consumers in order to maximize profit. As any marketing textbook will state, one way to do this is to "differentiate" basically similar products through advertising and market positioning. One can see this in the innumerable varieties of the same goods produced and marketed. For example, the average "Foot Locker" shoe store has hundreds of essentially similar products: athletic shoes. Of course, some variety is appropriate, but critics of capitalism insist that the amount of variety demanded by the market says something negative about the character of its consumers. This kind of consumerism leaves a person and a society spiritually impoverished.

A final criticism of capitalism is that the private accumulation of wealth is prohibited by the Bible. Old Testament commands such as those concerning the sabbatical year, the year of Jubilee, the redemption of the land (Levi. 25:1–55), and gleaning (Ruth 2) are designed to keep people from inordinately accumulating wealth. The rich young ruler is told to sell all he has and give the money to the poor (Matt. 9:16–26), poverty is a virtue and the poor are glorified (Luke 6:20), and the early church had all their goods in common (Acts 2:42–47). All of these passages suggest that the accumulation of wealth that is necessary to provide the capital for capitalism is in violation of biblical principles. Wallis insists that the gospel is biased for the poor and the rights of the rich are nonexistent in Scripture.

The defenders of capitalism have responded to each of these critiques of capitalism, arguing that its critics have misunderstood the system and misinterpreted the Bible. First, they insist that greed and self-interest are not the same thing. When Adam Smith wrote of self-interest fueling capitalism, he had nothing like *Wall Street* in mind. He advocated *enlightened* self-interest, that is, self-interest restrained by Judeo-Christian morality and a concern for the common good, in which everyone benefits. Capitalism was never intended to operate apart from the virtue of its participants. Yet the critics of capitalism reply that the conditions under which Smith envisioned capitalism are so foreign to today's conditions that perhaps capitalism is not capable of being a moral system, with self-interest properly restrained. Whether or not that is true is open to debate, but the key point here is that greed does not equal self-interest.

The second and third critiques, that the concentration of economic power inherent in capitalism is responsible for Third World poverty, assume that the world's supply of goods is a "zero-sum game." That is, when someone gains, inevitably someone else loses because the pie is the same size for everyone. So if someone gets a bigger slice of the economic pie, someone else will inevitably get a smaller slice. Those getting the bigger slice have been the rich in the First World who have profited at the expense of the poor in the Third World. The defenders of capitalism have responded that the world economy is not a zero-sum game. In fact, capitalism is capable of making the pie bigger for everyone. An honest assessment of capitalism should reveal that there are clearly some situations that can be categorized as win-lose. However, once again this is an indictment of unscrupulous participants who inhabit every system rather than of capitalism itself. In fact, the great majority of transactions in the free market create win-win conditions that increase the size of the economic pie for all parties when one participant profits. The genius of capitalism is that it is the only system capable of creating wealth as well as distributing it. For example, a recent study by Stanford economics professor Paul Krugman suggests that there is no simple cause-and-effect relationship between First World prosperity and Third World development.[2] Thus overconsumption is not inherently theft, nor has the First World necessarily become rich at the expense of the poor. No one has to lose when someone wins economically. In fact, economic development of all parts of the world is beneficial to all. Defenders of capitalism insist that the critics have fundamentally misunderstood capitalism at this point.

Capitalism's defenders point to decades of empirical data to show that capitalism is the best means of lifting the poor out of their poverty. They cite the Pacific Rim miracles of economic development as evidence. Nations known as the "Asian tigers" such as Singapore, South Korea, Taiwan, and Japan have little natural resources on which to build an economy. Yet they are all economic powers because of a system that allowed initiative and creativity to flourish. On the other

[2]Paul Krugman, "Does Third World Growth Hurt First World Prosperity?" *Harvard Business Review* (July–August 1994): 113–21.

welfare system. Rather, the individuals had to work for their welfare, making it more like the types of workfare proposed in many legislatures today.

It would be difficult to maintain that the Bible is neutral when it comes to evaluating different economic systems. For example, the prophets voiced searing criticism of the nation of Israel and its surrounding neighbors for their economic injustices, neglect of the poor, and exploitation of the economically vulnerable. Their critique was based on the foundation of the Mosaic law, which structured the social order, including economic life of the emerging nation of Israel. There were clearly ideals such as the Jubilee, that were to govern economic life, both individually and structurally, and the prophets held the nation accountable to them when they violated both the letter and the spirit of those laws. It may be that the Bible is not to be identified with any one economic system. Rather, it stands authoritative over all social and economic systems, proclaiming God's Word regarding them indiscriminately.

Although there are some aspects of capitalism that are clearly cause for concern, many of the critics of capitalism either misunderstand the way the system functions or misinterpret the Scripture. The Old Testament commands on economic life are probably better seen as mandates for a regular redistribution of opportunity rather than an indictment of wealth and income. The fifth commandment, "Thou shalt not steal," provides the basis for private ownership and property, and the church's having all things in common was a temporary response to the expected imminent return of Christ. The mandate at creation, as Novak and Sirico rightly maintain, gave mankind the opportunity to create wealth and so further exercise dominion over the creation. The emphasis on individual initiative, creativity, and economic freedom are rooted in the command to have responsible dominion over creation. The Bible places great emphasis on individual responsibility for one's own economic condition. The book of Proverbs stresses the role of diligence and its causal relationship to economic prosperity. Paul bluntly states that if someone does not want to work, they have no right to any of society's goods (2 Thess. 3:6). Thus it would appear that merit is a primary determinant of the distribution of society's goods.

Need surely counts for something as well, but the poor, the object of compassion and care in the Scripture, were those who were incapable of supporting themselves, not those who could work but did not, for whatever reason. Those who could claim need-based support appear to be quite a small group, and merit governed the distribution of wealth in the Bible. Whatever was redistributed was done so voluntarily, and clearly the Bible places great stress on generous giving to those in need. Finally, the high place the Bible gives to freedom suggests that a system that maximizes freedom, within the restraints of righteousness and virtue, is more consistent with biblical values than those systems that limit freedom.

However, there are some concerns that are raised by the collision of biblical values with capitalism. There is a well-placed concern about the overconsumption and the materialism that are encouraged by the system. The Bible saves some of its clearest condemnation for the person who has succumbed to the temptation of materialism. There is a further concern about the ability of capitalism to fairly distribute the goods of society. Even if one accepts a merit-based distribution of wealth, it should be troubling to see the wide disparities in the distribution of income, especially the accumulation of wealth that is way beyond what a person will ever need or is willing to give away. Indeed, it seems unfair that the citizens of the industrialized world have the privileges that only capitalism can provide. However, the means to economic justice for all is not less capitalism in the wealthy West, as some of capitalism's critics have suggested. Rather, it is more capitalism and democracy around the globe that will rectify the situation by providing unparalleled opportunities to escape poverty. The principles of justice balanced by mercy taught by the Old Testament mandates on economic life are still applicable to us today. Thus, while the inhabitants of wealthy countries are not to blame for Third World poverty, we have tremendous responsibilities to aid in the spread of free-market economy and its unique ability to create wealth. Finally, the potential abuses of capitalism illustrate the need for society in general and religious leaders specifically to encourage the development of virtue and character to provide the necessary internal restraints of self-interest and urge tempering self-interest in favor of the common good.

Part III

Business and Society

SIX

The Social Responsibilities
of Corporations

The social responsibility of business is to increase its profits.

Milton Friedman

Shameless exploitation in pursuit of the common good.

Motto of *Newman's Own Products*,
a company that gives all its profits to charity

INTRODUCTION

The actions of corporations have a tremendous impact on their surrounding communities. Consequently, the idea that corporations should be more "socially responsible" is appealing. In the wake of many recent scandals, especially those like the *Exxon Valdez* oil spill, most of us would like to see "soulless" corporations take on a greater concern for goals other than pure profit. In response to these concerns, many companies have altered their practices to become more "socially responsible."

During the past decade, the use of the label "socially responsible business" has sprung up like a cottage industry. Prevalent on store shelves are socially responsible products, made through "green manufacturing practices" and sold in environmentally friendly packaging. There is even an abundance of socially responsible services available to conscientious consumers. For example, one service provides travelers with a guide to "ecotravel: protecting the earth while you relax on vacation." There has also been an explosive growth in the number of mutual funds that exclude companies involved in such enterprises as tobacco, alcohol, and handgun manufacturing in their investment portfolios. In addition, there are even a host of publications devoted to the cause. One bimonthly magazine entitled *Business Ethics* carries the subtitle "The Magazine for Socially Responsible Business" on its cover.

Today, most consumers can readily name corporations that use slogans labeling themselves as "caring" or "sharing" companies in their promotional materials. Some firms, such as the retailer Target, state boldly in their advertising campaigns that they contribute large percentages of their profits back into their communities. Many others proclaim that they are "green" businesses that give priority to the health of the global environment in the manufacture and sales of their products and services. Undoubtedly, the strategic use of such concepts as public relations tools can be good for the bottom line. With all of the media attention on corporate corruption in the last two decades, many consumers will vote with their dollars and do business with corporations that they perceive to have social consciences.

Some corporations, however, do not appear to use such sloganeering for the sole purpose of long-term gains that will arise from public goodwill. A growing number of these firms claim to place social causes ahead of, or at least on a par with, profit making. For example, the recreational clothing manufacturing company Patagonia recently voluntarily downsized its operations and canceled an extremely popular and profitable line of garments because the materials in use were deemed to cause too much damage to the environment.[1] Consumer products company Tom's of Maine engages in many practices that voluntarily limit profit for the sake of the common good. Since both of these companies are privately held, no one is questioning the morality of their actions. However, controversy arises when publicly held companies engage in similar activities that may curtail profits for the sake of social causes.

To some critics, these types of actions are morally problematic on several grounds. First, they argue that while privately held companies such as Patagonia and Tom's of Maine can do as they like with the corporate treasury, managers of publicly held corporations have the sole "social responsibility" of maximizing profit for the owners of the companies, the shareholders. As employees of the shareholders, managers and executives are to do all that they can within the bounds of the law to increase the value of the company stock. To jeopardize the bottom line through "socially responsible" actions constitutes a serious breach of fiduciary duty to shareholders.

Second, there is widespread disagreement over just what it means to be "socially responsible" despite the prevalence of the current use of the term. To some, it means keeping an unprofitable plant in operation because of the jobs at stake and the harm to the local community caused by unemployment. To others, it may mean shutting down

[1] Peter Carlin, "Pure Profit," *Los Angeles Times Magazine* (February 5, 1995): 12f.

the same plant because the preservation of the environment takes precedence over profit or the well-being of local citizens.

Finally, disagreements have also arisen over corporate charitable contributions to social causes, as there is a definite lack of a consensus about what constitutes "a worthy cause." Shareholders from all over the political spectrum have protested when their companies have directly contributed to causes that they personally find deplorable. Furthermore, companies that have donated percentages of profits to organizations such as the Boy Scouts of America and Planned Parenthood have all been recent targets of consumer protest. In response, some have suggested that companies should stay away from charitable contributions altogether, since public relations damage can produce direct negative consequences for shareholder profits.

With all of these controversial aspects, the conflict that arises from the question over the "social responsibility of business" is one of the most foundational issues in business ethics. For example, debates over the environment, plant closings, employee rights, product safety, and a host of other issues usually place the pursuit of profit in direct conflict with other social aims. In each of these situations, a troubling question about the goals of publicly owned corporations and the employees within them is raised. Should a public corporation and its employees seek only to maximize profits for its owners? Or should it, at times, seek to serve its surrounding community by contributing to other social goals at the expense of direct financial profit to shareholders?

While situations in which profit competes with societal well-being can cause moral conflicts for all participants in business, they are even more problematic for Christians in the workplace. Such conflicts can bring about some vexing questions over the primacy of one's duties to higher morals over duties to employers when the two are in conflict. What is morally right when an employer demands that you engage in a practice that maximizes profit but goes against your beliefs because it is clearly harmful to members of the surrounding community? Do duties to one's employer override your other moral obligations? Does the "shareholder wealth" model proposed by Milton Friedman in this chapter provide a way out, or is another method of resolving these competing claims more appropriate?

Much has been written to address these questions by religious thinkers, philosophers, and economists. However, this has only served to heighten the controversy. On one side are those who, like Friedman, believe that since "business is not a charity" managers of publicly held corporations have a singular responsibility to maximize shareholder wealth. Friedman states that if shareholders want to contribute to the community, that is their right as private citizens. However, for managers to act in a "socially responsible" manner through the use of corporate funds constitutes a form of "taxation without representation." Despite its initial appearances, however, this position does not preclude behaviors that some would deem "socially responsible." In many instances, the socially responsible course of action is also the one that maximizes profit, perhaps through public relations or goodwill. The key issue, however, is whether or not such actions serve to enhance profit. Thus, for Friedman, actions that may benefit another social good at the short-term expense of profit is a matter of long-term strategy and not morality. However, if managers engage in actions that would harm long-term profit while contributing to another worthy social goal, this would be morally wrong. For example, unless there is an imminent threat to public relations, increasing production costs by abiding by environmental standards that go beyond the requirements of the law would be to steal from shareholders who have not approved such actions.

[2]See William M. Evan and R. Edward Freeman, "A Stakeholder Theory of the Modern Corporation: Kantian Capitalism," in *Ethical Theory and Business*, 4th ed., ed. Thomas Beauchamp and Norman Bowie (Engelwood Cliffs, N.J.: Prentice-Hall, 1993), 75–84.

An opposing viewpoint to this theory is the "stakeholder" model. Proponents of this alternate approach have proposed that the lone consideration of shareholder interests is morally insufficient. Rather, business must broaden its vision to include the consideration of a wide group of "stakeholders" in its determinations of specific actions. Arguing along Kantian lines, supporters of this viewpoint assert that stakeholders have rights not to be treated as a means to some end, namely profit for shareholders.[2]

Kenneth Goodpaster's article "Business Ethics and Stakeholder Analysis" lays out the basic contours of this position. While he is critical of this perspective and notes that stakeholder considerations present a "paradox," he does give an accurate account of the stakeholder model's basic claims in his description of the "multi-fiduciary approach." In essence, proponents of this model argue that corporations have responsibilities to those who have a "stake" in the company, rather than just to its owners. Since business transactions affect many constituent groups, business also has moral duties to such stakeholders as consumers, suppliers, employees, and other members of the community. Goodpaster, however, does not place the rights of shareholders and stakeholders on equal grounds. While stating that shareholder rights have primacy, he argues that other stakeholders also deserve moral consideration.

Addressing these questions from a markedly different paradigm, Pietra Rivoli targets the implicit assumptions in both the traditional "shareholder wealth" and "stakeholder" approaches in "Ethical Aspects of Shareholder Behavior." Rivoli operates from within the "communitarian" framework as conceived of by social thinkers such as Amitai

Etzioni.[3] Communitarians reject the individualist roots of conceiving of morality in the social order and business relationships as voluntary contracts between autonomous individuals. Rather than relying on the premises of John Locke's classical liberalism, such as the shareholder wealth and stakeholder models, communitarians base their claims on an Aristotelian conception of community. They reject the assumption that corporations are first autonomous individuals, who then consider the interests of the surrounding community as an afterthought. Instead, they believe that corporations are part and parcel of the communities and social networks that created them. Thus moral obligations are not purely voluntary agreements created by corporations through social contracts, but are rather intrinsic to their existence as social entities.

Rivoli uses empirical studies of investor behavior to show that shareholders are, in fact, "other interested" in terms of moral obligations. Her data reveals that shareholders will often vote in a manner that is more consistent with social responsibilities to stakeholders rather than pure wealth maximization. Thus she brings into question the accuracy of Friedman's assumption that investors are solely after profit maximization.

[3]See Amitai Etzioni, *The Spirit of Community* (New York: Touchstone, 1993) and *The Moral Dimension* (New York: Free Press, 1988). Also see Robert Solomon, *Ethics and Excellence* (New York: Oxford University Press, 1992).

READINGS

The Social Responsibility of Business Is to Increase Its Profits

Milton Friedman

New York Times Magazine, 13 September 1970, 33, 122–26. Copyright © 1970.

When I hear businessmen speak eloquently about the "social responsibilities of business in a free-enterprise system," I am reminded of the wonderful line about the Frenchman who discovered at the age of 70 that he had been speaking prose all his life. The businessmen believe that they are defending free enterprise when they declaim that business is not concerned "merely" with profit but also with promoting desirable "social conscience" and takes seriously its responsibilities for providing employment, eliminating discrimination, avoiding pollution and whatever else may be the catchwords of the contemporary crop of reformers. In fact they are—or would be if they or anyone else took them seriously—preaching pure and unadulterated socialism. Businessmen who talk this way are unwitting puppets of the intellectual forces that have been undermining the basis of a free society these past decades.

The discussions of the "social responsibilities of business" are notable for their analytical looseness and lack of rigor. What does it mean to say that "business" has responsibilities? Only people can have responsibilities. A corporation is an artificial person and in this sense may have artificial responsibilities, but "business" as a whole cannot be said to have responsibilities, even in this vague sense. The first step toward clarity in examining the doctrine of the social responsibility of business is to ask precisely what it implies for whom.

Presumably, the individuals who are to be responsible are businessmen, which means individual proprietors or corporate executives. Most of the discussion of social responsibility is directed at corporations, so in what follows I shall mostly neglect the individual proprietor and speak of corporate executives.

In a free-enterprise, private-property system, a corporate executive is an employee of the owners of the business. He has direct responsibility to his employers. That responsibility is to conduct the business in accordance with their desires, which generally will be to make as much money as possible while conforming to the basic rules of the society, both those embodied in law and those embodied in ethical custom. Of course, in some cases his employers may have a different objective. A group of persons might establish a corporation for an eleemosynary purpose—for example, a hospital or a school. The manager of such a corporation will not have money profit as his objective but the rendering of certain services.

In either case, the key point is that, in his capacity as a corporate executive, the manager is the agent of the individuals who own the corporation or establish the eleemosynary institution, and his primary responsibility is to them.

Needless to say, this does not mean that it is easy to judge how well he is performing his task. But at least the criterion of performance is straightforward, and the persons among whom a voluntary contractual arrangement exists are clearly defined.

Of course, the corporate executive is also a person in his own right. As a person, he may have many other responsibilities that he recognizes or assumes voluntarily—to his family, his conscience, his feelings of charity, his church, his clubs, his city, his country. He may feel impelled by these responsibilities to devote part of his income to causes he

regards as worthy, to refuse to work for particular corporations, even to leave his job, for example, to join his country's armed forces. If we wish, we may refer to some of these responsibilities as "social responsibilities." But in these respects he is acting as a principal, not an agent; he is spending his own money or time or energy, not the money of his employers or the time or energy he has contracted to devote to their purposes. If these are "social responsibilities," they are the social responsibilities of individuals, not of business.

What does it mean to say that the corporate executive has a "social responsibility" in his capacity as businessman? If this statement is not pure rhetoric, it must mean that he is to act in some way that is not in the interest of his employers. For example, that he is to refrain from increasing the price of the product in order to contribute to the social objective of preventing inflation, even though a price increase would be in the best interests of the corporation. Or that he is to make expenditures on reducing pollution beyond the amount that is in the best interests of the corporation or that is required by law in order to contribute to the social objective of improving the environment. Or that, at the expense of corporate profits, he is to hire "hard-core" unemployed instead of better-qualified available workmen to contribute to the social objective of reducing poverty.

In each of these cases, the corporate executive would be spending someone else's money for a general social interest. Insofar as his actions in accord with his "social responsibility" reduce returns to stockholders, he is spending their money. Insofar as his actions raise the price to customers, he is spending the customers' money. Insofar as his actions lower the wages of some employees, he is spending their money.

The stockholders or the customers or the employees could separately spend their own money on the particular action if they wished to do so. The executive is exercising a distinct "social responsibility," rather than serving as an agent of the stockholders or the customers or the employees, only if he spends the money in a different way than they would have spent it.

But if he does this, he is in effect imposing taxes, on the one hand, and deciding how the tax proceeds shall be spent, on the other.

✓This process raises political questions on two levels: principle and consequences. On the level of political principle, the imposition of taxes and the expenditure of tax proceeds are governmental functions. We have established elaborate constitutional, parliamentary and judicial provisions to control these functions, to assure that taxes are imposed so far as possible in accordance with the preferences and desires of the public—after all, "taxation without representation" was one of the battle cries of the American Revolution. We have a system of checks and balances to separate the legislative function of imposing taxes and enacting expenditures from the executive function of collecting taxes and administering expenditure programs and from the judicial function of mediating disputes and interpreting the law.

Here the businessman—self-selected or appointed directly or indirectly by stockholders—is to be simultaneously legislator, executive and jurist. He is to decide whom to tax by how much and for what purpose, and he is to spend the proceeds—all this guided only by general exhortations from on high to restrain inflation, improve the environment, fight poverty and so on and on.

> **The conflict of interest is clear when union officials are asked to subordinate the interest of their members to some more general social purpose.**

The whole justification for permitting the corporate executive to be selected by the stockholders is that the executive is an agent serving the interests of his principal. This justification disappears when the corporate executive imposes taxes and spends the proceeds for "social" purposes. He becomes in effect a public employee, a civil servant, even though he remains in name an employee of a private enterprise. On grounds of political principle, it is intolerable that such civil servants—insofar as their actions in the name of

social responsibility and real and not just window-dressing—should be selected as they are now. If they are to be civil servants, then they must be selected through a political process. If they are to impose taxes and make expenditures to foster "social" objectives, then political machinery must be set up to guide the assessment of taxes and to determine through a political process the objectives to be served.

This is the basic reason why the doctrine of "social responsibility" involves the acceptance of the socialist view that political mechanisms, not market mechanisms, are the appropriate way to determine the allocation of scarce resources to alternative users.

On the grounds of consequences, can the corporate executive in fact discharge his alleged "social responsibilities"? On the one hand, suppose he could get away with spending the stockholders' or customers' or employees' money. How is he to know how to spend it? He is told that he must contribute to fighting inflation. How is he to know what action of his will contribute to that end? He is presumably an expert in running his company—in producing a product or selling it or financing it. But nothing about his selection makes him an expert on inflation. Will his holding down the price of his product reduce inflationary pressure? Or, by leaving more spending power in the hands of his customers, simply divert it elsewhere? Or, by forcing him to produce less because of the lower price, will it simply contribute to shortages? Even if he could answer these questions, how much cost is he justified in imposing on his stockholders, customers and employees for this social purpose? What is his appropriate share and what is the appropriate share of others?

And, whether he wants to or not, can he get away with spending his stockholders', customers' or employees' money? Will not the stockholders fire him? (Either the present ones or those who take over when his actions in the name of social responsibility have reduced the corporation's profits and the price of its stock.) His customers and his employees can desert him for other producers and employers less scrupulous in exercising their social responsibilities.

This facet of "social responsibility" doctrine is brought into sharp relief when the doctrine is used to justify wage restraint by trade unions. The conflict of interest is naked and clear when union officials are asked to subordinate the interest of their members to some more general social purpose. If the union officials try to enforce wage restraint, the consequence is likely to be wildcat strikes, rank-and-file revolts and the emergence of strong competitors for these jobs. We thus have the ironic phenomenon that union leaders—at least in the U.S.—have objected to Government interference with the market far more consistently and courageously than have business leaders.

The difficulty of exercising "social responsibility" illustrates, of course, the great virtue of private competitive enterprise—it forces people to be responsible for their own actions and makes it difficult for them to "exploit" other people for either selfish or unselfish purposes. They can do good—but only at their own expense.

Many a reader who has followed the argument this far may be tempted to remonstrate that it is all well and good to speak of government's having the responsibility to impose taxes and determine expenditures for such "social" purposes as controlling pollution or training the hard-core unemployed, but that the problems are too urgent to wait on the slow course of political processes, that the exercise of social responsibility by businessmen is a quicker and surer way to solve pressing current problems.

Aside from the question of fact—I share Adam Smith's skepticism about the benefits that can be expected from "those who affected to trade for the public good"—this argument must be rejected on grounds of principle. What it amounts to is an assertion that those who favor the taxes and expenditures in question have failed to persuade a majority of their fellow citizens to be of like mind and that they are seeking to attain by undemocratic procedures what they cannot attain by democratic procedures. In a free society, it is hard for "good" people to do "good," but that is a small price to pay for making it hard for "evil" people to do "evil," especially since one man's good is another's evil.

I have, for simplicity, concentrated on the special case of the corporate executive, except only for the brief digression on trade unions. But precisely the same argument applies to the newer phenomenon of calling upon stockholders to require corporations to exercise social responsibility (the recent G.M. crusade for example). In most of these cases, what is in effect involved is some stockholders trying to get other stockholders (or customers or employees) to contribute against their will to "social" causes favored by the activists. Insofar as they succeed, they are again imposing taxes and spending the proceeds.

The situation of the individual proprietor is somewhat different. If he acts to reduce the returns of his enterprise in order to exercise his "social responsibility," he is spending his own money, not someone else's. If he wishes to spend his money on such purposes, that is his right, and I cannot see that there is any objection to his doing so. In the process, he, too, may impose costs on employees and customers. However, because he is far less likely than a large corporation or union to have monopolistic power, any such side effects will tend to be minor.

> *If the individual proprietor acts to reduce the returns of his enterprise in order to exercise his "social responsibility," he is spending his own money, not someone else's.*

Of course, in practice the doctrine of social responsibility is frequently a cloak for actions that are justified on other grounds rather than a reason for those actions.

To illustrate, it may well be in the long-run interest of a corporation that is a major employer in a small community to devote resources to providing amenities to that community or to improving its government. That may make it easier to attract desirable employees, it may reduce the wage bill or lessen losses from pilferage and sabotage or have other worthwhile effects. Or it may be that, given the laws about the deductibility of corporate charitable contributions, the stockholders can contribute more to charities they favor by having the corporation make the gift than by doing it themselves, since they can in that way contribute an amount that would otherwise have been paid as corporate taxes.

In each of these—and many similar—cases, there is a strong temptation to rationalize these actions as an exercise of "social responsibility." In the present climate of opinion, with its widespread aversion to "capitalism," "profits," the "soulless corporation" and so on, this is one way for a corporation to generate goodwill as a by-product of expenditures that are entirely justified in its own self-interest.

It would be inconsistent of me to call on corporate executives to refrain from this hypocritical window-dressing because it harms the foundations of a free society. That would be to call on them to exercise a "social responsibility"! If our institutions, and the attitudes of the public make it in their self-interest to cloak their actions in this way, I cannot summon much indignation to denounce them. At the same time, I can express admiration for those individual proprietors or owners of closely held corporations or stockholders of more broadly held corporations who disdain such tactics as approaching fraud.

Whether blameworthy or not, the use of the cloak of social responsibility, and the nonsense spoken in its name by influential and prestigious businessmen, does clearly harm the foundations of a free society. I have been impressed time and again by the schizophrenic character of many businessmen. They are capable of being extremely far-sighted and muddle-headed in matters that are outside their businesses but affect the possible survival of business in general. This short-sightedness is strikingly exemplified in the calls from many businessmen for wage and price guidelines or controls or incomes policies. There is nothing that could do more in a brief period to destroy a market system and replace it by a centrally controlled system than effective governmental control of prices and wages.

The short-sightedness is also exemplified in speeches by businessmen on social responsibility. This may gain them kudos in the short run. But it

helps to strengthen the already too prevalent view that the pursuit of profits is wicked and immoral and must be curbed and controlled by external forces. Once this view is adopted, the external forces that curb the market will not be the social consciences, however highly developed, of the pontificating executives; it will be the iron fist of Government bureaucrats. Here, as with price and wage controls, businessmen seem to me to reveal a suicidal impulse.

The political principle that underlies the market mechanism is unanimity. In an ideal free market resting on private property, no individual can coerce any other, all cooperation is voluntary, all parties to such cooperation benefit or they need not participate. There are no "social" values, no "social" responsibilities of individuals. Society is a collection of individuals and of the various groups they voluntarily form.

The political principle that underlies the political mechanism is conformity. The individual must serve a more general social interest—whether that be determined by a church or a dictator or a majority. The individual may have a vote and a say in what is to be done, but if he is overruled, he must conform. It is appropriate for some to require others to contribute to a general social purpose whether they wish to or not.

Unfortunately, unanimity is not always feasible. There are some respects in which conformity appears unavoidable, so I do not see how one can avoid the use of the political mechanism altogether.

But the doctrine of "social responsibility" taken seriously would extend the scope of the political mechanism to every human activity. It does not differ in philosophy from the most explicitly collectivist doctrine. It differs only by professing to believe that collectivist ends can be attained without collectivist means. That is why, in my book "Capitalism and Freedom," I have called it a "fundamentally subversive doctrine" in a free society, and have said that in such a society, "there is one and only one social responsibility of business—to use its resources and engage in activities designed to increase its profits so long as it stays within the rules of the game, which is to say, engages in open and free competition without deception or fraud."

Business Ethics and Stakeholder Analysis

Kenneth E. Goodpaster

Business Ethics Quarterly 1, no. 1 (January 1991): 53–73. Copyright © 1991.

*So we must think through what management should be accountable for;
and how and through whom its accountability can be discharged. The
stockholders' interest, both short- and long-term is one of the areas. But it
is only one.*

Peter Drucker, 1988, Harvard Business Review

What is ethically responsible management?
How can a corporation, given its economic mission, be managed with appropriate attention to
ethical concerns? These are central questions in
the field of business ethics. One approach to
answering such questions that has become popular during the last two decades is loosely referred
to as "stakeholder analysis." Ethically responsible
management, it is often suggested, is management
that includes careful attention not only to stockholders *but to stakeholders generally* in the decision-making process.

This suggestion about the ethical importance
of stakeholder analysis contains an important ker-
nel of truth, but it can also be misleading. Comparing the ethical relationship between managers
and stockholders with their relationship to other
stakeholders is, I will argue, almost as problematic
as ignoring stakeholders (ethically) altogether—
presenting us with something of a "stakeholder
paradox."

Definition

The term "stakeholder" appears to have been
invented in the early '60s as a deliberate play on
the word "stakeholder" to signify that there are
other parties having a "stake" in the decision-making of the modern, publicly-held corporation in
addition to those holding equity positions. Professor R. Edward Freeman, in his book *Strategic Management: A Stakeholder Approach* (Pitman, 1984),
defines the term as follows:

A stakeholder in an organization is (by definition) any group or individual who can
affect or is affected by the achievement of
the organization's objectives. (46)

Examples of stakeholder groups (beyond stockholders) are employees, suppliers, customers,
creditors, competitors, governments, and communities. . . .

Another metaphor with which the term "stakeholder" is associated is that of a "player" in a game
like poker. One with a "stake" in the game is one
who plays and puts some economic value at risk.[1]

Much of what makes responsible decision-making difficult is understanding how there can be an
ethical relationship between management and
stakeholders that avoids being too weak (making
stakeholders mere means to stockholders' ends) or
too strong (making stakeholders quasi-stockholders in their own right). To give these issues life, a
case example will help. So let us consider the case
of General Motors and Poletown.

The Poletown Case[2]

In 1980, GM was facing a net loss in income,
the first since 1921, due to intense foreign competition. Management realized that major capital
expenditures would be required for the company
to regain its competitive position and profitability.
A $40 billion five-year capital spending program
was announced that included new, state-of-the-art
assembly techniques aimed at smaller, fuel-effi-

cient automobiles demanded by the market. Two aging assembly plants in Detroit were among the ones to be replaced. Their closure would eliminate 500 jobs. Detroit in 1980 was a city with a black majority, an unemployment rate of 18% overall and 30% for blacks, a rising public debt and a chronic budget deficit, despite high tax rates.

The site requirements for a new assembly plant included 500 acres, access to long-haul railroad and freeways, and proximity to suppliers for "just-in-time" inventory management. It needed to be ready to produce 1983 model year cars beginning in September 1982. The only site in Detroit meeting GM's requirements was heavily settled, covering a section of the Detroit neighborhood of Poletown. Of the 3,500 residents, half were black. The whites were mostly of Polish descent, retired or nearing retirement. An alternative "green field" site was available in another midwestern state.

Using the power of eminent domain, the Poletown area could be acquired and cleared for a new plant within the company's timetable, and the city government was eager to cooperate. Because of job retention in Detroit, the leadership of the United Auto Workers was also in favor of the idea. The Poletown Neighborhood Council strongly opposed the plan, but was willing to work with the city and GM.

The new plant would employ 6,150 workers and would cost GM $500 million wherever it was built. Obtaining and preparing the Poletown site would cost an additional $200 million, whereas alternative sites in the midwest were available for $65–80 million.

The interested parties were many—stockholders, customers, employees, suppliers, the Detroit community, the midwestern alternative, the Poletown neighborhood. The decision was difficult. GM management needed to consider its competitive situation, the extra costs of remaining in Detroit, the consequences to the city of leaving for another part of the midwest, and the implications for the residents of choosing the Poletown site if the decision was made to stay. The decision about whom to talk to and *how* was as puzzling as the decision about *what* to do and *why*.

I. Stakeholder Analysis and Stakeholder Synthesis

Ethical values enter management decision-making, it is often suggested, through the gate of stakeholder analysis. But the suggestion that introducing "stakeholder analysis" into business decisions is the same as introducing ethics into those decisions is questionable. To make this plain, let me first distinguish between two importantly different ideas: stakeholder analysis and stakeholder synthesis. I will then examine alternative kinds of stakeholder synthesis with attention to ethical content.

The decision-making process of an individual or a company can be seen in terms of a sequence of six steps to be followed after an issue or problem presents itself for resolution.[3] For ease of reference and recall, I will name the sequence PASCAL, after the six letters in the name of the French philosopher-mathematician Blaise Pascal (1623–62), who once remarked in reference to ethical decision-making that "the heart has reasons the reason knows not of."

(1) PERCEPTION or fact-gathering about the options available and their short- and long-term implications;

(2) ANALYSIS of these implications with specific attention to affected parties and to the decision-maker's goals, objectives, values, responsibilities, etc.;

(3) SYNTHESIS of this structured information according to whatever fundamental priorities obtain in the mindset of the decision-maker;

(4) CHOICE among the available options based on the synthesis;

(5) ACTION or implementation of the chosen option through a series of specific requests to specific individuals or groups, resource allocation, incentives, controls, and feedback;

(6) LEARNING from the outcome of the decision, resulting in either reinforcement or modification (for future decisions) of the way in which the above steps have been taken.

. . . Now, by *stakeholder analysis* I simply mean a process that does not go beyond the first two steps mentioned above. That is, the affected parties caught up in each available option are identified and the positive and negative impacts on each stakeholder are determined. But questions having to do with processing this information into a decision and implementing it are *left unanswered*. These steps are not part of the *analysis* but of the *synthesis, choice,* and *action*.

Stakeholder analysis may give the initial appearance of a decision-making process, but in fact it is only a *segment* of a decision-making process. It represents the preparatory or opening phase that awaits the crucial application of the moral (or nonmoral) values of the decision-maker. So, to be informed that an individual or an institution regularly makes stakeholder analysis part of decision-making or takes a "stakeholder approach" to management is to learn little or nothing about the ethical character of that individual or institution. It is to learn only that stakeholders are regularly identified—*not why and for what purpose*. To be told that stakeholders are or must be "taken into account" is, so far, to be told very little. Stakeholder analysis is, as a practical matter, morally *neutral*. It is therefore a mistake to see it as a substitute for normative ethical thinking.[4]

What I shall call "stakeholder synthesis" goes further into the sequence of decision-making steps mentioned above to include actual decision-making and implementation (S, C, A). The critical point is that stakeholder synthesis offers *a pattern or channel by which to move from stakeholder identification to a practical response or resolution.* Here we begin to join stakeholder analysis to questions of substance. But we must now ask: What kind of substance? And how does it relate to *ethics*? The stakeholder idea, remember, is typically offered as a way of integrating *ethical* values into management decision-making. When and how does substance become *ethical* substance?

Strategic Stakeholder Synthesis

We can imagine decision-makers doing "stakeholder analysis" for different underlying reasons, not always having to do with ethics. A management team, for example, might be careful to take positive and (especially) negative stakeholder effects into account for no other reason than that offended stakeholders might resist or retaliate (e.g., through political action or opposition to necessary regulatory clearances). It might not be *ethical* concern for the stakeholders that motivates and guides such analysis, so much as concern about potential impediments to the achievement of strategic objectives. Thus positive and negative effects on relatively powerless stakeholders may be ignored or discounted in the synthesis, choice, and action phases of the decision process.[5]

In the Poletown case, General Motors might have done a stakeholder analysis using the following reasoning: our stockholders are the central stakeholders here, but other key stakeholders include our suppliers, old and new plant employees, the city of Detroit, and the residents of Poletown. These other stakeholders are not our direct concern as a corporation with an economic mission, but since they can influence our short- or long-term strategic interests, they must be taken into account. Public relations' costs and benefits, for example, or concerns about union contracts or litigation might well have influenced the choice between staying in Detroit and going elsewhere.

I refer to this kind of stakeholder synthesis as "strategic" since stakeholders outside the stockholder group are viewed instrumentally, as factors potentially affecting the overarching goal of optimizing stockholder interests. They are taken into account in the decision-making process, but as external environmental forces, as potential sources of either good will or retaliation. "We" are the economic principals and management; "they" are significant players whose attitudes and future actions might affect our short-term or long-term success. We must respect them in the way one "respects" the weather—as a set of forces to be reckoned with.[6]

It should be emphasized that managers who adopt the strategic stakeholder approach are not necessarily *personally* indifferent to the plight of stakeholders who are "strategically unimportant." The point is that in their role as managers, with a fiduciary relationship that binds them as agents to principals, their basic outlook subordinates other stakeholder concerns to those of stockholders. Market and legal forces are relied upon to secure the interests of those whom strategic considerations might discount. This reliance can and does take different forms, depending on the emphasis given to market forces on the one hand and legal forces on the other. A more conservative, market-oriented view acknowledges the role of legal compliance as an environmental factor affecting strategic choice, but thinks stakeholder interests are best served by minimal interference from the public sector. Adam Smith's "invisible hand" is thought to be the most important guarantor of the common good in a competitive economy. A more liberal view sees the hand of government, through legislation and regulation, as essential for representing stakeholders that might otherwise not achieve "standing" in the strategic decision process.

What both conservatives and liberals have in common is the conviction that the fundamental orientation of management must be toward the interests of stockholders. Other stakeholders (customers, employees, suppliers, neighbors) enter the decision-making equation either directly as instrumental economic factors or indirectly as potential legal claimants. . . . Both see law and regulation as providing a voice for stakeholders that goes beyond market dynamics. They differ about how much government regulation is socially and economically desirable.

During the Poletown controversy, GM managers as individuals may have cared deeply about the potential lost jobs in Detroit, or about the potential dislocation of Poletown residents. But in their role as agents for the owners (stockholders) they could only allow such considerations to "count" if they served GM's strategic interests (or perhaps as legal constraints on the decision). . . .

The essence of a strategic view of stakeholders is not that stakeholders are ignored, but that all but a special group (stockholders) are considered on the basis of their actual or potential influence on management's central mission. The basic normative principle is fiduciary responsibility (organizational prudence), supplemented by legal compliance. . . .

Multi-Fiduciary Stakeholder Synthesis

In contrast to a strategic view of stakeholders, one can imagine a management team processing stakeholder information by giving the same care to the interests of, say, employees, customers, and local communities as to the economic interests of stockholders. This kind of substantive commitment to stakeholders might involve trading off the economic advantages of one group against those of another, e.g., in a plant closing decision. I shall refer to this way of integrating stakeholder analysis with decision-making as "multi-fiduciary" since all stakeholders are treated by management as having equally important interests, deserving joint "maximization" (or what Herbert Simon might call "satisficing").

Professor Freeman, quoted earlier, contemplates what I am calling the multi-fiduciary view at the end of his 1984 book under the heading *The Manager as Fiduciary to Stakeholders*:

> Perhaps the most important area of future research is the issue of whether or not a theory of management can be constructed that uses the stakeholder concept to enrich "managerial capitalism," that is, can the notion that managers bear a fiduciary relationship to stockholders or the owners of the firm, be replaced by a concept of management whereby the manager *must* act in the interests of the stakeholders in the organization? (249)

As we have seen, the strategic approach pays attention to stakeholders as to factors that might affect economic interests, so many market forces to which companies must pay attention for competitive reasons. They become actual or potential legal challenges to the company's exercise of economic rationality. The multi-fiduciary approach, on the other hand, views stakeholders apart from their instrumental, economic, or legal clout. It does not see them merely as what philosopher John Ladd once called "limiting operating conditions" on management attention.[7] On this view, the word "stakeholder" carries with it, by the deliberate modification of a single phoneme, a dramatic shift in managerial outlook.

In 1954, famed management theorist Adolf Berle conceded a long-standing debate with Harvard law professor E. Merrick Dodd that looks in retrospect very much like a debate between what we are calling strategic and multi-fiduciary interpretations of stakeholder synthesis. Berle wrote:

> Twenty years ago, [I held] that corporate powers were powers in trust for shareholders while Professor Dodd argued that these powers were held in trust for the entire community. The argument has been settled (at least for the time being) squarely in favor of Professor Dodd's contention. (Quoted in Ruder, see below.)

The intuitive idea behind Dodd's view, and behind more recent formulations of it in terms of "multiple constituencies" and "stakeholders, not just stockholders" is that by expanding the list of those in whose trust corporate management must manage, we thereby introduce ethical responsibility into business decision-making.

In the context of the Poletown case, a multi-fiduciary approach by GM management might have identified the same stakeholders. But it would have considered the interests of employees, the city of Detroit, and the Poletown residents *alongside* stockholder interests, not solely in terms of how they might *influence* stockholder interests. This may or may not have entailed a different outcome. But it probably would have meant a different approach to the decision-making process in relation to the residents of Poletown (talking with them, for example).

We must now ask, as we did of the strategic approach: How satisfactory is multi-fiduciary stakeholder synthesis as a way of giving ethical substance to management decision-making? On the face of it, and in stark contrast to the strategic approach, it may seem that we have at least arrived at a truly moral view. But we should be cautious. For no sooner do we think we have found the proper interpretation of ethics in management than a major objection presents itself. And, yes, it appears to be a *moral* objection!

It can be argued that multi-fiduciary stakeholder analysis is simply incompatible with widely-held moral convictions about the special fiduciary obligations owed by management to stockholders. At the center of the objection is the belief that the obligations of agents to principals are stronger or different in kind from those of agents to third parties.

The Stakeholder Paradox

Managers who would pursue a multi-fiduciary stakeholder orientation for their companies must face resistance from those who believe that a strategic orientation is the only *legitimate* one for business to adopt, given the economic mission and legal constitution of the modern corporation. This may be disorienting since the word "illegitimate" has clear negative ethical connotations, and yet the multi-fiduciary approach is often defended on ethical grounds. I will refer to this anomalous situation as the *Stakeholder Paradox*:

> It seems essential, yet in some ways illegitimate, to orient corporate decisions by ethical values that go beyond strategic stakeholder considerations to multi-fiduciary ones.

I call this a paradox because it says there is an ethical problem whichever approach management takes. Ethics seems both to forbid and to demand a strategic, profit-maximizing mind-set. The argument behind the paradox focuses on management's *fiduciary* duty to the stockholder, essentially the duty to keep a profit-maximizing promise, and a concern that the "impartiality" of the multi-fiduciary approach simply cuts management loose from certain well-defined bonds of stockholder accountability. On this view, impartiality is thought to be a *betrayal of trust*. Professor David S. Ruder, a former chairman of the Securities and Exchange Commission, once summarized the matter this way:

> Traditional fiduciary obligation theory insists that a corporate manager owes an obligation of care and loyalty to shareholders. If a public obligation theory unrelated to profit maximization becomes the law, the corporate manager who is not able to act in his own self-interest without violating his fiduciary obligation, may nevertheless act in the public interest without violating that obligation.[8] (226)

Ruder continued:

> Whether induced by government legislation, government pressure, or merely by enlightened attitudes of the corporation regarding its long range potential as a unit in society, corporate activities carried on in satisfaction of public obligations can be consistent with profit maximization objectives. In contrast, justification of public obligations upon bold concepts of public need without corporate benefit will merely serve to reduce further the owner's influence on his corporation and to create additional demands for public participation in corporate management. (228-29)

Ruder's view appears to be that (a) multi-fiduciary stakeholder synthesis *need not* be used by management because the strategic approach is more accommodating than meets the eye; and (b) multi-fiduciary stakeholder synthesis should not be invoked by management because such a "bold" concept could threaten the private (*vs.* public) status of the corporation.

In response to (a), we saw earlier that there were reasonable questions about the tidy convergence of ethics and economic success. Respecting the interests and rights of the Poletown residents might really have meant incurring higher costs for GM (short-term as well as long-term).

Appeals to corporate self-interest, even long-term, might not always support ethical decisions. But even on those occasions where they will, we must wonder about the disposition to favor economic and legal reasoning "for the record." If Ruder means to suggest that business leaders can often *reformulate* or *re-present* their reasons for certain morally-grounded decisions in strategic terms having to do with profit maximization and obedience to law, he is perhaps correct. In the spirit of Milton Friedman's famous essay, we might not summon much indignation to denounce them. But why the fiction? Why not call a moral reason a moral reason?

This issue is not simply of academic interest. Managers must confront it in practice. In one major public company, the C.E.O. put significant resources behind an affirmative action program and included the following explanation in a memo to middle management:

> I am often asked why this is such a high priority at our company. There is, of course, the obvious answer that it is in our best interest to seek out and employ good people in all sectors of our society. And there is the answer that enlightened self-interest tells us that more and more of the younger people, whom we must attract as future employees, choose companies by their social records as much as by their business prospects. *But the one overriding reason for this emphasis is because it is right.* Because this company has always set for itself the objective of assuming social as well as business obligations. Because that's the kind of company we have been. And with your participation, that's the kind of company we'll continue to be.[9]

In this connection, Ruder reminds us of what Professor Berle observed over twenty-five years ago:

> The fact is that boards of directors or corporation executives are often faced with situations in which they quite humanly and simply consider that such and such is the decent thing to do and ought to be done.... They apply the potential profits or public relations tests later on, a sort of left-handed justification in this curious free-market world where an obviously moral or decent or humane action has to be apologized for one the ground that, conceivably, you may somehow make money by it. (*Ibid.*)

The Problem of Boldness

What appears to lie at the foundation of Ruder's cautious view is a concern about the "boldness" of the multi-fiduciary concept [(b) above].[10] It is not that he thinks the strategic approach is always satisfactory; it is that the multi-fiduciary approach is, in his eyes, much worse. For it questions the special relationship between the manager as agent and the stockholder as principal.

Ruder suggests that what he calls a "public obligation" theory threatens the private status of the corporation. He believes that what we are calling multi-fiduciary stakeholder synthesis *dilutes* the fiduciary obligation to stockholders (by extending it to customers, employees, suppliers, etc.) and he sees this as a threat to the "privacy" of the private sector organization. If public obligations are understood on the model of public sector institutions with their multiple constituencies, Ruder thinks, the stockholder loses status.

There is something profoundly *right* about Ruder's line of argument here, I believe, and something profoundly *wrong*. What is right is his intuition that if we treat other stakeholders on the model of the fiduciary relationship between management and the stockholder, we will, in effect, make them into quasi-stockholders. We can do this, of course, if we choose to as a society. But we should be aware that it is a radical step indeed. For it blurs traditional goals in terms of entrepreneurial risk-taking, pushes decision-making towards paralysis because of the dilemmas posed by divided loyalties and, in the final analysis, represents nothing less than the conversion of the modern private corporation into a public institution and probably calls for a corresponding restructuring of corporate governance (e.g., representatives of each stakeholder group on the board of directors). Unless we believe that the social utility of a private sector has disappeared, not to mention its value for individual liberty and enterprise, we will be cautious about an interpretation of stakeholder synthesis that transforms the private sector into the public sector.

On the other hand, I believe Ruder is mistaken if he thinks that business ethics requires this kind of either/or: either a private sector with a strategic stakeholder synthesis (business without ethics) or the effective loss of the private sector with a multi-fiduciary stakeholder synthesis (ethics without business).

Recent debates over state laws protecting companies against hostile takeovers may illustrate Ruder's concern as well as the new challenge. According to one journalist, a recent Pennsylvania anti-takeover law

does no less than redefine the fiduciary duty of corporate directors, enabling them to base decisions not merely on the interests of shareholders, but on the interests of customers, suppliers, employees and the community at large. Pennsylvania is saying that it is the corporation that directors are responsible to. Shareholders say they always thought they themselves were the corporation.

Echoing Ruder, one legal observer quoted by Elias[11] (*ibid.*) commented with reference to this law that it "undermines and erodes free markets and property rights. From this perspective, this is an anticapitalist law. The management can take away property from the real owners."

In our terms, the state of Pennsylvania is charged with adopting a multi-fiduciary stakeholder approach in an effort to rectify deficiencies of the strategic approach which (presumably) corporate raiders hold.

The challenge that we are thus presented with is to develop an account of the moral responsibilities of management that (i) avoids surrendering the moral relationship between management and stakeholders as the strategic view does, while (ii) not transforming stakeholder obligations into fiduciary obligations (thus protecting the uniqueness of the principal-agent relationship between management and stockholder).

II. Toward a New Stakeholder Synthesis

We all remember the story of the well-intentioned Doctor Frankenstein. He sought to improve the human condition by designing a powerful, intelligent force for good in the community. Alas, when he flipped the switch, his creation turned out to be a monster rather than a marvel! Is the concept of the ethical corporation like a Frankenstein monster?

Taking business ethics seriously need not mean that management bears *additional* fiduciary relationships to third parties (nonstockholder constituencies) as multi-fiduciary stakeholder synthesis suggests. It may mean that there are morally significant *nonfiduciary* obligations to third parties surrounding any fiduciary relationship (See *Figure 1*).

Such moral obligations may be owed by private individuals as well as private-sector organizations to those whose freedom and well-being is affected by their economic behavior. It is these very obligations in fact (the duty not to harm or coerce and duties not to lie, cheat, or steal) that are cited in regulatory, legislative, and judicial arguments for constraining profit-driven business activities. These obligations are not "hypothetical" or contingent or indirect, as they would be on the strategic model, wherein they are only subject to the corporation's interests being met. They are "categorical" or direct. They are not rooted in the *fiduciary* relationship, but in other relationships at least as deep.

	Fiduciary	Nonfiduciary
Stockholders	●	
Other Stakeholders		●

Figure 1. Direct Managerial Obligations

It must be admitted in fairness to Ruder's argument that the jargon of "stakeholders" in discussions of business ethics can seem to threaten the notion of what corporate law refers to as the "undivided and unselfish loyalty" owed by managers and directors to stockholders. For this way of speaking can suggest a multiplication of management duties *of the same kind* as the duty to stockholders. What we must understand is that the responsibilities of management toward stockholders are of a piece with the obligations that *stockholders themselves* would be expected to honor in their own right. As an old Latin proverb has it, *nemo dat quod non habet*, which literally means "nobody gives what he doesn't have." Freely translating in this context we can say: No one can expect of an *agent* behavior that is ethically less responsible than what he would expect of himself. I cannot (ethically) *hire* done on my behalf what I would not (ethically) *do* myself. We might refer to this as the "Nemo Dat Principle" (NDP) and consider it a formal requirement of consistency in business ethics (and professional ethics generally):

(NDP) Investors cannot expect of managers (more generally, principals cannot expect of their agents) behavior that would be incon-

sistent with the reasonable ethical expectations of the community.[12]

The NDP does not, of course, resolve in advance the many ethical challenges that managers must face. It only indicates that these challenges are of a piece with those that face us all. It offers a different kind of test (and so a different kind of stakeholder synthesis) that management (and institutional investors) might apply to policies and decisions.

The foundation of ethics in management—and the way out of the stakeholder paradox—lies in understanding that the conscience of the corporation is a logical and moral extension of the consciences of its principals. It is *not* an expansion of the *list* of principals, but a gloss on the principal-agent relationship itself. Whatever the structure of the principal-agent relationship, neither principal nor agent can ever claim that an agent has "moral immunity" from the basic obligations that would apply to any human being toward other members of the community.

Indeed, consistent with Ruder's belief, the introduction of moral reasoning (distinguished from multi-fiduciary stakeholder reasoning) into the framework of management thinking may *protect* rather than threaten private sector legitimacy. The conscientious corporation can maintain its private economic mission, but in the context of fundamental moral obligations owed by any member of society to others affected by that member's actions. Recognizing such obligations does *not* mean that an institution is a public institution. Private institutions, like private individuals, can be and are bound to respect moral obligations in the pursuit of private purposes.

Conceptually, then, we can make room for a moral posture toward stakeholders that is both *partial* (respecting the fiduciary relationship between managers and stockholders) and *impartial* (respecting the equally important non-fiduciary relationships between management and other stakeholders). As philosopher Thomas Nagel has said, "In the conduct of life, of all places, the rivalry between the view from within and the view from without must be taken seriously."[13]

Whether this conceptual room can be used *effectively* in the face of enormous pressures on contemporary managers and directors is another story, of course. For it is one thing to say that "giving standing to stakeholders" in managerial reasoning is conceptually coherent. It is something else to say that it is practically coherent.

Yet most of us, I submit, believe it. Most of us believe that management at General Motors *owed* it to the people of Detroit and to the people of Poletown to take their (nonfiduciary) interests very seriously, to seek creative solutions to the conflict, to do more than use or manipulate them in accordance with GM's needs only. We understand that managers and directors have a special obligation to provide a financial return to the stockholders, but we also understand that the word "special" in this context needs to be tempered by an appreciation of certain fundamental community norms that go beyond the demands of both laws and markets. There are certain class-action suits that stockholders ought not to win. For there is sometimes a moral defense.

Conclusion

The relationship between management and stockholders is ethically different in kind from the relationship between management and other parties (like employees, suppliers, customers, etc.), a fact that seems to go unnoticed by the multi-fiduciary approach. If it were not, the corporation would cease to be a private sector institution— and what is now called business ethics would become a more radical critique of our economic system than is typically thought. On this point, Milton Friedman must be given a fair and serious hearing.

This does not mean, however, that "stakeholders" lack a morally significant relationship to management, as the strategic approach implies. It means only that the relationship in question is different from a fiduciary one. Management may never have promised customers, employees, suppliers, etc. a "return on investment," but management is nevertheless obliged to take seriously its extra-legal obligations not to injure, lie to or cheat these stakeholders *quite apart from* whether it is in the stockholders' interests.

As we think through the *proper* relationship of management to stakeholders, fundamental features of business life must undoubtedly be recognized: that corporations have a principally economic mission and competence; that fiduciary obligations to investor and general obligations to comply with the law cannot be set aside; and that abuses of economic power and disregard of corporate stewardship in the name of business ethics are possible.

But these things must be recognized as well: that corporations are not solely financial institutions; that fiduciary obligations go beyond short-term profit and are in any case subject to moral criteria in their execution; and that mere compliance with the law can be unduly limited and even unjust.

The *Stakeholder Paradox* can be avoided by a more thoughtful understanding of the nature of moral obligation and the limits it imposes on the principal-agent relationship. Once we understand that there is a practical "space" for identifying the ethical values shared by a corporation and its stockholders—a space that goes beyond strategic self-interest but stops short of impartiality—the hard work of filling that space can proceed.

Notes

[1]Strictly speaking the historical meaning of "stakeholder" in this context is someone who literally *holds* the stakes during play.

[2]See Goodpaster and Piper, *Managerial Decision Making and Ethical Values,* Harvard Business School Publishing Division, 1989.

[3]See Goodpaster, *PASCAL: A Framework for Conscientious Decision Making* (1989).

[4]Actually, there are subtle ways in which even the stakeholder identification or inventory process might have *some* ethical content. The very process of *identifying* affected parties involves the use of the imagination in a way that can lead to a

natural empathetic or caring response to those parties in the synthesis, choice and action phases of decision-making. This is a contingent connection, however, not a necessary one.

[5]Note that including powerless stakeholders in the analysis phase may indicate whether the decision-maker cares about "affecting" them or "being affected by" them. Also, the inclusion of what might be called secondary stakeholders as advocates for primary stakeholders (e.g., local governments on behalf of certain citizen groups) may signal the values that will come into play in any synthesis.

[6]It should be mentioned that some authors, most notably Kenneth R. Andrews in *The Concept of Corporate Strategy* (Irwin, Third Edition, 1987) employ a broader and more social definition of "strategic" decision-making than the one implied here.

[7]Ladd observed in a now-famous essay entitled "Morality and the Ideal of Rationality in Formal Organizations" (*The Monist*, 54, 1970) that organizational "rationality" was defined solely in terms of economic objectives: "The interests and needs of the individuals concerned, as individuals, must be considered only insofar as they establish limiting operating conditions. Organizational rationality dictates that these interests and needs must not be considered in their own right or on their own merits. If we think of an organization as a machine, it is easy to see why we cannot reasonably expect it to have any moral obligations to people or for them to have any to it." (507)

[8]"Public Obligations of Private Corporations," *Univ. of Pennsylvania Law Review*, 114 (1965). Ruder recently (1989) reaffirmed the views in his 1965 article.

[9]Business Products Corporation—Part 1 HBS Case Services 9-377-077.

[10]"The Business Judgement Rule" gives broad latitude to officers and directors of corporations, but calls for reasoning on the basis of the long-term economic interest of the company. And corporate case law ordinarily allows exceptions to profit-maximization criteria only when there are actual or potential *legal* barriers, and limits charitable and humanitarian gifts by the logic of long term self-interest. The underlying rationale is accountability to investors. Recent work by the American Law Institute, however, suggest a rethinking of these matters. See *Exhibit 2*.

[11](Christopher Elias, "Turning Up the Heat on the Top," *Insight*, July 23, 1990).

[12]We might consider the NDP in broader terms that would include the relationship between "client" and "professional" in other contexts, such as law, medicine, education, government, and religion, where normally the community's expectations are embodied in ethical standards.

[13]T. Nagel, *The View from Nowhere*, Oxford Univ. Press (1986), p. 163.

Ethical Aspects of Investor Behavior

Pietra Rivoli

Journal of Business Ethics 14 (1955): 265–77. Copyright © 1955 Kluwer Academic Publishers.

Challenges to the neoclassical paradigm form much of the basis for scholarship in diverse fields including business ethics, management, and sociology. Two important challenges to the paradigm are the stakeholder duty concept and Etzioni's (1988) "I&We" construct. To what extent, and in what ways, are these views of the world mutually exclusive, incompatible, and irreconcilable? Alternatively, what is the common ground, either normative or positive, on which dialogue can proceed?

I will not attempt a complete statement of these views; this has been ably accomplished by others (Swanson, 1992; Preston and Sapienza, 1990). I will instead outline the features of each that are important to the subsequent discussion. The neoclassical model leads to the shareholder wealth (SWM) prescription for corporate decision-making. Shareholders are assumed to have a unidimensional utility function wherein their utility is solely a function of wealth. The model prescribes that management should operate in the interests of the shareholders. By assumption, the interests of the shareholders are best served by share price maximization.

The stakeholder concept is based on the normative premise that managers should balance competing claims by groups that include, but are not limited to, shareholders. Shareholders do not have innate preeminence among the groups competing for corporate resources. In brief, corporate decisions should consider the welfare of a range of constituencies.

The neoclassical model explicitly equates shareholder welfare with shareholder wealth. The stakeholder concept, on the other hand, does not explicitly define "welfare." Thus, while the stakeholder concept prescribes that the welfare of, for example, employees, should be considered in corporate decisions, it does not formally define welfare. However, the literature relating to the stakeholder concept leads readers to the conclusions that "welfare" and "economic welfare" are roughly interchangeable terms. For example, the welfare of employees is typically stated in terms of job security, wages, benefits, and so forth. The welfare of customers is stated in terms of a "good service" or "quality, competitive products." Stakeholder management attempts to balance the interests of competing groups, and these "interests" are assumed to be economic in nature. The key words of "balance" and "trade-off" emerge frequently in this literature: Should the firm increase dividends to shareholders, or wages to employees, or contributions to United Way, or built a child care center?

An important compatibility therefore emerges between the stakeholder management view and SWM: Both views assume that stakeholder groups are self-interested economic agents whose "utility" derives from wealth. The primary concerns of labor unions, customers, and shareholders are economic concerns, and management's charge is to arbiter or balance the competing economic claims of self-interested groups. The stakeholder construct does not challenge the neoclassical assumption that shareholder utility derives from wealth.

A central tenet of Etzioni's work, however, is that people are "other-interested" as well as self-interested, and are guided by moral duty as well as

economic self-interest. This is a positive claim, and poses a (by now) well-known challenge to the neoclassical paradigm. If Etzioni is correct, shareholder wealth and shareholder welfare are not equivalent, and managerial decisions that maximize the wealth of shareholders do not necessarily maximize shareholder welfare, because shareholders have concerns for others and moral duties to which they ascribe importance. The basis for the SWM decision rule is weakened substantially if Etzioni's description of human nature applies to shareholders.

The stakeholder view also assumes that shareholders are wealth maximizers, so that the challenge for management is to balance the economic welfare of shareholders against those of other groups. However, this challenge is ill-defined if Etzioni is correct in his view of human nature. If shareholders are to some extent "other-interested" and bound by a sense of moral duty, then much of the challenge of stakeholder management—balancing competing economic claims—becomes artificial. For example, if shareholders are interested in fair employment practices, truthful advertising, or environmental responsibility, as well as in their own economic welfare, then managers may not have to balance demands for such goods against demands for dividends. If shareholders are other-interested then they are interested in the well-being of other stakeholders, and will forego increases in wealth in order further the interests of others or to abide by moral duties.

Do shareholders have social and ethical concerns which affect their behavior as investors? The answer appears to be a qualified yes. I will argue that a broader definition of shareholder welfare, one which encompasses social and ethical concerns, is necessary to understand some recent developments in investment and corporate governance, and I will present empirical evidence supporting this argument.

I. Ethical and Economic Motives of Investors

It is necessary to distinguish clearly between ethical and social motives and economic motives of investors. Suppose that decisions can be made along two dimensions: ethics and economics. The economic decision will be made on the basis of the decision-maker's judgement regarding whether a course of action will increase or decrease the share price. The ethical decision will be made on the basis of the decision-maker's judgement regarding whether the course of action is right or wrong. In order to decide whether a course of action is right or wrong, the action is evaluated against ethical principles.

Ethical and economic decision-making may or may not conflict. The possible combinations are shown in Exhibit I.

EXHIBIT I

Conflicts and congruence between economic and ethical decisions

| | | **The Economic Decision: Course of Action will:** | |
		Increase share price	Decrease share price
The ethical decision Course of action is:	Right	**1A** No conflict— proceed with action	**1B** Conflict
	Wrong	**2A** Conflict	**2B** No conflict— Do not proceed with action

In boxes 1A and 2B the economic and ethical decisions do not conflict. Box 1A contains courses of action which the decision-maker believes to be both morally right (or at least morally neutral) and wealth-enhancing. Therefore, Box 1A contains all those "projects" which are expected to increase the share price and do not violate ethical principles or the rights of other stakeholders. Box 2B contains those actions which violate ethical principles and which will decrease the share price because they have negative NPVs. In these boxes, the neoclassical and stakeholder view would give the same prescription to management: the firm should proceed with action 1A and forego action 2B.

In boxes 1B and 2A, however, the economic and ethical dimensions of a decision conflict. In Box 2A are corporate activities which will increase the share price but violate ethical principles or the rights of other stakeholders. Examples of decisions with these attributes might include the export of hazardous U.S.-banned pesticides to developing countries, indirect marketing of tobacco to minors, failure to warn consumers of known product risks, certain forms of advertising to children, and certain forms of infant formula distribution.

Box 1B contains those actions which will reduce the share price, but are mandated by ethical principles or concern for other stakeholders. For example, in the early 1980s, many firms chose to voluntarily divest their South African operations for moral reasons. These firms suffered significant declines in share prices (Mukherjee *et al.*, 1991).

If we assume that shareholders are interested only in share price maximization, then a conflict will emerge between proponents of SWM and stakeholder management. In addition, there is an obvious challenge for stakeholder management. Shareholders will want the firm to pursue activity 2A, but managers must balance this demand against the rights of other stakeholders. Shareholders will want the firm to forego activity 1B, but managers must balance this preference against its benefits for other stakeholders. If, on the other hand, shareholders are concerned for the welfare of others and have ethical principles by which they wish to abide, then these conflicts may be less frequent, less important, and somewhat artificial. In brief, if shareholders are concerned about the welfare of (say) employees, then management's charge to balance the competing claims of shareholders and employees becomes less critical.

II. Shareholder Governance Behavior, 1988–1990

From a research perspective, the social and ethical concerns of investors are meaningful only to the extent that they affect behavior. Investor behavior may be influenced in two ways. First, ethical and social considerations may affect investors' decisions to buy or sell shares. Second, they may affect investors' shareholder governance and voting behavior.

The evidence relating to the ethical motivation behind buy and sell decisions is anecdotal, but collectively convincing. For example, in 1990 Harvard University announced the divestiture of $58 million in tobacco stocks from the University's portfolio. The decision was made with reference to ethical principles. Derek Bok, Harvard's President, said, "the University's decision was motivated by a desire not to be associated with as a shareholder with companies engaged in sales of products that create a substantial and unjustified risk of harm to other human beings." In explaining a similar decision, a Trustee of the City University of New York said that "It is hypocrisy for our institutions to own stocks in tobacco companies that make profits on the lives of people." Similar reasoning has been put forth to defend South African divestment.

Further evidence that shareholders consider ethical issues in their buy and sell decisions is found in the growth of mutual funds which screen firms using ethical and social criteria. In 1980, there were two such funds with total assets of under $4 million. By 1991, there were nine funds with assets of over $1 billion, an increase of over 250 percent. These funds, by definition, use ethical and social criteria in making buy and sell decisions.[1] In fact, the largest of these funds (Calvert) explicitly states that below market returns on some "socially desirable" investments will be accepted. Some observers estimate that 10 percent of investment capital in the U.S. is subject to social and ethical screens (IRRC, 1990).

The evidence suggests that screened mutual funds underperform the market, and that screening out firms involved in tobacco, weapons production, nuclear power, infant formula, forest products and other "offensive" industries eliminates some of the most profitable firms and industries from investor portfolios (Berss, 1991; Luck, 1992). Further, social or ethical screens severely limit diversification opportunities. The Domini Social Index, for example, screens out over half of the S&P 500 firms. Because "ethical investing" entails economic costs, the investors described above fall into Box 2A in Figure 1: the economically optimal portfolio conflicts with the investor's ethical principles.

While the growth in these mutual funds and decisions such as Harvard's can be cited as evidence of social concern on the part of investors, such evidence is necessarily anecdotal. Systematic analysis of the ethical motivation behind buy and sell decisions is not possible simply because while transactions are observable, the motivation behind them are not.

It is possible, however, to make inferences about shareholders' motives by observing voting behavior. Therefore, my objective is to examine shareholder voting behavior to determine whether the social and ethical considerations of shareholders help to explain this behavior. The most comprehensive source of information on proxy voting is the Investor Responsibility Research Center (IRRC), an organization promoting greater shareholder activism and involvement in corporate affairs. The IRRC's Corporate Governance Service tracks resolutions relating to corporate governance and control at approximately 1500 large American firms. According to the IRRC, 627 shareholder proposals relating to these issues control came to votes during the 1988–1990 period.

My first objective is to examine whether shareholder voting behavior is consistent with the wealth maximization view. I examined the content of the resolutions related to corporate governance and control introduced by shareholders during the 1988–1990 period. For some proposals, the effect on shareholder wealth is indeterminate. For example, some proposals called for the company to change the time or place of the annual meeting, to disclose executive compensation, to limit the terms of directors, or to require mandatory retirement for directors. However, any proposal that gives shareholders the option to exercise greater control over corporate affairs, any proposals which make wealth transfers from shareholders to outside parties more difficult, or any proposal which facilitates wealth transfers to shareholders or changes in corporate control, are in the economic interests of shareholders. Finance research has shown that these resolutions are wealth enhancing; that is, share prices increase when firms act in accordance with the resolutions:

Cumulative Voting: These proposals would allow shareholders to cast all of their votes for one director, or to divide them among two or more. These proposals, therefore, would increase the ability of shareholders to exercise influence. Evidence on the economic value of cumulative voting is provided by Bhagat and Brickley (1984).

Poison Pills: These proposals ask firms either to redeem poison pills, or to require that they be subject to shareholder votes. Poison pills are an impediment to the transfer of control, and a number of studies have shown that the adoption of the pills reduces shareholder wealth (Malatesta and Walking, 1988; Ryngaert, 1988).

Greenmail: The payment of greenmail impedes the transfer of control and results in a wealth transfer from shareholders to outside parties. These resolutions either ask management not to pay greenmail, or ask that greenmail be subject to a shareholder vote.

Confidential Voting: These proposals ask that shareholder voting behavior be confidential. Confidential voting is in the shareholder's interest for three reasons. First, some institutional shareholders have relationships with firms that may be jeopardized by opposing management. Second, institutional investors are often lobbied by management to influence their voting behavior, and some investors find this activity inappropriate. Finally, an investor would be free to disclose their voting behavior if such a disclosure were in their interest.

Repeal Classified Board: Classified Boards are an anti-takeover device. Under most classified board systems, only one third of the corporate directors are elected each year. As a result, it will take a minimum of two years for a majority of the directors to be replaced and classified boards are an impediment to changes in corporate control. Shareholders have proposed, therefore, that all directors be elected annually. The adoption of classified boards is associated with decreases in shareholder wealth (Jarrell and Poulson, 1987); the repeal of the boards benefits shareholders (Bhagat and Brickley, 1984).

Equal Access to Proxy Statement: Proxy materials now contain management's recommendation to shareholders on how each resolution should be voted. Generally, these recommendations include an argument in support of management's position, as well as the recommendation itself. The equal access resolutions would require that equal space be provided for shareholder views which dissent from management's. In other words, the proxy statement would present "both sides" of the arguments regarding the resolutions. Since this requirement would provide information to shareholders, it must have value.

Opt Out of Delaware Law: "Delaware Law" is an impediment to changes in corporate control. The law states that if an acquirer purchases 15 percent of a firm's shares, a merger between the firms may not occur for three years without the approval of the target's board, unless the purchase of the 15 percent caused the acquirer to own 85 percent of the voting shares. Since many firms control at least 15 percent of the voting shares through ESOPS or other mechanisms, it is very difficult for an acquirer to meet these requirements. A firm, however, may "opt out" of the law if a majority of the shareholders vote to do so. The value of the "opt out" proposals is evident. "Delaware type" laws reduce stock prices, and firms opting out experience increased prices (Szewczyk and Tsetsekos, 1992; Karpoff and Malatesta, 1989).

Golden parachutes: These proposals ask that golden parachute severance agreements be subject to shareholder vote.

Minimum Stock Ownership: These proposals would require that members of the board hold stock in the corporations. Such a proposal would align the interests of the board more closely with the interests of shareholders.

Institute or Restore Preemptive Rights: The preemptive right gives shareholders the right to purchase new stock issues in order to maintain their percentage ownership. The right is an option, and therefore has value to shareholders. Bhagat (1983) presents evidence of the economic value of preemptive rights.

Reduce or Repeal Supermajority Requirements: The supermajority requirements are an anti-takeover device which require between [fr2/3] and 90 percent of votes before a merger can be approved. The adoption of supermajority requirements are associated with decreases in shareholder wealth (Jarrell and Poulson, 1987).

Exhibit II shows the number (*n*) of each type of resolution brought to votes and the voting results for the 1988–1990 period. The vote is stated as an unweighted average of the percentage of shareholders voting in favor of the resolution. These resolutions garner 20–30 percent of shareholder votes. Therefore, these data show that the majority of shareholders do not vote in a manner consistent with price maximization.

Although these results show that shareholders do not use their votes in a manner consistent with share price maximization, they do not show that shareholders are not wealth-maximizing agents. That is, shareholders may be economically self-interested, but, at the same time vote in a manner inconsistent with wealth maximization. First, small investors are likely to be passive rather than active shareholders because they have little incentive to incur the information costs necessary for informed voting. As a result, they simply vote with management. The second explanation is that for some institutions, voting with management may be wealth-maximizing behavior in a global sense, even though the stock price effect of the resolutions would not suggest this. Some institutions have relationships with the firms in which they invest, and these relationships may be jeopardized by opposing management, because voting behavior is not confidential (Brickley *et al.*, 1988).

Some examination of the issue is possible by examining the behavior of shareholders who are known to be both active and knowledgeable. If investors are solely wealth-motivated, and they incur the costs associated with becoming informed voters on issues of corporate governance and control, they will vote in a manner consistent with

Exhibit II
Shareholder Governance and Control Resolutions, 1988–1990

Resolution type	1988		1989		1990	
	n	vote	n	vote	n	vote
Greenmail	5	28	4	26	0	–
Confidential voting	9	19	39	27	42	32
Repeal classified board	37	20	46	22	37	25
Equal access	6	12	3	6	0	–
Cumulative voting	32	14	39	16	16	39
Poison pills	19	36	19	34	28	39
Delaware law	0	–	4	16	5	27
Golden parachute	0	–	1	26	24	10
Min. stock ownership	11	13	17	9	20	12
Preemptive right	1	13	9	10	5	10
Reduce supermajority	3	30	4	26	3	34
Total/Wtd. average vote	132/20		186/21		203/23	

Exhibit III
Active investors' voting policies on shareholder governance and control proposals, 1988–1990

Type of resolution	Percentage saying that they "generally vote for" the proposal		
	1988	1989	1990
Redeem poison pill, or require vote	63	61	55
Confidential voting	43	70	72
Repeal classified board	43	59	60
Opt out of Delaware Law	na	44	49
Greenmail	70	74	75
Golden parachutes	na	71	57
Equal Access	35	43	na
Cumulative voting	30	38	41
Min. stock ownership	na	9	16
Average	47	49	48
Number of respondents	128	86	99

SWM. One of the services provided to institutional investors by the IRRC is the "Corporate Governance Service." For a fee, this subscription service provides impartial information to subscribers regarding the resolutions that relate to corporate governance and control. Subscribers receive information regarding the resolutions that will be introduced at particular companies, a description of the issues involved, statements by proponents and opponents, and voting results. It is reasonable to assume that subscribers to the Corporate Governance Service are active and knowledgeable regarding these issues, since the very act of subscribing implies interest and knowledge in shareholders governance, and implies that these investors do not blindly rubber stamp management's position. Survey data from these subscribers show that 87 percent of subscribers have special committees, for analyzing and voting proxies.[2]

Each year IRRC surveys its Corporate Governance Service subscribers to learn of the positions taken on shareholder and management resolutions. The questions do not relate to individual companies. Instead, the survey asks questions in general terms, for example, "How do you gener-

ally vote on resolutions calling for a shareholder vote on poison pills?" Survey respondents are not identified. A summary of the responses is shown in Exhibit III.

As we would expect, support for wealth-enhancing shareholder proposals is significantly higher among the active and knowledgeable shareholders than among the shareholder population at large. An admittedly rough measure of the activist sport for these resolutions is 47–49 percent, the average response. This support is approximately twice as high as that of the shareholder population. This suggests that the "shareholder apathy/information cost" explanation has some validity.

The "other hand" of these results is that 51–53 percent of activist shareholders do not "generally vote for" these proposals: a significant number of active and knowledgeable investors do not vote in accordance with their economic interests.

It may be, however, that the voting behavior results are wealth-enhancing in a global sense if there are costs associated with opposing management. Brickley *et al.* (1988) divided institutional investors into three categories depending upon their susceptibility to management pressure. At one end of the spectrum are the groups which may be susceptible to management pressure: insurance companies, banks, and non-bank trusts. These institutions may have other business relationships with the firms in which they invest. At the other end of the spectrum are groups for which opposing management will not be costly ("pressure-resistant groups"). These include public pension funds, mutual funds, endowments, and foundations. By definition, subscribers to the IRRC Corporate Governance Service are at least somewhat pressure-resistant. However, to examine this issue further, I separate the survey responses for pressure-resistant groups: public pension funds, foundations, endowments, and church groups.[3] The survey responses for the active and pressure-resistant shareholders are shown in Exhibit IV.

The average percentage of active and pressure-resistant shareholders voting for the resolutions is approximately 9 percentage points higher than that for the active investors in general. Investor susceptibility to management pressure therefore also has some explanatory power for voting behavior. However, much voting behavior (roughly 40 percent) remains unexplained by the share price maximization motive. Even when investors are informed, active, and immune to management pressure, many do not vote in a manner consistent with share price maximization.

III. Can the "I & We" Paradigm Help to Explain Investor Behavior?

The results presented in the previous section suggest that factors other than wealth maximization are needed to explain voting behavior for some active and knowledgeable investors; As Bhagat and Jefferis (1991) note, "... (Economics) does not explain shareholder support for wealth decreasing changes in corporate governance." What other factors might help to explain this behavior?

Most of the resolutions previously discussed would facilitate transfers of corporate control and it is well-known that takeovers benefit target shareholders. On average, target firm shareholders receive premiums of 40–80 percent above the market price of their shares. However, it is equally well-known that other stakeholders may be harmed in these transfers, particularly employees and local communities. As a result, some business ethicists have questioned various takeover-related activities (Richman, 1984; Woodstock Theological Center, 1988). They argue that from a moral

Exhibit IV
Percent of active and pressure-resistant shareholders saying that they "generally vote for" the proposal.

Resolution	1988	1989	1990
Greenmail	72.3	77.5	82
Confidential voting	62.4	75.5	87.0
Repeal classified board	57.4	55	69
Equal access	47.3	41	na
Cumulative voting	41	46.5	48
Poison pill	72	60	71.5
Delaware law	na	34	59
Min. stock ownership	na	na	23
Preemptive right	na	na	36.5
Supermajority	na	na	76
Average	59	56	56
Number of respondents	61	50	48

perspective, the well-being of other stakeholders must be considered in such decisions, and shareholder wealth and efficiency gains are not necessarily sufficient moral grounds for takeovers because these gains must be weighed against the effects on other stakeholders. In other words, a transfer of control is a decision residing in Box 2A: while the transfer will increase the share price, it may be morally suspect if it imposes significant costs on other stakeholders.

In 1989, nine resolutions were introduced by management that effectively asked shareholders to endorse the stakeholder view in the context of takeovers. These proposals authorized the Board of Directors to consider the "community impact," the "non-financial impact" or the "social and economic impact on communities, employees, customers and suppliers" when considering takeover offers. All of these proposals passed with a majority of the shareholder vote. The average shareholder vote in favor of these resolutions was 68 percent. The range at the nine companies was from 57 to 93 percent. Among the active investors referred to earlier, 20 percent generally vote against these resolutions, 23 percent generally vote in favor, and the remainder had no set policy but examined each resolution on a case by case basis.[4]

In effect, shareholders voted to consider the welfare of stakeholders, at the expense of share price maximization.

The results shown in Exhibits 3 and 4 suggest that some factors other than wealth are informing shareholder voting behavior. The voting behavior observed on the stakeholder proposals, together with that observed on takeover-related proposals, is consistent with Etzioni's paradigm. "Other interestedness" appears to explain at least some shareholder behavior on resolutions relating to corporate control.

A second phenomenon suggestive of the integration view is activism by shareholders to influence corporate behavior on moral and social issues. Increasingly, large institutions are introducing shareholder resolutions in an attempt to change firm behavior. During the past several years, the resolutions have dealt with the following broad issues:

South Africa: Requests that firms divest South African operations, cease sales to South Africa, or issue a report describing South African business activities.

CERES (or Valdez) Principles: Requests that the firms sign and adhere to the principles, which are an environmental code of conduct.

Northern Ireland: Asks firms to sign the MacBride principles prohibiting religious discrimination in Northern Ireland, or to take other steps relating to human rights.

Other environment: Reduce toxic emissions, establish environmental committee, or issue environmental report.

Military: Reduce or report on foreign military sales, reduce nuclear weapons business.

Tobacco: Research and report on effects of advertising on minors or other groups. Gradually withdraw from the tobacco business. Do not market without warning labels.

Equal employment: Report on progress in affirmative action and equal employment.

Animal Protection: Report on animal testing, cease live animal testing.

LDC Debt: Use social or human rights lending criteria; forgive debt that has been written off.

Infant Formula: Cease direct marketing to public.

The corporate actions described above are not mandated by law, they are voluntary and costly. Since they are not mandated, firms taking these actions will be at an economic disadvantage to its competitors. A health company ceasing animal testing, or a bank who forgives LDC debt, will be at a disadvantage relative to competitor firms. Shareholders advocating these proposals reside in Box 1B (they want the firm to do the "right" thing even if it is costly—e.g., forgive LDC debt), or box 2A (they do not want the firm to do the "wrong" thing even if it is profitable—e.g., directly market infant formula). These resolutions illustrate shareholder concern for other stakeholders.

The IRRC's Social Issues Service tracks "social policy" resolutions introduced by shareholders. Exhibit V shows the number of these resolutions brought to votes since 1973 and the number receiving more than 3 percent of the vote. The 3 percent hurdle is significant because a resolution must receive at least this percent of the shareholder vote in the first year it is introduced in order to be placed on the ballot in the following year. Both the number of these resolutions, and the support that they garner, is increasing.

Exhibit VI shows voting results by type in 1989–1991. There is wide variation in the voting results. Resolutions relating to South Africa, Northern Ireland and the environment garner the largest support, while those relating to human rights garner the least. Overall, the more successful resolutions garner approximately half as much shareholder support as do the wealth-enhancing shareholder resolutions. However, in several cases, support for the social issues resolutions exceeds that of the governance and control resolutions.

IV. The Influence of Social Voice Investors

The specter of the "little old man in tennis shoes" making a ruckus over social issues at annual meetings is largely a fallacy. Proponents of the social policy resolutions are likely to have significant influence on corporate activities. Virtually all of the social policy resolutions are introduced by (usually large) institutions. During 1989–91, institutions sponsored well over 90 percent of the social policy resolutions. Exhibit VII shows the sponsors of social policy resolutions, and the number of resolutions proposed by each group.

The Interfaith Center on Corporate Responsibility (ICCR) is the leader in the introduction of social policy shareholder resolutions. ICCR was formed in 1970 as a mechanism for American churches to influence corporate activities. ICCR directly controls approximately $12 billion in investment funds. In addition, other church groups often vote with ICCR on principle.

New York City and State, California, Minnesota, Connecticut, and Wisconsin Funds are the

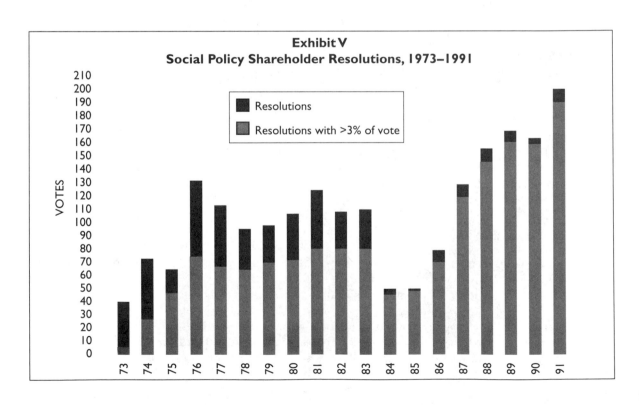

Exhibit VI
Social Policy Shareholder Resolutions, 1989–1991

Resolution	1989		1990		1991	
	n	vote	*n*	vote	*n*	vote
South Africa	88	12.65	85	12.78	78	13.00
N. Ireland	19	9.04	20	9.97	18	10.62
Valdez principles	0	-	5	12.52	32	8.21
Other environment	9	6.37	16	7.35	15	7.31
PACS	10	7.06	2	7.35	0	-
Weapons	15	4.77	8	5.51	14	4.39
Infant formula	1	4.5	2	6.45	2	7.35
EEO	4	5.5	2	4.7	5	5.76
Animal protection	13	8.32	8	8.13	7	3.95
LDC Debt	1	9.5	3	5.76	5	3.22
Human rights	3	2.83	1	3.20	2	2.90
Tobacco	0	-	5	3.14	8	5.05
Plant closings	1	8.1	0	-	1	9.40
Other	2	5.0	4	5.61	13	5.19

most active among public investors in introducing shareholder social policy resolutions. Along with TIAA-CREF, the financial resources of these funds are of course considerable. Four of the world's five largest pension funds (TAAA-CREF, New York City, New York State, California) have been active "social voice" investors during the past three years.

In general, these funds define their responsibilities as being somewhat broader than shareholder wealth maximization. In effect, wealth maximization is a constrained objective, and the constraints are ethical and social criteria. The following excerpt from the California Teacher's Fund Statement is illustrative:

> . . .In addition to its fiduciary responsibilities to its members, the Board has the social and ethical obligation to require that corporations in which securities are held meet a high standard of conduct in their operations. . . . The system is a large investor and, as such, is in a position to exert influence on the corporations in which it has invested. . . . The system establishes the following principles to govern the development of a responsible investment policy:

1. The preservation of principal and maximization of income will clearly be the primary and underlying criteria for the selection and retention of securities.
2. Non-economic factors will supplement (these criteria) in making investment decisions. . . . The consideration of non-economic factors is for the purpose of ensuring that the system, either through its actions or inaction, does not promote, condone, or facilitate social injury.
3. Social injury will be said to exist when the activities of a corporation serve to undermine basic human rights or dignities.
4. The extent of the responsibility of the System to engage in activity for the prevention, reduction, and elimination by the number of shares held in the corporation and the gravity of the social injury.

The statement suggests that while economic performance is the primary objective, "other-interestedness," in particular the avoidance of harm, is also important. It certainly suggests that the conventional wisdom which holds that ". . . The goals

Exhibit VII
Sponsors of Social Policy Resolutions, 1989–1991

	1989	1990	1991
ICCR*	101	153	161
Government funds	164	107	101
Other church groups	18	18	79
TIAA-CREF	12	14	19
Envir/animal groups	22	17	20
Unions	0	5	12
Other institutions	15	9	8
Individuals	11	11	19

*Interfaith Center on Corporate Responsibility

of institutional investors are purely financial and are focused on (short term) price appreciation ..." (Porter, 1992, p. 70) is an oversimplification. These institutions have significant influence on corporate behavior. The size of their holdings allows them to exercise voice directly to management, as well as through resolutions and voting. Unlike individuals, these institutions often negotiate directly with management before the introduction of social policy resolutions at shareholder meetings. Often, management agrees to change corporate behavior in a manner that is satisfactory to the proponents, rather than subject the issue to a shareholder vote. During the three year period, 28 percent of social policy resolutions were withdrawn by their sponsors after reaching satisfactory agreements with management regarding corporate behavior.[5] Clearly, individuals do not have such access to management. The 28 percent of resolutions that were withdrawn represent at least partial successes by their institutional proponents. On the other hand, only 2 percent of the wealth enhancing resolutions introduced in 1990 were withdrawn by their proponents. By some measures, then, shareholder voice on social issues is more effective than shareholder voice directed to economic issues; the social and ethical concerns of these investors have significant influence on corporate behavior.

VI. Concluding Comments

The assumption that investors are interested only in share price maximization is descriptive of much investor behavior. This assumption also underlies the neoclassical paradigm and the stakeholder concept. The assumption leads to the neoclassical prescription that corporate decisions should be made on the basis of shareholder wealth maximization, because shareholder welfare and shareholder wealth are assumed to be equivalent. However, if this assumption is not valid, then the justification for the SWM decision rule is substantially weakened. The assumption that shareholders are wealth maximizes also leads to the presumed challenge of stakeholder management—to balance the economic demands of shareholders against the welfare of other constituencies. If, however, shareholders are other-interested and bound by a sense of moral duty, then the challenge of stakeholder management becomes a more artificial construct. Shareholders are interested in the welfare of other constituencies as well.

The wealth maximization assumption fails to explain (1) why shareholders support wealth-decreasing changes in corporate governance, (2) why they support resolutions supporting the consideration of other stakeholders in takeovers at the expense of their economic interests, (3) why they lobby firms to undertake social activities that are costly, (4) why they lobby firms to cease activities which are profitable, or (5) why they divest or screen out certain firms and industries from their portfolios. If, however, we assume that some shareholders have ethical and social values, or in general, that they are "other-interested," this behavior is easily explained.

The evidence I have presented is consistent with the argument that investors who consider social and ethical concerns, and act on these concerns, represent a significant portion of equity investment in the United States. For these investors, wealth maximization is a constrained objective, and the constraints are ethical and social values. Etzioni's "I&We" paradigm is descriptive of much shareholder behavior. Therefore, management prescriptives—by both neoclassicists and stakeholder theorists—are based on a premise that is, at best, only partly accurate.[6]

References

Baker, J. C.: 1985, "The International Infant Formula Controversy: A Dilemma in Corporate Social Responsibility," *Journal of Business Ethics* 4, 181–90.

Berss, M.: 1991, "Socially Sensible Investing," *Forbes* (June 24), 164–65.

Bhagat, S.: 1983, "The Effect of Pre-emptive Right Amendments on Shareholder Wealth," *Journal of Financial Economics* 12, 289–310.

Bhagat, S., and J. A. Brickley: 1984, "Cumulative Voting: The Value of Minority Shareholder Voting Rights," *Journal of Law and Economics* 27, 339–65.

Bhagat, S., and R. H. Jefferis: 1991, "Voting Power in the Proxy Process: The Case of Anti-Takeover Charter Amendments," *Journal of Financial Economics* 30, 193–225.

Bowie, N. E.: 1988, "Fair Markets," *The Journal of Business Ethics* 7, 89–98.

Brickley, J. A., R. C. Lease, and C. W. Smith: 1988, "Ownership Structure and Voting on Antitakeover Amendments," *Journal of Financial Economics* 20, 267–91.

Coffey, B. S., and G. E. Fryxell: 1991, "Institutional Ownership of Stock and Dimensions of Corporate Social Performance: An Empirical Examination," *Journal of Business Ethics* 10, 437–44.

Cornel, B., and A. C. Shapiro: 1987, "Corporate Stakeholders and Corporate Finance," *Financial Management* 16 (Spring): 5–14.

Donaldson, T.: 1982, *Corporations and Morality* (Englewood Cliffs, N.J.: Prentice-Hall).

Donaldson, T., and P. Werhane: 1988, *Ethical Issues in Business: A Philosophical Approach* 3rd ed. (Englewood Cliffs, N.J.: Prentice-Hall).

Etzioni, A.: 1988, *The Moral Dimension: Toward a New Economics* (The Free Press, New York).

Evan, W. M., and E. Freeman: 1988, "A Stakeholder Theory of the Modern Corporation: Kantian Capitalism," *Ethical Theory and Business* (Englewood-Cliffs, N.J.: Prentice-Hall).

Investor Responsibility Research Center: 1990, "Portfolio Screening By Investment Professionals Grows. . .," *News for Investors* (Nov.), 205–17.

Investor Responsibility Research Center: *Voting by Institutional Investors on Corporate Governance Issues*, various dates (Investor Responsibility Research Center Corporate Governance Service, Washington, D.C.).

Investor Responsibility Research Center: *How Institutions Voted on Social Responsibility Resolutions*, various dates (Investor Responsibility Research Center Social Issues Service, Washington, D.C.).

Jarrell, G. A., and A. B. Poulson: 1987, "Shark Repellents and Poison Pills: The Effects of Anti-Takeover Amendments Since 1980," *Journal of Financial Economics* 19, 127–68.

Karpoff, J. M., and P. H. Malatesta: 1989, "The Wealth Effects of Second Generation State Anti-Takeover Legislation," *Journal of Financial Economics* 25, 292–322.

Luck, C.: 1992, "'Sinful' Industry Returns in the United States," *Barra Newsletter* (March/April), 1–4.

Malatesta P., and R. A. Walking: 1988, "Poison Pill Securities: Stockholder Wealth, Profitability, and Ownership Structure," *Journal of Financial Economics* 20, 347–76.

Mukherjee, T., V. Lokhande, and S. H. Lee: 1991, "Stock Price Reactions to Voluntary Versus Mandatory Social Actions—The Case of South Africa Divestiture," Presented at the meeting of the Financial Management Association.

Preston, L. E., and H. J. Sapienza: 1990, "Stakeholder Management and Corporate Performance," *Journal of Behavioral Economics* 19, 361–75.

Richman, J. D.: 1984, "Merger Decision Making: An Ethical Analysis and Recommendation," *California Management Review* 27 (Fall): 177–84.

Ryngaert, M.: 1988, "The Effect of Poison Pill Securities on Shareholder Wealth," *Journal of Financial Economics* 20, 377–417.

Simpson, A.: 1991, *The Greening of Global Investment* (The Economist Publications, London).

Swanson, D.: 1992, "A Critical Evaluation of Etzioni's Socioeconomic Theory: Implications for the Field of Business Ethics," *Journal of Business Ethics* 11, 545–53.

Szewczyk, S. H., and G. P. Tsetseko: 1992, "State Intervention in the Market for Corporate Control," *Journal of Financial Economics* 31 (Feb.): 3–23.

Woodstock Theological Center: 1988, *Ethical Considerations in Corporate Takeovers* (Washington: Georgetown University Press).

Notes

[1] An examination of fund prospectuses shows that the most common criteria are negative screens relating to South Africa, weapons, tobacco, nuclear power and environmental behavior, and the most common positive screens include substantial minority group members in leadership, environmental responsibility, and fair employment practices.

[2] *Voting by Institutional Investors on Corporate Governance Issues in the 1990 Proxy Season*, Washington, D.C.: IRRC (1990), p. 5.

[3] IRRC reports survey results for four categories of respondents: investment companies, private pension funds, public pension funds, and universities, foundations, and church groups.

[4] *How Institutions Voted on Corporate Governance Resolutions in the 1989 Proxy Season*, Washington, D.C.: IRRC (1989), p. 37.

[5] IRRC, *How Institutions Voted on Social Responsibility Shareholder Resolutions*, various dates. Washington, D.C.: IRRC.

[6] The helpful comments of Professors James Angel and Dennis Quinn are gratefully acknowledged.

CASES

Case 6.1: Violent Games

Rapidly evolving computer technology has spawned a new generation of "interactive" computer games with realistic sounds and visual effects. In one of the most popular games, "Doom 2," a shotgun, a chain saw, and a rocket launcher are among the weapons that a player can use to destroy human targets; this then results in the graphic spilling of blood and guts. In another game produced by Sega, "Night Trap," hooded killers chase and capture sorority sisters, drill their necks, and then drain their blood.

A newer game entitled "The Great Game"[4] places the participant in a covert CIA mission to protect the president from a plot to assassinate him. In one scene, the player is confronted with a situation in which a decision must be made to turn up the voltage on a screaming female Asian secret agent in order to extract critical information from her.

[4]Amy Harmon, "Fun, Games, and Gore," *Los Angeles Times*, 12 May 1995, A28.

While little research has been done to study the effect of simulated violence on real-world violence, experts say that computer interactivity is much more compelling than other forms of media because the players participate and become engaged in the game through the role of one of the characters. Pomona College professor Brian Stonehill claims that this is a big change from other types of spectator violence because "this takes you out of the role of spectator and into the role of murderer."

Some industry executives respond that their products ought not be taken so seriously. Steve Race, president of Sony Computer Entertainment, told a reporter, "I just sell games, lady. To make me responsible for the mores or values of America, I don't think I'm ready for that." Other manufacturers and consumers of these products defend themselves by adding that even children know the difference between games and reality.

While the social effects of exposure and participation in such violence are still relatively unknown, huge profits are a sure thing. Americans are expected to spend more than $10 billion on interactive entertainment in 1995 alone. Once the domain of adolescents, these games are now purchased by men in their 20s and 30s who enjoy the involvement and the action.

To be certain, not every highly profitable game is violent. Games such as "Myst" have been widely successful without the use of violence. However, one researcher found that nine of the ten top best-sellers had murder, abduction, or implied rape as a main theme. Industry wide, the top twenty sellers collect 80 percent of the revenues. Consequently, it makes sense from a financial perspective for manufacturers to stick with proven themes of violence in their games.

Outside of cyberspace, large profits are also being made on violence in the real world. Cable television operators see huge profits in a new sport called "ultimate fighting." Appearing to be inspired by such games as "Mortal Combat," ultimate fighting places two opponents into a fenced-in ring, with no rules or rounds. The fighter left standing is proclaimed the winner. While offering such games on cable is illegal in many states, cable company executives smell a winning combination of a violent "sport" and America's fascination with voyeuristic-type programming, which they can sell in a "pay-per-view" format.

Questions for Discussion:

1. Can executives of companies that manufacture violent video games or promote "ultimate fighting" be accused of being socially irresponsible? Are these legitimate ways of earning money, just because "there's a market for it"?

2. What obligations do these executives have to shareholders versus other stakeholders? How would Friedman, Goodpaster, and Rivoli respond to this case? How would you balance the interests?

Case 6.2: New Markets for Tobacco

Like other industries, executives of tobacco companies also feel the pressure to maximize shareholder wealth. However, the markets for their products appear to be shrinking as cigarette consumption among almost every age group in the United States has steadily declined in the last decade. Moreover, many smokers prematurely die each year. In fact, the surgeon general's office estimates that smoking causes 435,000 premature deaths annually in the United States.[5] Consequently, cigarette companies have to look for new markets in which to sell their products in order to maintain their profitability.

Allegedly, one of the markets to which they have looked to stimulate demand is that of underage smokers. Public health and consumer-affairs officials have accused companies such as R. J. Reynolds of utilizing cartoon figures to reach children and adolescents in order to persuade them to smoke. A series of articles in the December 1991

[5]Cited in Lauri Jones, "Surgeon General, AMA Snuff Out Old Joe Camel," *American Medical News* (23 March 1992): 1.

issue of the *Journal of the American Medical Association (JAMA)* presented research that pointed an accusing finger at the R. J. Reynolds Tobacco Co. for allegedly using the cartoon character "Old Joe Camel" to market cigarettes directly to minors. The studies claimed that among six-year-olds, Old Joe is almost as identifiable as Mickey Mouse.[6] Furthermore, the articles alleged that the ad campaign is more effective with children than with adults and that Camel is the stated brand of choice of many minors.

Another study claims that Camel's share of the underage smoking market is now 33 percent, up from the 1 percent share that it held prior to the campaign's commencement. In effect, this increased illegal sales of Camels to minors to $476 million from $6 million.[7] Using this data, the argument is advanced that because the tobacco industry must replace the share of the market that dies each year, it is alleged that the most vulnerable target market is children. Since 80 percent of adult smokers started smoking before or during their teen years, with the reported average age for first tobacco use at twelve, it is estimated that four or five thousand of those who begin smoking each day are underage.[8] Consequently, tobacco companies are under fire for using advertising to lure underage segments of the population to participate in an illegal and harmful activity.

Cigarette manufacturers respond by claiming that it would not be in their self-interest to target kids as this would invite public scrutiny and government regulation. They claim that their ads are not aimed at children but at adult smokers, "who change brands at least three times before the age of thirty-five."[9]

In addition to underage smokers, other markets can be found overseas where public health campaigns against smoking are not as prevalent as in the U.S. or are absent altogether. American cigarette manufacturers have aggressively targeted these areas as export markets for their products. For example, in Japan the consumption of cigarettes has risen dramatically in the last twenty years to the point where well over 50 percent of the adult male population are chainsmokers. American cigarette brands are in very high demand in some of these countries.

[6] Theme Issue on Tobacco Use, *Journal of the American Medical Association* (December 1991).

[7] *JAMA*, December 1991.

[8] J. J. Boddewyn, "Smoking Ads Don't Get People Hooked," *Wall Street Journal*, 21 November 1986.

[9] Kathleen Deveney, "R. J. Reynolds Battles the AMA, Defending Joe Camel Cartoon Ad," *Wall Street Journal*, 5 February 1992, B5.

Questions for Discussion:

1. Can the managers of these companies be rightly accused of being "socially irresponsible" in promoting harmful products in the quest for shareholder wealth? How would Milton Friedman respond? Would you agree with him? Why or why not?

2. How might the "stakeholder" and "communitarian" approaches differ in their assessments of this situation? Do you think that cutting back on such promotion and thereby causing a reduction in shareholder wealth would be justifiable?

Case 6.3: Controversial Corporate Contributions

Corporations often make charitable contributions to various social causes. Many museums, university buildings, academic research, and hospitals are funded with donations from large publicly held corporations. Recently, however, there have been strong conflicts that have arisen between management, shareholders, and consumers involving contributions to controversial causes. Some consumer groups have called for boycotts against companies that have contributed funds to the Boy Scouts of America because of its policy of excluding homosexuals from its leadership. When some companies, such as Levi Strauss, ended their financial support to the organization, they were in turn scrutinized by groups that were sympathetic to the Boy Scouts.[10] Other groups have called for similar boycotts against companies that have donated to causes on the other side of the political spectrum, such as Planned Parenthood and other agencies that are decidedly pro-choice.

The plight of the Dayton-Hudson corporation illustrates the difficult situation in which corporations are placed. When the Dayton-Hudson corporation withdrew its support from Planned Parenthood, protests came from pro-choice groups. The company then did a flip-flop and decided to resume such funding, thereby returning it to the list of companies being boycotted by pro-life groups.[11]

Compounding the apparent no-win nature of these controversies is the fact that many shareholders in the companies involved were angered that their profits were being hurt by the boycotts caused by the controversial practices and that companies in which they owned shares were contributing money to causes to which they were personally opposed.

[10]Woody Hochswender, "Boy Scouts Learn Levis Don't Fit," *New York Times*, 5 June 1992, A12.

[11]K. Kelly, "Dayton-Hudson Finds There Is No Graceful Way to Flip-Flop," *Business Week* (24 September 1990): 50.

Questions for Discussion:

1. In light of such controversies, do you think it would be better if public corporations simply stopped giving to charities? Or should they only give to charities that would help public relations and long-term profitability?

2. Do such contributions constitute "taxation without representation," as Friedman alleges? Or are they worthy sacrifices of profit for the common good?

COMMENTARY

Although the use of the phrase "socially responsible business" is prevalent in the commercial marketplace, its precise ramifications can be morally troubling for managers when they are asked to choose between profit for the shareholders and society's well-being. Unless one believes that good ethics is always synonymous with good business in the profit-making sense of the term, conflicts between profit and other goods will inevitably occur in the workplace.

These conflicts can be especially acute for Christian business people who may be torn in these situations between competing loyalties to one's employer and to God when profits seem to rival moral concerns. How should these claims be resolved? Is Friedman's suggestion that the "social responsibilities" of corporate managers is to maximize shareholder wealth within the bounds of the law morally adequate? Should other "stakeholders" or the surrounding community be considered when pondering a course of action, or does this constitute a breach of fiduciary duty to maximize profit for the owners of the company? In the following comments, we will address these critical questions and argue that managers do not have only wealth maximization duties to shareholders. We will begin by critiquing Milton Friedman's "custodian-of-wealth" model of social responsibility and pointing out some of its key limitations. We will then examine the stakeholder and communitarian approaches outlined by Kenneth Goodpaster and Pietra Rivoli respectively. Finally, we will conclude by offering some thoughts on practical ways that corporations can resolve controversies that surround charitable contributions.

The Limits of the Custodian-of-Wealth Model

Milton Freidman's provocative essay can be considered a classic in the field of business ethics if for no other reason than that it evokes strong responses. For those who view corporations solely as the engines of an efficient economy, Friedman's custodian-of-wealth model is the final word on the social responsibility question. However, many business ethicists and religious thinkers view his seeming deification of private property rights over other social goods as representative of the foundational shortcomings of our current business system. To them, his view is characteristic of an individualist acquisitive ethos characterized by a "gain at all cost" mentality that places profit as the highest social good.

While Friedman's thesis is controversial, it is a position that merits serious consideration since it is the most often used defense when employees of companies are accused of morally questionable practices. Indisputably, employees of a corporation have a fiduciary responsibility to a company's owners. They are hired with the goal, though in most cases it is not the only goal, of profit maximization. Indeed, a company must earn a profit in order to stay in business and provide for public well-being through job creation, products, and services, and monetary contributions to tax bases. Moreover, contrary to a cursory reading of this model, it does not necessarily preclude good actions on the part of corporations. Although Freidman's essay appears to support ruthless business practices, it actually provides ample room for corporations to do good in society while maximizing profit.

In many cases, engaging in socially responsible practices is not in conflict with profit. In fact, it can be the profit maximizing course of action because it can bring favorable publicity and goodwill to the firm. This can, in turn, benefit the prospects for long-term gain. For example, recent currency fluctuations have badly damaged the purchasing power of local workers in foreign-owned "Maquiladoras" manufacturing plants in Mexico. A large cost savings in labor through a 40 percent devaluation of the peso, coupled with a Mexican law that limits pay increases to 10 percent, would normally be a cause for celebration on the part of business owners. However, many managers of American-owned companies, including Mattel and Honeywell, reported ambivalence about the situation because of the effect on morale and the workplace climate. To get around the pay-raise limit, some of these companies resorted to giving away food and clothing and others helped with transportation costs in order to aid in the restoration of the financial well-being of their employees. While these actions appear to come at a cost to shareholder wealth, the managers of some of these companies explained their actions in self-interested profit-maximization terms, stating that such practices were necessary to enhance declining worker morale and decrease turnover.[12] Thus there are many instances in which there is only an apparent conflict between profit and the well-being of society. Goals that are on the sur-

[12]Chris Kraul, "Propping Up the Peso," *Los Angeles Times,* 20 March 1995, D1f.

face "socially responsible" can be accomplished within a consistent application of Friedman's profit-maximization model.

Moreover, proponents of this model assert that in a free-market economy, it is within the self-interest of companies to comply with the ethics of their surrounding culture since the market will punish those suppliers who engage in immoral activities. In theory, consumers will "vote" with their dollars and take their business to a more scrupulous operator. Consequently, some "socially responsible" actions are a must because they can stem the tide of a threat to profits through the curtailing of negative publicity. Clearly then, for Friedman, the underlying issue in deciding whether or not to act in apparent neglect of the bottom line is not a matter of ethics, but rather of long-term strategy. Such actions, then, which are on the surface "ethical," are just another means, like good advertising or customer service, to maximize profit.

While it has some strengths, Freidman's model has definite limits as an adequate guideline for morality in business. First, although this model does indeed leave ample room for good actions, these behaviors are for the wrong reasons. Any type of altruism is precluded, since self-interest in terms of profit is the foundational basis on which decisions are made. To be certain, the question about whether or not corporations can be expected to act in a manner other than in their own self-interest is up for debate, but the assumption that consumers can effectively influence ethics in the "enlightened self-interest" of companies through the regulatory force of the "invisible hand" is false. While it is true that competition in the free market will often act to punish immoral actors, consumers do not possess the "perfect information" about the marketplace necessary to consistently take steps to punish unethical actors, especially in the short term. Even with the advent of the information superhighway, there is always a time lag in the travel of information about unethical businesses in a global economy such as our own. Furthermore, average citizens do not have the financial resources necessary to support a publicity campaign designed to warn other consumers about the wiles of an unscrupulous actor. Thus, at the least, immoral practices can certainly go unpunished by the functioning of the market and may at times actually be in a company's best interests in terms of profit.

Second, the notion that managers have responsibilities only for maximizing shareholder wealth is much too narrow and relies on faulty premises about the fiduciary relationship between shareholders and employees. Friedman errs in his assumption that moneymaking is the only goal of a company. Most firms have mission statements that encompass broader social good than mere profit maximization.

Investors themselves should be well aware of these broader goals since they are often expressed in the company mission statement. Thus it is false to assume that shareholders can legitimately expect employees to pursue only the maximization of profits.

However, even if a case can be made that shareholders can hold employees to such a standard, Friedman errs in assuming that shareholders expect that managers of public corporations will do anything within the law to make money. While many investment vehicles today remove the direct sense of ownership responsibilities from shareholders, it is questionable as to how many investors would truly want the employees of their companies to engage in grossly immoral activities in order to increase earnings per share. Pietra Rivoli insightfully questions the truthfulness of this critical assumption made by Friedman through anecdotal and empirical evidence. Her conclusions are that many shareholders, even active and informed ones, will often vote for proposals that consider stakeholder welfare at the expense of share-price maximization. Even if Friedman is correct from a descriptive standpoint that investors' sole expectations are profit maximization, this still leaves the normative question of what investors *should* expect when they purchase shares in a company. With ownership come tremendous responsibilities. As Goodpaster rightly reminds us, it is immoral for owners of corporations to expect employees to engage in activities that they themselves would not carry out.

Furthermore, to expect profit maximization at all costs would violate the golden rule on the part of investors. Most people would not want companies, in the absence of specific legal restraints, knowingly to pollute the air or water in their own communities. This example points to a further false assumption on the part of Friedman, that is, that shareholders are often also stakeholders with other interests. Separating the two groups is not always an easy task particularly in light of the growing number of employee stock ownership programs.

Finally, the most serious shortcoming of this model can be seen where a morally unacceptable action would be one that would produce the greatest long-term profit for the firm. For example, case 6.1 presents a situation in which it is in the best financial interests of shareholders for companies to manufacture video games with an egregious amount of violent content. These companies have not violated any human laws. Yet, with escalating amounts of violence in society, the surrounding community, which ironically includes the shareholders themselves, would arguably be much better off without products with such minimal socially redeeming value.

In response to these types of controversies, Friedman would argue that as long as employees do not transgress the limits set by the law in the quest for profit, they cannot be accused of immorality. Clearly, Friedman's model is deficient for the task. The law is an insufficient standard for morality. Law merely tells us what we *cannot* do, while ethics instructs us in what we *ought* to do. Many actions that are permitted by law cannot be justified in terms of morality. Legal standards are also by nature reactionary, sometimes taking years to make their way from the initiative of harmed parties through legislatures and courts into enactment. Thus simply acting within the dictates of the law can create many unwitting victims while the law spends years catching up to practical reality. For example, as discussed in Case 6.2, advertising cigarettes to children through the use of cartoon characters is grossly immoral. Yet since underage smokers are the only growing domestic market segment for cigarettes, it would make logical sense from a profit perspective for tobacco manufacturers to target this group in order to maximize profit. While these actions are clearly harmful for society, their legality has yet to be determined, as cigarette advertisers claim that further restrictions would violate their First Amendment rights.

Furthermore, in other countries where there are unreasonably lax regulations for such things as employee and product safety, one can really be caught in a bind if the letter of the law is viewed as the ultimate source of moral authority. In fact, some ethicists have argued that the law should be the "moral minimum" rather than the final arbiter of one's actions and behaviors.

Christians are especially obligated to obey sources of moral authority that are higher than those of the surrounding culture or laws. While earthly authorities are indeed God-ordained, they are not to be obeyed in every instance. When God and Caesar are in clear conflict, it is God to whom ultimate loyalty must be pledged. Consequently, employers may be disobeyed, and in some extreme cases, it may in fact come down to a matter of leaving a position or career if the conflict is of a nature that these are the only options available.

These shortcomings in Freidman's model should lead one to conclude that simple profit maximization within the parameters of the law is an inadequate guideline to morality in business. Rather, profit maximization within the context of higher moral obligations and loyalties that go well beyond the law seems to be a better rule of thumb to follow.

Contributions From the Stakeholder and Communitarian Approaches

In response to Friedman, some thinkers have sought to mitigate the strength of fiduciary responsibilities to shareholders by putting them on a par with duties to other stakeholders. Since corporations are not private entities, but rather public institutions that interact with and influence and affect many more people than just the owners, other stakeholders also have rights due consideration by the employees. Furthermore, while shareholders may provide the capital, it is stakeholders that provide just about everything else, such as talent, supplies, purchases, etc.

This approach is gaining momentum and has made its way into the courts. Recently a state-level judge employed its basic contours to prevent the shutdown of a General Motors plant in Ypsilanti, Michigan. He argued that because the city had taken such measures as providing tax breaks and building roads to attract the plant, the company owed something to parties other than the shareholders.

Undoubtedly, practicing a stakeholder approach seems to be less destructive to other constituents affected by corporations. It also offers what appears to be a more heartfelt approach to capitalism. However, from our perspective, some applications of this theory can go too far. While the extreme individualism of personal-rights claims in our society is indeed leading to fragmentation and moral meltdown, profit is still a critical social good. Without the prospect of a reasonable profit and some defense of private property rights, the incentives to be creative and innovative will be destroyed and the engine of a growing economy will stall. With this in mind, Kenneth Goodpaster insightfully articulates a balanced theory of stakeholder analysis. In his model, he does not lessen property and ownership rights to the extreme that stakeholders and shareholders are entitled to equal consideration. Nonetheless, he rejects the Friedman thesis by arguing that stakeholders are worthy of moral consideration and of some obligations on the part of managers of publicly owned corporations.

Pietra Rivoli rejects both the shareholder-wealth and stakeholder approaches to corporate social responsibility on the ground that both make their claims based on the "social contract" model of the classical liberal tradition. In that tradition, parties are seen as actors who are seeking to maximize utility solely in a self-interested manner. Obligations to others is an afterthought that is the product of voluntary agreements in which natural rights are sacrificed for societal survival. As an alternative, Rivoli seeks to establish a "communitarian" paradigm in business in which corporations are viewed as creations and members of larger and prior social networks. In turn, moral obligations are intrinsic to a corporation's existence as a social entity rather than products of voluntary contracts.

Rivoli seeks empirical data to prove that Amitai Etzioni's "I&We" construct, which claims that humans are "other-interested" as well as self-interested, also holds true in investor behavior. She finds that shareholders are, in fact, concerned for the well-being of others. This is reflected in the ways they vote on various corporate resolutions. Thus she severely weakens Friedman's position by showing that it relies on faulty premises about shareholder expectations.

Both the stakeholder and communitarian models offer much in their critique of Friedman's shareholder-wealth model. While neither of these approaches offers situation-specific guidelines for managers, they do open the door for managers to consider moral obligations in situations where they conflict with profit maximization.

Charitable Contributions

While the preceding comments offer some clarity on the broader question of social responsibility, the issues surrounding charitable contributions from the corporate treasury are extremely problematic. As discussion case 6.3: "Controversial Corporate Contributions" illustrates, there are serious conflicts between shareholders and consumers as to what constitutes "worthy" causes. While some shareholders want to support the Boy Scouts of America, others are upset that the organization bans homosexuals from the ranks of its leaders. Some shareholders want funds to go to Planned Parenthood, while others do not want funds from their corporate treasury to go to this organization, which encourages abortion. Moreover, consumers of various political persuasions are as sharply divided and are not afraid to wield the boycott weapon to achieve their agendas.

Amid all of this conflict, the suggestion by Friedman that companies should make contributions only to causes that would bring favorable publicity seems attractive. Yet this is troubling since the values of the surrounding culture would then be the sole determinant of what are deemed morally worthy causes. Applying this logic, if pro-animal-rights groups are not a direct threat to the company and they are the public "flavor of the month," they should receive contributions. When they are out of style, another group, perhaps with a diametrically opposed agenda, will be deemed "worthy" of a contribution.

Obviously, the idea that corporations should simply follow culture is cowardly. We all find it morally praiseworthy that some companies fought local prejudice and hired women and members of ethnic minority groups in the face of public scrutiny and at the expense of profit long before civil rights legislation forced them to do so. Some adherents of Friedman's theory will undoubtedly criticize these and other socially responsible actions as theft of shareholder wealth. Conversely, adherents to the stakeholder and communitarian approaches would praise these actions as a worthy sacrifice of profits for a greater good. However, upon a closer examination of Friedman's thesis, an incredibly wide range of charitable contributions could be justified.

Many types of community giving may not have any immediate returns but may directly affect the corporation in the long term. For example, as we mentioned in the Commentary in chapter 3, corporations do not operate in a vacuum. Since their future employees, suppliers, consumers, etc., come from the surrounding culture, they are ever dependent on virtuous citizens for their long-term survival. Thus contributions to educational and citizenship efforts are essential to the long-run success of corporations. As such, managers can make decisions to donate corporate funds to a wide array of activities and still be within their fiduciary responsibilities to the shareholders.

McDonald's charitable contributions are an excellent case in point. In addition to the well-known Ronald McDonald houses, some franchise owners have instituted McPride programs in which employees are paid bonuses for attendance in school and getting good grades. Others offer an extra hour of pay if employees will come early to their shift to do their school work. McDonald's has also aggressively instituted programs in which senior citizens and physically and mentally challenged people are hired as workers. One franchise owner says that these actions are not a big deal as "the seniors and the special-ed kids in our stores create a special sense of humanity."[13] While these practices may be at the expense of short-term profits, they will undoubtedly have long-term positive ramifications for shareholders since positive models for academic achievement will enhance their future employee base.

Although contributions like those of McDonald's have a good chance of bettering companies' profitability in the future, the issue of controversial contributions that may have no such effect has still not been addressed. *Forbes* magazine reports in an article entitled "Biting the Hand That Feeds You" that managers of many companies donate corporate dollars to causes that are actually directly opposed to the goals of the corporations that employ them.[14] In the face of these controversies, suggestions that corporations stop making such donations altogether seem to make good sense. However, many people are uncomfortable with this notion since corporations have the resources to make such large-scale contributions to worthy causes.

While the issue is problematic, there are at least two better ways of addressing this situation that merit serious consideration. First, companies could simply state in their investment prospectuses and annual reports the causes to which they make contributions and the amounts of such contributions. Potential investors will then have

[13]Edwin Reingold, "America's Hamburger Helper," *Time* (29 June 1992): 66–67.

[14]Brigid McMenamin, "Biting the Hand That Feeds You," *Forbes* (19 December 1994): 122–26.

"informed consent" before choosing to purchase shares. Thus if individual investors are opposed to the fact that a company donates to some causes to which they are personally opposed, they can choose not to partake in ownership of the company. Second, corporations would do well to follow the suggestion and practice of one corporation of which we are aware, and let individual investors decide where they want corporate money to be donated. Shareholders in that firm designate various charities, and the company sends the checks. Many charities, including 347 churches and synagogues, that usually do not benefit from corporate donations received contributions under this company's plan in a recent year.[15]

[15]Ibid.

CONCLUSION

As we have seen, the concept of "social responsibility" is much more complex than a catchy marketing slogan. Indeed, there is wide disagreement about its implications for managers of publicly held corporations. While profit is an important social good and managers must take their fiduciary duties to shareholders seriously, Friedman is incorrect in assuming that managers may do anything within the law in order to increase profit. What we have tried to show is that Freidman's logic is flawed in that he makes some unfounded assumptions, because shareholders themselves may not expect employees to engage in immoral activities in order to increase their wealth. In fact, as Rivoli points out, investors will often vote against their own financial well-being for the sake of community interests.

Even in cases where they may want to maximize gain without regard for the social costs, managers, especially Christian managers, have ultimate duties to consider higher morals than those that prevail within a corporate culture or legal system. Furthermore, as Goodpaster argues, shareholders cannot legitimately expect the employees of companies in which they own shares to engage in activities to maximize profit if they themselves would not engage in such activities. We have also argued that Freidman's assertions that managers need only obey the law in order to be socially responsible is also dubious. The law is an inadequate guide to morality. Rather, it should serve only as the "moral minimum" and one must weigh other considerations when pondering a course of action. Thus the pursuit of profit, while a noble and necessary goal of business, should not be done at the direct expense of all other public good.

SEVEN

Employee Rights and Privacy

There is little consensus regarding the definition, nature, and justification of privacy rights in general. Statutory protection of privacy is a relatively recent development in American legal history.

Joseph R. Des Jardins, "Privacy in Employment"

INTRODUCTION

In the past twenty-five years, there has been an explosion of discussion on the subject of employee rights. This has corresponded with an increased emphasis in society in general on individual rights, particularly the rights to privacy and free speech. Understandably, this general societal emphasis has translated into a growing concern for protection of the rights of employees in the workplace. With the publication of David Ewing's classic employee "bill of rights" in 1977, the debate over exactly what rights employees have in the workplace was sharpened.[1] Questions of employee rights and privacy are more complicated today because of the growing use of electronic communication, the increasing concern over the use of illegal drugs, the spread of the HIV virus, and the growth of genetic testing for certain catastrophic diseases, some of which do not have their onset until later in life. In addition, with the extremely competitive business environment in the '90s, granting rights to workers will likely collide with the profit-maximization mandate more frequently, giving employers less financial flexibility to grant broad employee rights. When the exercise of employee rights affects a firm's profitability, as it often does, employers may feel less inclined to institute changes that protect the rights of workers at the expense of the company's bottom line.

Historically, employees have had to fight hard to gain certain rights in the workplace. Companies were commonly viewed as the owners' property, which they could dispose of in any way they saw fit.

[1] David Ewing, "A Proposed Bill of Rights," in *Freedom Inside the Organization* (New York: E. P. Dutton, 1977), 144–51. See Case 7:1 for more detail on the specifics of his bill of rights.

283

This idea came to be known more formally as "employment at will," that is, the employer had the right to hire and fire at his discretion. He owed virtually nothing to employees other than fair wages for work performed in a safe environment. For example, he did not owe workers due process when they had been fired. As a result, employees had few if any rights, and the differential in power favoring the employer effectively prevented employees from voicing concerns or otherwise pressuring employers to make changes in the way employees were treated. Labor unions were organized primarily to safeguard workers' rights, specifically the right to fair wages and a safe workplace. The National Labor Relations Act, passed in the mid-1930s prohibited companies from firing workers because of union membership and generally made it easier for workers to organize. In addition, other New Deal legislation in the 1930s extended worker rights by limiting the number of hours in the regular required workweek and prohibiting child labor.

In the first half of the twentieth century, the primary employee right for which employees fought was the right to organize into labor unions, helping balance the power differential between employer and employees. With the decline of union influence in the 1980s and '90s, employees must increasingly rely on the courts and government regulators to force employers to recognize the workplace rights they believe should be protected. One example of government stepping in to fill the void left by the weakened labor unions is the Occupational Safety and Hazard Administration (OSHA). It regulates safety in the workplace and though its critics insist that it has overreached its authority and unnecessarily increased the costs of conducting business, it is one of many instances in which government has taken responsibility for protecting worker rights.

The notion of employee rights and privacy is broad, encompassing many specific issues. There is great debate over what rights workers do possess when they enter the workplace and under what conditions these rights may be overridden. As an introductory exercise, consider the following short scenarios and decide whether management is justified in firing an employee when they occur. This will help you decide what rights employees have in the workplace.

- The president of the company has a "gut feeling" that an employee is not trustworthy.
- A high-ranking member of the company regularly and visibly purchases the competitor's products.
- An employee openly attacks and grumbles about company management to other employees.

- An employee "blows the whistle" on the employer for disseminating fraudulent information on product safety tests.
- An employee who is a pacifist refuses to service defense-industry clients on moral grounds.
- An employee refuses to service a pharmaceutical industry client that manufactures abortion-inducing drugs.
- An employee of a company with a conservative clientele participates in a televised gay-rights rally after work hours.
- An employee of a company with a liberal clientele participates in public anti-abortion demonstrations after work hours.

The issues in the above scenarios include the rights of employees to free speech, to follow their moral convictions, and to conduct themselves off company time however they see fit. Employee privacy is a bit more specific and is focused on what privacy rights employees possess while on the job. Again, consider the following brief scenarios and decide whether they constitute a justifiable invasion of the employee's privacy.

- An employee complains to another employee about management over the company "E-mail" system. Someone in management "reads" this and has the employee fired.
- Someone is stealing merchandise from a retail outlet, and the company mandates lie detector tests to try to catch the thief.
- The company president wants to clean up the company's image and orders random drug testing for all employees.
- For safety reasons, a company mandates HIV testing for all employees.
- A genetic test is developed that can screen a person for certain genetic diseases such as Alzheimer's, Lou Gehrig's disease, and Huntington's disease. Your employer wants you to be tested and wants access to the results.
- The employee handbook of the company states that "employees will not date co-workers or clients of the firm—a violation that could result in dismissal.
- The company has a policy that it will not hire smokers, because of the increased cost to the company for their health care.

The readings in this chapter will help you put employee rights and privacy in perspective. The central question they address is, What employee rights should be protected and under what conditions may these rights be overridden? Many are uncomfortable with a strict application of the employment-at-will doctrine, but there is wide variety in the degree to which these writers believe companies should protect worker rights and privacy. Max Ways comes the closest to defending employment at will in his article "The Myth of the 'Oppressive Corporation.'" He argues that corporations are unjustly criticized for ignoring important employee rights and that most companies actually allow significant latitude to employees in terms of privacy, personal behavior, and free speech. He criticizes Ewing's employee bill of rights for undermining a company's ability to remain competitive and unnecessarily involving government to enforce his version of workplace democracy. He maintains that current law protects most important employee rights adequately and he resists the need for further laws, not to mention a Constitutional amendment such as Ewing proposes to safeguard workers.

Philosopher Patricia Werhane rejects the notion of employment at will because of the change in employer property rights. Today many companies are not closely held private entities. They are large publicly held firms, in which management has taken over the property prerogatives of ownership, while at the same time being employees themselves. She further argues that the power differential between employers and employees makes employees more vulnerable, and thus employees merit more protection for their rights. They do not enter an employment contract on equal standing, since should the employee quit, he or she cannot inflict the same degree of harm to the company as the company can do to the employee if it fires him or her. She suggests a balance on employer and employee freedoms in the workplace because of the reciprocal nature of their relationship.

Joseph Des Jardins takes up the specific issue of employee privacy. He outlines two aspects of privacy that have relevance to the workplace: the right to be left alone, which would apply to privacy in off-work hours, and the right to control information about oneself. He distinguishes between a privacy that is rooted in the idea of liberty, of which an employee gives up a good deal by entering the workplace, and privacy rooted in the relationships between the persons involved. He concludes that the extent to which a person's privacy can be protected is dependent on the employer-employee relationship, which involves a contract that is free from fraud and willingly entered into by both parties. He comes down on the side of protecting employee privacy by insisting that employers should use only information gained with the consent of the employee. That is, the employee maintains substantial control over access to his or her personal information.

Finally, ethicist Sissela Bok tackles the thorny issue of whistle-blowing. This involves the important right of employees to follow the dictates of their conscience when faced with a conflict between loyalty to his or her employer and concern for the common good, when, for instance, he or she detects a safety flaw in the company's product. Bok provides a helpful overview of the motives for and consequences of whistle-blowing and suggests that different methods for reducing the risk of whistle-blowing are necessary, while at the same time protecting the company from malcontents wishing to get back at an employer. There is overlap in her discussion with other issues that will be addressed later in the book such as product safety and the environment.

READINGS

The Myth of the "Oppressive Corporation"

Max Ways

Fortune (October 1977): 149–53. Copyright © 1977.

From many angles these days fly charges that besmirch the good name of corporations. They are accused of polluting air, land, and water. They are taken to task for not providing enough jobs. Their level of profits, which determines their ability to create jobs and protect the environment, is assailed as obscenely high. Antitrusters say that in some industries competition is stifled; novelists depict the business world as a dog-eat-dog jungle. In almost every day's news at least one company is accused of bribery or unethical practice.

And the indictment does not end there. A growing body of writing, mainly academic in origin, addresses the corporation as a social unit, a theater of human relations, and it has little applause for what it sees. It finds corporate structure to be rigid, autocratic, and oppressive to those who work within it. The picture of the corporation that emerges recalls Thomas Hobbes's seventeenth-century description of the absolute sovereign. . . . But whereas Hobbes advanced an idea of the absolute state as a benign arbiter of social and moral order, critics of the business corporation believe that its overweening power

endangers employees' emotional health—and the mental and moral well-being of the whole society.

Most of these critiques are not Marxist. Their authors are reformers who profess, no doubt sincerely, to have the good of the corporation at heart. But the judgments they pronounce are so harsh and the implications for public policy so menacing that the business community could be forgiven for asking the classic question: With friends like these who needs enemies?

Unfair to (Almost) Everybody

A recently published specimen of this line of criticism is Rosabeth Moss Kanter's *Men and Women of the Corporation*. Kanter, an associate professor of sociology at Yale, has a twofold mission. She wants to diagnose the unequal treatment of women by corporations. Her book, however, is not one of the familiar feminist tracts against male chauvinism. She blames the inferior status of women in jobs on the corporate structure, which she sees as too rigid and autocratic to accommodate change of a magnitude that would achieve equality for women. In Kanter's eyes, inequality between the sexes is especially apparent in the better managerial and professional jobs.

And it is not only for the sake of women that she writes. Kanter's larger mission is to demonstrate that this same corporate structure also impedes other disadvantaged groups, and even white males. The corporate structure, in Kanter's view, is unfair not only to women but to everyone in it—except the small elite group holding power at the top.

Part of the blame for this slow pace of change in job distribution she attributes to the mind-set that shapes managers' thinking about jobs. They tend, Kanter says, to stress the qualities of individual employees; and their reliance on this "individual" model "serves to reinforce the present structure of organizations" and provides "a set of excuses for the slow pace of change." She wishes to substitute another model that does not take present organizational structure for granted, one that "would require organizations—not people—to change."

How Fast Is "Fast Enough"?

In principle, Kanter is surely correct in saying that business organizations, which have brought so much change to society, should themselves be not immune to change; present organization charts were not carved on Mount Sinai. But many other observers believe that in recent decades the widening of job opportunities has been rapid and the corporate structure, too, has been transforming itself.

Kanter's conclusions thus involve two intertwined issues about whether rates of change are adequate. Such questions cannot be settled by statistics. One side of the argument could show that women by the millions have recently entered the work force, and that a substantial number of them have better jobs than women had a generation ago. The other side would reply that women are still conspicuously underrepresented at the higher levels of corporations. . . .

The Post-Bureaucratic Corporation

. . . In the present stage in the evolution of organizations, they seem to be moving toward a new post-bureaucratic phase that will be less routinized, less "mechanical," more dependent on such highly personal qualities as "discretion" and "ability to communicate." In time, just as many women as men will be recognized as possessing these qualities.

Kanter has an excellent formulation of the ends toward which she thinks corporations ought to move: "the modification of hierarchy, the opening of opportunity, the broadening of participation in decisions, and the increase of worker discretion." Kanter, however, does not see that these are the directions in which many corporations have been moving for at least two decades. Almost certainly, they will continue to so move whether or not they are whipped by academic criticism.

Corporations pursue the four desiderata of her formulation for such fundamental reasons as the modern desire to reap the benefits of specialized knowledge, which requires that discretion (or "power") be distributed to the points, often far below the organization's top, where the relevant competence is found. The pace of this distribution may be considered "too slow," but managers have good reasons to move cautiously. As the number of "deciders" increases, problems of coordination and communication multiply. Corporations can and do increase employee participation where the change helps the organization. They do not and should not increase participation where confusion and inefficiency are likely consequences.

"The Job Makes the Person"

Kanter, like many other social scientists, emphasizes the psychological damage done to employees by the autocratic structure of corporations, which, she says, produces "stresses, tensions, and inequities." The workplace, all will agree, does indeed embrace a large part of human experience and exerts—for better and worse—a considerable influence on what people become. Kanter goes far beyond this. She says, "the job makes the person," and adds, "the corporation is the quintessential contemporary people-producer." She believes that this influence of corporations as they are today is mainly destructive of emotional health and personal growth.

This view allows little room for the influence of other "people-producing" institutions: the family, religion, the media, government, and, not least, a rather autocratic social form, the classroom.

Kanter's book, meant to be a helpful theoretical contribution to corporate policymaking, is deeply flawed by a tendency, often seen in missionaries, to exaggerate the vices and play down the virtues of the heathen cultures that are the objects of their solicitude. The damage done by such a book lies less in its policy recommendations than in the shaky observations that form its premise. If enough voices declare that the pace of change in the workplace is "too slow," and that this should be blamed on concentrated corporate power, then, obviously, somebody is going to limit the power of the corporate Leviathan.

Proposals along this line are set forth in *Freedom Inside the Organization* by David W. Ewing, an editor of the *Harvard Business Review*. Subtitled *Bringing Civil Liberties to the Workplace*, the book falls into a familiar pattern: generalizations about existing conditions are drawn from atrocity stories and selected opinions of employees. In the dark picture of corporate oppression that results, the author sees an urgent need for drastic legal remedies.

"For nearly two centuries," Ewing begins, "Americans have enjoyed freedom of press, speech, and assembly, due process of law, privacy, freedom of conscience, and other important rights—in their homes, churches, political forums, and social and cultural life. But Americans have not enjoyed these civil liberties in most companies, government agencies, and other organizations where they work. Once a U.S. citizen steps through the plant or office door at 9:00 a.m., he or she is nearly rightless until 5:00 p.m., Monday through Friday."

Ewing has in this opening passage disclosed a fundamental misconception about the nature of our cherished rights. A few pages later, this mistake leads him into a shocking distortion.

"For all practical purposes," he writes, "employees are required to be as obedient to their superiors, regardless of ethical and legal considerations, as are workers in totalitarian countries."

A writer so insensitive that he can equate U.S. corporate practices, even at their worst, with the system that produced the Gulag Archipelago is hardly qualified to lecture businessmen on their lack of concern for human rights.

Private Sanctions That Limit Speech

The historic rights enjoyed by Americans protect them against the abuse of government police power, not against all unpleasant consequences that may follow from their speech or action. Free speech, for instance, means that Americans cannot be fined or imprisoned for what they say; the exceptions are a small and shrinking number. It does not mean that they cannot be sued for slander. It does not mean that what they say may not deprive them of the respect of their children, the affection of their parents or spouses, the company of their friends. If an American's speech is rude enough, or malicious enough, or silly enough he may find that people don't listen to him and he may even be ostracized. Cases where such penalties are "unjust" do occur. But these instances are not violations of our right of free speech.

The human damage that can be done by words is so great and so plain that (most) children learn early to watch what they say. These inhibitions can be psychologically or socially hurtful, but civilized life would be impossible without them and the person-to-person sanctions by which they are maintained.

Most corporations today allow employees great latitude in their personal behavior, including speech. But corporations, like individuals, retain the power to employ all private sanctions that are not illegal in themselves (e.g., assault and battery) to express disapproval of an individual's speech. They can argue, remonstrate, and warn. The most extreme penalty at their disposal is to dissolve their association with the speaker by firing him. This can be, indeed, a serious penalty—but not necessarily more serious than divorce, which is frequently provoked by speech.

A Bill of Rights at I.B.M.

Reciting a number of instances where corporations have fired employees for what they said,

Ewing deems many, though not all, of these to be "unjust." He points out that some companies invoke penalties only after a scrupulously enforced "due process." He cites an I.B.M. policy that guarantees many freedoms to employees and establishes internal procedures to review penalties imposed by manager. More and more companies have moved in this direction.

Ewing's argument is that if some corporations choose to behave in this way then all corporations should be required by law to do likewise. The legal reasoning is reminiscent of that which produced the Eighteenth Amendment. First, the human damage done by alcohol was exaggerated, then "the power of the liquor interest" was blown up out of all proportion to reality, then attention was called to the fact that many Americans—perhaps half the adult population—hardly ever used alcohol. Ergo, let's have a law requiring everyone to conform to the best practice.

Sure enough, Ewing, too, wants an amendment to the Constitution of the United States. His draft starts, "No public or private organization shall discriminate against an employee for criticizing the ethical, moral, or legal policies and practices of the organization. . ."

In addition to protecting individual employees, Ewing frankly desires to encourage "whistle blowing" in cases of corporate wrongdoing. That might accomplish some desirable changes in corporate behavior. But this hypothesized advantage has to be weighed against some foreseeable disadvantages. Who is to distinguish between whistle blowing and spiteful accusation? Speech now is protected from government penalty, in most cases, even if the utterance is proved untrue. Would Ewing's amendment continue this broad protection? Or would courts have to sift evidence to discover whether the employee's charge against the corporation was true? In the first case an organization might be required to keep on its payroll an employee who continually lied about it. In the second case, courts, which are not winning much public applause for the way they discharge their present responsibilities, would have to take on a huge new burden of deciding not only whether charges were true or false, but whether ethical norms had or had not been violated by the defendant organization.

The incidence of these cases could become such a nuisance to companies that all employees might wind up having, in effect, life tenure in their jobs, like the Civil Service or the tenured faculty of universities. Neither of these examples is necessarily reassuring.

A Silly Idea That Feeds Leviathan

It's true, of course, that a company's right to fire has long been limited by the National Labor Relations Act, which has worked rather well in forbidding firing for union activity. In this narrow class of cases, it is relatively easy to determine whether the forbidden practice has occurred. In a much larger group of cases under equal-opportunity acts, corporations are forbidden to discriminate in respect to race or sex. Enforcement here has been less effective and has caused more confusion. Ewing's amendment is so much broader than the equal-opportunity laws, and its criteria so much vaguer, that the imagination boggles at the legal chaos that might ensue.

Such practical objections Ewing brushes aside with a quote from Judge Learned Hand: "To keep our democracy, there must be one commandment: Thou shalt not ration justice." The distinguished jurist said many wise things, but this was not one of them. In any society justice must always be less than perfect. A free society recognizes that its government should not pretend to dispense total justice. In that sense justice in a democracy must always be "rationed."

Much injustice that occurs among citizens is beyond the reach of courts or of any government instrument. The state in which that limitation is not recognized, the state that believes itself empowered to set all norms of conduct and to deal with every incident of ethical transgression, is the absolute state. Leviathan.

Employee and Employer Rights in an Institutional Context

Patricia H. Werhane

From *Ethical Theory in Business*, 3d ed., ed. Tom L. Beauchamp and Norman Bowie (Englewood Cliffs, N.J.: Prentice-Hall, 1988), 267–71. Copyright © 1988.

The common law principle of Employment at Will (EAW) states that in the absence of a specific contract or law, an employer may hire, fire, demote, or promote any employee (not covered by contract or law) when that employer wishes. The theory is that employers have rights—rights to control what happens in the workplace. These include decisions concerning all business operations, extending of course to the hiring and placement of employees. Although EAW is a common-law doctrine, until recently it virtually dictated employment relationships.

What are the justifications for EAW? How would one defend this idea? EAW is sometimes justified on the basis of property rights. It is contended that the rights to freedom and to property ownership are valid rights and that they include the right to use freely and to improve what one owns. According to this view, an employer has the right to dispose of her business and those who work for that business (and thus affect it) as she sees fit. Instituting employee rights such as due process or the protection of whistle blowers, for example, would restrict an employer's freedom to do what she wishes with her business, thus violating property rights.

In the twentieth century, employer property rights have changed. Businesses are mainly corporations owned by a large number of changing shareholders and managed by employees who usually own little or no stock in the company. The board of directors represents the owner-shareholder interests, but most business decisions are in the hands of managers. Despite this division of ownership from management, however, proprietary ownership rights of employers have translated themselves into management rights. Contemporary management sees itself as having the rights to control business and therefore to control employment. From a utilitarian perspective, control of a company by its managers is thought of as essential for maximum efficiency and productivity. To disrupt this would defeat the primary purpose of free enterprise organizations. Moreover, according to its proponents, EAW preserves the notion of "freedom of contract," the right of persons and organizations to enter freely into binding voluntary agreements (e.g., employment agreements) of their choice.

That managers see themselves in the role of proprietors is, of course, too simple a description. In complex organizations there is a hierarchy of *at-will* relationships. Each manager is an at-will employee, but sees himself as proprietor of certain responsibilities to the organization and as being in control of certain other employees whom the manager can dismiss at will, albeit within certain guidelines of legal restraint. That manager, in turn, reports to someone else who is herself an at-will employee responsible to another segment of the organization. These at-will relationships are thought to preserve equal employee and employer freedoms because, just as a manager can demote or fire an at-will employee at any time, so too an employee, any employee, can quit whenever he or she pleases for any reason whatsoever. Notice a strange anomaly here. Employees have responsibilities to their managers and are not free to make their own choices in the workplace. At the same time, employees are conceived of as autonomous person who are at liberty to quit at any time.

Notice, too, that there is sometimes a sort of Social Darwinist theory of management functioning in many of these relationships. Managers are so-titled because it is felt that they are the most capable. By reason of education and experience and from the perspective of their position, they allegedly know what is best for the organization or the part of the organization they manage. This gives them the right to manage other employees. The employees they manage (who themselves may be managers of yet other employees) have roles within the organization to carry out the directives of their managers, and so on.

The employee-manager hierarchy of at-will employment relationships is both more complex and more simple in union-management relationships. It is more complex because often the relationship is specified or restricted by a number of well-defined rules for seniority, layoffs, dismissals, and so on. It is more simple because by and large union employees are *employees*, not managers. Their role responsibilities defined by hierarchical relationships are clear-cut, and those wishing to change or move up to management usually must give up union membership.

This oversimplified, crude, overstated, overview of hierarchical employment relationships in business may not currently exist in the ways I have described in any business. Yet such relationships are at least *implicit* in many businesses and perpetuated in the law by a continued management or employer-biased interpretation of the principle of EAW.

Despite the fact that the principle of EAW is defended on a number of grounds—including that it allegedly protects equal employee and manager freedoms, that it promotes efficiency, and that it preserves the notion of freedom of contract—EAW violates all of these for the following reasons. EAW does not preserve equal freedoms because in most employment relationships employer-managers are in positions of greater power than employees. This in itself does not undermine EAW, but the potential abuse of this power is what is at issue. Employees and managers allegedly have equal rights—rights to be fired or to quit at any time for any reason. But an at-will employee is seldom in a position within the law to inflict harm on an employer. Legally sanctioned at-will treatment by employers of employees can, however, harm employees. This is because when an employee is fired arbitrarily

without some sort of grievance procedure, a hearing or an appeal, he cannot demonstrate that he was fired without good reason. Employees who have been fired have much more difficulty getting new jobs than those who have not been fired, even when that treatment was unjustified. Because arbitrarily fired employees are treated like those who deserved to lose their jobs, EAW puts such employees at an unfair disadvantage compared with other workers. The principle of EAW, then, does not preserve equal freedoms because it is to the advantage of the employer or manager and to the unfair disadvantage of the fired employee.

Worse, at-will practices violate the very right upon which EAW is allegedly based. Part of the appeal of EAW is that it protects the freedom of contract—the right to make employment agreements of one's choice. Abolishing EAW is coercive, according to its proponents, because this forces employers involuntarily to change their employment practices. But at-will employment practices too are or can be coercive. This is because when an employee is fired without sufficient reasons employers or managers place this person involuntarily in a personally harmful position unjustified by her behavior, a position that an employee would never choose. Thus the voluntary employment agreement according to which such practices are allowed is violated.

It is argued that EAW maximizes efficiency. But what is to prevent a manager from hiring a mentally retarded son-in-law or firing a good employee on personal grounds, actions that themselves damage efficiency? On a more serious level, if managers have prerogatives, these are based on a claim to the right to freedom—the freedom to conduct business as one pleases. But if this is a valid claim, then one must grant equal freedoms to everyone, including employees. Otherwise managers are saying that *they* have greater rights than other persons. This latter claim brings into question a crucial basis of democratic capitalism, namely that every person has *equal* rights, the most important of which is the equal right to freedom. The notion of equal rights does not necessarily imply that employees and managers have equal or identical prerogatives in business decision making or in managing a company. But what is implied is that the exercise of freedom requires a respect for the equal exercise of freedom by others, although the *kind* of exercises in each case may be different. EAW practices, then, are inconsistent practices because they do not preserve equal freedoms, they do not protect freedom of contract for both parties, and they do not guarantee efficiencies in the workplace. A number of thinkers contend that the principle should be abolished or disregarded in the law.

Interestingly, however, one can *defend* at least some employee rights from a consistent interpretation of the principle of EAW. This is because to be consistent the demands of EAW, principally the demand of management for the freedom to control business, require an equal respect for employee freedoms. In other words, if EAW is to be justified on the basis of the right to freedom, it can only be justified for that reason if it respects everyone's freedoms equally. Otherwise, managers' alleged freedoms are merely unwarranted licenses to do anything they please, even abridging employee rights, and thus have no moral or constitutional basis. Such equal respect for employee rights cannot always be interpreted as equal participation in management decisions. Extending and respecting employee freedoms requires balancing equal but not necessarily identical liberties. The free exercise of management employment decisions, however, does seem to require that employees be given reasons, publicly stated and verifiable, for management decisions that affect employees, including hiring and firing. In this way voluntary choices in the job market are truly equal to management employment choices. Moreover, freedom of choice in management decision making requires allowing legitimate whistle blowing, conscientious objection, and even striking without employer retaliation when an employee is asked to perform illegal, immoral, and /or socially dangerous jobs, or when such practices occur in the workplace. I am suggesting that a proper interpretation of EAW is not inconsistent with granting some employee rights. It is the misinterpretation of EAW that has served as a basis

for the exercise of management prerogatives at the expense of employee rights.

Employers and managers, of course, will not always be happy to grant these freedoms to employees, because such freedoms are often seen as giving employees too many rights. Others managers identify extending employee freedoms with participatory management programs that, they argue, would abridge management responsibilities. Neither of these consequences, however, necessarily follows from extending employee rights. On the other hand, continuing the present imbalance of freedoms in the workplace perpetuates injustices. Worse, from the perspective of management this is a highly risky policy in an age of employee enlightenment and a concern for employee rights. Many managers are sympathetic to arguments defending employee rights. However, they fear that instituting employee rights in the workplace entails government regulation of and intervention in the affairs of business, all of which is intrusive, expensive, and time-consuming. But there is no reason why businesses cannot voluntarily institute employment reforms, and in the climate of a surging interest in employee rights, such voluntary actions would help prevent government intervention and regulation.

Turning to a second moral justification for employee rights, balancing employee and employer freedoms in the workplace is also justified because of what I shall call the reciprocal nature of employment relationships. Employment relationships, which are by and large hierarchical role relationships, tend to be destructive of employee rights, yet this need not be so, and in fact quite the contrary is required. The reasons for this are the following. In the workplace both management and employees have role responsibilities that are a source of job accountability. A person holding a job is held accountable for a certain performance; it is sometimes not considered unjust to dismiss someone for failure to perform his or her job even if the employer pays poorly and sometimes even if the employer does not respect other employee rights. Employee job accountability in this context is usually described as first-party duties of the employee to a manager or to the organization for whom one works. However, this description is incomplete. There are, in addition, duties on the part of the manager or the institution to the employee who is held accountable. These obligations arise in part from the role responsibilities of the party to whom an employee is answerable and in part because of the nature of the relationship. These obligations, which are often neglected in an analysis of accountability, are reciprocal or correlative obligations implied by role responsibility to the employee in question. This notion of reciprocity, I shall argue, is crucial in employment relationships.

The notion of reciprocity in any social relationship is grounded on the basic fact that each party is a person or a group of persons. As the philosopher Carol Gould puts it,

> Reciprocity may be defined as a social relation among agents in which each recognizes the other as an agent, that is, as equally free, and each acts with respect to the other on the basis of a shared understanding and a free agreement to the effect that the actions of each with respect to the other are equivalent.[1]

This does not mean that each party must treat the other in the same way in every respect, but rather that each treats the other with equal respect and as equal possessors of rights and benefits. Because they are social relationships between persons or between persons and institutions developed by persons, accountability relationships entail this notion of reciprocity.

Reciprocity in accountability relationships operates in part, as follows. If I am accountable for my actions to a certain group or institution because of my role in that group or institution, this accountability implicitly assumes a reciprocal accountability to me on the part of the institution to whom I am answerable. The obligations in each relationship are not necessarily contractual, but the strength of my role obligations depends at least in part on equally forceful, though obviously not identical, role obligations of the second party to me. And if no such reciprocal obligations exist, or if they are not respected, my accountability to that individual, group, or institution weakens.

What this brief analysis of role accountability suggests in the workplace is that when taking a job an employee has responsibilities connected with that job, responsibilities that are often only implicitly stated. At the same time, accountability does not consist merely of first-party duties of employees to employers or managers; it is also defined in reciprocal relationships with the party to whom one is accountable. The reason for this is that employee-employer relationships are both social and contractual arrangements. They are social because they are relationships entered into between persons or between persons and organizations created and run by persons. They are at least implicitly contractual ones voluntarily entered into and freely dissolvable by both parties. Therefore, if employees are accountable to managers or employers, managers or employers are also accountable for upholding their part of the agreement by being reciprocally accountable, albeit in different ways, to their employees.

The reciprocal nature of employee-employer relationships entails some important employee rights, in particular the rights of fair treatment and respect. What might constitute such fair treatment and respect? Obviously, fair pay or a living wage in exchange for work is an essential part of just treatment in the workplace. But if, in addition to working, employees are expected to respect and be fair to their employers, then employers have reciprocal obligations that go beyond merely offering fair pay. Employee respect demands from a manager a correlative respect for employee privacy, employee information, and for due process in the workplace, even for at-will employees.

Due process demands not that employees not be dismissed, but rather than any employer action meet impartial standards of reasonableness, the same sort of reasonableness expected of employees. Similarly, if an employee is to respect his or her employer and the decisions of that employer, the employer needs to honor the privacy of the employee as a human being, including protecting with confidentiality personnel information and respecting the privacy of employee activities outside the workplace. Respect for the employee also involves keeping the employee well-informed about his or her job, the quality of his or her work, and the stability of the company. This is a two-pronged responsibility. It entails not only the requirement that all employees are equally entitled to information, but the recognition that all employees actually in fact *have* such information. Employees have rights not merely to be informed but also to be communicated with in ways they understand.

The employee rights just enumerated—the rights to privacy, to employee information, and the right to due process—are moral rights that result from the nature of role accountability in the workplace. Like the right to freedom that is implied by a consistent interpretation of EAW, these rights are moral rather than legal rights, so employers need not respect them. But if the reciprocal requirements of employment accountability relationships are not met by employers or managers, those employers or managers undermine the basis for employee accountability in the workplace.

Notes

[1] Carol Gould, "Economic Justice, Self-Management and the Principle of Reciprocity," in *Economic Justice*, ed. Kenneth Kipnis and Diana T. Meyers (Totowa, N.J.: Rowman and Allanheld, 1985), pp. 213–14.

Whistleblowing and Professional Responsibility

Sissela Bok

New York University Education Quarterly 11 (Summer 1980): 2–10. Copyright © 1980.

"Whistleblowing" is a new label generated by our increased awareness of the ethical conflicts encountered at work. Whistleblowers sound an alarm from within the very organization in which they work, aiming to spotlight neglect or abuses that threaten the public interest.

The stakes in whistleblowing are high. Take the nurse who alleges that physicians enrich themselves in her hospital through unnecessary surgery; the engineer who discloses safety defects in the braking systems of a fleet of new rapid-transit vehicles; the Defense Department official who alerts Congress to military graft and overspending: all know that they pose a threat to those whom they denounce and that their own careers may be at risk.

Moral Conflicts

Moral conflicts on several levels confront anyone who is wondering whether to speak out about abuses or risks or serious neglect. In the first place, he must try to decide whether, other things being equal, speaking out is in fact in the public interest. This choice is often made more complicated by factual uncertainties: Who is responsible for the abuse or neglect? How great is the threat? And how likely is it that speaking out will precipitate changes for the better?

In the second place, a would-be whistleblower must weigh his responsibility to serve the public interest against the responsibility he owes to his colleagues and the institution in which he works. While the professional ethic requires collegial loyalty, the codes of ethics often stress responsibility to the public over and above duties to colleagues and clients. Thus the United States code of Ethics for Government Servants asks them to "expose corruption wherever uncovered" and to "put loyalty to the highest moral principles and to country above loyalty to persons, party, or government."[1] Similarly, the largest professional engineering association requires members to speak out against abuses threatening the safety, health, and welfare of the public.[2]

A third conflict for would-be whistleblowers is personal in nature and cuts across the first two: even in cases where they have concluded that the facts warrant speaking out, and that their duty to do so overrides loyalties to colleagues and institutions, they often have reason to fear the results of carrying out such a duty. However strong this duty may seem in theory, they know that, in practice, retaliation is likely. As a result, their careers and their ability to support themselves and their families may be unjustly impaired.[3] A government handbook issued during the Nixon era recommends reassigning "undesirables" to places so remote that they would prefer to resign. Whistleblowers may also be downgraded or given work without responsibility or work for which they are not qualified; or else they may be given many more tasks than they can possibly perform. Another risk is that an outspoken civil servant may be ordered to undergo a psychiatric fitness-for-duty examination,[4] declared unfit for service, and "separated" as well as discredited from the point of view of any allegations he may be making. Outright firing, finally, is the most direct institutional response to whistleblowers.

Add to the conflicts confronting individual whistleblowers the claim to self-policing that many professions make, and professional responsibility is at issue in still another way. For an appeal to the public goes against everything that "self-policing" stands for. The question for the different professions, then, is how to resolve, insofar as it is possible, the conflict between professional loyalty and professional responsibility toward the outside world. The same conflicts arise to some extent in all groups, but professional groups often have special cohesion and claim special dignity and privileges.

The plight of whistleblowers has come to be documented by the press and described in a number of books. Evidence of the hardships imposed on those who chose to act in the public interest has combined with a heightened awareness of professional malfeasance and corruption to produce a shift toward greater public support of whistleblowers. Public service law firms and consumer groups have taken up their cause; institutional reforms and legislation have been proposed to combat illegitimate reprisals.[5]

Given the indispensable services performed by so many whistleblowers, strong public support is often merited. But the new climate of acceptance makes it easy to overlook the dangers of whistleblowing: of uses in error or in malice; of work and reputations unjustly lost for those falsely accused; of privacy invaded and trust undermined. There comes a level of internal prying and mutual suspicion at which no institution can function. And it is a fact that the disappointed, the incompetent, the malicious, and the paranoid all too often leap to accusations in public. Worst of all, ideological persecution throughout the world traditionally relies on insiders willing to inform on their colleagues or even on their family members, often through staged public denunciations or press campaigns.

No society can count itself immune from such dangers. But neither can it risk silencing those with a legitimate reason to blow the whistle. How then can we distinguish between different instances of whistleblowing? A society that fails to protect the right to speak out even on the part of those whose warnings turn out to be spurious obviously opens the door to political repression. But from the moral point of view there are important differences between the aims, messages, and methods of dissenters from within.

Nature of Whistleblowing

Three elements, each jarring , and triply jarring when conjoined, lend acts of whistleblowing special urgency and bitterness: dissent, breach of loyalty, and accusation.

Like all dissent, whistleblowing makes public a disagreement with an authority or a majority view. But whereas dissent can concern all forms of disagreement with, for instance, religious dogma or government policy or court decisions, whistleblowing has the narrower aim of shedding light on negligence or abuse, or alerting to a risk, and of assigning responsibility for this risk.

Would-be whistleblowers confront the conflict inherent in all dissent: between conforming and sticking their necks out. The more repressive the authority they challenge, the greater the personal risk they take in speaking out. At exceptional times, as in times of war, even ordinarily tolerant authorities may come to regard dissent as unacceptable and even disloyal.[6]

Furthermore, the whistleblower hopes to stop the game; but since he is neither referee nor coach, and since he blows the whistle on his own team, his act is seen as a violation of loyalty. In holding his position, he has assumed certain obligations to his colleagues and clients. He may even have subscribed to a loyalty oath or a promise of confidentiality. Loyalty to colleagues and to clients comes to be pitted against loyalty to the public interest, to those who may be injured unless the revelation is made.

Not only is loyalty violated in whistleblowing, hierarchy as well is often opposed, since the whistleblower is not only a colleague but a subordinate. Though aware of the risks inherent in such disobedience, he often hopes to keep his job.[7] At times, however, he plans his alarm to coincide with leaving the institution. If he is highly placed, or joined by others, resigning in protest may effectively direct public attention to the wrongdoing at issue.[8] Still another alternative, often chosen by those who wish to be safe from retaliation, is to leave the institution quietly, to secure another post, and then to blow the whistle. In this way, it is possible to speak with the authority and knowledge of an insider without having the vulnerability of that position.

It is the element of accusation, of calling a "foul," that arouses the strongest reactions on the part of the hierarchy. The accusation may be of neglect, of willfully concealed dangers, or of outright abuse on the part of colleagues or superiors. It singles out specific persons or groups as responsible for threats to the public interest. If no one could be held responsible—as in the case of an impending avalanche—the warning would not constitute whistleblowing.

The accusation of the whistleblower, moreover, concerns a present or an imminent threat. Past errors or misdeeds occasion such an alarm only if they still affect current practices. And risks far in the future lack the immediacy needed to make the alarm a compelling one, as well as the close connection to particular individuals that would justify actual accusations. Thus an alarm can be sounded about safety defects in a rapid-transit system that threaten or will shortly threaten passengers, but the revelation of safety defects in a system no longer in use, while of historical interest, would not constitute whistleblowing. Nor would the revelation of potential problems in a system not yet fully designed and far from implemented.[9]

Not only immediacy, but also specificity, is needed for there to be an alarm capable of pinpointing responsibility. A concrete risk must be at issue rather than a vague foreboding or a somber prediction. The act of whistleblowing differs in this respect from the lamentation or the dire prophecy. An immediate and specific threat would normally be acted upon by those at risk. The whistleblower assumes that his message will alert listeners to something they do not know, or whose significance they have not grasped because it has been kept secret.

The desire for openness inheres in the temptation to reveal any secret, sometimes joined to an urge for self-aggrandizement and publicity and the hope for revenge for past slights or injustices. There can be pleasure, too—righteous or malicious—in laying bare the secrets of co-workers and in setting the record straight at last. Colleagues of the whistleblower often suspect his motives: they may regard him as a crank, as publicity-hungry, wrong about the facts, eager for scandal and discord, and driven to indiscretion by his personal biases and shortcomings.

For whistleblowing to be effective, it must arouse its audience. Inarticulate whistleblowers are likely to fail from the outset. When they are greeted by apathy, their message dissipates. When they are greeted by disbelief, they elicit no response at all. And when the audience is not free to receive or to act on the information—when censorship or fear of retribution stifles response—then the message rebounds to injure the whistleblower. Whistleblowing also requires the possibility of concerted public response: the idea of whistleblowing in an anarchy is therefore merely quixotic.

Such characteristics of whistleblowing and strategic considerations for achieving an impact are common to the noblest warnings, the most vicious personal attacks, and the delusions of the paranoid. How can one distinguish the many acts of sounding an alarm that are genuinely in the public interest from all the petty, biased, or lurid revelations that pervade our querulous and gossip-ridden society? Can we draw distinctions between different whistleblowers, different messages, different methods?

We clearly can, in a number of cases. Whistleblowing may be starkly inappropriate when in malice or error, or when it lays bare legitimately private matters having to do, for instance, with political belief or sexual life. It can, just as clearly, be the only way to shed light on an ongoing unjust practice such as drugging political prisoners or subjecting them to electroshock treatment. It can be the last resort for alerting the public to an impending disaster. Taking such clear-cut cases as benchmarks, and reflecting on what it is about them that weighs so heavily for or against speaking out, we can work our way toward the admittedly more complex cases in which whistleblowing is not so clearly the right or wrong choice, or where different points of view exist regarding its legitimacy—cases where there are moral reasons both for concealment and for disclosure and where judgments conflict. Consider the following cases:[10]

A. *As a construction inspector for a federal agency, John Samuels (not his real name) had personal knowledge of shoddy and deficient construction practices by private contractors. He knew his superiors received free vacations and entertainment, had their homes remodeled and found jobs for their relatives—all courtesy of a private contractor. These superiors later approved a multimillion no-bid contract with the same "generous" firm.*

Samuels also had evidence that other firms were hiring nonunion laborers at a low wage while receiving substantially higher payments from the government for labor costs. A former superior, unaware of an office dictaphone, had incautiously instructed Samuels on how to accept bribes for overlooking subpar performance.

As he prepared to volunteer this information to various members of Congress, he became tense and uneasy. His family was scared and the fears were valid. It might cost Samuels thousands of dollars to protect his job. Those who had freely provided Samuels with information would probably recant or withdraw their friendship. A number of people might object to his using a dictaphone to gather information. His agency would start covering up and vent its collective wrath upon him. As for reporters and writers, they would gather for a few days, then move on to the next story. He would be left without a job, with fewer friends, with massive battles looming and without the financial means of fighting them. Samuels decided to remain silent.

B. *Engineers of Company "A" prepared plans and specifications for machinery to be used in a manufacturing process and Company "A" turned them over to Company "B" for production. The engineers of Company "B," in reviewing the plans and specifications, came to the conclusion that they included certain miscalculations and technical deficiencies of a nature that the final product might be unsuitable for the purposes of the ultimate users, and that the equipment, if built according to the original plans and specifications, might endanger the lives of persons in proximity to it. The engineers of Company "B" called the matter to the attention of appropriate officials of their employer who, in turn, advised Company "A." Company "A" replied that its engineers felt that the design and specifications for the equipment were adequate and safe and that Company "B" should proceed to build the equipment as designed and specified. The officials of Company "B" instructed its engineers to proceed with the work.*

C. A recently hired assistant director of admissions in a state university begins to wonder whether transcripts of some applicants accurately reflect their accomplishments. He knows that it matters to many in the university community, including alumni, that the football team continue its winning tradition. He has heard rumors that surrogates may be available to take tests for a fee, signing the names of designated applicants for admission, and that some of the transcripts may have been altered. But he has no hard facts. When he brings the question up with the director of admissions, he is told that the rumors are unfounded and asked not to inquire further into the matter.

Individual Moral Choice

What questions might those who consider sounding an alarm in public ask themselves? How might they articulate the problem they see and weigh its injustice before deciding whether or not to reveal it? How can they best try to make sure their choice is the right one? In thinking about these questions it helps to keep in mind the three elements mentioned earlier: dissent, breach of loyalty, and accusation. They impose certain requirements—of accuracy and judgment in dissent; of exploring alternative ways to cope with improprieties that minimize the breach of loyalty; and of fairness in accusation. For each, careful articulation and testing of arguments are needed to limit error and bias.

Dissent by whistleblowers, first of all, is expressly claimed to be intended to benefit the public. It carries with it, as a result, an obligation to consider the nature of this benefit and to consider also the possible harm that may come from speaking out: harm to persons or institutions and,

ultimately, to the public interest itself. Whistleblowers must, therefore, begin by making every effort to consider the effects of speaking out versus those of remaining silent. They must assure themselves of the accuracy of their reports, checking and rechecking the facts before speaking out; specify the degree to which there is genuine impropriety; consider how imminent is the threat they see, how serious, and how closely linked to those accused of neglect and abuse.

If the facts warrant whistleblowing, how can the second element—breach of loyalty—be minimized? The most important question here is whether the existing avenues for change within the organization have been explored. It is a waste of time for the public as well as harmful to the institution to sound the loudest alarm first. Whistleblowing has to remain a last alternative because of its destructive side effects: it must be chosen only when other alternatives have been considered and rejected. They may be rejected if they simply do not apply to the problem at hand, or when there is not time to go through routine channels, or when the institution is so corrupt or coercive that steps will be taken to silence the whistleblower should he try the regular channels first.

What weight should an oath or a promise of silence have in the conflict of loyalties? One sworn to silence is doubtless under a stronger obligation because of the oath he has taken. He has bound himself, assumed specific obligations beyond those assumed in merely taking a new position. But even such promises can be overridden when the public interest at issue is strong enough. They can be overridden if they were obtained under duress or through deceit. They can be overridden, too, if they promise something that is in itself wrong or unlawful. The fact that one has promised silence is no excuse for complicity in covering up a crime or a violation of the public's trust.

The third element in whistleblowing—accusation—raises equally serious ethical concerns. They are concerns of fairness to the persons accused of impropriety. Is the message one to which the public is entitled in the first place? Or does it infringe on personal and private matters that one has no right to invade? Here, the very notion of what is in the public's best "interest" is at issue: "accusations" regarding an official's unusual sexual or religious experiences may well appeal to the public's interest without being information relevant to "the public interest."

Great conflicts arise here. We have witnessed excessive claims to executive privilege and to secrecy by government officials during the Watergate scandal in order to cover up for abuses the public had every right to discover. Conversely, those hoping to profit from prying into private matters have become adept at invoking "the public's right to know." Some even regard such private matters as threats to the public: they voice their own religious and political prejudices in the language of accusation. Such a danger is never stronger than when the accusation is delivered surreptitiously. The anonymous accusations made during the McCarthy period regarding political beliefs and associations often injured persons who did not even know their accusers or the exact nature of the accusations.

From the public's point of view, accusations that are openly made by identifiable individuals are more likely to be taken seriously. And in fairness to those criticized, openly accepted responsibility for blowing the whistle should be preferred to the denunciation or the leaked rumor. What is openly stated can more easily be checked, its source's motives challenged, and the underlying information examined. Those under attack may otherwise be hard put to defend themselves against nameless adversaries. Often they do not even know that they are threatened until it is too late to respond. The anonymous denunciation, moreover, common to so many regimes, places the burden of investigation on government agencies that may thereby gain the power of a secret police.

From the point of view of the whistleblower, on the other hand, the anonymous message is safer in situations where retaliation is likely. But it is also often less likely to be taken seriously. Unless the message is accompanied by indications of how the evidence can be checked, its anonymity, however safe for the source, speaks against it.

During this process of weighing the legitimacy of speaking out, the method used, and the degree of fairness needed, whistleblowers must try to compensate for the strong possibility of bias on their part. They should be scrupulously aware of any motive that might skew their message: a desire for self-defense in a difficult bureaucratic situation, perhaps, or the urge to seek revenge, or inflated expectations regarding the effect their message will have on the situation. (Needless to say, bias affects the silent as well as the outspoken. The motive for holding back important information about abuses and injustice ought to give similar cause for soul-searching.)

Likewise, the possibility of personal gain from sounding the alarm ought to give pause. Once again there is then greater risk of a biased message. Even if the whistleblower regards himself as incorruptible, his profiting from revelations of neglect or abuse will lead others to question his motives and to put less credence in his charges. If, for example, a government employee stands to make large profits from a book exposing the iniquities in his agency, there is danger that he will, perhaps even unconsciously, slant his report in order to cause more of a sensation.

A special problem arises when there is a high risk that the civil servant who speaks out will have to go through costly litigation. Might he not justifiably try to make enough money on his public revelations—say, through books or public speaking—to offset his losses? In so doing he will not strictly speaking have *profited* from his revelations: he merely avoids being financially crushed by their sequels. He will nevertheless still be suspected at the time of revelation, and his message will therefore seem more questionable.

Reducing bias and error in moral choice often requires consultation, even open debate:[11] methods that force articulation of the moral arguments at stake and challenge privately held assumptions. But acts of whistleblowing present special problems when it comes to open consultation. On the one hand, once the whistleblower sounds his alarm publicly, his arguments will be subjected to open scrutiny: he will have to articulate his reasons for speaking out and substantiate his charges. On the other hand, it will then be too late to retract the alarm or to combat its harmful effects, should his choice to speak out have been ill-advised.

For this reason, the whistleblower owes it to all involved to make sure of two things: that he has sought as much and as objective advice regarding his choice as he can *before* going public; and that he is aware of the arguments for and against the practice of whistleblowing in general, so that he can see his own choice against as richly detailed and coherently structured a background as possible. Satisfying these two requirements once again has special problems because of the very nature of whistleblowing: the more corrupt the circumstances, the more dangerous it may be to seek consultation before speaking out. And yet, since the whistleblower himself may have a biased view of the state of affairs, he may choose not to consult others when in fact it would be not only safe but advantageous to do so; he may see corruption and conspiracy where none exists.

Applied Ethics: Institutional Questions

What changes, outside and inside business organizations, government agencies, and other places of work might serve to protect the rights of dissenters, cut down on endless breaches of loyalty and on false accusations, while assuring public access to needed information?

The most far-reaching set of changes, and the hardest to implement, involves the cutting down on legitimate causes for alarm. Reducing practices of corruption and cover-up, as well as opportunities for errors to go undiscovered, would reduce also the need to call attention to them. The needed changes in review procedures, incentives, and obstacles go far beyond the scope of this paper, but so long as improprieties remain serious and frequent, whistleblowing will remain a last resort for calling attention to them.

The need to resort to whistleblowing can be reduced by providing mechanisms for taking criticism seriously before it reaches the press and the courtroom. These mechanisms must work to counteract the blockage of information within an organization and the tendency to filter out negative information so that those who must make decisions ignore it.[12] The filtering process may be

simple or intricate, well-intentioned or malevolent, more or less consciously manipulated. Two examples of how it works follow:[13]

———

A. *A couple of years ago, when the Alaska pipeline was being built, some managers began ordering construction crews to take shortcuts in order to reduce costs and meet time deadlines for construction. According to reports confirmed by the Wall Street Journal and other sources, many batches of X-rays of weld joints were falsified so that flaws would not be detected. Some workers who objected were told to shut up. Nevertheless, news about the cover-up seeped out, and investigators were hired to look into the problem. Attempts were made to frustrate the investigation (one of the investigators died under mysterious circumstances), but the dreary mess finally came to the attention of responsible officials. It then became necessary for thousands of welds to be rechecked and a great many corrected at high costs in time and money.*

———

B. *On August 23, 1977, Glenn Greenwald, a chemist in the Public Utilities Department of the city of North Miami Beach, Florida, was called to 800 N.E. 182nd Terrace by a resident who complained that the water coming out of the tap tasted, smelled, and looked peculiar. Mr. Greenwald agreed, and his tests showed that the water contained an abnormally small amount of free chlorine as well as coliform bacteria.*

Unable to find his supervisor, he asked his department head for an immediate flushing of the water distribution system in the area. Mr. Greenwald's supervisor was irate when he learned of the flushing: he doubted that the action had been necessary; he feared that the residents of the affluent neighborhood where it had taken place might become unduly alarmed. He told Mr. Greenwald that he should consider resigning if he could not work through channels.

But the contamination problem had not been resolved by the flushing. Greenwald wanted officially to advise residents of the house not to drink their tap water. His supervisors agreed to the continued testing but refused to authorize the official notice.

Three days later, when a resident asked him why the testing was still going on, Mr. Greenwald explained about the contamination problem, and he suggested that the family not drink the water until the problem had been cleared up. When he told his supervisors of this conversation, he was summarily discharged for insubordination.

Mr. Greenwald promptly took his case to the city's Civil Service Board, which three months later upheld his firing. Then he took his case to the U.S. Department of Labor, appealing under the Safe Drinking Water Act of 1974, which states that no employer may discharge any employee or otherwise discriminate against any employee because the employee has participated in any action to carry out the purposes of this title. The Labor Department's administrative law judge who heard the case agreed that Mr. Greenwald's discharge was indeed a violation of the Act. But Mr. Greenwald's was an empty victory. His complaint had not been filed within a thirty-day statutory limit contained in the Act, so the judge recommended to the Secretary of Labor that the appeal be dismissed.

Ewing argues that industry has much to gain by not discouraging internal criticism.[14] A number of managements do welcome the views of dissenters and promise that no one will be unfairly dismissed or disciplined for having made his revelation.

Such an "open-door" policy may suffice at times; but it is frequently inadequate unless further buttressed. In the first place, the promises of protection given by top management cannot always be fulfilled. Though an employee may keep his job, there are countless ways of making his position difficult, to the point where he may be brought to resign of his own volition, or stay while bitterly regretting that he has spoken out. Second, it would be naïve to think that abuses in industry or in government are always unknown to top management and perpetrated against their will by subordinates. If the abuse—the secret bombardment of Cambodia, for instance, or corporate bribing, or conspiracy to restrict trade—is planned by those in charge, then the "open-door" policy turns out to be a trap for the dissenter.

For these reasons, proposals have been made to protect dissenters in more formal ways while giving serious consideration to their messages: independent review boards, ombudsmen, consumer or citizen representatives on boards of trustees, bills of rights for employees. These methods of protection spring up and sometimes die away with great rapidity. They are often instituted without careful comparison between different possibilities. Teaching and research could do much to study them, to compare their advantages and disadvantages, their differing suitability under different circumstances and possible disadvantages. The benefits from these methods, when they work, are strong. They allow for criticism with much less need for heroism; for a way to deflect the crank or the witch-hunter before their messages gain publicity; for a process of checking the accuracy of the information provided; for a chance to distinguish between urgent alarms and long-range worries; and for an arena for debating the moral questions of motive and of possible bias, of loyalty and responsibility to the public interest.

Many of these methods work well; others fail. They fail when they are but window dressing from the outset, meant to please or exhaust dissenters; or else they fail because, however independent at the outset, they turn into management tools. Such is the fate of many a patient representative in hospitals whose growing loyalty to co-workers and to the institution once again leaves the dissenter little choice between submission and open revolt. Still another reason for the failure of such intermediaries is their frequent lack of credibility. No matter how well-meaning, they will not be sought out if they cannot protect from retaliation those who turn to them for help. Even if they can give such protection but cannot inspire confidence in those with grievances, their role will be largely a ceremonial one.

A comparative study of such intermediaries and means of protection would have to seek out the conditions of independence, flexibility, separateness from management, institutional goodwill, fairness, and objectivity needed for success. Moreover, in looking at the protection given to dissenters, the entire system must be kept in perspective, so that changes in one area do not produce unexpected dislocations elsewhere. To what extent will increased due process make the entire institution more litigious? To what extent will protection in one place put increased pressure on another? Is it not possible, for example, that the increasing difficulties of firing incompetent federal employees have led to the growing resort to psychiatric fitness-for-duty examinations and that there, in turn, have become a new weapon with which to combat critics?

A different method for reducing the tension and risk of whistleblowing is to state conditions expressly under which those who learn about an abuse *must* blow the whistle: when, far from being disloyal, one is not only right to do so, but obliged. Laws or other regulations can require revelations and thus take the burden of choice off the individual critic.

Such requirements to report exist in a number of places. The Toxic Substances Control Act, for instance, enacted in January 1977, requires companies producing chemicals to instruct their employees and officials to report chemicals that pose a substantial risk to health or the environment. Once again, these requirements open up fields for study and for comparison.

In order to be effective, requirements to report must be specific and enforceable. It is therefore not appropriate for them to be as open-ended and exhortative as the U.S. Code of Ethics in urging government employees to "expose corruption wherever uncovered." They must be linked to clear-cut improprieties and used as a last resort only. Once again, here, the lines must be firmly drawn against requiring reporting on religious or political belief or purely personal matters. In many societies, citizens are asked to report "deviations," fellow workers to spy on one another, and students to expose the subversive views of their teachers. No society can afford to ignore these precedents in its enthusiasm for eradicating corruption.

Applied Ethics: Professional Responsibilities

The comparison between different types of work when it comes to whistleblowing forms part of a larger set of issues, recently highlighted in a number of articles,[15] that ought not to be ignored in courses on professional ethics: Must a professional sometimes act in such a way as to breach his personal ethical standards? Might professional and personal ethics actually conflict? John Noonan phrased the question for lawyers: "Can an honest person practice regularly as a criminal defense lawyer in the United States? Can a decent person serve as prosecutor for the state or federal government? Can an honest, decent person teach other persons to be criminal defense lawyers or prosecutors in the American system of criminal justice?"[16]

Such questions are not addressed to those who argue that professionals assume particular obligations to serve their clients as they do not serve all others, by protecting, say, their confidentiality more forcefully than would be their right were they *not* in a professional relationship with these clients. Such practices can be openly set forth and defended. Rather, Noonan's question addresses the means of acting as a professional: it asks whether professionals have special privileges of breaking common moral standards surreptitiously. Should they allow themselves to lie or cheat for their clients, for example? Should public officials overcome scruples about the covert use of force to further what they take as their nation's long-term interest? And at what point of threat to innocent bystanders should psychiatrists abandon their privilege of keeping confidential the plans of their patients?

These questions merit serious debate not only in courses on professional ethics but in preprofessional courses. Students should have an opportunity to think in advance of what will be expected of them and of how it might conflict with what they expect of themselves. Such consideration will in turn affect professional practices—if in no other way than to draw distinctions in what is now all too often an impossible tangle of diverging views. These distinctions will be clarified, too, if they are looked at from a perspective that includes a number of kinds of work; there is danger, otherwise, that the sense of mission and high purpose within any one calling might serve to undercut criticism and to reinforce the status quo.

Notes

[1]Code of Ethics for Government Service passed by the U.S. House of Representatives in the 85th Congress (1958) and applying to all government employees and office holders.

[2]Code of Ethics of the Institute of Electrical and Electronics Engineers, Article IV.

[3]For case histories and descriptions of what befalls whistle-blowers, see: Rosemary Chalk and Frank von Hippel, "Due Process for Dissenting Whistle-Blowers," *Technology Review* 81 (June–July 1979): 48–55. Alan S. Westin and Stephen Salisbury, eds., *Individual Rights in the Corporation* (New York: Pantheon, 1980); Helen Dudar, "The Price of Blowing the Whistle," *New York Times Magazine*, 30 October 1979, pp. 41–54; John Edsall, *Scientific Freedom and Responsibility* (Washington, D.C.: American Association for the Advancement of Science, 1975), p. 5; David Ewing, *Freedom Inside the Organization* (New York: Dutton, 1977); Ralph Nader, Peter Petkas, and Kate Blackwell, *Whistle-Blowing* (New York: Grossman, 1972); Charles Peter and Taylor Branch, *Blowing the Whistle* (New York: Praeger, 1972).

[4]Congressional hearings uncovered a growing resort to mandatory psychiatric examinations. See U.S., Congress, House Committee on Post Office and Civil Service, Subcommittee on Compensation and Employee Benefits, *Forced Retirement/Psychiatric Fitness for Duty Exams*, 95th Cong., 2nd sess., 3 November 1978, pp. 2–4. See also the Subcommittee hearings of 28 February 1978. Psychiatric referral for whistle-blowers has become institutionalized in government service, but it is not uncommon in private employment. Even persons who make accusations without being "employed" in the organization they accuse have been classified as unstable and thus as unreliable witnesses. See, e.g., Jonas Robitscher, "Stigmatization and Stone-Walling: The Ordeal of Martha Mitchell," *Psychohistory*, forthcoming.

[5]For an account of strategies and proposals to support government whistleblowers, see Government Accountability Project, *A Whistle-blower's Guide to the Federal Bureaucracy* (Washington, D.C.: Institute for Policy Studies, 1977).

[6]See, e.g., Samuel Eliot Morison, Frederick Merk, and Frank Friedel, *Dissent in Three American Wars* (Cambridge: Harvard University Press, 1970).

[7]In the scheme worked out by Albert Hirschman in *Exit, Voice and Loyalty* (Cambridge: Harvard University Press, 1970), whistleblowing represents "voice" accompanied by a preference not to "exit," though forced "exit" is clearly a possibility and "voice" after or during "exit" may be chosen for strategic reasons.

[8]Edward Weisband and Thomas N. Franck, *Resignation in Protest* (New York: Grossman, 1975).

[9]Future developments can, however, be the cause for whistleblowing if they are seen as resulting from steps being taken or about to be taken that render them inevitable.

[10]Case A is adapted from Louis Clark, "The Sound of Professional Suicide," *Barrister*, Summer 1980, p. 10; Case B is Case 5 in Robert J. Baum and Albert Flores, eds., *Ethical Problems of Engineering* (Troy, N.Y.: Rensselaer Polytechnic Institute, 1978), p. 186.

[11]I discuss these questions of consultation and publicity with respect to moral choice in chapter 7 of Sissela Bok, *Lying* (New York: Pantheon, 1978).

[12]John C. Coffee, "Beyond the Shut-Eyed Sentry: Toward a Theoretical View of Corporate Misconduct and an Effective Legal Response," *Virginia Law Review* 63 (1977): 1099–1278, gives an informed and closely reasoned account of such "information blockages" and "filtering out" and of possible remedies.

[13]Case A is from David W. Ewing, "The Employee's Right to Speak Out: The Management Perspective," *Civil Liberties Review* 5 (1978): 10–15; Case B is adapted from Chalk and von Hippel, "Due Process for Dissenting Whistle-Blowers."

[14]Ewing, "The Employee's Right to Speak Out."

[15]Benjamin Freedman, "A Meta-Ethics for Professional Morality," *Ethics* 89 (1974): 1–19; Stuart Hampshire, "Public and Private Morality," in *Public and Private Morality*, ed. Stuart Hampshire (Cambridge: Cambridge University Press, 1978), pp. 23–53; Thomas Nagel, "Ruthlessness in Public Life," in *Public and Private Morality*, pp. 75–91; Richard Wasserstrom, "Lawyers as Professionals: Some Moral Issues," *Human Rights* 5 (1975): 1–24; Bernard Williams, "Politics and Moral Character," in *Public and Private Morality*, pp. 55–73.

[16]John T. Noonan, Jr., "Professional Ethics or Personal Responsibility?" *Stanford Law Review* 29 (1977): 363.

Privacy in Employment

Joseph R. Des Jardins

From *Moral Rights in the Workplace*, ed. Gertrude Ezorsky (Albany: State University of New York Press). Copyright © 1987 State University of New York Press.

It would be convenient if we could begin a paper on privacy rights in employment by citing a commonly accepted definition of privacy and proceeding to develop the paper by applying that definition to employment situations. Unfortunately, there is little consensus regarding the definition, nature, and justification of privacy rights in general. Statutory protection of privacy is a relatively recent development in American legal history. The U.S. Constitution, for example, makes no explicit reference to a general right of privacy. It is not found among the numerous political rights mentioned in the Bill of Rights. The legal discussion of privacy typically is traced to the 1890 *Harvard Law Review* article by Samuel Warren and Louis Brandeis and the 1965 Supreme Court decision in *Griswold v. Connecticut*. Indeed, it was not until this 1965 decision that the Supreme Court recognized any Constitutional basis for privacy. Further, the very meaning of privacy is so confused that in 1977 the congressionally established Privacy Protection Study Commission reported that after two years of study its members could reach no consensus on a definition of privacy.

Fortunately, we do not need to settle upon one precise definition of the general civil right of privacy before considering the range of privacy rights in employment. In fact, one good way to sharpen a definition is to fix its context and reflect upon the use of the word within that particular situation. With this in mind, this paper considers the extent and justification of an employee's claim to privacy in the workplace.

There tend to be three general meanings to "privacy" used in the legal and philosophical literature on this topic: (1) the proprietary relationship that a person has to his/her own name or likeness; (2) the right to be "let alone" within one's own zone of solitude; and (3) the right to control information about oneself. There may be other ways to understand privacy, but these seem to cover the most obvious cases.

The origin of the first meaning of privacy is to tort law and often is traced to a New York statute passed after a well-publicized case involving the unauthorized use of a woman's likeness in a commercial endorsement. This use of a person's likeness or name without consent was said to involve an invasion of personal privacy. I will not be concerned with this sense of privacy here.

A more common understanding of privacy centers around the notion of being "let alone." Beginning with the Warren and Brandeis article in 1980 and the 1965 decision in *Griswold v. Connecticut*, this sense of privacy has dominated the legal discussions. Privacy as a right "to be let alone" is also the understanding typically found in ordinary linguistic usage. Since this is such a common understanding of privacy and since I will suggest that it is inadequate for employment contexts, it will be useful to consider this view in some detail.

In their article, Warren and Brandeis were concerned that certain technological advances and business practices, notably the practice among some newspapers of printing stories and photographs of private parties, were causing an increasing threat to the solitude of individual citizens. They defended the right of privacy as "the next step which must be taken for the protection of the person, and for securing to the individual . . . the right 'to be let alone.'"[1]

It was not until 1965, however, that the Supreme Court recognized Constitutional protection of this right to privacy. In *Griswold v. Connecticut*, the Court ruled that the Constitution guaranteed citizens a "zone of privacy" around their person that could not be violated by government. The Court found privacy within the "penumbra" of rights established by the First, Third, Fourth, and Fifth Amendments. By doing so, the Court found privacy implicit in the liberty-based rights established by the Bill of Rights.

Much of the discussion concerning the right of privacy in employment begins with this definition of privacy. The aim of some employee-rights advocates is to preserve the integrity of this zone within the workplace. According to this view, a citizen's right "to be let alone" should not be lost when he or she enters into an employment agreement. Some defenders of employee rights use this definition in developing extensive lists of privacy rights in the workplace. These lists include not only such issues as privacy of personnel records and freedom from polygraph and psychological testing, but also surveillance at work, restrictions upon after-hours activities, peace and quiet at work, employee lounges, privacy of personal property at work, and employee grooming, dress, and manners.[2]

Unfortunately there are problems with this definition of privacy. Phrases like *right to be let alone* and *zone of privacy* are quite vague, and their application tends to be much broader than is appropriate. It is difficult to see how a legitimate claim to be let alone can be consistently maintained at the same time in which one wishes to participate in an essentially social and cooperative activity like work. The difficulty with this second definition is that it confuses privacy with the more general right of liberty. Liberty, understood as the freedom from interference, can be used to generate a variety of specific rights. Free speech, freedom of religious worship, freedom of press, and private property have all been thought of as liberty-based rights. It seems that both Warren and Brandeis and the Griswold decision assume that privacy is simply another liberty-based right. It is understandable that they do so. In the *Griswold* case, the Court stated that the Connecticut law might require police searches of the bedrooms of married couples. Certainly this would be an unjustified interference with personal liberty. Being free from interference is virtually synonymous with Warren and Brandeis' definition of privacy as the right to be "let alone." Certainly privacy can be closely related to liberty. Indeed, in many cases a right to privacy can be justified by appeal to liberty. Nevertheless, the justification of a right claim is independent of the definition of that right. It seems a confusion between justification and definition may underlie much of the problem with this second definition of privacy.

Violating someone's liberty is neither necessary nor sufficient for violating privacy.

Violating someone's liberty is neither necessary nor sufficient for violating privacy. We can imagine a situation in which a "peeping tom" monitors someone's activities from a distance. While this would violate privacy it would not be an interference with their liberty, in any straightforward sense. Further, some coercive activities could well violate liberty without affecting the privacy of the person coerced. For example, subliminal advertising would, if effective, violate liberty without necessarily violating privacy. These examples show not only that privacy cannot be identified with liberty, but also that not all privacy claims can be justified by appeal to liberty.[3]

This brings us to the third understanding of privacy, privacy as involving information about oneself and the right to privacy as the right to control that information. To understand this view, let us return to the concerns of Warren and Brandeis. It seems that Mrs. Warren was troubled by the publicity that inevitably followed her social gatherings and parties. No doubt Mrs. Warren wanted to be "let alone," and Warren and Brandeis certainly were correct in identifying her concern as involving privacy. But surely Mrs. Warren's objections were to the publication of personal information and not simply with the violation of her liberty. No one was, after all, directly interfering with her parties. Her privacy was violated not by an interference with her actions, but when she lost control over information that was essentially private. More precisely, her privacy was violated when people who had no legitimate claim to this information (i.e., newspaper reporters and their readers) came to know the details of her parties. Her privacy was not violated when invited guests, for example, came to know about the party.

Despite the centrality of the Court's concern with the "fundamental liberties of citizens," it is also true that his informational sense of privacy played a crucial role in the *Griswold* case. Justice Douglas' majority opinion abhorred the violation of marital intimacy that would occur if government agents came to know the details of the sexual lives of married citizens.

These examples suggest that the right to privacy does not involve, as some have argued, merely the control that a person has over information about herself.[4] Rather, the relationship that exists between the person involved also plays a crucial role. Because they were invited guests, some people could claim that they were entitled to know certain things about Mrs. Warren's party. Since no such relationship existed between Mrs. Warren and the general public, the public was not entitled to that information. In the *Griswold* case, the relationship that exists between a citizen and a liberal-democratic state makes it illegitimate for that state to come to possess intimate information about its citizens' married lives.

In an insightful article, George Brenkert recently has developed this view.[5] Brenkert claims that the right to privacy involved a three place relation between person, A, some information, X, and another person, Z. The right of privacy is violated only when Z comes to possess information X, *and* no relationship exists between A and Z that would justify Z's coming to know X. Following Brenkert, I shall say that the right to privacy is the "right of individuals, groups, or institutions that [have] access to and information about themselves is [sic] limited in certain ways by the relationships in which they exist to others."[6]

Note that this definition will help resolve some of the difficulties associated with the liberty-based understanding of privacy. If privacy receives its value simply by being derived from the more general right of liberty, then it would seem that privacy could be seriously restricted in the workplace. After all, one of the things one gives up when entering an employment agreement is the freedom to do as one chooses. The cooperative nature of work will require, at least, some restrictions on employee liberties. If privacy were justified solely by its derivation from liberty, privacy in employment would be similarly limited. But a good case can be made for protecting employee privacy even though the employee has voluntarily accepted a general restriction upon her liberty. Brenkert's definition allows the employee to retain various privacy rights while relinquishing the general claim to liberty. It does this by recognizing that specific relationships between people can justify limiting access to information in certain ways. Consequently, even if an appeal to liberty cannot justify an employee's privacy claims, the nature of the employment relationship itself can.

The nature and extent of privacy rights in the workplace can be determined by identifying the relationship that exists between employer and employee.

Accordingly, the nature and extent of privacy rights in the workplace can be determined by identifying the relationship that exists between employer and employee. On one traditional view, the relationship that exists is that of an agent-principal. The employee is the agent of the employer and as such must comply with any legal request of the employer. On this view the only right that an employee can claim is the right to quit her job. At the same time, the employee has the obligations of obedience, loyalty, and confidentiality.[7] However, there are good reasons to reject this view. This model of the employer-employee relationship developed out of a common law tradition that viewed labor merely as one type of capital and the employee as merely one type of property. But surely this outdated model cannot be justified from a moral point of view since it does not treat both parties as autonomous moral agents. Consequently, the agent-principal model has come under increasing attack and is being replaced by a contractural model of the employer-employee relationship.[8]

The existence of a contractual relationship between employer and employee, whether the contract is implicit or explicit, will entail certain ground rules. These ground rules, in turn, can be used to generate the privacy rights that should exist within the workplace. Among these ground rules are, first, that contracts presuppose a legal framework to guarantee their enforcement. An unenforceable contract is an empty contract. Contracts also must be noncoercive, voluntary agreements between rational and free agents. Contracts involving children or mentally handicapped adults, or those involving a threat of force are invalid. Finally, contracts must be free from fraud and deception. This initial sketch can help us to begin to identify the nature of privacy rights in employment.

First, since the contract presupposes the existence of a legal framework, it must conform to the requirements of that legal system. In particular, obedience to tax, social security, equal opportunity, and health and safety laws would require an employer to collect and store certain information about all employees. Providing, of course, that this information is used only in the proper legal manner, an employer coming to know an employee's age, number of dependents, sex, race, social security number, and so on would not violate the employee's privacy.

There is much other information that an employer can come to know about employees without violating employee privacy. Certainly information needed to insure that the contract is voluntary and free from fraud or deception can be required. Accordingly, prior to the employment agreement, an employer can require, under the threat of not hiring the potential employee, information about job qualifications, work experience, educational background, and other information relevant to the hiring decision. However, this relevancy test should be taken seriously. There is no reason to require information concerning marital status, arrest records (as opposed to conviction records), credit or other financial data, military records (unless required by law), or such things as religious convictions and sexual or political preferences. This information is irrelevant for deciding whether or not the employee is capable of fulfilling her part of the employment contract. Further, as Brenkert argues, the use of polygraph tests prior to employment is also suspect since it seeks information in ways that bypass the employees' consent.[9]

Only after the employment agreement has been reached does other information about employees become relevant. Health and insurance plans, for example, may require information about the employee. However, since the contract is already in force, since, in other words, the relationship is grounded upon mutual consent, such information can only be requested with the consent of the employee. Thus, if an employee can choose not to participate in health or insurance packages, the medical examination required for such participation cannot be required (although, of course, there may be other reasons to require a medical examination). After the employment agreement has been reached, and the employer is satisfied with the employee's qualifications for the job, there is a prima facie prohibition against collecting or verifying evaluative information without the employee's consent. This would rule out such things as electronic or other covert surveillance, polygraph or psychological tests, background checks by third parties, and unconsented searches of an employee's desk, files, or locker.

Finally, since the contract does require the voluntary agreement of both parties, the use of third parties to gather or verify information about employees should be limited only to those cases in which the employee has given her uncoerced consent and in which the information sought is relevant to the employment relationship. Thus, checks with an employee's school to verify educational background can be justified, while credit agencies, private investigators, and police agencies are highly suspect as sources of information.

Two further issues need to be considered before this preliminary examination of privacy in employment will be complete. First, we need to consider how employers can use information about employees that has been legitimately collected, and second, we need to discuss employee access to and control over that information once the employer has come to know it.

Given the important function consent plays in the employment contract, we can say that, in general, employers should use personal information about employees only in those instances for which consent was granted. For example, social security numbers given to comply with legal requirements should not be used as employee identification numbers. Medical information released for insurance purposes should not be used during an evaluation for promotion. Information relevant for evaluations should not become the object of office gossip.

More importantly, the information an employer collects about an employee is not a commodity that can be exchanged, sold, or released in the marketplace. Accordingly, the release of information to a landlord, credit grantor, or any other third party without the employee's consent is a violation of that employee's privacy. Release of information to law enforcement agencies without either the employee's consent or a warrant also violates employee privacy. Releasing information about an employee to a credit agency, either in response to a credit check or in exchange for information about other present or potential employees, is another clear violation of employee privacy. In short, there is a prima facie prohibition against the release of any information about an employee to a third party without the employee's explicit consent.

Finally, the number of people within a company who have access to employee files should be strictly limited. Immediate supervisors ought not to have access to an employee's medical file, for example. Consent granted by employees should restrict not only the use to which personal information is put, but also the parties to whom that information is available. If an employee has not consented to release information to a particular person, release of that information again represents a prima facia violation of that employee's privacy.

The last issue to consider involves an employee's access to, and control over, information already released to an employer. In general, the rule here should be that employees ought to have access to all personal information within an employer's possession. A separate but equally important rule is that employees ought to be informed about the exact extent of the information an employer has. Access rights to personal information will prove empty unless employees know what files exist. Of course, third parties who come to possess information about an employee while providing services to the employer have similar obligations to make available the information they possess.

A morally legitimate contract must involve parties who are free and equal. An agreement between radically unequal parties can become coercive.

A morally legitimate contract must involve parties who are free and equal. An agreement between radically unequal parties easily can become coercive. To insure that this not occur in the employment agreement, it is important that neither party occupy a significantly superior position. When one party possesses a great deal more information about the other party, the relationship can become unequal and the agreement unfair. This needs special protection in employment relationships where employers typically have significant resources available for collecting and storing information about employees. Without knowledge of and access to their own personnel files, employees will be at an unfair "competitive disadvantage." As a result, this will undermine the legitimacy of the employment contract.

Of course, there can be exceptions to this rule. In some cases a third party (e.g., a physician or evaluating supervisor) may receive a pledge of confidentiality as a condition for providing information about an employee. In some cases, this pledge of confidentiality might restrict an employee's access. We should consider exactly why and when such restrictions are justified.

It may be the case that some information necessary to fulfill the employment contract can only be acquired with a promise of confidentiality to a third party. Its necessity to the contract would justify an employer coming to know this information, but does the promise of confidentiality justify restricting an employee's access? Consider two examples: In order to provide medical insurance, a medical examination might be required. The physician may request that the medical records be kept confidential. (Perhaps she thinks it unwise for the employee to have access without her being present to explain and interpret the report.) Or a supervisor is requested to evaluate an employee. The supervisor expects the evaluation to be kept confidential. Should the employee have access to such records? It seems to me that if the information is essential to the employment contract (as a medical exam might be necessary for insurance or an evaluation necessary for promotion), then access can be limited. However, if it is essential, then employee consent would be an appropriate precondition. Similar to standard practice with student recommendations, employees should be asked to sign a waiver of access rights. Employees who desire the medical insurance or promotion, for example, would waive their access rights. Those who choose not to waive their rights must acknowledge that they are jeopardizing these other goods. In general, there ought to be a presumption of access, but with employee consent confidential information can be excluded.

Before moving on, two caveats are in order. First, we should distinguish between evaluations made for promotion purposes from those made to determine satisfactory performance levels. Since the employee likely will desire the benefits of promotion, consent to limit access will be to everyone's advantage. However, we can imagine some workers who would rather not be evaluated on job performance at all. Unsatisfactory workers could hinder legitimate evaluations somewhat by refusing to waive their access rights. To overcome this potential problem, a time limit could be established, perhaps six months or a year, in which all evaluations could be kept confidential. After that time, we could assume that the employer is satisfied with job performance and make future evaluations open to employee inspection. (This latter issue may be more a concern of an employee's right to due process than a privacy concern.)

Second, some evaluations involve comparisons of employees. Since access here may involve violating another employee's privacy, some limitation may be in order. However, it would seem that if all parties consented, the same conditions should apply to these files that apply to single employee evaluation files.

Nevertheless, an employee's right to see, copy, challenge, respond to, and know about personal information held by an employer is very strong. Since numerous decisions involving an employee's life prospects are made on the basis of this information, simple justice requires that the information be accurate, complete, and relevant. To guarantee this, employees must have access to this information; they must be able to correct it when it is mistaken, and they must be allowed to challenge it when it is in question. To do otherwise would make the employment relationship radically unequal and unfair, and thereby make the contract fundamentally coercive.

More needs to be done to specify the exact extent of privacy rights in employment. Different employment situations will no doubt require different privacy rights. IBM employees, for example, likely will have different specific privacy rights than employees of the CIA. Government employees might have more extensive rights than employees in the private sector. This paper has attempted to sketch a framework into which the details of particular employment situations can be fit.

Notes

[1]Louis D. Brandeis and Samuel Warren, "The Right to Privacy," *Harvard Law Review* 4 (1890): p. 193.

[2]See, for example, the chapter on "Privacy in Employment" in Robert Ellis Smith, *Privacy* (New York: Anchor, Doubleday 1979).

[3]For more developed analyses of the relationship between privacy and liberty, see Hyman Gross, "Privacy and Autonomy," *Privacy: Nomos XIII*, ed. J. R. Pennock and J. W. Chapman (New York: Lieber Atherton, 1971) and H. J. McCloskey, "Privacy and the Right to Privacy," *Philosophy*, vol. 55, no. 211 (1980).

[4]For example, see Alan Westin, *Privacy and Freedom* (New York: Atheneum Publishers, 1976), p. 7.

[5]George Brenkert, "Privacy, Polygraphs, and Work," *Business and Professional Ethics Journal*, vol. 1, no. 1 (1982), 19–35.

[6]Ibid., 23.

[7]For a good discussion of this model, see Phillip Blumberg, "Corporate Responsibility and the Employee's Duty of Loyalty and Obedience: A Preliminary Inquiry," *Oklahoma Law Review*, vol. 24, no. 3 (August 1971).

[8]Besides the Blumberg article, also see David Ewing, "Your Right to Fire," *Harvard Business Review*, vol. 61, no. 2 (March–April 1983), 32–41, and Norm Bowie, "The Moral Contract Between Employer and Employee," *The Work Ethic in Business*, ed. W. M. Hoffman and T. J. Wyly (Cambridge, Mass.: Oelgeschlager, Gunn, and Hari, 1981), 195–202.

[9]Brenkert, "Privacy, Polygraphs, and Work."

CASES

Case 7.1: The Employee's Bill of Rights

To help safeguard workers' rights, David W. Ewing issued a proposed bill of rights to guide employers and empower employees in protecting proper worker rights. Modeled after the Bill of Rights to the Constitution, he suggests nine inviolable rights that employees have on the job:

1. No organization or manager shall discharge, demote or in other ways discriminate against any employee who criticizes in speech or in press, the ethics, legality, or social responsibility of management actions.

2. No employee shall be penalized for engaging in outside activities of his or her choice after working hours, whether political, economic, civic, or cultural, nor for buying products and services of his or her choice for personal use, nor for expressing or encouraging views contrary to top management's on political, economic, or social issues.

3. No organization or manager shall penalize an employee for not carrying out a directive that violates common norms of morality.

4. No organization shall allow audio or visual recordings of an employee's actions or conversations to be made without his or her prior knowledge and consent. Normally an organization requires an employee or applicant to take personality tests, polygraph examinations, or other tests that constitute, in his opinion, an invasion of privacy.

5. No employee's desk, files, or locker may be examined in his or her absence by anyone but a senior manager who has sound reason to believe that the files contain information needed for a management decision that must be made in the employee's absence.

6. No employer organization may collect and keep on file information about an employee that is not relevant and necessary for efficient management. Every employee shall have the right to inspect his or her personnel file and challenge the accuracy, relevance, or necessity of data in it, except for personal evaluations and comments by other employees which could not reasonably be obtained if confidentiality were not promised.

Access to an employee's file by outside individuals and organizations shall be limited to inquiries about the essential facts of employment.

7. No manager may communicate to prospective employers of an employee who is about to be or has been discharged gratuitous opinions that might hamper the individual from obtaining a new position.

8. An employee who is discharged, demoted, or transferred to a less desirable job is entitled to a written statement from management of its reasons for the penalty.

9. Every employee who feels that he or she has been penalized for asserting a right described in this bill shall be entitled to a fair hearing before an impartial official, board, or arbitrator. The findings and conclusions of the hearing shall be delivered in writing to the employee and management.

Questions for Discussion:

1. Do you think that Ewing's bill of rights is realistic in today's competitive business environment? Why or why not?
2. What employee rights do you think Ewing's bill appropriately protects? What rights does he propose to protect that you do not believe should be protected?

Case 7.2: Electronic Eavesdropping

With the advent of electronic mail technology, new privacy issues have arisen. In September 1992, Eugene Wang, a vice president of Borland International, a major computer software maker, left the company to join a competitor, Symantec. Borland executives suspected that Wang had been transmitting company secrets to Symantec in his last few months of employment at Borland. So they bypassed his password and opened his electronic mailbox, where they claimed they found evidence that Wang had delivered sensitive Borland memos, marketing plans, product release dates, and other Borland plans against their competitors to Symantec. The police were informed and searched the homes of both Wang and Symantec CEO Gordon Eubanks. Borland instituted a civil suit against Symantec and criminal charges against Wang.

The 1986 Electronic Communications Privacy Act (ECPA) generally prohibits phone and data-line taps, with two exceptions: law enforcement and employers. Outside electronic mail is protected in the same way that the regular postal service mail is. And most people believe that E-mail is just like a sealed letter. But the law is vague on how it protects in-house company electronic mail. Wang and Symantec argued that since he used MCI Mail, a commercial service, his messages were protected by his right to privacy. He further insisted that the messages were sent to someone out of the office, making his electronic mail the equivalent of a sealed letter. Borland countered by arguing that they paid for Wang's MCI account, that they owned the mail system, and thus had every right to read the messages, a position they believe is supported by the ECPA. They insisted that since each employee's password is on file with the network manager, there is no reasonable expectation of privacy. Further, since the password is given to the employee for company business by the company, such expectations of privacy are unwarranted.

A similar case involved two Nissan employees. They were fired from their jobs of installing E-mail software and training employees in their use at the dealerships, service centers, and administrative centers for complaining about management's reading of their E-mail. Their electronic correspondence included some racy conversations and complaints about management, the latter of which resulted in a confrontation in which they were admonished about using E-mail in this way. They then filed a complaint for violation of their privacy, arguing that they had an expectation of privacy while communicating on E-mail. Nissan fired them ostensibly for their performance and when they sued for reinstatement, the court ruled in Nissan's favor, agreeing that Nissan did not violate their privacy.[2]

²See Charles Piller, "Bosses With X-Ray Eyes," *Macworld* (July 1993): 118–23; Mitchell Kapor, "Computer Spies," *Forbes* (9 November 1992): 288; and "Whose Office Is This Anyhow?" *Fortune* (9 August 1993): 93.

Questions for Discussion:

1. Should electronic mail communications be treated just like sealed letters, which cannot be legally opened by an employer? Or does the fact that the company owns the system give them the right to monitor any employee's mail?

2. Does the company having probable cause to suspect an employee of harming the company, as in the case of Wang and Borland, justify invading someone's privacy and reading his or her electronic mail?

3. If the company informs employees up front that their E-mail will be monitored randomly, does that make it justifiable for the company to so monitor the E-mail?

Case 7.3: Romancing the Co-Worker

Many companies have policies that prohibit employees from dating co-workers or clients of the firm. The reason for this is that management does not want to deal with employees who continue to work together once a relationship has broken up. This is particularly true if there is a difference in position between the two people dating. If one is the boss and the other is a subordinate, then relations can become very complicated, and the boss leaves himself or herself open to retaliatory charges of sexual harassment. On the other hand, employees argue that their work relationships are the only place that they can regularly meet people and it is unduly burdensome to their social life to prohibit them from dating clients or co-workers.

Questions for Discussion:

1. Do you think that employers have the right to regulate employees' off-the-job social behavior by prohibiting dating among co-workers and clients? Is this an unjustified invasion of privacy or a common-sense policy to safeguard good working harmony in the office?

Case 7.4: Aerospace Whistle-Blowers

Roland Gibeault was a testing engineer for Genisco, a Southern California defense electronic firm that manufactured the Harm missile for the military in the mid-1980s. He alleged that the firm had falsified test data on the missiles; he worked undercover with federal agents for over a year gathering evidence against the company. Eventually his findings became public when he sued the company after his dismissal. The government recovered over $500,000 from the company, of which Gibeault was to receive $131,000, mostly in Genisco stock. Unfortunately for him, the stock price fell dramatically with the downturn in the aerospace industry and today the stock is worth less than the taxes he owes on the judgment. Although his findings saved the government a good deal of money, the stress of blowing the whistle cost him his job and his family. His wife divorced him in 1989.

Fred Clark owned a helicopter manufacturing company in Florida that did business with the Army, until an employee's allegations of fraud began an aggressive three-year investigation into the company's defense contracts. Clark's helicopters were judged satisfactory by Army standards, the government dropped its probe into the company

[3]See Ralph Vartabedian, "Heroes, Zealots or Victims?" *Los Angeles Times* (13 September 1993), A1; and Julie Miller, "For Blowing the Whistle," *New York Times* (12 February 1995), sec. 1, 1.

in early 1992, and the employee's lawsuit was also eventually dropped. But the costs of having to defend itself and the diversion of its time and energy from its business eventually forced Clark to cut the number of its employees from forty to two. Although the allegations were never proved, the company was seriously hurt by the investigation.[3]

Questions for Discussion:

1. Do you think whistle-blowers should be regarded as moral heroes, standing up for what's right regardless of the cost, or as disgruntled or greedy employees looking to strike back at the company?
2. If you were in a position in which you thought it necessary to blow the whistle on your employer, would you consider the costs (losing your job, likely being blackballed from your industry, loss of income) too heavy to bear, or would you follow your conscience and "let the chips fall where they will"?

COMMENTARY

What legitimate rights do employees have when they enter the workplace? And under what, if any, conditions can these rights be overridden by an employer? These questions are at the heart of the debate over employee rights. Although some states have employment at will as the law, many labor advocates are uncomfortable with its implications for employee rights. On the other hand, employers are uneasy with the way they feel their hands are tied in dealing with troublesome employees. New technologies such as electronic mail also raise new questions about how far an employer can go in addressing problems with employees. Employee rights usually fall into one of two broad categories: rights and privacy on the job, and privacy off the job. That is, what employee rights must the employer protect during work time, and, second, what latitude are employers allowed in dictating what an employee may do with his or her time off of the job?

Max Ways claims that in the impetus toward protecting employee rights, employers have often been cast in an overly negative light, causing vices to be exaggerated and virtues downplayed. Although there are certainly examples of corporate abuse of employees, most companies have a strong vested interest in keeping their employees satisfied. This surely involves protecting as many employee rights as they can without affecting the efficiency or profitability of the firm. Many management experts have rightly decried the autocratic style of leadership, and although clearly this style still characterizes some corporate settings, the management world of the 1990s is very different from that of the 1950s and earlier.

Ways rightly points out the assumption inherent in some of the most passionate defenses of employee rights. In his critique of Ewing's book *Freedom Inside the Organization: Bringing Civil Liberties to the Workplace*, in which his employee bill of rights is found, Ways exposes Ewing's presupposition that once a worker enters the workplace, he or she is nearly rightless until the end of the workday. Ewing extends this presumption by comparing the rights of employees under capitalism in the United States with that of workers in former Communist countries. Ways correctly points out that this assumption is greatly exaggerated, and since 1977, when Ways wrote his article, the work environment has improved significantly. That is not to say that some companies are not oppressive and blatantly ignore important employee rights, a point that Ways could have acknowledged, but the overgeneralized assumption of widespread neglect of employee rights is not accurate and not helpful to the discussion.

Ways specifically interacts with Ewing's bill of rights, particularly the right of employees to blow the whistle on practices they deem questionable. While acknowledging that encouragement such as is provided in Ewing's bill of rights would contribute to some welcome changes in corporate behavior, he rightly suggests a more complete consideration of the potential costs involved. He is anticipating cases like that of Clark Helicopter (Case 7.4), in which an abuse of whistle-blowing nearly closed down a company. He is skeptical of proposals that would protect the jobs of whistle-blowers by arguing that it would require a company to keep on the payroll employees who are continually lying about it. He correctly uncovers a flaw in Ewing's freedom-of-speech portion of his bill of rights. Companies should not be required to protect the right of free speech for employees whose speech is damaging the company's reputation or affecting its profitability. Their right to free speech is actually not violated when they are fired for something that they say about their employer. Employees do not have the right to remain employed by an organization when they exercise free speech against it. The First Amendment, which protects free speech, only protects individuals from government sanctions against what they say. It does not protect someone from the other consequences of their exercise of free speech, such as losing their jobs. Employers cannot prevent an employee from speaking his or her mind. But it does not follow from that that the employer is obligated to keep such an employee on the payroll. Nevertheless, corporate fraud is a serious problem, and the recent allegations against defense contractors are well-publicized examples of the need for moral courage in some cases. Companies should be encouraged to recognize people who exercise moral courage while at the same time insisting that such exercise be done through appropriate in-house channels. Ways understates the need for this kind of moral courage in today's corporate environment.

Werhane's rejection of employment at will is based on the changing role of ownership and the power differential between employers and employees. She rightly points out that ownership is more diffused today than in times past and management has taken over many of the former prerogatives of ownership. However, even though corporate ownership is more spread out among shareholders, the company is still their property, and the greater difficulty they have in exercising their will does not diminish the fact that they still own the company. But simply because they own the corporation, it does not follow that the employees are their property and that they can dispose of them as they choose. The Thirteenth Amendment to the Constitution, which outlawed slavery, made it clear that no human being is another's property. Employment at will is a flawed doctrine because the conclusion that employees can be hired and fired at will does not follow from the premise that the company is the property of those who own it. Employees have rights in the workplace because of their standing as human beings. They are not the company's property.

Werhane points out that the differential of power that exists in most employer-employee relationships undermines the original intent of employment at will. It was originally based on the notion of protecting equal freedoms in the workplace. EAW recognizes that the worker can quit at any time, and, to balance the freedom of contract, the employer should have the right to terminate his or her end of the contract similarly. But Werhane rightly recognizes that the power difference translates into a much higher degree of harm to the employee when fired than to the employer when someone quits. EAW does not protect equal freedom, but rather undercuts it. To protect equal freedoms at work involves seeing the hierarchical relationships as essentially reciprocal, protecting employee rights to resources such as due process when terminated.

Des Jardins contributes to the discussion in a helpful way by providing a framework in which to address employee privacy. The right of an employee to privacy involves the relationship with the employer as well as the information in question and the employee himself or herself. Thus an employee can give up a significant amount of liberty by agreeing to contract with an employer and still retain substantial privacy in the workplace because the right to privacy is dependent on the relationship with the person who wants access to the employee's private information. We would add that there are other factors that relate to employee privacy. Des Jardins holds to a presumption for privacy that is quite strong. In addition to the contract-related private information that he protects, such as personal information that is not necessary for determining whether or not the employee can perform his or her job, we suggest that any time informed consent is granted, privacy can be invaded. For example, if an employee is told up front, prior to starting a job, that his electronic mail can be read at any time, that surveillance cameras are used for security purposes, or that his phone calls will be monitored to insure quality control, then it is justifiable and not an invasion of privacy for the employer to do so. But if he does so without the knowledge and consent of the employee, that is quite different. Even so, the employer's action can still be justified, but only with probable cause that the employee is engaged in behavior that is detrimental to the company's profitability or reputation. Further, against Des Jardins, we suggest that pre-employment screening for drugs or pre-employment polygraphs are appropriate, since the prospective employee can simply choose not to be interviewed, and that is not an invasion of privacy.

Whistle-blowing is a much more difficult issue. Bok provides helpful background to this and gives it an educational twist, encouraging the use of these cases to educate the public and employees about the moral tensions they will face in the workplace. The dilemma for employees who think they have uncovered evidence of company wrongdoing is a difficult one. They feel loyalty to their moral principles, which pull them in the direction of exposing the problem. Yet the consequences suffered by whistle-blowers, even when they are vindicated, are often catastrophic. It is routine for them to lose their jobs and be blackballed from the industry, leaving them to be underemployed in some other field. If not fired, they may be put into some less desirable job in the company or find their lives made so difficult that they quit rather than work under such conditions. Many whistle-blowers suffer significantly from the stress involved, and it may cost them their families as well as their livelihood. Many corporate whistle-blowers have gone through all the proper channels in the company and have felt that they are left with no other option than to go public with their allegations, either to the press or the appropriate regulatory board. Once they go public, the consequences usually come down hard on them. The employee frequently calculates the costs associated with blowing the whistle and decides that the costs are too much to pay, choosing to keep his or her mouth shut, sometimes to the detriment of the consumer or the public in general.

Although we applaud the appropriate exercise of moral courage, whistle-blowers often prove to be extremists who may be somewhat unstable or disgruntled employees seeking an opportunity to strike back at the company they believe has wronged them. They can bring serious public relations and financial damage to a company by going public with their allegations. Companies can spend a good deal of money and time defending themselves from improper charges, and this drives up the costs of their products at the least and, at most, can drive them out of business, as was almost the case with Clark Helicopters. Protecting firms from unwarranted whistle-blowers and the damage they can cause needs to be carefully considered.

Bok correctly assesses the damage that can be done to firms falsely accused of some sort of corruption and the costs to the whistle-blower. To keep the damage to both at a minimum, she suggests that a person considering blowing the whistle on his or her company obtain as much objective input as possible on the issue at hand and on whistle-blowing in general to insure that bias and error have been minimized and to help the person calculate the costs as accurately as possible. Her conditions for justified whistle-blowing include a just cause, use of all other possible means to resolve the conflict, open acceptance of responsibility for one's allegations (instead of anonymously leaking them), and a character above reproach. These are all helpful and appropriate conditions that should be satisfied prior to blowing the whistle. But her conclusion that these conditions are rarely satisfied and thus whistle-blowing is rarely justifiable is a bit extreme. For example, without some morally heroic people inside defense contracting firms, the public would never have become aware of the extent of defense fraud. But the terms of the False Claims Act, also called the bounty-hunter law, amended in 1986 to encourage whistle-blowing by allowing individuals to sue contractors on behalf of the government and keep up to 30 percent of the money recovered, goes too far as well. Offering people financial incentives to blow the whistle on their employers invites abuse from people motivated by greed or disgruntled employees who now have an additional financial reason to get back at the company.[4]

[4]Vartabedian, "Heroes, Zealots, or Victims?" A1.

In the introduction to this chapter, you were introduced to a number of short scenarios that raised specific issues of employee rights. In view of the readings and commentary in this chapter, review these again and see if your answers change.

• *The president of the company has a "gut feeling" that an employee is not trustworthy.*

In EAW states, the president could fire this person legally and not have any questions asked. But employees have the right to due process in termination decisions, and management needs to have probable cause for such firings. At the least, this is probably a poor business decision, since it could hurt morale among the employees and make the president appear arbitrary and capricious in firing decisions.

• *A high-ranking member of the company regularly and visibly purchases the competitor's products.*

Although many companies provide financial incentives to employees to encourage purchase of their products, this is an aspect of privacy that rarely affects the reputation of the firm. It may be that this employee simply prefers a competitor's products because of factors besides quality. Thus his or her purchase of the product may actually say very little about the company. Even if it does, unless it clearly affects the profitability of the firm, the firm has no right to dictate product choice and would be unwise to attempt to do so.

• *An employee openly attacks and grumbles about company management to other employees.*

A discontented employee has the right to free speech but not to be exempt from the consequences of what he or she says. The First

Amendment protects people only from the government's imposing consequences for the exercise of free speech, not from individuals such as employers. Firms are under no obligation to tolerate employees who undermine morale and undercut legitimate authority. The firm has the responsibility to use all other means short of dismissal in an attempt to resolve the grievance, but if after these are exhausted, the public grumbling continues, the company has every right to fire the person.

• *An employee "blows the whistle" on the employer for disseminating fraudulent information on product safety tests.*

If the employee has a just cause (that is, the allegations are true), takes responsibility for uncovering the fault, exhausts all other in-house channels, and has motives that are above criticism, then such whistle-blowing is justified and his or her job should be protected. The employee should not be entitled to financial reward. If the whistle-blower is acting from impure motives, is incorrect about the charges, has not gone through all appropriate channels, or blows the whistle anonymously, the firm has every right to dismiss him or her because of the harm that was unjustly caused the company.

• *An employee who is a pacifist refuses to service defense-industry clients on moral grounds.*

• *An employee refuses to service a pharmaceutical industry client that manufactures abortion-inducing drugs.*

Both of these scenarios depend on how much of the company's business involves these clients. If it is a small part of the clientele and personnel and responsibility can be shifted without major disruption, then the firm should make reasonable efforts to accommodate the conscience of an otherwise valuable employee. If such employee action begins to happen more regularly and affects the profitability of the company, then it is under no obligation to accommodate the employee. The person should begin looking for other work that does not violate his or her moral standards as frequently.

• *An employee of a company with a conservative clientele participates in a televised gay-rights rally after work hours.*

• *An employee of a company with a liberal clientele participates in public anti-abortion demonstrations after work hours.*

Employees generally have the right to conduct themselves in their off-work time as they choose. Employers assume that in their off time the employees will not break the law. But if they are involved in legal activities that damage the reputation of the firm, the company is justified in taking certain steps, including dismissal of the employee, to protect its reputation. There is a presumption of privacy since the employee is not on company time. But that presumption can be overridden if the employee's activities affect the company's reputation or profitability. The burden of proof is on the employer to demonstrate that the employee's activity does indeed harm the company's interests and is not simply something that management finds personally objectionable.

• *An employee complains to another employee about management over the company "E-mail" system. Someone in management "reads" this and has the employee fired.*

Electronic mail should generally be treated as general postal service mail. The law is currently in flux when it comes to in-house E-mail, but the parallels to regular mail and the expectation of privacy in electronic mail should tilt employers in the direction of maintaining privacy. However, they do own the systems and, given probable cause, are justified in breaking into someone's mailbox and reading his or her mail. Companies may also do this randomly if they inform employees prior to their hiring that this is a company practice. That is, they may do so with the informed consent of the employee, which is presumed when the employee agrees to work at the office under those conditions. In the case of Wang and Borland International, Borland was justified in reading Wang's E-mail because they had reason to believe that he was passing important company information to a competitor. In the Nissan case, it appears that Nissan management was more randomly reading the employees' mail, a practice not justifiable unless probable cause exists.

• *Someone is stealing merchandise from a retail outlet, and the company mandates lie detector tests to try to catch the thief.*

Blanket lie detector tests are not legal, nor are they justifiable, partly because they lack reliability and could damage the careers and reputations of innocent people. Other measures can and should be taken to find the thieves such as hidden surveillance cameras. Pre-employment polygraphs are justifiable, since the prospective employee can refuse the interview if he or she does not want to be subject to a polygraph test. Random checking for employee theft can be best accomplished by hidden cameras or undercover employees. For this, no informed consent is necessary, since it would likely alert the guilty parties and defeat any effort to catch them.

• *The company president wants to clean up the company's image and orders random drug testing for all employees.*

Random drug testing is an unjustifiable invasion of privacy unless there is informed consent prior to one's beginning employment in the company. It is justifiable when used in pre-employment screening. In both cases, the employee has implicitly consented to the testing. In addition, given that the drug problem has reached epidemic proportions in society today, the common good is served by these "implicitly consented to" invasions of privacy. For people who serve in certain professions that require an added emphasis on safety, such as bus drivers and airline pilots, and those who work in sensitive governmental positions, such as security officers, both random and pre-employment drug testing are appropriate. In addition, if a supervisor has probable cause to believe that an employee's drug use is affecting his or her job performance, he or she may require the employee to submit to a drug test. The requirement is even stronger in some of the above safety-related occupations.

• *For safety reasons, a company mandates HIV testing for all employees.*

This is currently against the law in every state, and rightly so. The reasons for this are that the best scientific evidence indicates that the HIV virus cannot be spread by casual contact such as occurs in the workplace. In addition, the risk of discrimination is much higher than with people who fail drug tests. It could be argued that the fact that AIDS is a fatal disease and drug use is not suggests that stronger, not weaker, testing for AIDS is appropriate. But the virus is highly unlikely to be transmitted in the workplace, and thus the fatal nature of the disease is not a strong argument. However, for those who have jobs where there is contact with human fluids, such as hospital staff members, paramedics, and police officers, pre-employment HIV testing would be appropriate, and the law allows for that.

• *A genetic test is developed that can screen a person for certain genetic diseases such as Alzheimer's, Lou Gehrig's disease, and Huntington's disease. Your employer wants you to be tested and wants access to the results.*

This is one of the most difficult areas of employee privacy. The Human Genome Project, an international effort funded by governments in North America and Europe, is an attempt to map the entire human genetic code and find as many genetic links to disease as exist. Most people can be tested for a wide range of genetic diseases, some of which have their onset later in life. Employers understandably claim a right to an employee's genetic information so they can assess whether or not someone will be with the company long enough to justify the firm's investment in that person. Insurance companies also want to know this information. Individuals have a strong interest in keeping that information private, since it could lead to the most insidious form of discrimination, based on one's genetic endowment. This is similar to discrimination based on race and gender, and should not be allowed. Someone with the gene for Huntington's disease, for example, which does not begin to appear until the mid-thirties, could have years of productive work in a job they are denied because of their medical future.

• *The employee handbook states that "employees will not date co-workers or clients of the firm"—a violation that could result in dismissal.*

Many firms have dating policies, though the degree to which they are enforced varies widely. The reason for these restrictions is the effect on efficiency and morale in the office. If and when these in-house relationships break up, they have the potential of causing significant problems in workplace harmony. They can even lead to allegations of sexual harassment if the relationship was between a boss and a co-worker. Although these relationships are private, off-time activities, firms are justified in enforcing them out of a well-documented concern for maintaining smoothly functioning and positive work environments.

• *The company has a policy that it will not hire smokers, because of the increased cost to the company of their health care.*

This is commonly referred to as "lifestyle discrimination." Companies incur substantially higher health care costs for employees who smoke than for those who do not, even if the smoking is all done outside the office or on one's off time. Firms are justified in hiring only nonsmokers, given the statistical differential on health care costs. Care should be taken to insure that companies do not start down a slippery slope and begin restricting other behavior that may increase health care costs, such as certain high risk recreation, habits that may cause high blood pressure, and foods that increase the level of cholesterol. But since the link between smoking and disease is undeniable, firms have the right to cut their health care costs by not hiring smokers. However, in some states, this kind of restriction is illegal, as are all other off-the-job restrictions.

Conclusion

Companies should operate with the presumption of employee privacy. Morale is highest and companies operate best when there is an atmosphere of trust and respect for an individual's private matters. However, an employee's right to privacy both on and off the job may be overridden when there is informed consent, that is, when the employee is informed prior to employment and implicitly agrees to it by agreeing to begin work at the company. In addition, when there is probable cause to suspect an employee is doing something illegal or something that will negatively affect the firm's profitability, invasion of privacy is justified. Most pre-employment testing is also justifiable, except where it concerns HIV and other sensitive medical information such as a person's genetic record. An employee may be dismissed when activities engaged in during off time affect the reputation and profitability of the firm.

EIGHT

Workplace Discrimination and Affirmative Action

Preferential treatment, no matter how it is justified in the light of day, subjects blacks to a midnight of self-doubt, and so often transforms their advantage into a revolving door.

Shelby Steele, *The Content of Our Character*

*In order to get beyond racism, we must first take account of race....
And in order to treat some persons equally, we must treat them differently.*

Supreme Court Justice Harry A. Blackmun

INTRODUCTION

The subject of affirmative action raises heated debate whenever it is mentioned. When policies that have grown out of its aims have been implemented, communities, workplaces, and legislatures have been divided. It is one of the most controversial topics that we will address in this book. Nevertheless, it is germane to discussions about business ethics because it has important ramifications for corporations since it arguably interrupts the forces of the free market in hiring and other employment-related decisions. While almost all agree that companies that seek to be moral in their dealings will unequivocally prevent discrimination on the basis of gender and ethnicity, serious disagreements exist today with regard to the moral and practical viability of affirmative-action policies. Specifically, many critics argue that these policies have outlived their usefulness and are now actually detrimental forces in society. In fact, a recent *Wall Street Journal/NBC News* survey found that two out of three Americans, including half of those who voted for President Clinton, oppose affirmative action.[1]

[1]Cited in Steven Roberts et al., "Affirmative Action on the Edge," *U.S. News and World Report* (13 February 1995): 32.

327

damage done by discrimination will never be eradicated. Thus many of its supporters argue that affirmative action is a temporary, but necessary evil because members of some groups are still recovering from years of egregious discrimination. This position is taken by Thomas Nagel in his article "A Defense of Affirmative Action."

While much of the rhetoric surrounding the debate over affirmative action has focused on members of ethnic minority groups, women have also been victims of workplace discrimination and have recently been significant beneficiaries of affirmative action. Currently there is an increasing emphasis on gender equality in traditionally male dominated professions as women's rights groups have gained a stronger political voice. In response, many state and local governments have instituted controversial programs to correct statistical disparities in civil service occupations. For example, the city of Los Angeles has implemented programs in its city police department with specific numerical goals so that women will be represented in numbers that correspond to their makeup in the city's population. In order to achieve these goals, some of the physical "requirements" of the positions involved have been lowered, prompting arguments over the balance between public safety and gender equality.

Although this is a clear situation in which some physical requirements will be readjusted, there are many controversies surrounding employment in which women are only deemed "less qualified" than their male counterparts when they may possess equal merit. Laura Purdy insightfully addresses these situations in the context of college teaching positions in her article "In Defense of Hiring Apparently Less Qualified Women." Purdy argues that in many cases women only "appear" to be less qualified than they really are because of perceptual biases and other disadvantages women have in the workplace.

A related topic involving gender equality that is receiving much attention today is the concept of "comparable worth." Contrary to popular belief, comparable worth is not "equal pay for equal work." There are already laws mandating that men and women with the same qualifications who perform the same duties must be paid the same. "Comparable worth" is a much more radical proposition. Operating on the premise that gender discrimination has created unacceptable inequities in compensation in female-dominated positions in comparison with male-dominated ones, comparable worth programs attempt to rectify these pay differences. Instead of compensation through market value, these programs would pay employees according to the assigned "comparable worth" of their professions vis-à-vis other professions that demand similar levels of education and skill. June O'Neill describes these programs in detail in her article "An Argument Against

Comparable Worth." As the title of her article suggests, O'Neill is against these programs because they are based on false assumptions about the degree of discrimination involved in wage gaps between men and women. Furthermore, she argues that such programs would only perpetuate gender segregation in some professions since women would have the financial incentive to stay in traditionally female-dominated occupations.

READINGS

A Defense of Affirmative Action

Thomas Nagel

Testimony before the Subcommittee on the Constitution of the Senate Judiciary Committee, 18 June 1981.

The term "affirmative action" has changed in meaning since it was first introduced. Originally it referred only to special efforts to ensure equal opportunity for members of groups that had been subject to discrimination. These efforts included public advertisement of positions to be filled, active recruitment of qualified applicants from the formerly excluded groups, and special training programs to help them meet the standards for admission or appointment. There was also close attention to procedures of appointment, and sometimes to the results, with a view to detecting continued discrimination, conscious or unconscious.

More recently the term has come to refer also to some degree of definite preference for members of these groups in determining access to positions from which they were formerly excluded. Such preference might be allowed to influence decisions only between candidates who are otherwise equally qualified, but usually it involves the selection of women or minority members over other candidates who are better qualified for the position.

Let me call the first sort of policy "weak affirmative action" and the second "strong affirmative action." It is important to distinguish them, because the distinction is sometimes blurred in practice. It is strong affirmative action—the policy of preference—that arouses controversy. Most people would agree that weak or precautionary affirmative action is a good thing, and worth its cost in time and energy. But this does not imply that strong affirmative action is also justified.

I shall claim that in the present state of things it is justified, most clearly with respect to blacks. But I also believe that a defender of the practice must acknowledge that there are serious arguments against, it, and that it is defensible only because the arguments for it have great weight. Moral opinion in this country is sharply divided over the issue because significant values are involved on both sides. My own view is that while strong affirmative action is intrinsically undesirable, it is a legitimate and perhaps indispensable method of pursuing a goal so important to the national welfare that it can be justified as a temporary, though not short-term, policy for both public and private institutions. In this respect it is like other policies that impose burdens on some for the public good.

Three Objections

I shall begin with the argument against. There are three objections to strong affirmative action: that it is inefficient; that it is unfair; and that it damages self-esteem.

The degree of inefficiency depends on how strong a role racial or sexual preference plays in the process of selection. Among candidates meeting the basic qualifications for a position, those better qualified will on the average perform better, whether they are doctors, policemen, teachers, or electricians. There may be some cases, as in preferential college admissions, where the immediate usefulness of making educational resources available to an individual is thought to be greater because of the use to which the education will be put or because of the internal effects on the institution itself. But by and large, policies of strong affirmative action must reckon with the costs of some lowering in performance level: the stronger the preference, the larger the cost to be justified. Since both the costs and the value of the results will vary from case to case, this suggests that no one policy of affirmative action is likely to be correct in all cases, and that the cost in performance level should be taken into account in the design of a legitimate policy.

The charge of unfairness arouses the deepest disagreements. To be passed over because of membership in a group one was born into, where this has nothing to do with one's individual qualifications for a position, can arouse strong feelings of resentment. It is a departure from the ideal—one of the values finally recognized in our society—that people should be judged so far as possible on the basis of individual characteristics rather than involuntary group membership.

This does not mean that strong affirmative action is morally repugnant in the manner of racial or sexual discrimination. It is nothing like those practices, for though like them it employs race and sex as criteria of selection, it does so for entirely different reasons. Racial and sexual discrimination are based on contempt or even loathing for the excluded group, a feeling that certain contacts with them are degrading to members of the dominant group, that they are fit only for subordinate positions or menial work. Strong affirmative action involves none of this: it is simply a means of increasing the social and economic strength of formerly victimized groups, and does not stigmatize others.

There is an element of individual unfairness here, but it is more like the unfairness of conscription in wartime, or of property condemnation under the right of eminent domain. Those who benefit or lose out because of their race or sex cannot be said to deserve their good or bad fortune.

It might be said on the other side that the beneficiaries of affirmative action deserve it as compensation for past discrimination, and that compensation is rightly exacted from the group that has benefited from discrimination in the past. But this is a bad argument, because as the practice usually works, no effort is made to give preference to those who have suffered most from discrimination, or to prefer them especially to those who have benefited most from it, or been guilty of it. Only candidates who in other qualifications fall on one or the other side of the margin of decision will directly benefit or lose from the policy, and these are not necessarily, or even probably, the ones who especially deserve it. Women or blacks who don't have the qualifications even to be considered are likely to have been handicapped more by the effects of discrimination than those who receive preference. And the marginal white male candidate, who is turned down can evoke our sympathy if he asks, "Why me?" (A policy of explicitly *compensatory* preference, which took into account each individual's background of poverty and discrimination, would escape some of these objections, and it has its defenders, but it is not the policy I want to defend. Whatever its merits, it will not serve the same purpose as direct affirmative action.)

The third objection concerns self-esteem, and is particularly serious. While strong affirmative action is in effect, and generally known to be so, no one in an affirmative action category who gets a desirable job or is admitted to a selective university can be sure that he or she has not benefited from the policy. Even those who would have made it anyway fall under suspicion, from themselves and from others: it comes to be widely felt that success does not mean the same thing for women and minorities. This painful damage to esteem cannot be avoided. It should make any defender of strong affirmative action want the practice to end as soon as it has achieved its basic purpose.

Justifying Affirmative Action

I have examined these three objections and tried to assess their weight, in order to decide how strong a countervailing reason is needed to justify such a policy. In my view, taken together they imply that strong affirmative action involving significant preference should be undertaken only if it will substantially further a social goal of the first importance. While this condition is not met by all programs of affirmative action now in effect, it is met by those which address the most deep-seated, stubborn, and radically unhealthy divisions in the society, divisions whose removal is a condition of basic justice and social cohesion.

The situation of black people in our country is unique in this respect. For almost a century after the abolition of slavery we had a rigid racial caste system of the ugliest kind, and it only began to break up twenty-five years ago. In the South it was enforced by law, and in the North, in a somewhat less severe form, by social convention. Whites were thought to be defiled by social or residential proximity to blacks, intermarriage was taboo, blacks were denied the same level of public goods—education and legal protection—as whites, were restricted to the most menial occupations, and were barred from any positions of authority over whites. The visceral feelings of black inferiority and untouchability that this system expressed were deeply ingrained in the members of both races, and they continue, not surprisingly, to have their effect. Blacks still form, to a considerable extent, a hereditary social and economic community characterized by widespread poverty, unemployment, and social alienation.

When this society finally got around to moving against the caste system, it might have done no more than to enforce straight equality of opportunity, perhaps with the help of weak affirmative action, and then wait a few hundred years while things gradually got better. Fortunately it decided instead to accelerate the process by both public and private institutional action, because there was wide recognition of the intractable character of the problem posed by this insular minority and its place in the nation's history and collective consciousness. This has not been going on very long, but the results are already impressive, especially in speeding the advancement of blacks into the middle class. Affirmative action has not done much to improve the position of poor and unskilled blacks. That is the most serious part of the problem, and it requires a more direct economic attack. But increased access to higher education and upper-level jobs is an essential part of what must be achieved to break the structure of drastic separation that was left largely undisturbed by the legal abolition of the caste system.

Changes of this kind require a generation or two. My guess is that strong affirmative action for blacks will continue to be justified into the early decades of the next century, but that by then it will have accomplished what it can and will no longer be worth the costs. One point deserves special emphasis. The goal to be pursued is the reduction of a great social injustice, not proportional representation of the races in all institutions and professions. Proportional racial representation is of no value in itself. It is not a legitimate social goal, and it should certainly not be the aim of strong affirmative action, whose drawbacks make it worth adopting only against a serious and intractable social evil.

This implies that the justification for strong affirmative action is much weaker in the case of other racial and ethnic groups, and in the case of women. At least, the practice will be justified in a narrower range of circumstances and for a shorter span of time than it is for blacks. No other group has been treated quite like this, and no other group is in a comparable status. Hispanic-Americans occupy an intermediate position, but it seems to me frankly absurd to include persons of oriental descent as beneficiaries of affirmative action, strong or weak. They are not a severely deprived and excluded minority, and their eligibility serves only to swell the numbers that can be included on affirmative-action reports. It also suggests that there is a drift in the policy toward adopting the goal of racial proportional representation for its own sake. This is a foolish mistake, and should be resisted. The only legitimate goal of the policy is to reduce egregious racial stratification.

With respect to women, I believe that except over the short term, and in professions or institutions from which their absence is particularly marked, strong affirmative action is not warranted and weak affirmative action is enough. This is based simply on the expectation that the social and economic situation of women will improve quite rapidly under conditions of full equality of opportunity. Recent progress provides some evidence for this. Women do not form a separate hereditary community, characteristically poor and uneducated, and their position is not likely to be self-perpetuating in the same way as that of an outcast race. The process requires less artificial acceleration, and any need for strong affirmative action for women can be expected to end sooner than it ends for blacks.

I said at the outset that there was a tendency to blur the distinction between weak and strong affirmative action. This occurs especially in the use of numerical quotas, a topic on which I want to comment briefly.

A quota may be a method of either weak or strong affirmative action, depending on the circumstances. It amounts to weak affirmative action—a safeguard against discrimination—if, and only if, there is independent evidence that average qualifications for the positions being filled are no lower in the group to which a minimum quota is being assigned than in the applicant group as a whole. This can be presumed true of unskilled jobs that most people can do, but it becomes less likely, and harder to establish, the greater the skill and education required for the position. At these levels, a quota proportional to population, or even to representation of the group in the applicant pool, is almost certain to amount to strong affirmative action. Moreover it is strong affirmative action of a particularly crude and indiscriminate kind, because it permits no variation in the degree of preference on the basis of costs in efficiency, depending on the qualification gap. For this reason I should defend quotas only where they serve the purpose of weak affirmative action. On the whole, strong affirmative action is better implemented by including group preference as one factor in appointment or admission decisions, and letting the results depend on its interaction with other factors.

I have tried to show that the arguments against strong affirmative action are clearly outweighed at present by the need for exceptional measures to remove the stubborn residues of racial caste. But advocates of the policy should acknowledge the reasons against it, which will ensure its termination when it is no longer necessary. Affirmative action is not an end in itself, but a means of dealing with a social situation that should be intolerable to us all.

Affirmative Action: The Price of Preference

Shelby Steele

From *The Content of Our Character* (New York: HarperCollins, 1991), 111–25.
Copyright © 1991 Shelby Steele.

In a few short years, when my two children will be applying to college, the affirmative action policies by which most universities offer black students some form of preferential treatment will present me with a dilemma. I am a middle-class black, a college professor, far from wealthy, but also well-removed from the kind of deprivation that would qualify my children for the label "disadvantaged." Both of them have endured racial insensitivity from whites. They have been called names, have suffered slights, and have experienced firsthand the peculiar malevolence that racism brings out in people. Yet, they have never experienced racial discrimination, have never been stopped by their race on any path they have chosen to follow. Still, their society now tells them that if they will only designate themselves as black on their college applications, they will likely do better in the college lottery than if they conceal this fact. I think there is something of a Faustian bargain in this.

Of course, many blacks and a considerable number of whites would say that I was sanctimoniously making affirmative action into a test of character. They would say that this small preference is the meagerest recompense for centuries of unrelieved oppression. And to these arguments other very obvious facts must be added. In America, many marginally competent or flatly incompetent whites are hired everyday—some because their white skin suits the conscious or unconscious racial preference of their employer. The white children of alumni are often grandfathered into elite universities in what can only be seen as a residual benefit of historic white privilege. Worse, white incompetence is always an individual matter, while for blacks it is often confirmation of ugly stereotypes. The Peter Principle was not conceived with only blacks in mind. Given that unfairness cuts both ways, doesn't it only balance the scales of history that my children now receive a slight preference over whites? Doesn't this repay, in a small way, the systematic denial under which their grandfather lived out his days?

So, in theory, affirmative action certainly has all the moral symmetry that fairness requires—the injustice of historical and even contemporary white advantage is offset with black advantage; preference replaces prejudice, inclusion answers exclusion. It is reformist and corrective, even repentant and redemptive. And I would never sneer at these good intentions. Born in the late forties in Chicago, I started my education (a charitable term in this case) in a segregated school and suffered all the indignities that come to blacks in a segregated society. My father, born in the South, only made it to the third grade before the white man's fields took permanent priority over his formal education. And though he educated himself into an advanced reader with an almost professional authority, he could only drive a truck for a living and never earned more than ninety dollars a week in his entire life. So yes, it is crucial to my sense of citizenship, to my ability to identify with the spirit and the interests of America, to know that this country, however, imperfectly, recognizes its past sins and wishes to correct them.

Yet good intentions, because of the opportunity for innocence they offer us, are very seductive and can blind us to the effects they generate when implemented. In our society, affirmative action is, among other things, a testament to white goodwill and to black power, and in the midst of these heavy investments, its effects can be hard to see. But after twenty years of implementation, I think affirmative action has shown itself to be more bad than good and that blacks—whom I will focus on in this essay—now stand to lose more from it than they gain.

Good intentions, because of the opportunity for innocence they offer us, are very seductive and can blind us to the effects they generate when implemented.

In talking with affirmative action administrators and with blacks and whites in general, it is clear that supporters of affirmative action focus on its good intentions while detractors emphasize its negative effects. Proponents talk about "diversity" and "pluralism," opponents speak of "reverse discrimination," the unfairness of quotas and set-asides. It was virtually impossible to find people outside either camp. The closest I came was a white male manager at a large computer company who said, "I think it amounts to reverse discrimination, but I'll put up with a little of that for a little more diversity." I'll live with a little of the effect to gain a little of the intention, he seemed to be saying. But this only makes him a half-hearted supporter of affirmative action. I think many people who don't really like affirmative action support it to one degree or another anyway.

I believe they do this because of what happened to white and black Americans in the crucible of the sixties when whites were confronted with their racial guilt and blacks tasted their first real power. In this stormy time white absolution and black power coalesced into virtual mandates for society. Affirmative action became a meeting ground for these mandates in the law, and in the late sixties and early seventies it underwent a remarkable escalation of its mission from simple anti-discrimination enforcement to social engineering by means of quotas, goals, timetables, set-asides and other forms of preferential treatment.

Legally, this was achieved through a series of executive orders and EEOC guidelines that allowed racial discrimination. Once it could be assumed that discrimination explained racial imbalances, it became easy to justify group reme-

dies to presumed discrimination, rather than the normal case-by-case redress for proven discrimination. Preferential treatment through quotas, goals, and so on is designed to correct imbalances based on the assumption that they always indicate discrimination. This expansion of what constitutes discrimination allowed affirmative action to escalate into the business of social engineering in the name of anti-discrimination, to push society toward statistically proportionate racial representation, without any obligation of proving actual discrimination.

What accounted for this shift, I believe, was the white mandate to achieve a new racial innocence and the black mandate to gain power. Even though blacks had made great advances during the sixties without quotas, these mandates, which came to a head in the very late sixties, could no longer be satisfied by anything less than racial preferences. I don't think these mandates in themselves were wrong, since whites clearly needed to do better by blacks and blacks needed more real power in society. But, as they came together in affirmative action, their effect was to distort our understanding of racial discrimination in a way that allowed us to offer the remediation of preference on the basis of mere color rather than actual injury. By making black the color of preference, these mandates have reburdened society with the very marriage of color and preference (in reverse) that we set out to eradicate. The old sin is reaffirmed in a new guise.

But the essential problem with this form of affirmative action is the way it leaps over the hard business of developing a formerly oppressed people to the point where they can achieve proportionate representation on their own (given equal opportunity) and goes straight for the proportionate representation. This may satisfy some whites of their innocence and some blacks of their power but it does very little to truly uplift blacks.

A white female affirmative action officer at an Ivy League university told me what many supporters of affirmative action now say: "We're after diversity. We ideally want a student body where racial and ethnic groups are represented according to their proportion in society." When affirmative action escalated into social engineering, diversity became a golden word. It grants whites an egalitarian fairness (innocence) and blacks an entitlement to proportionate representation (power). *Diversity* is a term that applies democratic principles to races and cultures rather than to citizens, despite the fact that there is nothing to indicate that real diversity is the same thing as proportionate representation. Too often the result of this on campuses (for example) has been a democracy of colors rather than people, an artificial diversity that gives the appearance of an educational parity between black and white students that has not yet been achieved in reality. Here again, racial preferences allow society to leapfrog over the difficult problem of developing blacks to parity with whites and into a cosmetic diversity that covers the blemish of disparity—a full six years after admission, only about 26 percent of black students graduate from college.

> ### *Racial representation is not the same thing as racial development. Representation can be manufactured; development is always hard-earned.*

Racial representation is not the same thing as racial development, yet affirmative action fosters a confusion of these very different needs. Representation can be manufactured; development is always hard-earned. However, it is the music of innocence and power that we hear in affirmative action that causes us to cling to it and to its distracting emphasis on representation. The fact is that after twenty years of racial preferences, the gap between white and black median income is greater than it was in the seventies. None of this is to say that blacks don't need policies that ensure our right to equal opportunity, but what we need more is the development that will let us take advantage of society's efforts to include us.

I think that one of the most troubling effects of racial preferences for blacks is a kind of demoralization, or put another way, an enlargement of self-doubt. Under affirmative action the quality that earns us preferential treatment is an implied inferiority. However this inferiority is explained—and it is easily enough explained by the myriad deprivations that grew out of our oppression—it is still inferiority. There are explanations, and then there is the fact. And the fact must be borne by the individual as a condition apart from the explanation, apart even from the fact that others like himself also bear this condition. In integrated situations where blacks must compete with whites who may be better prepared, these explanations may quickly wear thin and expose the individual to racial as well as personal self-doubt.

All of this is compounded by the cultural myth of black inferiority that blacks have always lived with. What this means in practical terms is that when blacks deliver themselves into integrated situations, they encounter a nasty little reflex in whites, a mindless, atavistic reflex that responds to the color black with alarm. Attributions may follow this alarm if the white cares to indulge them, and if they do, they will most likely be negative—one such attribution is intellectual ineptness. I think this reflex and the attributions that may follow it embarrass most whites today, therefore, it is usually quickly repressed. Nevertheless, on an equally atavistic level, the black will be aware of the reflex his color triggers and will feel a stab of horror at seeing himself reflected in this way. He, too, will do a quick repression, but a lifetime of such stabbing is what constitutes his inner realm of racial doubt.

The effects of this may be a subject for another essay. The point here is that the implication of inferiority that racial preferences engender in both the white and black mind expands rather than contracts this doubt. Even when the black sees no implication of inferiority in racial preferences, he knows that whites do, so that—consciously or unconsciously—the result is virtually the same. The effect of preferential treatment—the lowering of normal standards to increase black representation—puts blacks at war with an expanded realm of debilitating doubt, so that the doubt itself becomes an unrecognized preoccupation that undermines their ability to perform, especially in integrated situations. On largely white campuses, blacks are five times more likely to drop out than whites. Preferential treatment, no matter how it is justified in the light of day, subjects blacks to a midnight of self-doubt, and so often transforms their advantage into a revolving door.

Another liability of affirmative action comes from the fact that it indirectly encourages blacks to exploit their own past victimization as a source of power and privilege. Victimization, like implied inferiority, is what justifies preference, so that to receive the benefits of preferential treatment one must, to some extent, become invested in the view of one's self as a victim. In this way, affirmative action nurtures a victim-focused identity in blacks. The obvious irony here is that we become inadvertently invested in the very condition we are trying to overcome. Racial preferences send us the message that there is more power in our past suffering than our present achievements—none of which could bring us a *preference* over others.

When power itself grows out of suffering, then blacks are encouraged to expand the boundaries of what qualifies as racial oppression, a situation that can lead us to paint our victimization in vivid colors, even as we receive the benefits of preference. The same corporations and institutions that give us preference are also seen as our oppressors. At Stanford University minority students—some of whom enjoy as much as $15,000 a year in financial aid—recently took over the president's office demanding, among other things, more financial aid. The power to be found in victimization, like any power, is intoxicating and can lend itself to the creation of a new class of super-victims who can feel the pea of victimization under twenty mattresses. Preferential treatment rewards us for being underdogs rather than for moving beyond that status—a misplacement of incentives that, along with its deepening of our doubt, is more a yoke than a spur.

But, I think, one of the worst prices that blacks pay for preference has to do with an illusion. I saw this illusion at work recently in the mother of a middle-class black student who was going off to his first semester of college. "They owe us this, so don't think for a minute that you don't belong there." This is the logic by which many blacks, and some whites, justify affirmative action—it is something "owed," a form of reparation. But this logic overlooks a much harder and less digestible reality, that it is impossible to repay blacks living today for the historic suffering of the race. If all blacks were given a million dollars tomorrow morning it would not amount to a dime on the dollar of three centuries of oppression, nor would it obviate the residues of that oppression that we still carry today. The concept of historic reparation grows out of man's need to impose a degree of justice on the world that simply does not exist. Suffering can be endured and overcome, it cannot be repaid. Blacks cannot be repaid for the injustice done to the race, but we can be corrupted by society's guilty gestures of repayment.

Affirmative action is such a gesture. It tells us that racial preferences can do for us what we cannot do for ourselves. The corruption here is in the hidden incentive *not* to do what we believe preferences will do. This is an incentive to be reliant on others just as we are struggling for self-reliance. And it keeps alive the illusion that we can find some deliverance in repayment. The hardest thing for any sufferer to accept is that his suffering excuses him from very little and never has enough currently to restore him. To think otherwise is to prolong the suffering.

Several blacks I spoke with said they were still in favor of affirmative action because of the "subtle" discrimination blacks were subject to once on the job. One photojournalist said, "They have ways of ignoring you." A black female television producer said, "You can't file a lawsuit when your boss doesn't invite you to the insider meetings without ruining your career. So we still need affirmative action." Others mentioned the infamous "glass ceiling" through which blacks can see the top positions of authority but never reach them. But I don't think racial preferences are a protection against this subtle discrimination; I think they contribute to it.

In any workplace, racial preferences will always create two-tiered populations composed of preferreds and unpreferreds. This division makes automatic a perception of enhanced competence for the unpreferreds and of questionable competence for the preferreds—the former earned his way, even though others were given preference, while the latter made it by color as much as by competence. Racial preferences implicitly mark whites with an exaggerated superiority just as they mark blacks with an exaggerated inferiority. They not only reinforce America's oldest racial myth but, for blacks, they have the effects of stigmatizing the already stigmatized.

> **Rather than asking affirmative action to ensure equal opportunity, we have demanded that it create parity between the races. But preferential treatment does not teach skills, or educate, or instill motivation.**

I think that much of the "subtle" discrimination that blacks talk about is often (not always) discrimination against the stigma of questionable competence that affirmative action delivers to blacks. In this sense, preferences scapegoat the very people they seek to help. And it may be that at a certain level employers impose a glass ceiling, but this may not be against the race so much as against the race's reputation for having advanced by color as much as by competence. Affirmative action makes a glass ceiling virtually necessary as a protection against the corruptions of preferential treatment. This ceiling is the point at which corporations shift the emphasis from color to competency and stop playing the affirmative action game. Here preference backfires for blacks and becomes a taint that holds them back. Of course, one could argue that this taint, which is, after all, in the minds of whites, becomes nothing more than an excuse to discriminate against blacks. And certainly the result is the same in either case—blacks don't get past the glass ceiling. But this argument does not get around the fact that racial preferences now taint this color with a new theme of suspicion that makes it even more vulnerable to the impulse in others to discriminate. In this crucial yet gray area of perceived competence, preferences make whites look better than they are and blacks worse, while doing noth-

ing whatever to stop the very real discrimination that blacks may encounter. I don't wish to justify the glass ceiling here, but only to suggest the very subtle ways that affirmative action revives rather than extinguishes the old rationalizations for racial discrimination.

In education, a revolving door; in employment, a glass ceiling.

I believe affirmative action is problematic in our society because it tries to function like a social program. Rather than ask it to ensure equal opportunity we have demanded that it create parity between the races. But preferential treatment does not teach skills, or educate, or instill motivation. It only passes out entitlement by color, a situation that in my profession has created an unrealistically high demand for black professors. The social engineer's assumption is that this high demand will inspire more blacks to earn Ph.D.'s and join the profession. In fact, the number of blacks earning Ph.D.'s has declined in recent years. A Ph.D. must be developed from preschool on. He requires family and community support. He must acquire an entire system of values that enables him to work hard while delaying gratification. There are social programs, I believe, that can (and should) help blacks *develop* in all these areas, but entitlement by color is not a social program; it is a dubious reward for being black.

It now seems clear that the Supreme Court, in a series of recent decisions, is moving away from racial preferences. It has disallowed preferences except in instances of "identified discrimination," eroded the precedent that statistical racial imbalances are *prima facie* evidence of discrimination, and in effect granted white males the right to challenge consent degrees that use preference to achieve racial balances in the workplace. One civil rights leader said, "Night has fallen on civil rights." But I am not so sure. The effect of these decisions is to protect the constitutional rights of everyone rather than take rights away from blacks. What they do take away from blacks is the special entitlement to more rights than others that preferences always grant. Night has fallen on racial preferences, not on the fundamental rights of black Americans. The reason for this shift, I believe, is that the white mandate for absolution from past racial sins has weakened considerably during the eighties. Whites are now less willing to endure unfairness to themselves in order to grant special entitlements to blacks, even when these entitlements are justified in the name of past suffering. Yet the black mandate for more power in society has remained unchanged. And I think part of the anxiety that many blacks feel over these decisions has to do with the loss of black power they may signal. We had won a certain specialness and now we are losing it.

But the power we've lost by these decisions is really only the power that grows out of our victimization—the power to claim special entitlements under the law because of past oppression. This is not a very substantial or reliable power, and it is important that we know this so we can focus more exclusively on the kind of development that will bring enduring power. There is talk now that Congress will pass new legislation to compensate for these new limits on affirmative action. If this happens, I hope that their focus will be on development and anti-discrimination rather than entitlement, on achieving racial parity rather than jerry-building racial diversity.

I would also like to see affirmative action go back to its original purpose of enforcing equal opportunity—a purpose that in itself disallows racial preferences. We cannot be sure that the discriminatory impulse in America has yet been shamed into extinction, and I believe affirmative action can make its greatest contribution by providing a rigorous vigilance in this area. It can guard constitutional rather than racial rights, and help institutions evolve standards of merit and selection that are appropriate to the institution's needs yet as free of racial bias as possible (again, with the understanding that racial imbalances are not always an indication of racial bias). One of the most important things affirmative action can do is to define exactly what racial discrimination is and how it might manifest itself within a specific institution. The impulse to discriminate *is* subtle and cannot be ferreted out unless its many guises are made clear to people. Along with this there should be monitoring of institutions and heavy

sanctions brought to bear when actual discrimination is found. This is the sort of affirmative action that America owes to blacks and to itself. It goes after the evil of discrimination itself, while preferences only sidestep the evil and grant entitlement to its *presumed* victims.

But if not preferences, then what? I think we need social policies that are committed to two goals: the educational and economic development of disadvantaged people, regardless of race, and the eradication from our society—through close monitoring and severe sanctions—of racial, ethnic, or gender discrimination. Preferences will not deliver us to either of these goals, since they tend to benefit those who are not disadvantaged—middle-class white women and middle-class blacks—and attack one form of discrimination with another. Preferences are inexpensive and carry the glamour of good intentions—change the numbers and the good deed is done. To be against them is to be unkind. But I think the unkindest cut is to bestow on children like my own an undeserved advantage while neglecting the development of those disadvantaged children on the East Side of my city who will likely never be in a position to benefit from a preference. Give my children fairness; give disadvantaged children a better shot at development—better elementary and secondary schools, job training, safer neighborhoods, better financial assistance for college, and so on. Fewer blacks go to college today than ten years ago; more black males of college age are in prison or under the control of the criminal justice system than in college. This despite racial preferences.

The mandates of black power and white absolution out of which preferences emerged were not wrong in themselves. What was wrong was that both races focused more on the goals of these mandates than on the means to the goals. Blacks can have no real power without taking responsibility for their own educational and economic development. Whites can have no racial innocence without earning it by eradicating discrimination and helping the disadvantaged to develop. Because we ignored the means, the goals have not been reached, and the real work remains to be done.

In Defense of Hiring Apparently Less Qualified Women

Laura M. Purdy

From *Journal of Social Philosophy* 15, no. 2 (Summer 1984): 26–33.

A Man's mind—what there is of it—has always the advantage of being masculine—as the smallest birchtree is of higher kind than the most soaring palm—and even his ignorance is of a sounder quality.

George Eliot, *Middlemarch*, chap. 2

There are relatively few women in academe, and it is reasonable to believe that discrimination—conscious and unconscious, subtle and overt, individual and institutional—is responsible for this state of affairs.[1] Affirmative action programs have been promoted to try to neutralize this discrimination. One form requires academic departments to search actively for female candidates; if a woman with qualifications at least as good as those of the leading male contender is found, she is to be hired.

Does this policy create new and serious injustice, as some contend?[2] If a woman and a man were equally qualified, and one could be sure that prejudice against women played no part in the decision to hire, such a policy would certainly be an imposition on the department's freedom to hire the most compatible-seeming colleague. (This is not to say that such an imposition could never be justified: we might, for example, believe that the importance of creating role models for female students justifies some loss of freedom on the part of departments.) However, it is widely conceded that there is prejudice against women among academics, with the result that women are not getting the appointments they deserve. My intent here is to consider how this happens. I will argue that women are often not perceived to be as highly qualified as they really are. Thus when the qualifications of candidates are compared, a woman may not be thought equally (or more highly) qualified, even when she is. Affirmative action programs which require hiring of equally qualified women

will therefore be ineffective: the hiring of women perceived to be less qualified is needed if discrimination against women is to cease.

Some people think that the latter course is both unnecessary and unfair. Alan Goldman, for instance, maintains that it is unnecessary because the procedural requirements of good affirmative action programs are sufficient to guarantee equal opportunity. He also believes it to be unfair because it deprives the most successful new Ph.D.'s of their just reward—a good job.[3] I will argue that neither of these claims is true and that there is a good case for hiring women perceived to be less well qualified than their male competitors.

The general difficulty of forming accurate assessments of candidates' merit is well-known, and it is probable that the better candidate has sometimes been taken for the worse. It is reasonable to believe, however, that the subjective elements in evaluations lead to systematic lowering of women's perceived qualifications. I have two arguments for this claim. The first is that past prejudice biases the evidence and the second is that present prejudice biases perception of the evidence. Let us examine each in turn.

Why then may women be better qualified than their records suggest? One principal reason is that many men simply do not take women seriously:

You might think that the evaluation of a specific performance would be an objective process, judged on characteristics of performance itself rather than on assumptions about the personality or ability of the performer. Yet performance is rarely a totally objective process. Two people may view the same event and interpret it differently. In the same way, it is possible for someone to view two people acting in exactly the same way and yet come to different conclusions about that behavior.[4]

Studies by Rosenthal and Jacobson provide experimental support for this claim. They found that students reported one group of rats to run mazes faster than another identical group, when they had previously been told that the first group was brighter. Ann Sutherland Harris quite plausibly concludes that such studies have important implications for women:

> If male scholars believe that women are intellectually inferior to men—less likely to have original contributions to make, less likely to be logical, and so on—will they not also find the evidence to support their beliefs in the women students in their classes, evidence of a far more sophisticated nature than the speed at which one rat finds its way through a maze? Their motives will be subconscious. Indeed, they will firmly believe that their judgment is rational and objective.[5]

What grounds are there for maintaining that this does not occur whenever women are evaluated? Other studies suggest additional hurdles for women that bias the evidence upon which they are judged. For instance, male students (though not female ones) rate identical course syllabi higher when the professor is said to be a man.[6]

Sociologist Jessie Bernard suggests that bias occurs whether women present accepted ideas or novel ones. In one study, a man and woman taught classes using the same material. The man engaged the students' interest: he was thought both more biased and more authoritative than the equally competent woman. According to Bernard, she was taken less seriously because she did not "look the part."[7] To support her position that novel ideas are less well received from women than men, Bernard mentions the case of Agnes Pockels, whose discoveries in physics were ignored for years. She cites this as an example of the general inability to see women in "the idea-man or instrumental role. We are simply not used to looking for innovation and originality from women."[8] The consequences of failing to take new ideas seriously may be even more detrimental to women than the failure to be taken seriously as a teacher. Bernard argues: "The importance of priority . . . highlights the importance of followers, or, in the case of science, of the public qualified to judge innovations. If an innovation is not recognized—even if recognition takes the form of rejection and a fight—it is dead."[9]

Additional persuasive evidence that women's ideas are not taken seriously by men comes from a study by Daryl and Sandra Bem, replicating a previous study by Philip Goldberg with women. A number of scholarly articles were submitted to a group of undergraduate men, who were to judge how good they were. Each paper was read by each man, but the paper read by half the students was attributed to a man, that read by the other half, to a woman. The results were striking: the "man's" article was rated higher than the "woman's" in most cases.[10] Does this prejudice continue to operate at more advanced levels?

One significant study showed more papers by women were chosen for presentation at the annual meeting of a national professional organization when they were submitted anonymously.[11] This suggests that whether a woman's work is published or not will also depend more on the reviewers' conception of women than upon the merits of the piece—at least until blind reviewing becomes the rule. Furthermore, there is evidence that even when a woman is recognized as having done a good job at some task, her performance is more likely than a man's to be attributed to factors other than ability. Hence others are less likely to expect future repeated success on her part.[12] And, unsuccessful performance by a male is more likely than that of a female to be attributed to bad luck.[13] Studies have also shown that male applicants for scholarship funds were judged more intelligent and likable than their female counterparts,[14] and that males were favored over females for study abroad programs.[15] In addition, until very recently, recommendations written for women were more likely to mention personal appearance in an undermining way (as well as marital status) than those written for men.[16] These facts have obvious repercussions for candidates' overall records. Hence if the hypotheses considered so far here are true, then women are systematically undervalued with respect to some of the most widely-used indicators of quality.

The existence of a first-rate mentor appears to be doubly important for women as for men.

Much of this bias could be neutralized if women were able to attract the best faculty as mentors. Bernard stresses the importance of mentors:

> The association of the graduate student with his mentor may make all the difference between success or lack of it in his subsequent career. If a top man takes him under his wing, doors will open for him and he will be in the club. If no one takes him on, he may never arrive professionally. He will not be recommended for the best jobs; he will not be in.[17]

The existence of a first-rate mentor is doubly important for women, if the results of a study by Gail Pheterson, Sara Kiesler, and Philip Goldberg are valid.[18] It suggests that women's performances will be taken seriously if an authority publicly recognizes their worth. This is because it is sometimes difficult to judge equality and in an ambiguous case, sexual stereotypes tend to step in to "help" the viewer decide. But there is no need for this when an individual acknowledged to be an expert has affirmed the value of the work.

Kay Deaux reports that this tendency is particularly evident when the judge has little training in the area to be evaluated. This is presumably not the case when faculties judge candidates within their own discipline. But it is plausible to believe that the uncertain nature of standards and the ambiguous performances in academe—especially in the conflict-ridden humanities—creates

some of the same pressures. Bernard provides more support for this hypothesis when, in another context, she comments: "Because there are so few objective criteria for judging the worth of a person and because so much competition is judgmental in nature, academic people depend on recognition from one another to a greater extent than do those in professions where autonomous competition is the rule."[19]

Thus graduate school mentors could help talented women achieve the professional recognition they deserve. Unfortunately women are less likely to enjoy the advantages of a good mentor. The best graduate schools have few women on their faculties and not every such woman will be interested in or capable of helping others advance. The men in such schools, with their poor record of hiring women, appear to be among the most prejudiced against them and hence cannot be counted on for help here.[20] The failure to take women seriously in graduate schools downgrades their apparent quality. This diminishes their chance of obtaining a prestigious post where they will have the opportunity to do significant research; in the current market, it also diminishes the probability that they will find any job in their field.

As if this were not enough, they run the risk of having their already undervalued qualifications devalued again when they are candidates for a position. This conclusion is supported by a study which showed that the same dossier was often ranked higher by academic departments when it was attributed to a man than when it was attributed to a woman.[21] Research on interviews also suggests that both men and women are systematically biased against women.[22]

I have been arguing that women are likely to be more highly qualified than they seem. This fact alone would support a policy of hiring women perceived to be less qualified. However, I think there is another sound argument for such a policy. Women may sometimes be less qualified than their male competitors because as students they faced stumbling-blocks the men did not. Hence some women probably deserve their weak recommendations and dearth of publications because their work is less fully developed and their claims less well supported than a man's might be. This can occur because women's social role often precludes opportunities for informal constructive criticism; it may also be the result of the lack of a mentor to push her to her limits. Finally a woman is likely to have had to work in a debilitating environment of lowered expectations.[23]

Goldman argues that it would be wrong to hire such a woman if there were a more qualified candidate: ". . . the white male who has successfully met the requirements necessary to attaining maximal competence attains some right to that position. It seems unjust for society to set standards of achievement and then to thwart the expectations of those who have met those standards."[24]

But surely hiring is ultimately intended to produce the best scholar and teacher, not to reward the most successful graduate student. Consequently, if there are grounds for believing that women turn into the former, despite not having been the latter according to the traditional criteria, it is reasonable to hold that they should sometimes be hired anyway. And there are such grounds.

The obstacles encountered by women in academe are well-documented and there is no need to elaborate at length upon them here. What matters is the nature of the person they create. Until very recently, at every stage of schooling, fewer girls than boys continued.[25] There is considerable evidence that women graduate students have higher academic qualifications than their male counterparts.[26] This appears to be because only the very highly qualified get into graduate school.[27] Harris argues that it ". . . is worth remembering that women candidates for graduate school are the survivors of a long sifting process—'only the very best of the good students' go on to graduate school."[28] A report issued by women at the University of Chicago supports this claim—the grade averages of women students entering graduate school were significantly higher than those of men.[29]

Once there, women have somewhat higher attrition rates than men. But Harris thinks that this is "largely explained by the lack of encouragement and the actual discouragement experienced by women graduate students for their career plans. . . . It is not surprising that some women decide that they are not cut out to be scholars and teachers."[30] She argues that if women were not highly committed, the attrition rate would be much higher: ". . . only the hardiest survive."[31]

In light of all these facts, a temporary policy of hiring women perceived to be less well qualified would be reasonable, to see if the hypothesis that they will bloom is borne out. Such a policy is less risky than it might seem since junior faculty members are on probation and can be fired if they do not start to fulfill their promise.

In conclusion, there are good grounds for at least a trial of the policy I am proposing with regard to hiring in academe, since existing affirmative action programs have not been and cannot be effective.[32] I have tried to show why women may often seem less qualified than they really are, and why they may be more promising than they seem. Unless faculty members take these factors into account, no improvement in the position of women can be expected, for women are likely to seem less worthy of being hired than their male competitors when they are judged in the usual manner. Requiring departments to hire women perceived to be less well qualified may well turn out to be the most efficacious way to force departments to recognize and remedy the situation. It might also have a more generally beneficial side-effect of promoting faculty-members' awareness of their own biases as they struggle to distinguish between truly mediocre women and those merely perceived to be so!

Notes

[1]The general trend continues to be that the more prestigious the post or institution, the fewer women there are to be found. See, for instance, "Status of Female Faculty Members, 1979–80," *The Chronicle of Higher Education*, 29 September 1980.

[2]See Alan Goldman, "Affirmative Action," *Philosophy and Public Affairs*, Vol. 5, n. 2 (Winter 1976), 178.

[3]Ibid.

[4]Kay Deaux, *The Behavior of Women and Men* (Monterey, Ca.: Brooks/Cole Publishing Co., 1976), 24.

[5]Ann Sutherland Harris reports this study in "The Second Sex in Academe" in *And Jill Came Tumbling After: Sexism in American Education*, ed. Judith Stacey et al. (New York: 1974), 299.

[6]Jessie Bernard, *Academic Women* (New York: Meridian Press, 1965), 255–57. "The 'teachers' were selected by the department as being of about equal competence in communications skills. They were given two written lectures to deliver to sections of Sociology 1 . . . both young people were given the lectures in advance, and they agreed on how to interpret all major points in their presentations, which were to be identical. One spoke to each section and a week later each spoke to the other section" (256).

[7]Ibid.

[8]Ibid.

[9]Ibid.

[10]Reported by Deaux, 25.

[11]This study appeared in "On Campus with Women," March 1977, Association of American Colleges, and was reported in *Ms.*, Vol. 7, n. 5 (November 1978), 87. *Ms.* writes: "In 1973, at the last annual conference held before the policy was initiated, 6.3 percent of the papers selected were from women scholars. In 1975, 17 percent of the papers selected were from women scholars. The organization in question is the Archaeological Institute of America."

[12]Veronica F. Nieva and Barbara Gutek, "Sex Effects on Evaluation," *Academy of Management Review*, Vol. 5, n. 2 (1980), 267.

[13]Ibid., 270.

[14]Ibid., 268.

[15]Ibid.

[16]Jennie Farley, "Academic Recommendations: Males and Females as Judges and Judged," *AAUP Bulletin*, Vol. 64, n. 2 (May 1978), 84.

[17]Bernard, 140.

[18]Reported by Deaux, 25.

[19]Bernard, 193.

[20]See Harris, above.

[21]L. S. Fidell, "Empirical Verification of Sex Discrimination in Hiring Practices in Psychology," *American Psychologist*, Vol. 60 (1970), 1049–98.

[22]Robert L. Dipboye, Richard D. Arvey, and David E. Terpstra, "Sex and Physical Attractiveness of Raters and Applicants as Determinants of Resume Evaluations," *Journal of Applied Psychology*, Vol. 62, n. 3 (June 1977), 288. This study was limited to undergraduate students, however, so it should not be assumed that it can be generalized to the educated population we are concerned with here.

[23]Nieva and Gutek, 271.

[24]Goldman, 191.

[25]See Harris and Barnard in Stacey et al., 302–05.

[26]Harris, 304–05.

[27]Ibid.

[28]Ibid.

[29]Ibid.

[30]Ibid.

[31]Ibid.

[32]Ibid., 297–98. My own experience at the prestigious Ivy League institution where I took my Ph.D. was far from encouraging. When I arrived, there were no women faculty members. The class before mine, numbering about 10, contained no women, and I was the only woman in my class of about 10. Twice in my first year I was present in groups addressed by professors as "Gentlemen." One of these occasions was especially fraught with emotion. I and four men gathered at a professor's office to return one of the crucial 4-hour field exams required of first-year students. The professor beamed at us and said, "Well, we'll see how you did, gentlemen!" See *Sex Discrimination in Higher Education*, ed. Jennie Farley, (Ithaca: ILR Publications, 1981).

An Argument Against Comparable Worth

June O'Neill

From *Comparable Worth: An Issue for the 80's*, vol. I (Washington, D.C.: U.S. Commission on Civil Rights, 1984).

The traditional goal of feminists has been equal opportunity for women—the opportunity for women to gain access to the schools, training, and jobs they choose to enter, on the same basis as men. This goal, however, basically accepts the rules of the game as they operate in a market economy. In fact the thrust has been to improve the way the market functions by removing discriminatory barriers that restrict the free supply of workers to jobs. By contrast, the more recent policy of "comparable worth" would dispense with the rules of the game. In place of the goal of equality of opportunity it would substitute a demand for equality of results, and it would do this essentially through regulation and legislation. It proposes, therefore, a radical departure from the economic system we now have, and so should be scrutinized with the greatest care.

The topics I will cover in this paper and the main points I will make are as follows:

1. The concept of comparable worth rests on a misunderstanding of the role of wages and prices in the economy.
2. The premises on which a comparable worth policy is based reflect a misconception about the reasons why women and men are in different occupations and have different earnings. Both the occupational differences and the pay gap to a large extent are the result of differences in the roles of women and men in the family and the effects these role differences have on the accumulation of skills and other job choices that affect pay. Discrimination by employers may account for some of the occupational differences, but it does not, as comparable worth advocates claim, lower wages directly in women's occupations.

3. Comparable worth, if implemented, would lead to capricious wage differentials, resulting in unintended shortages and surpluses of workers in different occupations with accompanying unemployment. Moreover, it would encourage women to remain in traditional occupations.
4. Policies are available that can be better targeted than comparable worth on any existing discriminatory or other barriers. These policies include the equal employment and pay legislation now on the books.

The Concept of Comparable Worth

By comparable worth I mean the view that employers should base compensation on the inherent value of a job rather than on strictly market considerations. It is not a new idea—since the time of St. Thomas Aquinas, the concept of the "just price," or payment for value, has had considerable appeal. Practical considerations, however, have won out over metaphysics. In a free market, wages and prices are not taken as judgments of the inherent value of the worker or the good itself, but reflect a balancing of what people are willing to pay for the services of these goods with how much it costs to supply them. Market prices are the efficient signals that balance supply and demand. Thus, in product markets we do not require that a pound of soybeans be more expensive than a pound of Belgian chocolates because it is more nutritious, or that the price of water be higher than that of diamonds because it is so much more important to our survival. If asked what the proper scale of prices should be for these products, most people—at least those who have taken Economics I—would give the sensible answer that there is no proper scale—it all depends on the tastes and needs of millions of consumers and the various conditions that determine the costs of production and the supplies of these products.

What is true of the product market is equally true of the labor market. There is simply no independent scientific way to determine what pay should be in a particular occupation without recourse to the market. Job skills have "costs of production" such as formal schooling and on-the-job training. Different jobs also have different amenities that may be more or less costly for the employer to provide—for example, part-time work, safe work, flexible hours, or a pleasant ambiance. And individuals vary in their talents and tastes for acquiring skills and performing different tasks. The skills required change over time as the demand for products changes and as different techniques of production are introduced. And these changes may vary by geographic region. In a market system, these changing conditions are reflected in changing wage rates, which in turn provide workers with the incentive to acquire new skills or to migrate to different regions.

The wage pattern that is the net outcome of these forces need not conform to anyone's independent judgment based on preconceived notions of comparability or of relative desirability. The clergy, for example, earn about 30 percent less than brickmasons.[1] Yet the clergy are largely college graduates; the brickmasons are not. Both occupations are more than 95 percent male—so one cannot point to sex discrimination. Possibly the reason for the wage disparity lies in unusual union power of construction workers and is an example of market imperfections. But other explanations are possible too. The real compensation to the clergy, for example, may include housing and spiritual satisfaction as fringe benefits. On the other hand, the high risk of unemployment and exposure to hazards of brickmasons may be reflected in additional monetary payments. If enough people require premiums to become brickmasons and are willing to settle for nonmonetary rewards to work as clergy, and if the buyers of homes are willing to pay the higher costs of brickmasons, while churchgoers are satisfied with

the number and quality of clergy who apply, the market solution may well be satisfactory.[2]

One can also think of examples of jobs that initially may seem quite comparable but that would not command the same wage, even in nondiscriminatory and competitive markets. The following example is based on a case that has been used before, but it illustrates the point so well it bears repeating.[3] Consider two jobs—one a Spanish-English translator and the other a French-English translator. Most job evaluators would probably conclude that these jobs are highly comparable and should be paid the same. After all, the skills required, the mental demands, the working conditions, and responsibility would seem to be nearly identical. But "nearly" is not equal, and the difference in language may in fact give rise to a legitimate pay differential. The demand for the two languages may differ—for example, if trade with Spanish-speaking countries is greater. But the supply of Spanish-English translators may also be greater. And this would vary by geographic area. It would be difficult to predict which job will require the higher wage and by how much in order to balance supply and demand.

What the market does is to process the scarcity of talents, the talents of heterogeneous individuals and the demands of business and consumers in arriving at a wage. The net outcome would only coincidentally be the same as a comparable worth determination. There are simply too many factors interacting in highly complex ways for a study to find the market clearing wage.

Why Abandon the Market?

The argument for abandoning market determination of wages and substituting "comparable worth," where wage decisions would be based on an independent assessment of the "value" of occupations, is based on the following premises: (1) the pay gap between women and men is due to discrimination and has failed to narrow over time; (2) this discrimination takes the form of occupational segregation, where women are relegated to low-paying jobs; and (3) pay in these female-dominated occupations is low simply because women hold them.

The Pay Gap

In 1983 the pay gap, viewed as the ratio of women's to men's hourly pay, was about 72 percent overall (table 1).[4] Among younger groups the ratio is higher (and the pay gap smaller)—a ratio of 89 percent for 20–24-year olds and 80 percent for the age 25–34 years old. Among groups age 35 and over the ratio is about 65 percent.

What accounts for the pay gap? Clearly, not all differentials reflect discrimination. Several minorities (Japanese and Jewish Americans, for example) have higher than average wages, and I do not believe anyone would ascribe these differentials to favoritism towards these groups and discrimination against others.

A growing body of research has attempted to account for the pay gap, and the researchers have come to different conclusions. These studies, however, use different data sources, refer to different populations and control for many, but not always the same set of variables. Even the gross wage gap—the hourly earnings differential before adjusting for diverse characteristics—varies from study to study, ranging from 45 to 7 percent depending on the type of population considered. Studies based on national samples covering the full age range tend to show a gross wage gap of 35 to 40 percent. Studies based on more homogeneous groups, such as holders of advanced degrees or those in specific professions, have found considerably smaller gross wage gaps.

After adjusting for various characteristics, the wage gap narrows. Generally, the most important variables contributing to the adjustment are those that measure the total number of years of work experience, the years of tenure on current job, and the pattern or continuity of previous work experience.

Traditional home responsibilities of married women have been an obstacle to their full commitment to a career. Although women are now combining work and marriage to a much greater extent than in the past, older women in the labor force today have typically spent many years out of the labor force raising their families. Data from the National Longitudinal Survey (NLS) indicate that in 1977 employed white women in their for-

ties had worked only 61 percent of the years after leaving school, and employed black women had worked 68 percent of the years.[5] By contrast, men are usually in the labor force or the military on a continuing basis after leaving school.

In a recent study I examined the contribution of lifetime work experience and other variables using the NLS data for men and women aged 25 to 34. White women's hourly wage rate was found to be 66 percent of white men's—a wage gap of 34 percent. This wage gap narrowed to 12 percent after accounting for the effects of male-female differences in work experience, job tenure, and schooling, as well as differences in plant size and certain job characteristics, such as the years of training required to learn a skill, whether the occupation was hazardous, and whether the occupation had a high concentration of women.

The gross wage gap between black men and black women was 18 percent. The gross wage gap was smaller for blacks than for whites because job-related characteristics of black women and black men are closer than those of white women and white men. Black women have somewhat fewer years of work experience in their teens and early twenties than white women, which may be related to earlier childbearing. They are more likely to work continuously and full time later on, however, and thus accumulate more total work experience and longer tenure on their current jobs than white women. The adjustment for differences in the measured characteristics cited above narrowed the wage gap of black men and women to 9 percent.

Are the remaining, unaccounted-for differences a measure of discrimination in the labor market?

If all the productivity differences between women and men are not accurately identified and measured, labor market discrimination would be overestimated by the unexplained residual. Many variables were omitted from this analysis and from other studies because relevant data are not available. These include details on the quality and vocational orientation of education; on the extent of other work-related investments, such as job search; and on less tangible factors, such as motivation and effort. Differences in these factors could arise from the priority placed on earning an income versus fulfilling home responsibilities. If women, by tradition, assume the primary responsibility for homemaking and raising children, they may be reluctant to take jobs that demand an intense work commitment.

On the other hand, the unexplained residual may underestimate discrimination if some of the included variables, such as years of training to learn a job, or the sex typicality of occupations, partially reflect labor market discrimination. Some employers may deny women entry into lengthy training programs or be reluctant to hire them in traditionally male jobs. It is difficult with available data to distinguish this situation from one where women choose not to engage in training because of uncertainty about their long-run career plans or choose female occupations because they are more compatible with competing responsibilities at home.

Occupational Segregation

Although occupational segregation clearly exists, it is in large part the result of many of the same factors that determine earnings: years of schooling, on-the-job training, and other human capital investments, as well as tastes for particular job characteristics. In a recently completed study, I found that women's early expectations about their future life's work—that is, whether they planned to be a homemaker or planned to work outside the home—are strongly related to the occupations they ultimately pursue.[6] Many women who initially planned to be homemakers, in fact, became labor force participants, but they were much more likely to pursue stereotyped female occupations than women who had formed their plans to work at younger ages. Early orientation influences early training and schooling decisions, and as a result women may be locked into or out of certain careers. Some women, however, by choice, maintain an ongoing dual career—combining work in the home with an outside job—and this leads to an accommodation in terms of the number of hours that women work and other conditions that influence occupational choice.

Women and men were also found to differ sharply in the environmental characteristics of their occupations. Women were less likely to be in jobs with a high incidence of outdoor work, noisy or hazardous work, or jobs requiring heavy lifting. These differences may reflect employer prejudice or the hostile attitudes of male coworkers. but they may also reflect cultural and physical differences.

In sum, a substantial amount of the differences in wages and in occupations by sex has been statistically linked to investments in work skills acquired in school or on the job. Varied interpretations of these results are possible, however. Thus, the precise amount that can be labeled as the result of choices made by women and their families rather than the result of discrimination by employers is not known.

The Trend in the Pay Gap

A major source of frustration to feminists and a puzzle to researchers has been the failure of the gap to narrow over the post–World War II period, despite large increases in women's labor force participation. In fact, the gap in 1982 is somewhat larger than it was in 1955.

The wage gap would not, however, narrow significantly over time unless the productivity or skill of women in the labor force increased relative to men's, or discrimination in the workplace diminished. Because the gross wage gap widened somewhat after 1955, either discrimination increased or women's skills decreased relative to men's. Findings from a recent study suggest that changes in skill, as measured by the changes in the education and work experience of men and women in the labor force, strongly contributed to an increase in the wage gap.[7]

In 1952 women in the labor force had completed 1.6 more years of schooling than men. This difference narrowed sharply so that by 1979 it had disappeared. One reason for this is that the educational level of men advanced more rapidly than that of women during the 1950s. Aided by the GI bill educational benefits, more men attended college. Another reason is that the labor force participation of less educated women

Table I
Female-Male Ratios of Median Usual Weekly Earnings of Full-Time
Wage and Salary Workers, by Age, 1971–1983

I. Unadjusted Ratios

Year Age	May 1971	May 1973	May 1974	May 1975	May 1976	May 1977	May 1978	2nd quarter 1979	Annual average 1979	1982	1983
Total, 16 years and over	.62	.62	.61	.62	.61	.61	.61	.62	.62	.65	.66
16–19	.89	.82	.82	.86	.86	.88	.86	.85	.87	.88	.94
20–24	.78	.77	.76	.76	.80	.78	.75	.75	.76	.83	.84
25–34	.65	.64	.65	.66	.67	.65	.66	.67	.66	.72	.73
35–44	.59	.54	.55	.57	.55	.56	.53	.58	.58	.60	.60
45–54	.57	.57	.57	.59	.57	.56	.54	.57	.56	.59	.58
55–64	.62	.63	.60	.63	.61	.59	.60	.60	.58	.60	.62

II. Adjusted for Male-Female Differences in Full-Time Hours[8]

Year Age	May 1971	May 1973	May 1974	May 1975	May 1976	May 1977	May 1978	2nd quarter 1979	Annual average 1979	1982	1983
Total, 16 years and over	.68	.68	.67	.68	.68	.67	.67	.68	.68	.71	.72
16–19	.94	.86	.87	.90	.90	.92	.91	.90	.92	.91	.96
20–24	.85	.83	.82	.82	.86	.84	.80	.81	.82	.88	.89
25–34	.73	.72	.72	.73	.74	.72	.73	.74	.73	.79	.80
35–44	.66	.61	.61	.63	.61	.62	.59	.64	.64	.66	.66
45–54	.62	.62	.62	.63	.62	.61	.59	.63	.61	.64	.63
55–64	.67	.69	.65	.67	.67	.65	.65	.66	.64	.65	.67

[8]Female-male earnings ratios were adjusted for differences in hours worked by multiplying by age-specific male-female ratios of average hours worked per week (for nonagricultural workers on full-time schedules).

Source: Earnings by age and sex are from unpublished tabulations from the Current Population Survey provided by the Bureau of Labor Statistics, U.S. Department of Labor. Hours data are from U.S. Bureau of Labor Statistics, Employment and Earnings series, January issues, annual averages.

increased more rapidly than the participation of highly educated women. Thus, the female labor force became increasingly less selective over time in terms of schooling attainment.

The rise in the number of women in the labor force may also have had an effect on the lifetime work experience of the average working women. A large number of less experienced women entering the labor force may have diluted the experience level of the working women. Although the total number of years of work experience of women is not available for periods of time before the late 1960s, data on job tenure—years with current employer—show that in 1951 men's job tenure exceeded women's job tenure by 1.7 years. This difference widened to 2.7 years in 1962 and

then slowly declined, reaching 1.9 years in 1978 and 1.5 years in 1981.

The decline in working women's educational level relative to men's alone would have caused the pay gap to widen by 7 percentage points. The initial widening in the job tenure differential contributed another 2 percentage points to the gap. Together the change in education and job tenure would have increased the wage gap by more than it actually increased. Possibly then, discrimination declined during this period even though the wage gap widened. Since the mid-1960s, educational and work experience differences have moved in different directions. Male educational attainment rose slightly more than that of working women, which alone would have widened the pay gap slightly. Difference in work experience declined overall. Recently (between 1979 and 1983), a narrowing has occurred in the wage gap, from 68 percent to 72 percent overall.

Evidence from the NLS and other sources suggests that the pay gap is likely to narrow perceptibly in the next decade. Not only are young women working more continuously, but they are also getting higher pay for each year of work experience than they were in the late 1960s. This could reflect a reduction in sex discrimination by employers or a greater willingness of women to invest in market skills, or both. Women's career expectations also seem to be rising. In response to an NLS question asked in 1973, 57 percent of women between 25 and 29 indicated their intention to hold jobs rather than be homemakers when they reach age 35. Among women reaching ages 25 to 29 in 1978, 77 percent expressed their intention to work.

Young women have also greatly increased their educational level relative to men. Female college enrollment increased significantly during the 1970s, while male enrollment fell between 1975 and 1980. Moreover, women have made impressive gains in professional degrees during the 1970s. Work roles and work expectations of women and men may well be merging. As these younger women become a larger component of the female labor force, it is anticipated that the overall wage gap will be reduced.

Are Women's Occupations Underpaid?

A major contention of comparable worth supporters is that pay in women's occupations is lower because employers systematically downgrade them. The argument differs from the idea that pay in women's occupations is depressed because of an oversupply to these occupations. An oversupply could arise either because large numbers of women entering the labor force choose these occupations (which is compatible with no discrimination) or because women are barred from some causing an oversupply in others (a discriminatory situation). Although comparable worth advocates have taken the view that overcrowding is caused by restrictive measures, they have lately come to believe that this explanation is not the whole cause of "low payment" in women's jobs.[9] The argument is made that employers can pay less to women's jobs regardless of supply considerations, simply reflecting prejudice against such jobs because they are held by women.

The ability of firms to wield such power is highly questionable. If a firm underpaid workers in women's occupations, in the sense that their wages were held below their real contributions to the firm's receipts, other firms would have a strong incentive to hire workers in these occupations away, bidding up the wages in these occupations. Thus, competition would appear to be a force curtailing employer power. This process could only be thwarted by collusion, an unrealistic prospect considering the hundreds of thousands of firms.

Killingsworth (1983) has suggested that the market for nurses may be an example of collusion by a centralized hospital industry that has conspired to hold wages down. Without more careful analysis of the hospital industry, it is difficult to verify whether this is a valid hypothesis. Basic facts about wages and supply in nursing, however, suggest that collusion either does not exist or is ineffective. Despite a perennial "shortage" of nurses that seems to have existed as far back as one can go, the number of nurses has increased dramatically, both absolutely and as a percentage of the population. In 1960 there were 282 registered nurses per 100,000 population. In 1980 there were 506 nurses per 100,000. This rate of increase is even more rapid than the increase in doctors over the past decade, and the supply of doctors has been rapidly increasing. Why did the increase occur? Were women forced into nursing because they were barred from other occupations? That does not seem to be the case in recent times. What has happened is that nursing, along with other medical professions, has experienced a large increase in demand since the middle 1960s when Medicare and Medicaid were introduced, and private health insurance increased. As a result, the pay of nurses increased more rapidly than in other fields. Between 1960 and 1978 the salary of registered nurses increased by 250 percent, while the pay of all men rose by 206 percent and the pay of all women rose by 193 percent. During the 1970s the rate of pay increase for nurses slowed, which is not surprising considering the increase in supply. And entry of women into nursing school has recently slowed, suggesting a self-correcting mechanism is at work.

Another way to attempt to evaluate the contention that lower pay in female-dominated occupations reflects discrimination is through statistical analysis of the determinants of earnings in occupations. In a recent study, I asked the question—after accounting for measurable differences in skill, do these predominantly female occupations still pay less? In an analysis of data on more than 300 occupations, I found that after adjusting for schooling training, part-time work, and environmental conditions (but not actual years of work experience or job tenure, which were not available), the proportion female in an occupation was associated with lower pay in that occupation for both women and for men. But the effect was not large. For each 10 percentage point increase in the percent female in an occupation, the wage in the occupation went down by 1.5 percent. Again, however, one is left with a question mark. Are there other characteristics of occupations that women, on the average, may value more highly than men because of home responsibilities or differences in tastes and for which women, more so than men, are willing to accept a lower wage in exchange? Characteristics that come to mind might be a long summer vacation, such as teaching provides, or a steady 9 to 5 job close to home that certain office or shop jobs may provide. The true effect of sex on occupational differences or wage rates is, therefore, another unresolved issue. There are many good reasons why women would be in lower paying occupations than men, even in the absence of sex discrimination on the part of employers. That does not rule out the existence of discrimination, but it weakens the case for seeking an alternative to the market determination of occupational wage rates.

Comparable Worth in Practice—The Washington State Example

What would happen if wages were set in accordance with comparable worth standards and independently of market forces? Any large-scale implementation of comparable worth would necessarily be based on job evaluations that assign points for various factors believed to be common to disparate jobs. For example, in the state of Washington, where a comparable worth study was commissioned, a job evaluation firm assisted a committee of 13 politically chosen individuals in rating the jobs used as benchmarks in setting pay in state employment. The committee's task was to assign points on the basis of knowledge and skills, mental demands, accountability, and working conditions. In the 1976 evaluation a registered nurse at level IV was assigned 573 points, the highest number of points of any job—280 points for knowledge and skills, 92 points for mental demands, 122 points for accountability, and no points for working conditions. In the market, however, computer systems analysts are among the highest paid workers. National data for 1981 show that they earn 56 percent more than registered nurses. The Washington job evaluation similarly differs radically from the market in its assessment of the value of occupations throughout the job schedule. A clerical supervisor is rated equal to a chemist in knowledge and skills and mental demands, but higher than the chemist in accountability, thereby receiving more total points. Yet the market rewards chemists 41 percent higher pay. The evaluation assigns an electrician the same points for knowledge and skills and mental demands as a level 1 secretary and 5 points less for accountability. Auto mechanics are assigned lower points than the lowest level homemaker or practical nurse for accountability as well as for working conditions. Truckdrivers are ranked at the bottom, assigned lower points on knowledge and skills, mental demands, and accountability than the lowest ranked telephone operator or retail clerk. The market, however, pays truckdrivers 30 percent more than telephone operators, and the differential is wider for retail clerks.

Should the market pay according to the comparable worth scale? Or is the comparable worth scale faulty? In Washington State, AFSCME, the American Federation of State, County, and Municipal Employees, brought suit against the state on the grounds that failure to pay women according to the comparable worth scale constituted discrimination. Judge Jack E. Tanner agreed and ruled in favor of the union. The decision was based largely on the fact that the state had conducted the study. Whether or not the study was a reasonable standard for nondiscriminatory wage patterns was never an issue. The state, in fact, was disallowed from presenting a witness who would have critically evaluated the study.

What would happen if comparable worth were to be adopted as a pay-setting mechanism? Take the example of registered nurses and computer systems analysts. Nurses are 95 percent female; systems analysts are 25 percent female. If a private firm employing both occupations were required to adopt the rankings from the Washington State comparable worth study, it would likely have to make a significant pay adjustment. It could either lower the salary of systems analysts below that of nurses or raise the pay of nurses above systems analysts. If it lowered the pay of systems analysts, it would likely find it impossible to retain or recruit them. The more popular remedy would be to raise the pay of nurses. If the firm did so, it would also be compelled to raise its prices. Most likely, demand for the firm's product would fall, and the firm would of necessity be required to cut back production. It would seek ways of lowering costs—for example, by reducing the number of registered nurses it employed, trying to substitute less skilled practical nurses and orderlies where possible. Some women would benefit—those who keep their jobs at the higher pay. But other women would lose—those nurses who become unemployed, as well as other workers who are affected by the cutback.

Of course, if the employer is a state government, the scenario may be somewhat different. The public sector does not face the rigors of competition to the same extent as a private firm. I suspect this is one reason why public sector employees seem to be in the forefront of the comparable worth movement. The public sector could not force workers to work for them if the remedy was to lower the wage in high-paying male jobs. But that is not usually what employee groups request. It can, however, pay the bill for the higher pay required to upgrade wages in female-domi-

nated occupations by raising taxes. But in the long run, the state may have financing problems, since taxpayers may not be willing to foot the bill, and the result would be similar to that in the private firm—unemployment of government workers, particularly women in predominantly female occupations, as government services are curtailed.

Concluding Remarks

Advocates of comparable worth see it as a way of raising women's economic status and, quite expectedly, tend to minimize costs. A typical comment is as follows (Center for Philosophy and Public Policy):

> Certainly, the costs incurred would vary widely depending on the scope of the approach chosen. But the economic costs of remedying overt discrimination should not prove staggering. Employers and business interests have a long history of protesting that fair treatment of workers will result in massive economic disruption. Similar claims were made preceding the abolishment of child labor and the establishment of the minimum wage, and none of the dire predictions came to pass.

Evidently the author is unaware of the numerous economic studies showing the disemployment effects of the minimum wage. However, what this statement fails to see is that comparable worth is in a bigger league than the child labor law or the minimum wage laws that have actually been implemented. It is far more radical. Instituting comparable worth by means of studies such as the one conducted in Washington State could be more like instituting a $15 an hour minimum wage or passing sweeping legislation like Prohibition. Moreover, the costs in terms of economic distortion would be much more profound than the dollars required to pay the bills. Curiously, this is recognized by one comparable worth proponent,[10] who then suggests "that we give very serious consideration to the idea that firms that do raise pay for 'disadvantaged occupations' get special tax incentives for capital equipment that will raise the productivity of these workers. We can't expect firms to swallow these losses; that's crazy." Barrett is willing to go to these lengths because she thinks it might be a way to raise the incomes of poor women heading families on welfare. Long-term welfare recipients, however, are not the women holding the jobs covered by comparable worth schemes. The work participation of women in this situation is very low. Moreover, the lesson of studies of minimum wage effects has been that those who are most vulnerable to disemployment as a result of wage hikes that exceed national market rates are the disadvantaged—those with little education, poor training, and little work experience. Comparable worth would hurt, not help, these women. Subsidies to try to prevent the effects from occurring would be impractical to implement and prohibitively costly.

With all the difficulties that would ensue from implementing comparable worth, it is striking that it would not achieve many of the original goals of the women's movement such as the representation of women as electricians, physicists, managers, or plumbers. In fact, it would likely retard the substantial progress that has been made in the past decade. Younger women have dramatically shifted their school training and occupational choices. They have been undertaking additional training and schooling because the higher pay they can obtain from the investment makes it worthwhile. Raising the pay of clerical jobs, teaching, and nursing above the market rates would make it less rewarding to prepare for other occupations and simply lead to an oversupply to women's fields, making it still harder to find a stable solution to the problem of occupational segregation.

Another byproduct of comparable worth is that it diverts attention away from the real problems of discrimination that may arise. Such problems need not be confined to women in traditional jobs. Pay differences between men and women performing the same job in the same firm at the same level of seniority may no longer be an important source of discrimination. The form discrimination more likely takes is through behavior that denies women entry into on-the-job training or promotions on the same basis as men. The obvious solution is the direct one—namely, allowing or encouraging women whose rights are being denied to bring suit. Existing laws were intended to cover this very type of problem.

The pay-setting procedure in all levels of government employment is another area where remedies other than comparable worth would be more direct and effective. Governments usually do not have the flexibility to meet market demands. The need to adhere to rigid rules under considerable political pressure may result in paying wages that are too high in some occupations and too low in others. (By "too high" I mean that an ample supply of workers could be obtained at a lower wage.) This could occur if the private plants covered in a pay survey for a particular occupation are themselves paying above market—for example, as the result of a powerful union. Such a situation could lead to unnecessary pay differentials between certain occupations that are male dominated (which are more likely to be represented by such strong unions) and other male, mixed, and female occupations whose private sector wages are more competitive. Comparable worth is not the solution, however, since it does not address the problem. Pay-setting procedures can be improved by changing the nature of the pay surveys and by introducing market criteria—for example, by considering the length of the queue to enter different government jobs and the length of time vacancies stay open. Such changes may help women and also improve the efficiency of government.

Dramatic changes have occurred in women's college enrollment, in labor force participation, and in entrance into formerly male occupations, particularly in the professions. These changes are taking place because of fundamental changes in women's role in the economy and in the family—changes that themselves reflect a response to rising wage rates as well as changing social attitudes. Pay set according to comparable worth would distort wage signals, inducing inappropriate supply response and unemployment. If women have been discouraged by society or barred by employers from entering certain occupations, the appropriate response is to remove the barriers, not try to repeal supply and demand. Comparable worth is no shortcut to equality.

References

Barrett, Nancy. 1984. "Poverty, Welfare and Comparable Worth," in Phyllis Schlafly, ed., *Equal Pay for Unequal Work, A Conference on Comparable Work*.

Hartmann, Heidi I. 1984. "The Case for Comparable Worth," in Phyllis Schlafly, ed., *Equal Pay for Unequal Work, A Conference on Comparable Work*.

Killingsworth, Mark. 1984. *Statement on Comparable Worth*. Testimony before the Joint Economic Committee, U.S. Congress, Apr. 10, 1984.

O'Neill, June. 1983. "The Determinants and Wage Effects of Occupational Segregation." Working Paper, The Urban Institute.

O'Neill, June. Forthcoming, 1984. "Earnings Differentials: Empirical Evidence and Causes," in G. Schmid, ed., *Discrimination and Equalization in the Labor Market: Employment Policies for Women in Selected Countries*.

O'Neill, June. 1984. "The Trend in the Male-Female Wage Gap in the United States." Forthcoming. *Journal of Labor Economics*, October.

Rytina, Nancy F. 1982. "Earnings of Men and Women: A Look at Specific Occupations." *Monthly Labor Review*, April 1982.

Notes

[1] These statistics are based on the median hourly earnings of workers in these occupations in 1981. Rytina, 1982.

[2] If brickmasons' wages are artificially high because of union power, the market would be unstable. More workers would desire to be brickmasons than would be hired at the artificially high wage. Would comparable worth policy help the situation? Not likely. A comparable worth solution would likely require higher pay for clergy than for brickmasons because of the heavy weight placed on readily measured items like education. A wage for clergy that is too high would also be unstable. Only the removal of the union power or restrictions on unions would satisfactorily resolve the issue.

[3] This example was originated by Sharon Smith and described in Killingsworth (1984), who notes it is cited in Gold (1983).

[4] The commonly cited pay gap—where women are said to earn 59 cents out of every dollar earned by men—is based on a comparison of the annual earnings of women and men who work year round and are primarily full time. In 1982 this ratio was 62 percent. This figure is lower than the figure of 72 percent cited above because the annual earnings measure is not adjusted for differences in hours worked during the year, and men are more likely than women to work overtime or on second jobs.

[5] O'Neill, 1984.

[6] O'Neill, 1983.

[7] O'Neill, 1984.

[8] Female-male earnings ratios were adjusted for differences in hours worked by multiplying by age-specific male-female ratios of average hours worked per week (for nonagricultural workers on full-time schedules).

[9] Hartmann, 1983.

[10] Barrett, 1983.

CASES

Case 8.1: Ann Hopkins and Price Waterhouse

In 1982 Ann Hopkins was denied a promotion to partnership in the Washington, D.C., office of the Big 6 accounting firm Price Waterhouse. Despite the fact that she had reached senior manager level, had brought in $34 million in consulting contracts, which was more than any other candidate had done that year, and had billed more hours in the preceding year than any other candidate, she was denied an invitation to join the partnership. Hopkins filed suit against the firm, alleging that she had been the victim of sexual discrimination based on unfair gender stereotypes. According to court documents, some partners (all of whom were males) described Ann as arrogant, abrasive, overbearing, impatient, and hard-nosed. They were also offended by her use of profanity. While these are legitimate criticisms of someone who will represent the firm as a partner, several other statements led Ann to believe that she was the victim of an unfair stereotype of what a female partner should be like. Some partners described her as "too macho" and "needing to go to charm school." One partner even advised her to "walk more femininely, talk more femininely, dress more femininely and wear makeup, wear jewelry and have her hair styled." Two lower courts ruled in favor of Ann Hopkins, declaring that gender bias came into play in their decision. The case was eventually heard by the United States Supreme Court in 1991.[2]

Note: The Court ruled that employers in sex-discrimination lawsuits have the burden of proving that they would have reached the same decision in the absence of bias. Moreover, the court affirmed that sexual stereotyping falls under Title VII of the 1964 Civil Rights Act against sex discrimination. However, the standard of proof of "clear and convincing" evidence was deemed to be too high of a standard under which Price Waterhouse could defend itself. Thus, the case was returned to a lower court and Price Waterhouse could free itself of liability with a "preponderance of evidence." Both sides claimed victory based upon this decision.

[2]Stephen Wermiel, "High Court Shifts Burden to Firms in Sex-Bias Case," *Wall Street Journal*, 2 May 1989, B1f.

Questions for Discussion:

1. Do you think the partners were justified in turning her application down for partnership? Why or why not? In your opinion, was she a victim of unfair gender stereotyping?

2. Some people believe that Ann was the victim of double standards for men and women. They would argue that the characteristics of "aggressive, abrasive," etc., would be viewed as favorable ones for a male candidate for promotion. Do you agree with this assessment? If so, do you think it is unfair to women in the workplace?

Case 8.2: Discrimination and Public Image

Your first position after graduating from college is at the branch of a major bank in a community with a good amount of racial tension. In three years, you advance to the position of assistant manager in charge of operations. Your bank wants to aggressively sell investment vehicles that give higher yields than traditional savings accounts and in order to do so contracts with a local mutual fund firm to have one of their employees work as a full-time investment counselor on the bank's premises. This investment counselor will occupy a desk in the lobby area and work by referrals from tellers and other officers of the branch. The mutual fund company sends one of its new hires to your branch. He is a black male with an MBA from a local state university. You find him to be trustworthy, well-spoken, and extremely knowledgeable about investments.

Over a three-month period, his sales are average. Confirming your suspicions, you hear several of your customers whispering to each other that they do not trust him with their investments because of his ethnic background. Your supervisor, the branch manager, calls you into his office and asks you to call the vice-president of the mutual fund company to have this investment counselor replaced with someone who "appears" more trustworthy to the customers. He remarks that several customers have lodged anonymous complaints with him and says, "After all, we don't run a charity around here. If our customers don't trust him because of the color of his skin, that's not our fault!" He adds, "I'm not racist; it's not our job to correct society's shortcomings. I'm just trying to do my job, which is to serve our customers and maximize profit for our shareholders, not to engage in social change!"

Questions for Discussion:

1. How would you handle the situation? How do you balance your responsibilities to your employer with your duties to another social good?

2. What responsibilities do you think business should have for positive social change, particularly when it may be at the expense of profit?

Case 8.3: Equal Pay in Collegiate Athletics

In August 1993 Marianne Stanley, women's basketball coach at the University of Southern California, filed an $8 million lawsuit against the university, alleging sex discrimination. Stanley asserted that she was promised a lucrative contract if she could successfully turn around the women's basketball program in her four years as coach. In her first year, the team achieved only 8–19. In her fourth year, a year in which she made $69,933, her team finished second in the Pacific Ten Conference with a record of 22–7.[3] Stanley was then offered a multiyear salary package in which she would earn $80,000 the first year, $90,000 the second, and $100,000 the third. The package also included a $6,000 housing allowance each year. Stanley reportedly called the offer an insult, rejected it twice, and subsequently filed the suit alleging sex discrimination. USC athletic director Mike Garrett then offered her a one-year deal worth $96,000 which she also rejected. Facing the prospect of starting the year without a coach, the university hired Cheryl Miller to replace Stanley.

Citing equal pay for equal work provisions that seek to eliminate gender bias in the workplace, Stanley said she wanted to be paid the same as then USC men's coach George Raveling, whose estimated salary was between $110,000–$150,000 per year, not including a lucrative shoe endorsement contract. Stanley's total four-year record at USC was 63–43, a winning percentage of .594 which included three NCAA tournament appearances. By contrast, Raveling's record for the first four years at USC was 38–78, a .328 percentage, and his total record at the university over seven years was 99–103, a .490 winning percentage, and two NCAA tournament appearances. Stanley's career record in sixteen years of coaching is 347–146, including three national championships at Old Dominion University. Raveling's career record in twenty-one seasons is 310–280.

Many other women coaches rose to Stanley's defense, arguing that the time had come to equalize pay across genders in collegiate sports programs. Betty Jaynes, the executive director of the Women's Basketball Coaches Association, remarked, "This is not the University of Southern California and Marianne Stanley, this is USC and the coaches of women's basketball."[4] At the time, several schools had already moved to equalized pay programs.

[3]Elliot Almond, "Stanley's Request Denied," *Los Angeles Times*, 27 August 1993, D1.

[4]Malcomb Moran, "Dispute Over Equality Leaves a Coach Jobless," *New York Times*, 14 September 1993, B1.

The university argued that the jobs were not the same so the salary differences did not violate equal-pay provisions. They claim that the higher profile and revenues generated by the men's programs contribute to greater pressures and responsibilities that mandate a higher salary for the men's coach.

Two years later, in March 1995, Los Angeles District Court Judge John G. Davies dismissed the suit, issuing a summary judgment in favor of the school, effectively stating that there were no grounds to continue the case. At the time of this decision, Stanley, who now works for the Stanford women's program, was expected to file an appeal.[5]

[5]Elliot Almond, "Stanley's Pay Discrimination Suit Dismissed," *Los Angeles Times*, 10 March 1995, C5.

Questions for Discussion:

1. Do you think the situation violated equal-pay-for-equal-work provisions? Why or why not?
2. The university's contention is that the jobs are different enough to warrant different salaries despite the fact that Stanley's qualifications seem better than Raveling's. Do you agree?
3. Is this a good case in which to ignore "market value" and institute a "comparable worth" program? Why or why not? In general, do you favor these types of programs?

COMMENTARY

No credible voice in the debate surrounding affirmative action can deny that our country has a long history of discrimination. Less than forty years ago, women and members of minority groups were denied access to such basic goods as equal education and employment opportunities, as exemplified by a well-known story about the plight of Sandra Day O'Connor, the first woman ever to serve as a United States Supreme Court justice. When she graduated from Stanford University Law School in the early 1950s, she was unable to find employment in a private law practice. Despite finishing second in her class, O'Conner had to settle for employment as a legal clerk for a judge. At the time, the legal profession was male-dominated and deemed an unfit place for women because of existing social conventions.

Another landmark case illustrates the plight of some members of minority groups in the recent past. Shortly after the 1964 Civil Rights Act was signed into law, fourteen black janitors of Duke Power Co. in North Carolina filed a complaint against the company for shutting them out of promotional opportunities. The men were initially told that high school diplomas, a rare possession for blacks in the rural South during the '60s, were needed for advancement. However, only fifteen whites in the whole plant had earned diplomas, and they held all of the advanced positions. As an alternative to a diploma, the janitors were told, they could take a test. Although most of the jobs in question involved manual labor, such as coal hauling, some very sophisticated questions were presented on the test. No black passed the test, but neither did any of the whites. Eventually the case became a landmark case that was heard before the Supreme Court in 1971. In the *Griggs v. Duke Power Co.* decision, the court unanimously sided with the fourteen janitors, arguing that the requirements were needless for the jobs in question and had the direct effect of discrimination against the black employees. Justice Warren Burger wrote the decision, which then placed the burden of proof on employers to prove that employment standards were essential to the work itself. In other words, there must be a "business necessity" for employment requirements to be legal.

While examples of flagrant discrimination such as O'Conner and the fourteen janitors faced occur with much less frequency today, most people readily acknowledge that discrimination is still prevalent, though manifested in much more subtle forms. Just a cursory examination will show that racism is prevalent even in the open Hollywood culture of film and television, where women and members of minority groups are regularly portrayed with the ugliest stereotypes available. For example, critics maintain that there are only three roles for Asian male actors. They regularly appear as either victims, scientists, or kung-fu-wielding gang members who are smart enough to dream up brilliant extortion schemes, but are too dumb to carry guns.

With respect to other employment settings, the Equal Employment Opportunity Commission received almost 90,000 job-discrimination charges in a recent year.[6] In addition, a recent *Business Week* article covering the debate over the 1991 Civil Rights Act cited an Urban Institute Study released in May 1991 that showed that in one out of five attempts to get an entry-level job, a white applicant advanced further than a black, all other things being equal.[7] While society has come a long way, acts of discrimination are far from eradicated.

Obviously, workplace discrimination is appalling. This is so for a number of reasons. To begin with, it unjustifiably interferes with the functioning of the economy as a significant portion of the population is restricted from full and equal participation in the marketplace. Second, and most important, it violates several scriptural mandates that we treat people with equality and dignity. Discrimination based on factors that people are born with is the deepest violation of dignity imaginable. Thus there is wide consensus that government interference in order to halt discriminatory practices on the basis of gender and ethnicity is not only morally justifiable but is morally demanded.

A Critical Evaluation of Race-and-Gender-Based Affirmative Action

Despite the presence of discrimination and racial tension in society, efforts to eradicate discrimination from the workplace are not necessarily corollary to programs of strong affirmative action that utilize preferences on the basis of race and gender. In light of recent data, many people are asking if the effectiveness of strong affirmative actions have not passed their time and if other measures would be more appropriate to realize the goal of equal opportunities for all members of society. To many, affirmative action made sense thirty years ago when it was clear that many identifiable victims of discrimination could not be expected to compete on an equal footing. But today many argue that the continuation of such policies benefits members of society who have not suffered at the hands of discrimination and, in the process, punishes others who have never discriminated and who may actually be disadvantaged themselves. Because of bills like the one proposed by the California state legislature that would have mandated quotas in the same proportion to the population of the state for college admissions *and* graduation, many are concerned that what

[6]Cited in Melanne Verveer, "The Quota Question," *Business and Society Review* (Spring 1991): 6.

[7]Proscella Painton, "Quota Quagmire," *Time* (27 May 1991): 22.

started out as equality of opportunity has become a quest for equality of results.

The statistical evidence seems to indicate that strong affirmative-action programs have largely failed. The number of black families earning under $15,000 per year is now nearly 40 percent. In the past twenty years, median income of African-American families has increased just over a mere $300 to $21,423, after adjustments for inflation.[8] Moreover, the wage gap has also failed to close: Although black and Hispanic women have made some gains, the average annual earnings of black men in comparison to white men has not gained any ground since 1975 and has actually grown worse for Hispanic men.[9]

In terms of employment, the percentage of blacks in the workforce has risen by 50 percent in the last twenty-five years. However, although about 5 percent of all managers in the U.S. are black, as a recent study by Korn/Ferry International shows, white males still control at least 95 percent of the real power positions in corporate America. While blacks make up 12.7 percent of the workforce, only 5 percent of all professionals are black. Additionally, only about 5 percent of students enrolled in law schools and 3 percent of doctors in the country are black.[10]

Dinesh D'souza, author of *Illiberal Education*, argues that these programs have contributed greatly to the alienation and failure of students admitted preferentially on America's college campuses. D'souza cites an internal report at Berkeley that shows that of the students admitted under affirmative action in 1982, only 22 percent of Hispanics and 18 percent of blacks had graduated by 1987. Blacks and Hispanics not admitted through these programs graduated at rates of 42 and 55 percent respectively.[11] However, on a positive note, a large number of minorities have risen to possess the once elusive middle-class status. For example, the proportion of black families earning over $50,000 per year has jumped from 10 to 15 percent.[12]

On the surface at least, the net effect of such programs is that they have not achieved their aims. While correlation is not causation, it would certainly be encouraging if there were more positive relationships between the resources spent on strong affirmative-action programs and the long-term success of their intended beneficiaries.

These modest results are indeed troubling. They are even more problematic when all of the relevant costs are considered. Noting that there is little research available on the real costs of these programs, the authors of a recent *Forbes* article on affirmative action attempted to determine the total yearly cost of regulating affirmative-action programs. The approach taken was to use cost categories that economists would consider, including direct costs, indirect costs, and opportunity

[8] Cited in Peter Brimelow and Leslie Spencer, "When Quotas Replace Merit, Everybody Suffers," *Forbes* (15 February 1993).

[9] Steven Roberts et al., "Affirmative Action of the Edge," *U.S. News and World Report* (13 February 1995): 35.

[10] Cited in Sylvester Monroe, "Does Affirmative Action Help or Hurt?" *Time* (27 May 1991): 22; see also Howard Gleckman et al., "Race in the Workplace: Is Affirmative Action Working? *Business Week* (8 July 1991): 52; also see Ann Quindlen, "The Great White Myth," *New York Times*, 15 January 1992.

[11] Dinesh D'souza, "Sins of Admission," *New Republic* (18 February 1991): 33.

[12] Gleckman et al., "Race in the Workplace," 52.

costs. In addition, they used some old figures and adjusted them for inflation. Their conclusion was that when all of these figures are added up, total costs are $225 million or 4 percent of 1991 GNP, about as much as the country spends on its public school system.[13] If these costs are accurate, this may suggest that America has spent trillions of dollars to achieve outcomes that fall far short of ideal.

University of Chicago professor Richard A. Epstein examines the costs versus the benefits and rejects the whole enterprise. In his book *Forbidden Grounds: The Case Against Employment Discrimination Laws*, he states that such legislation is wasteful, expensive, and covert redistributive legislation. In his most incriminating statement he writes that if it is a goal to subsidize a protected class, "it can be done more efficiently just by giving away grants."[14]

Aside from the statistical data, many sources of anecdotal evidence serve as the most serious indictments against strong affirmative-action policies. In some insidious ways, it seems as though these policies actually cause rather than heal racial tension. Through the consideration of the very factors that they have sought to eliminate, those involving ethnicity and gender, these policies have created many new victims of their good intentions.

First, in order to advance underqualified members of minority groups in college admissions and employment decisions, qualified younger white males who are not themselves guilty of discrimination have been forced to pay for the sins of the past. Through policies of preference, many members of this group have been victims of attempts at correcting statistical disparities in ethnic and gender makeup. For many civil service occupations such as law enforcement and fire fighting, it is not uncommon to hear discouraged white males complain that their plight is not that much different from that of excluded blacks prior to the civil rights movement. Furthermore, "set aside" programs that attempt to affirm minority-owned businesses that are presumed to be "disadvantaged" are favored in federal government contract bids. Typically, a minority-owned firm can win a government contract even if it is not the lowest bidder. These companies usually receive a "bid preference" of a certain percentage as a provision of the set-aside program. For example, with a 10 percent bid preference, a minority-owned business can win a contract as long as its bid isn't more than 10 percent higher than the next lowest bid. Aside from the obvious higher costs to taxpayers, it is not uncommon for white-owned firms to object to the fact that at least in some parts of the country, they don't have a chance at winning federal contracts.[15]

Furthermore, some minority groups who have been oppressed themselves are victims of affirmative action. For example, in some

[13]Brimelow and Spencer, "When Quotas Replace Merit, Everybody Suffers."

[14]Cited in ibid.

[15]Paul Barrett, "Federal Preferences for Minority Firms Illustrate Affirmative Action Dispute," *Wall Street Journal*, 14 March 1995, A20.

employment and college admissions situations, Asian-Americans are considered "over represented," given their representation in the surrounding population size. They then lose out as a result of preferential hiring, promotion, and layoff practices. In a sense, Asian-Americans are the ones decapitated by the back swing of the affirmative-action sword. This has become most evident in some prominent California universities.

D'souza writes that although universities strenuously deny a ceiling on Asian admittees, "it is mathematically impossible to raise the percentage of students from underrepresented groups without simultaneously reducing students from overrepresented groups."[16] Indeed, Ira Heyman, the former chancellor of Berkeley, has admitted to and apologized for discrimination against Asians. In addition, in 1991 the U.S. Department of Education found the University of California, Los Angeles, guilty of illegal ceilings on Asians.

What is ironic is the factor of double victimization. As D'souza states it,

> For Asian-Americans, the cruel irony is that preferential policies, which are set up to atone for discrimination, seem to have institutionalized and legitimized discrimination against a minority group that is itself a victim of continuing prejudice in America. Moreover, for Asians, minority quotas that were intended as instruments of inclusion have become instruments of exclusion.[17]

Finally, as exemplified by Shelby Steele's essay, many vocal critics from within the African-American community argue that the intended beneficiaries of affirmative action are themselves the most serious victims since these practices actually serve more to hinder than to help the very groups that they are attempting to assist. It is alleged that these policies damage self-esteem, hurt self-reliance by creating a dependency effect, and stigmatize all members of the group as inferior.

Concurring with D'souza, Shelby Steele, who considers himself a political liberal, comments on the costs of artificial diversity by pointing out the self-doubt that such programs can create:

> Here again, racial preferences allow society to leapfrog over the difficult problem of developing blacks to parity with whites and into a cosmetic diversity that covers that blemish of disparity—a full six years after admission, only 26% of black students graduate from college. . . . Preferential treatment, no matter how it is justified in the light of day, subjects blacks to a midnight of self-doubt, and so often transforms their advantage into a revolving door.[18]

[16]D'souza, "Sins of Admission," 30.

[17]Ibid.

[18]Shelby Steele, "Affirmative Action: The Price of Preference," in *The Content of Our Character* (New York: HarperCollins, 1990), 106.

He further asserts that since the quality that earns preferential treatment is an "implied inferiority," it leads to "demoralization," no matter how it is explained away. Thomas Nagel, an avowed supporter of such policies, agrees that, since "this painful damage to esteem cannot be avoided, it should make any defender of strong affirmative action want the practice to end as soon as it has achieved its basic purpose."[19]

Steele further argues that affirmative action creates a self-defeating spiral by encouraging blacks to blame racism rather than their own shortcomings for their failures. By creating incentives for blacks to exploit past victimization into power and privilege, preference policies communicate that they can do for blacks what blacks can't do for themselves. Moreover, it can create incentives for members of preferred groups to rely on others rather than themselves and can create a great incentive for underachievement. An attitude of "getting in on a quota" is too easily fostered when the system openly discourages excellence by rewarding mediocrity.

University of California regent Ward Connerly, a black conservative who is currently leading a campaign to abolish affirmative-action policies in the University of California system, echoes Steele's assertions. Connerly argues that these policies create an *illusion* of progress because of the lower standards that are set. This illusion disappears quickly, he argues, when the beneficiaries are forced to compete with those who have qualified without a preference policy.[20] Economist Thomas Sowell calls this process "mismatching," for in it the competition for talented minorities is so fierce in college recruitment that many are pushed into environments for which they are not ready.[21] Thus the problems of high drop-out rates and lower standards are further perpetuated.

Another significant problem with these policies is that they unintentionally perpetuate stigmas that their beneficiaries are inferior. Several studies, most notably a 1992 investigation that was published in the *Journal of Applied Psychology*, concludes that stigmatization because of affirmative-action efforts in organizations does in fact lead to "presumed incompetence" on the part of its beneficiaries.[22] Furthermore, they can promote the deep stain of stigmas or the widespread belief that all members of specific groups who are hired, promoted, or gain admission into elite colleges are less qualified. Like Steele, who states his position in his essay included in this chapter, Allan Bloom, author of *The Closing of the American Mind*, lays the responsibility for such beliefs at the doorstep of the policies themselves. He argues that preferential treatment programs lead to the stigmatization of minority groups as being quota qualifiers. He reasons that since employment recruiters at major universities know that

[19] Thomas Nagel, "A Defense of Affirmative Action," testimony before the Subcommittee on the Constitution of the Senate Judiciary Committee, 18 June 1981.

[20] Joe Klein, "The End of Affirmative Action," *Newsweek* (13 February 1995): 36–37.

[21] Steven Roberts et al., "Affirmative Action of the Edge," 33.

[22] Madeline E. Heilman, Jonathan A. Lucas, and Caryn J. Brock, "Presumed Incompetent? Stigmatization and Affirmative Action Efforts," *Journal of Applied Psychology* 77, no. 4 (1992): 536–44.

[23]Allan Bloom, "Race," in *The Closing of the American Mind* (New York: Simon & Schuster, 1987).

many members of protected groups are enrolled as a result of preferential treatment, a pall is cast on all members of those groups, even those who have qualified as a result of merit. Thus they are viewed with suspicion and stigmatized along with those who entered on lower standards.[23]

With all of the evidence that points to the current shortcomings of strong affirmative-action policies, it seems reasonable to conclude that they have achieved their basic purpose and have now run their course. To its credit, race-based aggressive affirmative action has rushed members of minority groups into the economic mainstream. But, beyond this basic accomplishment, the damage it causes seems unjustifiable from a moral perspective. In addition, current trends indicate that it may no longer be necessary as the economic self-interest of employers is already working to ensure diversity in hiring practices.

Since the U.S. population now is made up of about 28 percent minorities, companies would be foolish not to utilize a workforce of similar proportions in order to capture these growing markets. Furthermore, the makeup of the current workforce is rapidly changing. Minorities now make up 22 percent of the workforce and, according to most studies, women, immigrants, and minorities will constitute over 80 percent of new hires by the year 2000. To ignore this rapidly growing segment of the labor market is to let a valuable talent pool go untapped. According to AT&T chairman Robert Allen, "affirmative action is not just the right thing to do, it's a business necessity."[24] Indeed, Allstate voluntarily increased the number of women and minorities on its staff while motivated by profit through the search for new customers for its insurance products.[25]

[24]Gleckman et al., "Race in the Workplace," 53.

[25]Peter Annin, "The Corporation: Allstate Saw the Light When It Started Following the Money," *Newsweek* (3 April 1995): 32–33.

[26]Tom L. Beauchamp, "Goals and Quotas in Hiring and Promotion," in *Ethical Theory and Business*, 4th ed., ed. Tom L. Beauchamp and Norman Bowie (Englewood Cliffs, N.J.: Prentice-Hall, 1992), 387–90.

Along these lines of reasoning, business ethicist Tom Beauchamp cites three specific benefits to corporations when they maintain voluntary programs of strong affirmative action. First, because of the aforementioned demographics, these practices will lead to an improved workforce. Second, they will contribute to the stability of good working conditions and maintenance of a bias-free work environment. Finally, they are congenial to managerial planning, since quotas have been successful for the companies that have adopted them. In fact, Beauchamp cites a survey of three hundred executives in which 72 percent of the respondents said that minority hiring improves rather than hinders performance.[26]

Furthermore, in what appears to confirm Beauchamp's theories, 86 percent of executives responding to a recent *Business Week* survey answered that they felt it was "somewhat" or "very" important for companies to increase the hiring of women and minorities because of "the benefits of having different types of people in the workforce." Similarly, 88 percent answered with like enthusiasm for reasons of "the changing makeup of labor supply."[27]

[27]Gleckman et al., "Race in the Workplace," 63.

It is important to note that while such practices are commonly referred to as voluntary "affirmative-action" programs, this label is a misnomer. Since companies are acting on behalf of profit, "qualifications" are not being lowered to accommodate members of minority groups as has been the practice in many traditional affirmative-action programs. If the bottom line is the measuring stick for "qualifications," the women and minorities hired are by definition in these situations "better qualified" to serve these employers.

Thus if these trends continue, the fortunes of members of minority groups will be advanced greatly without government-mandated quotas or percentages. However, this is not to deny that some disadvantaged members of society still need help in order to meet some of the minimum qualifications that would allow them access to good educational and employment opportunities. We will address this further in our concluding comments.

Gender Issues

Although we have focused so far on ethnic minorities in this debate, women have also faced discrimination in the workplace and have been significant beneficiaries of affirmative-action programs. Laura Purdy argues that in many employment situations women only "appear" to be less qualified than men. Thus hiring or promoting them is not really an act of "affirmative action" in the traditional sense of lowering the requirements. Purdy insightfully brings to light the perceptual biases and other disadvantages that women face in employment situations that are traditionally male dominated. Purdy's argument is not so much an argument for affirmative action as it is a challenge for employers to continually review their stated qualifications and performance review practices to assure that they are fair to members of both genders. Undoubtedly, ethical workplaces will also seek to eradicate subtle forms of discrimination based on gender.

However, many other voices are calling for affirmative-action policies that go beyond just eliminating discrimination. It is common to hear advocacy for affirmative action in the form of lower qualifications in order to accommodate more women in traditionally male-dominated professions. For example, some local governments have recently announced policies in which they intend to hire women as police and fire department officers in proportions representative of their makeup in the surrounding population.

Qualifications that are frivolous and have no reasonable "business necessity," in the sense of correlation to the performance of the jobs themselves, but only serve to discriminate should be reexamined. However, some positions that involve public safety should not be places for social experimentation in equality. If specific minimum physical requirements for certain tasks are indeed necessary to best serve the public, they should be upheld as standards. The discriminating factor in some of these situations is not based on gender at all. Rather, the issue at stake is physical since there are many men who also do not have the physical abilities necessary to be combat pilots and police and fire department officers.

In addition to hard numbers as goals for the hiring of women, there has been a strong discussion of comparable-worth programs. Based on the assumption that gender discrimination has created unacceptable inequities in compensation in female-dominated positions in comparison with male-dominated ones, these programs attempt to redress these differences through the "comparable-worth" of different professions. June O'Neill describes and argues against these programs in detail in her article "An Argument Against Comparable Worth." She rightly argues that the factor of discrimination in the wage gap is largely exaggerated. Upon closer examination, we find that many professions pay differently for reasons other than discrimination. Furthermore, she questions the power of firms in a free market to be able to underpay women in the manner in which they are accused of doing since women could move to other employers who would bid up wages in exchange for their talents. Finally, she argues that such programs would only serve to further segregate professions, as women would have no financial incentives to crack the barriers of traditionally male-dominated professions.

O'Neill seems correct in her arguments against comparable-worth programs and in her assertion that the wage gap will close over time. Moreover, the overall plight of women in the workforce seems to be improving at a rapid pace. Employers are enacting many enlightened policies to help women strike the difficult balance between family and career. Many of these employers are undoubtedly acting out of self-interest. They realize the costs involved in losing good employees and having to hire and train their replacements. Thus market forces are working in favor of gender equality in the workplace.

However, it would be naive to believe that self-interest and a blind trust in the "invisible hand" of the free market alone are enough to totally eradicate discrimination on the basis of gender or ethnicity. If jobs are left totally to market forces, some instances of unfair discrimination will undoubtedly occur. Thus existing laws against such discrimination must be stringently enforced. Much care must be taken to ensure that hiring practices are not arbitrary and discriminatory in practice, such as in the case of *Griggs v. Duke Power*. As such, there must be a legitimate "business necessity" and correlation between job performance and the stated "qualifications."

Ethnicity and Gender Blind Affirmative Action

One of the most compelling reasons that we can find in favor of affirmative action comes from the fact that many members of disadvantaged groups are in no position to acquire many of the stated qualifications for college admissions and employment. For example, it is common knowledge that black, Hispanic, and Native American students can gain admission into top-level schools with SAT scores that are far short of the level that must be attained by students with other backgrounds. However, the differences in test scores is not a reflection of genetics, nor in many cases are they indicative of effort. Children of many families from these backgrounds attend schools plagued by violence and low academic achievement, making learning extremely difficult. The average SAT scores of students from such schools can be several hundred points lower than those of schools in wealthier neighborhoods. Thus even if a student were to work as diligently as possible, the odds are highly stacked against his or her ability to ever achieve the "required" score for admission into top-level schools. Proponents of affirmative action argue that without these policies many of these students will never have the opportunity to attend good schools. The same arguments are advanced with respect to many employment situations.

Undoubtedly, an honest assessment shows that many poor children, through no fault of their own, do not have the same opportunities to achieve as children of wealthy parents. Thus if our society is to take seriously the scriptural mandates to care for the poor and for our children, something has to be done to ensure that all start on an equal footing. Help in the form of outreach at an early age to assist them to meet qualifications would truly provide equality of opportunity. Undoubtedly, people will finish the metaphorical race at different places, but if there is early intervention, there will be no excuses in the end.

However, these examples argue more for class-based rather then race- or gender-based policies of affirmative action. Since many beneficiaries of current policies are not themselves identifiable victims of past discrimination, the argument from a compensatory justice perspective that only minorities and women should benefit seems dubious. Indeed, there are many poor disadvantaged members of society that are children of white families. Shelby Steele remarks that it seems quite unfair that his daughter may benefit from preference policies at the expense of the son of a poor white family. Since the most significant factor in "disadvantage" in society seems to be poverty rather than ethnicity, class-based and race-blind policies seem best fitted for our current conditions.

Along with color-blind affirmative-action programs, other reforms have been suggested by public figures such as Ward Connerly that make much sense. In a day where public sentiment is focused on "merit" rather than preference, admissions or employment based on stated qualifications must be consistently applied. Many find it hypocritical that no one makes an outcry when underqualified children of alumni are admitted under "legacies" programs at prestigious colleges. With approximately 12 percent of all admissions at elite colleges going to these students, one wonders why there isn't the same type of protest as when underqualified minorities are admitted. Thus for the sake of consistency, Connerly suggests that these types of programs must also be eliminated in order to level the playing field from the top down.[28]

In light of the seemingly weighty evidence of the failures of strong affirmative-action programs and the extreme costs to society, public funds would be much better placed into programs that create equality of opportunity in other arenas. While simultaneously investigating and remedying arbitrary and subtly discriminatory "qualifications," we should put finances into early-age intervention policies that attempt to bring all disadvantaged members of society into full qualification.

Although the use of funds in this manner would not completely serve to eradicate the stigmatization factors mentioned previously, the focus is on equality of opportunity and not a guarantee of results. This will surely lean toward true justice and serve to lessen resentment on the part of those who lose out and suspicion on the part of those who are in the position of observing qualifications.

Although such "softer" policies are open to criticism that they will not move fast enough, gradual progress is the only true outcome that can be accomplished without radical moves toward central planning and redistribution. Furthermore, "strong" affirmative-action policies have certainly done no better than the achievement of gradual change over the last thirty years. In fact, in the minds of many, they have actually worked to the detriment of society.

[28]Klein, "The End of Affirmative Action," 37.

NINE

Sexual Harassment

Sexual harassment, then, seems to be just one more ugly manifestation of the sexism and sexual inequality which is rampant in public life.

Lucy Dodds et al., "Sexual Harassment"

In the feminist Salem that the corporate American workplace has become, men and women must relate to one another like humanoids.

Barbara Amiel, "Feminist Harassment"

INTRODUCTION

In the confirmation hearings of Justice Clarence Thomas before the Senate Judiciary Committee, sexual harassment was again at the forefront in the media and the attention of the public. Although we may never know the truth of what actually took place between Thomas and Anita Hill, and although he was eventually confirmed to the United States Supreme Court, his reputation was tarnished by the charges, perhaps beyond repair. The case illustrates many of the difficult and complex issues in this area that must be resolved before laws can be crafted that will both protect victims from harassment and enable those charged with harassment to confront the charges against them. There is little doubt that women have been subject to sexual harassment in the workplace over the years and that they are more empowered today to stop it. But some wonder about the effects of such empowerment on the relationships between men and women in general at work and whether the new awareness of sexual harassment in the workplace has encouraged women to file charges when no harassment has actually occurred.

There is perhaps no other charge that strikes such fear and dread into the hearts of individuals in the workplace than the charge of sexual harassment. It is one of the few "infractions" of which a person can be considered guilty until proven innocent. Companies frequently feel the need to take harassment claims seriously, since the firm can be held liable for not stopping harassment of which it has knowledge. But this desire to take it seriously tends to undermine the rights of the accused to due process, which includes the opportunity to confront one's accuser and rebut the charges. Often employees accused of harassment are fired first, and the company asks questions later. As a result, all it takes is the charge of sexual harassment to ruin a person's reputation at the least, and it may take years to rebuild it. At most, the charge alone can ruin a person's career with that particular company. This has resulted in a chilling effect on relations between men and women at work, precisely the opposite effect from that which feminist advocates desired when they began to confront sexual harassment in the workplace.

There are several issues that must be resolved before fair and adequate laws can be put into place to safeguard both the victims of sexual harassment and those accused of it. The first and perhaps the most difficult one is the definition of sexual harassment. Many people cannot define it precisely, but they surely know it when it occurs, particularly if it should happen to them. But an intuitive sense of when it occurs is inadequate because it is much too subjective and gives the alleged victim too much power. More objective criteria are needed to adequately assess when sexual harassment has genuinely occurred. One of the cases in this chapter involves the Stroh's brewery, in which the female employees charged that the commercial featuring the "Swedish bikini team" created a hostile work environment for them and contributed to their being sexually harassed. Cases like these reveal the need for clear criteria for identifying harassment when it occurs. Think about how you would define sexual harassment if you were a company's human resource manager responsible for drafting a policy for addressing sexual harassment.

A second issue is whether or not the current emphasis on sexual harassment has gone too far, resulting in frivolous accusations and a general stifling of interaction between men and women at work. There is no more effective way for employees to strike back at a boss or fellow employee who has hurt them than to charge them with harassment. As a result, there is a growing atmosphere of fear and distrust surrounding gender relations in the workplace. Has the trend toward correcting sexual harassment in the workplace been pushed too far, or is the problem being addressed in proportion to the frequency with which it occurs? Has it produced unanticipated and unintended consequences that are not helpful to workplace morale and harmonious relationships between men and women at work?

A third critical issue is the way in which companies balance two legitimate concerns. It is clear that firms must take sexual harassment claims seriously, and a company that fails to do so is rightly held liable. But the firm must also be committed to using due process for employees accused of harassment. The fire-first-and-ask-questions-later approach surely indicates decisiveness about sexual harassment, but one must ask at what price? If the price is the loss of due process for accused employees, is that too high a price to pay? Or is giving an employee access to due process only delaying dealing with the problem and giving companies a way to sweep employees' complaints about harassment under the rug?

Perhaps the most difficult aspect of sexual harassment is defining it. To help you wrestle with this complex area, take each of the following brief scenarios. Which of these constitutes sexual harassment? Indicate whether you think the scenario is "definitely not" sexual harassment, "possibly" sexual harassment, or "definitely" sexual harassment. Once you have decided which situations are harassment, think about what your choices indicate about your criteria for defining harassment.

1. A co-worker asking you repeatedly for a date and in each instance being turned down
2. Putting your hand on a female co-worker's shoulder for a brief moment during a conversation
3. Having calendar pinups of scantily clad women on the shop floor's bulletin board
4. Reading soft porn in an out-of-the-way place at work during the lunch hour
5. Consenting to sex with a co-worker and having it used against you later
6. Telling sexual jokes in the presence of women co-workers
7. Making slightly suggestive complimentary comments about a woman's appearance
8. Giving hints that one's career would be well served by going out with the boss
9. Looking a co-worker up and down during a conversation

Most of these examples involve men sexually harassing women. This reflects the large majority of cases of harassment in the workplace. But women can also be guilty of sexually harassing men, though it happens far less frequently. The best-selling book and later a movie entitled *Disclosure* by Michael Crichton, though fictional, is nevertheless a realistic account of how men can also be victimized by sexual harassment. Thus most of the above scenarios could occur with the genders of the participants reversed.

Philosopher Susan Dodds and her colleagues in their article "Sexual Harassment" attempt a comprehensive definition of sexual harassment. Through the use of an extended case study, they distinguish between gender discrimination and sexual harassment, which is to point out that not every case of sexist discrimination involves sexual harassment. They provide what they call a behavioral account of sexual harassment. They underscore that a person's behavior toward a co-worker, if it meets the criteria that define sexual harassment, constitutes the problem. They hold that the causes, intentions, and consequences of the behavior are all irrelevant for determining whether or not sexual harassment has occurred. The behavior itself is both the necessary and the sufficient condition for harassment to have occurred. Only if the definition is behavior oriented can it provide a workable guideline for a company's policy on sexual harassment.

Journalist Barbara Amiel, in her article "Feminist Harassment," defines sexual harassment more narrowly and laments the way in which feminists have overreacted to sexual harassment in the workplace. She holds that what legitimately constitutes sexual harassment in the workplace, demanding sexual favors in return for job security or promotion, had little to do with the charges that Anita Hill brought against Clarence Thomas in his Supreme Court nomination hearings. Further, she charges that the current emphasis on sexual harassment actually amounts to feminists harassing men with their radical views on gender relations.

While acknowledging that sexual harassment must be addressed, J. H. Foegen insightfully points out that one of the unfortunate side effects of the efforts to rid the workplace of sexual harassment has been the chilling effect on relations between men and women in the office. It has promoted unhealthy fears of relating to the opposite sex and encouraged men to ignore women co-workers out of a paranoiac fear of saying or doing something that could be construed as harassment. Thus all the appropriate emphasis on sexual harassment, which was designed to bring men and women together, has actually worked to further isolate them. One of the most significant challenges for a company trying to deal with sexual harassment responsibly is to have a policy that is workable but does not stifle interaction between men and women.

READINGS

Sexual Harassment

Susan Dobbs et alia

Social Theory and Practice 14, no. 2 (Summer 1988). Copyright © 1988.

Mary has a problem. Her boss, Bill, gives her a bad time. He is constantly making sexual innuendoes and seems always to be blocking her way and brushing against her. He leers at her, and on occasions has made it explicitly clear that it would be in her own best interests to go to bed with him. She is the one woman in the office now singled out for this sort of treatment, although she hears that virtually all other attractive women who have in the past worked for Bill have had similar experiences. On no occasion has Mary encouraged Bill. His attentions have all been unwanted. She has found them threatening, unpleasant and objectionable. When on some occasions she has made these reactions too explicit, she has been subjected to unambiguously detrimental treatment. Bill has no genuinely personal feelings for Mary, is neither truly affectionate nor loving: his motivation is purely sexual.

Surely this is a paradigmatic case of sexual harassment. Bill discriminates against Mary, and it seems that he would also discriminate against any other attractive woman who worked for him. He misuses his power as an employer when he threatens Mary with sex she does not want. His actions are clearly against her interests. He victimizes her at present and will probably force her to leave the office, whatever the consequences to her future employment.

Not all cases of sexual harassment are so clear. Indeed, each salient characteristic of the paradigmatic case may be missing and yet sexual harassment still occurs. Even if all the features are missing, it could still be a case of sexual harassment.

We aim to explicate the notion of sexual harassment. We note that our aim is not to provide an analysis of the ordinary language concept of sexual harassment. Rather we aim to provide a theoretical rationale for a more behavioral stipulative definition of sexual harassment. For it is an account of this kind which proves to be clearly superior for policy purposes. It provides the basis for a clear, just and enforceable policy, suitable for the workplace and for society at large. Of course ordinary language intuitions provide important touchstones. What else could we use to broadly determine the relevant kind of behavior? But this does not mean that all ordinary language considerations are to be treated as sacrosanct. Sexual harassment is a concept with roots in ordinary language, but we seek to develop the concept as one suitable for more theoretical purposes, particularly those associated with the purposes of adequate policy development.

1. Sexual Harassment and Sexual Discrimination

It seems plausible that minimally harassment involves discrimination, and more particularly, sexual harassment involves sexism. Sexual discrimination was clearly part of the harassment in the case of Mary and Bill.

The pull towards viewing sexual harassment as tied to sexual discrimination is strengthened by consideration of the status of most harassers and most harassees. In general, the roles of these men and women are reinforced by historical and cultural features of systematic sexual discrimination against women. Generally, men have control of greater wealth and power in our society, while women are economically dependent on men. Men are viewed as having the (positive) quality of aggression in sexual and social relations, while women are viewed as (appropriately) passive. These entrenched attitudes reflect an even deeper view of women as fundamentally unequal, that is in some sense, less fully person than men. Sexual harassment, then, seems to be just one more ugly manifestation of the sexism and sexual inequality which is rampant in public life.

Closer consideration reveals, however, that while discrimination may be present in cases of harassment, it need not be. More specifically, while sexual discrimination may be (and often is) present in cases of sexual harassment, it is not a necessary feature of sexual harassment.

The fact that in most cases women are (statistically, though not necessarily) the objects of sexual harassment, is an important feature of the issue of sexual harassment, and it means that in many cases where women are harassed, the harassment will involve sexual discrimination. However, sexual harassment need not entail sexual discrimination.

2. Negative Consequences and Interests

Perhaps sexual harassment always involves action by the harasser which is against the interest of the harassee, or has overall negative consequences for the harassee.

However consider Mary B who is sexually harassed by Bill B. Mary B gives in, but as luck would have it, things turn out extremely well; Mary B is promoted by Bill B to another department. The long-term consequences are excellent, so clearly it has been in Mary B's best interests to be the object of Bill B's attentions. One could also imagine a case where Mary B rejects Bill B, with the (perhaps unintentional) effect that the overall consequences for Mary B are very good.

In general, harassment need not be against the interests of the harassee. You can be harassed to stop smoking, and harassed to give up drugs. In these cases the consequences may well be good, and the interests of the harassee adequately considered and served, yet it is still harassment. This general feature seems equally applicable to sexual harassment.

3. Misuse of Power

Bill has power over Mary and it is the misuse of this power which plays an important role in making his treatment of Mary particularly immoral. For, on almost any normative theory, to misuse power is immoral. But is this misuse of power what makes this action one of sexual harassment?

If it is, then it must not be restricted to the formal power of the kind which Bill has over Mary—the power to dismiss her, demote her, withhold benefits from her, and so on. We also usually think of this sort of formal power in cases of police harassment. But consider the harassment of women at an abortion clinic by Right-to-Lifers. They cannot prevent the women having abortions and indeed lack any formal power over them. Nonetheless, they do possess important powers—to dissuade the faint-hearted (or even the oversensitive), and to increase the unpleasantness of the experience of women attending the clinic.

Now consider the case of Mary C. Bill C and Mary C are co-workers in the office, and Bill C lacks formal power over Mary C. He sexually harasses her—with sexual innuendoes, touches, leers, jokes, suggestions, and unwanted invitations. To many women Bill C's actions would be unpleasant. But Mary C is a veteran—this has happened to her so many times before that she no longer responds. It is not that she desires or wants the treatment, but it no longer produces the unpleasant mental attitudes it used to produce—it just rolls off her. She gives the negative responses automatically, and goes on as though nothing had happened.

It would still seem to us that Mary C has been sexually harassed. But what power has Bill C misused against Mary C? He has not used even some informal power which has caused her some significantly unpleasant experience.

4. Attitudes, Intentions and Experiences

In our discussions so far, it seems that we have not taken into account, to any significant extent, how Mary and Bill feel about things. It may be argued that what defines or characterizes sexual harassment is the mental state of the harasser, or harassee, or both.

Bill wanted to have sex with Mary. He perceived her as a sex object. He failed to have regard for her as a person. He failed to have regard for how she might feel about things. And his actions gave him egotistical pleasure. These attitudes, intentions and experiences may help constitute Bill's action as a case of sexual harassment.

Mary also had very specific kinds of mental states. She found Bill's actions unpleasant, and unwanted. She wished Bill would not act in that way towards her, and she disliked him for it. She was angry that someone would treat her in that way, and she resented being forced to cope with the situation. So again we have attributed attitudes and mental experiences to Mary in describing this case as one of sexual harassment.

We do not want to have to label as sexual harassment all sexual actions or approaches between people in formally structured relationships. Cases of sexual harassment and non-harassing sexual interaction may appear very similar (at least over short time intervals.) It seems that in the two kinds of cases only the mental features differ. That is, we refer to attitudes, intentions or experiences in explaining the difference between the two cases. But attention to this feature of sexual harassment is not enough in itself to identify sexual harassment.

The actual mental states of the people involved cannot be what is definitive of sexual harassment. They are not even necessary for sexual harassment.

5. A Behavioral Account of Sexual Harassment

The case of Mary E and Bill E persuades us that we require a behavioral account of sexual harassment. For a harasser to sexually harass a harassee is for the harasser to behave in a certain way towards the harassee. The causes of that behavior are not important, and what that behavior in turn causes is not important. The behavior itself constitutes the harassment.

But how then are we to specify the behavior that is to count as sexual harassment? We shall borrow a technique from the functionalist theory of the mind.

Functionalists usually identify mental states in terms of the functional roles they play. However some functionalist theories allow a variation on this. If we talk instead of the kind of mental state which *typically* fills a functional role or the functional role *typically* associated with a mental state, we maintain the functionalist flavor, but allow unusual combinations of kinds of inner states and kinds of functional roles to be accommodated. We shall follow a similar technique when describing the kinds of behavior associated with sexual harassment.

Consider the behavior which is typically associated with a mental state representing an attitude which seeks sexual ends without any concern for the person from whom those ends are sought, and which typically produces an unwanted and unpleasant response in the person who is the object of the behavior. Such behavior we suggest is what constitutes sexual harassment. Instances of the behavior are instances of sexual harassment even if the mental states of the harasser or harassee (or both) are different from those typically associated with such behavior. The behavior constitutes a necessary and sufficient condition for sexual harassment.

According to this view, the earlier suggestion that attitudes, intentions and experience are essential to an adequate characterization of sexual harassment is correct. It is correct to the extent that we need to look at the mental states typical of the harasser, rather than those present in each actual harasser, and at those typical of the harassee, rather than those present in each actual harassee. The empirical claim is that connecting these typical mental states is a kind of behavior—behavior not incredibly different from instance to instance, but with a certain sameness to it. Thus it is a behavior of a definite characteristic *type*. This type of behavior is sexual harassment.

This proffered account may at first appear surprising. But let us look at some of its features to alleviate the surprise, and at the same time increase the plausibility of the account.

Most importantly, the account satisfies our three desiderata: to show the connection between harassment in general and sexual harassment, to distinguish between sexual harassment and legitimate sexual interaction, and to assist in guiding policy on sexual harassment.

The relationship between harassment and sexual harassment is to be accounted for in terms of a behavioral similarity. This at first may seem to be a sweeping suggestion, since *prima facie*, there need be no descriptive similarity between sexual harassment, harassment by police, harassment of homosexuals, harassment of Jews, and so on. But the behavioral elements on which each kind of harassment supervenes will have enough in common to explain our linking them all as harassment, while at the same time being sufficiently different to allow for their differentiation into various kinds of harassment. The most plausible similarity, as we shall argue later, will be in the presence of certain behavioral dispositions, though the bases for these dispositions may differ.

Our approach allows for an adequate distinction between sexual harassment and legitimate sexual approaches and interactions. The approach requires that this be a behavioral difference. There is something intrinsically different about the two kinds of activity. Given that the typical causal origin of each of the kinds of behavior is different and so too is the typical reaction it in turn produces, it is to be expected that there would be a difference in the behavior itself. It is important to note that the constitutive behavior will be within a particular context, in particular circumstances. (The importance of this is well illustrated in cases such as a student and her lecturer at a university.[1]) Further it will include both overt and covert behavior (subtle differences count). In many cases it will also be behavior over a time interval, not just behavior at a time.

From the policy guiding perspective the account is very attractive. It is far easier to stipulate a workable, practical, defensible, and legally viable policy on harassment if it is totally definable in behavioral terms. Definition in terms of mental experiences, intentions and attitudes spells nothing but trouble for a viable social policy on sexual harassment.

The analysis we have offered entails that if there were no such characteristic kind of behavior there would be no sexual harassment. This seems to be right. In this case no legislation to ground a social policy would be possible. We would instead condemn individual actions on other moral grounds—causing pain and distress, acting against someone's best interests, misusing power and so on.

In addition to satisfying these three desiderata, our account has numerous other positive features. First our account is culturally relative. It is highly likely that the kind of behavior constitutive of sexual harassment will vary from culture to culture, society to society. That is, it will be a culture-relative kind of behavior that determines sexual harassment. In any culture our reference to the typical mental states of the harasser and harassee will identify a kind of behavior that is constitutive of sexual harassment in that culture. This kind of behavior matches well with the empirical observations. There is so much variation in human behavior across cultures that behavior which may be sexual harassment in one need not be in another. The same is true of other kinds of human behavior. In the middle east, belching indicates appreciation of a meal. In western society, it is considered bad manners. The practice of haggling over the price of a purchase is acceptable (indeed expected) in some societies, and unacceptable in others. But in almost any culture, some kind of behavior may reasonably be judged to be sexual harassment.

Second, while we have cast our examples in terms of a male harasser and female harassee, there is nothing in the account which necessitates any gender restriction on sexual harassment. All that is required is that the behavior is sexual in nature and has other behavioral features which make it an instance of sexual harassment. The participants could be of either sex in either role, or of the same sex.

We acknowledge that we use the notion of an action being sexual in nature without attempting any explication of that notion. Such an explication is a separate task, but we believe that for our purposes there is no problem in taking it as primitive. Third, the account allows for the possibility of sexual harassment without the presence of the mental states typical of the harasser or the harassee. There is an important connection between these typical mental states and sexual harassment, but it does not restrict instances of sexual harassment to instances where we have these typical mental states.

Further as the account focuses on behavior, rather than mental states, it explains why we feel so skeptical about someone who behaves as Bill behaves, yet pleads innocence and claims he had no bad intentions. The intentions are not essential for the harassment, and such a person has an obligation to monitor the responses of the other person so that he has an accurate picture of what is going on. Moreover, he has an obligation to be aware of the character of his own behavior. He also has an obligation to give due consideration to the strength and the weight of the beliefs upon which he is operating before he makes a decision to act in a manner that may have unpleasant consequences for others. Strength of belief concerns the degree of confidence it is rational to have in the belief, given the evidence available. Weight of belief concerns the quality of the evidential basis of the belief, and the reasonableness of acting on the evidence available.[2] If a person is acting in a way which has a risk of bad consequences for others, that person has an obligation to be aware of the risks and to refrain from acting unless he has gained evidence of sufficient strength and weight to be confident that the bad consequences will not arise. In the case of someone who wishes to engage in legitimate sexual interaction and to avoid sexual harassment, he must display a disposition to be alive to the risks and to seek appropriate evidence from the other person's behavior, as to whether that person welcomes his attentions. He must also display a disposition to refrain from acting if such evidence is lacking.

In the case of Mary E and Bill E, Bill E relies on the harassing behavior of other men as a guide to his actions regarding Mary E. Mary E has displayed standard forms of avoidance behavior (although she has ulterior motives). Bill E does not pay sufficient heed to the strength and weight of the beliefs which guide his actions, and it is just fortunate that Mary E is not harmed by what he does. Given Bill E's total disregard of Mary E's interest and reactions, it seems that his behavior could have

caused, just as easily, significant distress to any other Mary who might have filled that role. A policy intended to identify sexual harassment should not rely on such luck, although the actual mental states (where they are as atypical as Mary E's) may mitigate blameworthiness. Bill E's harassing behavior should be checked and evaluated, regardless of any of Mary's actual mental states.[3]

Consider an example taken from an actual case[4] which highlights this obligation. Suppose Tom is married to Jane. He invites Dick (an old friend who has never met Jane) home to have sex with Jane. He tells Dick that Jane will protest, but that this is just part of the game (a game she very much enjoys). Dick forces Jane, who all the time protests violently, to have sex with him. Jane later claims to have been raped. Dick has acted culpably because he has acted without giving due consideration to the weight of the belief which guided his action, that is, to how rational it was to act on the belief given such a minimal evidential base. The only evidence he had that Jane did consent was Tom's say-so, and the consequences of acting on the belief were very serious. All of Jane's actions indicated that she did not consent.

In the case of Bill E and Mary E, Bill has an obligation to consider the strength and weight of the beliefs which guide his action before he acts. He is not justified in claiming that he is innocent, when he has been provided with signals that indicate that Mary does not welcome his attentions.

We acknowledge that it will be difficult in many situations to obtain sufficient evidence that a proposed act will not be one of sexual harassment. This will be true especially in cases where the potential harassee may believe that any outward indication of her displeasure would have bad consequences for her. The awareness of this difficulty is probably what has led others to promote the policy of a total ban on sexual relationships at the office or work place. While we acknowledge the problem, we feel that such a policy is both unrealistic and over restrictive.

Fourth, the account allows an interesting stance on the connection between sexual harassment and morality. For consequentialist theories of morality, it is possible (though unlikely) that an act of sexual harassment may be, objectively, morally right. This would be the case if the long term good consequences outweighed the bad effects (including those on the harassee at the time of the harassment). For other moral theories it is not clear that this is a possibility, except where there are sufficiently strong overriding considerations present, such as to make the sexual harassment morally permissible. From the agent's point of view, it would seem that the probable consequences of sexual harassment (given the typical harasser and the typical effects on the typical harassee) will be bad. Hence it is very likely, on any moral theory, that the agent evaluation for a harasser will be negative. The possible exceptions are where the harasser's actual mental state is not typical of a harasser, or the harassee's is not typical of a harassee.

Further, on this account many of the salient features of the case of Mary and Bill—such as misuse of power, discrimination, unfair distribution of favors, and so on—are not essential features of sexual harassment. They are usually immoral in their own right, and their immorality is not explained by their being part of the harassment. But the behavior characteristic of sexual harassment will be constituted by features which we commonly find in particular instances of sexual harassment. For sexual harassment must supervene on the behavioral features which constitute its instances, but there is a range of such behavior, no one element of which need to present on any particular occasion. Similarly the morality of an instance of sexual harassment (at least for the consequentialist) will supervene on the morality of those same features of behavior.

6. Objections to the Behavioral Account

We have made two claims about behavior constitutive of sexual harassment, and we should now see how they relate. The behavior is identified in terms of its typical causes and typical effects, that is, in terms of the typical mental states of harassers and harassees. But harassment is recognized by references to features of the behavior itself, and any legislation to ground social policy will also refer to such features. The philosophical claim is that there will be a range of such behavior features some combination of which will be present in each case of sexual harassment. The empirical job is to tell us more about the nature of such behavior and help determine the practical social policy and legislation.[5]

Notes

[1]See, for example, Billie Wright Dzeich and Linda Weiner, *The Lecherous Professor: Sexual Harassment on Campus* (Boston: Beacon Press, 1984).

[2]For a discussion of this concept of weight see Barbara Davidson and Robert Pargetter, "Weight" *Philosophical Studies* 49 (1986): 219–30.

[3]Some might say that this behavioristic account of sexual harassment is similar to having strict liability for murder, that is to say, that mental states do need to be taken into account when judging and penalizing someone's actions. What we are arguing for is a way of *identifying* sexual harassment, not how (or even if) it should be *penalized*. The appropriate response to a case of sexual harassment may very well take mental states into account, along with the harm caused, or likely to be caused, and so forth. One advantage of our account is that it demands that potential harassers become aware of their behavior and to be alert to the responses of those around them. The response of Bill E (that he thought women liked to be treated that way) ought not be considered adequate especially in public life where a person's livelihood could hang in the balance.

[4]This example is based on the British case, D.P.P. v Morgan (1975), 2 All E.R. 347 (House of Lords): Morgan (1975), 1 All E.R. 8 (Court of Appeal); see also Frank Jackson, "A Probabilistic Approach to Moral Responsibility," in Ruth Barcan Marcus, *et al.* (eds.), *Logic, Methodology and Philosophy of Science VII* (North Holland, 1986), 351–66.

[5]We acknowledge useful comments from Robert Young and various readers for this journal.

The Double Jeopardy of Sexual Harassment

J. H. Foegen

Business and Society Review 82 (Summer 1992). Copyright © 1992.

Biology prevents men and women from ignoring one another—in the workplace as elsewhere. Heightened sensitivity regarding sexual harassment has resulted from the Clarence Thomas confirmation hearings last year. Despite the admitted positive aspects, new awareness risks a productivity-reducing chill in the workplace climate. Most American companies can ill afford this as they compete internationally and pursue total quality management.

Last October, after controversial hearings concerning allegations of sexual harassment, the United States Senate confirmed Judge Clarence Thomas to the Supreme Court. The vote was fifty-two to forty-eight. Workplace fallout from those hearings will undoubtedly continue for a long time, as employers, supervisors, and workers of both genders try to accommodate greater sensitivity to an old problem made newly urgent. A potential danger is that either deliberately, or as an unconscious, knee-jerk reaction, males will in self-defense tend to ignore women coworkers. Wary of even possible charges of harassment, they will try to play it safe.

Much of the problem hinges upon definition; existing laws are helpful but hardly satisfactory. Though improving gradually, the laws remain less than helpful in specific situations. Equal Employment Opportunity Commission (EEOC) guidelines, which have been updated several times since 1980, flag two basic kinds of sexual impropriety. The blatant, now relatively uncontroversial kind involves a quid pro quo: sleep with me or else. The more subtle type, still arguable in its near-infinite ramifications, concerns "hostile environment." Offensive behavior not yet addressed satisfactorily under the law includes jokes, leers, displays of girlie calendars, and refusing to take "no" for an answer in dating.

In the typical legalese, the EEOC defined sexual harassment as: "unwelcome sexual advances, requests for sexual favors, and other verbal or physical contact or communication of a sexual nature when submission to such conduct is made either explicitly or implicitly a term or condition of an individual's employment; submission to or rejection of such conduct by an individual is used as a basis for employment decisions affecting such individual; or such conduct has the purpose or effect of unreasonably interfering with an individual's work performance, or creating an intimidating, hostile, or offensive work environment." Bringing such language down to earth, one of the nation's major labor unions, the United Auto Workers, spells things out more clearly in a brochure available from its women's department.

Noting that harassment violates Title VII of the Civil Rights Act, the union stresses that represented employees are also protected by the union's constitution, and often by negotiated contract language. All this is meaningless, however, unless the individual takes a stand, and says "no." The UAW also notes that, while most of this undesirable contact is aimed at women, its policies also cover incidents in which men are victims, either of women or of other men.

Examples of nonverbal harassment are also cited. They include certain looks, gestures, leering, ogling, pictures, and cartoons. Physical offensiveness includes touching, pinching, rubbing, or "accidentally" brushing breasts or buttocks. The union advises members that, in addition to saying no, they should tell the offender they do not like what is going on. They should also document times, dates, and locations where harassment occurs, what was said or done to them, and their responses. Looking for other victims, sometimes people who were fired or who quit suddenly, is also advised, as is supporting others facing the problem.

Perhaps even more practical is the common-sense approach taken by Corning, the well-known kitchenware manufacturer. The company recommends that employees consider four questions, according to *The Economist*: Would you do it before your spouse or parents? Would you do it in front of a same-sex colleague? Would you like it reported in the local newspaper? Does it need saying or doing at all?

The courts, meanwhile, have tried to refine their concept of what is allowable. The test first evolved from a "reasonable man" standard to a more restrictive "reasonable person" one. And early last year a federal court in Florida ruled that the standard was what would be offensive in the perception of a reasonable woman.

Earlier, in the 1986 case, *Meritor Savings Bank v. Vinson*, the Supreme Court flagged possible employer liability if a policy on sexual harassment was absent. Many agree, however, that formal statements are not enough; preventative action is needed. Training sessions for both sexes are highly desirable, recognizing that too many people still do not realize that once-common practices are no longer acceptable.

The change impacting both genders today seems to hinge upon different perceptions between the sexes. During and after the Thomas confirmation hearings, countless stories were reported in the press. One consultant told *Business Week*, for example, that "When men look at sexual harassment, they tend to think of touching. Women tend to consider the hostile work environment—her chest being stared at, the sexual jokes." And syndicated columnist Ellen Goodman quoted a political scientist and law professor from the University of Michigan, who sees a related contrast: "Men see the sex first and miss the coercion. Women see the coercion and miss the sex." Regardless of seemingly intractable differences, the professor is not fatalistic about change. He says our justice system is convinced that empathy is possible. People can "get in another's head," given a willingness to do so.

Ignoring one another completely in the workplace, regardless of motivation, is of course unlikely, if not impossible. Such an extreme, however, is far from necessary. Even a degree of wariness can hinder productivity; people sense intuitively when interpersonal tension exists. Ample evidence can be found that such wariness is present already, with the end of the harassment controversy nowhere in sight.

Bewilderment about what is permissible continues to be reported—and what appears in print is undoubtedly only the tip of the iceberg. One manager, for example, told *Business Week* about a female colleague putting her hand lightly on a man's shoulder. Another woman rushed up and said excitedly, "Oh, no, don't do that!" Another woman at a large insurance company told the magazine, "In my office now, if we say something that could be misconstrued as sexist, the guys pop up and say, 'That's sexual harassment.'"

While the Hill-Thomas controversy was at its height, a *Washington Post* editor pointedly asked, "Can we women and men of the work force never again laugh together at the latest off-color joke? Can we not exchange compliments or (discreetly) discuss the physical attributes of passersby in the office halls?" Similarly, as Ellen Goodman reported, one boss greeted his secretary, "Good morning—or is that sexual harassment?" More likely than not, he was only half kidding; the question can be seen as symbolic of a chilled atmosphere.

Perhaps most representative was the observation of an employee of the Union Pacific Railroad shortly after the Thomas hearings. "I have already noticed the difference at work. As a matter of fact, I asked a couple of ladies—they had even noticed the difference. Men are not speaking to them as . . . in the past," he told the Associated Press. He said he thought coworkers of both sexes were made nervous by the harassment issue.

Sex-Saturated Society

Behind the short-run feelings of unease created by greater awareness are at least two broad-scale problems that together offer a meaningful framework. The climate in which workplace harassment occurs is itself an issue. One editorial, which appeared in *The National Catholic Register*, was right on target: "Society cannot have it both ways.

It cannot encourage and subsidize sleaze in art, film, literature, advertising, and television—and then expect to have work atmospheres that are free of sexual harassment. Our entire culture is so saturated and obsessed with sexual imagery that no one should be surprised when that obsession is expressed in the workplace." Individuals can, of course, control their actions; even in a sex-saturated society they do not have to harass coworkers. Still, a valid point is made.

Another wide-ranging aspect of the harassment issue concerns communication generally. Whatever deficiencies exist in an organization are magnified when an emotional issue like sexual behavior surfaces. Intentions are often misinterpreted; it is often hard to tell whether comments are innocent, intended to demean, or somewhere between. Unfortunately, this can also provide a handy rationalization for any who intend to harass. On the other hand, having to watch every word said can be irritating too, especially when no offense is meant. It seems as though the presumption of innocence until proved guilty has been turned on its head. It can be disconcerting.

Being on guard constantly against giving offense sexually inhibits all other communication too. You can never tell when someone might take something the wrong way. The situation can even deteriorate into another us-versus-them confrontation, much like that which exists between some labor unions and management. When total quality management is being stressed widely, such an atmosphere is counterproductive. Output, teamwork, competitiveness, and a pleasant work environment all suffer.

Without denying the problem's seriousness, it is instructive that confusion and wariness can fuse in a superficially humorous way. In one poll, for example, one in seven men responded that they would be offended if they were the object of sexual advances in the workplace; three-quarters of the polled women said so. But three-quarters of the men said they would be flattered.

This discussion should not be interpreted as defending sexual harassment by anyone at any time. The whole situation should, in fact, be a nonissue. For whatever perverse reasons, however, it remains one. Perhaps the bottom line must rest ultimately upon goodwill, once sufficient understanding has been achieved. While biology cannot be ignored, it controls intelligent employees of integrity only in a primitive sense. Those who, in fairness and good conscience, conduct themselves properly, can set the pace by being good examples. Any initial chill can disappear or remain negligible, given goodwill all around.

Feminist Harassment

Barbara Amiel

National Review (4 November 1991). Copyright © 1991.

Did Clarence Thomas tell Anita Hill the size of his penis? When the two of them worked together ten years ago, did he use office time to tell her about his preferences in pornographic films? Would Miss Hill, the youngest of 13 from a dirt-poor black family, ruin the career of Judge Thomas, the prodigal son of another impoverished black family?

These weighty matters were pondered by a Senate committee that includes such stalwarts of the new moral order as Edward Kennedy (Chappaquiddick) and Joseph Biden, the man who plagiarized Neil Kinnock's speech. We will never know whether Judge Thomas or Professor Hill is telling the truth. After watching them give evidence, live and complete on CNN, I defy anyone but the good Lord to say what actually happened between that man and that woman. Which brings me to the core of the matter. Let us assume that every word Professor Hill is saying is true. What on earth does this have to do with Judge Thomas's fitness for the Supreme Court?

As I understand it, feminism notwithstanding, we have not yet made it illegal to discuss sex. Since Professor Hill chose not to complain about the conversations and, indeed, followed Thomas when he changed jobs, it is possible that he did not realize she disliked this sort of chat. If he did what she alleges, we can convict him at worst of bad taste and possibly poor judgment of another person's reactions. Perhaps he is so full of himself that he does not notice the effect of his conversation on others. This may make him a rotten dinner companion, but it has nothing to do with character or fitness for the Supreme Court. What then is this fuss all about?

If we forget the pointless "who is telling the truth" and simply assume Professor Hill is, one can see the real story. Judge Thomas's nomination had infuriated the left-wing lobby. It tried to discredit

him by labeling him an "arch-conservative" because of his reservations about affirmative-action policies and a suspicion that he did not favor abortion on demand. Since Thomas's views in these matters concurred with those of about three-quarters of Americans, the block-Thomas campaign failed. The more conservative he was said to be, the more support he was getting.

At this point, someone on the losing side leaked the FBI report on sexual-harassment charges, hoping it would stop the "conservative" Thomas. What needs to be said very loudly to the left-wing/liberal lobby in America is this: If you want a soulmate on the Supreme Court, do it through the ballot box rather than smear tactics. You have no innate right to a political appointment of your choice without first getting a political victory. If you can elect a President who reflects your views, then, you will be able to have Supreme Court nominees who reflect your views.

One wondered, after the defeat of Communism, where the totalitarian impulse would next emerge. My bet was on the feminist movement or environmentalism, and sure enough we can see it in the kangaroo trial of Clarence Thomas, who had no due process of law to protect him.

There is such a thing as sexual harassment in the workplace. It involves a person demanding sexual favors in return for job security or promotion. That is extortion. But that is a far cry from the charges against Judge Thomas. If he had appealed to Professor Hill's idea of an interesting man, his requests for a date would have been pleasurable, not abominable. His conversation might have been teasing, not revolting. As it was, Professor Hill tolerated the alleged conversations because, she says, they guaranteed her job. If she had been promoted, would the conversations have been okay or totally forgotten? And if an action can be legal when performed by someone I think is attractive and a crime when performed by someone who is unappealing, well, the mote is in thine own eye, isn't it?

I was amused to see an executive of a large U.S. oil company commenting on the Thomas affair with the rueful remark: "Corporate America has had to put up with this, why shouldn't Washington?" In the feminist Salem that the corporate American workplace has become, men and women must relate to one another like humanoids. Take this sequence from a training video depicting the horror of sexual harassment:

Woman (at a photocopying machine): "Sorry, I'll be out of your way in a second."

Man (leaning on counter): "Take your time. I'm enjoying the view."

Who, but disturbed human beings, would see this as sexual harassment? The answer came from a female attorney on CNN. "We must," she said after viewing the video approvingly, "make the response on the reasonable woman's behavioral standard, not the reasonable man's." What she really meant, of course, was that the response of the pathologically neurotic woman has become the standard.

Extreme feminism is now a state religion in America. People are being disentitled to their own sexuality, which, in the case of men, allows them to initiate courtship, make compliments—and the occasional pass. This all goes fundamentally against a free society, but that, one fears, may be part of the feminists' agenda as they rearrange social structures. Meanwhile, about the only relevant argument Professor Hill might have made was that anyone crazy enough to ask her out is not fit to be a Supreme Court Justice.

CASES

Case 9.1: Sex in the Bank Vault

Approximately one year after she began working for Capital City Savings and Loan outside Washington, D.C., Ms. Vinson, a female employee of the S & L, began having sex with her male supervisor, Mr. Taylor. According to Vinson, she submitted to his requests because Taylor suggested that she was obligated to him because he had helped her get her current job. She initially refused his requests but finally consented. They continued their sexual involvement for the next three years, both during work hours and during their off time and in some daring places such as the bank's vault and other hidden storage areas in the bank. She claimed in court that some of those times she had been assaulted or raped but that she continued to have sex with Taylor because failure to do so would have put her job in jeopardy. Taylor denied even having sex with her and claimed that her harassment allegations were her way of getting back at him for other job-related complaints that she had.

The federal district court ruled in Taylor's favor, holding that sexual relations, assuming they had occurred, were voluntary and thus not harassment. In addition, the company was not liable because it did not know that the presumed harassment had taken place. The court of appeals overruled the lower court and ruled that even if sex was voluntary, that had no bearing on whether or not it constituted harassment, since sex could still be a condition of her employment, thus constituting harassment. Further, the court ruled that the employer did not have to have notice of the incidents to be held liable.

Questions for Discussion:

1. Which court do you think made the right decision, the lower court or the court of appeals? Do you think that harassment can occur even when the person consents to sex? Does consent to sex always mean that the person is a willing participant? What else could Vinson have done if she did not want to have sex with Taylor?

2. What responsibility should employers have in creating an environment that discourages sexual harassment? Should they be liable for harassment episodes for which they have not been notified?

Case 9.2: The Swedish Bikini Team

In 1991 Stroh's Brewery in St. Paul, Minnesota, released an ad for its Old Milwaukee beer that featured a group of blond, bikini-clad women who parachuted into a campsite with cases of beer to be served to the men who were camped there. Before the women came into the campsite, the men were sitting around saying, "It doesn't get any better than this," a line from other ads for Old Milwaukee. As the women parachuted into the camp bearing cases of beer, they interrupted the men by saying, "It gets better," and the male fantasy of beautiful, blond, and buxom women serving them beer was portrayed. The ad campaigns were very popular at first, then began to spin out of control when the team was featured in the January 1992 issue of *Playboy* and some of the team participated in a *Playboy*-sponsored 900 number on which they talked with callers in broken Swedish accents in all kinds of sexually suggestive language such as one might expect on 900 numbers. Early in 1992 Stroh's pulled the ad because of the criticism it received.

Some of the critics were female employees of the St. Paul brewery. They filed a sexual harassment lawsuit in November 1991. The employees contended that the ads contributed to sexual harassment at the brewery and further encouraged an already hostile environment in which they worked. The suit was based on a 1986 Supreme Court ruling that sexual harassment occurs when a hostile work environment is created by employees' sexually related actions. The attorney for the women insisted that the ad "produces, encourages and condones the hostile workshop environment." The brewery was defended by the ACLU, who argued that commercial speech that is not obscene or misleading is legal and that a ban on the ads would constitute censorship where no significant harm is occurring. They argued that the First Amendment protects a company's right to speak freely in the marketplace.

In contrast, in March 1994 Coca-Cola released a new ad that became known as "The Diet Coke Break." In it a young, well-sculpted construction worker, at a certain time each day, stripped off his shirt and flexed his rippling muscles as he drank a Diet Coke, prompting the ogling stares of the secretaries in an office a few floors above. When he finished, they returned to work, promising to meet again the next day for their Diet Coke break.[1]

[1]The sources for this case are as follows: "Bikini Team Lawsuit," *Wall Street Journal*, 11 November 1991, B4; Arthur S. Hayes, "Stroh's Case Pits Feminists Against ACLU," *Wall Street Journal*, 14 November 1991, B6; Ronald K. L. Collins, "Bikini Team: Sexism for the Many," *Los Angeles Times*, 20 November 1991, B7; "Stroh Ad Campaign Spins Out of Control," *Wall Street Journal*, 12 December 1991, B6; "No Bikini Team in New Stroh Ads," *New York Times*, 13 February 1992, D10; Robin Abcarian, "Despite Giggles and Leers, It's Sexism Stripped Bare," *Los Angeles Times*, 16 March 1994, E1; Jean Kilbourne, "Gender Bender Ads: Same Old Sexism," *New York Times*, 15 May 1994, C13.

Questions for Discussion:

1. Do you think that Stroh's female employees were justified in bringing a sexual harassment suit against the company? Why or why not?
2. Do you think that the ads contribute to a hostile environment for female employees at the brewery? Is that enough to constitute sexual harassment even if there may be no increase in the occurrences of sexual harassment between individual employees?
3. Do you think a double standard is being used when society objects to the Stroh's ads and accepts the Diet Coke ads? Or does the Diet Coke ad, in its portrayals of the women as secretaries in a pink-collar ghetto, mindlessly lusting after the construction worker, actually reinforce existing gender stereotypes?

Case 9.3: Reading That Is Cause for Alarm?

The Los Angeles County Fire Department, in an effort to make the firehouses comfortable for female employees, instituted a policy in late 1992 that prohibited firefighters from possessing or reading sexually explicit literature while on duty at the firehouse. The rule was challenged by one of the firefighters in the Antelope Valley north of Los Angeles. He argued that his First Amendment rights were violated by the policy. He insisted that there are often long stretches of time between emergency calls and that he had the right to read in private whatever he chose. The county denied his complaint and his case was taken up by the ACLU, who filed a lawsuit on his behalf. The county held that possession of pornographic literature in the workplace produced a hostile work environment for female firefighters, and extended the 1986 Supreme Court ruling in the case of a Florida shipyard, which prohibited employees from displaying pornographic posters in the workplace.[2]

[2]See "Alarming Reading?" *Los Angeles Times*, 18 December 1993, B7; and Tracey Kaplan, "County Fire Dept. Ends Ban on Playboy Magazines," *Los Angeles Times*, 22 September 1994, B3.

Questions for Discussion:

1. Did the county's policy amount to an unjustified invasion of an individual firefighter's right to privacy, or was it an appropriate policy to curb occurrences of sexual harassment and make firehouses a comfortable work environment for female employees?

2. Should employees be prohibited from displaying sexually explicit material in their private work areas? Does that constitute a sexually hostile workplace for female employees? What if the material is posted on the centrally located company bulletin board? Does that constitute sexual harassment of female employees?

COMMENTARY

There is little doubt that society in general and business in particular are becoming justifiably more sensitive about sexual harassment. With such flagrant examples as the 1992 Tailhook scandal (at Tailhook, female navy officers were required to run a humiliating gauntlet in which they were touched and grabbed in various sexually explicit ways) to the more subtle forms of private interoffice interactions with sexual overtones, it is time that companies and other institutions no longer look the other way and pretend that sexual harassment is not occurring. Women are becoming more empowered to say no to colleagues who harass them because their allegations are taken very seriously in the courts and the media. However, in all efforts to rid the workplace of sexual harassment and make it safe for women and men to interact together, companies must follow two principles. The first is to allow the accused due process before any penalties are assessed. The second is to insure that the chilling effect on gender relations is not an unfortunate side effect of taking sexual harassment charges seriously.

Defining sexual harassment is a bit like defining pornography. As one judge in a pornography case put it, "I can't define it, but I know it when I see it." Most people would probably agree with that assessment of sexual harassment—difficult to define, but intuitively obvious when one sees it, or especially when a person experiences it. One of the primary problems in defining it is that women and men tend to perceive it very differently. What may be simply innocent joking and teasing for men may be offensive to women. What may be culturally acceptable ways of interacting for men may actually be threatening for women. This may explain why very few men objected to the "Diet Coke Break" commercial, which portrayed the male construction worker as the object of sexual fantasies for the women working in the offices above the construction site. Many men would be complimented if women looked at them with such desire and fantasy, whereas many women would consider being viewed as such a blatant sex object highly offensive and even threatening, since women are frequently the victims of sexual assault. So one of the primary questions about the definition of sexual harassment is "From whose perspective should harassment be defined?"

Dodds and her colleagues are surely correct in defining sexual harassment according to the behavior, not necessarily the consequences, misuse of power, or intentions by themselves. They are also right to distinguish between sexual harassment and sexual discrimination, since the latter does not necessarily involve the former. They define sexual harassment as "behavior . . . which seeks sexual ends without any concern for the person from whom those ends are sought, and which typically produces an unwanted and unpleasant response in the person who is the object of the behavior." In this definition, they see sexual harassment from the perspective of the victim, typically a woman. While admitting that there may be some cultural variety in what people see as sexual harassment, when the cultural notions clash, the victim's perception should determine what constitutes harassment. Since men and women frequently perceive the definition of sexual harassment differently, this definition implies that the victim's perception should set the standard.

The definition of Dodds and colleagues is a helpful place to begin, but it probably does not go far enough in order to protect women in the workplace. The courts have defined two primary types of sexual harassment. The first is what is called "quid pro quo" harassment, in which sexual favors are demanded in exchange for job security or promotion. Barbara Amiel rightly calls this sexual extortion, and virtually everyone agrees that this constitutes the clearest and most egregious form of sexual harassment. But a second type has also been clarified. When the harassment produces a hostile working environment for the person victimized, that also may be labeled sexual harassment, and in most cases justifiably so. The courts have held that a person who works in such an environment does not have to prove that he or she has been harmed in any way, either physically or emotionally, to establish that sexual harassment has occurred. While acknowledging that this aspect of the definition can be abused, we agree that unwanted sexual attention creates a hostile work environment, particularly but not exclusively for women, and constitutes sexual harassment; it certainly should be stopped. Although we agree with Amiel that some harassment charges are frivolous and amount to feminist harassment of men, her definition of sexual harassment surely does not go far enough. She is probably right in saying that we may never know what actually transpired between Clarence Thomas and Anita Hill, but if Hill's allegations are true, then she can make a good case for sexual harassment. However, her case is substantially undermined by her unwillingness to confront Thomas at the time the allegedly offensive remarks occurred and by her following Thomas when he changed jobs. One wonders about how hostile the work environment was when she willingly continued silently in them, especially after Thomas had changed jobs and she went with him. However, Amiel is wrong when she holds that the man who is "enjoying the view" of his female co-worker at the copy machine is not guilty of harassment. The standard of the reasonable woman when it comes to defining harassment is a sound one;

it keeps the situation from being problematic, as it would be had it been entirely subjective. The reasonable-woman standard is not necessarily the "pathologically neurotic woman" standard that she portrays. She fails to point out that men and women see sexual harassment differently and that what is innocent for men is often offensive to many women.

Of course, if the reasonable-woman standard is used, then women must give fair warning to those who are treading on thin sexual-harassment ice. It is unrealistic to expect men to be mind readers, particularly since the specifics of a reasonable standard are usually not spelled out, nor is it wise for any company's policy to become too specific in defining harassment. When it becomes too specific, a firm runs the risk of being legalistic about sexual harassment—obeying the letter of the law and neglecting its spirit. Thus before any charge of sexual harassment can be taken seriously, the alleged victim must take responsibility for saying no to any behavior that she finds sexually offensive. Once warned, alleged perpetrators are informed and can be held accountable for any similar violations with the same person in the future. The victim who suffers in silence cannot reasonably expect sexual harassment to stop, nor can the person hold any individual or company liable for harassment they have not been made aware of. Of course, many people who do sexually harass women know it even without any warning. They know it is offensive, and frequently that is precisely the reason they engage in such behavior. Still, many co-workers, once warned, not only stop the offensive behavior, but appreciate being told that their behavior was offensive. It is further incumbent on any company that purports to be sensitive to sexual harassment to have an adequate reporting system in place to help empower victims to voice their complaints and warn both the company and the perpetrator.

Thus, in general, sexual harassment is defined as behavior that either demands sexual favors in exchange for favorable treatment on the job or creates a hostile working environment according to a reasonable-woman standard. With this working definition, let's look back at the brief scenarios mentioned in the introduction and try to label them definitely harassment, possibly harassment, and definitely not harassment.

1. *A co-worker asks you repeatedly for dates, all of which you turn down.* In most cases, this is probably a nuisance, but not sexual harassment unless the person doing the asking is in a more powerful position in the company and is connecting the request for a date with some favor on the job. A person who is not in a position of power but repeatedly asks for dates may not be guilty of sexual harassment but simply cannot properly read the signals that the other person is not

interested in a date. He may be somewhat relationally inept, which is bothersome but not illegal or unethical.

2. *Putting your hand on a female co-worker's shoulder for a brief moment during a conversation.* This could possibly be sexual harassment; however, it is appropriate in such an event both to use the reasonable-woman standard and to give a warning before charging sexual harassment. Some people are more tactile in their approach and place great value on an affirming touch. Often touch is merely casual and has no sexual overtones, but some touching is more sensual and therefore is sexual harassment. It would be unfortunate if the emphasis on sexual harassment caused affirming people to be afraid to use touch as an affirming gesture; surely tactile people are more careful about using casual touch than they were a decade ago. The hand on the shoulder for a brief moment is probably not sexual harassment, but if the recipient is uncomfortable with such touching, she is responsible for communicating that to the other person.

3. *Having calendar pinups of scantily clad women on the shop floor's bulletin board.* This is probably sexual harassment, because it could easily contribute to a hostile environment for women working there. Since the pictures are posted in a public area within the shop and not in someone's private work station, the female employees who might be offended constitute a "captive audience" as it is difficult for them to avoid seeing that material. However, it is incumbent on those offended to make a complaint through appropriate channels before going further with any charges of sexual harassment.

4. *Reading soft porn in an out-of-the-way place at work during the lunch hour.* This is not sexual harassment, and the right to read such materials in private on off time is actually protected by the First Amendment. In Case 9.3, the Los Angeles County Fire Department rescinded the prohibition against reading this kind of material in the firehouses because the prohibition violated the individual's right to privacy and his right to read whatever he chose. But if such material is flaunted, exposed to other employees, or left on the table in plain view, then it is no longer purely private. But when this reading is done in private in an out-of-the-way place in the work area, any offended employees can easily avoid seeing the material and are responsible for doing so.

5. *Consenting to sex with a co-worker and having it used against one later.* This could possibly be sexual harassment if the information is used to "blackmail" or slander one of the persons involved. But generally if a person consents to sex, it cannot be called sexual harassment. Although the court ruled in the Vinson case that consent does not necessarily exempt someone from sexual harassment charges, we consider

this to be incorrect. Given the current sensitivity in many companies to sexual harassment, quid pro quo sexual extortion is a dangerous thing. The woman who suffers in silence and submits to sexual relations surely is responsible for voicing a complaint to the one requesting sex and if necessary to others in the appropriate chain of command in the company. People are responsible for saying no to sexual extortion, and the current atmosphere in many companies has empowered employees to do so. People who attempt to "sleep their way to the top" and then, when they do not get there, complain of sexual harassment are guilty of some of the worst abuses of society's increased emphasis on sexual harassment. Further, anyone who consents to sex and later uses the charge of harassment to get back at the person for whatever reason is guilty of similar abuse.

6. *Telling sexual jokes in the presence of women co-workers.* This scenario presumes that men tell most of the sexually suggestive jokes in the workplace, something that is not necessarily the case. In general, although it is in bad taste, it is not sexual harassment unless a particular employee is "targeted" with such jokes. However, if the people involved are a captive audience and cannot walk away, and if they give fair warning about being offended by such conversation, then they may be victims of sexual harassment if it continues.

7. *Slightly suggestive complimentary comments about a woman's appearance.* This is similar to the brief touch on the shoulder mentioned in scenario #2. It is possibly sexual harassment, depending on exactly what is said. The more explicit the compliment, the more likely it is sexual harassment. However, the offended person is responsible for giving fair warning and not expecting the alleged perpetrator to read her mind. If the "compliments" continue after the warning has been issued, then she has grounds for filing a complaint.

8. *Hints that your career would be well served by going out with the boss.* This is clearly a case of quid pro quo sexual extortion and no one should have to tolerate it. In the rare cases in which nothing sexual is expected, and the person is only establishing a better relationship, then it is not harassment. But when unwelcome hints are dropped, especially by the boss, one senses that sexual expectations are attached. This is the most obvious form of sexual harassment.

9. *Looking a co-worker up and down during a conversation.* This may be sexual harassment if the woman finds it offensive and has given fair warning. Most men would likely consider it a compliment and would not find it a problem. One must be careful about this since in meetings or presentations a manager may be observing body language in order to become aware of audience response to what he is saying, or a negotiator may observe the body language of others around the table

in order to gain maximum advantage in negotiations. Many men are not aware that they are looking a woman up and down, and, if the woman finds it offensive, they would appreciate the warning. If they ignore the warning and repeatedly engage in this behavior, then it would likely constitute sexual harassment and should be stopped.

Companies that are trying to take sexual harassment seriously need to balance the concern for harassment with the effect that such concern has on employees. J. H. Foegen is surely correct in his observations about what the emphasis on sexual harassment has done to gender relations. He calls this a "productivity reducing chill in the workplace climate" that has undermined the original intent behind sexual harassment laws. Many men are justifiably nervous about relating to women at work and some men are finding themselves going out of their way to avoid women in the workplace when they can. This is not only unfortunate for gender relations, but it also inhibits productivity and morale. Foegen points out that companies like Corning have issued some helpful general guidelines for avoiding sexual harassment situations by asking four questions—"Would you do it before your spouse or parents? Would you do it in front of another same-sex colleague [we would add to this "a colleague you respect," since some colleagues may actually encourage you in such behavior]? Would you like it reported in the newspaper? Does it need saying or doing at all?" These are very insightful questions that help eliminate harassment by putting responsibility on the one tempted to harass. Companies that are dealing with sexual harassment seriously have an interest in avoiding the chilling effect. One way to help alleviate the chill is to insist on clear, firm, and civil communication among employees when one or more are sexually offended. Both this emphasis on communication and an intolerance of sexual harassment must come from the top, both by example and policy. Foegen also insightfully points out the double standard that exists in a society that sponsors sex saturation in the media and expects the workplace to be free of sexual harassment.

Companies must also balance taking sexual harassment complaints seriously with due process for those charged with harassment. The "fire first and ask questions later" policy is unethical because it deprives employees of their rights to confront their accusers and rebut the charges. It also potentially victimizes innocent employees and empowers people to use sexual harassment charges for other purposes besides stopping sexual harassment. It is unconscionable for people to use false sexual harassment charges to strike back at people with whom they have grievances. To be fair to all concerned, companies must institute a process for insuring that people are not pronounced guilty before the evidence is heard. The tragic side effect of the recent sexual harassment sensitivity is that those unjustly charged or charged prior to fair warning have suffered severe and perhaps irreparable damage to their reputations. When that happens, genuinely innocent people may be victimized. In the workplace, as in the legal system, people should be considered innocent until proven guilty, particularly when the charge is sexual harassment.

TEN

Advertising: Creating Desire or Informing the Public?

In the factory, we make cosmetics, in the store we sell hope.

Charles Revson, quoted by Theodore Levitt
in "The Morality (?) of Advertising"

We buy all the right stuff and yet have no more friends, lovers, excitement, or respect than before.

John Waide, "The Making of Self and World in Advertising"

INTRODUCTION

Advertising is all around us. Experts estimate that by the age of twenty-one, the average American has been exposed to an estimated 1 to 2 million advertising messages.[1] Some of the most effective campaigns grab our attention, elicit laughter, and even become a part of our culture. So powerful are some ads that young children can often be heard singing commercial jingles along with nursery rhymes. And, as if billboards and electronic media ads weren't enough, we are now inundated with commercials while we sit in movie theaters. After slides that promote everything from local businesses to popcorn at the concessionaire are projected onto the screen before the lights dim, previews of two or three upcoming attractions are shown. Once the movie itself finally starts, we are insidiously bombarded with more promotions as companies regularly pay for their products to be used by the actors in the film itself.

The advertising industry is big business. Companies pay advertisers large sums of money with a singular goal in mind: to get you to buy a product or service that you might otherwise neglect. This is the clear aim despite the creativity and unquestionable entertainment value of many ads. By 1988, advertisers were already spending well

[1]Craig N. Smith and John A. Quelch, *Ethics in Marketing* (Boston: Irwin, 1993), 607.

[2]Paul Farhi, "Madison Avenue Adrift in Advertising Doldrums," *San Francisco Chronicle*, 9 May 1989, C5; cited in William Shaw and Vincent Barry, *Moral Issues in Business* (Belmont, Calif.: Wadsworth, 1992), 491.

[3]Richard V. Pierard, "Where America Missed the Way," *Journal of the American Scientific Affiliation* (29 March 1979): 19; cited in Craig M. Gay, *With Liberty and Justice for Whom?* (Grand Rapids: Eerdmans, 1991), 37.

[4]Ronald K. Collins and David M. Skover, "Commerce and Communication," *Texas Law Review* (March 1993): 697–746.

[5]John Kenneth Galbraith, *The New Industrial State*, 2d ed. (Boston: Houghton Mifflin, 1971).

[6]Karen Kaplan, "Suit Charges PC Firms Cheat on Monitor Sizes," *Los Angeles Times*, 29 March 1995, D4.

over a total of $100 billion on all forms of advertising. This amounts to around $5,000 for every person in the country.[2]

With this type of presence, advertising as an industry receives an inordinate amount of criticism, which comes in two main forms. First, in terms of the big picture, advertising as a total enterprise is criticized for its alleged detrimental effects on society. Second, the specific contents of one form of advertising, persuasive, are regularly criticized for misleading and manipulating consumers into product purchases.

With respect to the first criticism, many argue that as a total enterprise, advertising spurs the conspicuous consumption of many unnecessary goods. In doing so, it leads people into an endless cycle of consumerism that keeps them economically and spiritually impoverished.[3] To some, this is not merely shallow but also grossly immoral in view of the standard-of-living inequities in the wealthy West in contrast to other parts of the globe. Viewed in this light, advertising is often attacked as the engine of a system of greed, waste, and materialism. In fact, some pundits argue that the predominance of persuasive commercial communications on airwaves has undermined conditions for a healthy democracy. For example, some legal scholars argue that modern advertising has not only ceased to provide information, it is now also manipulative and actually replaces a "citizenship democracy" with a "consumer democracy."[4]

Economist John Kenneth Galbraith echoes this notion by suggesting in his book *The New Industrial State* that because private enterprise has the ability and the resources to advertise and persuade consumers, far too many of society's financial resources fall into the pursuit of private goods. In turn, since public goods such as public transportation, parks, and schools do not reinforce consumer choices through advertising, they are left neglected and strapped for resources.[5]

While the morality of advertising as a total enterprise is debatable, the specific contents of advertising also comes under regular controversy. Companies are regularly challenged by consumer groups and/or the Federal Trade Commission for engaging in "false and misleading" advertising campaigns that are accused of duping even "reasonable" consumers. For example, case 10.3 discusses computer manufacturers who have been recent targets of a Merced County, California, district attorney's lawsuit for regularly overstating the size of monitors to consumers. The suit alleges that companies overinflate the size of monitors by about 13 to 19 percent on average because vendors count the entire glass area rather than just the size of the image in their ads. The suit also claims that some monitors were up to 33.7 percent smaller than advertised. The State of California may soon bring similar charges.[6] Airlines also find themselves amid controversy for advertising low fares, making such fantastic claims as "50% off" rates. These ads allegedly fool reasonable consumers into believing that the percentage deducted was from the latest price of a fare. Instead, the real prices are often a percentage off of the full fare, so consumers don't save what they believe they will.

Many advertisers are also regularly criticized for gross exaggeration in the use of less misleading but highly ambiguous product claims such as the "best," "finest," "most," "original," and other immeasurable superlatives in their campaigns. Advertising executives respond to these charges by noting that most ads are mere instances of "puffery" or embellishment and not deception because most reasonable consumers do not expect objective information in ads. In fact, as Theodore Levitt argues in his classic article "The Morality (?) of Advertising," consumers want excitement to enliven their otherwise mundane lives. Quoting T. S. Eliot, he notes that "human kind cannot bear very much reality." As such, consumers are after much more that the pure functional utility of particular products and services. A car, for example, is not just a car to a consumer but a symbol of sexuality. And, as he states it, cosmetics "are not cosmetics, but the satisfactions of allurements they promise." Thus, he argues, advertisers are not engaged in duplicity at all, they are merely responding to true consumer wants, which are often latent, but nonetheless real.

In addition to making misleading claims, advertisers fall under constant scrutiny for manipulating consumers through messages that appeal to the subconscious levels of the human psyche. This is perhaps the most serious criticism of advertising. If true, advertising would go beyond the legitimate fulfillment of a need and cross over into the process of "needs creation" and the undermining of consumer autonomy. In Adam Smith's vision of capitalism, the marketplace is filled with "rational" consumers who make free choices to purchase products or services based solely on their needs, the price, and the perceived quality. Thus the legitimate meeting of a healthy need is not morally questionable. Rather than informing buyers in order to equip them to make informed rational choices, however, persuasive advertising is accused of manipulation through the creation of a need where none previously existed. One way advertising is accused of accomplishing this is through the use of sexual persuasion. For example, sex is often used to place a product in the subconscious mind of consumers through association of the product with sexual power and pleasure. This can be readily seen in the number of companies whose products have very little to do with sex, yet employ these themes with regularity. Beer commercials regularly utilize scantily clad women to promote products. Often, mention of the product itself is made only in the last few seconds of the spot. Virginia Slims and other cigarette brands often (ironically) portray their products in the context of healthy social lifestyles.

Consumer persuasion can also be accomplished successfully through psychological appeals to common human insecurities. For example, it appears that the whole fashion industry is based on the exploitation of the common human desire to "fit in." Changing fashions rarely outlast the true life of garments. Every season many useful clothes are tossed away (though not by some of your professors) in the name of keeping up with the latest.

Defenders of advertising disagree that it has the power to undermine human choice as its critics maintain. They argue that most consumers recognize the exaggerated claims made in ads for what they are. Moreover, they argue that persuasive ads do not have the power to overcome free will as critics have suggested. Consumers can and do say no regularly to most ads. Robert Arrington comes to this conclusion in his article "Advertising and Behavior Control" in which he examines the condition of human freedom and the limits of advertising to subvert it.

Breaking the boundaries of the traditional debate over the morality of advertising, John Waide offers an insightful article that disagrees with both Levitt and Arrington. Although he does not take issue with Arrington's assertions about the limits of the power of advertising to coerce, Waide offers a strong critique of "associative" advertising through the lens of the development of character in human life using a virtue-based approach to ethics. Waide refreshingly notes that he is not so much concerned with autonomy and behavior control as he is with what kind of people and the type of world that are made through the creation and proliferation of associative advertising.

READINGS

The Morality (?) of Advertising

Theodore Levitt

Harvard Business Review (July–August 1970): 84–92. Copyright © 1970.

In curbing the excesses of advertising, both business and government must distinguish between embellishment and mendacity.

The present controversy over the regulation of advertising may well result in restrictive legislation of some kind, but it is by no means clear how this should be set up. This article presents a philosophical treatment of the human values of advertising as compared with the values of other "imaginative" disciplines. It is designed to provoke thought about the issues at stake. . . .

***

This year Americans will consume about $20 billion of advertising, and very little of it because we want it. Wherever we turn, advertising will be forcibly thrust on us in an intrusive orgy of abrasive sound and sight, all to induce us to do something we might not ordinarily do, or to induce us to do it differently. This massive and persistent effort crams increasingly more commercial noise into the same, few strained 24 hours of the day. It has provoked a reaction as predictable as it was inevitable: a lot of people want the noise stopped, or at least alleviated.

And they want it cleaned up and corrected. As more and more products have entered the battle for the consumer's fleeting dollar, advertising has increased in boldness and volume. Last year, industry offered the nation's supermarkets about 100 new products a week, equal, on an annualized basis, to the total number already on their shelves. Where so much must be sold so hard, it is not surprising that advertisers have pressed the limits of our credulity and generated complaints about their exaggerations and deceptions.

Only classified ads, the work of rank amateurs, do we presume to contain solid, unembellished fact. We suspect all the rest of systematic and egregious distortion, if not often of outright mendacity.

The attack on advertising comes from all sectors. Indeed, recent studies show that the people most agitated by advertising are precisely those in the higher income brackets whose affluence is generated by the industries that create the ads.[1] While these studies show that only a modest group of people are preoccupied with advertising's constant presence in our lives, they also show that distortion and deception are what bother people most.

This discontent has encouraged Senator Philip Hart and Senator William Proxmire to sponsor consumer-protection and truth-in-advertising legislation. People, they say, want less fluff and more fact about the things they buy. They want description, not distortion, and they want some relief from the constant, grating, vulgar noise.

Legislation seems appropriate because the natural action of competition does not seem to work, or, at least not very well. Competition may ultimately flush out and destroy falsehood and shoddiness, but "ultimately" is too long for the deceived—not just the deceived who are poor, ignorant, and dispossessed, but also all the rest of us who work hard for our money and can seldom judge expertly the truth of conflicting claims about products and services.

The consumer is an amateur, after all; the producer is an expert. In the commercial arena, the consumer is an impotent midget. He is certainly not king. The producer is a powerful giant. It is an uneven match. In this setting, the purifying power of competition helps the consumer very little—especially in the short run, when his money is spent and gone, from the weak hands into the strong hands. Nor does competition among the sellers solve the "noise" problem. The more they compete, the worse the din of advertising.

A Broad Viewpoint Required

Most people spend their money carefully. Understandably, they look out for larcenous attempts to separate them from it. Few men in business will deny the right, perhaps even the wisdom, of people today asking for some restraint on advertising, or at least for more accurate information on the things they buy and for more consumer protection.

Yet, if we speak in the same breath about consumer protection and about advertising's distortions, exaggerations, and deceptions it is easy to confuse two quite separate things—the legitimate purpose of advertising and the abuses to which it may be put. Rather than deny that distortion and exaggeration exist in advertising, in this article I shall argue that embellishment and distortion are among advertising's legitimate and socially desirable purposes; and that illegitimacy in advertising consists only of falsification with larcenous intent. And while it is difficult, as a practical matter, to draw the line between legitimate distortion and essential falsehood, I want to take a long look at the distinction that exists between the two. This I shall say in advance—the distinction is not as simple, obvious, or great as one might think.

The issue of truth versus falsehood, in advertising or in anything else, is complex and fugitive. It must be pursued in a philosophic mood that might seem foreign to the businessman. Yet the issue at base *is* more philosophic than it is pragmatic. Anyone seriously concerned with the moral problems of a commercial society cannot avoid this fact. I hope the reader will bear with me—I believe he will find it helpful, and perhaps even refreshing.

What Is Reality?

What, indeed? Consider poetry. Like advertising, poetry's purpose is to influence an audience; to affect its perceptions and sensibilities; perhaps even to change its mind. Like rhetoric, poetry's intent is to convince and seduce. In the service of that intent, it employs without guilt or fear of criticism all the arcane tools of distortion that the literary mind can devise. Keats does not offer a truthful engineering description of his Grecian urn. He offers, instead, with exquisite attention to the effects of meter, rhyme, allusion, illusion, metaphor, and sound, a lyrical, exaggerated, distorted, and palpably false description. And he is thoroughly applauded for it, as are all other artists, in whatever medium, who do precisely this same thing successfully.

Commerce, it can be said without apology, takes essentially the same liberties with reality and literality as the artist, except that commerce calls its creations advertising, or industrial design, or packaging. As with art, the purpose is to influence the audience by creating illusions, symbols, and implications that promise more than pure functionality. Once, when asked what his company did, Charles Revson of Revlon, Inc. suggested a profound distinction: "In the factory we make cosmetics; in the store we sell hope." He obviously has no illusions. It is not cosmetic chemicals women want, but the seductive charm promised by the alluring symbols with which these chemicals have been surrounded—hence the rich and exotic packages in which they are sold, and the suggestive advertising with which they are promoted.

Commerce usually embellishes its products thrice: first, it designs the product to be pleasing to the eye, to suggest reliability, and so forth; second, it packages the product as attractively as it feasibly can; and then it advertises this attractive package with inviting pictures, slogans, descriptions, songs, and so on. The package and design are as important as the advertising.

The Grecian vessel, for example, was used to carry liquids, but that function does not explain why the potter decorated it with graceful lines and elegant drawings in black and red. A woman's compact carries refined talc, but this does not explain why manufacturers try to make these boxes into works of decorative art.

Neither the poet nor the ad man celebrates the literal functionality of what he produces. Instead, each celebrates a deep and complex emotion which he symbolizes by creative embellishment—a content which cannot be captured by literal description alone. Communication, through advertising or through poetry or any other medium, is a creative conceptualization that implies a vicarious experience through a language of symbolic substitutes. Communication can never be the real thing it talks about. Therefore, all communication is in some inevitable fashion a departure from reality.

Everything Is Changed . . .

Poets, novelists, playwrights, composers, and fashion designers have one thing more in common. They all deal in symbolic communication. None is satisfied with nature in the raw, as it was on the day of creation. None is satisfied to tell it exactly "like it is" to the naked eye, as do the classified ads. It is the purpose of all art to alter nature's surface reality, to reshape, to embellish, and to augment what nature has so crudely fashioned, and then to present it to the same applauding humanity that so eagerly buys Revson's exotically advertised cosmetics.

Few, if any, of us accept the natural state in which God created us. We scrupulously select our clothes to suit a multiplicity of simultaneous purposes, not only for warmth, but manifestly for such other purposes as propriety, status, and seduction. Women modify, embellish, and amplify themselves with colored paste for the lips and powders and lotions for the face; men as well as women use devices to take hair off the face and others to put it on the head. Like the inhabitants of isolated African regions, where not a single whiff of advertising has ever intruded, we all encrust ourselves with rings, pendants, bracelets, neckties, clips, chains, and snaps.

Man lives neither in sackcloth nor in sod huts—although these are not notably inferior to tight clothes and overheated dwellings in congested and polluted cities. Everywhere man rejects nature's uneven blessings. He molds and repackages to his own civilizing specifications an otherwise, crude, drab, and generally oppressive reality. He does it so that life may be made for the moment more tolerable than God evidently designed it to be. As T. S. Eliot once remarked, "Human kind cannot bear very much reality."

. . . Into Something Rich and Strange

No line of life is exempt. All the popes of history have countenanced the costly architecture of St. Peter's Basilica and its extravagant interior decoration. All around the globe, nothing typifies man's materialism so much as the temples in which he preaches asceticism. Men of the cloth have not been persuaded that the poetic self-denial of Christ or Buddha—both men of sackcloth and sandals—is enough to inspire, elevate, and hold their flocks together. To amplify the temple in men's eyes, they have, very realistically, systematically sanctioned the embellishment of the houses of the gods with the same kind of luxurious design and expensive decoration that Detroit puts into a Cadillac.

One does not need a doctorate in social anthropology to see that the purposeful transmutation of nature's primeval state occupies all people in all cultures and all societies at all stages of development. Everybody everywhere wants to modify, transform, embellish, enrich, and reconstruct the world around him—to introduce into an otherwise harsh or bland existence some sort of purposeful and distorting alleviation. Civilization is man's attempt to transcend his ancient animality; and this includes both art and advertising.

. . . And More Than "Real"

But civilized man will undoubtedly deny that either the innovative artist or the *grande dame* with *chic* "distorts reality." Instead, he will say that artist and woman merely embellish, enhance, and illuminate. To be sure, he will mean something quite different by these three terms when he applies them to fine art, on the one hand, and to more secular efforts, on the other.

But this distinction is little more than an affectation. As man has civilized himself and developed his sensibilities, he has invented a great variety of subtle distinctions between things that are objectively indistinct. Let us take a closer look at the difference between man's "sacred" distortions and his "secular" ones.

The man of sensibility will probably canonize the artist's deeds as superior creations by ascribing to them an almost cosmic virtue and significance. As a cultivated individual, he will almost certainly refuse to recognize any constructive, cosmic virtues in the productions of the advertisers, and he is likely to admit the charge that advertising uniformly deceives us by analogous techniques. But how "sensible" is he?

And by Similar Means . . .

Let us assume for the moment that there is no objective, operational difference between the embellishments and distortions of the artist and those of the ad man—that both men are more concerned with creating images and feelings than with rendering objective, representational, and informational descriptions. The greater virtue of the artist's work must then derive from some subjective element. What is it?

It will be said that art has a higher value for man because it has a higher purpose. True, the artist is interested in philosophic truth or wisdom, and the ad man in selling his goods and services. Michelangelo, when he designed the Sistine chapel ceiling, had some concern with the inspirational elevation of man's spirit, whereas Edward Levy, who designs cosmetics packages, is interested primarily in creating images to help separate the unwary consumer from his loose change.

But this explanation of the differences between the value of art and the value of advertising is not helpful at all. For is the presence of a "higher" purpose all that redeeming?

Perhaps not; perhaps the reverse is closer to the truth. While the ad man and designer seek only to convert the audience to their commercial custom, Michelangelo sought to convert its soul. Which is the greater blasphemy? Who commits the greater affront to life—he who dabbles with man's erotic appetites, or he who meddles with man's soul? Which act is the easier to judge and justify?

. . . For Different Ends

How much sense does it really make to distinguish between similar means on the grounds that the ends to which they are directed are different—

"good" for art and "not so good" for advertising? The distinction produces zero progress in the argument at hand. How willing are we to employ the involuted ethics whereby the ends justify the means?

Apparently, on this subject, lots of people are very willing indeed. The business executive seems to share with the minister, the painter, and the poet the doctrine that the ends justify the means. The difference is that the businessman is justifying the very commercial ends that his critics oppose. While his critics justify the embellishments of art and literature for what these do for man's spirit, the businessman justifies the embellishment of industrial design and advertising for what they do for man's purse.

Taxing the imagination to the limit, the businessman spins casuistic webs of elaborate transparency to the self-righteous effect that promotion and advertising are socially benign because they expand the economy, create jobs, and raise living standards. Technically, he will always be free to argue, and he *will* argue, that his ends become the means to the ends of the musician, poet, painter, and minister. The argument which justifies means in terms of ends is obviously not without its subtleties and intricacies.

The executive and the artist are equally tempted to identify and articulate a higher rationale for their work than their work itself. But only in the improved human consequences of their efforts do they find vindication. The aesthete's ringing declaration of "art for art's sake," with all its self-conscious affirmation of selflessness, sound shallow in the end, even to himself; for, finally, every communication addresses itself to an audience. Thus art is very understandably in constant need of justification by the evidence of its beneficial and divinely approved effect on its audience.

The Audience's Demands

This compulsion to rationalize even art is a highly instructive fact. It tells one a great deal about art's purposes and the purposes of all other communication. As I have said, the poet and the artist each seek in some special way to produce an emotion or assert a truth not otherwise apparent. But it is only in communion with their audiences that the effectiveness of their efforts can be tested and truth revealed. It may be academic whether a tree falling in the forest makes a noise. It is *not* academic whether a sonnet or a painting has merit. Only an audience can decide that.

The creative person can justify his work only in terms of another person's response to it. Ezra Pound, to be sure, thought that "... in the [greatest] works the live part is the part which the artist has put there to please himself, and the dead part is the part he has put there ... because he thinks he *ought* to—i.e., either to get or keep an audience." This is certainly consistent with our notions of Pound as perhaps the purest of twentieth-century advocates of art for art's sake.

But if we review the record of his life, we find that Pound spent the greater part of his energies seeking suitable places for deserving poets to publish. Why? Because art has little merit standing alone in unseen and unheard isolation. Merit is not inherent in art. It is conferred by an audience.

The same is true of advertising: if it fails to persuade the audience that the product will fulfill the function the audience expects, the advertising has no merit.

Where have we arrived? Only at some common characteristics of art and advertising. Both are rhetorical, and both literally false; both expound an emotional reality deeper than the "real"; both pretend to "higher" purposes, although different ones; and the excellence of each is judged by its effect on its audience—its persuasiveness, in short. I do not mean to imply that the two are fundamentally the same, but rather that they both represent a pervasive, and I believe *universal*, characteristic of human nature—the human audience *demands* symbolic interpretation in everything it sees and knows. If it doesn't get it, it will return a verdict of "no interest."

To get a clearer idea of the relation between the symbols of advertising and the products they glorify, something more must be said about the fiat the consumer gives to industry to "distort" its messages.

Symbol and Substance

As we have seen, man seeks to transcend nature in the raw everywhere. Everywhere, and at all times, he has been attracted by the poetic imagery of some sort of art, literature, music, and mysticism. He obviously wants and needs the promises, the imagery, and the symbols of the poet and the priest. He refuses to live a life of primitive barbarism or sterile functionalism.

Consider a sardine can filled with scented powder. Even if the U.S. Bureau of Standards were to certify that the contents of this package are identical with the product sold in a beautiful paisley-printed container, it would not sell. The Boston matron, for example, who has built herself a deserved reputation for pinching every penny until it hurts, would unhesitatingly turn it down. While she may deny it, in self-assured and neatly cadenced accents, she obviously desires and needs the promises, imagery, and symbols produced by hyperbolic advertisements, elaborate packages, and fetching fashions.

The need for embellishment is not confined to personal appearance. A few years ago, an electronics laboratory offered a $700 testing device for sale. The company ordered two different front panels to be designed, one by the engineers who developed the equipment and one by professional industrial designers. When the two models were shown to a sample of laboratory directors with Ph.D.'s, the professional design attracted twice the purchase intentions that the engineer's design did. Obviously, the laboratory director who has been baptized into science at M.I.T. is quite as responsive to the blandishments of packaging as the Boston matron.

And, obviously, both these customers define the products they buy in much more sophisticated terms than the engineer in the factory. For a woman, dusting powder in a sardine can is not the same product as the identical dusting powder in an exotic paisley package. For the laboratory director, the test equipment behind an engineer-designed panel just isn't as "good" as the identical equipment in a box designed with finesse.

Form Follows the Ideal Function

The consumer refuses to settle for pure operating functionality. "Form follows function" is a resoundingly vacuous cliché, which like all clichés, depends for its memorability more on its alliteration and brevity than on its wisdom. If it has any truth, it is only in the elastic sense that function extends beyond strict mechanical use into the domain of imagination. We do not choose to buy a particular product; we choose to buy the functional expectations that we attach to it, and we buy these expectations as "tools" to help us solve a problem of life.

Under normal circumstances, furthermore, we must judge a product's "nonmechanical" utilities before we actually buy it. It is rare that we choose an object after we have experienced it; nearly always we must make the choice before the fact. We choose on the basis of promises, not experiences.

Whatever symbols convey and *sustain* these promises in our minds are therefore truly functional. The promises and images which imaginative ads and sculptured packages induce in us are as much the product as the physical materials themselves. To put this another way, these ads and packagings describe the product's fullness for us: in our minds, the product becomes a complex abstraction which is, as Immanuel Kant might have said, the conception of a perfection which has not yet been experienced.

But all promises and images, almost by their very nature, exceed their capacity to live up to themselves. As every eager lover has ever known, the consummation seldom equals the promises which produced the chase. To forestall and suppress the visceral expectation of disappointment that life has taught us must inevitably come, we use art, architecture, literature, and the rest, and advertising as well, to shield ourselves, in advance of experience, from the stark and plain reality in which we are fated to live. I agree that we wish for unobtainable unrealities, "dream castles." But why promise ourselves reality, which we already possess? What we want is what we do *not* possess!

Everyone in the world is trying in his special personal fashion to solve a primal problem of life—the problem of rising above his own negligibility, of escaping from nature's confining, hostile, and unpredictable reality, of finding significance, security, and comfort in the things he must do to survive. Many of the so-called distortions of advertising, product design, and packaging may be viewed as a paradigm of the many responses that man makes to the conditions of survival in the environment. Without distortion, embellishment, and elaboration, life would be drab, dull, anguished, and at its existential worst.

Symbolism Useful and Necessary

Without symbolism, furthermore, life would be even more confusing and anxiety-ridden than it is *with* it. The foot soldier must be able to recognize the general, good or bad, because the general is clothed with power. A general without his stars and suite of aides-de-camp to set him apart from the privates would suffer authority and credibility as much as perfume packaged by Dracula or a computer designed by Rube Goldberg. Any ordinary soldier or civilian who has ever had the uncommon experience of beginning in the same shower with a general can testify from the visible unease of the latter how much clothes "make the man."

Similarly, verbal symbols help to make the product—they help us deal with the uncertainties of daily life. "You can be sure . . . if it's Westinghouse" is a decision rule as useful to the man buying a turbine generator as to the man buying an electric shaver. To label all the devices and embellishments companies employ to reassure the prospective customer about a product's quality with the pejorative term "gimmick," as critics tend to do, is simply silly. Worse, it denies, against massive evidence, man's honest needs and values. If religion must be architectured, packaged, lyricized, and musicized to attract and hold its audience, and if sex must be perfumed, powdered, sprayed, and shaped in order to command attention, it is ridiculous to deny the legitimacy of more modest, and similar, embellishments to the world of commerce.

But still, the critics may say, commercial communications tend to be aggressively deceptive. Perhaps, and perhaps not. The issue at stake here is more complex than the outraged critic believes. Man wants and needs the elevation of the spirit produced by attractive surroundings, by handsome packages, and by imaginative promises. He needs the assurances projected by well-known brand names, and the reliability suggested by salesmen who have been taught to dress by Oleg Cassini and to speak by Dale Carnegie. Of course, there are blatant, tasteless, and willfully deceiving salesmen and advertisers, just as there are blatant, tasteless, and willfully deceiving artists, preachers, and even professors. But, before talking blithely about deception, it is helpful to make a distinction between things and descriptions of things.

The Question of Deceit

Poetic descriptions of things make no pretense of being the things themselves. Nor do advertisements, even by the most elastic standards. Advertisements are the symbols of man's aspirations. They are not the real things, nor are they intended to be, nor are they accepted as such by the public. A study some years ago by the Center for Research in Marketing, Inc. concluded that deep down inside the consumer understands this perfectly well and has the attitude that an advertisement is an ad, not a factual news story.

Even Professor Galbraith grants the point when he says that "... because modern man is exposed to a large volume of information of varying degrees of unreliability ... he establishes a system of discounts which he applies to various sources almost without thought.... The discount becomes nearly total for all forms of advertising. The merest child watching television dismisses the health and status-giving claims of a breakfast cereal as 'a commercial.'"[2]

This is not to say, of course, that Galbraith also discounts advertising's effectiveness. Quite the opposite: "Failure to win belief does not impair the effectiveness of the management of demand for consumer products. Management involves the creation of a compelling image of the product in the mind of the consumer. To this he responds more or less automatically under circumstances where the purchase does not merit a great deal of thought. For building this image, palpable fantasy may be more valuable than circumstantial evidence."[3]

Linguists and other communications specialists will agree with the conclusion of the Center for Research in Marketing that "advertising is a symbol system existing in a world of symbols. Its reality depends upon the fact that it is a symbol ...

the content of an ad can never be real, it can only say something about reality, or create a relationship between itself and an individual which has an effect on the reality life of an individual."

Consumer, Know Thyself!

Consumption is man's most constant activity. It is well that he understands himself as a consumer.

The object of consumption is to solve a problem. Even consumption that is viewed as the creation of an opportunity—like going to medical school or taking a singles-only Caribbean tour—has as its purpose the solving of a problem. At a minimum, the medical student seeks to solve the problem of how to lead a relevant and comfortable life, and the lady on the tour seeks to solve the problem of spinsterhood.

The "purpose" of the product is not what the engineer explicitly says it is, but what the consumer implicitly demands that it shall be. Thus the consumer consumes not things, but expected benefits—not cosmetics, but the satisfactions of the allurements they promise; not quarter-inch drills, but quarter-inch holes; not stock in companies, but capital gains; not numerically controlled milling machines, but trouble-free and accurately smooth metal parts; not low-cal whipped cream, but self-rewarding indulgence combined with sophisticated convenience.

The significance of these distinctions is anything but trivial. Nobody knows this better, for example, than the creators of automobile ads. It is not the generic virtues that they tout, but more likely the car's capacity to enhance its user's status and his access to female prey.

Whether we are aware of it or not, we in effect expect and demand that advertising create these symbols for us to show us what life *might* be, to bring the possibilities that we cannot see before our eyes and screen out the stark reality in which we must live. We insist, as Gilbert put it, that there be added a "touch of artistic verisimilitude to an otherwise bald and unconvincing narrative."

Understanding the Difference

In a world where so many things are either commonplace or standardized, it makes no sense to refer to the rest as false, fraudulent, frivolous, or immaterial. The world works according to the aspirations and needs of its actors, not according to the arcane or moralizing logic of detached critics who pine for another age—an age which, in any case, seems different from today's largely because its observers are no longer children shielded by protective parents from life's implacable harshness.

To understand this is not to condone much of the vulgarity, purposeful duplicity, and scheming half-truths we see in advertising, promotion, packaging, and product design. But before we condemn, it is well to understand the difference between embellishment and duplicity and how extraordinarily uncommon the latter is in our times. The noisy visibility of promotion in our intensely communicating times need not be thoughtlessly equated with malevolence.

Thus the issue is not the prevention of distortion. It is, in the end, to know what kinds of distortions we actually want so that each of our lives, is, without apology, duplicity, or rancor, made bearable. This does not mean we must accept out of hand all the commercial propaganda to which we are each day so constantly exposed, or that we must accept out of hand the equation that effluence is the price of affluence, or the simple notion that business cannot and government should not try to alter and improve the position of the consumer vis-à-vis the producer. It takes a special kind of perversity to continue any longer our shameful failure to mount vigorous, meaningful programs to protect the consumer, to standardize product grades, labels, and packages, to improve the consumer's information-getting process, and to mitigate the vulgarity and oppressiveness that is in so much of our advertising.

But the consumer suffers from an old dilemma. He wants "truth," but he also wants and needs the alleviating imagery and tantalizing promises of the advertiser and designer.

Business is caught in the middle. There is hardly a company that would not go down in ruin if it refused to provide fluff, because nobody will buy pure functionality. Yet, if it uses too much fluff and little else, business invites possibly ruinous legislation. The problem therefore is to find a middle way. and in this search, business can do a great deal more than it has been either accustomed or willing to do:

- It can exert pressure to make sure that no single industry "finds reasons" why it should be exempt from legislative restrictions that are reasonable and popular.
- It can work constructively with government to develop reasonable standards and effective sanctions that will assure a more amenable commercial environment.
- It can support legislation to provide the consumer with the information he needs to make easy comparison between products, packages, and prices.
- It can support and help draft improved legislation on quality stabilization.
- It can support legislation that gives consumers easy access to strong legal remedies where justified. It can support programs to make local legal aid easily available, especially to the poor and undereducated who know so little about their rights and how to assert them.
- Finally, it can support efforts to moderate and clean up the advertising noise that dulls our senses and assaults our sensibilities.

It will not be the end of the world or of capitalism for business to sacrifice a few commercial freedoms so that we may more easily enjoy our own humanity. Business can and should, for its own good, work energetically to achieve this end. But it is also well to remember the limits of what is possible. Paradise was not a free-goods society. The forbidden fruit was gotten at a price.

Notes

[1] See Raymond A. Bauer and Stephen A. Greyser, *Advertising in America: The Consumer View* (Boston, Division of Research, Harvard Business School, 1968), see also Gary A. Steiner, *The People Look at Television* (New York, Alfred A. Knopf, Inc., 1963).

[2] John Kenneth Galbraith, *The New Industrial State* (Boston, Houghton Mifflin Company, 1967), 325–26.
[3] Ibid., 326.

The Making of Self and World in Advertising

John Waide

Journal of Business Ethics 6 (1987), 73–79. Copyright © 1987 D. Reidel Publishing Co.

In this paper I will criticize a common practice I call associative advertising. The fault in associative advertising is not that it is deceptive or that it violates the autonomy of its audience—on this point I find Arrington's arguments persuasive.[1] Instead, I will argue against associative advertising by examining the virtues and vices at stake. In so doing, I will offer an alternative to Arrington's exclusive concern with autonomy and behavior control.

Associative advertising is a technique that involves all of the following:

1. The advertiser wants people[2] to buy (or buy more of) a product. This objective is largely independent of any sincere desire to improve or enrich the lives of the people in the target market.

2. In order to increase sales, the advertiser identifies some (usually) deep-seated non-market good for which the people in the target market feel a strong desire. By "non-market good" I mean something which cannot, strictly speaking, be bought or sold in a marketplace. Typical non-market goods are friendship,

acceptance and esteem of others. In a more extended sense we may regard excitement (usually sexual) and power as non-market goods since advertising in the U.S.A. usually uses versions of these that cannot be bought and sold. For example, "sex appeal" as the theme of an advertising campaign is not the market-good of prostitution, but the non-market good of sexual attractiveness and acceptability.

3. In most cases, the marketed product bears only the most tenuous (if any) relation to the non-market good with which it is associated in the advertising campaign. For example, soft drinks cannot give one friends, sex, or excitement.

4. Through advertising, the marketed product is associated with the non-market desire it cannot possibly satisfy. If possible, the desire for the non-market good is intensified by calling into question one's acceptability. For example, mouthwash, toothpaste, deodorant, and feminine hygiene ads are concocted to make us worry that we stink.

5. Most of us have enough insight to see both (a) that no particular toothpaste can make us sexy and (b) that wanting to be considered sexy is at least part of our motive for buying that toothpaste. Since we can (though, admittedly, we often do not bother to) see clearly what the appeal of the ad is, we are usually not lacking in relevant information or deceived in any usual sense.

6. In some cases, the product actually gives at least partial satisfaction to the non-market desire—but only because of advertising.[3] For example, mouthwash has little prolonged effect on stinking breath, but it helps to reduce the intense anxieties reinforced by mouthwash commercials on television because we at least feel that we are doing the proper thing. In the most effective cases of associative advertising, people begin to talk like ad copy. We begin to sneer at those who own the wrong things. We all become enforcers for the advertisers. In general, if the advertising images are effective enough and reach enough people, even preposterous marketing claims can become at least partially self-fulfilling.

Most of us are easily able to recognize associative advertising as morally problematic when the consequences are clear, extreme, and our own desires and purchasing habits are not at stake. For example, the marketing methods Nestlé used in Africa involved associative advertising. Briefly, Nestlé identified a large market for its infant formula—without concern for the well-being of the prospective consumers. In order to induce poor women to buy formula rather than breastfeed, Nestlé selected non-market goods on which to base its campaigns—love for one's child and a desire to be acceptable by being modern. These appeals were effective (much as they are in advertising for children's clothing, toys, and computers in the U.S.A.). Through billboards and radio advertising, Nestlé identified parental love with formula feeding and suggested that formula is the modern way to feed a baby. Reports indicate that in some cases mothers of dead babies placed cans of formula on their graves to show that the parents cared enough to do the very best they could for their children, even though we know the formula may have been a contributing cause of death.[4]

One might be tempted to believe that associative advertising is an objectionable technique only when used on the very poorest, most powerless and ignorant people and that it is the poverty, powerlessness, and ignorance which are at fault. An extreme example like the Nestlé case, one might protest, surely doesn't tell us much about more ordinary associative advertising in the industrialized western nations. The issues will become clearer if we look at the conceptions of virtue and vice at stake.

Dewey says "the thing actually at stake in any serious deliberation is not a difference of quantity [as utilitarianism would have us believe], but what kind of person one is to become, what sort of self is in the making, what kind of a world is making."[5] Similarly, I would like to ask who we become as we use or are used by associative advertising. This will not be a decisive argument. I have not found clear, compelling, objective principles—only considerations I find persuasive and which I expect many others to find similarly persuasive. I will briefly examine how associative advertising affects (a) the people who plan and execute marketing strategies and (b) the people who are exposed to the campaign.

(a) Many advertisers[6] come to think clearly and skillfully about how to sell a marketable item by associating it with a non-market good which people in the target market desire. An important ingredient in this process is lack of concern for the well-being of the people who will be influenced by the campaign. Lloyd Slater, a consultant who discussed the infant formula controversy with people in both the research and development and marketing divisions of Nestlé, says that the R & D people had made sure that the formula was nutritionally sound but were troubled or even disgusted by what the marketing department was doing. In contrast, Slater reports that the marketing people simply did not care and that "those guys aren't even human" in their reactions.[7] This evidence is only anecdotal and it concerns an admittedly extreme case. Still, I believe that the effects of associative advertising[8] would most likely be the same but less pronounced in more ordinary cases. Furthermore, it is quite common for advertisers in the U.S.A. to concentrate their attention on selling something that is harmful to many people, e.g., candy that rots our teeth, and cigarettes. In general, influencing people without concern for their well-being is likely to reduce one's sensitivity to the moral motive of concern for the well-being of others. Compassion, concern, and sympathy for others, it seems to me, are clearly central to moral virtue.[9] Associative advertising must surely undermine this sensitivity in much of the advertising industry. It is, therefore, *prima facie* morally objectionable.

Associative advertising tends to desensitize its practitioners to the compassion, concern, and sympathy for others that are central to moral virtue and it encourages its audience to neglect the cultivation of non-market virtues.

(b) Targets of associative advertising (which include people in the advertising industry) are also made worse by exposure to effective advertising of this kind. The harm done is of two kinds:

(1) We often find that we are buying more but enjoying it less. It isn't only that products fail to live up to specific claims about service-life or effectiveness. More often, the motives ("reasons" would perhaps not be the right word here) for our purchases consistently lead to disappointment. We buy all the right stuff and yet have no more friends, lovers, excitement or respect than before. Instead, we have full closets and empty pocket books. Associative advertising, though not the sole cause, contributes to these results.

(2) Associate advertising may be less effective as an advertising technique to sell particular products than it is as an ideology[10] in our culture. Within the advertising which washes over us daily we can see a number of common themes, but the most important may be "You are what you own."[11] The quibbles over which beer, soft drink, or auto

to buy are less important than the over-all message. Each product contributes its few minutes each day, but we are bombarded for hours with the message that friends, lovers, acceptance, excitement, and power are to be gained by purchases in the market, not by developing personal relationships, virtues, and skills. Our energy is channeled into careers so that we will have enough money to *be* someone by buying the right stuff in a market. The not very surprising result is that we neglect non-market methods of satisfying our non-market desires. Those non-market methods call for wisdom, compassion, skill, and a variety of virtues which cannot be bought. It seems, therefore, that insofar as associative advertising encourages us to neglect the non-market cultivation of our virtues and to substitute market goods instead, we become worse and, quite likely, less happy persons.

To sum up the argument so far, associative advertising tends to desensitize its practitioners to the compassion, concern, and sympathy for others that are central to moral virtue and it encourages its audience to neglect the cultivation of non-market virtues. There are at least five important objections that might be offered against my thesis that associative advertising is morally objectionable.

First, one could argue that since each of us is (or can easily be if we want to be) aware of what is going on in associative advertising, we must want to participate and find it objectionable. Accordingly, the argument goes, associative advertising is not a violation of individual autonomy. In order to reply to this objection I must separate issues.

(a) Autonomy is not the main, and certainly not the only, issue here. It may be that I can, through diligent self-examination neutralize much of the power of associative advertising. Since I can resist, one might argue that I am responsible for the results—*caveat emptor* with a new twist.[12] If one's methodology in ethics is concerned about people and not merely their autonomy, then the fact that most people are theoretically capable of resistance will be less important than the fact that most are presently unable to resist.

(b) What is more, the ideology of acquisitiveness which is cultivated by associative advertising probably undermines the intellectual and emotional virtues of reflectiveness and self-awareness which would better enable us to neutralize the harmful effects of associative advertising. I do not know of specific evidence to cite in support of this claim, but it seems to me to be confirmed in the ordinary experience of those who, despite associative advertising, manage to reflect on what they are exposed to.

(c) Finally, sneer group pressure often makes other people into enforcers so that there are penalties for not going along with the popular currents induced by advertising. We are often compelled even by our associates to be enthusiastic participants in the consumer culture. Arrington omits consideration of sneer group pressure as a form of compulsion which can be (though it is not always) induced by associative advertising.

So far my answer to the first objection is incomplete. I still owe some account of why more people do not complain about associative advertising. This will become clearer as I consider a second objection.

Second, one could insist that even if the non-market desires are not satisfied completely, they must be satisfied for the most part or we would stop falling for associative advertising. This objection seems to me to make three main errors:

(a) Although we have a kind of immediate access to our own motives and are generally able to see what motives an advertising campaign uses, most of us lack even the simple framework provided by my analysis of associative advertising. Even one who sees that a particular ad campaign is aimed at a particular non-market desire may not see how all the ads put together constitute a cultural bombardment with an ideology of acquisitiveness—you are what you own. Without some framework such as this, one has nothing to blame. It is not easy to gain self-reflective insight, much less cultural insight.

(b) Our attempts to gain insight are opposed by associative advertising which always has an answer for our dissatisfactions—buy more or newer or different things. If I find myself feeling let down after a purchase, many voices will tell me that the solution is to buy other things too (or that

I have just bought the wrong thing). With all of this advertising proposing one kind of answer for our dissatisfactions, it is scarcely surprising that we do not usually become aware of alternatives.

(c) Finally, constant exposure to associate advertising changes[13] us so that we come to feel acceptable as persons when and only when we own the acceptable, fashionable things. By this point, our characters and conceptions of virtue already largely reflect the result of advertising and we are unlikely to complain or rebel.

Third, and perhaps most pungent of the objections, one might claim that by associating mundane marketable items with deeply rooted non-market desires, our everyday lives are invested with new and greater meaning. Charles Revson of Revlon once said that "In the factory we make cosmetics: in the store we sell hope."[14] Theodore Levitt, in his passionate defense of associative advertising, contends that[15]

> Everyone in the world is trying in his [or her] special personal fashion to solve a primal problem of life—the problem of rising above his [or her] own negligibility, of escaping from nature's confining, hostile, and unpredictable reality, of finding significance, security, and comfort in the things he [or she] must do to survive.

Levitt adds, "Without distortion, embellishment, and elaboration, life would be drab, dull, anguished, and at its existential worst."[16] This objection is based on two assumptions so shocking that his conclusion almost seems sensible.

(a) Without associative advertising would our lives lack significance? Would we be miserable in our drab, dull, anguished lives? Of course not. People have always had ideals, fantasies, heroes, and dreams. We have always told stories that captured our aspirations and fears. The very suggestion that we require advertising to bring a magical aura to our shabby, humdrum lives is not only insulting but false.

(b) Associative advertising is crafted not in order to enrich our daily lives but in order to enrich the clients and does not have the interests of its audience at heart. Still, this issue of intent, though troubling, is only part of the problem. Neither is the main problem that associative advertising images somehow distort reality. Any work of art also is, in an important sense, a dissembling or distortion. The central question instead is whether the specific appeals and images, techniques and products, enhance people's lives.[17]

A theory of what enhances a life must be at least implicit in any discussion of the morality of associative advertising. Levitt appears to assume that in a satisfying life one has many satisfied desires—*which* desires is not important.[18] To propose and defend an alternative to his view is beyond the scope of this paper. My claim is more modest—that it is not enough to ask whether desires are satisfied. We should also ask what kinds of lives are sustained, made possible, or fostered by having the newly synthesized desires. What kind of self and world are in the making, Dewey would have us ask. This self and world are always in the making. I am not arguing that there is some natural, good self which advertising changes and contaminates. It may be that not only advertising, but also art, religion, and education in general, always synthesize new desires.[19] In each case, we should look at the lives. How to judge the value of these lives and the various conceptions of virtue they will embody is another question. It will be enough for now to see that it is an important question.

> **There is another legitimate concern besides that of autonomy and behavior control—whether the advertising will tend to influence us to become worse persons.**

Now it may be possible to see why I began by saying that I would suggest an alternative to the usual focus on autonomy and behavior control.[20] Arrington's defense of advertising (including, as near as I can tell, what I call associative advertising) seems to assume that we have no standard to which we can appeal to judge whether a desire enhances a life and, consequently, that our only legitimate concerns are whether an advertisement violates the autonomy of its audience by deceiving them or controlling their behavior. I want to suggest that there is another legitimate concern—whether the advertising will tend to influence us to become worse persons.[21]

Fourth, even one who is sympathetic with much of the above might object that associative advertising is necessary to an industrial society such as ours. Economists since Galbraith[22] have argued about whether, without modern advertising of the sort I have described, there would be enough demand to sustain our present levels of production. I have no answer to this question. It seems unlikely that associative advertising will end suddenly, so I am confident that we will have the time and the imagination to adapt our economy to do without it.

Fifth, and last, one might ask what I am proposing. Here I am afraid I must draw up short of my mark. I have no practical political proposal. It seems obvious to me that no broad legislative prohibition would improve matters. Still, it may be possible to make small improvements like some that we have already seen. In the international arena, Nestlé was censured and boycotted, the World Health Organization drafted infant formula marketing guidelines, and finally Nestlé agreed to change its practices. In the U.S.A., legislation prohibits cigarette advertising on television.[23] These are tiny steps, but an important journey may begin with them.

Even my personal solution is rather modest. *First*, if one accepts my thesis that associative advertising is harmful to its audience, then one ought to avoid doing it to others, especially if doing so would require that one dull one's compassion, concern, and sympathy for others. Such initiatives are not entirely without precedent. Soon after the surgeon general's report on cigarettes and cancer in 1964, David Ogilvy and William Bernbach announced that their agencies would no longer accept cigarette accounts and *New Yorker* magazine banned cigarette ads.[24] *Second*, if I am even partly right about the effect of associative advertising on our desires, then one ought to expose oneself as little as possible. The most practical and effective way to do this is probably to banish commercial television and radio from one's life. This measure, though rewarding,[25] is only moderately effective. Beyond these, I do not yet have any answers.

In conclusion, I have argued against the advertising practice I call associative advertising. My main criticism is two-fold: (a) Advertisers must surely desensitize themselves to the compassion, concern, and sympathy for others that are central emotions in a virtuous person, and (b) associative advertising influences its audience to neglect the non-market cultivation of our virtues and to substitute market goods instead, with the result that we become worse and, quite likely, less happy persons.

Notes

[1]Robert L. Arrington, "Advertising and Behavior Control," *Journal of Business Ethics*, 3–12.

[2]I prefer not to use the term "consumers" since it identifies us with our role in a market, already conceding part of what I want to deny.

[3]Arrington, 8.

[4]James B. McGinnis. *Bread and Justice* (New York: Paulist Press, 1979), 224. McGinnis cites as his source INFACT Newsletter, September 1977, 3. Formula is often harmful because poor families do not have the sanitary facilities to prepare the formula using clean water and utensils, do not have the money to be able to keep up formula feeding without diluting the formula to the point of starving the child, and formula does not contain the antibodies which a nursing mother can pass to her child to help immunize the child against common local bacteria. Good accounts of this problem are widely available.

[5]John Dewey, *Human Nature and Conduct* (New York: Random House, 1930), 202.

[6]This can be a diverse group including (depending upon the product) marketing specialists, sales representatives, or people in advertising agencies. Not everyone in one of these positions, however, is necessarily guilty of engaging in associative advertising.

[7]This story was told by Lloyd E. Slater at a National Science Foundation Chatauqua entitled "Meeting World Food Needs" in 1980–1981. It should not be taken as a condemnation of marketing professionals in other firms.

[8]One could argue that the deficiency in compassion, concern, and sympathy on the part of advertisers might be a result of self-selection rather than of associative advertising. Perhaps people in whom these moral sentiments are strong do not commonly go into positions using associative advertising. I doubt, however, that such self-selection can account for all the disregard of the audience's best interests.

[9]See Lawrence A. Blum, *Friendship, Altruism and Morality* (Boston: Routledge and Kegan Paul, 1980) for a defense of moral emotions against Kantian claims that emotions are unsuitable as a basis for moral judgment and that only a purely rational good will offers an adequate foundation for morality.

[10]I use "ideology" here in a descriptive rather than a pejorative sense. To be more specific, associative advertising commonly advocates only a part of a more comprehensive ideology. See Raymond Guess, *The Idea of a Critical Theory* (Cambridge University Press, 1981), 5–6.

[11]For an interesting discussion, see John Lachs, "To Have and To Be," *Personalist* 45 (Winter 1964), 5–14; reprinted in John Lachs and Charles Scott, *The Human Search* (New York: Oxford University Press, 1981), 247–55.

[12]This is, in fact, the thrust of Arrington's arguments in "Advertising and Behavior Control."

[13]I do not mean to suggest that only associative advertising can have such ill effects. Neither am I assuming the existence of some natural, pristine self which is perverted by advertising.

[14]Quoted without source in Theodore Levitt, "The Morality (?) of Advertising," *Harvard Business Review*, July-August 1970; reprinted in Vincent Barry, *Moral Issues in Business*, (Belmont, CA: Wadsworth Publishing Company, 1979), 256.

[15]Levitt (in Barry), 252.

[16]Levitt (in Barry), 256.

[17]"Satisfying a desire would be valuable then if it sustained or made possible a valuable kind of life. To say this is to reflect the argument that in creating the wants he [or she] can satisfy, the advertiser (or the manipulator of mass emotion in politics or religion) is necessarily acting in the best interests of his [or her] public." Stanley Benn, "Freedom and Persuasion," *Australasian Journal of Philosophy* 45 (1969); reprinted in Beauchamp and Bowie, *Ethical Theory and Business*, second edition (Englewood Cliffs, NJ: Prentice-Hall, 1983), 374.

[18]Levitt's view is not new. "Continual success in obtaining those things which a man from time to time desires—that is to say, continual prospering—is what men call felicity." Hobbes, *Leviathan* (Indianapolis: Bobbs-Merrill, 1958), 61.

[19]This, in fact, is the principal criticism von Hayek offered of Galbraith's argument against the "dependence effect." F. A. von Hayek, "The Non Sequitur of the 'Dependence Effect,'" *Southern Economic Journal*, April 1961; reprinted in Tom L. Beauchamp and Norman F. Bowie, *Ethical Theory and Business*, second edition (Englewood Cliffs, New Jersey: Prentice-Hall, 1983), 363–66.

[20]Taylor R. Durham, "Information, Persuasion, and Control in Moral Appraisal of Advertising," *The Journal of Business*

Ethics 3, 179. Durham also argues that an exclusive concern with issues of deception and control leads us into errors.

[21]One might object that this requires a normative theory of human nature, but it seems to me that we can go fairly far by reflecting on our experience. If my approach is to be vindicated, however, I must eventually provide an account of how, in general, we are to make judgments about what is and is not good (or life-enhancing) for a human being. Clearly, there is a large theoretical gulf between me and Arrington, but I hope that my analysis of associative advertising shows that my approach is plausible enough to deserve further investigation.

[22]The central text for this problem is *The Affluent Society* (Houghton Mifflin, 1958). The crucial passages are reprinted in many anthologies, e.g., John Kenneth Galbraith. "The Dependence Effect," in W. Michael Hoffman and Jennifer Mills Moore, *Business Ethics Readings and Cases in Corporate Morality* (New York: McGraw-Hill, 1984), 328–33.

[23]"In March 1970 Congress removed cigarette ads from TV and radio as of the following January. (The cigarette companies transferred their billings to print and outdoor advertising. Cigarette sales reached new records.)" Stephen Fox, *The Mirror Makers: A History of American Advertising and Its Creators* (New York: William Morrow and Co., 1984), 305.

[24]Stephen Fox, 303–4.

[25]See, for example, Jerry Mander, *Four Arguments for the Elimination of Television* (New York: Morrow Quill Paperbacks, 1977).

Advertising and Behavior Control

Robert L. Arrington

Journal of Business Ethics 1 (1982): 3–12. Copyright © 1982 D. Reidel Publishing Co.

Consider the following advertisements:

(1) "A woman in *Distinction Foundations* is so beautiful that all other women want to kill her."

(2) Pongo Peach color from Revlon comes "from east of the sun ... west of the moon where each tomorrow dawns." It is "succulent on your lips" and "sizzling on your finger tips (and on your toes, goodness knows)." Let it be your "adventure in paradise."

(3) "Musk by English Leather—The Civilized Way to Roar."

. . .

These are instances of what is called puffery—the practice by a seller of making exaggerated, highly fanciful or suggestive claims about a product or service. Puffery, within ill-defined limits, is legal. It is considered a legitimate, necessary, and very successful tool of the advertising industry. Puffery is not just bragging; it is bragging carefully designed to achieve a very definite effect. Using the techniques of so-called motivational research, advertising firms first identify our often hidden needs (for security, conformity, oral stimulation) and our desires (for power, sexual dominance and dalliance, adventure) and then they design ads which respond to these needs and desires. By associating a product, for which we may have little or no direct need or desire, with symbols reflecting the fulfillment of the other, often subterranean interests, the advertisement can quickly generate large numbers of consumers eager to purchase the product advertised. What woman in the sexual race of life could resist a fountain which would turn other women envious to the point of homicide? Who can turn down an adventure in paradise, east of the sun where tomorrow dawns?

Who doesn't want to be civilized and thoroughly libidinous at the same time? . . . It doesn't take very much motivational research to see the point of these sales pitches. Others are perhaps a little less obvious. The need to feel secure in one's home at night can be used to sell window air conditioners, which drown out small noises and provide a friendly, dependable companion. The fact that baking a cake is symbolic of giving birth to a baby used to prompt advertisements for cake mixes which glamorized the "creative" housewife. And other strategies, for example involving cigar symbolism, are a bit too crude to mention, but are nevertheless very effective.

Don't such uses of puffery amount to manipulation, exploitation, or downright control? In his very popular book *The Hidden Persuaders*, Vance Packard points out that a number of people in the advertising world have frankly admitted as much:

> As early as 1941 Dr. Dichter (an influential advertising consultant) was exhorting ad agencies to recognize themselves for what they actually were—"one of the most advanced laboratories in psychology." He said the successful ad agency "manipulates human motivations and desires and develops a need for goods with which the public has at one time been unfamiliar—perhaps even undesirous of purchasing." The following year *Advertising Agency* carried an ad man's statement that psychology not only holds promise for understanding people but "ultimately for controlling their behavior."[1]

Such statements lead Packard to remark: "With all this interest in manipulating the customer's subconscious, the old slogan 'let the buyer beware' began taking on a new and more profound meaning."[2]

B. F. Skinner, the high priest of behaviorism, has expressed a similar assessment of advertising and related marketing techniques. Why, he asks, do we buy a certain kind of car?

Perhaps our favorite TV program is sponsored by the manufacturer of that car. Perhaps we have seen pictures of many beautiful or prestigeful persons driving it—in pleasant or glamorous places. Perhaps the car has been designed with respect to our motivational patterns: the device on the hood is a phallic symbol; or the horsepower has been stepped up to please our competitive spirit in enabling us to pass other cars swiftly (or, as the advertisements say, "safely"). The concept of freedom that has emerged as part of the cultural practice of our group makes little or no provision for recognizing or dealing with these kinds of control.[3]

In purchasing a car we may think we are free, Skinner is claiming, when in fact our act is completely controlled by factors in our environment and in our history of reinforcement. Advertising is one such factor.

A look at some other advertising techniques may reinforce the suspicion that Madison Avenue controls us like so many puppets. TV watchers surely have noticed that some of the more repugnant ads are shown over and over again, *ad nauseam*. My favorite, or most hated, is the one about A-1 Steak Sauce which goes something like this: Now, ladies and gentlemen, what *is* hamburger? It has succeeded in destroying my taste for hamburger, but it has surely drilled the name of A-1 Sauce into my head. And that is the point of it. Its very repetitiousness has generated what ad theorists call *information*. In this case it is indirect information, information derived not from the content of what is said but from the fact that it is said so often and so vividly that it sticks in one's mind—i.e., the information yield has increased. And not only do I always remember A-1 Sauce when I go to the grocers, I tend to assume that any product advertised so often has to be good—and so I usually buy a bottle of the stuff.

Still another technique: On a recent show of the television program "Hard Choices" it was demonstrated how subliminal suggestion can be used to control customers. In a New Orleans department store, messages to the effect that shoplifting is wrong, illegal, and subject to punishment were blended into the Muzak background music and masked so as not to be consciously audible. The store reported a dramatic drop in shoplifting. The program host conjectured whether a logical extension of this technique would be to broadcast subliminal advertising messages to the effect that the store's $15.99 sweater special is the "bargain of a lifetime." Actually, this application of subliminal suggestion to advertising has already taken place. Years ago in New Jersey a cinema was reported to have flashed subthreshold ice cream ads onto the screen during regular showings of the film—and, yes, the concession stand did a landslide business.[4]

Puffery, indirect information transfer, subliminal advertising—does the success of these techniques show that many of us have forfeited our autonomy and become a herd of packaged souls?

Puffery, indirect information transfer, subliminal advertising—are these techniques of manipulation and control whose success shows that many of us have forfeited our autonomy and become a community, or herd, of packaged souls?[5] The business world and the advertising industry certainly reject this interpretation of their efforts. *Business Week*, for example, dismissed the charge that the science of behavior, as utilized by advertising, is engaged in human engineering and manipulation. It editorialized to the effect that "it is hard to find anything very sinister about a science whose principle conclusion is that you get along with people by giving them what they want."[6] The theme is familiar: businesses just give the consumer what he/she wants; if they didn't they wouldn't stay in business very long. Proof that the consumer wants the products advertised is given by the fact that he buys them, and indeed often returns to buy them again and again.

The techniques of advertising we are discussing have had their more intellectual defenders as well. For example, Theodore Levitt, Professor of Business Administration at the Harvard Business School, has defended the practice of puffery and the use of techniques depending on motivational research.[7] What would be the consequences, he asks us, of deleting all exaggerated claims and fanciful associations from advertisements? We would be left with literal descriptions of the empirical characteristics of products and their functions. Cosmetics would be presented as facial and bodily lotions and powders which produce certain odor and color changes; they would no longer offer hope or adventure. In addition to the fact that these products would not then sell as well, they would not, according to Levitt, please us as much either. For it is hope and adventure we want when we buy them. . . . He maintains that "everybody everywhere wants to modify, transform, embellish, enrich and reconstruct the world around him." Commerce takes the same liberty with reality as the artist and the priest—in all three instances the purpose is "to influence the audience by creating illusions, symbols, and implications that promise more than pure functionality." For example, "to amplify the temple in men's eyes, (men of cloth) have, very realistically, systematically sanctioned the embellishment of the houses of the gods with the same kind of luxurious design and expensive decoration that Detroit puts into Cadillac." A poem, a temple, a Cadillac—they all elevate our spirits, offering imaginative promises and symbolic interpretations of our mundane activities. Seen in this light, Levitt claims, "Embellishment and distortion are among advertising's legitimate and socially desirable purposes." To reject these techniques of advertising would be "to deny man's honest needs and values."

Philip Nelson, a Professor of Economics at SUNY-Binghamton, has developed an interesting defense of indirect information advertising.[8] He argues that even when the message (the direct information) is not credible, the fact that the brand is advertised, and advertised frequently, is valuable indirect information for the consumer. The reason for this is that the brands advertised most are more likely to be better buys—losers won't be advertised a lot, for it simply wouldn't pay to do so. Thus even if the advertising claims made for a widely advertised produce are empty, the consumer reaps the benefit of the indirect information which shows the product to be a good buy. Nelson goes so far as to say that advertising, seen as information and especially as indirect information, does not require an intelligent human response. If the indirect information has been received and has had its impact, the consumer will purchase the better buy even if his explicit reason for doing so is silly, e.g., he naively believes an endorsement of the product by a celebrity. Even though his behavior is overtly irrational, by acting on the indirect information he is nevertheless doing what he ought to do, i.e., getting his money's worth. "'Irrationality' is rational," Nelson writes, "if it is cost-free." . . .

The defense of advertising which suggests that advertising simply is information which allows us to purchase what we want, has in turn been challenged. Does business, largely through its advertising efforts, really make available to the consumer what he/she desires and demands? John Kenneth Galbraith has denied that the matter is as straightforward as this.[9] In his opinion the desires to which business is supposed to respond, far from being original to the consumer, are often themselves created by business. The producers make both the product and the desire for it, and the "central function" of advertising is "to create desires." Galbraith coins the term "The Dependence Effect" to designate the way wants depend on the same process by which they are satisfied.

David Braybrooke has argued in similar and related ways.[10] Even though the consumer is, in a sense, the final authority concerning what he wants, he may come to see; according to Braybrooke, that he was mistaken in wanting what he did. The statement "I want x," he tells us, is not incorrigible but is "ripe for revision." If the consumer had more objective information than he is provided by product puffing, if his values had not been mixed up by motivational research strategies (e.g., the confusion of sexual and automotive values), and if he had an expanded set of choices instead of the limited set offered by profit-hungry corporations, then he might want something quite different from what he presently wants. This shows, Braybrooke thinks, the extent to which the consumer's wants are a function of advertising and not necessarily representative of his real or true wants.

The central issue which emerges between the above critics and defenders of advertising is this: do the advertising techniques we have discussed involve a violation of human autonomy and a manipulation and control of consumer behavior, *or* do they simply provide an efficient and cost-effective means of giving the consumer information on the basis of which he or she makes a free choice. Is advertising information, or creation of desire?

To answer this question we need a better conceptual grasp of what is involved in the notion of autonomy. This is a complex, multifaceted concept, and we need to approach it through the more determinate notions of (a) autonomous desire, (b) rational desire and choice, (c) free choice, and (d) control or manipulation. In what follows I shall offer some tentative and very incomplete analyses of these concepts and apply the results to the case of advertising.

(a) Autonomous desire. Imagine that I am watching T.V. and see an ad for Grecian Formula 16. The thought occurs to me that if I purchase some and apply it to my beard, I will soon look younger—in fact I might even be myself again. Suddenly I want to be myself! I want to be young again! So I rush out and buy a bottle. This is our question: was the desire to be younger manufactured by the commercial, or was it "original to me" and truly mine? Was it autonomous or not?

F. A. von Hayek has argued plausibly that we should not equate nonautonomous desires, desires which are not original to me or truly mine, with those which are culturally induced.[11] If we did equate the two, he points out, then the desires for music, art, and knowledge could not properly be attributed to a person as original to him, for these are surely induced culturally. The only desires a person would really have as his own in this case would be the purely physical ones for food, shelter, sex, etc. But if we reject the equation of the nonautonomous and the culturally induced, as von Hayek would have us do, then the mere fact that my desire to be young again is caused by the T.V. commercial—surely an instrument of popular culture transmission—does not in and of itself show that this is not my own, autonomous desire. Moreover, even if I never before felt the need to look young, it doesn't follow that this new desire is any less mine. I haven't always liked 1969 Aloxe Corton Burgundy or the music of Satie, but when the desires for these things first hit me, they were truly mine.

This shows that there is something wrong in setting up the issue over advertising and behavior control as a question whether our desires are truly ours *or* are created in us by advertisements. Induced and autonomous desires do not separate into two mutually exclusive classes. To obtain a better understanding of autonomous and nonautonomous desires, let us consider some cases of a desire which a person does not *acknowledge* to be his own even though he *feels* it. The kleptomaniac has a desire to steal which in many instances he repudiates, seeking by treatment to rid himself of it. And if I were suddenly overtaken by a desire to attend an REO concert, I would immediately disown this desire, claiming possession or momentary madness. These are examples of desires which one might have but with which one could not identify. They are experienced as foreign to one's character or personality. Often a person will have what Harry Frankfurt calls a second-order desire, that is to say, a desire *not* to have another desire.[12] In such cases, the first-order desire is thought of as being nonautonomous, imposed on one. When on the contrary a person has a second-order desire to maintain and fulfill a first-order desire, then the first-order desire is truly his own, autonomous, original to him. So there is in fact a distinction between desires which are the agent's own and those which are not, but this is not the same as the distinction between desires which are innate to the agent and those which are externally induced.

If we apply the autonomous/nonautonomous distinction derived from Frankfurt to the desires brought about by advertising, does this show that advertising is responsible for creating desires which are not truly the agent's own? Not necessarily, and indeed not often. There may be some desires I feel which I have picked up from advertising and which I disown—for instance, my desire for A-1 Steak Sauce. If I act on these desire it can be said that I have been led by advertising to act in a way foreign to my nature. In these cases my autonomy has been violated. But most of the desires induced by advertising I fully accept, and hence most of these desires are autonomous. The most vivid demonstration of this is that I often return to purchase the same product over and over again, without regret or remorse. And when I don't it is more likely that the desire has just faded than that I have repudiated it. Hence, while advertising may violate my autonomy by leading me to act on desires which are not truly mine, this seems to be the exceptional case.

Note that this conclusion applies equally well to the case of subliminal advertising. This may generate subconscious desires which lead to purchases, and the act of purchasing these goods may be inconsistent with other conscious desires I have, in which case I might repudiate my behavior and by implication the subconscious cause of it. But my subconscious desires may not be inconsistent in this way with my conscious ones; my id may be cooperative and benign rather than hostile and malign.[13] Here again, then, advertising may or may not produce desires which are "not truly mine."

What are we to say in response to Braybrooke's argument that insofar as we might choose differently if advertisers gave us better information and more options, it follows that the desires we have are to be attributed more to advertising than to our own real inclinations? This claim seems empty. It amounts to saying that if the world we lived in, and we ourselves, were different, then we would want different things. This is surely true, but it is equally true of our desire for shelter as of our desire for Grecian Formula 16. If we lived in a tropical paradise we would not need or desire shelter. If we were immortal, we would not desire youth. What is true of all desires can hardly be used as a basis for criticizing some desires by claiming that they are nonautonomous.

(b) Rational desire and choice. Braybrooke might be interpreted as claiming that the desires induced by advertising are often irrational ones in the sense that they are not expressed by an agent who is in full possession of the facts about the products advertised or about the alternative products which might be offered him. Following this

line of thought, a possible criticism of advertising is that it leads us to act on irrational desires or to make irrational choices. It might be said that our autonomy has been violated by the fact that we are prevented from following our rational wills or that we have been denied the "positive freedom" to develop our true, rational selves. It might be claimed that the desires induced in us by advertising are false desires in that they do not reflect our essential, i.e., rational, essence.

The problem faced by this line of criticism is that of determining what is to count as rational desire or rational choice. If we require that the desire or choice be the product of an awareness of *all* the facts about the product, then surely every one of us is always moved by irrational desires and makes nothing but irrational choices. How could we know all the facts about a product? If it be required only that we possess all of the *available* knowledge about the product advertised, then we still have to face the problem that not all available knowledge is *relevant* to a rational choice. If I am purchasing a car, certain engineering features will be, and others won't be, relevant, *given what I want in a car*. My prior desires determine the relevance of information. Normally a rational desire or choice is thought to be one based upon relevant information, and information is relevant if it shows how other, prior desires may be satisfied. It can plausibly be claimed that it is such prior desires that advertising agencies acknowledge, and that the agencies often provide the type of information that is relevant in light of these desires. To the extent that this is true, advertising does not inhibit our rational wills or our autonomy as rational creatures.

It may be urged that much of the puffery engaged in by advertising does not provide relevant information at all but rather makes claims which are not factually true. If someone buys Pongo Peach in anticipation of an adventure in paradise, or Old Charter in expectation of increasing the value of his holdings, then he/she is expecting purely imaginary benefits. In no literal sense will the one product provide adventure and the other increased capital. A purchasing decision based on anticipation of imaginary benefits is not,

it might be said, a rational decision, and a desire for imaginary benefits is not a rational desire.

In rejoinder it needs to be pointed out that we often wish to purchase subjective effects which in being subjective are nevertheless real enough. The feeling of adventure or of enhanced social prestige and value are examples of subjective effects promised by advertising. Surely many (most?) advertisements directly promise subjective effects which their patrons actually desire (and obtain when they purchase the product), and thus the ads provide relevant information for rational choice. Moreover, advertisements often provide accurate indirect information on the basis of which a person who wants a certain subjective effect rationally chooses a product. The mechanism involved here is as follows.

To the extent that a consumer takes an advertised product to offer a subjective effect and the product does not, it is unlikely that it will be purchased again. If this happens in a number of cases, the product will be taken off the market. So here the market regulates itself, providing the mechanism whereby misleading advertisements are withdrawn and misled customers are no longer misled. At the same time, a successful bit of puffery, being one which leads to large and repeated sales, produces satisfied customers and more advertising of the product. The indirect information provided by such large-scale advertising efforts provides a measure of verification to the consumer who is looking for certain kinds of subjective effect. For example, if I want to feel well dressed and in fashion, and I consider buying an Izod Alligator shirt which is advertised in all of the magazines and newspapers, then the fact that other people buy it and that this leads to repeated advertisements shows me that the desired subjective effect is real enough and that I indeed will be well dressed and in fashion if I purchase the shirt. The indirect information may lead to a rational decision to purchase a product because the information testifies to the subjective effect that the product brings about.[14]

Some philosophers will be unhappy with the conclusion of this section, largely because they have a concept of true, rational, or ideal desire which is not the same as the one used here. A Marxist, for instance, may urge that any desire felt by alienated man in a capitalistic society is foreign to his true nature. Or an existentialist may claim that the desires of inauthentic men are themselves inauthentic. Such concepts are based upon general theories of human nature which are unsubstantiated and perhaps incapable of substantiation. Moreover, each of these theories is committed to a concept of an ideal desire which is normatively debatable and which is distinct from the ordinary concept of a rational desire as one based upon relevant information. But it is in the terms of the ordinary concept that we express our concern that advertising may limit our autonomy in the sense of leading us to act on irrational desires, and if we operate with this concept we are driven again to the conclusion that advertising may lead, but probably most often does not lead, to an infringement of autonomy.

> ### How do we distinguish between an impulse we do not resist and one we could not resist, between freely giving in to a desire and succumbing to one?

(c) Free choice. It might be said that some desires are so strong or so covert that a person cannot resist them, and that when he acts on such desires he is not acting freely or voluntarily but is rather the victim of irresistible impulse or an unconscious drive. Perhaps those who condemn advertising feel that it produces this kind of desire in us and consequently reduces our autonomy.

This raises a very difficult issue. How do we distinguish between an impulse we *do* not resist and one we *could* not resist, between freely giving in to a desire and succumbing to one? I have argued elsewhere that the way to get at this issue is in terms of the notion of acting for a reason.[15] A person acts or chooses freely if he does so for a reason, that is, if he can adduce considerations which justify in his mind the act in question. Many of our actions are in fact free because this condition frequently holds. Often, however, a person will act from habit, or whim, or impulse, and on these occasions he does not have a reason in mind. Nevertheless he often acts voluntarily in these instances, i.e., he could have acted otherwise. And this is because if there *had been* a reason for acting otherwise of which he was aware, he would in fact have done so. Thus acting from habit or impulse is not necessarily to act in an involuntary manner. If, however, a person is aware of a good reason to do x and still follows his impulse to do y, then he can be said to be impelled by irresistible impulse and hence to act involuntarily. Many kleptomaniacs can be said to act involuntarily, for in spite of their knowledge that they likely will be caught and their awareness that the goods they steal have little utilitarian value to them, they nevertheless steal. Here their "out of character" desires have the upper hand, and we have a case of compulsive behavior.

Applying these notions of voluntary and compulsive behavior to the case of behavior prompted by advertising, can we say that consumers influenced by advertising act compulsively? The unexciting answer is: sometimes they do, sometimes not. I may have an overwhelming, T.V. induced urge to own a Mazda Rx-7 and all the while realize that I can't afford one without severely reducing my family's caloric intake to a dangerous level. If, aware of this good reason not to purchase the car, I nevertheless do so, this shows that I have been the victim of T.V. compulsion. But if I have the urge, as I assure you I do, and don't act on it, or if in some other possible world I could afford an Rx-7, then I have not been the subject of undue influence by Mazda advertising. Some Mazda Rx-7 purchasers act compulsively; others do not. The Mazda advertising effort *in general* cannot be condemned, then, for impairing its customers' autonomy in the sense of limiting free or voluntary choice. Of course the question remains what should be done about the fact that advertising may and does *occasionally* limit free choice. We shall return to this question later.

In the case of subliminal advertising we may find an individual whose subconscious desires are activated by advertising into doing something his calculating, reasoning ego does not approve. This would be a case of compulsion. But most of us have a benevolent subconsciousness which does not overwhelm our ego and its reasons for action. And therefore most of us can respond to subliminal advertising without thereby risking our autonomy. To be sure, if some advertising firm developed a subliminal technique which drove all of us to purchase Lear jets, thereby reducing our caloric intake to the zero point, then we would have a case of advertising which could properly be censured for infringing our right to autonomy. We should acknowledge that this is possible, but at the same time we should recognize that it is not an inherent result of subliminal advertising.

(d) Control or manipulation. Briefly let us consider the matter of control and manipulation. Under what conditions do these activities occur? In a recent paper on "Forms and Limits of Control" I suggested the following criteria:[16]

A person C controls the behavior of another person *P if*

(1) C intends *P* to act in a certain way *A*;
(2) C's intention is causally effective in bringing about *A*; and
(3) C intends to ensure that all of the necessary conditions of *A* are satisfied.

These criteria may be elaborated as follows. To control another person it is not enough that one's actions produce certain behavior on the part of that person; additionally one must intend that this happen. Hence control is the intentional production of behavior. Moreover, it is not enough just to have the intention; the intention must give rise to the conditions which bring about the intended effect. Finally, the controller must intend to establish by his actions any otherwise unsatisfied necessary conditions for the production of the intended effect. The controller is not just influencing the outcome, not just having input; he is as it were guaranteeing that the sufficient conditions for the intended effect are satisfied.

Let us apply those criteria of control to the case of advertising and see what happens. Conditions (1) and (3) are crucial. Does the Mazda manufacturing company or its advertising agency intend that I buy an Rx-7? Do they intend that a certain number of people buy the car? *Prima facie* it seems

more appropriate to say that they *hope* a certain number of people will buy it, and hoping and intending are not the same. But the difficult term here is "intend." Some philosophers have argued that to intend *A* it is necessary only to desire that *A* happen and to believe that it will. If this is correct, and if marketing analysis gives the Mazda agency a reasonable belief that a certain segment of the population will buy its product, then, assuming on its part the desire that this happen, we have the conditions necessary for saying that the agency intends that a certain segment purchase the car. If I am a member of this segment of the population, would it then follow that the agency intends that I purchase an Rx-7? Or is control referentially opaque? Obviously we have some questions here which need further exploration.

Let us turn to the third condition of control, the requirement that the controller intends to activate or bring about any otherwise unsatisfied necessary conditions for the production of the intended effect. It is in terms of this condition that we are able to distinguish brainwashing from liberal education. The brainwasher arranges all of the necessary conditions for belief. On the other hand, teachers (at least those of liberal persuasion) seek only to influence their students—to provide them with information and enlightenment which they may absorb *if they wish*. We do not normally think of teachers as controlling their students, for the students' performances depend as well on their own interests and inclinations.

Now the advertiser—does he control, or merely influence, his audience? Does he intend to ensure that all of the necessary conditions for purchasing behavior are met, or does he offer information and symbols which are intended to have an effect only *if* the potential purchaser has certain desires? Undeniably advertising induces some desires, and it does this intentionally, but more often than not it intends to induce a desire for a particular object, *given* that the purchaser already has other desires. Given a desire for youth, or power, or adventure, or ravishing beauty, we are led to desire Grecian Formula 16, Mazda Rx-7's, Pongo Peach, and Distinctive Foundations. In this light, the advertiser is influencing us by appealing to independent desires we already have. He is not creating those basic desires. Hence it seems appropriate to deny that he intends to produce all of the necessary conditions for our purchases, and appropriate to deny that he controls us.[17]

Let me summarize my argument. The critics of advertising see it as having a pernicious effect on the autonomy of consumers, as controlling their lives and manufacturing their very souls. The defense claims that advertising only offers information and in effect allows industry to provide consumers with what they want. After developing some of the philosophical dimensions of this dispute, I have come down tentatively in favor of the advertisers. Advertising may, but certainly does not always or even frequently, control behav-

ior, produce compulsive behavior, or create wants which are not rational or are not truly those of the consumer. Admittedly, it may in individual cases do all of these things, but it is innocent of the charge of intrinsically or necessarily doing them or even, I think, of often doing so. This limited potentiality, to be sure, leads to the question whether advertising should be abolished or severely curtailed or regulated because of its potential to harm a few poor souls in the above ways. This is a very difficult question, and I do not pretend to have the answer. I only hope that the above discussion, in showing some of the kinds of harm that can be done by advertising and by indicating the likely limits of this harm, will put us in a better position to grapple with the question.

Notes

[1]Vance Packard, *The Hidden Persuaders* (Pocket Books, New York, 1958), 20–21.

[2]*Ibid.*, 21.

[3]B. F. Skinner, "Some Issues Concerning the Control of Human Behavior: A Symposium" in Karlins and Andrews (eds.), *Man Controlled* (The Free Press, New York, 1972).

[4]For provocative discussions of subliminal advertising, see W. B. Key, *Subliminal Seduction* (The New American Library, New York, 1973), and W. B. Key, *Media Sexploitation* (Prentice Hall, Inc., Englewood Cliffs, N.J., 1976).

[5]I would like to emphasize that in what follows, I am discussing these techniques of advertising from the standpoint of the issue of control and not from that of deception. For a good and recent discussion of the many dimensions of possible deception in advertising, see Alex C. Michalos, "Advertising: Its Logic, Ethics, and Economics" in J. A. Blair and R. H. Johnson (eds.), *Informal Logic: The First International Symposium* (Edgepress, Pt. Reyes, Calif., 1980).

[6]Quoted by Packard, *op. Cit.*, 220.

[7]Theodore Levitt, "The Morality (?) of Advertising," *Harvard Business Review* 48 (1970), 84–92.

[8]Philip Nelson, "Advertising and Ethics," in Richard T. De George and Joseph A. Pichler (eds.), *Ethics, Free Enterprise, and Public Policy* (Oxford University Press, New York, 1978), 187–98.

[9]John Kenneth Galbraith, *The Affluent Society*; reprinted in Tom L. Beauchamp and Normal E. Bowie (eds.), *Ethical Theory and Business* (Prentice-Hall, Englewood Cliffs, 1979), 496–501.

[10]David Braybrooke, "Skepticism of Wants, and Certain Subversive Effects of Corporations on American Values," in Sidney Hook (ed.), *Human Values and Economic Policy* (New York University Press, New York, 1967); reprinted in Beauchamp and Bowie (eds.), *op. Cit.* 502–08.

[11]F. A. von Hayek, "The *Non Sequitur* of the 'Dependence Effect,'" *Southern Economic Journal* (1961); reprinted in Beauchamp and Bowie (eds.), *op. Cit.*, 598–612.

[12]Harry Frankfurt, "Freedom of the Will and the Concept of a Person," *Journal of Philosophy* LXVIII (1971), 5–20.

[13]For a discussion of the difference between a malign and a benign subconscious mind, see P. H. Nowell-Smith, "Psychoanalysis and Moral Language," *The Rationalist Annual* (1954); reprinted in P. Edwards and A. Pap (eds.), *A Modern Introduction to Philosophy*, Revised Edition (The Free Press, New York, 1965), 86–93.

[14]Michalos argues that in emphasizing a brand name—such as Bayer Aspirin—advertisers are illogically attempting to distinguish the indistinguishable by casting a trivial feature of a product as a significant one which separates it from other brands of the same product. The brand name is said to be trivial or unimportant "from the point of view of the effectiveness of the product or that for the sake of which the product is purchased" (*op. Cit.*, 107). This claim ignores the role of indirect information in advertising. For example, consumers want an aspirin *they can trust* (trustworthiness being part of "that for the sake of which the product is purchased"), and the indirect information conveyed by the widespread advertising effort for Bayer Aspirin shows that this product is judged trustworthy by many

other purchasers. Hence the emphasis on the name is not at all irrelevant but rather is a significant feature of the product from the consumer's standpoint, and attending to the name is not at all an illogical or irrational response on the part of the consumer.

[15]Robert L. Arrington, "Practical Reason, Responsibility and the Psychopath," *Journal for the Theory of Social Behavior* 9 (1979), 71–89.

[16]Robert L. Arrington, "Forms and Limits of Control," delivered at the annual meeting of the Southern Society for Philosophy and Psychology, Birmingham, Alabama, 1980.

[17]Michalos distinguishes between appealing to people's tastes and molding those tastes (*op. Cit.*, 104), and he seems to agree with my claim that it is morally permissible for advertisers to persuade us to consume some article *if* it suits our tastes (105). However, he also implies that advertisers mold tastes as well as appeal to them. It is unclear what evidence is given for this claim, and it is unclear what is meant by *tastes.* If the latter are thought of as basic desires and wants, then I would agree that advertisers are controlling their customers to the extent that they intentionally mold tastes. But if by molding tastes is meant generating a desire for the particular object they promote, advertisers in doing so may well be appealing to more basic desires, in which case they should not be thought of as controlling the consumer.

CASES

Case 10.1: Diamonds Are Forever

One popular advertisement for engagement rings sponsored by the DeBeers Diamond company poses the following question to men planning proposal: "Is two months' salary too much to spend?" Many suitors take "two months' salary" as an unwritten rule of etiquette and as a measuring stick of how well they've fared in the jewelry aspect of courtship. However, "two months" is not written in any well-known traditional books on wedding etiquette. It seems to be simply an extremely effective creation of the DeBeers company, which controls 80 percent of the world market in diamonds.

While wedding rings were traditionally regarded as symbols of vows to lifelong commitment, today they symbolize wealth and, to some, how much the suitor loves his bride-to-be. Givers and receivers of the glimmering objects can be regularly comparing the caret weight, cost, etc., of their "symbols" with friends and family members. This seems like a clear situation in which the diamond business has violated consumer autonomy by "creating" a new need through exploiting basic human needs to fit in and impress others. For some potential suitors, simply saying no in the face of social pressures to value his bride-to-be in this manner is difficult. Advertisers would probably respond by saying that they are simply "fulfilling" latent human desires rather than creating them. Indeed, it appears that the "need" or desire to impress peers and the bride-to-be is already in existence.

Questions for Discussion:

1. Is the prevalence of the belief of the "two months' salary" rule proof of the power of advertisers to create needs by exploiting human insecurity? Why or why not?
2. If so, does this unjustly violate the autonomy of consumers?

Case 10.2: Sex in Advertising

In a popular television commercial, several attractive young women are in a giggly conversation in a fashionable living room. Soon one of them announces, "He's back!" The young women then rush over to a telescope to spy on a well-built man in a building across the way as he removes his clothes and steps into the shower. As he steps out of the shower, he finally puts on his jeans, which, though barely shown (no pun intended), are the subject of this commercial. Another television advertisement for a popular soft drink has several women staring out of an office building window at a shirtless construction worker as he drinks his Diet Coke. In the spirit of camaraderie and bonding, the women agree to be back at the same time tomorrow for more. While controversial, these ads are effective because they engage in a role-reversal of what advertisers have used to appeal to male members of the audience for years, that is, raw appeals to sexual power and libido.

Consider commercials for one popular beer in which the opening of one bottle of this company's brew usually paves the way for men to party with beautiful women in bikinis at bars or in some tropical location. In other beer company ads, some members of the audience may wonder if it is swimsuits that are being promoted, since the real product doesn't even appear until the last few seconds of the spot. Perhaps most flagrant, though, are ads for fashion and perfumes. Promotions for Calvin Klein's Obsession perfume barely show the actual product. Instead, photos of nude and semi-dressed models in provocative poses are used to draw attention to the ad and create a sexual association with the product. Ads for Guess jeans and Wilke-Rodriguez fashions have also used overtly sexual themes in order to be effective.

In addition to decrying the sexual contents of these ads, critics claim that they are manipulative and may undermine autonomy through appeals to subconscious drives. Advertisers respond that they are merely reflecting society's norms and appealing to desires that people already have. Perfume would not sell if advertised for its chemical content and few people would buy certain fashions in the absence of the adventure associated with it.

Questions for Discussion:

1. Do you think that these ads are immoral? Why or why not?
2. Can these ads truly undermine consumer autonomy through unconscious associations with pleasure and sexual power? Or are most consumers stronger than to allow this to happen?
3. Do you find anything morally objectionable to appealing to the "least common denominator" of a male audience in order to sell items such as beer?

Case 10.3: Undersized Computer Monitors

When is 13 inches not 13 inches? This is not a tricky math question. Rather, it is the subject of a recent lawsuit filed on behalf of consumers by Merced County District Attorney Gordon Spencer. The suit alleges that computer manufacturers such as IBM, Compaq, Apple, and ten others regularly overstate the size of their computer monitors in their advertisements. Spencer accuses the companies of inflating the size of the monitors by an average of 13 to 19 percent, with some monitors being as much as 33.7 percent smaller than advertised. The suit claims that the overstating occurs because manufacturers measure the total glass area of the screen rather than just the image size. "They should only measure the viewable areas of a computer screen, but sometimes they were measuring the stuff that's behind the plastic housing," Spencer said. "If I buy a pound of hamburger, I expect a pound of hamburger—and I don't expect the wrapping to go into it [the weight]," he further stated.

In contrast to the advertised sizes of screens on television sets, computer screens are not strictly regulated. Since the products are similar, it is alleged that most reasonable consumers would expect the same standards of measurement from computers. The suit started in 1993, when a resident of Merced County complained that his monitor was much smaller than the advertisement declared it to be. The State of California's attorney general's office has launched its own investigation and may file similar charges in the near future.[7]

[7]See Karen Kaplan, "Suit Charges PC Firms Cheat on Monitor Sizes," *Los Angeles Times*, 29 March 1995, D4.

Questions for Discussion:

1. Do these practices constitute outright deception of even reasonable consumers? Are these ads blatantly false and misleading?
2. Do consumers have any responsibility to be informed by making their own measurements?

Is it a false assumption on the part of consumers, and thus their own fault for being misled, that computer monitors and television screens are measured and advertised in the same fashion?

COMMENTARY

Questions over the morality of advertising have been the subject of public debate for decades. The proliferation of another highly anticipated source of more commercial communication, worldwide networking through computer technology, will only make this debate more intensive in the years ahead. Since its inception, advertising as an industry has received a tremendous amount of criticism from groups with various agendas along the political and moral spectrum. It has been accused of everything from perpetuating conspicuous consumption and materialism to leading young women to develop self-esteem disorders through an irresponsible portrayal of a "beauty myth" that is both unrealistic and unhealthy.

While these are significant causes for concern, a question that is more foundational to these criticisms is whether or not the contents of many campaigns can actually undermine consumer autonomy and free choice through deception and manipulation. If they can, this goes against Adam Smith's vision of capitalism in which autonomous actors engage in voluntary and rational exchange. In his vision of the market, he theorized that supply would be guided by demand and producers of goods and services would profit only through meeting the needs of consumers. This is in sharp contrast to how some believe the current system works. It is alleged that today's economy is one that is dominated by advertising in which producers allegedly stimulate artificial demand by "creating" needs where none previously existed. If in fact advertising can truly undermine the autonomy and rationality of consumers through deception and manipulation, using it for this purpose would make it an immoral enterprise that would mandate more stringent regulations in order to protect consumer interests.

Upon a deeper investigation, many of these specific claims of advertising's power to subvert autonomy seem largely exaggerated. However, there are other significant moral concerns about some of the practices of Madison Avenue. Before we get to these concerns, we will first resolve two critical questions: First, is advertising inherently deception, since very little information is ever presented about the products and services promoted? Second, does advertising really have the power to manipulate and undermine the autonomy of rational consumers through the creation of artificial needs as some of its critics allege?

Many critics have claimed that by only emphasizing the positive aspects of products and services, almost all advertising misleads consumers. Referring to the "bluffing" example discussed in chapter 1, deception does not take place in very specific contexts in which lesser standards of veracity are expected. Thus we must ask if most consumers are really deceived by advertising. The answer seems dubious in light of the fact that most of us were admonished since preschool days by our parents to be skeptical of the claims made by advertisers. Thus we do not expect advertising to be "truthful" in the sense of offering both sides of the story. The great majority of adult consumers are more sophisticated than the pundits allege. Most can "read" through ads and see them for what they are. No reasonable consumer believes that by wearing a specific brand of athletic shoe, he will be able to play basketball like Shaquille O'Neal or Michael Jordan. In fact, some advertisements even offer tongue-in-cheek parodies of themselves. A recent jingle for Sprite claims that by drinking the product, "you will make friends, beautiful women will surround you . . . violins will play to you . . ., etc." It is doubtful that such a benign poke at the industry would work if consumers were not sophisticated enough to laugh along with the ad.

Undoubtedly, some consumers will be misled and will have their autonomy undermined by some campaigns, but consumers must take some responsibility to become educated and aware of the marketplace. As such, current legislation rightfully protects only "reasonable" consumers from deceiving and misleading claims. Policies that protect irresponsible consumers are too paternalistic and circumvent responsible citizenship. However, in cases where even reasonable consumers are readily deceived, current laws must be rigorously enforced because in those cases consumer autonomy is truly being subverted. For example, the 1994 Fair Labeling and Packaging Act was signed into law because many grocery store items offered nutritional information on packages that would mislead even sophisticated consumers. Prior to the act, there were no standard measurements for terms such as "low-fat" "fat-free" and "low-sodium." Some product packages, which is another form of advertising, made claims such as "98% fat free." Most health-conscious consumers assumed that this meant that only 2 percent of the calories came from fat, the standard dietary interpretation of this claim. Some products were deceptive because the 2 percent of fat referred to was measured in terms of volume or weight. In some cases, up to 40 percent or 50 percent of the actual calories came from fat. While the act has helped to make nutritional information much easier to understand, consumers still must be careful. Some wily producers state very low quantities of sodium and fat, but in the context of unrealistic serving sizes. While some of the loopholes of the new law still need to be closed, this is a clear case of the law reasonably stepping in to protect consumer interests. However, it seems certain that in the majority of cases, no reasonable consumer is being truly deceived by advertising.

Let's move to the second question: Does advertising truly have the power to undermine autonomy? John Kenneth Galbraith and a host of other critics of advertising have argued that the industry as a whole can "create" needs in order to sell their products and services to unwitting consumers. The allegation is made that many campaigns undermine autonomy by exploiting deep human insecurities and needs and associating products with answers for those needs. Are these critics right? Can ads manipulate and undermine freedom? It seems obvious that some ads do indeed exploit the darker aspects of human nature. However, experiments suggest that despite the fact that we are inundated with ads, we readily dismiss them. Each of us on average is exposed to 1,600 advertisements a day, notices about 1,200 of them, and responds to only about 12. We also seem to pay more attention to ads for products we already own, possibly to soothe post-purchase dissonance.[8]

Equally lost in the barrage of criticisms is the fact that many, perhaps even most, advertisements are nonmanipulative in nature and are for products that meet genuine needs in the marketplace. For example, advertisements for overnight mail services, telecommunications companies, and computer firms meet the need that individuals and businesses have always had; that is, the need to communicate more efficiently and effectively. While the ads may create the desire for a product or service, the need to communicate was there long before the ad ever appeared.

Furthermore, as Theodore Levitt asserts, advertisements for products such as cosmetics appeal to often latent, but nonetheless real, desires of consumers. As such, he exonerates the industry as a whole by arguing that it does not create needs at all. Rather, advertising merely offers products that are directed to needs that already exist within consumers. He asserts that there would be dire consequences if all forms of "puffery" and association were removed from advertisements. For example, cosmetics would be promoted as chemicals rather than the hope or adventure that they offer. Quoting T. S. Eliot's famous claim that "human kind cannot bear very much reality," Levitt states that advertising is merely reflective of the human journey to transcend "an otherwise harsh or bland existence." Consumers indeed want much more than the utility or intended purpose of a product. Rather, they want "not cosmetics, but expectations of the allurements they promise . . . not low-cal whip cream but self-rewarding indulgence."

Robert Arrington takes a similar position with respect to advertising's alleged powers to control human behavior. Arrington argues that if the hope offered by such advertisements for products are not corollary with rational consumer desires, many products would not be repeatedly purchased by the same consumers. Furthermore, he

[8]Roger Draper, "The Faithless Shepherd," *New York Review of Books* (26 June 1986): 16; cited in William Shaw and Vincent Barry, *Moral Issues in Business*, 5th ed. (Belmont, Calif.: Wadsworth, 1992), 500.

asserts that ads may create demand for a specific product such as Grecian Formula 16, but only if the purchaser already has the desire to look or feel youthful. Thus the advertiser does not create this need, he is merely "influencing us by appealing to independent desires we already have."

The "Diamonds Are Forever" case in this chapter further illustrates Arrington's point, and at the same time introduces our most serious concerns about the content of some forms of associative advertising. To summarize the case, the often heard "two-months' salary" rule for engagement rings has taken on the credibility of a long-held social norm. However, as far as we can tell, it is the successful creation of advertisers for the DeBeers company, which controls approximately 80 percent of the world's diamond market. On the surface, the prevalence of the belief in the two-months rule would seem to indicate that the campaign has in fact created a need that did not previously exist. Without commercial influence, rings are symbols of vows of commitment. In most parts of the world, diamond engagement and wedding rings are far from the norm. As such, it appears that at least in the United States, advertisers have successfully created an artificial demand for their product. However, upon a deeper examination, the real "need" was there all along. Men have always "needed" to impress their future spouses and their peers. Diamonds merely provide another means for this desire to be fulfilled. The same can be said for almost every product and service that exists in the marketplace.

However, just because advertising is limited in its power to create needs and thereby undermine autonomy, this does not mean that advertising does not alter some forms of behavior. While ads may not subvert freedom and autonomy, they do successfully influence behavior through the power of persuasion and association. Indeed, advertising works successfully to get consumers to buy products that they may otherwise choose to avoid. If it did not, companies would not pay Madison Avenue the exorbitant sums that they do to promote their products. Advertising may not subvert choice, but it can surely limit it. John Waide points out that society becomes the best enforcers of the claims of ads through peer and social pressure. The diamond example is a case in point. Many men have their choices artificially limited because some members of society measure their success by how close they come to meeting the two-months rule. While many men can and do simply say no to that rule, an even clearer example with respect to the power of advertising to limit choices is in the fashion industry. Certainly consumers can say no, but at what cost? In many instances, it is difficult to even procure a job in the absence of conforming to socially acceptable fashion trends.

While advertisers accomplish their goals of persuasion through appeals to human needs, desires, and insecurities that already exist, there are still serious criticisms that can be levied at advertising. John Waide brings to light a most serious concern by insightfully pointing out that Levitt takes as a given that a satisfactory life is one in which many desires are satisfied, but falsely assumes that "*which* desires is not important." Indeed, it seems critical to ask if appeals to *any* emotion, insecurity, or need is as morally neutral as Levitt and Arrington implicitly assume in their discussions.

Most of us would agree that appeals to healthy needs that can be met with good products serve an important function in a robust and growing economy. For example, commercials for long-distance telephone-communication carriers in which keeping in touch with friends and family is emphasized is a legitimate social function that these companies can meet. Furthermore, many public-service advertisements appeal to fear in portraying the consequences of drug and alcohol abuse. There is no debate over whether or not the prevention of substance abuse is a "product" worth selling through appeals to healthy amounts of human fear.

Some advertisements, however, clearly traverse the bounds of healthy persuasion into the realm of appealing to what one of our former students has labeled "the least common denominator" in the target audience. For example, appeals to sexual power feed on the most base elements of the human psyche. Advertisements for Guess clothes and Calvin Klein perfumes are among the most blatant examples of campaigns that use sexual arousal rather than the product itself in order to promote brand awareness. In many of these ads, the product itself is never even shown. Instead, barely dressed, and in some cases nude, models are placed in provocative situations in order to grab attention. Advertisements for some beer companies also make similar appeals. Many of their television spots use scantily clad women in sketches in which the product is barely mentioned. Undoubtedly, these types of ads attempt to lead the consumer to "associate" the product with sexual power and promiscuity or to correlate the product with perhaps unconscious pleasurable feelings of sex. While these ads are "smart business" from a marketing perspective, appeals to such base appetites are morally deficient.

The most disturbing aspects of many of these examples is that appeals to these parts of the psyche seem so unnecessary. There are countless examples of ad campaigns that rely on entertainment value and creativity rather than on sexual appeals. Even within the alcoholic beverage industry itself are examples of ads that seem to capture the audience without appeals to sex. Most sports fans can recall television commercials in which beer brands rely on cleverness rather than sex to place their product in the minds of consumers. Furthermore, the wine industry offers a sharp contrast to irresponsible appeals among beer advertisers. Wine makers have voluntarily agreed to responsible advertising of their product in the form of a self-imposed code of conduct. To avoid portraying wine as a means to drunkenness, their code states that it will only be advertised in the context of food. This code is consistently adhered to, as wine is rarely, if ever, advertised outside of this context.

Undoubtedly some advertisers would defend their use of sexual appeals by stating that they are only mirroring society's values, rather than creating them. Thus in reality they are simply giving society what it wants. But should advertisers simply give society what it wants? Are they free from any moral responsibilities to take the higher ground and appeal to healthier parts of the psyche? In one sense the answer to this difficult question gets back to the age-old question that asks whether it is moral for someone to provide a product or service just because there is a market for it. Certainly we can all think of some things that are so grossly immoral that no one ought to supply the demand. Legal products such as pornography, hard alcohol, and tobacco are of such dubious social value that we would all readily state to manufacturers of these products that their gains are "ill-gotten." A corollary argument can be advanced with respect to advertisers. Just because an insecurity, fear, or desire can be successfully appealed to, this does not make it morally right to do so. And just because advertisers do not create immoral societal values, they can and do powerfully and readily reinforce them.

Furthermore, the claim that advertising merely reflects reality is untruthful. No one we know has ever been anywhere where everyone was as physically fit or beautiful as portrayed in some ads. Computer technology in mass media can also create "unreality." Print ads regularly use graphic techniques such as airbrushing to cover blemishes and other less than "ideal" physical features of models. Newer technologies even allow for the changing of eye color, the thickening of hair, and the augmentation of the shape and size of various body parts. Thus the models appearing in magazines really don't exist as we see them. To some extent then, advertising can in fact create a world of unreality, as most reasonable consumers are not aware of some of these enhancement techniques.

John Waide correctly inquires about the type of world we are making through associative advertising. He asks if advertising "will tend to influence us to become worse persons." Instead of the cultivation of virtues, he asserts that advertising contributes to a culture in which people seek security in material goods that promise nonmarket goods such as friendship, joy, etc. It is obvious that there is no way for market goods to fulfill these deep needs of human beings.

Waide's criticisms are particularly true where we live in Southern California. In many parts of the greater Los Angeles area, the emphasis is on what you own and what you look like rather than who you are. It is not uncommon to come across people who seem to invest all of their resources in looks and material possessions rather than on the cultivation of character. While advertising cannot be blamed for creating such shallow values, it undoubtedly perpetuates an ethos of shallow materialism.

It is obvious, then, that advertisers have great responsibilities with respect to being accountable in the appeals they are making in order to persuade consumers. There is a high road and a low road in business. Companies and advertisers that seek to be ethical must respect human well-being and the "world" they are making; they must be cautious about the types of appeals they are making to their target audience.

While the content of some ads must be cleaned up in order to better society, it is unrealistic to expect voluntary compliance on the part of advertisers. However, further governmental regulation outside of the blatantly false and misleading runs into all sorts of thorny questions about the freedom of speech protected by the First Amendment. Thus the only practical solution for Christians and other members of society who object to such advertising is to influence societal norms or to make their positions known in such a way that morally objectionable ads become unprofitable to use. Other groups have clearly shown that this has already been effective. Various ads have been pulled or changed by major corporations amidst public protest for too much violent or sexual content.

A case can be made, however, for further legislation to protect one group that cannot be deemed reasonable consumers in the marketplace—young children. Children under a certain age are constant targets of ads for products such as cereals, toys, and perhaps even cigarettes. They do not and cannot be expected to bear the responsibilities accorded to a rational consumer in the marketplace. Thus, some further legislative measures, especially for products like cigarettes, can be justified in order to protect their interests.

With all of the criticism that advertising receives, it comes as no surprise that many Christians believe that advertising is one arena that believers are better off staying away from. Undoubtedly, there are some ad campaigns that Christians should not participate in creating. As John Waide states, creating ads that "influence people without concern for their well-being is likely to reduce one's sensitivity to the moral motive of concern for the well-being of others." Yet, once again we must emphasize that many ads and the products and services they promote are not manipulative and/or destructive for society in general. Commercial communications serve a critical role in a robust economy. Furthermore, Christians once took similar strategies of withdrawal from the realm of radio and television. These mass communication media were left almost exclusively to secular minds and perspectives, and the result is that many Christians are today crying for change. In our opinion, one of the best ways to minimize the amount of morally objectionable advertising is if people who have higher morals and convictions get into the business and create campaigns that can appeal to higher parts of the human psyche and, in the process, serve to help "make a better world."

ELEVEN

Product Safety and Quality

Profoundly effective countermeasures to epidemic assaults on human health cannot be left to the whim of sales campaigns of the 'competitive' marketplace where only those with enough money can buy health and safety."

Benjamin Kelley, "How the Auto Industry Sets Roadblocks to Safety"[1]

The proliferation of product liability lawsuits is taking a terrible toll on the economy by hurting American firms trying to compete against foreign rivals.

Former Vice President Dan Quayle and former Solicitor General
Kenneth Starr, "Not Guilty"

[1]Quoted in the account of the safety record of the Suzuki Samurai, in *Business and Society Review* 83 (Fall 1992): 50–53.

INTRODUCTION

Product safety is perhaps the one issue in business ethics that stirs the emotions and generates rhetoric like no other. The visions of people forever scarred or even killed by use of unsafe products are indelibly imprinted on the minds of many people. Similarly there are companies that have been victimized by frivolous lawsuits, charging that the company was responsible for any injury associated with its product, no matter how the buyer misused it or tampered with it. Product safety touches people individually, both those who have been hurt by unsafe products and those who have lost their jobs as a result of the dramatic increase in litigation related to product safety in the past decade.

In the past few years there has been an explosion of product liability lawsuits. To be sure, some companies have egregiously put their customers at risk when they use their products. The Ford Pinto in the 1970s with its exploding rear gas tank is perhaps the most well-publicized example of a company's neglect of consumer safety and poor use

437

of cost-benefit analysis to outline its options. This case is probably what gave the discipline of business ethics its real start. Similar charges have been raised against General Motors for its trucks, and one family of a teenager who died when the gas tank exploded received a $105 million judgment from a jury.[2] But other companies argue that hypersensitivity about product safety has crippled their ability to compete in the marketplace. The costs of defending themselves in such litigation is very high, and the threat of liability often inhibits the innovation necessary for companies to remain competitive. They further hold that many of these lawsuits are either frivolous, filed by people simply out for the money, or unreasonable. They insist that they cannot be held responsible for safety risks that they could not have reasonably foreseen and risks that do not come from normal and intended use of the product.

Think about the product-safety cases that have been prominently featured in the media in the past few years. Perhaps the longest-running product liability case has been the frequent and still ongoing litigation over asbestos, which was widely used long before anyone became aware of its health risks. Most companies stopped using it after the risks became well known in the 1960s and 1970s. Yet decades later, some companies are still defending themselves in court from people claiming damage from asbestos. The asbestos scenario raises an important question about the degree to which a company can be held liable for health risks that were not known at the time the product was produced and would not become known for some time.

Many product-safety issues arise in medicine in regard to drugs and medical devices. Consider the widely publicized intrauterine birth-control device (IUD) the Dalkon Shield, which caused severe pelvic infections, miscarriages, and even death in a few cases. Its manufacturer, A. H. Robins, never acknowledged that it caused these problems, even though it took it off the market in the mid-seventies, and in 1990 set aside $2.4 billion to compensate women hurt from its use.[3] Robins actually filed for bankruptcy while still a profitable company in anticipation of future litigation. Similarly, and more recently, the silicone-gel breast implants produced by Dow Corning and a handful of others were found to be defective; they have set aside a similar trust to compensate women harmed by them. Corning has consistently maintained that the implants were safe and that they have been victimized by overzealous lawyers who are pursuing these suits in their own financial interest, not in the interests of the women involved.[4] Johnson & Johnson, maker of the pain reliever Tylenol, avoided a public relations disaster when it pulled the product off the market after some capsules were discovered to have been tampered with and laced with cyanide.

[2]This case became notorious for its exposure on NBC's *Dateline*, whose producers later admitted rigging the gas tanks in the truck with small explosives to facilitate the explosion for television purposes. See Donald W. Nauss, "GM Wins Appeal Over Side-Saddle Gasoline Tanks," *Los Angeles Times*, 14 June 1994, O1.

[3]Milo Geyelin, "Dalkon Shield Trust Hailed as Innovative, Stirs a Lot of Discord," *Wall Street Journal*, 3 June 1991, A1.

[4]Michele Galen, "Debacle at Dow Corning: How Bad Will It Get?" *Business Week* (2 March 1992): 36–37.

The most recent well-publicized case involved McDonald's fast-food chains. They are well known for their piping hot coffee, and in 1994 an eighty-one-year-old woman was holding a cup of their coffee between her legs while she was parked in her car. The coffee spilled onto her lap, causing second-degree burns to her groin and thigh regions. She sued the company and won a $2.9 million award, later reduced to $480,000 on appeal.[5] Many people reacted to the award with incredulity, insisting that hot coffee was not meant to be carried between someone's legs and that the woman should bear the responsibility for something as foolish as that. For many, this case epitomized an out-of-control legal system in which people can win judgments from a jury for practically any product that causes them injury, irrespective of their misuse of the product and in spite of the company's warnings. Some of these cases will be developed further, and you will get the chance to deal with them in more detail in the "Cases" section in this chapter.

Virtually everyone agrees that companies should be held liable for knowingly placing unsafe products on the market without warning the consumer about the risks. And virtually everyone agrees that consumers have to take responsibility for using products in the way they were intended to be used. Business, government, and consumers all have a role in insuring that the market is filled with safe products. But how should that responsibility be shared? Should consumers take more responsibility, punishing companies that market unsafe products through their purchasing power and through punitive lawsuits? Or should companies take further responsibility, perhaps at the cost of stifling innovation and further driving up the costs of product development? Or should government take a more active role in regulating business to insure product safety, as is done in most of Europe and Japan? The article entitled "Who Should Pay? The Product Liability Debate" is a helpful overview of the issues in this matter. It outlines the arguments for each sector's taking more or less responsibility for product safety.

A second issue concerns the degree of autonomy and freedom that consumers should have as opposed to the responsibility (some would call it paternalism) of the government to protect them from unsafe products. Given that all the attention given to product safety, both by regulators and by the courts, has driven up the costs of many products, should consumers be able to make the choice to purchase less safe products that are more cost effective for them? What responsibility does government have for protecting consumers from their informed, yet foolish choices? For example, should the government, in the name of product safety, prohibit the marketing of cigarettes? Or should

[5]Andrea Gerlin, "How a Jury Decided That a Coffee Spill Is Worth $2.9 Million," *Wall Street Journal*, 1 September 1994, A1.

consumers, informed about the risks, be able to make those decisions for themselves, without government interference? The same questions could be asked about other types of risky behavior, such as skydiving and riding a motorcycle without a helmet. To what degree should individual freedom be balanced by government regulation designed to protect people from foolish exercise of that freedom? To those of a more libertarian bent, who would argue for less government involvement in business and individuals' lives, Ian Maitland points out that there are significant limits to business's ability to regulate itself, given its overarching mandate for profit maximization and the way that firms are isolated from many of the impacts of their actions.

A third issue concerns the actual damage to companies from all the emphasis on product safety. Companies argue that they are bearing an excessive share of the responsibility for product safety, which is dangerously hindering their competitive stance in a global marketplace in which are companies of many other countries that do not have such rigorous safety standards. Recent investigators have insisted that the competitive disadvantage to companies has been overstated and should not be a basis for cutting back on product-safety litigation or regulation. Two of the articles in this chapter argue that case. Glenn W. Bailey, chairman of the New York–based Keene Corporation, which is still involved in asbestos litigation for a firm it acquired, argues that product liability litigation is entirely out of control and is threatening the competitiveness of many companies, who are delaying or canceling introducing new products and spending millions in settlements and other costs to defend themselves from liability actions. On the other hand, and in response to the $105 million award in the GM trucks case, the article from *The Economist* entitled "Not Guilty" argues that though product liability litigation is significantly greater in the United States than in Europe and Japan, it has not hurt American companies as significantly as some claim. The author argues that the costs for insuring product safety are imposed differently in the United States than in other parts of the world, where they are assessed primarily through more extensive regulation. Try to decide where you stand on the costs to business after reading these two articles.

READINGS

Who Should Pay? The Product Liability Debate

Issues in Ethics (Winter–Spring 1991): 4–6. Copyright © 1991 Markkula Center for Applied Ethics at Santa Clara University.

In 1977 Esther Kociemba began wearing the "Cu-7," a copper intrauterine contraceptive device (IUD) manufactured by G. D. Searle & Co. A year and a half later, hoping to become pregnant, she removed the device only to find she had become infertile. Doctors blamed her sterility on pelvic inflammatory disease (PID), a condition frequently associated with the use of IUDs. Kociemba hired a lawyer and brought a product liability suit against G. D. Serle, stating that the company should be held liable for her infertility. The company countered that PID was also associated with certain sexual activities, activities in which Kociemba might have engaged. In addition, corporate representatives said that the risks of IUDs were well known to her doctor. Therefore, the company asserted, she and her doctor should be held responsible for her injuries.

Every year, 34 million people are injured or killed as a result of product-related accidents. Such injuries are the major cause of death for people between the ages of 1 and 36, outnumbering deaths from cancer or heart disease. The estimated cost of these injuries is $12 billion annually.

Tens of thousands of product injury lawsuits are filed each year. As the number of claims has risen, so too have the number of companies forced to file bankruptcy because of massive suits. Moreover, an increasing number of companies are claiming that they have pulled established products off the market and halted research on promising products for fear of liability.

Manufacturers claim that they are victims of a system gone haywire. According to strict liability laws, a manufacturer can be held liable for injuries even when he or she had no way of preventing those injuries. Holding manufacturers responsible for injuries caused by products known to be defective or potentially dangerous is one thing, but today manufacturers face lawsuits—often bordering on the outrageous—for injuries they could not have prevented.

Consumer activists, on the other hand, claim that the threat of product liability suits forces manufacturers to make product safety a priority and that those who suffer injuries caused by products should be compensated for their injuries by the manufacturers of those products.

Product injuries represent a major cost of introducing products into a society. Since virtually every new product carries some unknown risk, a possibility always exists that the product may cause injuries or impose other costs on users. This raises an important moral question: How should these costs be distributed among the members of our society?

Should Consumers Bear More Responsibility?

Manufacturers contend that consumers should bear more responsibility for product injuries because the costs of placing full liability onto companies far outweigh the benefits. Since the 1960s, there has been a steady increase of product liability cases. According to one study, 13,500 product liability suits were filed in federal court in 1986, compared to only 1,500 in 1974. Due to this barrage of litigation, the cost of doing business has risen dramatically. Insurance premiums have skyrocketed, where insurance is available at all. Manufacturers' legal costs have also soared: about 60% of the average corporation's litigation expenses today are product liability cases. The rising cost of product liability insurance and lawsuits has led, in turn, to great increases in consumer prices.

The economy also has suffered from the boom in product liability claims. When companies facing massive lawsuits have been forced to scale down their operations, the result is a loss of jobs. In a recent report by the Conference Board, 15% of corporations surveyed had laid off workers because of product liability costs, while 8% had been forced to close plants altogether. In addition, the threat of liability has affected American businesses' ability to compete internationally. In other countries, there are severe limits on what manufacturers can be held responsible for and there is less tendency to sue. By not having to contend with a morass of lawsuits, these companies can offer cheaper products, and put American manufacturers at a competitive disadvantage.

It is also argued that the fear of being hit with a liability claim keeps many lifesaving drugs and devices off the market, and stifles creativity and innovation. Even the most rigorous conformity to safety regulations doesn't prevent liability. One report found that 39% of the companies surveyed delayed introducing new products or had discontinued products because of product liability suits. The pharmaceutical industry has been hit the hardest. Only one company in the U.S. now manufactures vaccines, a product often targeted in lawsuits. Vaccines for AIDS will certainly not reach the market without protection against lawsuits. Said one spokesperson from the drug industry, "Decisions [are] already being made on [AIDS] research priorities for liability reasons."

The costs to manufacturers and to society will only increase as technologies grow more complex and their applications more varied. Testing products for safety under every possible condition of use will not only impose great testing costs on manufacturers but will result in enormous delays in the introduction of new products that could benefit society.

Manufacturers also maintain that it is morally unjust to hold someone liable for injuries that he or she could not have prevented. Through extensive research and repeated testing, companies do all that they possibly can to ensure product safety. And, to prevent harm, warnings and instructions are plastered over each piece of merchandise.

Finally, some manufacturers point out that in a free market system, businesses have the right to make and sell whatever products they choose and consumers have the right to choose what they buy. But rights carry with them responsibilities. When consumers choose to buy risky products rather than safe ones (both of which businesses may offer in a free market) or when they choose not to inform themselves about products, they must accept the consequences, including the responsibility for any injuries resulting from those choices.

Should Manufacturers Bear More Responsibility?

Those who hold that manufacturers should bear more of the responsibility for product injuries argue that the benefits of holding companies liable for these injuries outweigh the costs. In a recent year, more than 200,000 infants were hospitalized for injuries resulting from the use of toys, or nursery or recreational equipment. About 1,777,000 people required emergency treatment because of injuries involving home furnishings; more than 1,200 of these injuries involving home construction materials; 1,300 of them died from the injuries. Society has an obligation to minimize such tragedy and suffering. Without the threat of liability, manufacturers would have little incentive to ensure product safety, and the number of product-related injuries would escalate.

The costs of holding manufacturers responsible for product injuries are not as great as company representatives would have us believe. For example, the so-called "explosion" in product liability suits, "crippling American business," is a myth. A recent study by the RAND Corporation found that although the number of product liability lawsuits had increased nearly eight-fold during the last decade, more than half of these lawsuits involved only a handful of companies, reflecting mass litigation against a few asbestos and pharmaceutical companies. A report by the Government Accounting Office also concluded that, except for cases involving a few drug or asbestos companies, product liability suits "do not appear to have been rapidly accelerating or explosive."

Furthermore, it cannot be claimed that product litigation makes domestic companies any less competitive internationally. Foreign companies that sell in the U.S. have to abide by the same product liability laws that American companies face. And when American companies compete abroad, they have the same advantages that foreign companies have.

Those who hold manufacturers liable for product-related injuries also claim that justice is on their side. Since the defective product that caused the injury was produced by the manufacturer, it is fair that the manufacturer bear the costs of that injury. Moreover, they argue, justice requires that the party that is most able to pay for an injury be the party that bears most of the financial burden. Manufacturers know in advance that there is always a risk of liability in introducing new products, and can therefore build the cost of potential lawsuits into the price of those products. Manufacturers also have the research expertise and laboratories, the engineering and technical knowledge, and the budgets to assess the risks of product use and to ensure that these products are safe. Consumers lack these. It is just to place greater burdens on those who are better able to bear these burdens.

Consumer activists also challenge the corporate claim that consumers "freely" choose to buy unsafe products. Consumers, they argue, are woefully uninformed about the products they buy because they don't have access to information about the products. Others lack a comprehensive understanding of the seriousness of the printed warning. Still others may be functionally illiterate or too young to make informed choices. It is manufacturers, not consumers, who make the "free" choices to compromise product safety and it is manufacturers who must therefore accept the consequences.

As long as products are produced, product injuries will occur. Who should bear the costs of those injuries? Our answer requires that we weigh the claims of consumers against those of manufacturers—claims which appeal, in different ways, to our desire to minimize harm, our ideal of justice, and our commitment to taking responsibility for the choices we make.

For Further Reading

Andrew Eiler, *The Consumer Protection Manual* (New York: Facts on File, 1983).

Peter Huber, "Are We Afraid of the Future?" *Reader's Digest*, Vol. 133 (December 1988), 191–92, 194.

Peter Huber, "Litigation Thwarts Innovation in the U.S.," *Scientific American*, Vol. 260 (March 1989), 120.

Deborah Johnson, *Computer Ethics* (Englewood Cliffs: Prentice Hall, Inc., 1985), 39–55.

Carolyn Lockhead, "Liability's Creative Clamp Holds Firms to the Status Quo," *Insight* (August 29, 1988), 38–40.

"Unsafe Products: The Great Debate Over Blame and Punishment," *Business Week* (April 30, 1984), 96–104.

Litigation Is Destroying American Companies

Glenn W. Bailey

USA Today (January 1994): 76–77. Copyright © *USA Today*.

The spectre of punitive damages, unnecessary and expensive pre-trial discovery, and the filing of "junk" lawsuits all contribute to the wasting of our nation's resources.

A survey that was conducted by a congressman among his constituents showed that, while most of them were concerned deeply about the economy, very few seemed to be worked up about America's competitiveness, even though competitive superiority in the world made the U.S. prosperous. The economy depends on it. Americans take U.S. manufacturing superiority for granted. However, the country is losing it, and litigation is one of the big reasons why.

Litigation impedes productivity. Forty-seven percent of the nation's manufacturers threw in the towel on some product they were making or planning to produce because lawyers have a chance to sue over a customer misusing the product or improperly handling it. Losses due to litigation might be endless, explaining why 25% of manufacturers discontinued some forms of product research and 15% laid off workers. Americans have forgotten that their rights are dependent on the willingness to take responsibility for their actions.

Compare Japanese and American cultures. The Japanese are motivated by a cooperative system that benefits all. A struggle for power in the Japanese culture is paramount. He who has the power, has the right.

Now look at Americans. They all ought to be proud of their individual rights, but, somewhere over the past decade or two, one's responsibility for his or her actions has been forgotten. People now look at power and perceive it as immoral. Americans say power works against the average person. How did that attitude come about? It's partly because we are becoming a nation of crybabies and busybodies, as an August 1991 article in *Time* magazine stated.

Individuals forget their responsibilities, demand rights and entitlements, blame others for their problems, and don't want to pay for what happens to them as a result of their own actions. Lawyers exploit these trends and become rich. A number of them are obscenely greedy. As a result, the American civil justice system is breaking down, businesses are becoming less competitive, and jobs are disappearing.

What exists today is a lawsuit lottery that leads to legalized extortion. Lawyers feed on the "entitlement generation" to create panic over asbestos and other products. Attorneys blame the suppliers of the products despite the fact that warnings on packages were ignored by workers, their unions, and their employers. Lawyers wrongly claim that suppliers were concerned about profits over people. They preach that they are taking from rich companies and giving to the poor, yet two-thirds of the money goes to attorneys.

A Roper poll of the American people reported in the *Wall Street Journal* showed that 70% agree that liability suits give lawyers more money than they deserve, and 63% agree that some people start frivolous lawsuits because the awards are so big and there's so little to lose. Almost 70% would limit punitive damage awards. By contrast, a survey of lawyers and judges also reported by the *Wall Street Journal* found that only 22% viewed the civil justice system negatively, while 77% blamed the media for clogging the courts and the breakdown of the system.

The *New York Times* reported that the American Bar Association rejects all limits on fact-finding before trial, appeals on convicted criminals, punitive damages, fees they charge, and so-called "junk science experts." Instead, the *Times* said, the ABA calls for more taxpayer funds for legal aid lawyers, tax benefits for payments to attorneys, a halt to Federal crime statutes, and additional judges appointed to handle more cases.

What has been the reaction to proposals for civil justice reform recommended by the President's Council on Competitiveness? Non-lawyers support them by 100 to one. Perhaps surprisingly, individual attorneys back the civil justice reform package by four to one. So, who's more in touch with reality, the public or America's largest organization of attorneys?

The fact is, lawyers are overwhelming America. The U.S. has one lawyer for every 300 people—about 70% of the world's attorneys—while Japan has one for every 10,000 of its population. With all of the lawyers we have in America, some of them have found it expedient to inspire panic to promote litigation through which they can build income for themselves.

Keene Corporation's experience with asbestos litigation is a perfect example of the civil justice system run amok as well as the negative effect litigation has on competitiveness. Keene bought Baldwin-Ehret-Hill in 1968 for $8,000,000. A small percentage of BEH's sales were in asbestos-containing products, made to meet U.S. Navy, utility, and construction project requirements. BEH placed warnings on its packaging before Keene purchased the company. In 1972, BEH stopped production of these products, which never produced a profit for Keene, and the company was shut down completely by 1975. Yet, despite this minimal involvement with a company it owned for a mere seven years, Keene is a major defendant in prohibitively expensive asbestos litigation.

Through 1992, Keene and its insurance carriers had spent about $415,000,000 on this litigation, even though the company never did anything illegal or improper. Keene has expressed willingness to provide total settlements up to $500,000,000—and lawyers will get more than $300,000,000 of that amount.

All of this has occurred even though it is undisputed that, when properly handled, asbestos products are safe and of great social utility. The U.S. Navy maintained as late as 1979 that it was impossible to build efficient naval vessels without asbestos.

While asbestos is number 90 on the Environmental Protection Agency's list of items that should concern people, asbestos litigation is number one as a cause of court clogging, number one in number of claimants, number one in causing bankruptcies of otherwise healthy and productive companies, and number one in generating lawyers' fees for damage litigation.

Judges' efforts to resolve cases all too often have resulted in a perverse incentive—causing more cases and more backlog.

The existing format for processing asbestos claims—through the tort system—is the most inefficient way to get money to claimants. In asbestos litigation, less than 35% of the funds go to the plaintiff. Because a system has evolved that establishes different legal standards for asbestos claimants—making it easier for unimpaired claimants to obtain grossly inflated damage awards—as few as five to 10 cents on the dollar are delivered to the truly impaired plaintiffs.

Judges' efforts to resolve cases all too often have resulted in a perverse incentive—causing more cases and more backlog. The opportunity for contingency fees that yield some attorneys returns of well over $5,000 per hour drive them to recruit more plaintiffs, many of whom are not sick. When cases are settled, these lawyers recruit still more plaintiffs and file still more cases, resulting in even more serious docket clogging and the further depletion of funds needed for truly impaired plaintiffs in the future.

Today's trials limit the plaintiffs' responsibility for ignoring warnings and the employer's responsibility for not providing a safe workplace and enforcing the company's then-existing requirement to wear respirators in areas where dust could not be controlled by the use of ventilation and dust collection equipment. Instead, they focus solely on the supplier and permit the introduction of irrelevant and inflammatory evidence, resulting in verdicts not related to the extent of the plaintiffs' injury, but to the heat of the lawyers' rhetoric. This combination inevitably leads to more cases and more trials.

Various cases yield unpredictable, inequitable, and arbitrary results. Juries, confronted with essentially the same facts, have awarded damages ranging from zero to millions of dollars! This "asbestos lottery" and its attendant high contingency fee payments have motivated plaintiff lawyers to recruit increasing numbers of unimpaired claimants to perpetuate their fee-feeding frenzy.

In some jurisdictions, defendants have been "gagged" from commenting on matters of public concern and presenting historical facts while judges and attorneys publicly have aired frequently prejudicial opinions.

Since the bankruptcy of Johns-Manville and other major suppliers, plaintiffs' law firms have scrambled to retool their practice and target smaller companies like BEH. The burden of larger and larger "lottery" type awards now falls on fewer and fewer companies with less and less money. For example, in a current case, with 8,555 plaintiffs, approximately 85% of the 100-plus original defendants are not in the courtroom. Furthermore, though BEH had less than a few percent of the market and never mined or milled asbestos, Keene currently has more than 90,000 cases pending against it.

The asbestos litigation thus far has cost the American economy around $20,000,000,000, with about $12,000,000,000 going to lawyers. Those billions could have been used to invest in and create more than 200,000 jobs or 90,000 housing units.

Finding a Better System

If the goal is to run the litigation until every defendant has been bankrupted, thousands of people left uncompensated, and thousands of workers without jobs, then the legal system should continue what now is being done. On the other hand, if the goal is to do justice to the concerned parties and the public, what is needed is a system—uniform all over the U.S.—that will provide fair compensation to truly impaired plaintiffs promptly, stop unfounded new case filings, control transactional costs—mainly lawyers' fees, both plaintiff and defendant, and keep defendants in business to provide compensation for future meritorious claimants.

First, it is necessary to make sure that the money gets only to sick people. The best way to ensure that is by the establishment of court-mandated pleural registries, or some similar non-trial track docket. By establishing a pleural registry and ordering cases to it, judges could make the trial track litigation more manageable and unclog court dockets overnight.

A pleural registry would take the cases of all claimants who do not have any asbestos-associated impairment off the court's active docket and suspend the statute of limitations until the plaintiff becomes impaired. Only then would he or she have the right to return to court and have his or her case processed. It already is being done in some places, but to accomplish the above-stated goals, pleural registries must be implemented everywhere. Otherwise, there simply isn't enough money to pay these claims nor enough courts to process them.

Second, punitive damages must be stopped. Historically, they have been imposed on defendants as punishment for intentionally causing harm and as a deterrent to bad conduct. All punitive damage awards punish, but in the asbestos cases they don't act as a deterrent because these products haven't been made in decades and no harm was caused intentionally. What else can further awards of punitive damages deter?

Third, there must be a stop to consolidating cases, which is being used increasingly by trial judges to force settlements and control their dockets. This device actually is counterproductive and has resulted in a significant increase in the rate of new asbestos claims filed. Large consolidations make it impossible for a defendant to get a fair trial, resulting in inflated jury verdicts. That, in turn, creates more incentive to file more cases.

The Limits of Business Self-Regulation

Ian Maitland

California Management Review 27, no. 3 (Spring 1985): 132–47. Copyright © 1985,
The Regents of the University of California.

In a liberal democracy, there are limits to the extent to which socially responsible behavior can be ordered by law. Beyond a certain point, the costs of expanding the apparatus of state control become prohibitive—in terms of abridged liberties, bureaucratic hypertrophy, and sheer inefficiency. This fact probably accounts for the lasting appeal of the concept of self-regulation—the idea that we would be better off if we could rely on the promptings of a corporate "conscience" to regulate corporate behavior instead of the heavy hand of government regulation.

To its advocates, the virtues of self-regulation—or "corporate social responsibility"—seem self-evident. It promises simultaneously to allay business fears of further government encroachment and to restore the public's faith in business. What is more, it asks of business only that it behave in its own enlightened self-interest. While this entails a radical break with the way managers have conceived of their role in the past, it does not make any impossible or self-contradictory demands that an imaginative manager cannot adapt to. In any case, such things as the new awareness of the fragility of the physical environment, the quantum leap in the power of large corporations, and a New American Ideology, all demand no less.

The period from the mid-1950s to the mid-1970s saw a stream of proposals for the moral reconstruction of the corporation. The principal obstacle to self-regulation was diagnosed as managers' single-minded preoccupation with profit maximization. This, in turn, was attributed to intellectual shortcomings—managers' insularity, their failure to keep up with changing values, their inability to see their role in a system-wide perspective, and their attachment to an outmoded ideology which defined the public interest as the unintended outcome of the pursuit of selfish interests. Also implicated were the organizational structure and culture of the modern corporation which supposedly embodied and perpetuated this orientation to profit. The advocates of self-regulation saw their task as being the proselytizing and scolding of managers into a broader definition of their role and the drawing up of blueprints for the socially responsible corporation.

This most recent wave of enthusiasm for self-regulation has largely receded, leaving behind it few enduring achievements. By and large, the exhortations appear to have fallen on deaf ears, or at best to have had only a marginal impact on corporate conduct. The primacy of profit maximization remains unchallenged and we continue to rely—and will do so for the foreseeable future—on legal compulsion administered by the state to regulate the undesirable consequences of economic activity.

If the marriage between the corporation and self-regulation was made in heaven, why has it not been consummated? The failure of self-regulation to live up to its promise is attributable to factors that have, for the most part, been overlooked by its advocates. In their attempts to make over managers' value systems and restructure the modern corporation, they have largely neglected the very real limits on managers' discretion that result from the operation of a market economy. As a consequence of these limits, managers are largely *unable* to consider their firms' impact on society or to subordinate profit-maximization to social objectives, no matter how well-intentioned they are.

A Game Theoretic Analysis of Self-Regulation

The crux of this argument is the recognition that an individual firm's interests as a competitor in the marketplace often diverge from its interests as a part of the wider society (or, for that matter, as a part of the business community). In this latter role, the firm is likely to welcome a cleaner environment, but as a competitor in the marketplace it has an interest in minimizing its own pollution abatement costs. It may philosophically favor a free market, but it will probably lobby in favor of protection for itself. This observation is a commonplace one, but its implications are rarely fully explored.

The firm's interests as part of a broader group typically take the form of collective or public goods. Using a rational choice model of behavior, Mancur Olson has demonstrated that it is not in the interest of a group member (let us say, the firm) to contribute to the costs of providing such goods.[1] Public goods (e.g., a cleaner environment or the free market) are goods that are available to all firms irrespective of whether or not they have contributed to their upkeep or refrained from abusing them. Since their availability is not contingent on a firm having contributed, each firm has a rational incentive to free-ride, i.e., to leave the costs of providing them to other firms. However, if each firm succumbs to this temptation, as it must if it acts in its own rational self-interest, then the public good will not be provided at all. Thus, even when they are in agreement, "rational, self-interested individuals will not act to achieve their common or group interests."[2] In a rational world, Olson concludes, "it is certain that a collective good will *not* be provided unless there is coercion or some outside inducement."[3]

The typical objectives of business self-regulation and responsible corporate behavior-such as a cleaner environment—are public goods. Olson's theory therefore provides a basis for explaining why business self-regulation appears so hard to achieve.

Russell Hardin has pointed out that the logic underlying Olson's theory of collective action is identical to that of an n-person prisoner's dilemma (PD).[4] The strategy of not contributing toward the cost of a public good dominates the strategy of paying for it, in the sense that no matter what other firms do, any particular firm will be better off if it does not contribute.

Both Olson's theory and the PD have been criticized on the grounds that their assumptions regarding human motivations (i.e., that they are invariably rational and self-interested) are unduly strict. A modified version of the PD relaxes its harsh motivational assumptions. Ford Runge (following A. K. Sen) has argued that what appears to be a prisoner's dilemma proves, on closer inspection, to be an "assurance problem" (AP).[5] According to this theory, the group member (i.e., firm) does not withhold its contribution to a public good based on a rational calculation of the costs and benefits involved (as with the PD) but rather does so because it is unable to obtain the necessary assurance that other firms will contribute their fair share. In other words, the AP substitutes the more lenient assumption that firms prefer equal or fair shares for the PD's assumption that they invariably try to maximize their individual net gain. Under the AP, we can expect firms to regulate their own behavior in some larger interest so long as they are confident that other firms are doing the same.

But in a market economy, where decision making is highly dispersed, the prediction of other firms' behavior becomes problematic. As a consequence, no individual firm can be sure that it is not placing itself at a competitive disadvantage by unwittingly interpreting its own obligations more strictly than its competitors do theirs. In these circumstances, all firms are likely to undertake less self-regulation than they would in principle be willing (indeed, eager) to accept.

In spite of their differences, both the PD and the AP involve problems of collective action. In the case of the PD, the problem is that it is always in the rational interest of each firm to put its own individual interest ahead of its collective interests. In the case of the AP, the problem is that of coordinating firms' expectations regarding fair shares.

The sub-optimal supply of business self-regulation can be explained largely in terms of the barriers to collective action by firms. There are three levels of self-regulation: the firm level (corporate social responsibility); the industry level (industry self-regulation); and the level of the economy (business-wide self-regulation). It is only at the third level that the necessary collective action is likely to be of a socially benign variety.

Three Levels of Self-Regulation

Corporate Social Responsibility—Contemporary advocates of corporate social responsibility acknowledge the difficulties of implementing it, but they go on to proclaim its inevitability anyway. In their view, it has to work because nothing else will; at best, the law elicits grudging and literal compliance with certain minimal standards when what is needed is corporations' spontaneous and whole-hearted identification with the *goals* of the law.[6] As Christopher Stone says, there are clear advantages to "encouraging people to act in socially responsible ways because they believe it the 'right thing' to do, rather than because (and thus, perhaps, only to the extent that) they are ordered to do so."[7]

Advocates of social responsibility have offered a number of prescriptions for curing firms' fixation on profit maximization. The weakness of these proposals lies in their assumption that social responsibility can be produced by manipulating the corporation. They overlook the extent to which the firms' behavior is a function of market imperatives rather than of managers' values or corporate structure.

The irony is that corporate "irresponsibility" is largely a product of our own making. The principal means we (the people) rely on to regulate corporate conduct in the public interest—namely the competitive market—undercuts the ability of firms to regulate themselves in cases of market failure. In effect, we have sought to make the logic of the prisoner's dilemma work for us (much as the D.A. does in the paradigmatic case of the PD).[8] We have isolated firms from one another so that they cannot coordinate their behavior to our detriment. While we have been successful at creating truly competitive markets, we have in the process limited firms' capacity to take into consideration anything but profits.

The decentralized structure of the U.S. economy makes the provision of *any* public goods problematic. The point is not just that firms find it difficult to act in the public interest; they find it no less difficult to act in the interests of their industry or of the business community. According to James Q. Wilson, trade associations have been beset with free-rider problems.[9] For example, trade association attempts to restrain price competition have been frustrated by the absence of "sanctions with which to ensure that collective benefits would override individual rationality."[10] Wilson concludes that "business associations have on the whole been . . . least successful when they have had to rely on voluntary agreements."[11]

This point is also illustrated by cases where competitive pressures have prevented firms from acting responsibly even where it would be in their economic interest to do so. Robert Leone has described how aerosol spray manufacturers were reluctant to abandon the use of fluorocarbon propellants (which were suspected of depleting the ozone layer in the stratosphere) even though the alternative technology was cheaper. The problem was that "any individual company that voluntarily abandoned the use of such propellants ran the risk of a sizable loss of market share as long as competitors still offered aerosol versions of their products [which the public valued for their convenience]."[12] In situations of this kind it is not unusual for responsible firms, aware of their own helplessness, to solicit regulation in order to prevent themselves being taken advantage of by competitors who do not share their scruples about despoiling the environment or injuring the industry's reputation. Thus aerosol manufacturers did not oppose the ban on fluorocarbons in spite of the tenuous scientific evidence of their dangers. Similarly, following the Tylenol poisonings, the pharmaceutical industry sought and obtained from the FDA a uniform national rule on tamper-resistant packaging, because no individual firm had wanted to unilaterally incur the expense of such packaging.[13] The list of examples is endless.

In a market economy, firms are usually *unable* to act in their own collective interests because "responsible" conduct risks placing the firms that practice it at a competitive disadvantage unless other firms follow suit. Where there is no well-defined standard that enjoys general acceptance, it will take some sort of tacit or overt coordination by firms to supply one. Even if that coordination survives the attentions of the Antitrust Division and the FTC, compliance will still be problematic because of the free-rider problem. Arrow has pointed out that a "code [of behavior] may be of value to . . . all firms if all firms maintain it, and yet it will be to the advantage of any one firm to cheat—in fact the more so, the more other firms are sticking to it."[14] We are therefore faced with the paradox that the voluntary compliance of the majority of firms may depend on the coercive imposition of the code of behavior on the minority of free riders. Thus, although it is fashionable to view voluntarism and coercion as opposites—and to prefer the former for being more humane and, ultimately, effective—they are more properly seen as interdependent.[15]

Industry Self-Regulation—If responsible corporate conduct must ultimately be backed by coercion, there remains the question of who is to administer the coercion. Is self-regulation by a trade association or other industry body a practical alternative to government regulation? The classic solution to the public goods dilemma is "mutual coercion, mutually agreed upon."[16] The possibility of "permitting businesses to coerce themselves" has been raised by Thomas Schelling who adds that such an approach "could appeal to firms which are prepared to incur costs but only on condition that their competitors do also."[17]

The record of industry self-regulation in the United States suggests that it does indeed commonly arise in response to the public goods problem. David A. Garvin explains the development of self-regulation in the advertising industry in this way.[18] Michael Porter has noted that self-regulation may be of particular importance to an emerging industry which is trying to secure consumer acceptance of its products. At this stage of its life cycle, an industry's reputation could be irretrievably injured by the actions of a single producer.[19] Thus the intense self-regulation in the microwave industry is understandable in terms of the industry's need to "overcome the inherent suspicion with which many people view 'new' technology like microwave ovens."[20] Nevertheless, industry self-regulation remains the exception in the United States. This is so because it is a two-edged sword: the powers to prevent trade abuses are the same powers that would be needed to restrain trade.

Because of the potential anti-competitive implications of industry self-regulation, its scope has been strictly limited. Anti-trust laws have significantly circumscribed the powers of trade associations. Legal decisions have proscribed industry-wide attempts to eliminate inferior products or impose ethical codes of conduct. Major oil firms were frustrated by the anti-trust statutes when they tried to establish an information system to rate the quality of oil tankers in an attempt to reduce the incidence of oil spills from substandard vessels.[21] Airlines have had to petition the civil Aeronautics Board for antitrust immunity so that they could discuss ways of coordinating their schedules in order to reduce peak-hour overcrowding at major airports.[22]

In short, industry or trade associations appear to hold out little promise of being transformed into vehicles for industry self-regulation. The fear is too entrenched that industry self-regulation, however plausible its initial rationale, will eventually degenerate into industry protectionism.

Business Self-Regulation—If self-regulation at the level of the individual firm is of limited usefulness because of the free-rider problem, and if industry self-regulation is ruled out by anti-trust considerations, we are left with self-regulation on a business-wide basis, presumably administered by a confederation or peak organization. An "encompassing" business organization of this sort would be less vulnerable to the anti-trust objections that can be leveled at industry associations. This is so because the diversity of its membership would inhibit such an organization from aligning itself with the sectional interest of particular firms or industries. Because it would embrace, for example, both producers and consumers of steel, it would be unable to support policies specifically favoring the steel industry (such as a cartel or tariffs) without antagonizing other parts of its membership that would be injured by such policies. A business peak organization would thus be constrained to adopt a pro-competitive posture.[23]

How might a peak organization contribute to resolving the assurance problem and the prisoner's dilemma? In the case of the AP, we saw that the principal impediment to cooperation is the difficulty of predicting others' behavior—without which coordination is impossible. By defining a code of responsible corporate conduct—and/or making authoritative rulings in particular cases—a peak organization might substantially remove this difficulty. In particular, if it is equipped to *monitor* compliance with the code, it could provide cooperating firms with the necessary assurance that they were not shouldering an unfair burden.

The point here is not that a peak organization would necessarily be more competent to make ethical judgments or that its code would be ethically superior; it is that the code would be a *common* one that would enable firms to coordinate their behavior. As we have seen, where there is a multiplicity of standards, there is effectively no standard at all, because no firm can be confident that its competitors are playing by the same rules.

A common external code would also help defuse two contentious issues in top management's relations with the firm's stockholders. First, managers would be at least partly relieved of the task of making subjective (and often thankless) judgments about the firms' obligations to various stakeholders—a task for which they are generally not equipped by training, by aptitude, or by inclination. Second, such a code would permit them to heed society's demands that the firm behave responsibly while at the same time protecting them from the charge that their generosity at the stockholders' expense was jeopardizing the firm's competitive position.[24]

So far we have assumed that each firm *wants* to cooperate (i.e., to contribute to the realization of the public good, in this case by acting responsibly) provided other firms do the same. As long as there is some means of coordinating their behavior, then firms can be counted on to cooperate. What happens if we allow for the likelihood that, while most firms may be disposed to comply with the code, some number of opportunistic firms will choose to defect?

A code of conduct—even if only morally binding—can be expected to exert a powerful constraining influence on the behavior of would-be defectors. Such a code would embody "good practice" and so would serve as a standard against which corporate behavior could be judged in individual cases. Consequently, firms which violated the code would be isolated and the spotlight of public indignation would be turned on them. In the cases where moral suasion failed, the code would still offer certain advantages (at least from business's standpoint). First, an adverse ruling by the peak organization would serve to distance the business community as a whole from the actions of a deviant firm and so would counter the impression that business was winking at corporate abuses.[25] Second, the standards defined by the peak organization might become the basis for subsequent legislation or regulatory rule-making. By setting the agenda in this fashion, the peak organization might forestall more extreme or onerous proposals.

However, the defection of even a handful of firms (if it involved repeated or gross violation of the code) would undermine the social contract on which the consent of the majority was based. Their continued compliance would likely be conditional on the code being effectively policed. Therefore, it seems inconceivable that business self-regulation could be based on moral suasion alone. As John Rawls says, "Each person's willingness to contribute is contingent upon the contribution of the others. Therefore, to maintain public confidence in (a common agreement) that is superior from everyone's point of view, or better anyway than the situation that would obtain in its absence, some device for administering fines and penalties must be established. . . . In a well-ordered society the required sanctions are no doubt mild and they may never be applied. Still, the existence of such devices is a normal condition of human life even in this case."[26]

Thus, if we modify the AP to reflect the real-world probability that some number of opportunistic firms will disregard the code, the case for investing the peak organization with some powers of compulsion becomes unanswerable. The case is stronger still if we accept the axiom of the

PD that firms will invariably defect when it is in their narrow self-interest to do so. Some form of sovereign to enforce the terms of the social contract then becomes indispensable.

To sum up, under the original AP a peak organization (or some functional equivalent) is essential to self-regulation because it provides a means by which firms can coordinate their behavior. Under both the modified AP (in which the heroic assumption that firms universally want to cooperate is abandoned) and the PD, a peak organization is also necessary; but if it is to administer a system of self-regulation effectively, it must be given teeth in order to secure firms' compliance. Before discussing the prospects of such an organization evolving or being created in the American context, we must address the objections that

- such a formidable concentration of power would be as likely to be used in an irresponsible manner as a responsible one, and
- a powerful peak organization would weaken representative democracy.

Since no true peak organizations exist in the United States, these questions can best be answered in the light of the experience of other countries.

The Consequences of Peak Organization

Peak (or "encompassing") organizations are not merely larger special interest organizations. By virtue of the breadth and heterogeneity of their membership, they are transformed into a qualitatively different phenomenon. Indeed, peak organizations are likely to exert pressure on the behavior of their members in the direction of the public interest.

In the interests of its own stability, any organization must resist efforts by parts of its membership to obtain private benefits at the expense of other parts. It follows that the more inclusive or encompassing the organization, the larger the fraction of society it represents, and so the higher the probability that it will oppose self-serving behavior (by sections of its membership) that inflicts external costs on the rest of society. By virtue of its size, it will necessarily internalize many of the resulting external costs. The costs of

pollution or workplace injuries, for example, are not just borne by some undifferentiated "public" or "society," but by other managers, stockholders, workers, and so on. According to Mancur Olson, encompassing organizations are less likely than narrowly based ones to further the economic interests of their members in ways that reduce overall levels of social income and wealth.

> The incentives facing an encompassing . . . organization are dramatically different from those facing an organization that represents only a narrow segment of society. . . . The members of the highly encompassing organization own so much of the society that they have an important incentive to be actively concerned about how productive it is. . . . The [encompassing] organization has not only an incentive to at least consider the effect of its policies on the efficiency of the society, but also an incentive to bargain with other substantial organized groups in the interests of a more productive society. The really narrow special-interest group usually does not have an incentive to do even that.[27]

If Olson is correct, we should expect the existence of a powerful business peak organization to promote convergence between the interests of business and other social groups and so lessen the need for coercive regulation.

The officers of business peak organizations in Germany, Japan, and Sweden have a quasi-public conception of their role that is far removed from the American interest group model. According to Andrew Shonfield, Germany's two business *Spitzenverbände* "have typically seen themselves as performing an important public role, as guardians of the long-term interest of the nation's industries."[28] The same finding is reported by an American scholar who evidently has difficulty in taking at face value the claims made by leaders of the BDI (Confederation of German Industry): "To avoid giving an impression that it is an interest group with base, selfish and narrow aims, the BDI constantly identifies its own goals with those of the entire nation."[29] Finally, David Bresnick recently studied the role of the national confederation of employers and trade unions of six countries in the formation and implementation of youth employment policies. In Germany, these policies were largely made and administered by the confederations themselves. In Bresnick's words, "The system in Germany has evolved with minimal government regulation and maximum protection of the interests of the young, while promoting the interests of the corporations, trade unions and the society in general. It has reduced the government role to one of occasional intervenor. It has taken the government out of the business of tax collector and achieved a degree of social compliance that is extraordinary."[30]

A similar account is given by Ezra Vogel of the role of the Japanese business peak organization, *Keidanren*.[31] Keidanren concentrates on issues of interest to the business community as a whole and "cannot be partial to any single group or any industrial sector." Vogel reports that Japanese business leaders are surprised at "the extent to which American businessmen thought only of their own company and were unprepared to consider business problems from a broader perspective." In Japan, this "higher level of aggregation of interests within the business community tends to ensure that the highest level politicians also think in comparably broad terms."[32]

Perhaps the fullest account of the role played by a peak organization in the regulatory process is to be found in Steven Kelman's comparative case-study of occupational safety and health rule making in Sweden and the United States.[33] Remarkably, Kelman found that the content of the regulations in the two countries was rather similar and in both cases tended to favor more protective alternatives over less protective ones. But the resemblances ended there. According to Kelman:

- The regulations were fought persistently in the U.S. but accepted meekly in Sweden.
- OSHA was bound by a detailed set of procedural requirements while ASV (its Swedish counterpart) was bound by virtually none.
- OSHA adopted a far more punitive approach to compliance than ASV did.

- Lawyers and courts were pervasively involved in both rule making and compliance in the United States and virtually uninvolved in Sweden.[34]

In short, American business got a set of regulations no less strict than the Swedish ones, but only after a rancorous and costly rule-making process. What is more, the American regulations were then administered in a more coercive, inflexible, and adversarial manner. In his introduction to Kelman's study, James Q. Wilson notes the irony of the finding that social democratic Sweden showed "a willingness to accommodate business views, an inclination to make policy behind closed doors, and a readiness to accept business assurances of compliance that, if they occurred in this country, would bring forth immediate charges of collusive behavior and irresistible demands for congressional investigations."[33]

A key factor in the ability of business and government in Sweden to reach agreement on health and safety standards was the dominant role played by SAF, the Swedish employers' federation. SAF enjoyed a virtual monopoly on the representation of business's interests in the rule-making process. It is noteworthy that on the rare occasions when individual firms or industry associations participated, the likelihood of agreement being reached decreased markedly.[36]

But why should SAF have been more ready to agree with government? For Kelman, the answer is to be found in the political culture of the Swedish elite, particularly the deference it shows to the state. Deferent values "are . . . more widely held at the elite level . . . [and] encourage elites to lean more toward government views . . . than followers do."[37]

In Kelman's view, business leaders (and the leaders of other organized interests) are coopted by the state in Sweden. He is plainly disturbed by the unabashed elitism of the Swedish system (interest group leaders reportedly believe they "should act accordingly to the 'real' or 'long-term' interests of those they represent (or society as a whole) independent of how followers themselves define their interests") and he fears that one of its effects is to disenfranchise parts—possibly the majority—of the population.[38]

But was it in fact the case that business's views were inadequately weighed in the rule-making process? On Kelman's own evidence, firms got health and safety standards that were no stricter than U.S. ones. More fundamentally, Kelman overlooks the possibility that the U.S. system of interest representation disenfranchises a whole class of interests. This arises from the fact that firms (and other interested parties) have an incentive to intervene in the regulatory process only if the rule under consideration would impose substantial costs on them (e.g., by requiring that they modify their workplaces). The benefits of such a rule (e.g., a healthier workforce, lower workers' compensation rates) are likely to be public goods—for which it is in no one's rational interest to lobby or litigate. Thus, the incidence of pressure does not reflect the actual underlying distribution of interests and, as a consequence, the system is not truly representative.

In making his claim that SAF did not faithfully represent business's viewpoint, Kelman apparently relied on the evidence that agreement on safety and health regulation was harder to achieve when individual firms and industries were involved. But that is to confuse the positions that firms took on specific regulations whose costs they themselves would have to bear with their positions on safety and health regulation in general. It is quite possible that a majority of firms reckoned that the system's indirect benefits to them outweighed its direct costs. Kelman's account contains no evidence concerning firms' evaluation of the system as a whole.[39]

According to the logic of the prisoner's dilemma, even if each firm supported the system of safety and health regulation, it would still have had an incentive to try to avoid paying its share of the system's costs. If each firm then successfully lobbied to have the regulations directly affecting it withdrawn or watered down, there would be no regulation of safety and health, and each firm would be left worse off than before. In Sweden, the SAF provides a mechanism for overcoming such prisoner's dilemmas; in the U.S. they are vir-

tually inescapable because, outside the government, there exists no effective means of providing public goods.

Moreover, by consulting only firms' particularistic interests (e.g., in avoiding the costs associated with regulation) and neglecting general interests (e.g., in safer workplaces) which firms share with the rest of society, the American system of interest representation magnifies conflict. The Swedish system, by contrast, promotes accommodation by emphasizing interests that are shared both within and between broad constituencies.

While the data on Swedish, German, and Japanese peak organizations are too unsystematic to constitute a strict test concerning the consequences of peak organizations, they do shed a revealing light on the role such an organization might play in the U.S. In particular, in administering a system of self-regulation, a peak organization would be in a position to take into account a broader range of interests than is catered for by our present structures of interest representation. Also, a peak organization might promote more harmonious business-government relations without entailing the co-optation or capture of either one by the other.

Prospects

What are the prospects of a system of business self-regulation administered by a peak organization taking root in the U.S.? What incentives would an American peak organization be able to rely on to secure firms' compliance with its standards and rulings? We have seen that, by itself, recognition of the mutuality of gains to be had from a peak organization cannot guarantee such compliance. In order to overcome the free-rider problem, the would-be peak organization must be able to offer firms private benefits or "selective incentives" that are unavailable outside the organization but that are sufficiently attractive to induce firms to comply.[40]

Students of organizations have identified an array of incentives—both positive and negative—that have been used to attract and hold members. These include: selective access to information (e.g., about government actions, technical developments, and commercial practices) under the organization's control; regulation of jurisdictional disputes between members; predatory price-cutting; boycotts; withdrawal of credit; public disparagement; fines; social status; and conviviality. According to James Q. Wilson, "some trade associations did emerge out of a common recognition of the gains that will accrue to combined efforts . . . [but all] suffered from the problem of the 'free-rider.'" Finally, purposive incentives—"intangible rewards that derive from the sense of satisfaction of having contributed to the attainment of a worthwhile cause"—have provided at least a transient basis for organization. But, in the absence of major external threats, organizations relying on such incentives have typically recruited only a fraction of their potential members.[41]

For the most part, trade associations have found these incentives to be of limited usefulness in influencing members' behavior. Wilson says of the cotton industry in the early 1900s that "though it was in the interest of the industry as a whole to have a uniformly high price level, it was to the advantage of each individual firm to undercut that level, and the association had no sanctions with which to ensure that collective benefits would override individual rationality."[42] The use of some incentives was ruled out by anti-trust considerations; other incentives involved services which firms could just as easily obtain through the market; and still other incentives were used sparingly because of the fear that they would create bitterness and distrust within the organization.

Associations have been much more successful when they have enlisted the government to underwrite their agreements for them. The upsurge in associational activity stimulated by the National Recovery Administration and its decrease following NRA's dissolution suggest the difficulties of maintaining purely voluntary agreements.

The difficulties encountered by trade associations that try to influence their members' behavior are compounded in the case of a would-be peak organization. A peak organization has access to fewer selective benefits with which to maintain members' allegiance, and its goals are even further removed from the immediate concerns of most

firms. Moreover, these goals tend to be public goods (e.g., maintaining the private enterprise system or avoiding higher taxes). Wilson notes that "no single businessman has an incentive to contribute to the attainment of what all would receive if the organized political efforts are successful." In these circumstances, "the creation and maintenance of an association such as the [U.S.] Chamber, which seeks to represent all business in general and no business in particular, has been a considerable achievement."[43]

The Chamber, of course, seeks only to speak for business's collective interest. It is not difficult to imagine how much more precarious its existence would be if it also tried to set and enforce standards of conduct. It follows that if trade associations have generally been ineffective except when their powers have been underwritten by the government, a peak organization is *a fortiori* likely to be dependent on government support. And, in fact, in Western Europe, it appears that "many of the peak associations . . . reached their hegemonic status with major contributions from the more or less official recognition of key government agencies."[44]

What form would such public support have to take in the U.S.? It might involve waiving antitrust laws in the case of the peak organization, e.g., by permitting it to punish free-riding behavior by imposing fines or administering boycotts. Government might grant it certain prerogatives— e.g., privileged access to key policy deliberations or agency rule-making, which it might in turn use to obtain leverage over recalcitrant firms. The government might require—as in Japan[45]—that every firm be a registered member of the peak organization. All these actions would serve to strengthen the peak organization vis-à-vis its members.

However, the chances are slight that actions of this kind could be taken in the U.S. In the first place, as Salisbury says, "American political culture is so rooted in individualist assumptions that [interest] groups have no integral place."[46] In contrast with Europe, associations have not been officially incorporated into the process of policy formation; bureaucrats in the U.S. deal directly with constituent units (individual firms, hospitals, universities, etc.) not with associations.[47] Given the dubious legitimacy of interest organizations in general, it seems improbable that semi-official status or privileged access would be granted to a peak organization.

A second obstacle is the structure of American government. The fragmentation of power in the American system—federalism, separation of powers, legislators nominated and elected from single-member districts—has created multiple points of access for interests that want to influence the policy process. Wilson has persuasively argued that a country's interest group structure is largely a reflection of its political structure. Thus a centralized, executive-led government is likely to generate strong national interest associations and, conversely, "the greater decentralization and dispersion of political authority in the United States helps explain the greater variety of politically active American voluntary associations."[48] In the American context, then, it is virtually inconceivable that a peak organization could secure a monopolistic or privileged role in public policy-making in even a few key areas; but without superior access of this sort it is deprived of one of the few resources available to influence its members' behavior.

Conclusion

"Responsible" corporate conduct cannot simply be willed or exhorted into existence by appeals to the public interest or firms' so-called enlightened self-interest. Instead, it depends on the creation and maintenance of particular institutional conditions under which business can behave responsibly as a matter of self-interest.

In our atomistic market economy, firms are bound to take a partial or parochial view of their behavior and its consequences. For the most part, their actions—seen in isolation—have imperceptible impacts for better or for worse on the general welfare. Firms may well deplore the consequences that result when all firms engage in such actions, but so long as they have no control over other firms' behavior they have no incentive to behave responsibly themselves. In such circumstances, social responsibility is not rational but irrational: The firm that practiced it would be doubly penalized, first by forgoing the benefits of irresponsible behavior, and second by having to share in the decline in general welfare regardless.

In this dilemma inescapable? This article has examined the ways it might be possible for firms to coordinate their behavior (both in their own larger interests and the public interest) while at the same time minimizing the risk that this coordination would be exploited for anti-social purposes. Such a benign outcome could be obtained by permitting collective action to be administered by a business-wide peak organization. At this level of coordination, a competitive market economy could coexist with effective self-regulation. However, the United States—given its distinctive political political institutions—is not likely to provide a congenial soil for such an organization to take root.

Notes

[1]Mancur Olson, *The Logic of Collective Action* (Cambridge, MA: Harvard University Press, 1965).

[2]Ibid., p. 2.

[3]Ibid., p. 44.

[4]Russell Hardin, "Collective Action as an Agreeable n-Prisoner's Dilemma," *Behavioral Science*, vol. 16 (1971), pp. 472–79.

[5]C. Ford Runge, "Institutions and the Free Rider: The Assurance Problem in Collective Action," *Journal of Politics*, vol. 46 (1984), pp. 154–81.

[6]Cf. Henry Mintzberg, "The Case for Corporate Social Responsibility, *Journal of Business Strategy*, vol. 14 (1983), pp. 3–15.

[7]Christopher Stone, *Where the Law Ends* (New York, NY: Harper Torchbooks, 1975), p. 112.

[8]In the prisoner's dilemma, two prisoners are interrogated separately about an armed robbery they are charged with committing. Given the strength of the case against them, each can expect to get one year in jail for fire-arms possession, but only so long as neither confesses. The D.A. offers each of them a

deal: if either turns state's evidence against the other, all charges against him will be dropped, but his partner will be convicted and will face a ten-year sentence. However, if *both* confess, both will be convicted and will receive reduced sentences of six years each. Plainly, what is in the narrow self-interest of each prisoner (each is better off confessing no matter what his partner does) is in conflict with what is in their collective interest (between them they serve a total of only two years if neither squeals). See Russell Hardin, op. cit., p. 2.

[9]James Q. Wilson, *Political Organizations* (New York, NY: Basic Books, 1973), chapter 8.

[10]Ibid., p. 149.

[11]Ibid., p. 151.

[12]Robert A. Leone, "Competition and the Regulatory Boom," in Dorothy Tella, ed., *Government Regulation of Business: Its Growth, Impact, and Future* (Washington, D.C.: Chamber of Commerce of the United States, 1979), p. 34.

[13]Susan Bartlett Foote, "Corporate Responsibility in a Changing Legal Environment," *California Management Review*, vol. 26 (1984), pp. 217–28.

[14]Kenneth J. Arrow, "Social Responsibility and Economic Efficiency," *Public Policy*, vol. 21 (1973), p. 315.

[15]See Thomas Schelling on "the false dichotomy of voluntarism and coercion," in "Command and Control," in James W. McKie, ed., *Social Responsibility and the Business Predicament* (Washington, D.C.: Brookings, 1974), p. 103.

[16]The phrase is from Garrett Hardin's "The Tragedy of the Commons," *Science*, vol. 162 (1968), p. 1247.

[17]Schelling, op. cit., p. 103.

[18]David Garvin, "Can Industry Self-Regulation Work?" *California Management Review*, vol. 25 (1983), p. 42.

[19]Michael Porter, *Competitive Strategy* (New York, NY: Free Press, 1980), p. 230.

[20]Thomas P. Grumbly, "Self-Regulation: Private Vice and Public Virtue Revisited," in Eugene Bardach and Robert Kagan, eds., *Social Regulation: Strategies for Reform* (San Francisco, CA: Institute for Contemporary Studies, 1982), p. 97.

[21]Garvin, op. cit., p. 155, 156.

[22]Christopher Conte, "Transport Agency's Dole Vows to Restrict Traffic at 6 Busy Airports if Carriers Don't," *Wall Street Journal*, August 16, 1984, p. 10.

[23]Mancur Olson, *The Rise and Decline of Nations* (New Haven CT: Yale University Press, 1982), pp. 47–48.

[24]These objections lie at the heart of the complaint that the doctrine of corporate social responsibility provides no operational guidelines to assist managers in making responsible choices. The most sophisticated (but, I think, ultimately unsuccessful) attempt to supply an objective, external standard (located in what they call the public policy process) is Lee Preston and James Post, *Private Management and Public Policy* (Englewood Cliffs, NJ: Prentice-Hall, 1975).

[25]See on this point the remarks of Walter A. Haas, Jr., of Levi Strauss quoted in Leonard Silk and David Vogel, *Ethics and Profits* (New York, NY: Simon & Schuster, 1976), pp. 25–27.

[26]John Rawls, *A Theory of Justice* (Cambridge, MA: Harvard University Press, 1971), pp. 270, 269.

[27]Olson, *Rise and Decline*, op. cit., pp. 47–48.

[28]Andrew Shonfield, *Modern Capitalism* (New York and London: Oxford University Press, 1965), pp. 56–57.

[29]Gerard Baunthal, *The Federation of German Industries in Politics* (Ithaca, NY: Cornell University Press, 1965), pp. 56–57.

[30]David Bresnick, "The Youth Employment Policy Dance: Interest Groups in the Formulation and Implementation of Public Policy," paper presented at the American Political Science Association meetings in Denver, September 2–5, 1982, p. 33.

[31]Ezra Vogel, *Japan as Number 1* (New York, NY: Harper Colophon, 1979), chapter 5.

[32]Ibid.

[33]Steven Kelman, *Regulating America, Regulating Sweden: A Comparative Study of Occupational Safety and Health Policy* (Cambridge, MA: MIT Press, 1981).

[34]Ibid., p. 6.

[35]Ibid., p. x.

[36]Ibid., pp. 117 and 158–61.

[37]Ibid., pp. 154–55.

[38]Ibid., p. 151, 233.

[39]In Bauer, Pool and Dexter's classic study, a lopsided majority of the businessmen with opinions on the subject supported free trade, but when they contacted members of Congress it was invariably to ask for protection. Raymond A. Bauer, Ithiel de S. Pool, and Lewis Dexter, *American Business and Public Policy: The Politics of Foreign Trade* (New York: Atherton, 1963), p. 221. The *odyen* of the pluralist school in American political science has recently remarked that "by emphasizing aspects of the self that are enhanced by segmented gains, organizational pluralism helps to produce in political actors a set of perceptions and beliefs, even a persistent political culture, in which the absence of a common, public or widely shared set of interests is a self-fulfilling prophecy." Robert A. Dahl, *Dilemmas of Pluralist Democracy* (New Haven: Yale University Press, 1982), p. 44.

[40]This is, of course, the essence of the argument in Olson's *Logic*, op. cit. This section draws heavily on James Q. Wilson, *Political Organizations*, op. cit.; Robert H. Salisbury, "Why No Corporatism in America?," in Philippe Schmitter and Gerhard Lehmbruch, *Trends Toward Corporatist Intermediation* (Beverly Hills: Sage, 1979); and Philippe Schmitter and Donald Brand, "Organizing Capitalists in the United States: The Advantages and Disadvantages of Exceptionalism," presented at a workshop at the International Institute of Management, Berlin, November 14–16, 1979.

[41]Wilson, op. cit., pp. 146–47, 34, 153–56 and passim.

[42]Ibid., p. 149.

[43]Ibid., p. 153, 161.

[44]Salisbury, op. cit., p. 215. See also Wilson, op. cit., p. 82.

[45]Vogel, *Japan as Number 1*, op. cit., p. 112.

[46]Salisbury, op. cit., p. 222.

[47]Schmitter and Brand, op. cit., p. 71.

[48]Wilson, op. cit., p. 83; see generally chapter 5.

Not Guilty

The Economist (13 February 1993): 63–64. Copyright © 1993.

*General Motors faces a $105m bill for damages. That does not mean that
American competitiveness is being destroyed by product-liability lawsuits.*

Rare is the big-money lawsuit in which the first judgment is also final. On February 4th an Atlanta jury found General Motors responsible for the death in 1989 of a teenager in the fiery crash of one of its pick-up trucks. GM was ordered to pay his parents $105 million in damages. But the case is not closed. Federal safety regulators are deciding whether to tell GM to recall 4.7 million pick-ups made between 1973 and 1987, which could cost more than $500 million. On February 8th GM, which will appeal against the judgment, launched a fierce public-relations campaign to persuade people that its trucks have always been safe. The next day car-safety groups replied, demanding the "GM firebombs" be recalled.

Despite the slew of claims and counterclaims, GM's loss of the case was no surprise to those who followed the trial. Witnesses, including one of the company's own safety inspectors, told the jury that the firm had known for years that its fuel-tank design was dangerously defective and yet had failed to change it. But it is not the verdict itself that has made the GM decision so controversial. It is the size of the award (if upheld, the biggest ever in a car-safety suit), coupled with GM's precarious financial condition, which has rekindled a long-simmering debate about America's product-liability regime.

That debate reached boiling-point last year, when Dan Quayle attacked America's legal system as a "self-inflicted competitive disadvantage" costing $300 billion a year. In the past critics have blamed a "litigation explosion" detonated by ambulance-chasing lawyers for crises in the medical profession, the insurance business and certain other industries. But the charges made by Mr. Quayle and buttressed by Kenneth Starr, then solicitor-general and now one of the lawyers handling GM's appeal, are far more sweeping: that the proliferation of product-liability lawsuits is taking a "terrible toll" on the economy by hurting American firms trying to compete against foreign rivals.

To many managers and politicians, especially those convinced that American firms are falling behind their competitors abroad, this is seductive talk. But the trouble is that, although the effects of the liability system on competitiveness are not entirely clear, there is scant evidence of the catastrophic damage described by Mr. Quayle and other critics. Indeed, much of the conventional wisdom about product liability that lies behind the alarmist talk is plain wrong.

Start with the widely held myth that there is more of such litigation than ever before, and that it is proliferating wildly. Apart from asbestos cases, the number of product-liability lawsuits filed in federal courts has fallen since 1985. . . . And from 1974 to 1985 asbestos—a carcinogen whose dangers were concealed for years by its manufacturers—accounted for fully half the surge in product litigation. Nor is there evidence that other product liability suits have increased in state courts, where perhaps 60% of all cases are heard.

However, the level of product-liability litigation in America dwarfs that in Europe and Japan. More important to firms, so does its cost. General-liability premiums more than tripled in the 1980s, to $20 billion, and some companies found it hard to buy insurance at any price. Contrast this with Europe, where some firms pay one-tenth as much for the same insurance coverage. Tillinghast, an insurance-industry consultancy, calculates that American liability-loss payments (including those for medical malpractice and car accidents) totaled $132 billion last year, or 2.3% of GDP—about twice the percentage in other rich countries.

These are big figures, though nowhere close to Mr. Quayle's $300 billion—which is impossible to justify, even if indirect costs are taken into account. Nevertheless, is the "tort tax" too high? The answer is another question: compared with what? America's liability system is an easy target because its costs are visible. Many countries impose similar costs through regulation.

Nowhere is the difference more plain than in product liability. In America, newspapers are full of stories about jackpot verdicts and looming epidemics of litigation over such issues as silicone breast-implants. In other countries, such tales are rare. Yet it is far from clear that America's system costs companies more. If it did, many products sold there would be more expensive than elsewhere. Or American firms would be, on average, less profitable than those abroad. Neither is the case. Even though foreigners are governed by local liability law when doing business in America, they are keen to manufacture and sell. By contrast, Japan is under pressure from foreign companies to make it easier to sue. These firms prefer more lawsuits to the high costs of complying with Japanese safety regulations.

Litigation and regulation do more than impose costs. They also produce benefits, mainly by deterring firms from making unduly risky products. It is not clear whether tough product-liability is a more efficient way to encourage safety than stringent regulation. But America's tort system does double duty: it deters risky behavior and compensates for losses that in other countries would be financed with higher taxes to support more generous social programs. Although the United States has emphasized product liability while European countries have plumped for safety regulation, standards of product safety have not diverged much.

Yet critics of America's product-liability regime do not claim that it fails to make firms care enough about safety; rather, that it forces them to worry too much. They argue that the unpredictability of juries and their ability to make multi-million-dollar awards—like the one in the GM Case—discourage firms from introducing new products or cost-saving technologies.

The horror stories are familiar to businessmen: litigation over Bendectin, a morning-sickness drug, has stopped all development of that kind of medicine; lawsuits over DTP have greatly slowed research on vaccines; those over IUDs, research on contraceptives. America's light-aircraft industry has collapsed under soaring liability costs. Monsanto has kept a patented phosphate-fibre substitute for asbestos off the market because it fears potential lawsuits.

Such anecdotes are vivid, and often valid, cases against the imperfections in America's product-liability system. But there are counter examples—drugs such as Halcion, a sleeping pill, that can be bought in America but not in Britain. Other facts are often ignored. America's Environmental Protection Agency believes that Monsanto's asbestos substitute may be as carcinogenic as asbestos. The company's decision not to sell it may be correct.

Nor have economists found much evidence that America's liability laws systematically stifle innovation. Robert Litan of the Brookings Institution, a Washington think-tank, and Kip Viscusi of Duke University are two economists who favor product-liability reform. Both agree that the "innovation effect" of litigation on certain industries has been negative. But Mr. Litan says that, even in the industries hit most frequently by lawsuits from 1974 to 1986, R & D spending increased; in the drug industry, where suits were especially prevalent, it more than doubled.

Mr. Viscusi looked at the relationship between liability-insurance premiums and various measures of innovation, especially new patents. He concluded that, for firms with low product-liability costs (i.e., the vast majority), increases in those costs actually foster innovation as firms invest in making better, safer products. Only at extremely high levels do the costs of liability keep firms from launching new products.

If the American system seriously discouraged innovation, many products that can be bought elsewhere in the world would be unavailable in America. That is patently not the case. Firms that want to compete globally must alter their products to the safety standards of different markets. But this is hardly a competitive disadvantage to

American producers. Foreign companies that want access to the world's biggest market must play by its rules, just as American firms have to tailor their products for foreign markets.

None of this means that lawsuits are not a burden on American firms. But much of it is self-inflicted. The type of litigation that is growing fastest is not "frivolous" product-liability suits brought by "greedy" consumers, but the kind of cases in which businesses sue other businesses in complex disputes over antitrust, intellectual property, broken contracts and the like. When firms act this way, they do not call it frivolous or greedy. They call it strategic.

CASES

Case 11.1: Leaking Breast Implants and Faulty IUDs

Karen Reid was one of thousands of women who received silicone-gel breast implants from Dow Corning Corporation in the seventies and eighties. Within a few weeks of getting the implants, she knew something was drastically wrong when she felt shoulder pains and had developed nodules on her arms and legs. She felt sure that her implants had ruptured and leaked silicone gel into her body, giving her health problems and causing her to fear for her life. She and numerous other women sued Dow Corning and are waiting to hear from the courts on their fate. They are encouraged by the case of Mariann Hopkins, a Texas woman who won a $7.34 million judgment against Dow in 1992.

Dow has consistently denied that the implants were unsafe, but in Hopkins's case, several documents were unearthed that described uneasiness about problems with the implants. Since 1992, thousands of women have joined in a class-action suit against Dow and three other manufacturers of the implants. These companies set aside a combined pool of roughly $4 billion to satisfy the claims, amounting to approximately $105,000 per woman in the group. However, in May 1995, a federal judge ruled that the settlement pool was likely to be inadequate, due to the unexpected flood of claims from women who allegedly have suffered damage from the implants. If the fund is not adequately capitalized, then the amount paid to each woman will decrease, prompting more women to opt out of the settlement and pursue their claims in court on their own, a scenario that the manufacturers want to avoid and one of the principal reasons they created the settlement pool. Approximately three thousand women are believed to be opting out of the settlement. In May 1995 Dow announced that they are filing for bankruptcy protection, in much the same way that A. H. Robins, maker of the Dalkon Shield intrauterine contraceptive device, did in the 1970s. However, the federal bankruptcy judge who heard the case refused Dow's request to freeze lawsuits against the larger parent company, Dow Chemical, whom plaintiffs were also attempting to hold responsible.

Robins began making the IUD in 1971, and within a few years women began complaining of pelvic infections and miscarriages. At least eighteen people died from complications arising from its use. In 1985 the company filed for bankruptcy while still a profitable

[6]See David R. Olmos and Henry Weinstein, "Breast Implant Settlement in Peril," *Los Angeles Times*, 5 May 1995, A1; John Carey, "I'm Frightened for My Life," *Business Week* (20 January 1992): 32; Linda Williams, "$2.4 Billion Dalkon Shield Payout Options Disclosed," *Los Angeles Times*, 18 March 1990, A1; Milo Geyelin, "Dalkon Shield Trust, Hailed as Innovative, Stirs a Lot of Discord," *Wall Street Journal*, 3 June 1991, A1; David R. Olmos and Henry Weinstein, "Maker of Implants Seeks Bankruptcy, Freezing Lawsuits," *Los Angeles Times*, 16 May 1995, A1.

company, in anticipation of the rising tide of lawsuits. In 1990, in a move hailed in the business community as innovative, Robins set aside nearly $2.4 billion for roughly 100,000 women who claimed injury from the Dalkon Shield. The settlement is designed to enable the company to settle the majority of claims quickly and for less money, reserving the brunt of the pool for women with more severe damage and the medical records to back up their claim. Women who have been more seriously harmed complained that the terms of the settlement provide far too little money for most women and require an inordinate amount of paperwork and medical records to prove their case. This is particularly problematic for women who were treated through public health clinics that frequently destroy old medical records and hospitals that have closed in the last twenty years and no longer have records available.[6]

Questions for Discussion:

1. Should companies be allowed to create these settlement pools to settle the claims of people allegedly damaged by their products? Do these pools enable the company to underpay people who have been hurt? Or are they a fair way of insuring that people are compensated without the long and expensive appeal to a court?

2. Should companies be allowed to declare bankruptcy in anticipation of future litigation claims?

3. To what degree should companies be held responsible for defects in a product of which they had no knowledge prior to putting it on the market, if they pulled it off the market when the defects came to light?

4. Are the thousands of women in these suits evidence of a widely used defective product or a litigation-happy society in which everyone is trying get money from a deep-pockets corporation?

Case 11.2: Crying Over Spilled Coffee?

Stella Liebeck, an eighty-one-year-old Albuquerque, New Mexico, woman was burned when she opened her McDonald's coffee in her parked car to add cream and sugar. As she was holding the 49-cent cup of coffee between her legs, it spilled in her lap, causing burns on her thighs, groin, and buttocks, for which she spent eight days in the hospital and received skin grafts as treatment. She sued McDonald's, and in August 1994 she won a $2.9 million award (which was later reduced to $480,000 in punitive damages upon appeal) to go with the $160,000 in compensatory damages she was awarded. In December 1994, the company settled out of court with her. Terms of the settlement were not disclosed.

McDonald's coffee is roughly 180–190 degrees, some twenty degrees hotter than coffee served at most other restaurants and fast-food outlets. They had been receiving complaints for some time, and jurors who awarded Liebeck her damages were outraged at the callous way in which McDonald's ignored complaints about their coffee (there were close to 700 reports of coffee burns, which they settled for a total of roughly $500,000), particularly since they admitted that they kept coffee hotter than most competitors and too hot to be ingested when first poured. On the other hand, some argued that coffee is supposed to be hot, and the difference between coffee at 160 degrees and 180–190 degrees is not significant. Further, people who are handling hot materials like a cup of coffee should be careful when handling it. They argued that the company should not be held liable for carelessness on Ms. Liebeck's part and that she should have known what could happen if she opened the coffee while holding it between her legs. Others were sympathetic with Ms. Liebeck but were appalled at the amount of the money she received. They saw it as a symptom of a product liability system that has gone out of control. Shortly after the verdict was announced, McDonald's posted warning signs on their drive-through windows about the temperature of their coffee.[7]

[7]See Andrea Gerlin, "How a Jury Decided That a Coffee Spill Is Worth $2.9 Million," *Wall Street Journal*, 1 September 1994, A1; "McDonald's Coffee Award Reduced 75% by Judge," *Wall Street Journal*, 15 September 1994, A3; Charles Allen, "Fighting Over More Than Just Spilled Coffee," *Los Angeles Times*, 23 March 1995, B5.

Questions for Discussion:

1. Do you think that Ms. Liebeck was justified in holding McDonald's liable for the temperature of their coffee? Or should she have expected her coffee to be that hot and not held them responsible?
2. Do you think that this case is evidence of properly holding a company responsible for its products or of the product-liability litigation system gone out of control?
3. Do you think that the amount of money Ms. Liebeck was awarded was appropriate, given her injuries, or was it excessive? Do you think she should be entitled to any compensatory damages from McDonald's? Any punitive damages?

Case 11.3: General Motors' Flammable Gas Tanks

Seventeen-year-old Shannon Moseley was driving a 1985 GMC pickup truck when he was hit by a drunk driver. The gas tank exploded upon impact, allegedly causing Shannon's death. His family sued GM, and in January 1993 a Fulton County state court awarded them $105 million—$4 million in compensatory damages and $101 million in punitive damages. The decision was reversed on appeal to the Georgia Court of Appeals in June 1994, and if further appeals are not attempted or fail, the case will be remanded back to the state court for retrial.

Safety advocates allege that the GMC truck has one of the worst safety records of cars and trucks on the road. The Federal Department of Transportation had been conducting a lengthy investigation of GM pickups from the model years 1973 to 1987. They have not required GM to recall the trucks, which they normally do when there are clear safety hazards, but in 1993 they did request the company to voluntarily recall the vehicles, because of an alleged flaw in design. The gas tank is located outside the main frame of the truck, presumably making it more prone to explosion. GM refused the recall, which would have included over 4 million pickup trucks, and instead offered $1,000 coupons toward purchase of a new truck (labeled as a marketing ploy by safety advocates). The company insists that the vehicles are some of the safest on the road. They point out that at the time of manufacture, they met all federal crash-safety standards in effect and thus should not be held liable for any alleged design flaw. In court, GM argued that Moseley was killed on impact when struck by the drunk driver, that the gas tank explosion did not cause the boy's death. In the lower court, the jury found for the family and held GM liable for Moseley's death. The appeals court overturned the verdict, a major victory for GM.[8]

[8]See Donald W. Nauss, "GM Wins Appeal Over Side-Saddle Gasoline Tanks," *Los Angeles Times,* 14 June 1994, 1.

Questions for Discussion:

1. If you were sitting on the jury hearing this case, would you hold GM liable for Shannon Moseley's death? Why or why not?
2. If you decided to hold GM liable, do you think that the $105 million award to Moseley's family is appropriate compensation or excessive?
3. Should companies be held liable for products that meet federal safety standards in effect at the time of manufacture but still cause injury or death?

COMMENTARY

In May 1995 the United States Congress took up the controversial and emotionally charged issue of reforming the nation's product liability system. Legislators were responding to the rapidly increasing number of product liability lawsuits and the enormous sums of money being awarded to plaintiffs. They realized that something had to be done to keep business from being overwhelmed by product liability litigation. Some of the suggested reforms include limiting the amount of punitive damages that a person can collect from a company he or she is suing for defective products, limiting the time period in which a person can sue a company to two years after any alleged injury occurs, and limiting a company's liability if the consumer misused or altered the product in an unforeseen manner.[9] Business has been seeking this kind of reform for decades but such reforms had been successfully resisted by consumer-advocacy groups; the reaction to some of the proposed reforms was predictable. Business leaders hailed the measures as necessary to keep them competitive, while consumer groups complained that the measures give companies the freedom to pursue profit at the expense of the consumer's safety. They suggest that the system is not broken and actually protects consumers quite well, and should not be fixed.[10] Business leaders, particularly those in medical products and pharmaceuticals, often respond that they can even be sued and punished for manufacturing products that have gained approval of the Food and Drug Administration, as was the case with silicone-gel breast implants.

How should society insure that the products on the market are safe? Who ultimately is responsible for making sure that the products and devices sold are safe for consumers? Some argue that business is responsible and should be charged with greater accountability for product safety. But Ian Maitland is surely correct when he suggests that there are significant limits on the self-regulation that can be expected from companies engaged in profit maximization. He cites the problem of the "free rider," whereby some companies in a particular industry can benefit from others' increased safety measures without undertaking such measures themselves. He further suggests that firms inevitably take a limited view of their behavior and its consequences. He states that "firms may well deplore the consequences that result when all firms engage in such actions, but so long as they have no control over other firms' behavior, they have no incentive to behave responsibly themselves." Thus for business to insure product safety it must be in their self-interest to do so, and by implication it must be coerced, either by consumers who vote with their dollars, by courts that by punitive damages deter companies from producing unsafe

[9] Edwin Chen, "Senate Set for Major Reform of Product-Liability Laws," *Los Angeles Times*, 10 May 1995, A1.

[10] David C. Vladek, "Trust the Judicial System to Do Its Job," *Los Angeles Times*, 30 April 1995, M5.

products, or by government regulation, with compliance forced by the threat of fines or other more drastic sanctions. Since the company is the one that manufactured the product, it is ultimately responsible, but how to insure that proper responsibility is taken is a different and more difficult question.

Surely consumers can and should take responsibility for some degree of product safety. "Let the buyer beware" is still a good maxim, and consumers should be responsible for any injury when they tamper with a product or use it in a way in which it was not intended. Furthermore, consumers have substantial power to punish companies by voting with their pocketbooks and boycotting a company's products.[11] However, consumer responsibility has one important limit: attempting through the market to influence a company to change its behavior probably will, at best, be a longer-run influence. The reason for this is that it takes time for the information about the product and the company to become public enough to enlist enough consumers to affect the company's bottom line. In the short run, prior to the information about the product getting out to the public and prior to any action being taken through the market, people are still at risk and the likelihood of their being injured is real. Thus it seems that though it is proper to encourage consumers to take more responsibility for safe products, their impact is limited by this information lag time. A further limit is that it is unrealistic to expect consumers to fully research the products they are buying. That is the job of state and federal regulators. Consumers rightly expect the items they purchase to be safe and should not be held responsible for unearthing information that is not easily accessible.

However, many consumers want to have more responsibility for using products that they purchase. They explicitly do not want the regulatory system or the government telling them what products they should or should not purchase. They charge that such restrictions on what products may be brought to the market are an unjustified form of paternalism, treating adults as children and restricting their freedom unnecessarily.[12] They generally raise a good question: To what degree is society responsible for protecting consumers from their poor, yet informed choices? To put it another way, should consumers be able to make the choice to purchase less safe products because they are less expensive, or to purchase unsafe products generally? For example, some suggest that tobacco companies should be prohibited from marketing cigarettes because of their clear, proven harm to smokers. Yet smokers argue that if they want to take the risk of smoking and be responsible for the damage it produces, then they should be able to do so. However, in reality, they do not bear all the costs for lung can-

[11]Todd Putnam and Timothy Much, "Wielding the Boycott Weapon for Social Change," *Business and Society Review* 78 (Summer 1991): 5–8.

[12]For a detailed discussion of this issue related to product safety and regulation, see Steven Kelman, "Regulation and Paternalism," *Public Policy* 29, no. 2 (Spring 1981): 219–54.

cer and other damage created by smoking. The public bears much of that cost in the form of higher insurance premiums and increased use of scarce medical resources to treat them.

Or consider the Honda three-wheeler all-terrain vehicle (ATV). It is great fun to ride, and many suggest that it is more fun to use than the safer four-wheeler that Honda now makes. But the law presently prohibits Honda from manufacturing the three-wheeler because of its propensity to overturn when used in rough terrain, where it was intended to be used. Off-road enthusiasts contend that if they knowingly want to take the risks of using it, they should be free to do so, and their liberty to take informed risks should be maintained. Yet they are prevented from taking such risks because of what they call paternalistic government regulation. Consider also experimental drugs that have yet to gain the lengthy Food and Drug Administration approval, a process that can take as long as a decade. Many cancer patients would readily take the risks involved in using laetrile, yet they cannot, because the drug cannot yet be legally marketed in the United States, and they must go to Mexico or other parts of the world where it is legally available. Surely in the next decade there will be a myriad of experimental cures for AIDS that many AIDS patients would gladly try, irrespective of the risks involved. In addition, there has been a great outcry among motorcycle riders when helmet laws have been passed. They claim that if they want to engage in risky behavior such as riding a motorcycle, they should have the right to do so, in the same way that no one prohibits people from doing risky things such as skydiving, hang gliding, and being employed as a stunt person for the film industry. Generally if the costs can be limited to the individual engaging in the risky behavior and not spill over to the rest of society, people should have the right to take risks if they so desire, and society should rightly be concerned about government encroaching on people's freedom. But with smoking and the freedom to ride motorcycles without helmets, the costs are most often borne by society in general through increased medical costs. Therefore there appears to be a basis for limiting a person's freedom to use a product that poses these kinds of risks to others besides the one using it.[13]

There is substantial debate about whether companies themselves should take further responsibility for insuring product safety. Glenn W. Bailey is surely correct when he speaks from personal experience that the threat of litigation ties up a company's time and resources and inhibits them in the pursuit of innovation necessary to continually introduce new products to the market. For example, the recent case involving Dow Corning and the silicone-gel breast implants has already encouraged some medical suppliers to abandon that market,

[13]Although it might seem that on the basis of this argument smoking should be prohibited, that would probably be unwise and counter productive to the overall goal of limiting a harmful behavior such as smoking. If the law made smoking illegal, there would undoubtedly be a sizable black market for cigarettes, similar to what occurred during Prohibition. For this reason, we hold that smoking should continue to be legal and that education about the dangers of smoking be continued.

as well as making other medical-device manufacturers more hesitant to either continue in the market or launch new products. Silicone is used to make a wide variety of medical devices and implants, and as a result of the costs of litigation against some of the principal suppliers, the costs of the materials have increased dramatically and forced some suppliers to stop making other types of medical implants. Not only does the threat of litigation discourage innovation but it may also deter a company from improving its product, since earlier versions of the product that are still on the market and are less than perfect may be the basis for liability lawsuits.

It is debatable whether or not these rising costs actually make American business less competitive internationally. The article entitled "Not Guilty" insightfully points out that in other countries the costs of insuring product safety are imposed primarily by the government, not primarily by the courts. It is much more difficult to sue a company for product liability in Europe and Japan, but the regulatory burden borne by firms in those countries is much higher. American firms and their counterparts in other parts of the world have much the same safety standards, but these standards are enforced by a different mixture of means. Even though the direct costs of insuring product safety may be roughly the same, there is mounting evidence that the threat of litigation does deter companies from introducing some products to the market. It may be that this threat does not deter certain industries, but, as the reading "Not Guilty" points out, there is clear evidence that this negative effect is occurring. That is clearly cause for concern and should prompt thoughtful observers to ask if the emphasis on product liability lawsuits has gone too far. The excessive amounts of money being awarded to injured individuals usually comes in the form of punitive, not compensatory damages. It may be that limiting punitive damages may be appropriate while maintaining compensatory damages for the victims. In this way the injured parties are compensated for their injuries and companies are not at risk of frivolous lawsuits that tie up their time and resources.

In terms of general guidelines for a sound product liability policy, we would reject the notion of "strict liability," which suggests that firms should be held responsible for any injury that occurs with any use of their product. If someone uses a product in a way different from its intended use or tampers with the product and makes it less safe, then the company should not be held liable for such unreasonable use. Many states do have a strict liability standard, which we suggest is unfair to manufacturers. Companies can and should be held accountable for injuries suffered when their products are used reasonably and in the way they are intended. Companies can and should be assessed punitive damages for knowingly putting unsafe products on the market without warning the consumer about the risks. Certainly, with fair warning, if consumers choose to take the risks inherent in the use of particular products, that is their prerogative, as long as they pay any costs associated with their injuries from such risky behavior.[14] But when the costs are likely to be shared with the public through public hospital services or increased insurance premiums, then it is reasonable to restrict people's freedom to engage in such risky behavior. That is why laws such as those requiring motorcycle helmets are good laws. The public should not be able to buy certain products even when they are informed of the risks because the individual is not the only one who shares the costs should accident and injury occur. For most products, fair warning of the risks to the consumer should be adequate to safeguard a company from liability. If it is legal to produce the product and the manufacturer met the appropriate regulatory standards in effect at the time of manufacture, then it is hard to see how companies should be liable for punitive damages for defects in their products. Compensatory damages are appropriate for injuries received through use of a company's products, even if unforeseen. Surely companies should be held liable for continuing to market an unsafe product after they discover the safety flaws. But to punish companies for producing a product in accordance with all safety and regulatory standards in effect at the time of manufacture is unfair and unreasonable.

We support some of the efforts at product-liability reform that have been proposed in Congress, such as exemption of products from punitive liability if they have been approved by the Food and Drug Administration, limited liability if the product has been tampered with, and the two-year time period from the date of injury in which a person could file a liability lawsuit. In order to deter frivolous lawsuits and still assess punitive damages when appropriate, we suggest that the money from punitive damages be given to charities of the injured person's choice. If they were not able to keep the money themselves, they might be less motivated to sue. But companies would still be forced to pay if they have violated the public trust and knowingly put unsafe products on the market. Compensatory damages would still be paid to the injured individual. For example, the $101 million in punitive damages assessed to General Motors in the death of Shannon Moseley would have gone to charities of the family's choice instead of into their pockets. They would still be awarded the $4 million compensation for the death of their son. For reasonable intended use with fair warning of the risks, consumers are responsible. For unforeseen risks, companies can be liable for compensatory damages. For knowingly putting unsafe products on the market or keeping unsafe products on the market after

[14]A recent example of the trend toward making consumers pay for the costs incurred by engaging in risky behavior is that the national park services in many areas will charge people who need to be rescued after accidents in risky activities such as rock climbing, rappelling, mountain climbing, and hang gliding. They will rescue a person from virtually any situation, but he or she will be billed up to $500 for the service.

a firm knows they are unsafe, punitive damages are appropriate. Both consumers and companies must take responsibility if business is to avoid further regulatory burdens.

This area of product liability illustrates the need for virtue on the part of both consumers and business. Consumers should not be looking to exploit a company's deep pockets or for public sympathy to get money to which they are not entitled. Companies, by contrast, should restrain their profit maximization if the pursuit of profit leads them to disregard public safety. It is unfortunate that it takes coercion of the law or punitive damages to compel some firms to make safe products. But we should not lose sight of the numerous (and the majority of) companies that produce safe products every day. These are unfortunately not often newsworthy, and thus they remain out of the public eye.

TWELVE

The Environment and Economic Growth

The message was ominous, somewhat akin to God warning Noah. It spoke through droughts, heat waves, and forest fires. . . .

W. Michael Hoffman, "Business and Environmental Ethics"

There's no doubt that the environment makes for good politics. . . . The problem, however, is that the environment has become a hostage to politics.

Doug Bandow, "Environmentalism: The Triumph of Politics"

INTRODUCTION

In the past twenty-five years, the environmental movement has succeeded in raising public awareness of the various dangers to the environment posed by industry, development, and population growth. Movements such as Greenpeace and Earth First reflect more radical views, but it is clear that even movements such as these have made significant inroads with the general public and particularly with those who make environmental policy. The result has been both substantial progress in halting the spread of environmental damage and a backlash against what is becoming more widely perceived as environmental extremism. Although the environmentalists have been routinely opposed by business and industry leaders, the public has recently become more aware of the extremes of environmentalism and appears to desire a more balanced view of society's environmental responsibility. For example, the way in which endangered species such as the gnatcatcher, the spotted owl, and the kangaroo rat are protected at the expense of jobs, communities, and individual property rights has become troubling for many who see that the environment has become an end in itself and is being protected to an extreme at the expense of other important goods of society.

To be sure, there have been cases of egregious environmental negligence in recent years, and these have justifiably stimulated a growing concern for the environment. The oil spill of the *Exxon Valdez* in Prince William Sound off the coast of Alaska left damage that will likely never be fully repaired despite the millions of dollars that Exxon committed to the cleanup efforts. The nuclear disasters at Three Mile Island and Chernobyl illustrate the dangers of nuclear power and the need for extremely careful control of such power plants. The destruction of the Amazon rain forests seems to many to be a rampant and random destruction of a unique environmental habitat to make room for economic development in Latin America. Even the recent North American Free Trade Agreement (NAFTA) passed in 1994 was controversial because of what many people perceive to be lower environmental standards in Mexico. They fear that the agreement will allow American businesses to export their air and water pollution along with their products and jobs to areas that care more about economic development than environmental protection.

Environmental awareness is even becoming more fashionable, with a wide variety of "green products" that are advertised for their environmental sensitivity. These products range from biodegradable laundry detergent and other types of household cleaners to many types of recycled products, particularly paper products made from recycled paper. Some green products are even considered chic, such as certain environmentally sensitive fashions and cosmetics.[1] The well-publicized British body products chain called "The Body Shop" specializes in environmentally sensitive facial and body care products and has been very profitable in the late 1980s and early 1990s. The success of these products has prompted the charge that many of these companies are simply using environmental awareness as a slick marketing strategy and actually care very little for the environment. But the CEOs of many companies such as these appear genuinely concerned for the environment and have developed their products accordingly.

The central issue that this chapter addresses is how to maintain a proper balance between environmental protection and economic growth. Most radical environmental measures come at the expense of economic growth and development, and clearly some development does come at the expense of the environment. Environmental issues are often stated in terms of jobs versus the environment. There seems to be an almost inherent conflict between an expanding business and the environment. This is particularly acute for the underdeveloped countries of the Third World, who argue that they should be able to

[1] Rose Marie Turk, "Lean, Mean and Green," *Los Angeles Times*, 25 April 1995, E1.

set their own priorities and not be bound to the developed First World's standards of environmental protection. How one balances concern for the environment, particularly endangered species, with concerns about human well-being is at the heart of this issue that pits business against environmental activists all too frequently. Many of the cases in this chapter will challenge you to articulate how you would balance economic growth and the environment.

Two of the three articles in this chapter directly address this key issue. Michael Hoffman, in his provocative article "Business and Environmental Ethics," suggests a new paradigm for viewing the environment. He rejects what he calls a "homocentric" view of the environment (that human beings ought to protect the environment out of concern for human interests) in favor of what he calls "biocentrism." Also known as "deep ecology," the biocentrist's view is that natural things other than human beings have intrinsic value and rights that merit protection. He accuses business of environmental chauvinism and argues that the best interests of the environment, not the best interests of human beings, should be the primary consideration in making environmental policy.

By contrast, Doug Bandow, in his critique of current environmental policy, "Environmentalism: The Triumph of Politics," argues that a policy such as Hoffman suggests actually is self-defeating, because environmentalism has become hostage to politics. He cites several examples of how certain well-intended environmental policies have backfired, actually resulting in further harm to the part of the environment that the policy was designed to protect. He points out the religious overtones of the deep-ecology movement, which treats the earth as sacred, even to the point of sometimes developing an eco-spirituality that has parallels with ancient and modern forms of pantheism.

The Bible has a great deal to say about the environment in a way that differs from its contribution to other issues addressed in this book such as product safety and insider trading. Peter J. Leithart develops a Judeo-Christian ethic of the environment in his theologically penetrating article "Snakes in the Garden: Sanctuaries, Sanctuary Pollution, and the Global Environment." He attempts to balance the biblical emphasis on the dominion over the environment given to human beings at creation with the responsibility to be stewards of what God has entrusted to their care. He develops an interesting analogy between polluting the sanctuary of God with sin and polluting the environment with the byproducts of economic activity. This article is helpful for developing a theology of the environment.

READINGS

Business and Environmental Ethics[1]

W. Michael Hoffman

Business Ethics Quarterly 1, no. 2 (1991): 169–84. Copyright © 1991.

Business has an ethical responsibility to the environment which goes beyond obeying environmental law.

The business ethics movement, from my perspective, is still on the march. And the environmental movement, after being somewhat silent for the past twenty years, has once again captured our attention—promising to be a major social force in the 1990s. Much will be written in the next few years trying to tie together these two movements. This is one such effort.

Concern over the environment is not new. Warnings came out of the 1960s in the form of burning rivers, dying lakes, and oil-fouled oceans. Radioactivity was found in our food, DDT in mother's milk, lead and mercury in our water. Every breath of air in the North American hemisphere was reported as contaminated. Some said these were truly warnings from Planet Earth of eco-catastrophe, unless we could find limits to our growth and changes in our lifestyle.

Over the past few years Planet Earth began to speak to us even more loudly than before, and we began to listen more than before. The message was ominous, somewhat akin to God warning Noah. It spoke through droughts, heat waves, and forest fires, raising fears of global warming due to the buildup of carbon dioxide and other gases in the atmosphere. It warned us by raw sewage and medical wastes washing up on our beaches, and by devastating oil spills—one despoiling Prince William Sound and its wildlife to such an extent that it made us weep. It spoke to us through increased skin cancers and discoveries of holes in the ozone layer caused by our use of chlorofluorocarbons. It drove its message home through the rapid and dangerous cutting and burning of our primitive forests at the rate of one football field a second, leaving us even more vulnerable to greenhouse gases like carbon dioxide and eliminating scores of irreplaceable species daily. It rained down on us in the form of acid, defoliating our forests and poisoning our lakes and streams. Its warnings were found on barges roaming the seas for places to dump tons of toxic incinerator ash. And its message exploded in our faces at Chernobyl and Bhopal, reminding us of past warnings at Three Mile Island and Love Canal.

Senator Albert Gore said in 1988: "The fact that we face an ecological crisis without any precedent in historic times is no longer a matter of any dispute worthy of recognition."[2] The question, he continued, is not whether there is a problem, but how we will address it. This will be the focal point for a public policy debate which requires the full participation of two of its major players—business and government. The debate must clarify such fundamental questions as: (1) What obligation does business have to help with our environmental crisis? (2) What is the proper relationship between business and government, especially when faced with a social problem of the magnitude of the environment crisis? And (3) what rationale should be used for making and justifying decisions to protect the environment? Corporations, and society in general for that matter, have yet to answer these questions satisfactorily. In the first section of this paper I will briefly address the first two questions. In the final two sections I will say a few things about the third question.

I.

In a 1989 keynote address before the "Business, Ethics and the Environment" conference at the Center for Business Ethics, Norman Bowie offered some answers to the first two questions.

Business does not have an obligation to protect the environment over and above what is required by law; however, it does have a moral obligation to avoid intervening in the political arena in order to defeat or weaken environmental legislation.[3]

I disagree with Bowie on both counts.

Bowie's first point is very Friedmanesque.[4] The social responsibility of business is to produce goods and services and to make profit for its shareholders, while playing within the rules of the market game. These rules, including those to protect the environment, are set by the government and the courts. To do more than is required by these rules is, according to this position, unfair to business. In order to perform its proper function, every business must respond to the market and operate in the same arena as its competitors. As Bowie puts this:

An injunction to assist in solving societal problems [including depletion of natural resources and pollution] makes impossible demands on a corporation because, at the practical level, it ignores the impact that such activities have on profit.[5]

If, as Bowie claims, consumers are not willing to respond to the cost and use of environmentally friendly products and actions, then it is not the responsibility of business to respond or correct such market failure.

Bowie's second point is a radical departure from this classical position in contending that business should not lobby against the government's process to set environmental regulations. To quote Bowie:

Far too many corporations try to have their cake and eat it too. They argue that it is the job of government to correct for market failure and then they use their influence and money to defeat or water down regulations designed to conserve and protect the environment.[6]

Bowie only recommends this abstinence of corporate lobbying in the case of environmental regulations. He is particularly concerned that politicians, ever mindful of their reelection status, are already reluctant to pass environmental legislation which has huge immediate costs and in most cases very long-term benefits. This makes the obligations of business to refrain from opposing such legislation a justified special case.

I can understand why Bowie argues these points. He seems to be responding to two extreme approaches, both of which are inappropriate. Let me illustrate these extremes by the following two stories.

At the Center's First National Conference on Business Ethics, Harvard Business School Professor George Cabot Lodge told of a friend who owned a paper company on the banks of a New England stream. On the first Earth Day in 1970, his friend was converted to the cause of environmental protection. He became determined to stop his company's pollution of the stream, and marched off to put his new-found religion into action. Later, Lodge learned his friend went broke, so he went to investigate. Radiating a kind of ethical purity, the friend told Lodge that he spent millions to stop the pollution and thus could no longer compete with other firms that did not follow his example. So the company went under, 500 people lost their jobs, and the stream remained polluted.

When Lodge asked why his friend hadn't sought help from the state or federal government for stricter standards for everyone, the man replied that was not the American way, that government should not interfere with business activity, and that private enterprise could do the job alone. In fact, he felt it was the social responsibility of business to solve environmental problems, so he was proud that he had set an example for others to follow.

The second story portrays another extreme. A few years ago "Sixty Minutes" interviewed a manager of a chemical company that was discharging effluent into a river in upstate New York. At the time, the dumping was legal, though a bill to prevent it was pending in Congress. The manager remarked that he hoped the bill would pass, and that he certainly would support it as a responsible citizen. However, he also said he approved of his company's efforts to defeat the bill and of the firm's policy of dumping wastes in the meantime. After all, isn't the proper role of business to make as much profit as possible within the bounds of law? Making the laws—setting the rules of the game—is the role of government, not business. While wearing his business hat the manager had a job to do, even if it meant doing something that he strongly opposed as a private citizen.

Both stories reveal incorrect answers to the questions posed earlier, the proof of which is found in the fact that neither the New England stream nor the New York river was made any cleaner. Bowie's points are intended to block these two extremes. But to avoid these extremes, as Bowie does, misses the real managerial and ethical failure of the stories. Although the paper company owner and the chemical company manager had radically different views of the ethical responsibilities of business, both saw business and government performing separate roles, and neither felt that business ought to cooperate with government to solve environmental problems.[7]

If the business ethics movement has led us anywhere in the past fifteen years, it is to the position that business has an ethical responsibility to become a more active partner in dealing with social concerns. Business must creatively find ways to become a part of solutions, rather than being a part of problems. Corporations can and must develop a conscience, as Ken Goodpaster and others have argued—and this includes an environmental conscience.[8] Corporations should not isolate themselves from participation in solving our environmental problems, leaving it up to others to find the answers and to tell them what not to do.

Corporations have special knowledge, expertise, and resources which are invaluable in dealing with the environmental crisis. Society needs the ethical vision and cooperation of all its players to solve its most urgent problems, especially one that involves the very survival of the planet itself. Business must work with government to find appropriate solutions. It should lobby for good environmental legislation and lobby against bad legislation, rather than isolating itself from the legislative process as Bowie suggests. It should not be ethically quixotic and try to go it alone, as our paper company owner tried to do, nor should it be ethically inauthentic and fight against what it believes to be environmentally sound policy, as our chemical company manager tried to do. Instead business must develop and demonstrate moral leadership.

There are examples of corporations demonstrating such leadership, even when this has been a risk to their self-interest. In the area of environmental moral leadership one might cite DuPont's discontinuing its Freon products, a $750-million-a-year-business, because of their possible negative effects on the ozone layer, and Proctor and Gamble's manufacture of concentrated fabric softener and detergents which require less packaging. But some might argue, as Bowie does, that the real burden for environmental change lies with consumers, not with corporations. If we as consumers are willing to accept the harm done to the environment by favoring environmentally unfriendly products, corporations have no moral obligation to change so long as they obey environmental law. This is even more the case, so the argument goes, if corporations must take risks or sacrifice profits to do so.

This argument fails to recognize that we quite often act differently when we think of ourselves as *consumers* than when we think of ourselves as *citizens*. Mark Sagoff, concerned about our over-reliance on economic solutions, clearly characterizes this dual nature of our decision making.[9] As consumers, we act more often than not for ourselves; as citizens, we take on a broader vision and do what is in the best interests of the community. I often shop for things I don't vote for. I might support recycling referendums, but buy products in nonreturnable bottles. I am not proud of this, but I suspect this is more true of most of us than not. To stake our environmental future on our consumer willingness to pay is surely shortsighted, perhaps even disastrous.

I am not saying that we should not work to be ethically committed citizen consumers, and investors for that matter. I agree with Bowie that "consumers bear a far greater responsibility for preserving and protecting the environment than they have actually exercised,"[10] but activities which affect the environment should not be left up to what we, acting as consumers, are willing to tolerate or accept. To do this would be to use a market-based method of reasoning to decide on an issue which should be determined instead on the basis of our ethical responsibilities as a member of a social community.

Furthermore, consumers don't make the products, provide the services, or enact the legislation which can be either environmentally friendly or unfriendly. Grass roots boycotts and lobbying efforts are important, but we also need leadership and mutual cooperation from business and government in setting forth ethical environmental policy. Even Bowie admits that perhaps business has a responsibility to educate the public and promote environmentally responsible behavior. But I am suggesting that corporate moral leadership goes far beyond public educational campaigns. It requires moral vision, commitment, and courage, and involves risk and sacrifice. I think business is capable of such a challenge. Some are even engaging in such a challenge. Certainly the business ethics movement should do nothing short of encouraging such leadership. I feel morality demands such leadership.

II.

If business has an ethical responsibility to the environment which goes beyond obeying environmental law, what criterion should be used to guide and justify such action? Many corporations are making environmentally friendly decisions where they see there are profits to be made by doing so. They are wrapping themselves in green where they see a green bottom line as a consequence. This rationale is also being used as a strategy by environmentalists to encourage more businesses to become environmentally conscientious. In December 1989 the highly respected Worldwatch Institute published an article by one

of its senior researchers entitled "Doing Well by Doing Good" which gives numerous examples of corporations improving their pocketbooks by improving the environment. It concludes by saying that "fortunately, businesses that work to preserve the environment can also make a buck."[11]

In a recent Public Broadcast Corporation documentary entitled "Profit the Earth," several efforts are depicted of what is called the "new environmentalism" which induces corporations to do things for the environment by appealing to their self-interest. The Environmental Defense Fund is shown encouraging agribusiness in Southern California to irrigate more efficiently and profit by selling the water saved to the city of Los Angeles. This in turn will help save Mono Lake. EDF is also shown lobbying for emissions trading that would allow utility companies which are under their emission allotments to sell their "pollution rights" to those companies which are over their allotments. This is for the purpose of reducing acid rain. Thus the frequent strategy of the new environmentalists is to get business to help solve environmental problems by finding profitable or virtually costless ways for them to participate. They feel that compromise, not confrontation, is the only way to save the earth. By using the tools of the free enterprise system, they are in search of win-win solutions, believing that such solutions are necessary to take us beyond what we have so far been able to achieve.

I am not opposed to these efforts; in most cases I think they should be encouraged. There is certainly nothing wrong with making money while protecting the environment, just as there is nothing wrong with feeling good about doing one's duty. But if business is adopting or being encouraged to adopt the view that good environmentalism is good business, then I think this poses a danger for the environmental ethics movement— a danger which has an analogy in the business ethics movement.

As we all know, the position that good ethics is good business is being used more and more by corporate executives to justify the building of ethics into their companies and by business ethics consultants to gain new clients. For example, the

Business Roundtable's *Corporate Ethics* report states:

> The corporate community should continue to refine and renew efforts to improve performance and manage change effectively through programs in corporate ethics ... corporate ethics is a strategic key to survival and profitability in this era of fierce competitiveness in a global economy.[12]

And, for instance, the book *The Power of Ethical Management* by Kenneth Blanchard and Norman Vincent Peale states in big red letters on the cover jacket that "Integrity Pays! You Don't Have to Cheat to Win." The blurb on the inside cover promises that the book "gives hard-hitting, practical, *ethical* strategies that build profits, productivity, and long-term success."[13] Whoever would have guessed that business ethics could deliver all that! In such ways business ethics gets marketed as the newest cure for what ails corporate America.

Is the rationale that good ethics is good business a proper one for business ethics? I think not. One thing that the study of ethics has taught us over the past 2500 years is that being ethical may on occasion require that we place the interests of others ahead of or at least on par with our own interests. And this implies that the ethical thing to do, the morally right thing to do, may not be in our own self-interest. What happens when the right thing is not the best thing for the business?

Although in most cases good ethics may be good business, it should not be advanced as the only or even the main reason for doing business ethically. When the crunch comes, when ethics conflicts with the firm's interests, any ethics program that has not already faced up to this possibility is doomed to fail because it will undercut the rationale of the program itself. We should promote business ethics, not because good ethics is good business, but because we are morally required to adopt the moral point of view in all our dealings—and business is no exception. In business, as in all other human endeavors, we must be prepared to pay the costs of ethical behavior.

There is a similar danger in the environmental movement with corporations choosing or being wooed to be environmentally friendly on the grounds that it will be in their self-interest. There is the risk of participating in the movement for the wrong reasons. But what does it matter if business cooperates for reasons other than the right reasons, as long as it cooperates? It matters if business believes or is led to believe that it only has a duty to be environmentally conscientious in those cases where such actions either require no sacrifice or actually make a profit. And I am afraid this is exactly what is happening. I suppose it wouldn't matter if the environmental cooperation of business was only needed in those cases where it was also in business self-interest. But this is surely not the case, unless one begins to really reach and talk about that amorphous concept "long-term" self-interest. Moreover, long-term interests, I suspect, are not what corporations or the new environmentalists have in mind in using self-interest as a reason for environmental action.

I am not saying we should abandon attempts to entice corporations into being ethical, both environmentally and in other ways, by pointing out and providing opportunities where good ethics is good business. And there are many places where such attempts fit well in both the business and environmental ethics movements. But we must be careful not to cast this as the proper guidelines for business' ethical responsibility. Because when it is discovered that many ethical actions are not necessarily good for business, at least in the short-run, then the rationale based on self-interest will come up morally short, and both ethical movements will be seen as deceptive and shallow.

III.

What is the proper rationale for responsible business action toward the environment? A minimalist principle is to refrain from causing or prevent the causing of unwarranted harm, because failure to do so would violate certain moral rights not to be harmed. There is, of course, much debate over what harms are indeed unwarranted due to conflict of rights and questions about whether some harms are offset by certain benefits. Norm Bowie, for example, uses the harm principle, but contends that business does not violate it as long as it obeys environmental law. Robert Frederick, on the other hand, convincingly argues that the harm principle morally requires business to find ways to prevent certain harm it causes even if such harm violates no environmental law.[14]

However, Frederick's analysis of the harm principle is largely cast in terms of harm caused to human beings and the violation of rights of human beings. Even when he hints at the possible moral obligation to protect the environment when no one is caused unwarranted harm, he does so by suggesting that we look to what we, as human beings, value.[15] This is very much in keeping with a humanistic position of environmental ethics which claims that only human beings have rights or moral standing because only human beings have intrinsic value. We may have duties with regard to nonhuman things (penguins, trees, islands, etc.) but only if such duties are derivative from duties we have toward human beings. Nonhuman things are valuable only if valued by human beings.

Such a position is in contrast to a naturalistic view of environmental ethics which holds that natural things other than human beings are intrinsically valuable and have, therefore, moral standing. Some naturalistic environmentalists only include other sentient animals in the framework of being deserving of moral consideration; others include all things which are alive or which are an integral part of an ecosystem. This latter view is sometimes called a biocentric environmental ethic as opposed to the homocentric view which sees all moral claims in terms of human beings and their interests. Some characterize these two views as deep *versus* shallow ecology.

The literature on these two positions is vast and the debate is ongoing. The conflict between them goes to the heart of environmental ethics and is crucial to our making of environmental policy and to our perception of moral duties to the environment, including business. I strongly favor the biocentric view. And although this is not the place to try to adequately argue for it, let me unfurl its banner for just a moment.

A version of R. Routley's "last man" example[16] might go something like this: Suppose you were the last surviving human being and were soon to die from nuclear poisoning, as all other human and sentient animals have died before you. Suppose also that it is within your power to destroy all remaining life, or to make it simpler, the last tree which could continue to flourish and propagate if left alone. Furthermore you will not suffer if you do not destroy it. Would you do anything wrong by cutting it down? The deeper ecological view would say yes because you would be destroying something that has value in and of itself, thus making the world a poorer place.

It might be argued that the only reason we may find the tree valuable is because human beings generally find trees of value either practically or aesthetically, rather than the atoms or molecules they might turn into if changed from their present form. The issue is whether the tree has value only in its relation to human beings or whether it has a value deserving of moral consideration inherent in itself in its present form. The biocentric position holds that when we find something wrong with destroying the tree, as we should, we do so because we are responding to an intrinsic value in the natural object, not to a value we give to it. This is a view which argues against a humanistic environmental ethic and which urges us to channel our moral obligations accordingly.

Why should one believe that nonhuman living things or natural objects forming integral parts of ecosystems have intrinsic value? One can respond to this question by pointing out the serious weaknesses and problems of human chauvinism.[17] More complete responses lay out a framework of concepts and beliefs which provides a coherent picture of the biocentric view with human beings as a part of a more holistic value system. But the final answer to the question hinges on what criterion one decides to use for determining moral worth—rationality, sentience, or a deeper biocentric one. Why should we adopt the principle of attributing intrinsic value to all living beings, or even to all natural objects, rather than just to human beings? I suspect Arne Naess gives as good an answer as can be given.

Faced with the ever returning question of "Why?," we have to stop somewhere. Here is a place where we well might stop. We shall admit that the value in itself is something shown in intuition. We attribute intrinsic value to ourselves and our nearest, and the validity of further identification can be contested, and *is* contested by many. The negation may, however, also be attacked through a series of "whys?" Ultimately, we are in the same human predicament of having to start somewhere, at least for the moment. We must stop somewhere and treat where we then stand as a foundation.[18]

In the final analysis, environmental biocentrism is adopted or not depending on whether it is seen to provide a deeper, richer, and more ethically compelling view of the nature of things.

If this deeper ecological position is correct, then it ought to be reflected in the environmental movement. Unfortunately, for the most part, I do not think this is being done, and there is a price to be paid for not doing so. Moreover, I fear that even those who are of the biocentric persuasion are using homocentric language and strategies to bring business and other major players into the movement because they do not think they will be successful otherwise. They are afraid, and undoubtedly for good reason, that the large part of society, including business, will not be moved by arguments regarding the intrinsic value and rights of natural things. It is difficult enough to get business to recognize and act on their responsibilities to human beings and things of human interest. Hence many environmentalists follow the counsel of Spinoza:

> . . . it is necessary that while we are endeavoring to attain our purpose . . . we are compelled . . . to speak in a manner intelligible to the multitude. . . . For we can gain from the multitude no small advantages. . . .[19]

I understand the temptation of environmentalists employing a homocentric strategy, just as I understand business ethicists using the rationale that good ethics is good business. Both want their important work to succeed. But just as with the good ethics is good business tack, there are dangers in being a closet ecocentrist. The ethicists in both cases fail to reveal the deeper moral base of their positions because it's a harder sell. Business ethics gets marketed in terms of self-interest, environmental ethics in terms of human interest.

A major concern in using the homocentric view to formulate policy and law is that nonhuman nature will not receive the moral consideration it deserves. It might be argued, however, that by appealing to the interests and rights of human beings, in most cases nature as a whole will be protected. That is, if we are concerned about a wilderness area, we can argue that its survival is important to future generations who will otherwise be deprived of contact with its unique wildlife. We can also argue that it is important to the aesthetic pleasure of certain individuals or that, if it is destroyed, other recreational areas will become overcrowded. In this way we stand a chance to save the wilderness area without having to refer to our moral obligations to respect the intrinsic value of the spotted owl or of the old-growth forest. This is simply being strategically savvy. To trot out our deeper ecological moral convictions runs the risk of our efforts being ignored, even ridiculed, by business leaders and policy makers. It also runs head-on against a barrage of counter arguments that human interests take precedence over nonhuman interests. In any event it will not be in the best interest of the wilderness area we are trying to protect. Furthermore, all of the above homocentric arguments happen to be true—people will suffer if the wilderness area is destroyed.

In most cases, what is in the best interests of human beings may also be in the best interests of the rest of nature. After all, we are in our present environmental crisis in large part because we have not been ecologically intelligent about what is in our own interest—just as business has encountered much trouble because it has failed to see its interest in being ethically sensitive. But if the environmental movement relies only on arguments based on human interests, then it perpetuates the danger of making environmental policy and law on the basis of our strong inclination to fulfill our immediate self-interests, on the basis of our consumer viewpoints, on the basis of our willingness to pay. There will always be a tendency to allow our short-term interests to eclipse our long-term interest and the long-term interest of humanity itself. Without some grounding in a deeper environmental ethic with obligations to nonhuman natural things, then the temptation to view our own interests in disastrously short-term ways is that much more encouraged. The biocentric view helps to block this temptation.

Furthermore, there are many cases where what is in human interest is not in the interest of other natural things. Examples range from killing leopards for stylish coats to destroying a forest to build a golf course. I am not convinced that homocentric arguments, even those based on long-term human interests, have much force in protecting the interests of such natural things. Attempts to make these interests coincide might be made, but the point is that from a homocentric point of view the leopard and the forest have no morally relevant interests to consider. It is simply fortuitous if nonhuman natural interests coincide with human interests, and are thereby valued and protected. Let us take an example from the work of Christopher Stone. Suppose a stream has been polluted by a business. From a homocentric point of view, which serves as the basis for our legal system, we can only correct the problem through finding some harm done to human beings who use the stream. Reparation for such harm might involve cessation of the pollution and restoration of the stream, but it is also possible that the business might settle with the people by paying them for their damages and continue to pollute the stream. Homocentrism provides no way for the stream to be made whole again unless it is in the interests of human beings to do so. In short it is possible for human beings to sell out the stream.[20]

I am not saying that human interests cannot take precedence over nonhuman interests when there are conflicts. For this we need to come up with criteria for deciding on interspecific conflicts of interests, just as we do for intraspecific conflicts of interest among human beings.[21] But this is a different problem from holding that nonhuman nat-

ural things have no interests or value deserving of moral consideration. There are times when causing harm to natural things is morally unjustifiable when there are no significant human interests involved and even when there are human interests involved. But only a deeper ecological ethic than homocentrism will allow us to defend this.

Finally, perhaps the greatest danger that biocentric environmentalists run in using homocentric strategies to further the movement is the loss of the very insight that grounded their ethical concern in the first place. This is nicely put by Lawrence Tribe:

> What the environmentalist may not perceive is that, by couching this claim in terms of human self-interest—by articulating environmental goals wholly in terms of human needs and preferences—he may be helping to legitimate a system of discourse which so structures human thought and feeling as to erode, over the long run, the very sense of obligation which provided the initial impetus for his own protective efforts.[22]

Business ethicists run a similar risk in couching their claims in terms of business self-interest.

The environmental movement must find ways to incorporate and protect the intrinsic value of animal and plant life and even other natural objects that are integral parts of ecosystems. This must be done without constantly reducing such values to human interests. This will, of course, be difficult, because our conceptual ideology and ethical persuasion is so dominantly homocentric; however, if we are committed to a deeper biocentric ethic, then it is vital that we try to find appropriate ways to promote it. Environmental impact statements should make explicit reference to nonhuman natural values. Legal rights for nonhuman natural things, along the lines of Christopher Stone's proposal, should be sought.[23] And naturalistic ethical guidelines, such as those suggested by Holmes Rolston, should be set forth for business to follow when its activities impact upon ecosystems.[24]

At the heart of the business ethics movement is its reaction to the mistaken belief that business only has responsibilities to a narrow set of its stakeholders, namely its stockholders. Crucial to the environmental ethics movement is its reaction to the mistaken belief that only human beings and human interests are deserving of our moral consideration. I suspect that the beginnings of both movements can be traced to these respective moral insights. Certainly the significance of both movements lies in their search for a broader and deeper moral perspective. If business and environmental ethicists begin to rely solely on promotional strategies of self-interest, such as good ethics is good business, and of human interest, such as homocentrism, then they face the danger of cutting off the very roots of their ethical efforts.

Notes

[1] This paper was originally presented as the Presidential Address to the *Society for Business Ethics*, August 10, 1990, San Francisco, CA.

[2] Albert Gore, "What Is Wrong With Us?" *Time* (January 2, 1989), 66.

[3] Norman Bowie, "Morality, Money, and Motor Cars," *Business, Ethics, and the Environment: The Public Policy Debate*, edited by W. Michael Hoffman, Robert Frederick, and Edward S. Petry, Jr. (New York: Quorum Books, 1990), 89.

[4] See Milton Friedman, "The Social Responsibility of Business Is to Increase Its Profits," *The New York Times Magazine* (September 13, 1970).

[5] Bowie, 91.

[6] Bowie, 94.

[7] Robert Frederick, Assistant Director of the Center for Business Ethics, and I have developed and written these points together. Frederick has also provided me with invaluable assistance on other points in this paper.

[8] Kenneth E. Goodpaster, "Can a Corporation Have an Environmental Conscience," *The Corporation, Ethics, and the Environment*, edited by W. Michael Hoffman, Robert Frederick, and Edward S. Petry, Jr. (New York: Quorum Books, 1990).

[9] Mark Sagoff, "At the Shrine of Our Lady of Fatima, or Why Political Questions Are Not All Economic," found in *Business Ethics: Readings and Cases in Corporate Morality*, 2nd edition, edited by W. Michael Hoffman and Jennifer Mills Moore (New York: McGraw-Hill, 1990), 494–503.

[10] Bowie, 94.

[11] Cynthia Pollock Shea, "Doing Well By Doing Good," *World-Watch* (November/December, 1989), 30.

[12] *Corporate Ethics: A Prime Business Asset*, a report by The Business Roundtable, February, 1988, 4.

[13] Kenneth Blanchard, and Normal Vincent Peale, *The Power of Ethical Management* (New York: William Morrow and Company, Inc., 1988).

[14] Robert Frederick, "Individual Rights and Environmental Protection," presented at the Annual Society for Business Ethics Conference in San Francisco, August 10 and 11, 1990.

[15] Frederick.

[16] Richard Routley, and Val Routley, "Human Chauvinism and Environmental Ethics," *Environmental Philosophy*, Monograph Series, No. 2, edited by Don Mannison, Michael McRobbie, and Richard Routley (Australian National University, 1980), 121ff.

[17] See Paul W. Taylor, "The Ethics of Respect for Nature," found in *People, Penguins, and Plastic Trees*, edited by Donald VanDe Veer and Christine Pierce (Belmont, California: Wadsworth, 1986), 178–83. Also see R. and V. Routley, "Against the Inevitability of Human Chauvinism," found in *Ethics and the Problems of the 21st Century*, edited by K. E. Goodpaster and K. M. Sayre (Notre Dame: University of Notre Dame Press, 1979), 36–59.

[18] Arne Naess, "Identification as a Source of Deep Ecological Attitudes," *Deep Ecology*, edited by Michael Tobias (San Marcos, California: Avant Books, 1988), 266.

[19] Benedict de Spinoza, "On the Improvement of the Understanding," found in *Philosophy of Benedict de Spinoza*, translated by R. H. M. Elwes (New York: Tudor Publishing Co., 1936), 5.

[20] Christopher D. Stone, "Should Trees Have Standing?—Toward Legal Rights for Natural Objects," found in *People, Penguins, and Plastic Trees*, 86–87.

[21] Stone, 83–96.

[22] Lawrence H. Tribe, "Ways Not to Think about Plastic Trees: New Foundations for Environmental Law," found in *People, Penguins, and Plastic Trees*, 257.

[23] Stone, 83–96.

[24] Holmes Rolston, III, *Environmental Ethics* (Philadelphia: Temple University Press, 1988), 301–13.

Environmentalism: The Triumph of Politics

Doug Bandow

The Freeman: Ideas on Liberty (September 1993), 332–39. Copyright © 1993.

There's no doubt that the environment makes for good politics. Eight of ten Americans call themselves environmentalists. Overwhelming majorities say that gasoline should be less polluting, cars should be more efficient, trash should be recycled, and lifestyles should be changed.

This increasing sensitivity is reflected in business' growing emphasis on environmental products. Such catalogues as *Real Goods, Seventh Generation*, and *Earth Care Paper* offer recycled paper, vegetable-based dishwashing liquid, battery chargers, and fluorescent light bulbs. Even many mainstream firms are labeling their products CFC-free, biodegradable, and environmentally friendly. While the environmental benefits of these activities are unclear, they apparently help sell products.

Increasing numbers of people are taking an interest in environmental issues in part in response to their own concerns and in part in response to social pressure—including from their children. The schools have launched what for a less politically correct goal would be called indoctrination programs. And the campaign seems to be working: The *New York Times* ran one story about parents who were relieved when their children went off to camp so they could again use Styrofoam cups and toss out used plastic.

The law is also playing a greater role in people's lives. An unaccountable bureaucracy in southern California, for instance, proposed banning use of lighter fluid for barbecues and prohibiting drive-in facilities. Federal agencies have essentially seized control of millions of acres of land arbitrarily designated as wetlands. And the Washington, D.C., suburb of Tacoma Park employs what it euphemistically calls "recycling coordinators" to comb through people's trash and hand out tickets—with fines ranging up to $500—for not properly sorting garbage.

In the abstract, greater attention to environmental matters would seem to be a positive trend. After all, no one wants to breathe polluted air. No one wants to visit an Everglades that is dying or see Yellowstone's Old Faithful replaced by condominiums. And who could not be concerned about the possibility of a warming environment, threatening ozone holes, and the specter of acid rain?

The problem, however, is that the environment has become a hostage to politics. Many environmental activists want more than a clean environment. Their commitment to conservation and political action is religious, and their goals are often far-reaching: to transform what they consider to be a sick, greedy, and wasteful consumer society. As a result, many otherwise well-meaning people have proved quite willing to use state power to force potentially draconian social changes irrespective of numerous important alternative values, including freedom, health, and prosperity.

The real political divide is not between right and left, conservative and liberal, or Republican and Democrat. Rather, it is between market process and central planning, the free market and command and control by the government. Most politicians believe in government solutions. They may not be consistent in the specific ways they want the state to intervene, but they like government involvement. Although liberal enthusiasm for state action is best known, conservatives, too, often want government to rearrange environmental outcomes arbitrarily. There are no more fervent supporters of irrigation projects that deliver below-cost water to farmers, subsidies to promote logging on public lands, and cut-rate range fees on federal grazing land for ranchers than Republican legislators. Conservative western senators have fervently opposed selling federal lands.

Where Do We Stand?

Much of today's concern for new environmental restrictions comes from the perception that the sky is falling. In the view of Lester Brown of Worldwatch, for instance, we're in a "battle to save the earth's environmental support systems." He worries about global warming, growing populations, disappearing species, expanding deserts, depleting topsoil, and so on. We face "the wholesale collapse of ecosystems," he claims.

Yet somehow the world seems rather less bleak than he suggests. Between 1970 and 1986, for instance, the amount of particulates spewed into the air fell by 64 percent, carbon monoxide emissions dropped 38 percent, and releases of volatile organic compounds fell by 29 percent. Ocean dumping of industrial wastes was reduced 94 percent. There were 80 percent fewer cities without adequate sewage treatment plants. Rivers unfit for swimming dropped 44 percent. Hazardous waste sites such as Love Canal and Times Beach now appear far less dangerous than once thought. Cars built in 1988 produced 96 percent less carbon monoxide and hydrocarbons than those made in the early 1980s. Population continues to grow sharply in some Third World states, but these increases reflect lower infant mortality rates and longer life expectancies. Total recoverable world oil reserves grew by 400 billion barrels between 1985 and 1990. Global warming trends may lengthen growing seasons. And extensive product packaging, falsely derided as wasteful, makes Americans among the most efficient eaters on earth.

The point is not that there are no environmental problems. But claims of imminent disaster are simply not supported by the facts. To the contrary, they reflect the politicization of the environment, because only claims of imminent disaster can galvanize popular support for the sort of exceedingly harsh policy changes advocated by many people for ideological—or even religious—reasons. Some environmental apocalyptics have admitted as much.

Politics has infected environmental policymaking in two different ways. The first is to create real environmental problems. The second is to generate unfounded hysteria.

Poor Environmental Stewardship

For all of the enthusiasm of environmentalists for government programs, the government has proved to be a remarkably poor resource steward. Consider Uncle Sam's 191 million acres of forestland. The Wilderness Society estimates that losses on federal timberland amounted to $400 million annually during the 1980s, while losses on Alaska's Tsongass rain forest have hit 99 cents on the dollar. The problem is that the government both undertakes expensive investments, such as road-building in mountainous wilderness terrain, and underprices the timber that is produced. Washington's reason for doing so is to "create" a few jobs. The cost, however, is both needless environmental destruction and the squandering of taxpayers' money.

Federal water projects and management of rangeland have consistently led to similar results. The government has expended billions of dollars to subsidize such influential groups as farmers and ranchers, all the while leaving environmental despoliation in its wake. In fact, the greatest threat to wetlands across the country is not private development, but federal efforts like the $1.2 billion Garrison Diversion project, which destroyed some 70,000 acres of wetlands to benefit a few thousand farmers.

Nearly 90 percent of all federal water in the west is sold at heavily subsidized prices to heavily subsidized farmers. In California's San Joaquin Valley, for instance, irrigation projects typically cost $300–$500 an acre foot, yet the water is marketed to farmers for less than a tenth that much—even as Los Angeles and other parts of the state until recently were suffering from severe water shortages. Only the government would subsidize the production of a water-intensive crop like rice in a desert.

The federal government similarly mismanages its 307 million acres of rangeland. The Bureau of Land Management (BLM) has typically charged ranchers half of what it costs the government to administer its land, and one-tenth the rental price for comparable private lands. The BLM also spent millions of dollars "chaining" land—ripping out trees to create more rangeland on which it would lose more money. Not surprisingly, federal lands are generally in poor condition—and continue to generate a flood of red ink.

It is not just Uncle Sam who is to blame. Local governments have distorted the trash market, leading to pressure for a federal garbage law. Many localities have essentially socialized trash collection and disposal, barring any private competition which increases efficiency and innovation. Moreover, few cities charge citizens based upon how much garbage they generate, providing no incentive for people either to recycle or to change their buying habits. (Localities that have implemented fees for each can or bag have made people more environmentally conscious without a trash Gestapo.) Political restrictions on the placement of new landfills and construction of incinerators, both of which are quite safe with new technologies, have exacerbated the problem.

But the U.S. government is the most culpable party. World Bank loans, underwritten by American taxpayers, have financed the destruction of Brazilian rain forests; federally subsidized flood insurance has encouraged uneconomic construction on the environmentally sensitive Barrier Islands. Years of energy price controls inflamed demand and discouraged conservation.

This sort of special-interest driven environmental abuse is not new, and the only solution is to eliminate political malfeasance. Unfortunately, as public choice economists have so effectively pointed out, the political process tends to be biased toward taxpayer exploitation and against sound policy.

Unfounded Hysteria

The second form of environmental politicization is more recent. That is the manufacture of false crises and the exaggeration of more limited problems to achieve other ideological ends, such as banning chemicals, closing incineration plants, and eliminating chlorofluorocarbons (CFCs). Unfortunately, examples of this sort of problem now abound.

For instance, in 1989 the Natural Resources Defense Council (NRDC) used a public relations agency to launch a campaign against the chemical Alar, a pesticide used on some 15 percent of apples in the United States. The charges received wide attention and demand for apples dropped dramatically—prices fell almost in half, ruining some farmers. Yet the furor was based on one 1973 study, where mice were fed very high levels of Alar. Two recent reviews, by Great Britain's Advisory Committee on Pesticides and the California Department of Food and Agriculture, concluded that the risk of ingesting Alar was minimal. As Dr. Joseph Rosen of Rutgers University explained, "There was never any legitimate scientific study to justify the Alar scare."

But skillful manipulation of the media to inflame people's fears—and the enlistment of such knowledgeable environmental experts as Hollywood's Meryl Streep—enabled one activist group to create a crisis. The NRDC's public relations agent later circulated a memo to other organizations describing his efforts.

Indeed, pesticides have long been subject to counterfactual demagogic attacks. Natural pesticides—nature's way of protecting plants—may cause cancer, and they occur in far higher quantities in at least 57 food varieties than do man-made pesticides. A National Center for Policy Analysis study estimates that the risk of getting cancer from chloroform in tap water is greater than that of getting it from pesticides in food. A person is more than three times as likely to be killed by lightning than to contract cancer from pesticides. The risk of cancer from all pesticides in the food consumed by the average person in one day is one-twentieth of the risk from the natural carcinogens in a single cup of coffee.

Another apocalyptic vision emerged from the EPA, which in 1980 claimed that acid rain, caused by sulfur dioxide emissions, had increased the average acidity of northeast lakes one hundredfold over the last 40 years and was killing fish and trees alike. A year later the National Research Council predicted that the number of acidified lakes would double by 1990, so Congress included stringent provisions to cut SO_2 emissions (already down 50 percent from the 1970s) at a cost of billions of dollars annually when it re-authorized the Clean Air Act three years ago.

Yet in 1987 EPA research raised doubts about the destructiveness of acid rain: A congressional firestorm forced the study's director to quit. Then came the most complete study of acid rain ever conducted, the half billion dollar National Acid Precipitation Assessment Project (NAPAP), which concluded that the allegedly horrific effects of acid rain were largely a myth. Among other things, the study found that lakes were on average no more acidic than before the industrial era; just 240 of 7,000 northeast lakes, most with little recreational value, were critically acidic, or "dead"; most of the acidic water was in Florida, where the rain is only one-third as acidic; there was only very limited damage to trees, far less than that evident elsewhere in the world where SO_2 emissions are minimal; half of the Adirondack lakes were acidified due to natural organic acids; and crops remained undamaged at acidic levels ten times present levels. In the end, NAPAP's scientists figured that applying lime to the few lakes that were acidic would solve the problem at a mere fraction of the cost of the Clean Air Act's acid rain provisions.

Perhaps the most famous form of the "sky is falling" claim today is global warming—the so-called "Greenhouse Effect." The U.N.'s 1992 Rio summit focused on this issue. The fear is that pollution, particularly such "greenhouse gases" as carbon dioxide, will stay within the atmosphere, leading to a rise in the earth's temperature, which will create deserts, melt the polar icecaps, and flood coastal nations.

In fact, warnings of global warming are not new: The theory was first advanced in the 1890s and re-emerged in the 1950s. But soon thereafter a new theory gained sway—that we were entering a new Ice Age. In 1974 the U.S. National Science Board stated that "during the last 20 to 30 years, world temperature has fallen, irregularly at first but more sharply over the last decade." In the same year, *Time* magazine opined that "the atmosphere has been growing gradually cooler for the past three decades. The trend shows no indication of reversing." Similarly, observed Dr. Murray

Mitchell of the National Oceanic and Atmospheric Administration in 1976, "Since about 1940 there has been a distinct drop in average global temperature. It's fallen about half a degree Fahrenheit."

Five years later Fred Hoyle's *Ice: The Ultimate Human Catastrophe* appeared, warning that a new Ice Age was long overdue, and "when the ice comes, most of northern America, Britain, and northern Europe will disappear under the glaciers. . . . The right conditions can arise within a single decade." He advocated warming the oceans to forestall this "ultimate human catastrophe." Another two years passed and *Rolling Stone* magazine declared that: "For years now, climatologists have foreseen a trend toward colder weather—long range, to be sure, but a trend as inevitable as death. . . . According to [one] theory, all it would take is a single cold summer to plunge their earth into a sudden apocalypse of ice."

A decade later we have passed into a new crisis. Climatologists like Stephen Schneider, who two decades ago was warning of a cooling trend that looked like "one akin to the Little Ice Age," now berates the media for covering scientists who are skeptical of claims that global warming is occurring. He is, at least, refreshingly honest, admitting that "to avert the risk we need to get some broad-based support, to capture public imagination. . . . So we have to offer up some scary scenarios, make some simplified dramatic statements and little mention of any doubts one might have."

And he does this precisely because the doubts about global warming are serious, so serious that both *The Washington Post* and *Newsweek* recently ran stories debunking the apocalyptic predictions of everyone from Vice President Gore to Greenpeace. Observed *The Post*:

> Scientists generally agree that it has been getting warmer over the last hundred years, but the average rate of change is no greater than in centuries past, and there is no consensus that human activity is the cause. And while there is no doubt that continued emissions of "greenhouse gases" tend to aid warming, it is not clear that cutting back on

emissions could do much to stop a natural trend, if that is what is happening.

Indeed, a survey by Greenpeace, one of the most radical environmental organizations, of scientists involved in the Intergovernmental Panel on Climate Change found that only 13 percent of them believed there was probably a point-of-no-return in the future leading to a runaway greenhouse effect. Just 17 percent of climatologists in a broader Gallup poll believed that human-induced warming had occurred at all, while 53 percent did not.

The problems with the theory are many. First, there is no reason to assume that any change in temperature is undesirable. In fact, people living in colder climates would benefit from small increases; higher temperatures at night also would likely have a positive impact.

Second the evidence does not support the contention that human activity is raising temperatures. We have seen slight warming over the last century, but 90 percent of it occurred before 1940, when greenhouse gas emissions started rising dramatically. The assumptions suggest that daytime temperatures should rise in the northern hemisphere, but most of the limited warming so far observed has occurred at night in the southern hemisphere. The ice caps have been growing, not shrinking. And so on. Even those predicting a much hotter future have had to lower their forecasts over the last decade. In the end, it is obvious both that mankind, which produces just a couple percent of total CO_2, has only a limited impact on the earth's climate, and that the globe has a dramatic ability to adjust. For instance, increased pollution may help shield the earth from sunlight, counteracting any temperature increase. Higher temperatures at the poles actually allow more precipitation. Since serious warming could cause serious damage, there is cause to monitor changes in climate, but not yet to implement the sort of draconian changes demanded by the greenhouse crowd.

The ozone issue has been similarly politicized. The fear is that chlorofluorocarbons are thinning atmospheric ozone, allowing in more ultraviolet (UV) rays. In January 1992 a Harvard university chemist, James Anderson, held a press conference warning of a "hole" in the ozone in the so-called polar vortex, the upper atmosphere over New England and Canada. His claims were based on the initial findings from a scientific expedition monitoring atmospheric conditions and received wide attention. Yet four months later he was forced to admit that "the dreaded ozone hole never materialized."

A decade ago apocalyptic environmentalists were warning of a reduction of 18 percent in ozone levels. Today the predictions are down to 2 to 4 percent. Even if these forecasts are borne out, the impact may not be dramatic: It would be like moving roughly 60 miles south, from Palm Beach to Miami in Florida. And, oddly, UV radiation levels have dropped over the last decade, even as the ozone layer was supposedly thinning. Moreover, there is some question as to whether CFC's—inexpensive, safe chemicals that have no obvious replacement—are really villainous destroyers of ozone after other factors are taken into account. Such things as ocean salt spray may help counteract increasing CFC levels. Explains Dr. Melvyn Shapiro of the National Oceanic and Atmospheric Administration, in making their claims even many atmospheric chemists "have little regard for the impact of atmospheric variability on chemical processes." In fact, the higher levels of chlorine monoxide detected in January did not create an ozone hole because temperatures were higher than expected.

Population growth has been cited as an impending disaster for nearly two centuries. Recent apocalyptics include Paul Ehrlich of Stanford University, who predicted mass famine and death in the 1970s, and former World Bank President Robert McNamara, who went so far as to compare the threat of population pressure to that of nuclear war.

Their argument is simple: More people mean the use of more resources and more waste. The end result is lower incomes and disaster.

This apocalyptic scenario ignores the fact that some part of the population "explosion" is short term, since infant mortality rates have fallen more swiftly than have fertility rates. Moreover, people normally produce more than they consume—

otherwise even one person would be too many. Further, fears of population growth assume a static view of the world, that economics is a zero-sum game. Yet the market naturally adjusts as the number of people and demand for goods and services increase; technological innovation and behavioral changes work together to allow better and more efficient resource use.

In practice we see no adverse relationship between population or population density and economic growth. Population density is very high in such places as Hong Kong, Singapore, and Taiwan, yet their economies have grown faster. The population of the Netherlands is 50 percent denser than India, Great Britain's is twice as dense as that of Thailand, and South Korea possesses less territory but twice the population of North Korea. In all of these cases the more populated states have achieved much higher levels of development.

The issue of population growth, then, is a red herring. The central issue is economic growth. The most important means of adaptation is the marketplace: If governments prevent people from freely producing goods and services, charging prices that reflect changing resource values, and responding to diverse human needs, then worsening poverty will result. Third World countries are impoverished not because they are populous, but because their governments have enforced anti-capitalistic economic policies.

Related to the supposed problem of too many people is that of too few resources. Such reports as the Club of Rome's 1972 *Limits to Growth* and the Carter Administration's 1980 *Global 2000* predicted that we would soon run out of key resources. Indeed, much of the Carter energy program was predicated on the assumption that we would soon run out of fossil fuels. (Since oil was first discovered in the United States 130 years ago people have been predicting that reserves would soon be depleted.)

The Club of Rome, which imagined the imminent exhaustion of such resources as gold, lead, and zinc, has already been proved wrong. Even more significant, however, is the fact that real resource prices fell consistently throughout the 1980s. According to Stephen Moore, in a study for the Institute for Policy Innovation, "of 38 natural resources examined in this study, 34 declined in real price" between 1980 and 1990. Prices for two remained constant, while only the cost of manganese and zinc rose. Moore found that American and international prices of food, energy, timber, and minerals, for instance, all fell.

Again, the doomsayers have ignored the powerful adjustment process that occurs through the marketplace. As goods become scarcer, prices rise, encouraging entrepreneurs to locate new supplies, manufacture synthetic equivalents, find substitutes, use products more efficiently, and reduce consumption. As long as prices can rise freely, the market will ensure that shortages will not occur. The fact that real resource prices fell during the 1980s indicates that relative scarcity has not increased but decreased.

Apocalyptic predictions regarding a number of other issues, such as toxic wastes and desertification, have proved to be equally flawed. The point is not that there are not environmental problems, but rather that environmental issues tend to be quite complex and that one should not make long-run predictions based on short-term trends. Unfortunately, many activists are willing to distort the facts because they have either political or religious reasons for proclaiming that disaster is imminent.

The New Theology

The environment has become as much a spiritual as a political issue for some people. Many churches now recycle products, install solar power, and pray for endangered animal species. Moreover, religious leaders who once busily promoted social and economic "justice" are now turning to ecological concerns. Global warming "is a spiritual issue, not just a technical problem," explained Bruce McLeod, president of the Canadian Council of Churches, after his organization endorsed the U.N.'s World Climate Convention last year.

Indeed, a variety of religious environmental organizations have formed—the North American Coalition on Religion and Ecology (NACRE), Religion and Science for the Environment, and the Presbyterian Eco-Justice Task Force, for instance. The 1990 NACRE Intercontinental Conference on Caring for Creation presented a Liturgy for the Earth, in which "Mother Earth" spoke to her "children."

Much church activism is based on false scientific theories, such as global warming. More significant, however, is the theological contamination from much of the new conservation ethic. Christianity and Judaism hold man to be a steward of the earth, which King David declared to be "the Lord's, and everything in it" (Psalm 24:1). Because man thereby "subdues" or exercises dominion over the planet (Genesis 1:28), many environmentalists view these faiths as largely responsible for the plight of the earth today. Historian Lynn White, for one, has criticized Christianity for being "the most anthropocentric religion the world has ever seen." He further argued that "since the roots of our [environmental] trouble are so largely religious, the remedy must also be essentially religious." Many other environmentalists have made similar charges.

Strangely, some churchmen seem to agree. James Nash, Executive Director of the Churches' Center for Theology and Public Policy, writes that "without doubt, Christian traditions bear some responsibility for propagating" destructive environmental perspectives. Thus, "for the Christian churches," he argues, "the ecological crisis is more than a biophysical challenge. It is also a theological-ethical challenge." The obvious solution, then, is to make Christianity "green." We now have a similarly minded ecologian in the White House. "Both conservative and liberal theologians have every reason, scriptural as well as ideological, to define their spiritual mission in a way that prominently includes the defense of God's creation," argues Vice President Gore in his apocalyptic book, *Earth in the Balance*.

But some environmentalists go further, turning ecology into a separate religion by mixing ancient and modern forms of pantheism. John Muir and a host of other early environmentalists experimented with different forms of Earth and nature worship. More recently, environmentalism has joined New Age thinking to produce a vibrant Neo-Pagan movement, including such practices as witchcraft, which has always had a heavy ecological emphasis, and goddess (Earth) worship. Moreover, explains Lesley Phillips, "the growing awareness of the urgent need to honor and heal Mother Earth has drawn many Unitarian Universalists to a contemporary pagan approach to religion."

Another religious strand is deep ecology, which treats the planet as sacred. Philosophy professors Bill Devall and George Sessions advocate "the revival of Earth-bonding rituals." Some deep ecologists even support the use of violence to protect their "god." Dave Forman, co-founder of Earth First! and later convicted of attempting to blow up power pylons for an Arizona nuclear plant, explains that so-called ecoterrorism is "a form of worship toward the earth." He has also advocated allowing the poor in Third World countries to starve, "to just let nature seek its own balance."

The new eco-spiritualism does more than threaten traditional faiths, which are being pressed to accept doctrines contrary to their basic tenets. More broadly, treating the earth as sacred distorts public policy. Our objective should be to balance environmental preservation with economic growth and personal freedom, and to rely on market forces to make any environmental controls as efficient and as flexible as possible. Unfortunately, however, treating the environment as a goddess has caused environmental activists to advance the most frightening theories, irrespective of the evidence, and demand the most draconian controls possible, irrespective of the cost.

The Reds and the Greens

Many other environmentalists have radical philosophical rather than theological agendas. Most of the activists are implicitly anti-capitalist, anti-profit, and, frankly, anti-freedom, since it is people acting freely that leads, in some conservationists' views, to consumerism, greed, pollution, and waste. In fact, it has been jokingly said that the only remaining socialists in the world are in the environmental movement, since they are promoting a centrally planned system based on government command-and-control regulation. The Reds have been replaced by the Greens.

The problem is not so much the motives of such activists, but the fact that their ideological biases lead them to ignore evidence questioning the genuineness of alleged environmental problems and to refuse to make compromises in drafting solutions to real concerns. While a doctrinal environmentalist might be happy with the policy result for religious or philosophical reasons, it is foolish for the rest of us to waste resources on non-problems and on unnecessarily inefficient clean-up strategies.

Environmental protection is important, and good people can disagree on the best policies to adopt. But today the public discussion over conservation is being distorted by politics and pagan theology, making the American public poorer and less free and the environment dirtier.

We need to look for private strategies to protect the environment. Privatizing federal timber and rangeland, for instance, would end subsidized development, since no private individual or company would willingly turn a dollar investment into a few cents in revenue. Establishing full private property rights in water would help conserve this precious resource in the western United States. We need to develop equally creative solutions for such "common pool" problems as air and water pollution. In short, we need to depoliticize the environment, making the issue one of balancing competing interests rather than imposing ideological or religious dogmas. If we succeed in doing so, we will end up with not only a cleaner society, but also a wealthier and freer one.

Snakes in the Garden: Sanctuaries, Sanctuary Pollution, and the Global Environment

Peter J. Leithart

Stewardship Journal (Fall 1993): 24–32. Copyright © 1993.

The Bible is full of instruction concerning the environment. Land, work, plants and animals, population growth and decline, and environmental devastation are recurring themes particularly in the Old Testament. In the space of this paper, I can give only the most superficial sketch of the Bible's teaching on this topic. My purpose is not to answer specific policy questions, but rather to explore in broad outline some aspects of the Bible's teachings as it relates to the environment. I have focused on the sanctuary both in order to make the subject more manageable and because the sanctuary is, from the perspective of Scripture, the central environment of human life. I hope that this approach will yield some fruitful and fresh insights into how Christians should address contemporary problems.

In creating the world, God first made an environment and then placed Adam and Eve in it. Following this pattern, I will first discuss the environments of creation and then examine humanity's role.

Three Environments

Biblical theologian James B. Jordan has noted that God created the world in three basic environments.[1] First, there was the Garden, which God planted on the east side of the land of Eden (Genesis 2:8). Second, there was the land of Eden itself, which included the Garden but was not identical to it (Genesis 2:8). Finally, there were other lands, such as Pishon, Havilah, and Cush (Genesis 2:11–13). Jordan describes these three environments as sanctuary (Garden), home (Eden), and world. Our attention will particularly be devoted to the relationships between the sanctuary and the world.

Several details indicate that the Garden of Eden was a sanctuary. It was the place where God was present in glory (Genesis 3:8),[2] and the glory of God consecrates space (Exodus 29:43). Later sanctuaries, moreover, incorporated garden imagery: cherubim (Genesis 3:24; Exodus 26:1), flowers (1 Kings 6:18), a water source (Genesis 2:10–14; Exodus 30:18–21), a tree-like lampstand (Genesis 2:16–17; Exodus 25:31–37), animals (Genesis 2:18–20; Leviticus 1–5), and a priest (Genesis 2:15).[3]

Though the Bible distinguishes these three environments, it does not sharply separate them. The sanctuary is a specially designated place of worship, but men are to worship God in everything they do in the world (Romans 12:1–2; 1 Corinthians 10:31). Men rest both in their homes and in the Sabbath worship of the sanctuary. The tabernacle was a "micro-cosmos" as well as a place of worship. As Jordan explains,

> The Most Holy Place itself was a model of the highest heavens, with the firmament or earthly heavens pictured in the Holy Place, and the earth pictured in the courtyard. The courtyard altar was the holy mountain that reached toward the sky, pictured in the Holy Place behind the veil, a veil of sky blue.[4]

Thus, there are analogies between the garden and the home, and between the garden and the world. The three environments overlap, interpenetrate, and parallel one another.

In the Bible's hierarchy of environments, the sanctuary holds first place. On the first day of his life, Adam was placed in the Garden; God's seventh day was Adam's first. Worship, further, was to be the source of life and blessing for the home and the world. Finally, the sanctuary provides the blueprint or model for other environments. God's heavenly sanctuary provided the pattern for the tabernacle and temple (Hebrews 8:5; 9:23–25), and the earthly sanctuaries in turn provided models for the home and the world.

Thus, though the home is not the same as the sanctuary, the home can become something like the sanctuary. A good wife is like an olive tree at a man's table, making his home a garden (Psalm 128:3). When Micah prophesied the salvation of the last days, he pictured every man sitting under his own vine and his own fig tree (Micah 4:4). The Biblical ideal is for every man to have his own garden, his own "sanctuary."

The world, likewise, is analogous to the garden. When the prophets speak of a renewed heaven and earth, they often depict it as a garden of Eden extended to global proportions:

> The wilderness and the desert will be glad, and the Arabah will rejoice and blossom; like the crocus it will blossom profusely and rejoice with rejoicing and shout of joy. . . . And the scorched land will become a pool, and the thirsty ground springs of water; in the haunt of jackals, its resting place, grass, weeds and rushes (Isaiah 35:1–2, 7).

Revelation 21–22, where John recorded his vision of the heavenly city of God established on earth, reinforces this point. The entire city has the form of a sanctuary. Like the Most Holy Place of the tabernacle, the city is a cube (Revelation 21:16). The temple is no longer separate from the city, since city and sanctuary have been united (Revelation 21:22).

Consideration of Revelation 21–22 leads us to a further observation. God intends real progress in history. The final form of the world will be a city rather than a garden. Contrary to Rousseauian environmentalism, the Lord's plan is not a reconstruction of the pristine environment of the original creation; God's plan is for the creation to be transformed into an image of the heavenly *city* of God (see Matthew 6:10). In this transformation of the world from Garden to city, the leading role is played by the human race. We therefore, turn to a consideration of the creation mandate given to Adam and Eve.

King and Guardian

The fact that the creation was divided into multiple environments opposes any simplistic notion of man's role in "the" environment. Adam and Eve's roles and activities differed from environment to environment. Our attention here will be confined to the different duties assigned to Adam and Eve in the Garden and in the world.

Genesis 1:28 issues this command: "Be fruitful, multiply, and fill the earth, and subdue it, and rule over the fish of the sea and over the birds of the sky, and over every living thing that moves on the earth." In five imperatives, the Lord outlined His program for man's labors in the world, and the passage provides the fundamental material for Christian reflection on the environment. For example, this verse challenges contemporary assumptions about population growth and control. Clearly too, man and woman, as images of God, are set by the Lord over the creation. Under God, human beings rule the earth and all living creatures. These applications of the text have been well developed by others.

I am concerned, however, with the force of the last two verbs, since this will eventually lead to a deeper understanding of the relation of sanctuary and world. The Hebrew verb *kabash*, translated "subdue," is frequently used in military contexts (Numbers 32:22, 29; Joshua 18:1). To "subdue" frequently means "to subject to slavery" (2 Chronicles 28:10; Nehemiah 5:5) and *kabash* sometimes has the sense of "trample" (Micah 7:19; Zechariah 9:15). The verb implies that the subduer uses force, and that what is subdued resists in some measure.[5] It is perhaps significant that the object of "subduing" is the "earth," not living things. It is surely noteworthy that this commandment was issued before the fall. Even if Adam had not sinned, the world would not have been to human rule apart from human labor. Eden was not the Land of Cockaigne, that imaginary place of great luxury and ease of living. The explanation for this seems to be that maturity comes, even for sinless creatures, only through labor and struggle.

According to S. R. Hirsch, "subdue" implies mastery, acquisition, and transformation of the earth.

To "subdue" means to bring something into one's power, to press one's stamp upon a thing.[6] Adam and Eve were commanded to bring the earth, its resources, and the other creatures into service to mankind and, ultimately, to borrow the Ignatian motto, to promote the greater glory of God.

The verb translated as "rule" or "take dominion" has less aggressive connotations. It is used of Solomon's peaceable rule over Israel (1 Kings 4:24). "Ruling" certainly implies authority to use coercion, but this verb does not necessarily connote severity or harshness; instead, it has the basic meaning of headship, leadership, direction, and authority. Where it is used to connote oppressive rule, it is qualified adverbially (e.g., Exodus 1:13; Leviticus 25:43, 46, 53). Again, it seems significant that this word is used to describe Adam and Eve's relationship to living creatures. They were to guide and lead but not to "trample" them.

Meredith Kline describes the goal of humanity's subduing and ruling as "maximal, global mastery." Kline explains,

> The cultural mandate put all the capacity of human brain and brawn to work in a challenging and rewarding world to develop his original paradise home into a universal city. . . . The citizens of the city would come into being through the process of procreation. Its physical-architectural form would take shape as a product of man's cultural endeavors. And the governmental dimension of the city was provided for in the community authority structure that was appointed as a further creation ordinance [i.e., marriage]. . . . The city is mankind culturally formed.[7]

In the Garden, by contrast, Adam's task was to guard, a priestly duty (Genesis 2:15).[8] All Biblical sanctuaries had guardian priests, who established and protected the boundaries of holy space and were authorized to use force to prevent trespass by "strangers." Adam was especially to guard his bride from seduction by the serpent (see 2 Corinthians 11:2–3), a duty in which he miserably failed. As the priestly warrior and guardian, Adam should have subdued the serpent; instead, he was subdued. As a result, he was replaced by guardian cherubim (Genesis 3:24). Practically, Genesis 1–2 shows that there are zones of life where man's task is mainly "guarding" and zones where man's focus is on "development." There are zones of safety and zones of risk. The basic zone of safety is the sanctuary. Throughout the Psalms, the sanctuary is the place where men find refuge in the Lord's presence, under the shadow of the wings of the cherubim that covered the ark of God (Psalm 17:8; 36:7; 57:1; etc.). The basic zone of development and progress is the world: development is necessarily a risky undertaking. Adam and Eve's role in the world was primarily aggressive, but their role in the sanctuary primarily defensive.

As we have seen, however, the Bible also indicates that the world is to be transformed into a sanctuary. The city that lies at the end point of humanity's aggressive "subduing and ruling" is a sanctuary that must be guarded. To understand what this means more concretely, let us examine the characteristics of the sanctuary. The sanctuary, as we have seen, was a place of refuge and safety. It was also a place of nourishment. The tree of life was a special provision of food through which Adam and Eve had communion with the God who is the Lord and Giver of life. The Garden, finally, was a place of beauty. The description in Ezekiel 28 informs us that the garden was filled with precious "stones of fire" (v. 14). Later sanctuaries—the tabernacle and the temple—were likewise wondrously beautiful. The environment of the garden-sanctuary, then, was characterized by three qualities: safety, fruitfulness, and beauty.

As Adam and his descendants fulfilled the calling to subdue the earth and rule the lower creation, the entire world was to become more and more like the sanctuary. The goal of human action was to make the world more secure, more productive, more beautiful—that is, more like a sanctuary. Thus, given the analogies between the sanctuary and the world, we may say that man is both to guard and develop the world; he is priest as well as king of the creation.

More precisely, in God's wisdom, man best guards the world precisely by subduing it; he fulfills his priestly charge by pursuing his royal mis-

sion. Several uses of the verb *kabash*, translated as "subdue" in Genesis 1:28, underline this point. Once Israel had "subdued" the land (Joshua 18:1), they were able to live in safety, peace, and prosperity; their military efforts, under the blessing of God, made the land a "sanctuary" or holy land (Psalm 114:2). David encouraged the people of Israel to donate to the construction of the temple by reminding them that the Lord had "given you rest on every side" and "given the inhabitants of the land into my hand, and the land is subdued before the Lord and before His people" (1 Chronicles 22:18). More generally, it is frequently stated that the sanctuary would be erected only after Israel had subdued her enemies and achieved "rest" (Deuteronomy 12:10; 1 Kings 8:56). These passages suggest the following conceptual pattern: subjugation leads to rest, and rest is a prerequisite for the erection of the sanctuary.

This pattern is clearly evident in everyday, ordinary reality. Wild animals become safe and serviceable only after they are made submissive to human rule. Land becomes more productive under human care. Art and architecture are possible only because of human effort to transform the material of creation. Subduing the earth brings safety, prosperity, and beauty. As the earth is subdued, it becomes something worth guarding: it becomes a sanctuary. By contrast, should man fail to exercise the royal mandate, the world will be less productive, safe, and beautiful. This pattern implies a very different perspective from that of contemporary environmentalism. Instead of guarding the pristine creation, humanity is called to guard the world once it has been subdued to human rule, conceit has been transformed by human labor into something like a sanctuary. Man guards the garden and the city, not the wilderness.

These reflections doubtless seem naive and idealistic, and indeed they are. While humanity's original commission was to form the earth into a sanctuary-city, sin has disrupted man's efforts to attain that goal. Sin, of course, does not deprive man of his humanity. Sinful human beings continue to subdue, rule, and guard; they continue to function as kings and priests. But instead of subduing the earth in righteousness and for the glory of God, they rule in rebellion and to make a name for themselves. Instead of forming creation into an image of the heavenly Jerusalem, they erect Babel.

By union to the Last Adam, men and women are "put back on track," restored to their Adamic calling. By the recreating power of the Spirit, they are redeemed from the power of sin and death, and enabled to live in righteousness, holiness, and peace to the glory of God. Thus, as Christianity influences the world, the world becomes more like a sanctuary. When the world submits to the teaching and discipline of the Lord of the Church, the nations beat their swords into plowshares, and their spears into pruning hooks, and they devote themselves to peaceful labor (see Isaiah 2:2–4; 65:17–25). The world becomes a safer, more fruitful, more beautiful place as it comes under the influence of the Gospel. This does not mean that the world will reach a state of sinless perfection before the return of Jesus Christ, but it does mean that the redeemed are called to construct a world that approximates the eschatological city.

This may seem rather fanciful, but it is simple historical fact that the Church has been deeply involved in efforts to make the world a more productive, safer, and more beautiful place. Medieval monks were in the forefront of technology, applying water power to increase the output of flour mills and introducing innovations in agriculture. R. J. Rushdoony has noted that "a remarkable record of reclamation and conservation marks church history. Desert areas of Europe were made productive, dikes built, and amazing acts of changing the face of the continent [of Europe] were made by the medieval monks and their successors." The Church also beautified the world, forming stone and sand into some of the most spectacular buildings ever constructed. In the contemporary world, the same point may be made by even a superficial comparison of the environmental management of the once-Christian nations of the West with that of India or the former Soviet Union.

Stewardship

God redeemed His people so that they might live to honor Him in obedience to His Word. God has not left His people without instruction about how they are to form the creation into a sanctuary. In relation to the environment, this means that redeemed man is called to be a steward of his portion of the creation. Sinners reject God's lordship of the environment. In the order of creation and redemption, however, man is a steward, not an owner (Psalm 24:1). Though man is lord of the creation, he is a vassal of God. As *the* Lord of creation, God controls the creation.[9] He causes the earth to bring forth grass and plants, feeds the animals, and brings floods, volcanoes, and other environmental catastrophes. He has promised that "While earth remains, seedtime and harvest, and cold and heat, and summer and winter, and day and night shall not cease" (Genesis 8:22). It is impossible for man to destroy completely the world that God has given to him.

Yet man is not free to rape and pillage the creation. This is true because as Lord of creation, God has authority over how the creation is to be used. Development does not mean that God gives humanity free rein to lay waste to the world. This basic perspective—that the creation serves man, but that man is bound to use the creation in submission to God—is filled out in detail throughout Scripture. God gives many specific commands about how the earth and its resources are to be used. Only a few relevant texts can be cited here:

It is clear that *animals* are under human authority (Genesis 1:26–28). After God had named the day and night, the sun, moon, and stars, God delegated authority to name the animals to Adam (2:19–20). It is equally clear that animals are given to man to be used. The Lord Himself slaughtered animals to make coverings for Adam and Eve (Genesis 3:21). Noah was given explicit permission to eat meat of animals (Genesis 9:3). Throughout Scripture, animals are used for plowing, transportation, and other work.

Yet, Scripture gives guidelines for man's use of animals. The Proverbs tell us that the righteous man is kind to his beasts (Proverbs 12:10). Because animals symbolize men, a man's treatment of his animals will tell us something about his treatment of other men. For the same reason, many of the rulers of Israel (Moses and David, for example) trained for leadership by shepherding.

The threshing ox is not to be denied his sustenance (Deuteronomy 25:4). God forbade sacrificing a mother and her young on the same day (Leviticus 22:28), and required the Israelites to return a straying animals to its master (Exodus 23:4–5). Animals were to be given rest on the Sabbath day (Exodus 20:10). God showed compassion to the animals of Nineveh (Jonah 4:11), and directed Noah to preserve members of each "kind" of animal, bird, and creeping thing (Genesis 6:19–7:3). There is some indication in Scripture that the diet and dress of the new creation is vegetarian: Bread and wine, not the flesh of bulls and goats, are the foods of the kingdom; white linen, not animals skins, is the eschatological dress (Revelation 19:8, 14).

Plants are given to man for food (Genesis 1:29), and are used as medication (Ezekiel 47:12; Revelation 22:2). Wood was used for building the tabernacle and temple, transformed to reflect Gods' glory more brightly. But plants are also protected. Even during a protracted siege, the Israelites were forbidden to make war against fruit-bearing trees as if they were enemies (Deuteronomy 20:10–20).

The same pattern applies to the *land*. Land was Israel's most basic resource. The land provided grains and fruits for food and trees for lumber. Canaan was a land flowing with milk and honey, full of resources for the use and enjoyment of the people of God. Gold, silver, and other metals were mined from the earth. Yet, the land was not to be exploited and abused. It was given rest every seven years (Exodus 23:10–11).

These few passages indicate something of the breadth of God's instruction concerning the proper use of the environment. Understanding these laws in their original historical and literary context, and applying them to the very different concerns that dominate modern environmental discussions, is no easy task. But faithfulness to the Lord requires that the effort be made.

Pollution

If you look up "pollute" in an English Bible concordance, you will discover that the words are used exclusively of "moral" or "ritual" pollution.

The most dangerous kind of pollution is of the sanctuary. The Bible speaks frequently about clean and unclean, abominable things and pollution. Invariably, however, environmental pollution as we know it is not in view; rather, in the Bible pollution has mainly to do with transgressions of God's laws, and particularly laws governing man's approach to Gods' sanctuary. Human waste in Israel's war camp was an "indecent thing" (Deuteronomy 23:14; lit., a "thing of nakedness"), but even here the main concern is not sanitation but maintenance of a holy environment.

The Bible thus provides little direct revelation concerning environmental pollution. If we hope to move toward a Biblical conception of pollution, therefore, we need to think through the analogies between the sanctuary and the world. Under the Old Testament system, sanctuary pollution resulted from transgression of the moral and ritual boundaries that God established between Himself and His people (Numbers 35:33; Isaiah 24:5; Jeremiah 3:1–2; 23:11). Preventing pollution of the sanctuary meant guarding against unqualified intruders, idolatry, and sin. It meant keeping the snakes out of the garden.

To a polluted man or nation, the sanctuary took on qualities opposite to the qualities of the original, undefiled garden. After Adam became polluted by sin, the sanctuary was no longer a refuge; instead it was a dangerous place, with cherubim stationed at the entrance to prevent his return (Genesis 3:24). It was no longer a place Adam could flee to, but a place he had to flee from. Later, because the Israelites polluted His house with their sin, the Lord abandoned it and left it desolate (Ezekiel 10:1–11:25). Bereft of the protective covering that the Lord provided, the remaining inhabitants of the land were vulnerable to judgment by sword, famine, wild beasts, and plague (Ezekiel 14:6–13). A polluted sanctuary provides no refuge. Ultimately God is the refuge of His people, and God does not give sanctuary to a polluted people.

Nor was the Garden a place where defiled Adam could be nourished. Instead, he was denied access to the tree of life. The sanctuary was no longer a fruitful and productive environment for him. Similarly, the Lord warned Israel that if they broke covenant, the good land would become hard as iron (Deuteronomy 28:23).

Finally, sins defile and disfigure the sanctuary. Every year, the priest had to enter the Holy of Holies to sprinkle the cleansing blood on the "mercy seat," which the sins of the people had dirtied (Leviticus 16). Ezekiel's tour of the temple revealed "wicked abominations . . . every form of creeping things and beasts and detestable things, with all the idols of Israel, were carved on the wall all around" (Ezekiel 8:9–10). Instead of being a reflection of God's glorious beauty, the sanctuary became ugly and dirty, a place of abominable idols.

The primary connection between sanctuary and environmental pollution is that sanctuary desecration pollutes the world. Bloodshed not only disfigured the sanctuary, but also polluted the land, and only the blood of the one who shed blood could cleanse it (Numbers 35:33). Isaiah said that the earth was polluted by those who transgressed laws, violated statutes, and broke the everlasting covenant (Isaiah 24:5). Jeremiah warned that the sins of God's Bride, Israel, had polluted the land, and that her efforts to return to her first husband would only bring further pollution (Jeremiah 3:1–9; cf. Deuteronomy 24:1–5). Idolatry especially polluted the land (Jeremiah 16:18).

Thus, the most dangerous form of pollution is pollution of God's sanctuary, which in the New Testament is the Christian Church. When the Church and the world are filled with sin and idolatry, God intervenes in judgment, and His judgment often takes the form of an environmental catastrophe. Prior to God's coming, the area around Sodom and Gomorrah was like the Garden of Eden, well-watered and fertile (Genesis 13:10). Because of the sin of the people of Sodom, God rained fire and burning sulphur on the earth, and the Garden was turned into a salt waste (cf. Psalm 107:34). God's judgment against Israel turned the Edenic land into a wilderness (Joel 2:3). Similarly, God destroyed the world and all living creatures in the flood, saving only eight people and representatives of each animal species. Ten plagues left Egypt ravaged. In each case, the Lord Himself wasted the environment as punish-

ment for sin. If we face real environmental catastrophes, our first response should be to turn to God in repentance and humility, pleading for His mercy. The fear of the Lord is the beginning of wise environmental policy.

Man is therefore responsible for environmental devastations, but not always in the way that environmentalists believe. Environmentalist rhetoric suggests that man has ultimate control over the creation, as if the human race could bring the world to an end by its own power. This is obviously contrary to Scripture, which everywhere asserts that God, not man, is sovereign. The Bible does teach, however, that man is responsible for environmental turmoil. Man alone sins and calls forth God's judgment. If men keep covenant with the Lord, He promises to bless them and their world with productivity, safety, and beauty (see Deuteronomy 28:1–14). When they sin, however, God turns creation against them. The creation itself is "on God's side" and "helps" God execute His judgments against impenitent men. Creation was and remains good (1 Timothy 4:4–5); the lower creatures do what God commands and do not rebel. Man alone is evil. Man alone is culpable for the judgments that God brings to the earth.

It is a mistake to suggest that we can discern a one-to-one correspondence between sin and particular environmental devastations. Yet, all environmental degradation is, in a general sense, a judgment on human rebellion because if there were no sin there would be no judgment. Thus, the relationship between human action and environmental consequence is not: Human technology violates some natural harmony and thereby brings environmental catastrophe. The dynamic is rather: Sinful man violates God's laws, angers God, and God brings judgments that may involve destruction of the environment.

In this context, it is significant, for example, that there has been a marked increase in volcanic activity in recent years. Dixy Lee Ray says, "The earth, at present, appears to be in a period of active volcanism, with volcanic eruptions occurring at a rate of about 100 per year." Occasionally, the eruptions directly threaten populated areas. Even when, as is more often the case, volcanoes occur in remote areas, they spew thousands of tons of gases into the atmosphere, gases that have as yet undetermined effects on the environment.[10] Christians do not have the option of saying that this increase in volcanic activity is accidental or part of a natural "cycle." Instead, we must say that it is a judgment of the Just and Awesome God, calling the nations (and His church especially) to repentance, faith, and obedience. Even when such judgments cannot be traced to specific violations of God's law, they are judgments on mankind's general sinfulness intended to confront men with the holiness of God.

Since the sanctuary is not only the center of the world but also a model of the world, we can extrapolate a Biblical notion of environmental pollution from our reflections on sanctuary pollution. As noted above, sanctuary pollution involves trespass of boundaries. Similarly, Gary North points out that environmental pollution likewise involves trespass of property boundaries.[11] We have seen that sanctuary pollution has three effects: It makes the sanctuary unsafe, unfruitful, and ugly. Similarly, we can define environmental pollution in these terms:

Pollution is a foreign substance that causes a resource or a part of the world to become hazardous, unfruitful, or ugly.

Polluted *water* is water that is unsafe to drink, or water that is incapable of supporting plant or animal life, or water that is unappealing to the sight, smell, or taste, because of the presence of a foreign substance.

Polluted *land* is land that is unsafe to have direct contact with (e.g., due to chemical dumping), or unproductive (e.g., due to overuse of chemical fertilizers), or that is unattractive (e.g., due to litter).

Polluted *air* is air that is unsafe to breathe, or air that blackens buildings and causes other aesthetic irritations, due to the presence of dangerous gases.

A polluted environment is an environment that is unsafe to live in, one that cannot produce necessary goods, or one that is unattractive in an aesthetic sense, due to the presence of foreign substances.

These three effects of pollution are obviously of varying degrees of importance. A pollutant that causes grave health risks is a more serious problem than one that is harmless but aesthetically unappealing. Generally, the first thing people want from their environment is sufficient resources to survive. Yet, a genuinely clean environment is one that is safe, productive, and beautiful.

Many of the most obvious pollutants are relatively minor irritations that make our environment ugly: paper cups along the highway, discarded tires in the creek at the park, the odor from the sewage treatment plant on the other side of town. Some may claim that the forms of pollution are irrelevant, but Christians should see them as legitimate causes for concern and remedy. God wants us to glorify His creation not "uglify" it. We should strive not only to make the world safe and productive, but to make it beautiful. At the same time, we should recognize that not all the peoples of the world have the luxury of spending time worrying about the environment's appearance. We should recognize that productivity and safety are presently higher priorities than beauty for many of the world's nations.

Guarding Boundaries

Exploring environmental issues from the perspective of the sanctuary and sanctuary pollution holds practical implications for environmental economics. As we have seen, the analogies between the sanctuary and the world indicate that it is valid for men to talk about "guarding" and protecting the environment, especially that portion of the world that has been subdued to human rule. Since sanctuary pollution involves trespass, we ought to think of environmental pollution in similar terms.

Private property is basic to a Biblical view of economics. The Bible forbids theft, and theft assumes that men have a right to the property they lawfully possess. Property owners have a right and responsibility to protect and guard the boundaries of their property. Wise environmental policy would ensure that each man's property is treated as his sanctuary, the boundaries of which he has a right to defend against harmful intruders.

Civil government thus has the same role in regulating pollution that it has in enforcing property boundaries in general. Exodus 22:5–6 is important in this connection:

> If a man shall cause a field or vineyard to be eaten, and shall put in his beast, and shall feed in another's field; of the best of his own field, and of the best of his own vineyard, shall he make restitution. If a fire break out, and catch in thorns, so that the stacks of corn, or the standing corn, or the field, be consumed therewith; he that kindleth the fire shall surely make restitution.

Gary North explains that just as "the firestarter is responsible for all subsequent fires that his original fires starts," so also a polluter is responsible for harm done to his neighbor's property.[12] The basic principle is that no one should be able to impose costs on his neighbor without his neighbor's permission; to do so is theft.[13] North concludes,

> Pollution should be seen as a form of trespassing. It is an invasion of private property.

The State has a responsibility to enforce property rights against trespassers; similarly, it has a responsibility of enforcing laws against polluters. This would include legislating fire codes (pre-pollution restrictions) and automobile emissions and noise-reduction devices.[14]

Conclusion

In the final analysis, a productive, safe, and beautiful environment is a blessing of the Lord. Scientific study of environmental problems is important and necessary, but in the end no amount of technical expertise will shield rebellious men from the judgment of a Holy God. As Nineveh found, only a penitent appeal to the God of all compassion can save the city, and its animals, from destruction (Jonah 3; 4:11). Only water flowing from the sanctuary can transform the barren land into a Garden (Ezekiel 47:1ff.).

Notes

[1]Jordan, *Through New Eyes: Developing a Biblical View of the World* (Brentwood, TN: Wolgemuth & Hyatt, 1988), 152–55.

[2]See Meredith G. Kline, *Images of the Spirit* (self-published, 1986), 97–115, for the argument that Genesis 3:8 describes a theophany of the glory of God.

[3]Jordan, *Through New Eyes*, 181–279, for explorations of the transformations of Garden imagery in various sanctuaries. See also William J. Dumbrell, *The End of the Beginning: Revelation 21–22 and the Old Testament* (Homebush West, Australia: Lancer, 1985), 52.

[4]Jordan, *Through New Eyes*, 207–12. For similar associations, see Meredith G. Kline, *Images of the Spirit*, 39. The notion that sanctuaries were microcosms was widespread in the Ancient Near East.

[5]John N. Oswalt, "*Kabash*," in *Theological Wordbook of the Old Testament* (2 vols.; R. Laird Harris, ed.; Chicago: Moody, 1980), 1:430.

[6]S. R. Hirsch, *The Pentateuch* (6 vols.; 2nd ed.; trans. by Isaac Levy; London: Judaica Press, 1989), 1:35.

[7]Kline, *Kingdom Prologue*, 1:55.

[8]Jacob Milgrom has demonstrated that the word translated "keep" (Hebrew, *shamaar*) connotes a priest's guard duty at a sanctuary (Milgrom, *Studies in Levitical Terminology, I: The Encroacher and the Levite; The Term Aboda* [Berkeley: University of California Press, 1970], 8–16). See Kline, *Kingdom Prologue*, 1:64–69.

[9]See the discussion of lordship in John M. Frame, *The Doctrine of the Knowledge of God* (Phillipsburg, NJ: Presbyterian and Reformed, 1987).

[10]Dixy Lee Ray with Lou Guzzo, *Trashing the Planet* (Washington, D.C.: Regnery Gateway, 1990), 37.

[11]North, *Tools of Dominion: The Case Laws of Exodus* (Tyler, TX: Institute for Christian Economics, 1990), 606. Human property is analogous to God's property, so trespass of property rights is analogous to sanctuary desecration. See my "Levitical Economy 101," *Stewardship Journal* 3 (1993), 19–24.

[12]North, *op. cit.*, 551.

[13]*Ibid.*, 548.

[14]*Ibid.*, 606.

CASES

Case 12.1: Pacific Northwest Loggers and the Spotted Owl

The northern spotted owl lives in many of the old-growth forests in the Pacific Northwest, in small town areas dominated by the logging industry. Many of these towns are heavily dependent on logging to sustain their communities. Environmentalists are pushing for the spotted owl to be placed on the government's endangered species list, which would prevent loggers from cutting the trees in the designated areas. The amount of land that would be off-limits to loggers amounts to roughly 65 percent of Western wood production. Logging companies claim that the owl nests just as comfortably in the new-growth forests that the loggers replant as they cut the old-growth forests for the timber. If the owl is named as an endangered species, many of the logging mills will be closed, and the U.S. Forest Service estimates that it will throw close to 30,000 people out of jobs and threaten the livelihood of many small logging-dependent communities. For example, Gregory Forest Products, in Glendale, Oregon, bought only a fraction of the normal amount of timber from the federal government, which controls the land on which the company cuts trees. This was because court injunctions initiated by environmentalists limited the amount of timber the owner was permitted to cut. He has had to cut his work force and insists that if the injunctions are not lifted, he will be out of business within a year. Roughly 25 percent of the population of the community is either employed by the mill or dependent on it for a living. However, if logging continues at the current pace, most of the spotted owl's habitat will be gone, claim environmentalists, and the bird will be in danger of becoming extinct. Roughly 4,000 of them remain in the Pacific Northwest. Emotions are running high on both sides of this issue.[2]

[2]See Jonathan B. Levine, "The Spotted Owl Could Wipe Us Out," *Business Week* (18 September 1989): 94, 99; Michael Satchell, "The Endangered Logger," *U.S. News and World Report* (25 June 1990): 27–29; Ted Gup, "Owl and Man," *Time* (25 June 1990): 56–62; and "Ethics and the Spotted Owl Controversy," *Issues in Ethics* 4, no. 1 (Winter–Spring 1991): 1, 6–7.

Questions for Discussion:

1. Who do you think is more endangered, the spotted owl or the logger?
2. How would you balance the conflict between jobs and the environment in this case? Explain why you lean toward the option you chose.

3.   Does proper stewardship of the environment mean that all species of animals be protected from extinction because they are God's creation? Or since some species of animals become extinct naturally, does it really matter if certain other species become extinct?

Case 12.2: The Gnatcatcher and the Developers

The black-tailed gnatcatcher is a small songbird that has recently become a symbol of the conflict between real estate developers and environmentalists, and between slow-growth advocates and business development advocates. Once common throughout Southern California, today it is found only in small parts of three different counties. Roughly 65–90 percent of its coastal sage scrub habitat has already been destroyed by development, and the remainder is scheduled for development in the next few years. Its primary habitat is in inland south Orange County, an area in which major development, including freeways, is planned or already under way. Two of the largest developers in Orange County, the Irvine Company and the Santa Margarita Company, own most of the gnatcatcher's prime habitat.

The arid scrub is widely recognized as some of the most rapidly disappearing types of vegetation due to development, and with its decrease comes the demise of many different types of birds, reptiles, and mammals. Environmentalists insist that the gnatcatcher is on the edge of becoming extinct, and unless it is protected, the bird will become extinct within the next two decades. Roughly three thousand to four thousand of the birds are left today. Environmentalists strongly support listing the bird as an endangered species, which would put its habitat off limits to developers. They cite the need for immediate action to prevent further destruction of the bird's habitat, since during the deliberations of the state Fish and Game Commission, the county toll road authority plowed under forty acres of the bird's prime habitat to continue construction of a freeway that developers claim is crucial to their plans.

Developers insist that land that doesn't interfere with their plans can be set aside for the bird, a compromise about which environmentalists are skeptical. Developers hold that thousands of jobs will be affected if the bird is listed as endangered and that housing prices will rise, as developers will have less land on which to build and would be required to not use land they already own. In addition, they may even be responsible for restoring some of the bird's habitat that they have already plowed under.

One option is to declare the bird a "threatened" species, requiring less stringent measures than if it were declared endangered. But some environmentalists insist that nothing less than the endangered species listing is enough to stop the onslaught of development. Developers likewise insist that there is nothing to stop the environmentalists from urging that all of the habitat be left alone. Others hold that this is a compromise that saves both the bird and the region's jobs.[3]

[3]See Eric Bailey, "Small Bird at the Heart of a Big Ruckus," *Los Angeles Times*, 5 August 1991, A3; Robert Reinhold, "U.S. to Protect a Songbird But Give Builders Leeway," *New York Times*, 25 March 1993, A20; William Fulton, "How to Have Environmental Protection and Jobs That Enable People to Eat Too," *Los Angeles Times*, 11 April 1993, M6.

Questions for Discussion:

1. How would you balance the critical "jobs versus environment" conflict in this case?
2. Do you think that listing the gnatcatcher as "threatened" is an acceptable compromise? Why or why not?
3. How important do you think it is to save the gnatcatcher, given the hard economic times experienced in Southern California recently?

Case 12.3: Profit Versus Environmental Concern

You are the manager of a toxic waste dump that is located outside of Sacramento, California. The parent company is located in downtown Los Angeles. Some years ago, a cement "pond" was built in supposedly impermeable soil to house toxic waste from the firm's operations throughout northern California. When the toxic waste was combined with other chemicals, the waste was broken down, thereby rendering it considerably less toxic and therefore safe to be contained in the pond. This operation has worked well for a number of years.

A few months ago, you noticed a change in the taste of the drinking water in your office and home. As a result, you ordered some tests to be run, and to your dismay the tests revealed that some leakage from the pond was moving toward the water table. The engineers who conducted the tests were not able to determine with certainty if the waste was leaking into the water table, since the soil outside the pond acts as a partial filtering agent.

Being a responsible manager and concerned about the community, you report this to your boss in L.A. He consults with the top management of the company, and their response is the same as his. Since the facility passed the state inspection only a few months earlier, they choose to ignore the problem because of the cost involved in its cleanup and their continuing compliance with the standards of the state.

You maintain that the state's standards clearly are not adequate, but the company is adamant. They will do nothing about the problem unless they are found to be in violation of state standards. You protest that decision, and they warn you to keep to managing the facility and leave these other decisions to the appropriate people.

Your dilemma is compounded by the fact that "whistle-blowers" almost always lose their jobs (something you can ill afford, since you have a wife and three school-age children dependent on your income) and frequently are blackballed from the industry.[4]

*This case is adapted from a case used by Dr. William W. May, School of Religion, University of Southern California.

Questions for Discussion:

1. As the manager of the facility, what would you do in this situation? How would you justify your actions?
2. What are the various options that you have as the manager? How would you balance environmental concern with concern for your job and family?

COMMENTARY

The conflict between business and the environment involves maintaining the difficult balance between jobs/economic growth and environmental protection. Clearly there are extremes in rhetoric on both sides of the issue. Environmentalists are wrong when they insist on predicting doomsday scenarios, suggesting that society is at the brink of an environmental Armageddon. Business leaders are likewise wrong when they insist that there is no environmental problem worth sacrificing economic growth for. It is a given that there are environmental problems that need urgent attention, particularly in Eastern Europe and the Third World, though, to be sure, some problems such as global warming and ozone depletion have been overstated and may not even be issues at all. It is true that in many ways the environment is healthier today than at any time in the past fifty years. For example, the air in smog-ridden Southern California is likely cleaner than at any other time in the past four decades. Environmentalists point out that results like this mean that their emphasis and strong government regulation are working and should be continued just as aggressively as in the past. But business leaders point to the condition of the environment as evidence that the days of grave environmental concern are past, thus justifying a rethinking of the balance, tilting it back toward economic growth, development, and less government interference to protect the environment at the expense of business.

The Bible sets the primary parameters for a Judeo-Christian environmental ethic. In the creation account in Genesis 1–2, God clearly gives mankind dominion over the creation. That is, it is God's gift to human beings to be used for their benefit. But the gift is always balanced by their responsibility to be good stewards over that which has been entrusted to them. Humans were commanded by God to subdue the earth, for their benefit. To be sure, this has been abused because of the entrance of sin into the world. Greed has replaced legitimate self-interest and dominion over the environment and has repeatedly motivated mankind to rape the environment, thereby abandoning the human being's rightful place as a steward and caretaker of the creation for the sake of profit. Strip-mining, clear-cutting of forests, and gill netting the ocean floor are examples of greed-motivated neglect of the environment that leaves it blighted and its inhabitants in jeopardy.

God's giving mankind dominion over creation and the command to subdue the earth clearly imply that development that brings creation under the control of human beings for their benefit is a good thing. Peter J. Leithart insightfully points out that the environmentalist ideal of a return to the pristine undeveloped wilderness is not necessarily a biblical ideal. In an important section of his article he suggests a contrast between the biblical notion of dominion and the contemporary environmentalist ideal. He states,

> More precisely, in God's wisdom, man best guards the world precisely by subduing it. . . . Wild animals become safe and serviceable only after they are made submissive to human rule. Land becomes more productive under human care. Art and architecture are possible only because of human effort to transform the material of creation. Subduing the earth brings safety, prosperity and beauty. As the earth is subdued, it becomes something worth guarding; it becomes a sanctuary. By contrast, should man fail to exercise this royal mandate, the world will be less productive, safe and beautiful. This pattern implies a very different perspective from that of contemporary environmentalism. Instead of guarding the pristine creation, humanity is called to guard the world once it has been subdued to human rule, once it has been transformed by man into something like a sanctuary. Man guards the garden and the city, not the wilderness.

umanity's dominion is clearly seen as a good thing from the per-
e of Scripture. It is debatable how much development con-
to the beauty of creation, and Leithart likely overstates how
eauty comes out of development. Most people would prefer an
oped wilderness to the city for sheer aesthetics. That is why
ple get away for leisure and relaxation to less-developed areas.
loes not undermine his primary point, that development was
a good thing, though, like everything else in creation, it has
come corrupted by sin, which makes abuses and excesses inevitable.
This point can probably be taken a step further. A good case can be
made that the environmental ideal of a pristine, undisturbed wilderness is actually parallel in the Bible to land that is under God's
curse.[5] For example, when the prophets describe the land of Israel and
the land of many of its neighbors as under God's curse, there is a
remarkable similarity to the ideal held up by environmentalists as the
goal of their movement and the environmental policy they hope to
shape. Furthermore, Leithart suggests that the ultimate ideal in the
Bible, the eternal state, is crafted out of the metaphor not of the undisturbed wilderness but of the *city*. The eternal state is referred to as the
heavenly *city* (Rev. 21–22). Thus it would appear that development is
not inherently problematic, nor is the pristine environment inherently
as good as the environmental movement seems to assume. Again, that
is not to suggest that human dominion has not been corrupted by sin
and the environment abused. But to insist that development is somehow inherently a problem is not consistent with the biblical account of
humanity's relationship with creation.

This biblical emphasis on human dominion over the creation
helps us to evaluate the new and popular paradigm for environmentalism suggested by Michael Hoffman, known as biocentrism, or deep
ecology. Deep ecologists hold that the environment can and should be
protected for its own sake, not for what it can benefit human beings.
Many environmentalists and religious groups with environmental concern have adopted this view and have given it strongly spiritual overtones. As Doug Bandow points out in his article, things like creation
spirituality, the Mother Earth movement, and treating the planet as a
sacred thing to be worshiped—all outgrowths of biocentrism—are
actually a form of ancient paganism, in which the creation was revered
and worshiped. Eco-terrorism—that is, acts of sabotage against business, such as placing spikes in trees to cause injury to loggers—is sometimes referred to as a form of worship and there is an emphasis on
bonding with the earth in many of these movements.

All of these manifestations of biocentrism have much in common
with various forms of idolatry condemned by the Bible. To be sure,

[5] For further details on this see E. Calvin Beisner, *Prospects for Growth: A Biblical View of Population, Resources and the Future* (Westchester, Ill.: Cross-way, 1990).

God reveals himself in the creation (Ps. 19:1) and the earth does belong to the Lord (Ps. 24:1). But the earth is not the Lord. Nowhere does the Bible or any Judeo-Christian ethic that is consistent with the Bible equate worship of the creation with worship of the Creator. In fact, one of the purposes of the Genesis account of creation was to distance Hebrew theology from the Canaanite religions of the Middle East, most of which worshiped the creation or parts of it. The creation account in the Bible is very clear that God stands over and above the creation. He is not to be identified with creation, nor is creation to be worshiped instead of him. To be sure, we honor God when we properly care for his creation, exercising our role as stewards over it. But we also honor God when we exercise our dominion over creation, developing it and harnessing it for the benefit of humanity. The biblical notion of humanity's dominion over creation would appear to indicate that a homocentric view of the environment is more consistent with Judeo-Christian ethics than a biocentric ethic. Some of the idolatrous leanings of biocentrism should be cause for concern for the adherent of a Judeo-Christian ethic rather than an emphasis that should be enlisted to support environmental concern. There is no reason why a proper homocentric view of the environment, balanced by the clear biblical responsibility to be stewards of creation, cannot produce a genuine environmental concern. Most people are motivated to take care of the environment so that there is something left to pass on to the next generations. The idea of good stewardship mandates this.

A second concern with biocentrism is that it appears to lead to the notion that trees, plants, and animals have parallel rights with human beings. Hoffman suggests that nonhuman living things are also integral parts of the ecosystem and have intrinsic value. Human beings with rights do not stand above animals and plants, which lack such rights. Rather, all are part of a more holistic system in which all things are valued equally. This seems to lead to the idea that animals and trees have rights that should be protected. We would not want to suggest that animals, for example, have no interests that are not worthy of protection. We hold that cruelty to animals is immoral, but we stop short of insisting that animals have rights. There is a good deal of debate over animal rights that is beyond the scope of this discussion, but at the least we suggest that animals and plants are not rights-bearers; however, animals have some interests that should compel us to protect them from cruelty. The problem with the way in which biocentrists view plants and animals is that it presents a system that is very difficult to live with consistently. If plants and trees have rights, then basic questions about what one will have for dinner are problematic. To be fair, Hoffman does hold that with clear criteria, human interests can take precedence over the environment, but he does not spell out these criteria. Once one admits that animals and trees have rights, it becomes difficult to draw the necessary lines that would justify promoting human interests ahead of those of the rest of the ecosystem. In our view, a homocentric view balanced by the responsibility of stewardship for the creation avoids many of those problems.

However, the broad biblical parameters of dominion and stewardship are not particularly helpful when it comes to balancing jobs with the environment in specific cases. The cases of the spotted owl and the gnatcatcher are difficult ones, and balancing jobs and the environment is a challenge in both of those cases. What makes them particularly difficult is that the birds in view are threatened with extinction for the sake of economic development. How should the extinction of certain species of animals be viewed by someone committed to stewardship of the environment? A good case can be made for protecting species threatened by extinction because each species is a part of God's creative order and has a part to play in maintaining it. But others argue that there is no moral obligation to protect species of animals and plants.

⁶Published in *Public Utilities Fortnightly* (26 September 1974): 357–62.

Wilfred Beckerman, in "The Case for Economic Growth,"[6] argues that thousands of species of animals have naturally become extinct over the ages, and that if it happens naturally without any intervention of human beings, how can it be so problematic when it happens in the process of economic development for the benefit of humanity? Further, he insists that even if the world does run out of some natural resources, society will likely get along just fine without them, as it did for centuries before these raw materials were discovered. Many people apply this kind of reasoning to the spotted owl and the gnatcatcher, suggesting that in a few years, no one will notice the disappearance of these birds. Certainly compromises such as the one reached in the gnatcatcher case that allowed developers to use some of the bird's habitat in exchange for protecting other parts of the habitat was a way to have environmental protection and economic development at the same time, though neither to the degree that its advocates desired. New studies have demonstrated that the spotted owl nests just as well in new-growth forests as in the old-growth ones, again providing a basis for compromise that lets loggers stay in business and protects the owl at the same time. When no compromise is available and when the existence of a species is in conflict with the existence of communities dependent on an industry affected by the presence of the species, then one can argue that the people thrown out of work will recover from their fate. They will get new jobs, relocate if necessary, and get on with their lives. But the extinct species will not recover from extinction.

On the other hand, it can also be argued that the communities that are destroyed by endangered species listings may not recover, and with their loss something valuable to human society and community will have been lost.

This conflict between jobs and the environment is particularly acute in developing countries. Many Third World countries insist that it is unfair to hold them to developed countries' standards of environmental protection. They argue that they should be allowed to set their own standards for protecting the environment, reflecting their national priorities, presumably biased toward economic growth at the expense of the environment. They suggest that it is hypocritical of the developed world to impose their standards on the developing nations, since the developed countries had the benefits of developing without current environmental standards. This is perhaps one area in which economic growth can and should be pursued and environmental protection be allowed to take a lower place on the scale of priorities, since the livelihood of many people living on the precipice of poverty is at stake. If a nation's pollution could all be contained within its borders and if it would pay all the costs of cleanup or live with the consequences, that would probably be fair. However, a nation's pollution inevitably spills over beyond its borders, affecting people who had no say in the matter. Economists call these "externalities," and a significant problem in Third World environmental ethics is, Who pays for the externalities?

However one balances jobs and the environment, there is also debate over the most effective means to accomplish that balance. As Doug Bandow points out, one of the primary conflicts over the environment concerns the means. The essential difference is between those who advocate a command-style approach to environmental protection and those who advocate a market-style approach. He cites the repeated failures of government to protect the environment and suggests that in many cases, government policy has actually produced the opposite effect from what was intended. He rightly highlights the ideological basis for much of the environmental movement in transforming "a sick, greedy and wasteful consumer society." There is an element of social engineering that appears to be inherent in the environmental movement, at least in the more radical fringes of it, that Bandow correctly suggests violates people's liberty to make important life choices for themselves.

Although market incentives are probably not available to address every environmental problem, the market can be very effective in encouraging environmental protection by offering incentives for people to safeguard it. For example, in some countries in sub-Saharan

Africa, elephants are prized for their ivory tusks and are thus endangered. Some countries take a command approach and prohibit the poaching of elephants and the sale of ivory. Since the sale of ivory is highly profitable, there are more poachers than the government can police. But some countries have taken a market approach and allowed the villages around the elephants' habitat to trade in ivory and share the profit. This gives them a financial incentive to keep the herds well populated, and in those countries the number of herds is rising. To be sure, there are limits on how much ivory can be "harvested," but this arrangement gives the people a more powerful incentive, financial self-interest, to safeguard the herds.

A second example of market incentives involves air pollution. The Los Angeles basin is one of the most heavily polluted areas in the United States, and the local Air Quality Management District has set guidelines for businesses and automobiles in conjunction with the federal Clean Air Act. These guidelines set limits on the total amount of air pollution allowed in the area. But the AQMD also allocates to the businesses in a given area "pollution credits" that indicate their acceptable pollution level. The AQMD also allows companies to buy and sell their pollution credits, so that companies would have an incentive to reduce pollution and sell their credits to those who need them. Thus the net amount of pollution being created remains the same.

Bandow suggests a similar approach to recycling and reducing the amount of trash with fees for trash collection based on the amount of trash a household generates. Likewise, for protecting other environmentally sensitive land areas, the government should either sell the land or turn over its maintenance to the environmental groups intent on seeing the land remain undeveloped. This approach enabled environmentalists to safeguard the wilderness area of Laguna Canyon in Southern California and keep it free from development. At the least, when the government lists a species of bird or animal as endangered and declares its habitat off-limits, it should compensate those who own the land by paying them fair market value for it. This is the normal procedure when the government appropriates land to build highways. It is called the right of "eminent domain." Fairness dictates that the same procedure should be followed in dealing with environmentally sensitive areas.

THIRTEEN

The Ethics of Insider Trading, Mergers, and Acquisitions

Greed is good.

Gordon Gekko in the film *Wall Street*

Corporate raiders have yet to make their first widget, grow their first carrot, or deliver their first lunch.

Lisa Newton, "The Hostile Takeover: An Opposition View"

INTRODUCTION

The 1980s have often been labeled "the decade of greed" by pundits who point to material excess and unscrupulous moneymaking on Wall Street. In the minds of most people, the faces of Ivan Boesky and Michael Milken, key figures on insider trading headlines, are synonymous with the avarice associated with this period in American history. Although scandals in business have long been a part of business culture, the fall of investment industry heroes Boesky and Milken seemed to symbolize a new degree of collapsing morality in business and society. What stood out was that even the best and brightest heroes of free enterprise fell into making millions of dollars through illegal and immoral means. The type of shady dealings in which they were involved were well chronicled in the Oliver Stone film *Wall Street* in which actor Michael Douglas, portraying corporate raider Gordon Gekko, paraphrased the famous "greed is good" speech that Ivan Boesky once delivered in real life.

The competitive and materialistic spirit of Wall Street during the 1980s undoubtedly contributed to this ethos of greed. To be sure, there is a great temptation to make a fast buck in almost any industry. However, the securities industry provides unparalleled opportunities

509

to make large amounts of money swiftly. This was especially true during the 1980s when young college and business school graduates could easily (and legally) earn six-figure salaries in exchange for hundred-hour-plus workweeks as analysts, brokers, and dealers with various investment firms. Some top producers were earning yearly salaries in the multimillions. For example, Michael Milken's slated bonus from his employer—Drexel Burnham Lambert—was $350 million the year he was indicted on insider trading charges. Within this atmosphere, money became the sole measuring stick for success, creating pressure to earn even more. One reporter poignantly describes the culture of Wall Street during the 1980s:

> Carl Icahn, then an arbitrageur and discount stockbroker, told me that it was Boesky that was making the real money. . . . A couple years later, Boesky, with maybe $100 million by then, lamented that he could not bid on a movie studio as a few other moguls had. "The Tisches, now they're rich," he said. A short time later I sat next to Robert Tisch on an airplane. "That Eddie DeBartolo," Tisch said, referring to the shopping-center magnate, "he's really rich."[1]

[1]Jeff Madrick, "What Milken Really Did," *M.* (April 1991), 88–96.

Within this environment, it was evidently easy to fall into temptation to become the biggest fish in the pond regardless of the means. Two particular methods of accomplishing these goals, insider trading and hostile takeover bids, eventually rocked the industry and raised concerns about ethics in business to new heights.

Before proceeding to discuss the specific ethical issues involved with these two activities, we should note that although the public uproar has died down, both of these types of activities still regularly occur today. The Securities and Exchange Commission (SEC) is as busy as ever investigating and filing complaints against transgressors for insider trading. Recent insider trading allegations have been made against individuals involved in such companies as AT&T, Hilton Hotels, Garnett Company, L.A. Gear, and Motel 6 in recent months. In the Motel 6 case, illegal profits were alleged to be $5.6 million and thirty people were charged, a record for the SEC involving insider trading for a single security.[2] In addition, several large hostile takeover bids have made news recently. Most noteworthy is the attempt by billionaire Kirk Kerkorian and former chairman Lee Iacocca to buy out the Chrysler Corporation. We will now proceed to examine the ethical debate involved in these two types of practices.

[2]Francis A. McMorris and Jonathan Welsh, "SEC Files Charges of Insider Trading Against Six Men," *Wall Street Journal*, 7 March 1995, B10.

Insider Trading

Although the concept sounds technically complex, the practice of "insider trading" is relatively easy. With large amounts of money at stake, tidbits of private information about company activities become invaluable. All one has to do is find out about important developments shortly before they are announced to the public and either purchase or "sell short" some shares of the company stock—and a fortune can be made instantly. Ivan Boesky paid hundreds of thousands of dollars for such information and allegedly made $28.3 million on just one transaction.[3] Other "insiders" have been more than willing to steal tips, sell them, tip off friends and relatives, and trade on them for their own profit.

Insider trading is generally defined as using significant facts about a company that have not been made public and then trade securities or release such information for a profit. These activities are legally prohibited, based on two main principles. The first is the narrower issue of property rights, which argues that the corporation has a protected property right in confidential information. As such, private information should be treated in the same manner as other corporate assets. Since the information "belongs" to the corporation, employees who trade on it or disseminate it are engaging in theft of company property. The second principle is the much broader one of fairness and equity. Insider trading is prohibited to ensure that all investors who trade on the securities market are playing on a "level playing field" in terms of access to information. From this perspective, it is wrong for anyone to trade on this type of information, regardless of how it is acquired. Thus, though this point is controversial, "remote tippees" can be held legally accountable for insider trading even if the information has not been stolen and no fiduciary duties have been breached.[4]

The first two articles in this chapter address the morality of insider trading and debate whether such practices should remain illegal. Bill Shaw argues in defense of insider trading and believes that the prohibition against such activities is needless. He asserts that permitting insider trading would actually contribute to overall economic efficiency because stock prices would more accurately reflect their real value since insiders have better information with which to make investment decisions. This more accurate information would then offer better market signals to common investors and improve overall efficiency.

Patricia Werhane disagrees strongly with Shaw's perspective. Basing her claims on Adam Smith's vision of "restrained self-interest" in the marketplace, she argues that permitting insider trading would in fact circumvent, rather than facilitate, competition and a truly efficient economy. Werhane believes that insider trading permits only a

[3]Anthony Bianco and Gary Weiss, "Suddenly the Fish Get Bigger," *Business Week* (2 March 1987): 28–32.

[4]"Insider Case Is Rejected," *New York Times*, 28 April 1992, D10.

privileged few to be privy to the rules, violating Smith's ideal of competition between "two equally matched parties." Within this framework, she further argues against the claim that insider trading is a "victimless crime."

Mergers and Acquisitions

Gains made through activities surrounding mergers and acquisitions can also be large and swift. Although legal, many of the practices associated with such activities are morally questionable. In fairness, we must say that not all mergers and acquisitions are ethically suspect. Many of them are actually good for employees, shareholders, and society at large. For example, when two companies can join together in a strategic alliance enabling the production of better products at lower prices, consumers and the economy receive substantial benefits. Furthermore, today's realities of global competition mandate that some companies in either rapid-growth or maturing industries join forces in preventative moves to ensure future survival. While some jobs will inevitably be lost in these maneuvers, this is preferable to a long-term situation in which many more would be laid off as a result of a failure to anticipate change.

However, these were not the types of takeover and merger activities that brought public criticism to bear in the '80s. During that time period, "corporate raiders" made large sums of money through "hostile takeovers" and leveraged buyouts that placed employees and sometimes the companies themselves at great financial risk. In these situations, a takeover artist targets a firm and offers a premium to stockholders to purchase their shares on the open market without approval from the target company's management. Some of these "raiders" then gain control of the target company and drain its cash reserves or sell off its most valued divisions and assets in order to make a quick profit. Sometimes the companies taken over are severely weakened and many employees may lose jobs in the course of such actions. Even more controversial were those who engaged in "greenmail," a practice in which a raider bought up large of amounts of a company's stock and announced a takeover to the public with no real intention of buying the company. Knowing that the company would probably defend itself against takeover, the raider could then exact a premium from the target company who would buy back its shares at inflated prices.

Other defensive tactics used by corporations are equally controversial. They include swallowing a "poison pill," a move by which a company uses impediments to transfer of control in order to make itself a less attractive target for takeover. Courting a "white knight,"

"Pac-Man defense," "selling off the crown jewels," and "golden parachutes" are other controversial maneuvers that are discussed in the last two articles in this chapter.

In response to the public criticism, Michael Jensen defends many of these practices on the grounds of economic efficiency in his article "Takeovers: Folklore and Science." Jensen cites numerous empirical studies in order to address what he claims to be "the myths that swirl around the controversy" and defends his position that hostile takeovers are actually beneficial to stockholders and the economy as a whole.

Lisa Newton offers a refutation of Jensen and other "shark defenders" in her essay "The Hostile Takeover: An Opposition View." Newton brings to light many of the noneconomic effects of these activities by focusing on the human costs. She then proceeds to address the weaknesses of the empirical evidence that supports the claims that these activities are beneficial to society and arrives at the exact opposite conclusion. She asserts that hostile takeovers severely weaken corporations, hurt shareholders, and may even jeopardize the competitiveness of U.S. corporations. Most poignant, however, is her statement that "corporate raiders have yet to make their first widget, grow their first carrot, or deliver their first lunch. All they do is turn money into money, cantilevering the profit off the shell of responsible ownership."

READINGS

Should Insider Trading Be Outside the Law?

Bill Shaw

Business and Society Review 66 (1988): 34–37. Copyright © 1988.

Insider trading is good for the U.S. economy, for the corporation that is traded, and for the insiders (of course), and it does not necessarily amount to fraud on investors. Looking beyond the financial pages, and certainly beyond the 6:00 news, you can find a number of economic, legal, and moral arguments supporting this view.

Professor Henry G. Manne, now dean of the George Mason University School of Law, crystallized the most radical position on this topic with his 1966 *Insider Trading and the Stock Market*. Essentially, Manne sought a return to simpler times—common law, pre-1934 Securities Exchange Act times. He saw knowledge as a valuable thing, whether it be knowledge that advances our cultural well-being or, more practically, knowledge that takes a business from marginal solvency to Fortune 500 status. This widely recognized insight led Manne and others to assign property rights to this information. The originator of the information (the individual or corporation that spent hard-earned bucks producing it) owns and controls this asset just as it does other proprietary goods—securities, real estate, patents, or copyrights. This assignment of ownership and exclusive use is essential to encouraging the production of additional information.

In a society that values freedom, especially economic freedom, self-interested owners of information ought to be permitted to use this asset to its highest and best use.

By employing information in the most efficient manner, as we do with all other privately owned goods, private wealth is maximized, and, in the spirit of Adam Smith, social wealth is thus maximized as well.

Societal Effects

A reconsideration and revision of the insider trading prohibition would have a number of positive effects. It would also have a downside. The changes would make themselves felt on three levels: societal or systemic, corporate, and individual.

Without getting too technical, it should at least be noted that the securities industry operates on the proposition that information relating to the performance of a firm affects its stock price. The price increase/decrease will depend on how market experts perceive that information. If it appears that fourth quarter earnings will be much higher than expected, or that an innovative new product will soon be released, one would expect the stock price of that firm to increase when the information is made public; the opposite result would follow from the publication of an unfavorable court action or the loss of key personnel.

This evaluative process, led by market professionals, enhances the efficiency of our national and regional exchanges by moving securities prices close to, if not perfectly in line with, a stock's real or intrinsic value. These adjustments take place quickly and in an unbiased (i.e., impersonal, objective) way. Thus, traders cannot expect to make a "quick kill" in the market unless they control nonpublic, inside information.

The paradigm just described is known as the "efficient capital market hypothesis." It is a given

in the investment community, and it admits to the reality of insiders earning above-normal returns. Proponents of insider trading argue that the social value of such trades is immense. By pumping new information into the market, stock prices adjust quickly to real values. The insider's message—encoded in "who's buying, who's selling signals" rather than in volume trades per se—contributes more in the way of social benefits than it extracts in price.

Dogs and Gems

This same positive account may be rendered in another way. If insiders enter the market buying or selling, the traders with whom they deal will either profit more or lose less than they would have if the insider had abstained. By bidding up the price of a "gem" the insider is preventing the seller from experiencing the full, post-announcement gain, but the seller is making some gain, and in fact more than would have been made in the absence of such trading. By the same token, in depressing the price of a "dog," the insider is protecting the buyer from experiencing the full, post-announcement loss; the buyer's purchase is made at a price below that which would have been quoted in the absence of insider trades. Since the investors who are selling to or buying from the insider obviously do not know of the nonpublic, inside information, their perspective on the market remains the same.

Still, if it doesn't seem quite "fair" for insiders to utilize their positional advantage, trading on an informational disparity, consider the situation that exists today in the absence of such trading.

Even when insiders sit tight with the nonpublic information they possess, they at least know when not to sell and when not to buy. We tolerate that situation because it seems preferable to the alternative. If full and immediate disclosure of all nonpublic information were compelled by law, the economic freedom of the firm would be compromised and its economic interests would be diminished. For example, if an energy firm was compelled to announce its oil discoveries before it contracted for drilling rights, the loss of control over the information it developed would be extremely costly to the firm when it sought mineral leases. It appears then that our society is going to have to buy into some level of unfairness. The creation of a system of informational parity seems unlikely.

A New Paradigm

Suppose now that the corporate proprietor of insider information, a computer chip firm, believed it to be in the company's best interest to license or permit insider trading. It could operate in the following way: The board of directors, or some appropriate committee thereof, could be charged with the responsibility of selecting employees who had notably contributed to the success of the firm. Permitting these selected employees to inside trade would be a way of rewarding their efforts over and above their base salary and fringe package. This licensing process permits the firm to cut its wage bill to a minimum while still attracting to its employ the brightest and most creative minds.

In effect, the firm is making entrepreneurs out of managers. Managers are notoriously risk-averse. They need to be nudged, encouraged, and booted into a more aggressive posture if the firm is to achieve and maintain a winning edge.

As an alternative to a board-designated list of insiders, the firm could simply adopt a hands-off policy, not involving itself in the selection process. This approach gives implicit approval to those who created the information to trade on it. It takes the lid off and allows employees to rewrite their compensation package whenever the opportunity arises to trade on nonpublic information.

The Downside

There is the possibility that the "candidates" for insider trading permits (or in firms with a hands-off policy, all employees) will create such turmoil as they jockey for position that the efficient operation of the firm will suffer. They will be so concerned with creating mega trade events that the long-term viability of the firm will be sacrificed to the short-term goal. The rate of development of promising projects and the timing of new releases could become secondary to efforts to line up

financial backers and tippees in order to take advantage of the trading opportunities. At the very least, it must be said that the culture of such a firm would be significantly impacted by this strategy, and it is by no means certain that this work environment would attract and hold the most talented and productive work force.

With regard to the financing of this strategy, although the debits may not show up on the balance sheet, it is not without its price. Just as compensation packages, with their mix of salary, insurance, retirement, stock options, and other fringes, come out of someone's pocket, so, too, do inside trade profits. Investors will find themselves with less of a good stock or more of a bad one.

Once the lid is off, insiders will have the same opportunity to sell on nonpublic bad news, by emptying their portfolios or selling short, as they will to buy on undisclosed good news. There is a moral hazard lurking within this brew; the deliberate creation of bad news, or a perverse incentive to advance high-risk projects. If the insider locks into a no-lose or risk-neutral position, the genius of this strategy is undone.

Cost of Compensation

There is a question mark as well with regard to the cost of insider compensation. In the normal compensation scheme, shareholders can choose among different benefits packages. But if the ban on insider trading is lifted, there is scarcely any means of accounting for the cost or controlling it.

Whereas in theory this strategy is an attractive way of inducing employee zeal, there is really no sound method of determining the marginal contribution that is purchased by each new dollar of inside trade profit. Is the amount of trade profits appropriate, or do employees become like proverbial "kids in the candy store?" Cost-benefit analysis, so dear to the calculations of the business community, flies out the window. The likelihood of tipping friends, relatives, and financial backers exacerbates the problem, bringing into the picture a whole contingent of free riders who have contributed nothing to the success of the firm.

Finally, in a system that rolls back the ban on insider trading, you can be assured that the message will not be lost on the financial community. Before a single sale is made, specialists and market makers will adjust their bid and ask prices, and traders their reservation prices. The initial adjustment is likely to be a negative one; it will have a discounting effect on the price of the security to account for the possibility of insider trading. Market experts have always taken positions against this possibility, but never to such a great extent.

A long-term price depression could spell hard times for the firm—an increase in the cost of capital and an increase in the number of takeover bids are just two possibilities.

Nudging Effect

A price depression, however, is not an inevitable result. It really depends on how the market perceives the alleged productivity gains that are touted by insider trade proponents. If indeed the firm performs consistently above its historical levels, if there is some evidence that the strategy is working, one might safely guess that stock prices will be adjusted upward accordingly.

Clearly, neither the SEC nor the Justice Department is much impressed by efficiency arguments. If the "nudging" effect of insider trading is good, full disclosure would be that much better, the government contends. Further, the government insists, there are many different mixes of incentive packages, and, on balance, not all of them could be worse than letting an insider write his or her own. The bottom line is that the legislative and judicial branches in this country consider disclosure or abstinence from trading on the basis of nonpublic information to be fraudulent. No one in Washington is going to challenge this position in an election year or in any other.

Form Over Substance

There is an opening, nevertheless, for the argument that insider trading is not fraudulent. Suppose that firm X, convinced of the economic soundness of insider trading, announced loudly and publicly that it intended to license such trading in its securities. It is difficult to see, under these circumstances, that such trading would be considered fraudulent.

Prior to the 1934 Act, common-law courts did not invoke insider trading unless there was some exceptional circumstance, such as express or implied misrepresentation of value or of the identity of the trader. Judges reasoned that fraud was an intentional tort that required, first of all, the breach of some duty to the plaintiff. In what has been described as a "triumph of form over substance," common-law judges found that the duty of corporate officers and employees was owed to the corporation, not to the stockholders; the fact that they traded on unequal information was simply the way of the world. Even today in the federal courts, trading on a disparity of information, even unfairness in the treatment of shareholders by fiduciaries, is not fraud and is not regarded as a violation of SEC rules.

If firm X announces its intentions and investors are forewarned of what lies ahead, how can it be said that they are defrauded? How can the firm or its insiders breach a duty toward shareholders if they have no such duty to breach? How can investors prove that they have suffered damages as a result of stock prices which are adjusted to account for inside information. In our scenario, shareholders have received all the normal attributes of stock ownership, minus only the assurance that the stock will not be traded on inside information. They got what they paid a discounted price for—no one deceived them, no one breached a duty toward them, and no one compelled them to make a purchase.

Looking Abroad

In Japan, insider trading is an unspoken part of the business culture—there has been only one reported case under the limited insider trading prohibition currently in effect. Hong Kong has repealed the insider prohibitions it put into effect in 1974. France has a narrow prohibition against such trading, but it is hardly considered immoral, and the total number of suits and sanctions is negligible. West Germany relies on voluntary inside trading guidelines—the practice is proscribed but not illegal. These guidelines are enforced, or not, through employment contracts; it is a choice the firm makes itself. Great Britain, like common-law jurisdictions in the United States prior to 1934, applied no sanctions against insider trading until recently—in fact, too recently to analyze the level of enforcement.

These examples are relevant only for the purpose of documenting the official versus the real attitudes toward insider trading in other nations. Both sets of attitudes seem to be more tolerant. Insider trading probably would not be much different or more harmful in the United States. This is not to say that we should pattern our legal institutions after theirs, nor is it a suggestion that practices regarded as moral in other countries are the best that we are capable of achieving. It is important to note, however, that insider trading is not regarded as an abomination throughout the world, and since most countries do have legal and moral proscriptions against fraud, one must admit the possibility that our judgment is faulty.

The American people are indignant about insider trading because they view it as fraud and theft. While this is not necessarily the case, the efficiency agreement is not likely to sway anybody's opinion. Moreover, there is surely no moral compulsion to insider trade; there is no cause for righteous indignation at the ban. Ivan Boesky is no modern-day hero—he just wanted to make a few million dollars. For now, live with the law. Don't break it. Get it changed.

The Ethics of Insider Trading

Patricia H. Werhane

Journal of Business Ethics 8 (1989): 841–45. Copyright © 1989.

Insider trading is the reverse of speculation. It is reward without risk, wealth generated—and injury done to others—by an unfair advantage in information.... [T]he core principle is clear: no one should profit from exploitation of important information not available to the public.[1]

Insider trading in the stock market is characterized as the buying or selling of shares of stock on the basis of information known only to the trader or to a few persons. In discussions of insider trading it is commonly assumed that the privileged information, if known to others, would affect their actions in the market as well, although in theory this need not be the case. The present guidelines of the Securities and Exchange Commission prohibit most forms of insider trading. Yet a number of economists and philosophers of late defend this kind of activity both as a viable and useful practice in a free market and as a practice that is not immoral. In response to these defenses I want to question the value of insider trading both from a moral and an economic point of view. I shall argue that insider trading both in its present illegal form and as a legalized market mechanism violates the privacy of concerned parties, destroys competition, and undermines the efficient and proper functioning of a free market, thereby bringing into question its own raison d'etre. It does so and therefore is economically inefficient for the very reason that it is immoral.

That insider trading as an illegal activity interferes with the free market is pretty obvious. It is like a game where there are a number of players each of whom represents a constituency. In this sort of game there are two sets of rules—one ostensive set and another, implicit set, functioning for some of the players. In this analogy some of the implicit rules are outlawed, yet the big players manage to keep them operative and actually often in control of the game. But not all the players know all the rules being played or at least they are ignorant of the most important ones, ones that determine the big wins and big losses. So not all the players realize what rules actually manipulate the outcome. Moreover, partly because some of the most important functioning rules are illegal, some players who do know the implicit rules and could participate do not. Thus not everyone in a position to do so plays the trading game the same way. The game, then, like the manipulated market that is the outcome, is unfair—unfair to some of the players and those they represent—unfair not only because some of the players are not privy to the most important rules, but also because these "special" rules are illegal so that they are adopted only by a few of even the privileged players.

But suppose that insider trading was decriminalized or not prohibited by SEC regulations. Then, one might argue, insider trading would not be unfair because anyone could engage in it without impunity. Although one would be trading on privileged knowledge, others, too, could trade on *their* privileged information. The market would function more efficiently since the best-informed and those most able to gain information would be allowed to exercise their fiscal capabilities. The market itself would regulate the alleged excesses of insider trading. I use the term "alleged" excesses because according to this line of reasoning, if the market is functioning properly, whatever gains or losses are created as a result of open competition are a natural outcome of that competition. They are not excesses at all, and eventually the market will adjust the so-called unfair gains of speculators.

There are several other defenses of insider trading. First, insider information, e.g., information about a merger, acquisition, new stock issue, layoffs, etc., information known only to a few, *should* be and remain private. That information is the property of those engaged in the activity in question, and they should have the right to regulate its dissemination. Second and conversely, even under ideal circumstances it is impossible either to disseminate information to all interested parties equally and fairly, or alternately, to preserve absolute secrecy. For example, in issuing a new stock or deciding on a stock split, a number of parties in the transactions from brokers to printers learn about that information in advance just because of their participation in making this activity a reality. And there are always shareholders and other interested parties who claim they did not receive information of such an activity or did not receive it at the same time as other shareholders even when the information was disseminated to everyone at the same time. Thus it is, at best, difficult to stop insider trading or to judge whether a certain kind of knowledge is "inside" or privileged. This is not a good reason to defend insider trading as economically or morally desirable, but it illustrates the difficulties of defining and controlling the phenomenon.

Third, those who become privy to inside information, even if they take advantage of that information before it becomes public, are trading on probabilities, not on certainties, since they are trading before the activity actually takes place. They are taking a gamble, and if they are wrong the market itself will "punish" them. It is even argued that brokers who do not use inside information for their clients' advantage are cheating their clients.

Finally, and more importantly, economists like Henry Manne argue that insider trading is beneficial to outsiders. Whether it is more beneficial than its absence is a question Manne admits he cannot answer. But Manne defends insider trading because, he argues, it reduces the factor of chance in trading both for insiders and outsiders. When shares are traded on information or probabilities rather than on rumor or whim, the market reflects more accurately the actual economic status of that company or set of companies. Because of insider trading, stock prices go up or down according to real, factual information. Outsiders benefit from this because stock prices more closely represent the worth of their company than shares not affected by insider trading. Insider trading, then, actually improves the fairness of the market, according to this argument, by reflecting in stock prices the fiscal realities of affected corporations thereby benefiting all traders of the stocks.[2]

> ## *The misinterpretation is that the free market works something like the law of gravity—autonomously and anonymously in what I would call a no-blooded fashion.*

These arguments for insider trading are persuasive. Because outsiders are allegedly not harmed from privileged information not available to them and may indeed benefit from insider trading, and because the market punishes rash speculators, insider trading cannot be criticized as exploitation. In fact, it makes the market more efficient. Strong as these arguments are, however, there is something amiss with these claims. The error, I think, rests at least in part with the faulty view of how free markets work, a view which stems from a misinterpretation that derives from a misreading of Adam Smith and specifically a misreading of Smith's notions of self-interest and the Invisible Hand.

The misinterpretation is this. It is sometimes assumed that an unregulated free market, driven by competition and self-interest, will function autonomously. The idea is that the free market works something like the law of gravity—autonomously and anonymously in what I would call a no-blooded fashion. The interrelationships created by free market activities based on self-interested competition are similar to the gravitational relationships between the planets and the sun: impersonal, automatic interactions determined by a number of factors including the distance and competitive self-interest of each of the market components. The free market functions, then, despite the selfish peculiarities of the players just as the planets circle the sun despite their best intentions to do otherwise. Given that picture of the free market, so-called insider trading, driven by self-interest but restrained by competi-

tive forces, that is, the invisible hand, is merely one gravitational mechanism—a complication but not an oddity or an aberration in the market.

This is a crude and exaggerated picture of the market, but I think it accounts for talk about the market *as if* it functioned in this independent yet forceful way, and it accounts for defenses of unrestrained self-interested actions in the market place. It allows one to defend insider trading because of the positive market fall-out from this activity, and because the market allegedly will control the excesses of self-interested economic activities.

The difficulty with this analysis is not so much with the view of insider trading as a legitimate activity but rather with the picture of economic actors in a free market. Adam Smith himself, despite his 17th century Newtonian background, did not have such a mechanical view of a laissez-faire economy. Again and again in the *Wealth of Nations* Smith extols the virtues of unrestrained competition as being to the advantage of the producer and consumer.[3] A system of perfect liberty he argues, creates a situation where "[t]he whole of the advantages and disadvantages of the different employments of labour and stock . . . be either perfectly equal or continually tending to equality."[4] Yet for Smith the greatest cause of inequalities of advantage is any restrictive policy or activity that deliberately gives privileges to certain kinds of businesses, trades, or professions.[5] The point is that Smith sees perfect liberty as the necessary condition for competition, but perfect competition occurs only [when] both parties in the exchange are on more or less on equal grounds, whether it be competition for labor, jobs, consumers, or capital. This is not to imply that Smith favors equality of outcomes. Clearly he does not. But the market is most efficient and most fair when there is competition between equally matched parties.

Moreover, Smith's thesis was that the Invisible Hand works because, and only when, people operate with restrained self-interest, self-interest restrained by reason, moral sentiments, and sympathy, in Smith's case the reason, moral sentiments and sympathies of British gentlemen. To operate otherwise, that is, with unrestrained self-interest, where that self-interest causes harm to others would "violate the laws of justice"[6] or be a "violation of fair play,"[7] according to Smith. This interferes with free competition just as government regulation would because the character of competition, and thus the direction of the Invisible Hand, depends on the manner in which actors exploit or control their own self-interests. The Invisible Hand, then, that "masterminds" the free market is not like an autonomous gravitational force. It depends on the good will, decency, self-restraint, and fair play of those parties engaging in market activities.[8] When self-interests get out of hand, Smith contends, they must be regulated by laws of justice.[9]

Similarly, the current market, albeit not Smith's ideal of laissez-faire, is affected by how people operate in the market place. It does not operate autonomously. Unrestrained activities of insider traders affect competition differently than Smithian exchanges which are more or less equal exchanges between self-interested but restrained parties. The term "insider trading" implies that some traders know more than others, that information affects their decision-making and would similarly affect the trading behavior of others should they become privy to that information. Because of this, the resulting market is different than one unaffected by insider trading. This, in itself, is not a good reason to question insider trading. Henry Manne, for example, recognizes the role of insider trading in influencing the market and finds that, on balance, this is beneficial.

Insider trading, however, is not merely a complication in the free market mechanism. Insider trading, whether it is legal or illegal, affects negatively the ideal of laissez-faire of *any* market: competition, just as "insider" rules affect the fairness of the trader even if that activity is not illegal and even if one could, in theory, obtain inside information oneself. This is because the same information, or equal information, is not available to everyone. So competition, which depends on the availability of equal advantage by all parties is precluded. Insider trading allows the insider to indulge in greed (even though she may not) and that, by eschewing stock prices, works against the very kind of market in which insider trading might be allowed to function.

If it is true, as Manne argues, that insider trading produces a more efficient stock market because stock prices as a result of insider trading better reflect the underlying economic conditions of those companies involved in the trade, he would also have to argue that competition does not always produce the best results in the marketplace. Conversely, if competition creates the most efficient market, insider trading cannot, because competition is "regulated" by insiders. While it is not clear whether outsiders benefit more from insider trading than without that activity, equal access to information would allow (although not determine) every trader to compete from an equal advantage. Thus pure competition, a supposed goal of the free market and an aim of most persons who defend insider trading, is more nearly obtained without insider trading.

Insider trading does not protect the privacy of information it is supposed to protect.

Insider trading has other ethical problems. Insider trading does not protect the privacy of information it is supposed to protect. To illustrate, let us consider a case of a friendly merger between Company X and Company Y. Suppose this merger is in the planning stages and is not to be made public even to the shareholders for a number of months. There may be good or bad reasons for this secrecy, e.g., labor problems, price of shares of acquired company, management changes, unfriendly raiders, competition in certain markets, etc. By law, management and others privy to knowledge about the possible merger cannot trade shares of either company during the negotiating period. On the other hand, if that information is "leaked" to a trader (or if she finds out by some other means), then information that might affect the merger is now in the hands of persons not part of the negotiation. The alleged privacy of information, privacy supposedly protected by insider traders, is now in the hands of not disinterested parties. While they may keep this information a secret, they had no right to it in the first place.

Moreover, their possession of the information has three possible negative effects.

First, they or their clients in fact may be interested parties to the merger, e.g., labor union leaders, stockholders in competing companies, etc., the very persons for whom the information makes a difference and therefore are the objects of Company X's and Y's secrecy. Second, insider trading on privileged information gives unfair advantages to these traders. Even if outsiders benefit from insider trading, they are less likely to benefit as much nor as soon as insider traders for the very reason of their lack of proximity to the activity. Insider traders can use information to their advantage in the market, an advantage neither the management of X or Y nor other traders can enjoy. Even if the use of such information in the market makes the market more efficient, this is unfair competition since those without this information will not gain as much as those who have such knowledge. Even if insider trading does contribute to market stabilization based on information, nevertheless, one has also to justify the fact that insider traders profit more on their knowledge than outsiders, when their information becomes an actuality simply by being "first" in the trading of the stock. Do insider traders deserve this added profit because their trading creates a more propitious market share knowledge for outsiders? That is a difficult position to defend, because allowing insider trading also allows for the very Boeskyian greed that is damaging in any market.

Third, while trading X and Y on inside information may bring their share prices to the value most closely reflecting their real price-earnings ration, this is not always the case. Such trading may reflect undue optimism or pessimism about the possible outcome of the merger, an event that has not yet occurred. So the prices of X and Y may be overvalued or undervalued on the basis of a probability, or, because insider traders seldom have all the facts, on guesswork. In these cases insider trading deliberately creates more risk in the market since the stock prices of X and Y are manipulated for not altogether solid reasons. So market efficiency, the end which allegedly justifies insider trading is not guaranteed.

What Henry Manne's defenses of insider trading do show is what Adam Smith well knew, that the market is neither independent nor self-regulatory. What traders do in the market and how they behave affects the direction and kind of restraint the market will exert on other traders. The character of the market is a product of those who operate within it, as Manne has demonstrated in his defense of insider trading. Restrained self-interest creates an approximation of a self-regulatory market, because it is that that allows self-interested individuals and companies to function as competitively as possible. In the long run the market will operate more efficiently too, because it precludes aberrations such as those exhibited by Ivan Boesky's and David Levine's behavior, behavior that created market conditions favorable to no one except themselves and their clients.

Notes

[1]George Will, "Keep Your Eye on Guiliani," *Newsweek*, March 2, 1987, 84.

[2]See Henry Manne, *Insider Trading and the Stock Market* (The Free Press, New York, 1966), especially Chapters X and XI.

[3]Adam Smith, *The Wealth of Nations*, ed. R. A. Campbell and A. S. Skinner (Oxford University Press, Oxford, 1976), I.x.c, II. v. 8–12.

[4]*Wealth of Nations*, I.x.a.1.

[5]*Wealth of Nations*, I.x.c.

[6]*Wealth of Nations*, IV. ix. 51.

[7]Adam Smith, *The Theory of Moral Sentiments*, ed. D. D. Raphael and A. L. Macfie (Oxford University Press, Oxford, 1976), II. ii. 2.1.

[8]See Andrew Skinner, *A System of Social Science* (Clarendon Press, Oxford, 1979), especially 237ff.

[9]See, for example, *The Wealth of Nations*, II. ii. 94, IV, v. 16

Takeovers: Folklore and Science

Michael C. Jensen

Harvard Business Review (November–December 1984): 109–21. Copyright © 1984.

[1]From 1981 to 1983, the number of large U.S. corporate acquisitions grew at a rate roughly double that of the 1970s and even exceeded the one realized during the famous merger wave of the 1960s. The drama of 2,100 annual takeovers valued at more than $1 million—much of it played out in heated, public battles—has generated an enormous amount of criticism, not only from politicians and the media but also from high-level corporate executives.

Commenting in the *Wall Street Journal* on the Bendix and Martin Marietta takeover battle, for example, Lee Iacocca, chairman of Chrysler, argued:

"It's not a merger. It's a three-ring circus. If they're really concerned about America, they'd stop it right now. It's no good for the economy. It wrecks it. If I were in the banking system I'd say no more [money] for conglomerates for one year."

A former director at Bendix added:

"I think . . . it's the kind of thing corporate America ought not to do, because the poor stockholder is the one whose interest is being ignored in favor of the egos of directors and executives. And who . . . is running the show—the business of making brakes and aerospace equipment—while all of this is going on?"

In a 1984 *New York Times* piece on the "surge of corporate mergers," Felix Rohatyn noted:

"All this frenzy may be good for investment bankers now, but it's not good for the country or investment bankers in the long run. We seem to be living in a 1920s, jazz age atmosphere."

Just as the public outcry over excesses on Wall Street in the early 1930s led to the Glass Steagall Act regulating banking, so the latest criticisms of mergers have brought enormous political pressure to bear on Congress to restrict takeovers. The July 1983 report of the SEC Advisory Committee on Tender Offers contained 50 recommendations for new regulations. Democratic Representative Peter Rodino has cosponsored a bill that would require advance notice of proposed acquisitions resulting in assets of $5 billion and 25,000 employees and a judgment by the Antitrust Division of the Justice Department or the FTC whether such acquisitions "serve the public interest."

The popular view underlying these proposals is wrong, however, because it ignores the fundamental economic function that takeover activities serve. In the corporate takeover market, management teams compete for the right to control—that is, to manage—corporate resources. Viewed in this way, the market for control is an important part of the managerial labor market, which is very different from, and has higher stakes than, the normal labor market. After all, potential chief executive officers do not simply leave their applications with personnel officers. Their on-the-job performance is subject not only to the normal internal control mechanisms of their organizations but also to the scrutiny of the external market for control.

Imagine that you are the president of a large billion-dollar corporation. Suddenly, another management team threatens your job and prestige by trying to buy your company's stock. The whole world watches your performance. Putting yourself in this situation leads to a better understanding of the reasons behind the rhetoric, maneuverings, and even lobbying in the political and regulatory sectors by managers for protection from unfriendly offers.

The Bendix attempt to take control of Martin Marietta in 1982 gained considerable attention because of Marietta's unusual countertakeover offer for Bendix, called the "Pac-Man defense," whose principle is: "My company will eat yours before yours eats mine."[2] Some describe this kind of contest as disgraceful. I find it fascinating because it makes clear that the crucial issue is not whether the two companies will merge but which managers will be in control.

At the end of the contest, Bendix held 67% of Martin Marietta while Martin Marietta held 50% of Bendix. United Technologies then entered as Martin Marietta's friend and offered to buy Bendix. But it was Allied, coming in late, that finally won the battle with its purchase of all of Bendix's stock, 39% of Martin Marietta's, and a promise not to buy more. When the dust had cleared, shareholders of Bendix and Martin had both won; their respective shares gained roughly 38% in value (after adjusting for marketwide stock price change). Allied's shareholders, on the other hand, lost approximately 8.6%.[3]

Given the success and history of the modern corporation, it is surprising how little the media, the legal and political communities, and even business executives understand the reasons behind the complexities and subtleties of takeover battles. Prior to the last decade, the academic community made little progress in redressing this lack of understanding. But research efforts in business schools across the country have recently begun to overcome it.

In this article I summarize the most important scientific evidence refuting the myths that swirl around the controversy. The research shows that:

- Takeovers of companies by outsiders do not harm shareholders of the target company; in fact, they gain substantial wealth.
- Corporate takeovers do not waste resources; they use assets productively.
- Takeovers do not siphon commercial credit from its uses in funding new plant and equipment.
- Takeovers do not create gains for shareholders through creation of monopoly power.
- Prohibition of plant closings, layoffs, and dismissals following takeovers would reduce market efficiency and lower aggregate living standards.

- Although managers are self-interested; the environment in which they operate gives them relatively little leeway to feather their nests at shareholders' expense. Corporate control-related actions of managers do not generally harm shareholders, but actions that eliminate actual or potential takeover bids are most suspect as exceptions to this rule.
- Golden parachutes for top-level executives are, in principle, in the interest of shareholders. Although the practice can be abused, the evidence indicates that shareholders gain when golden parachutes are adopted.
- In general, the activities of takeover specialists benefit shareholders.

Before exploring the evidence, I consider why shareholders are the most important constituency of the modern corporation and why their interests must be held paramount when discussing the current wave of acquisitions and mergers.

The Nature of the Corporation

Stockholders are commonly portrayed as one group in a set of equal constituencies, or "stakeholders," of the company. In fact, stockholders are not equal with these other groups because they are the ultimate holders of the rights to organization control and therefore must be the focal point for any discussion concerning it.

The public corporation is the nexus for a complex set of voluntary contracts among customers, workers, managers, and the suppliers of materials, capital, and risk bearing. The rights of the interacting parties are determined by law, the corporation's charter, and the implicit and explicit contracts with each individual.

Corporations, like all organizations, vest control rights in the constituency bearing the residual risk.[4] (Residual risk is the risk associated with the difference between the random cash inflows and outflows of the organization.) In partnerships and privately held companies, for example, these residual claims and the organizational control rights are restricted to major decision agents (directors and managers); in mutuals and consumer cooperatives, to customers; and in supplier cooperatives, to suppliers.

Corporations are unique organizations because they make no restrictions on who can own their residual claims and this makes it possible for customers, managers, labor, and suppliers to avoid bearing any of the corporate residual risk. Because stockholders guarantee the contracts of all constituents, they bear the corporation's residual risk. The absence of restrictions on who can own corporate residual claims allows specialization in risk bearing by those investors who are most adept at the function. As a result, the corporation realizes great efficiencies in risk bearing that reduce costs substantially and allow it to meet market demand more efficiently than other organizations.

Although the identities of the bearers of residual risk may differ, all business organizations vest organizational control rights in them. For control to rest in any other group would be equivalent to allowing that group to "play poker" with someone else's money and would create inefficiencies that lead to the possibility of failure. Stockholders as the bearers of residual risk hold the right to control of the corporation, although they delegate much of this control to a board of directors who normally hire, fire, and set the compensation of at least the CEO.

Proof of the efficiency of the corporate organizational form shows dramatically in market performance. In principle, any marketer can supply goods and services. In reality, all organizational forms compete for consumers, managers, labor, and supplies of capital and other goods. Those that supply the goods demanded by customers at the lowest price win out. The dominance of the corporate form of organization in large-scale nonfinancial activities indicates that it is winning much of this competition.

Acquisition Folklore

Takeovers can be carried out through mergers, tender offers, and proxy fights, or sometimes through elements of all three. A tender offer made directly to the stockholders to buy some or all of their shares for a specified price during a specified time period does not require the approval of the target company's management or board of directors. A merger, however, is negotiated with the company's management and, when approved by its board of directors, is submitted to the shareholders for approval. In a proxy contest the votes of the stockholders are solicited, generally for the election of a new slate of directors.

Takeovers frequently begin with what is called a "friendly" merger offer from the bidder to the target management and board. If management turns down the offer, the bidder can, and often does, take the offer directly to the shareholders in the form of a tender offer. At this point, target company managers usually oppose the offer by issuing press releases condemning it as outside the shareholders' best interest, by initiating court action, by requesting antitrust action against the bidder, by starting a countertakeover move for the bidder, and by other actions designed to make the target company a less desirable acquisition.

Target company management often casts about for a "white knight"—a friendly merger partner who will protect the "maiden" from the advances of the feared raider and more important, who will pay a higher price. When the company doesn't find a white knight, and an unfriendly bidder takes it over, its leaders will likely look for new jobs. The takeover process penalizes incompetent or self-serving managers whose actions have lowered the market price of their corporation's stock. Although the process operates with a lag, the forces are strong and persistent. Of course—as a result of economies of scale or other efficiencies—some efficient managers lose their jobs after a takeover through no fault of their own.

This kind of romantic language has been used to offer comic relief, but it contributes to the atmosphere of folklore that surrounds a process fundamental to the corporate world. The resulting myths and misunderstandings distort the public's perception and render a meaningful dialogue impossible.

Folklore: Takeovers harm the shareholders of target companies.

Fact: The pejorative term *raider* used to label the bidding company in an unfriendly takeover suggests that the bidder will buy control of a company, pillage it, and leave the stockholders with only a crumbling shell.

More than a dozen studies have painstakingly gathered evidence on the stock price effect of successful takeovers (see *Exhibit I* for a summary of the results).[5] According to these studies, companies involved in takeovers experience abnormal increases in their stock prices for approximately one month surrounding the initial announcement of the takeover. (Abnormal stock price changes are stock price changes customarily adjusted by regression analysis to eliminate the effects of marketwide forces on all corporations.)[6] The exhibit shows that target company shareholders gain 30% from tender offers and 20% from mergers.

Exhibit I
Abnormal stock price increases
from successful takeovers*

	Target companies	Bidding companies
Tender offers	30%	4%
Mergers	20%	0%
Proxy contests	8%	N.A.†

* Adjusted to eliminate the effects of marketwide price changes.
† Not applicable.

Because tender offers are often extended for less than 100% of the outstanding shares and because not all takeover announcements result in acquisitions, stock prices do not increase at the announcement of the offer by the full amount of the premium offered. Consequently, average target stockholder returns in takeovers are actually higher than the estimates in *Exhibit I* because the abnormal stock price changes it summarizes generally exclude the purchase premiums shareholders receive when they surrender their shares.

The shareholders of bidding companies, on the other hand, earn only about 4% from tender offers and nothing from mergers. If the much feared raiding has taken place, it seems to be of a peculiar, Robin Hood Variety.

When an insurgent group, led by a dissatisfied manager or a large stockholder, attempts to gain controlling seats on the board of directors of a company (thereby taking over the company through an internal proxy fight), shareholders also gain. As *Exhibit I* shows, the stock prices of these companies gain 8% on average.

Because target companies are usually a lot smaller than the bidders, you cannot calculate total returns to both parties from the data in *Exhibit I*. An analysis of more than 180 tender-offer acquisitions, however, indicates statistically significant gains to target and acquiring company shareholders equal to an average 8.4% of the total market value of the equity of both companies.[7]

In sum, contrary to the argument that merger activity wastes resources without benefiting stockholders, stockholders earn substantial gains in successful takeovers. In the Texaco takeover of Getty, for example, Getty Oil shareholders realized abnormal stock price gains of $4.7 billion, or 78.6% of the total equity value, and Texaco shareholders, abnormal returns of $1.3 billion or 14.5%. Gains for both totaled $6 billion, 40% of the sum of their equity values. Gulf stockholders earned abnormal returns of $6.2 billion (79.9%) from the Social takeover, and Social stockholders earned $2.8 billion (22.6%). The total gains of $9 billion in this merger represent a 44.6% increase in the total equity values of both companies.

In light of these shareholder benefits, the cries to eliminate or restrain unfriendly takeovers seem peculiar (and in some cases self-serving). In a January 5, 1983 *Wall Street Journal* article, Peter Drucker called for such controls: "The question is no longer whether unfriendly takeovers will be curbed but only when and how." He went on to say:

"The recent shoot-out between Bendix and Martin Marietta has deeply disturbed even the staunchest laissez-faire advocates in the business community. And fear of the raider and his unfriendly takeover bid is increasingly distorting business judgment and decisions. In company after company the first question is no longer: Is this decision best for the business? But, will it encourage or discourage the raider?"

Such arguments may comfort concerned managers and board members who want protection from the discipline of competition in the market for managers. But they are based on false premises. The best way to discourage the competing manager (that's what *raider* means) is to run a company to maximize its value. "Will this decision help us obtain maximum market value?" is the only logically sensible interpretation of "What is best for the business?"

Folklore: Takeover expenditures are wasted.

Fact: Purchase prices in corporate takeovers represent the transfer of wealth from the stockholders of bidding companies to those of target organizations, not the consumption of wealth. In a takeover, the resources represented in the cash received by the target shareholders can still be used to build new plant and equipment or for R & D.

The only resources consumed are those used to arrange the transaction, such as the time and fees of managers, lawyers, economists, and financial consultants. These expenses are often large in dollar terms; the financial fees of the U.S. Steel/Marathon Oil merger were more than $27 million, and those received by four investment banking firms in the Getty takeover hit a record by exceeding $47 million. But they are a tiny fraction of the dollar value of the acquisition; total financial and legal fees usually amount to only about .7%. More significantly, they help shareholders achieve their much larger gains of 4% to 30%.

In fact, the stock price change is the best measure of the takeover's future impact on the organization. The vast scientific evidence on the theory of efficient markets indicates that, in the absence of inside information, a security's market price represents the best available estimate of its true value.[8] The evidence shows that market prices incorporate all current public information about future cash flows and the value of individual assets in an unbiased way. Stock prices change, of course, in response to new information about individual assets. Because market prices are efficient, however, the new information is equally likely to cause them to decrease or increase, after allowing for normal returns. Positive stock price changes, then, indicate a *rise* in the total profitability of the merged companies. Furthermore, because evidence indicates it does not come from the acquisition of market power, this increased

profitability must come from the company's improved productivity.

Folklore: The huge bank credit lines used to carry out large takeovers siphon credit from the financial system, and crowd out "legitimate" borrowing for productive investments.

Fact: First, the increases in shareholder wealth I've discussed indicate that takeover activities are productive investments; credit lines are not wasted. Second, companies that make acquisitions with stock or other securities, or with cash on hand or capital acquired from the sale of assets, do not use bank credit.

More important, even when companies accomplish takeovers with bank loans, they do not waste credit because most, if not all, of it is still available for real investment such as new plant and equipment. Let me illustrate the point by using a simple example.

When an acquiring company borrows from a bank for an acquisition, it receives the funds in the form of a credit to its bank account. When target company stockholders deposit receipts from the takeover in their accounts, the bank's total deposits remain unchanged because the acquirer's deposits are reduced by the same amount.

Now, however, the portfolios of the target company shareholders are unbalanced. In response, they can make new investments either directly or by purchasing newly issued shares, and if they do so the credit goes directly into productive real investments. If they take the opposite course of action and reduce their bank debt, the bank will have the same amount of loans and deposits as before the acquisition; total outstanding credit is unchanged and there is no waste.

Alternatively, target company shareholders can purchase securities from other investors, but the sellers then are in the same position as the target company shareholders after the acquisition.

If the recipients of the funds from the takeover don't make new investments or pay down debt, they must increase either their cash holdings or their consumption. If their wealth hasn't changed, they have no reason to change either their cash balances or their consumption, and, therefore, the proceeds will go to make new investments and/or reduce debt. If investor wealth increases, investors will increase their consumption and their cash balances. The value of the consumption and cash balance increases will only be a small fraction of the wealth increase (the capital gains, not the proceeds) from the takeover; the remainder will go for new investments and/or debt reduction. The increase in cash balances and consumption will be the same as that coming from increases in wealth generated by any other cause. Thus, takeovers waste no more credit than any other productive investment.

Folklore: By merging competitors, takeovers create a monopoly that will raise product prices, produce less, and thereby harm consumers.

Fact: The evidence from four studies of the issue indicates that takeover gains come not from the merger's creation of monopoly market power but from its productive economies and synergy.

If the gains did come from the creation of companies with monopolistic powers, industry competitors would benefit, in turn, from the higher prices and would enjoy significant increases in profits and stock prices. Furthermore, the stock prices of rivals would fall if the FTC or the Antitrust Division of the Justice Department canceled or challenged the merger.

The evidence indicates, however, that competitors gain when two other companies in the same industry merge. But these gains are not related to the creation of monopolistic power or industry concentration. Moreover, the stock prices of competitors do not fall on announcement of antitrust prosecution or cancellation of the acquisition. This evidence supports the hypothesis that takeover gains stem from real economies in production and distribution realized through the takeover and that it signals the availability of similar gains for rival companies.[9]

In fact, the evidence raises serious doubts about the wisdom of FTC or Justice Department policies concerning mergers. The cancellation of an acquisition erases virtually all the stock price increases occurring on its announcement—with no apparent offsetting benefits to anyone.[10]

Folklore: Consolidating facilities after a takeover leads to plant closings, layoffs, and employee dismissals—all at great social cost.

Fact: No evidence with which I am familiar indicates that takeovers produce more plant closings, layoffs, and dismissals than would otherwise have occurred.

This charge raises a serious question, however, about the proper criteria for evaluation of the social desirability of takeovers. The standard efficiency yardstick measures increases in the aggregate real standard of living. By these criteria the wealth gains from takeovers (and their associated effects) are good as long as they do not come from the creation of monopolistic market power. Therefore, even if takeovers lead to plant closings, layoffs, and dismissals, their prohibition or limitation would generate real social costs and reduce aggregate human welfare because of the loss of potential operating economies.

Some observers may not agree that the standard efficiency criterion is the best measure of social desirability. But the adoption of any other criterion threatens to paralyze innovation. For example, innovations that increase standards of living in the long run initially produce changes that reduce the welfare of some individuals, at least in the short run. The development of efficient truck and air transport harmed the railroads and their workers; the rise of television hurt the radio industry. New and more efficient production, distribution, or organizational technology often imposes similar short-term costs.

The adoption of new technologies following takeovers enhances the overall real standard of living but reduces the wealth of those individuals with large investments in older technologies. Not surprisingly, such individuals and companies, their unions, communities, and political representatives will lobby to limit or prohibit takeovers that might result in new technologies. When successful, such politics reduce the nation's standard of living and its standing in international competition.

Folklore: Managers act in their own interests and are in reality unanswerable to shareholders.

Fact: Because executive compensation is related to company size, critics charge that a top officer's desire for wealth and an empire drives merger activity while the stockholders pay the bill. But as *Exhibit I* shows, there is no systematic evidence that bidding company managers are harming shareholders to build empires. Instead, the evidence is consistent with the synergy theory of takeovers. This theory argues that the stock price increases for target companies come from the increase in value obtained by consolidating or altering control of the assets of the companies involved, perhaps because of cost savings from economies of scale or from a highly complementary combination of employees and assets in production and distribution.

The evidence shows that target companies get a large share of the gains; indeed, the gains in mergers to go the target companies while virtually none accrue to bidding companies on the average. Bidding wars such as the DuPont-Seagram-Mobil competition for control of Conoco push up the gain for target companies.

The zero returns to bidders in mergers noted in *Exhibit 1* are puzzling. For several reasons, however, this particular estimate has more uncertainty built into it and is probably biased downward. My own assessment is that the returns to bidding companies in mergers are closer to the 4% shown for bidders in tender offers. An examination of the total dollar gains to both bidding and target company shareholders shows that both get about the same amount of dollars but not of percentage gains. The disparity results because bidding companies are generally larger than target companies and the same dollar gains translate into different percentage gains. Because the stock prices of larger companies vary more widely relative to gains in an acquisition than do the stock prices of target companies, their returns, cannot be estimated as precisely.

Furthermore, bidders often engage in a prolonged acquisition program. The benefits for target companies from a particular merger occur around the time of the takeover announcement and therefore can be more easily estimated than the bidders' benefits, which may be spread out over several acquisitions.

Often the stock price of a company that seeks several acquisitions reflects the projected benefits of future deals at an early date.[11] When a particular acquisition is announced, the bidder's stock

price will change only to the extent that there is a difference between the actual and the previously expected profitability of their merger and on average this will be zero in an efficient market. And because mergers involve negotiations that do not occur in tender offers, more information about the intentions of bidders will leak than will information about the identity of the target; the effect on the bidder's price will therefore be spread out over time.

The record of several large takeovers shows mixed evidence on the returns to acquiring shareholders. In the $13.2 billion takeover of Gulf, Social shareholders earned $2.77 billion (22.6%) after adjustment for the effects of marketwide price changes (from January 23, 1984 to May 3, 1984). Similarly, in the $10.1 billion takeover of Getty Oil, Texaco shareholders earned $1.3 billion (14.5%, from December 13, 1983 to February 7, 1984). In contrast, Allied shareholders lost $100 million (-8.6%) in the acquisition of Bendix; DuPont lost $800 million (-10%) in the takeover of Conoco, while Conoco shareholders realized a gain of 71%, or about $3.2 billion.[12]

On the other hand, Occidental Petroleum shareholders did not lose in Occidental's takeover of Cities Service, whose shareholders gained about $350 million (12.5%).[13] Mesa Petroleum initiated the Cities Service war with a bid of $45 per share. Cities Service countered with a bid for Mesa Petroleum. Gulf Oil then announced completion of negotiations to merge with Cities Service for $63 per share; Cities Service stock immediately gained over 43%, or $1.25 billion. In contrast, the Gulf stock price fell over 14%, or slightly over $900 million. The $350 million difference between the gain to Cities Service shareholders and the loss to Gulf shareholders measures the market's estimate of the net increase in value from the merger.

Citing antitrust difficulties with the FTC, Gulf canceled its acquisition of Cities Service seven weeks later. Cities Service countered with a breach of contract suit against Gulf for $3 billion. All the earlier gains in the price of Cities Service stock were eliminated, but only one-third of the Gulf loss was recovered—perhaps because the market forecast that legal action might hold Gulf liable for part of the premium offered to Cities Service shareholders or that Gulf would make more overpriced takeover attempts. Within four weeks of the Gulf cancellation, Cities Service merged with Occidental for a $350 million premium—an amount identical to the estimated value of the net merger gains from the aborted combination of Cities Service and Gulf.

A good way for a company to become a takeover target is to make a series of acquisitions that reduce value but allow the value to be recovered through divestiture. A bidder that realizes it can make money by selling off the pieces at a profit will likely seize the initiative. Victor Posner's attack on Marley Company in 1981 is an extreme example. Marley, which manufactured water-cooling towers and heat exchangers, took control of Wylain, a manufacturer of air conditioning, heating, and pumping systems, for an 87% premium over Wylain's previous market value. Marley's stock price fell 21%. Posner bought 11.2% of Marley during the first six months of 1980. Unable to find a white knight, Marley sold its assets, dissolved, and distributed the proceeds in June 1981. Posner received $21.9 million for his investment of $12.5 million in Marley.[14]

Exhibit II
Abnormal stock price increases from unsuccessful bids*

	Target companies	Bidding companies
Tender offers	-3%	-1%
Mergers	-3%	-5%
Proxy contests	8%	N.A.†

* Adjusted to eliminate the effects of marketwide price changes.
† Not applicable.

Manager-Shareholder Conflicts

The interests of managers and shareholders conflict on many, but certainly not all, issues. The divergence intensifies if the company becomes the target of an unfriendly takeover. *Exhibit I* indicates that target shareholders benefit when the bidders offer substantial premiums over current market value. During a takeover top managers of target companies can lose both their jobs and the value of their talents, knowledge, and income that are particular to the organization. Threatened with these losses, such officers may try to reduce the probability of a successful unfriendly takeover and benefit themselves at the expense of shareholders.

Management Struggles

The attempt by Carter Hawley Hale to acquire Marshall Field is an interesting example of a management struggle to retain control. Marshall Field, a high-quality department and specialty store chain, enjoyed less growth than other retailers but consistently rejected merger bids. In early 1978, Carter Hawley Hale, another retailer, offered $42 per share for Marshall Field stock, which was selling for less than $20. Resisting, Marshall Field filed a lawsuit that argued the acquisition would violate securities and antitrust laws. It informed shareholders that the asking price was inadequate and made several defensive acquisitions that aggravated potential antitrust problems and made it less attractive to Carter Hawley. Marshall Field's board authorized top officials to take "such action as they deemed necessary" to defeat the offer. After Carter Hawley withdrew the offer, Marshall Field's stock fell back to $20 per share.

In April 1984, another retailer, The Limited, tried to take over Carter Hawley Hale, whose stock then experienced abnormal gains of 49% in the ensuing conflict. Carter Hawley filed suit against The Limited, claiming securities law violations and antitrust problems, and gave up 33% of its voting rights through the sale of $300 million of convertible preferred stock to General Cinema Corporation. Carter Hawley then gave General Cinema a six-month option to buy the Waldenbook chain, one of its most profitable subsidiaries, and repurchased 51% of its own shares. As a result The Limited withdrew its offer in May and Carter Hawley stockholders lost $363 million—the entire 49% abnormal stock price gain.

Both of these cases show what happens to stock prices when acquisition bids fail. *Exhibit II* summarizes the general evidence obtained from ten studies on stock price behavior during unsuccessful takeover attempts. The average abnormal stock price changes surrounding unsuccessful takeover bids are uniformly small and negative, ranging from -1% to -5%. The exception is the 8% positive return to shareholders of companies subjected to unsuccessful proxy contests. It is interesting that a proxy contest causes an abnormal stock price gain even when the challengers fail, perhaps because the contest threat motivates incumbent managers to change their strategies.

The uncertainty of the estimates, however, means that only the -5% return for unsuccessful bidders is statistically significantly different from zero. The other negative returns can arise by chance if the true returns from such unsuccessful offers are actually zero. In conclusion, the Marshall Field experience that target company shareholders essentially lose all the offered premiums when an acquisition bid fails, fits the general evidence.

Exhibit II, however, simplifies the story. Sometimes stockholders benefit greatly from opposition to takeover bids.

Uncoordinated, independent decisions by individual shareholders regarding the acceptance or rejection of a tender offer can cause most of the takeover gains to go to bidding company stockholders.[15] If target managers act as the agents for all target shareholders in negotiating with the bidder for a higher price, however, this "free rider" problem can be alleviated.

Empirical evidence also indicates that some managerial opposition benefits target shareholders. For example, on the failure of a tender offer, target stock prices do not on average immediately lose the 30% average increase in price they earned when the offer was made. In fact, they generally stay up, apparently in anticipation of future bids. And target companies that receive at least one more bid in the two years following the failure of a tender offer on average realize another 20% increase in price. Those targets that do not receive another bid, however, lose the entire initial price increase.[16] Apparently, a little opposition in a merger battle is good, but too much can be disastrous if it prohibits takeover of the company.

The Corporate Charter

Corporate charters specify governance rules and establish conditions for mergers, such as the percentage of stockholders who must approve a takeover. Since constraints on permissible charter rules differ from state to state, changing the state of incorporation will affect the contractual arrangement among shareholders and the probability that a company will be a takeover target. It is alleged that some states desiring to increase their corporate charter revenues make their statutes appealing to corporate management. Allegedly, in doing so they provide management with great freedom from stockholder control and therefore provide little shareholder protection. Delaware, for example, has few constraints in its rules on corporate charters and hence provides much contractual freedom for shareholders. William L. Cary, former chairman of the Securities and Exchange Commission, has criticized Delaware and argued that the state is leading a "movement towards the least common denominator" and "winning a race for the bottom."[17]

But a study of 140 companies switching their state of incorporation reveals no evidence of stock price declines at the time of the change, even though most switched to Delaware.[18] In fact, small abnormal price increases are usually associated with the switch. This evidence is inconsistent with the notion that such charter changes lead to managerial exploitation of shareholders.

Without switching their state of incorporation, companies can amend corporate charters to toughen the conditions for the approval by shareholders of mergers. Such antitakeover amendments may require a "super majority" for approval or for the staggered election of board members and can thus lower the probability that the company will be taken over and thereby reduce shareholder wealth. On the other hand, the amendments can also benefit shareholders by increasing the plurality required for takeover approval and thus enable management to better represent their common interests in the merger negotiations.

Two studies of adoption of antitakeover amendments in samples of 100 and 388 companies reveal no negative impact on shareholder wealth.[19] One exception may arise if the super-majority provisions grant effective power to block mergers to a manager-stockholder. The market value of R. P. Scherer, for example, fell 33.8% when shareholders adopted an 80% super-majority merger approval provision. Because the wife of Scherer's CEO owned 21.1% of the stock, she then had the power to block a proposed takeover by FMC. In fact, FMC withdrew its offer after Scherer stockholders approved the 80% majority provision and the price of Scherer stock plummeted.

Repurchase Standstill Agreements

Currently available evidence suggests that management's opposition to takeovers reduces shareholder wealth only when it eliminates potential takeover bids. In a privately negotiated or targeted repurchase, for example, a company buys a block of its common stock from a holder at a premium over market price—often to induce the holder, usually an active or a potential bidder, to cease takeover activity. Such repurchases, pejoratively labeled "greenmail" in the press, generate statistically significant abnormal stock price declines for shareholders of the repurchasing company and significantly positive returns for the sellers.[20] These stock price declines contrast sharply with the statistically significant abnormal stock price increases associated with *nontargeted* stock repurchases found in six studies.[21]

The managers of target companies also may obtain standstill agreements, in which one company agrees to limit its holdings in another. Announcements of such agreements are associated with statistically significant abnormal stock price declines for target companies. Because these agreements almost always lead to the termination of an acquisition attempt, the negative returns seem to represent the merger gains lost by shareholders.

Again, however, the issue is not clear-cut because closer examination of the evidence indicates that these takeover forays by competing managers benefit target shareholders. Within ten days of an acquisition of 5% or more of a company's shares, the SEC requires the filing of information giving the identity of the purchaser, purpose of acquisition, and size of the holding. The significantly positive increase in stock price that occurs with the initial purchase announcement indicates that potential dissident activity is expected to benefit shareholders even given the chance that the venture will end in a targeted repurchase. Moreover, this is confirmed by the fact that on average during the period from the SEC filing through the targeted repurchase of the shares, target company shareholders earn statistically significant positive abnormal returns.[22]

Thus, when you look at the whole process, repurchase agreements are clearly not "raiding" or "looting" but are profitable as a takeover. The stock price decline at repurchase seems due to the repurchase premium that is effectively paid by the nonselling shareholders of the target firm and to the unraveling of takeover expectations with consequent loss of the anticipated takeover premium.

Because, on average, target shareholders lose the anticipated takeover premiums shown in *Exhibit I* when a merger or takeover fails for any reason, we cannot easily tell whether they were hurt by a repurchase. If the takeover would have failed anyway and if the target company's stock price would have fallen even more without the repurchase, then the repurchase benefited target company shareholders. Such additional price declines might be caused, for example, by the costs of dealing with a disgruntled minority shareholder.

Although the issue requires further study, current evidence implies that prohibition of targeted large-block repurchases advocated by some may hurt target shareholders. Moreover, since shareholders can amend corporate charters to restrict targeted repurchases, there is little justification for regulatory interference by the state in the private contractual arrangements among shareholders. Such repurchase restrictions might well restrict the vast majority of stock repurchases that clearly benefit shareholders. In addition, by reducing the profitability of failed takeovers, such restrictions would strengthen the position of entrenched managers by reducing the frequency of takeover bids. Doing so would deprive shareholders of some of the stock price premiums associated with successful mergers.

Going Private

The phrase *going private* means that publicly owned stock is replaced with full equity ownership by an incumbent management group and that the stock is delisted. On occasion, when going private is a leveraged buy out, management shares the equity with private investors. Some believe that incumbent managers as buyers are exploiting outside shareholders as sellers in these minority freeze outs.

Advocating restrictions on going-private transactions, in 1974 Securities and Exchange Commissioner A. A. Sommer, Jr., argued:

"What is happening is, in my estimation, serious, unfair, and sometimes disgraceful, a perversion of the whole process of public financing, and a course that inevitably is going to make the individual shareholder even more hostile to American corporate mores and the securities markets than he already is."[23]

Study of stockholder returns in 72 going-private transactions, however, reveals that the average transaction offers a premium 56% over market price and that abnormal stock price increases on announcement of the offer average 30%. The gains apparently arise from savings of registration and other public ownership expenses, improved incentives for decision makers under private ownership, and increased interest and depreciation tax shields. Outside shareholders are not harmed in going-private transactions.[24]

Golden Parachutes

Some companies provide compensation in employment contracts for top-level managers in the event that a takeover occurs—that is, golden parachutes. Allied agreed, for example, to make up the difference for five years between Bendix CEO William Agee's salary in subsequent employment and his former annual $825,000 salary in the event of a change in control at Bendix. Much confusion exists about the propriety and desirability of golden parachutes, even among senior executives.

But the detractors fail to understand that the parachutes protect stockholders as well as managers. Think about the problem in the following way: top-level managers and the board of directors act as stockholders' agents in deals involving hundreds of millions of dollars. If the alternative providing the highest value to stockholders is sale to another company and the retirement of the current management team, stockholders do not want the managers to block a bid in fear of losing their own jobs. Stockholders may be asking managers to sacrifice position and wealth to negotiate the best deal for them.

Golden parachutes are clearly desirable when they protect stockholders' interests. Like anything else, however, they may be abused. For example, a stockholder doesn't want to pay managers so much for selling the company that they hurry to sell at a low price to the first bidder. But that is a problem with the details of the parachute's contractual provisions and not with the existence of the parachute itself. An analysis of 90 companies shows that adoption of golden parachutes on average has no negative effect on stock prices and provides some evidence of positive effects.[25]

The thing that puzzles me about most golden parachute contracts is that they pay off only when the manager leaves his job and thus create an unnecessary conflict of interest between shareholders and executives. Current shareholders and the acquiring company will want to retain the services of a manger who has valuable knowledge and skills. But the officer can collect the golden parachute premium only by leaving; the contract rewards him or her for taking an action that may well hurt the business. As the bidder assimilates the knowledge that turnover among valuable top-level managers after the acquisition is highly likely, it will reduce its takeover bid. A company can eliminate this problem by making the award conditional on transfer of control and not on the manager's exit from the company.

Selling the "Crown Jewels"

Another often criticized defensive tactic is the sale of a major division by a company faced with a takeover threat. Some observers claim that such sales prove that managers will do anything to preserve their tenure, even to the extent of crippling or eliminating major parts of the business that appear attractive to outside bidders. Such actions have been labeled a "scorched earth policy."

Studies of the effects of corporate spin-offs, however, indicate they generate significantly positive abnormal returns.[26] Moreover, when target managers find a white knight to pay more for the entire company than the initial, hostile bidder, shareholders clearly benefit.

In the same way, when an acquirer is interested mainly in a division rather than the whole company, shareholders benefit when target management auctions off the unit at a higher price. Brunswick's sale of its Sherwood Medical Industries division to American Home Products shows how the sale of a crown jewel can benefit shareholders. Whittaker Corporation made a hostile takeover bid for Brunswick in early 1982. In defense, Brunswick sold a key division, Sherwood Medical, to American Home Products through a negotiated tender offer for 64% of Brunswick's shares. American Home Products then exchanged these shares with Brunswick for Sherwood's stock. Because its main interest lay in acquiring Sherwood, Whittaker withdrew its offer.[27]

The value of the Whittaker offer to Brunswick shareholders ranged from $605 million to $618 million, depending on the value assigned to the convertible debentures that were part of the offer. The total value to Brunswick shareholders of the management strategy, selling off the Sherwood division, was $620 million. Moreover, because of the structure of the transaction, the cash proceeds went directly to the Brunswick shareholders through the negotiated tender offer. The $620 million value represents a gain of $205 million (49%) on the total equity value of Brunswick prior to the initial Whittaker offer. The Brunswick shareholders were $2 million to $15 million better off with the management strategy, hardly evidence of a scorched-earth policy.

Takeover Artists

Recently, criticism has been directed at corporate takeover specialists who are said to take advantage of a company's vulnerability in the market and thus ultimately harm shareholders. While acting in their own interests, however, these specialists also act as agents for shareholders of companies with entrenched managers. Returning to the Marshall Field story, for example, Carl Icahn launched a systematic campaign to acquire the chain after it had avoided takeover. When it looked as if he would achieve the goal, Marshall Field initiated a corporate auction and merged with BATUS (British American Tobacco Company, U.S.) for $30 per share in 1982. After adjustment for inflation, that price was slightly less than the $20 price of Fields' stock in 1977, when it defeated Carter Hawley's $42 offer.

Takeover specialists like Icahn risk their own fortunes to dislodge current managers and reap part of the value increases available from redeploying the assets or improving the management. Evidence from a study of 100 such instances indicates that when such specialists announce the purchase of 5% or more of a company's shares, the stockholders of that company on average earn significantly positive abnormal returns of about 6%.[28]

The Effectiveness of the Market

The corporation has contributed much to the enhancement of society's living standards. Yet the details of how and why this complex institution functions and survives are poorly understood, due in part to the complexity of the issues involved and in part to the political controversy that historically surrounds it. Much of this controversy reflects the actions of individuals and groups that wish to use the corporation's assets for their own purposes, without purchasing them.

One source of the controversy comes from the separation between managers and shareholders— a separation necessary to realize the large efficiencies in risk bearing that are the corporation's comparative advantage. The process by which internal control mechanisms work so that professional managers act in the shareholders' interest is subtle and difficult to observe. When internal control mechanisms are working well, the board of directors will replace top-level managers whose talents are no longer the best ones available for the job.[29]

When these mechanisms break down, however, stockholders receive some protection from the takeover market, where alternative management teams compete for the rights to manage the corporation's assets. This competition can take the form of mergers, tender offers, or proxy fights. Other organizational forms such as nonprofits, partnerships, or mutual insurance companies and savings banks do not benefit from the same kind of external market.

The takeover market also provides a unique, powerful, and impersonal mechanism to accomplish the major restructuring and redeployment of assets continually required by changes in technology and consumer preferences. Recent changes occurring in the oil industry provide a good example.

Scientific evidence indicates that activities in the market for corporate control almost uniformly increase efficiency and shareholders' wealth. Yet there is an almost continuous flow of unfavorable publicity and calls for regulation and restriction of unfriendly takeovers. Many of these appeals arise from managers who want protection from competition for their jobs and others who desire more controls on corporations. The result, in the long run, may be a further weakening of the corporation as an organizational form and a reduction in human welfare.

Notes

[1]Author's note: I am indebted to Armen Alchian, Karl Brunner, Harry DeAngelo, Leo Herzel, Charles Plosser, Richard Rosett, Richard Ruback, Clifford Smith, Jr., Robert Sproull, Alan Underberg, and Ned Wass for comments and assistance.

[2]For further analysis, see Leo Herzel and John R. Schmidt, "SEC is Probing 'Double Pac-Man' Takeover Defense," *Legal Times*, April 18, 1983, 27.

[3]For further insight, see Claude W. McAnally, III, "The Bendix-Martin Marietta Takeover and Stockholder Returns," unpublished masters thesis, Massachusetts Institute of Technology, 1983.

[4]The only exception is the nonprofit organization, against which there are no residual claims. For a discussion of the critical role of donations in the survival of nonprofits, the nature of the corporation, and competition and survival among organizational forms, see Eugene F. Fama and Michael C. Jensen, "Separation of Ownership and Control," *Journal of Law and Economics*, June 1983, 301, and also "Agency Problems and Residual Claims," *Journal of Law and Economics*, June 1983, 327.

[5]For a summary, see Michael C. Jensen and Richard S. Ruback, "The Market for Corporate Control: The Scientific Evidence," *Journal of Financial Economics*, April 1983, 5. . . . [Editor's note: See original source for the list of studies cited.]

[6]Financial economists have used abnormal price changes or abnormal returns to study the effects of various events on security prices since Eugene F. Fama, Lawrence Fisher, Michael C. Jensen, and Richard Roll used them to measure the impact of stock splits in "The Adjustment of Stock Prices to New Information," *International Economic Review*, February 1969,

1. Stephen J. Brown and Jerold B. Warner provide a detailed discussion in "Measuring Security Price Performance," *Journal of Financial Economics*, September 1980, 205, and in "Using Daily Stock Returns in Event Studies," *Journal of Financial Economics*, forthcoming.

[7]Bradley, Desai, and Kim, "Determinants of the Wealth Effects of Corporate Acquisitions Via Tender Offer."

[8]For an introduction to the literature and empirical evidence on the theory of efficient markets, see Edwin J. Elton and Martin J. Gruber, *Modern Portfolio Theory and Investment Analysis* (New York: Wiley, 1984), chapter 15, 375, and the 167 studies referenced in the bibliography. For some anomalous evidence on market efficiency, see the symposia in the *Journal of Financial Economics*, June/September 1978, 95.

[9]B. Espen Eckbo, "Horizontal Mergers, Collusion, and Stockholder Wealth," *Journal of Financial Economics*, April 1983, 241; Robert Stillman, "Examining Antitrust Policy Towards Horizontal Mergers," *Journal of Financial Economics*, April 1983, 225; B. Espen Eckbo and Peggy Wier, "Antimerger Policy and Stockholder Returns: A Reexamination of the Market Power Hypothesis," University of Rochester Managerial Economics Research Center Working Paper No. MERC 84–109 (Rochester, N.Y.: March 1984); and B. Espen Eckbo, University of Rochester Managerial Economics Research Center Working Paper No. MERC 84–108, "Horizontal Mergers, Industry Structure, and the Market Concentration Doctrine," (Rochester, N.Y.: March 1984).

[10]Wier, "The Costs of Antimerger Lawsuits: Evidence from the Stock Market."

[11]Schipper and Thompson, "Evidence on the Capitalized Value of Merger Activity for Acquiring Firms."

[12]For a further look, see Richard S. Ruback, "The Conoco Takeover and Stockholder Returns," *Sloan Management Review*, Winter 1982, 13.

[13]This discussion is based on Richard S. Ruback, "The Cities Service Takeover: A Case Study," *Journal of Finance*, May 1983, 319.

[14]For a detailed analysis, see David W. Mullins, Jr., *Managerial Discretion and Corporate Financial Management*, Chapter 7, unpublished manuscript, Harvard Business School, 1984.

[15]See S. Grossman and O. Hart, "Takeover Bids, the Free-Rider Problem and the Theory of the Corporation," *Bell Journal of Economics*, Spring 1980, 42; and Michael Bradley, "Interfirm Tender Offers and the Market for Corporate Control," *Journal of Business*, October 1980, 345.

[16]See Bradley, Desi, and Kim, "The Rationale Behind Interfirm Tender Offers."

[17]William L. Cary, "Federalism and Corporate Law: Reflections upon Delaware," *Yale Law Journal*, March 1974, 663.

[18]Peter Dodd and Richard Leftwich, "The Market for Corporate Charters: 'Unhealthy Competition' Versus Federal Regulation," *Journal of Business*, July 1980, 259.

[19]Harry DeAngelo and Edward M. Rice, "Antitakeover Charter Amendments and Stockholder Wealth," *Journal of Financial Economics* April 1983, 329; and Scott C. Linn and John J. McConnell, "An Empirical Investigation of the Impact of 'Antitakover' Amendments on Common Stock Prices," *Journal of Financial Economics*, April 1983, 361.

[20]Larry Y. Dann and Harry DeAngelo, "Standstill Agreements, Privately Negotiated Stock Repurchases, and the Market for Corporate Control," *Journal of Financial Economics*, April 1983, 275; and Michael Bradley and L. MacDonald Wakeman, "The Wealth Effects of Targeted Share Repurchases," *Journal of Financial Economics*, April 1983, 301.

[21]Bradley and Wakeman, "The Wealth Effects of Targeted Share Repurchases"; Larry Dann, "The Effect of Common Stock Repurchase on Stockholder Returns," unpublished dissertation, University of California, Los Angeles, 1980; Larry Dann, "Common Stock Repurchases: An Analysis of Returns to Bondholders and Stockholders," *Journal of Financial Economics*, June 1981, 113; Ronald Masulis, "Stock Repurchase by Tender Offer: An Analysis of the Causes of Common Stock Price Changes," *Journal of Finance*, May 1980, 305; Ahron Rosenfeld, University of Rochester, Managerial Economics Research Center Monograph and Theses No. MERC MT-82-01, 1982, "Repurchase Offers: Information Adjusted Premiums and Shareholders' Response"; Theo Vermaelen, "Common Stock Repurchases and Market Signaling," *Journal of Financial Economics*, June 1981, 139.

[22]Richard S. Ruback and Wayne H. Mikkelson, "Corporate Investments in Common Stock," Sloan School of Management Working Paper #1559-84 (Cambridge: M.I.T., 1984); and Clifford G. Holderness and Dennis Sheehan, University of Rochester Managerial Economics Research Center Working Paper No. MERC 84-06, "Evidence on Six Controversial Investors" (Rochester: N.Y.: August 1984).

[23]A. A. Sommer, Jr., " 'Going Private': A Lesson in Corporate Responsibility," Law Advisory Council Lecture, Notre Dame Law School, reprinted in *Federal Securities Law Reports*, Commerce Clearing House, Inc., 1974, 84.

[24]Harry De Angelo, Linda DeAngelo, and Edward M. Rice, "Going Private: Minority Freezeouts and Stockholder Wealth," *Journal of Law and Economics*, October 1984; and Harry DeAngelo, Linda DeAngelo, and Edward M. Rice, "Going Private: The Effects of a Change in Corporate Ownership Structure," *Midland Corporate Finance Journal*, Summer 1984.

[25]Richard A. Lambert and David E. Larcker, "Golden Parachutes, Executive Decision-Making and Shareholder Wealth," *Journal of Accounting and Economics*, forthcoming.

[26]See Katherine Schipper and Abbie Smith, "Effects of Recontracting on Shareholder Wealth: The Case of Voluntary Spin-offs," *Journal of Financial Economics*, December 1983, 437; Gailen Hite and James Owers, "Security Price Reactions Around Corporate Spin-off Announcements," *Journal of Financial Economics*, December 1983, 409; J. Miles and J. Rosenfield, "The Effect of Voluntary Spin-off Announcements on Shareholder Wealth," *Journal of Finance*, December 1983, 1597; Gailen Hite and James E. Owers, "The Restructuring of Corporate America: An Overview," *Midland Corporate Finance Journal*, Summer 1984; Scott C. Linn and Michael Rozeff, "The Effects of Voluntary Spin-offs on Stock Prices: The Energy Hypothesis," *Advances in Financial Planning and Forecasting*, Fall 1984; Scott C. Linn and Michael Rozeff, "The Corporate Sell-off," *Midland Corporate Finance Journal*, Summer 1984; Scott C. Linn and Michael Rozeff, "The Effects of Voluntary Sell-offs on Stock Prices," unpublished manuscript, University of Iowa, 1984; and Abbie Smith and Katherine Schipper, "Corporate Spin-offs," *Midland Corporate Finance Journal*, Summer 1984.

[27]For a further analysis, see Leo Herzel and John R. Schmidt, "Shareholders Can Benefit from Sale of 'Crown Jewels,' " *Legal Times*, October 24, 1983, 33.

[28]For analysis of the effects of purchases by six so-called raiders, Bluhdorn, Icahn, Jacobs, Lindner, Murdock, and Posner, see Holderness and Sheehan, "The Evidence on Six Controversial Investors."

[29]For evidence on the relation between poor performance and executive turnover, see Anne Coughlan and Ronald Schmidt, "Executive Compensation, Management Turnover and Firm Performance: An Empirical Investigation," *Journal of Accounting and Economics*, forthcoming.

The Hostile Takeover: An Opposition View

Lisa Newton

From *Ethical Theory and Business*, 3d ed., ed. Tom L. Beauchamp and Norman E. Bowie (Englewood Cliffs, N. J.: Prentice-Hall, 1987), 501–10. Copyright © 1987 by Lisa Newton.

I. Rights and Consequences

Given the nature and prestige of the players, we might be tempted to think that the *hostile takeover* is just one more game businessmen play. But the business literature on the subject sounds atypically harsh notes, describing this activity in the unbusinesslike language of threat and attacks, followed by occasionally desperate and increasingly sophisticated defenses—the junk-bond bust-up takeover versus the Pac-Man, Poison Pill, Crown Jewel Option defenses ranged against the two-tier tender offer and finally the launching of the golden parachutes.

In this colorful literature, the most noticeable feature of a corporate takeover is its terrible human cost. *Fortune* magazine entitled a 1984 article, "Help! My Company Has Just Been Taken Over," and began the article with the story of the suicide of a corporate executive precipitated by his termination following a takeover. "There are more mergers than ever these days," the author warns, "and their human toll is higher than ever too."[1] A more recent *New York Times* article, entitled "'People Trauma' in Mergers" documents the anxiety and feelings of betrayal experienced by employees—increasingly, down to the hourly level—when the prospect of takeover looms into view. Trust is broken, loyalty ebbs, and, if none of the above is of any interest to managers, productivity plummets.[2] The fact that these alarms come from publications inside the business world is significant; outsiders might be expected to see human effects more clearly than the economic realities that underlie the takeover activity, yet here are the insiders suddenly concluding that the realities of profit may actually be less important than the injuries to the people caught up in it

against their will. The hostile corporate takeover is simply *not* business as usual. It is assault with a deadly weapon; and the question seems to be, how can it be right?

Let us backtrack for the moment. A practice requires moral scrutiny if it regularly derogates from human dignity, causes human pain, or with no apparent reason treats one class of human beings less well than another. Any practice that regularly throws people out of work does at least the first two of those (work being possibly the largest factor in self-worth and the major instrument to creature satisfactions), and unless we find the raider's urgent need for self-aggrandizement as a worthy reason for dismembering working units, it probably does the third also. To be sure, all manner of evil things can happen to people in non-takeover situations; part of the fun of being alive is the risk, and part of being in business is knowing that your livelihood may depend on the next quarter's earnings. But as a general moral principle, if I, by my voluntary act and for my own profit, increase the riskiness of your life, no matter how high the base risk and no matter how small the increment by which I raise it for you, then I owe you an explanation. The hostile takeover regularly disemploys at least some people who would not have been unemployed absent the takeover; that makes it, by the above, a proper candidate for moral scrutiny, without presumption one way or another on the results of the scrutiny.

A further problem, if it is a problem, is that a takeover deliberately destroys something—a company, corporation, an instance of human association. In the other cases, it can be said that the association itself "decided" to do something to make itself better, or more efficient. But when it is taken over, it does nothing—it is killed, and the atmosphere of the threat of death hangs over the entire proceeding, from the raider's first phone call to the final resolution (usually the acquisition of the company by some party other than the raider). Does it make any difference, that a company is destroyed? Is that an evil over and above all the other disruptions that takeovers occasion? Or is it, strictly speaking, meaningless, beyond the sufferings of the individuals?

We have, in short, two very separate and distinct questions. First, does the hostile corporate takeover serve some ordinary and necessary role in the economy? Whatever the present injuries, is the practice justified in the long run as improving the economic condition of the greatest number? That very pragmatic question is accompanied by a second, metaphysical one: Is the corporation the type of thing whose demise could or should be regretted? Could it have some right to live, to persevere in existence—a right appropriately exercised in management's series of "defenses"? Ordinarily we assume that only individual human beings have dignity, worth, or rights (beyond the uninteresting legal "rights" bestowed on the corporation to permit it to conduct business). But that assumption fits poorly with the fact that people will willingly die for their associations when they will not willingly sacrifice their lives for personal interests; that fact needs further examination before we dismiss the association as a merely instrumental good. We will pursue, then, two separate and logically independent lines of inquiry: First, on straightforward utilitarian reasoning, does the business practice that we know as the *hostile takeover* serve the public interest by performing some useful role in the economy, or are there good utilitarian reasons for limiting or prohibiting it? Second, does the corporation have some right to exist that is violated by any business practice that ends its existence without the consent of its present governors? Along the line of the first inquiry, we will argue, first, that the hostile takeover is damaging to the economy (and the people in it) in the short and middle run and, second, that this practice is a deadly symptom of a

long-term process in our relation to material goods, a loss of "ownership," which ought to be noted and, as far as possible, reversed. On the line of the second inquiry, we will argue that "the association," usually the political association, has been invested with dignity since Aristotle's day, and that its right to self-defense is firmly grounded in individual rights of undisputed worth. Therefore the corporation, acting through its present management, has the right and (sometimes) the duty to defend itself when its existence is threatened, apart from any arguments about immediate effects on the wealth of individuals.

II. Responsible Ownership Profits

Takeovers are generally defended on the utilitarian grounds that they are in the public interest. The "takeover" is simply capital flowing from one sector of the economy to a more profitable one, in this instance, to buy up the stock of a company the value of whose assets is significantly greater than the value of its outstanding stock. Where stock is undervalued, an inefficiency exists in the economy; whether through management ineptness or other market conditions, the return on the shareholder's investment is not as high as it could be. It would be maximized by selling off the assets and distributing the proceeds among the owners; but then, by the above, it is management's duty to do that. The takeover merely does the job that the managers were supposed to do, and the prospect of a takeover, should the stock become undervalued, is an excellent incentive to management to keep the shareholders' interest in mind.

Moreover, defenses against takeovers often involve managers in apparent conflicts of interest. They are protecting their jobs rather than meeting their fiduciary obligations to stockholders. Theory in this instance concurs with current case law; there should be no regulation of takeovers beyond (not very rigorous) anti-trust scrutiny, and defensive moves on the part of management are morally and probably legally illegitimate. To be sure, people get hurt in takeovers, but the shareholders profit, and control of the corporation belongs by statute to them. Against these considerations, what arguments can be raised that unregulated takeover activity is harmful, wrong, contrary to the public interest, and ought to be stopped by new legislation?

The best approach to a response may be to peel an onion: All of the evils seem to be related, differing primarily in the level of analysis suited to elicit them. Beginning with the surface, then, we may note the simple disruption caused by hostile takeover activity: The raider's announcement that a certain percentage of shares of a company have been purchased, more to follow, immediately puts the company in play in a deadly game from which it will not emerge intact. Productive activity, at least at the upper levels of the target (where salaries are highest), stops. Blitzkrieg raider tactics are met with poison pills, sales of crown jewels and other defenses—often of questionable legality. Orderly planning disappears. Employees, terrified for their jobs, spend their days in speculation and the search for another job.[3] Other bidders emerge from the Midwest, from abroad, from next door. Nobody sleeps. All the players hire lawyers, financiers, banks, and start paying them incredible amounts of money. (In the takeover of Revlon by Pantry Pride in the fall of 1985, the investment bankers' share alone came to over $100 million, legal fees to over $10 million, and the negotiated "golden parachutes" to $40 million. Added up, the costs of the takeover—not one penny of which went to shareholders—came to close to 9 percent of the $1.83 billion deal.)[4] However the game ends, people are exhausted, betrayed, out of work, and demoralized. The huge debt incurred by the acquiring company, secured by the assets of the target (by the infamous *junk bonds*), require the immediate dismemberment of the company for financial survival (more on this later), and financial health, under those circumstances, is out of the question. And all this to what end?

"Hostile takeovers create no new wealth," Andrew Sigler pointed out to the House Committee on Energy and Commerce, "They merely shift ownership, and replace equity with large amounts of debt." He continues:

More and more companies are being pushed—either in self-defense against the raiders or by the raiders once they achieve control—into unhealthy recapitalizations that run contrary to the concepts of sound management I have learned over thirty years. This type of leveraging exposes companies to inordinate risks in the event of recession, unanticipated reverses, or significant increases in interest rates. . . . Generation after generation of American managers have believed that there *must* be a solid equity basis for an enterprise to be successful in the long term. This long-term equity base absorbs—in exchange for the expectation of higher returns—the perils of depression, product failure, strikes, and all the other dangers that characterize business in a free economy. That healthy conservatism is now being replaced by a new game in which the object is to see how far that equity base can be squeezed down by layers of debt. And too much of this debt is carrying interest rates far in excess of those a prudent manager can possibly be comfortable with.[5]

At a second level, then, the takeover has two deleterious effects on the management of corporations: First, when the takeover materializes, equity is inevitably transformed into debt, leaving the company terribly vulnerable to foreseeable reverses; second, anticipating takeover attempts, management may well be tempted to aim for short-term profits and engage in aggressive accounting practices to show higher current earnings. These practices may weaken the company and deceive long-term investors, but they will be reflected in a higher stock price and thus one more resistant to attack.[6] As Peter Drucker put it, "Fear of the raider and his unfriendly takeover bid is increasingly distorting business judgment and decisions. In company after company the first question is no longer: Is this decision best for the business? But, will it encourage or discourage the raider?"[7] Fear of the raider may encourage the managers of a company to put up their own money as well as to incur debts well beyond prudence, to take the company privately in a "leveraged buyout." All the same risks, including bankruptcy in the event of any reversal, attend the buyout as attend the takeover.[8] Nor is it clear that the damaging effects of these maneuvers are limited to the domestic scene: As Harold Williams (chairman of the Securities and Exchange Commission during the Carter administration) points out,

> The pursuit of constantly higher earnings can compel managers to avoid needed write-downs, capital programs, research projects, and other bets on the long term. The competitiveness of U.S. corporations has already been impaired by the failure to make long-term commitments. To compound the problem because of fears of takeovers is a gift to foreign competitors that we cannot afford.[9]

The alarms, confusions, and pains first noted as the result of hostile takeover activity, are then compounded by what seems to be very imprudent business practice. But imprudent for whom? Do the target shareholders, at least, get some profit from the takeover—and if they do, does that not justify it? Michael Jensen, one of a new breed of scholar known as the "shark defenders," argues that they do and that it does. He dismisses worries about shareholders' welfare as "folklore," and insists that "science" shows otherwise.[10] His evidence for this claim is interesting:

> More than a dozen studies have painstakingly gathered evidence on the stock price effect of successful takeovers. . . . According to these studies, companies involved in takeovers experience abnormal increases in their stock prices for approximately one month surrounding the initial announcement of the takeover. . . . The evidence shows that target company shareholders gain 30% from tender offers and 20% from mergers.[11]

But isn't the raider's effect pure artifice? Let his initiative be withdrawn—because of government opposition, or because he has agreed to purchase one more stock for whatever reason—and the same studies show that the stock immediately reverts to its previous value.[12] So it was not, really, that the company's stock was too low. It was

rather that the flurry of activity, leading to speculation that the stock might be purchased at an enormous premium, fueled the price rise all by itself. Or could it be that certain professional investors find out about the raid before the public does, buy the target's stock at the lowest point, sending it up before the announcement, wait for the announcement, ride the stock to the top, then sell off before the defense moves, government action, or "targeted repurchase" (see the section on "greenmail," below) stop the takeover bid and send the stock back down to its true market value? As Jensen's figures confirm,[13] that value is often a bit *lower* than the starting value of the stock; after all those payouts we are dealing with a much poorer company. Nothing but evil, for all concerned except professional fund managers and investment bankers, seems to come of this takeover activity.

Current law does not recognize, or even have any language to describe, the rights possessed by those who have contributed to the growth of an association, have participated in it and loved it, and now see it threatened.

Hence, at the first level there is disruption and tens of millions of dollars' worth of unproductive expense; at the second level there is very dubious business practice. At a third, there is the betrayal of the stakeholders. Current laws, as discussed earlier, force the directors of the target company to consider only shareholder rights and interests, to the probable disadvantage of the other stakeholders: employees, retirees, creditors, host communities, customers, and suppliers. But each of these has helped to build the company to its present state, relying on the company's character and credit-worthiness; the employees and retirees, especially, have worked in expectation of future benefits that may depend in part on the good faith of management, good faith that can hardly be presumed in a raider.[14] The mid-career, upper middle-level managers are especially vulnerable to redundancy and the least likely to be able to transfer their acquired skills and knowledge elsewhere.

Some elimination of positions resulting from duplication is inevitable in any merger, of course, hostile or otherwise, and when carried out under normal conditions succeeds at least in making the company more efficient, even if the cost to the individual is very high. But only some of the people-cutting in these extravagant takeovers stems from real redundancy. Companies are paying such high takeover prices that they have to engage in deep cost-cutting immediately, even to the elimination of personnel crucial to continued operations. The "efficiency" achieved may not serve the company well in the long run, but the raider's calculations rarely run very long. As a consequence, middle-management employees (who are, on the whole, not stupid, and read the same business publications as we do) seem to have taken all this into account and reoriented their work lives accordingly:

> Management turnover at all levels is on the rise and employee loyalty is at a low, according to consultants, executive recruiters and the companies themselves. And there is growing evidence, they say, that merger mania is an important reason for both problems, spreading fear about layoffs and dissatisfaction with other changes in the corporate environment. These problems, in turn, promise to make it harder for companies to realize the anticipated efficiencies that many of them pointed to in justifying their acquisitions. . . . Critics of the takeover binge maintain that the short shrift given to "people issues" . . . [is] one reason why perhaps half to two-thirds of mergers and acquisitions ultimately fail.[15]

Do we owe anything to people who have worked for a company and who may actually love the company and may be devastated by its dismemberment or transformation? At present, our law does not recognize, or even have any language to describe, the rights possessed by those who have contributed to the growth of an association, have participated in it and loved it, and now see it

threatened. The fact that such rights are by no means absolute does not mean they are not there. Classical political theory has the vocabulary to discuss them, under the rubric of the "just war"; discussion of the implications of that doctrine for the hostile takeover issue will occupy the final section of this paper. Rights or no rights, and prudential considerations (as discussed earlier) aside, the condition of the stakeholders ought not, in charity, to be ignored; yet our institutions make no provision for them. Here we have, in the center of the most civilized sector of the civilized world, an open wound, a gap of institutional protection most needed by those who have worked hardest, which we struggle to paper over with the "unemployment benefits" fashioned for different people in different circumstances. Law and business practice seem to require a callousness toward human need and human desert that is incompatible with our notions of justice.

Inevitable disruption, mandated imprudence, and legally required injustice are the first three levels of palpable wrong in the hostile takeover phenomenon. It may be that the fourth layer, the last under consideration in this section, has more worrisome implications that all of the above. The thesis is simple: At primary risk in all of this is our concept of ownership. For all of human history, we have been able to trust property owners (individuals or groups) to take care of their property, because it was in their interest to do so, and outside of military and government property, that was how the property of the world was cared for. With the corporate takeover, that may no longer be the case for the kind of property that looms so large in Western economies, the publicly held corporation. And this development is very alarming.

To begin with the concepts: Ordinarily we use the concepts of *ownership* and *property* interchangeably; even etymologically, they are indistinguishable. But the concept does have two distinct aspects: the primary aspect of a legally protected complex of rights and duties obtaining between the owner and other *persons* and the less prominent aspect of a diffuse set of nonlegal duties, or imperatives, incumbent upon the owner to take care of the *owned thing*, itself. This duty of care has a history of its own; the duty to the thing, analogous to the duty of *stewardship* when the property of others is in question, attaches naturally to the legal owner.

Ownership has the longest history of any concept still extant in the West, certainly longer than its ultimate derivative, *personhood*. Aristotle assumed that the union of man and property, along with the union of man and woman, lay at the foundation of the household and hence of all society. Ownership is presupposed, and discussed, throughout the earliest books of the Bible. The list of *what* was owned was very short: animals, people (slaves), land, tools, buildings, and personal effects. Except for the last item, all were essential to survival, and all required care. The duty arises from that fact.

Whether ownership is single or shared, the duty corresponds to personal interest. If I own a sheep, it is very much in my interest, and incumbent upon me, to take care of the beast and see that it thrives. If you and I together own a sheep, the same interest applies to both of us, the same imperative follows, and we shall divide up the responsibilities of caring for it. If you and I and 998 others own it, enormous practical difficulties attend that care. But however small my interest in that sheep, it is still in my interest that the animal should thrive. Similarly, partial ownership in a whole herd of sheep, or a farm, or a factory, or a business that owns several factories, does not necessitate a change in the notion of *ownership*.

Liquidation consumes something that is owned, or turns it into money that can be spent on consumption. The easiest way to liquidate a sheep is to eat it. The way to liquidate most owned things is to sell them. Then you no longer own the thing, and your responsibilities terminate; but so, of course, does all future good you might have gotten of the thing. Part of the cultural evolution of ownership has been the elaboration of a tension between retention and liquidation, saving and spending, with the moral weight of the most successful cultures on the side of thrift and preservation. The business system probably depends as much on Ben Franklin's "A penny saved is a penny earned" as it does on Adam Smith's "invisible hand." The foreseen result of the *hand*, we may remember, was to increase the wealth, the assets, of a nation. For the herdsman it is self-evident that if you slaughter or sell all your sheep, you will starve in the next year; for Smith, it was equally self-evident that it is in a businessman's interest, whatever business he may be in, to save his money and invest it in clearing more land, breeding more beasts, or building more plants, to make more money in the future. Hence the cleared land, the herds, and the factories—the assets of the nation—increase without limit, and all persons, no matter how they participate in the economy, in fact share in this increased wealth. Presupposed is the willingness of all players in the free enterprise game to acquire things that need care if they are to yield profit, hence to render that care, and to accept that responsibility, over the long run. Should that willingness disappear, and the population suddenly show a preference for liquidation, all bets are off for the wealth of the nation.

And the problem is, of course, that the developments of ownership made possible in the last century create excess tendencies toward liquidation. If several thousand of us jointly own several thousand shares of stock, we may in theory bear the traditional responsibilities of owners for those companies, but we shall surely not *feel* them. And if we purchased those shares not for the sake of investing in the companies, but for the sake of having money available to us at some future time (say, in a pension fund), we will have acquired them for a purpose that is directly contrary to our concerns as owners. We will be involved in a conflict of interest and obligation with ourselves: on the one hand, we should be protecting and nurturing the company(s) we (partially) own, plowing profit back into improvements in plant on occasion, even if that means no profit this year; on the other, if it seems we could get more money if the company were liquidated and the proceeds shared around, we should work toward that end. Suppose that we several thousand owners hire a fund manager to make sure our pension fund provides us with as much pension as possible. That manager, hired with those instructions, is not an owner, and has *no* responsibility toward the companies. On the contrary, his entire obligation is to us and the increase of our money. Where liquidation serves that purpose, it is his job to bring it about. Ownership, for such a manager, is no more than present legal title to property, a way station between sums of money, and its whole moral framework has become totally irrelevant. To complete the picture, let only the tax structure subsidize that liquidation in cases of takeover:

> Accounting procedure and tax laws ... shift much of the cost of acquisitions to taxpayers through the deductibility of interest payments and the revaluation of assets in ways that reduce taxes. I suspect that many of the acquisitions that proved profitable for acquirers did so largely because of tax benefits and the proceeds from busting up the target company. If liquidation is subsidized by the tax system, are we getting more liquidations than good business would dictate?[16]

The answer is probably yes.

It must be unprecedented in human history that majority ownership of such entities lies with "owners" whose interests may be best served by the destruction of the object owned.

Institutional investors—those gargantuan funds—now own up to 70 percent of the stock of the publicly owned corporations. It must be unprecedented in human history that majority ownership of such entities lies with "owners" whose interests may be best served by the destruction of the object owned. In the case of companies that own large holdings of natural resources, forests, or oil reserves, it is usually the case that the assets sold separately will yield more than the companies' stock. (As Minow and Sawyer grimly put it, under current practices such companies "are worth more dead than alive.")[17] Any company, in fact, that regularly works for the long term (funding research and development, for

example), can be profitably liquidated: Whatever those raiders may be, they do not need to be geniuses to figure out which companies to attack. The only limits on the process of liquidation of the country's assets by the managers hired by those investors, or by the raiders that cater to their own interests, might be the success of new and inventive defenses.

The evils of the takeover market, then, go to the philosophical base of our market system, striking at the root of moral habits evolved over 2500 years. The corporate raiders have yet to make their first widget, grow their first carrot, or deliver their first lunch. *All* they do is turn money into money, cantilevering the profit off the shell of responsible ownership. No doubt capital is more productively lodged in some places than others, but it follows from no known economic theory that it is more beneficial to the world when lodged in T. Boone Picken's bank account than when lodged wherever it was before he got it. Possibly it will end up facilitating some industrial projects—he has no intention of keeping it in a mattress, after all—but only in those that promise quick profits. We need not look to him to revitalize our smokestack industries and make them competitive on the world markets. The whole productive capacity of the American economy seems at the mercy of moneymen on the rampage, with all productive companies under threat of being taken over, taken apart, and eradicated. Surely this condition cannot be healthy or good.

In sum: This section has tried to provide a series of pragmatic arguments that the present rash of corporate takeover activity is harmful to the stakeholders, to the economy, and the general public, from all of which it would follow that regulation is justified. In the next section we attempt to provide a defense for the proposition that a corporation has a real right to exist, hence to resist takeover.

III. The Association as Worth Keeping

Individuals may be hurt by the corporate takeover. The corporation, on the other hand, is usually killed. Does this fact add anything to the list of injuries, or is it simply a shorthand way of saying that the individuals are no longer part of it? Does the corporation have a right to life—a right to persevere in existence, as itself, under its own laws and practices, at least to the extent that would give it a presumptive right to mount a defense against hostile takeover?

The disutility of unregulated takeover activity, implying the desirability of some regulation in the public interest, was the theme of the last section. In this section we ask a different question: Can the corporation be seen as an entity analogous to an individual human being, with rights, including the right to defend itself (through the actions of its officers) regardless of the utilities involved in each case? The law is unsympathetic to defensive moves in takeover situations, suggesting that the right in question here is not derivable from any acknowledged legal rights or present powers of the corporation. It must be found, if it is to be found anywhere, as a logical derivation from other recognized rights of the corporation or, more likely, of the individuals who make it up.

We may begin the inquiry by noting that over the last decade, philosophical students of the corporation have been moving cautiously in the direction of grounding their moral discourse, in the assumption that the corporation is a moral individual like other moral individuals.

It is possible, however, that a corporation may be capable of assuming moral responsibility and still not have rights, but it is not likely. Our attribution of rights rests heavily on the attribution of moral agency, which alone confers worth or dignity on the human, and moral agency is the condition for attribution of moral responsibility. In the literature, the development continues, and recent work (e.g., Patricia Werhane's *Persons, Rights, and Corporations*) accepts that corporations have, indeed, moral rights, even if only "secondarily."[18]

There is, however, one body of literature precisely on the point of our question, albeit not one that deals with "the corporation" as this paper understands the corporation. Since Saint Augustine, the right of a nation to defend itself against foreign aggression has been recognized. While the political association, as Aristotle and Augustine

understood it, may seem an odd model for Phillips Petroleum and Continental Group, it is possible that the literature articulating any collectivity's right of defense may help us formulate one for the modern corporation.

The queerness of attributing a "right" to a collectivity rather than to an individual was not generally noticed in discussions of the Just War, most likely because its recognition predates the theory of individual rights by several centuries; nations had rights long before we did. But if we are to make sense of this right in a modern political context, it must be restated in terms compatible with individual rights theory. Michael Walzer undertakes this task in *Just and Unjust Wars*. For Walzer, the right of the political association to exist comes from the general right of *social contract*—the right of people to join together in any voluntary association, preeminently the state, the association charged with the whole governance of a people. (This is the right primarily challenged in *aggression*, which threatens to abrogate it permanently.) Like Burke before him, Walzer does not understand the agreement that binds the state as a set of real "contracts."

> What actually happens is harder to describe. Over a long period of time, shared experiences and cooperative activity of many different kinds shape a common life. . . . The moral standing of any particular state depends on the reality of the common life it protects and the extent to which the sacrifices required by that protection are willingly accepted and thought worthwhile.[19]

Again,

> The right of a nation or people not to be invaded derives from the common life its members have made . . . and not from the legal title they hold or don't hold.[20]

So the fact of the common life, which has been made by the participants in it, is the immediate source of the right to defend it, presumably necessarily mediated by the desire of participants to defend it. Walzer is likely correct that the right of the state to defend itself stems from the right of a people to create a common life, to adorn and embellish it, to examine and reform it, and by spending themselves on it, to make it valuable—a variety of the rather prosaic right of association. And the reason why people exercise that right in the formation of permanent associations, which build up a history for themselves, is that associations extend individual life in dimensions that the individual otherwise cannot control—in time, in space, in power. To the limited and partial individual, participation in an association provides immortality, global reach, and collective power. The individual needs the association for these benefits, and in this way the right of association is grounded in human nature. When my association is attacked, my basic security in these insecurity-ridden areas is very much endangered, and that is why I so justifiably resent any attacks on it.

Has this argument any validity for the corporation? Here the relatively recent moves to articulate the internal order of a corporation precisely as a historical culture, with a set of values and commitments all its own, may have some relevance. It would be tempting to argue that a corporation that has, as have the best companies of the recent literature, earnestly pursued excellence in all respects, taken care of its employees, stayed close to its customers, produced the highest quality product, and really cared about its customers, produced the highest quality product, and really cared about its communities, has somehow earned the right to exist, while the others have not.[21] Temptation must be resisted: the difficulties of discerning the "excellent" companies from the others are insurmountable. But maybe we don't have to make a judgment: If a corporation, even in theory, can be the kind of collectivity that the state is, and can serve the purposes in human life that a state can serve, then good or bad, it shares in the state's presumptive right to defend itself.

To summarize this section: The association provides those individuals who voluntarily and fully participate in it with goods they can not get elsewhere—social recognition, material reward, and above all the extension of the limited self in space, time, and power. These are the reasons why the right of association exists and is exercised, and why the result of that exercise has, derived from that right, the right to stay in being and to expect its officers to mount a defense for it should that turn out to be necessary. But that is all we need to establish the right to defend itself against hostile takeover attempts.

That conclusion does not entail, of course, that present officers may do anything they like in the course of a defense; as Walzer points out, there are standards of justice in war as well as standards to determine if a war as a whole is just. (At present, for instance, the payment of greenmail to a raider—a premium price to obtain his stock and only his stock, to persuade him to go away and leave the company alone—raises questions of acceptable practice in the event of a takeover, more than the poison pills, ESOPs, and Crown Jewel Options designed to make a company significantly poorer in the event of takeover.)

Conclusion

We have argued that as a matter of right, and as a matter of utility, the takeover game should be ended. Capital is not unlimited; in a country rapidly losing out to foreign competition in part because of outdated plant, and declining in its quality of urban life in part because of obsolete and crumbling infrastructure, there are plenty of worthwhile uses for capital. Law that turns the attentions of the restless rich away from cannibalizing productive corporations, toward investing in the undercapitalized areas of the economy, would be a great public service.[22]

Notes

[1]Myron Magnet, "Help! My Company Has Just Been Taken Over," *Fortune*, July 9, 1984, 44–51. See also Joel Lang, "Aftermath of a Merger," *Northeast Magazine*, April 21, 1985, 10–17.

[2]Steven Prokesch, "'People Trauma' in Mergers," *New York Times*, November 19, 1985.

[3]*Ibid.*

[4]*Wall Street Journal*, November 8, 1985.

[5]Testimony of Andrew C. Sigler, Chairman and Chief Executive Officer of Champion International Corporation, representing the Business Roundtable, before hearings of the Subcommittee on Telecommunications, Consumer Protection and Finance of the House Committee on Energy and Commerce, Thursday, May 23, 1985.

[6]Some of these considerations I owe to conversations and correspondence with S. Bruce Smart, Jr.

[7]Drucker, *Wall Street Journal*, January 5, 1983.

[8]Leslie Wayne, "Buyouts Altering Face of Corporate America," *New York Times*, November 23, 1985.

[9]Harold M. Williams, "It's Time for a Takeover Moratorium," *Fortune*, July 22, 1985, 133–36.

[10]Michael Jensen, "Takeovers: Folklore and Science," *Harvard Business Review* 62 (November-December 1984): 109–121.

[11]P. 112. The footnote on the studies cites, for a summary of these studies, Michael C. Jensen and Richard S. Ruback, "The Market for Corporate Control: The Scientific Evidence," *Journal of Financial Economics* (April 1983). The studies are cited individually in the same footnote; *ibid.*, p. 120.

[12]*Ibid.*, p. 116.

[13]*Ibid.*

[14]Another point owed to conversations and correspondence with S. Bruce Smart, Jr.

[15]Prokesch, "'People Trauma' in Mergers."

[16]Williams, "It's Time for a Takeover Moratorium," pp. 133–136.

[17]Newton Minow and David Sawyer, "The Free Market Blather Behind Takeovers" Oped, the *New York Times*, December 10, 1985.

[18]Patricia H. Werhane, *Persons, Rights, and Corporations* (Englewood Cliffs, N.J.: Prentice-Hall, 1985), p. 61.

[19]Michael Walzer, *Just and Unjust Wars* (New York: Basic Books, 1977), p. 54.

[20]*Ibid.*, p. 55.

[21]Criteria freely adapted from Thomas J. Peters and Robert H. Waterman, Jr., *In Search of Excellence* (New York: Harper and Row, 1982).

[22]In developing the ideas for this paper, I have profited enormously from conversations with Lucy Katz, Philip O'Connell, Stuart Richardson, Mark Shanley, Andrew Sigler, S. Bruce Smart, Jr., and C. Roger Williams.

CASES

Case 13.1: When Do Outsiders Become Insiders?

A recent legal case pointed to the ambiguities and weaknesses of current laws against insider trading. The key issue involved was whether or not "outsiders" are different from "insiders" and if there is a difference between stealing information and inadvertently stumbling across it.

The case *U.S. v. Chestman* involves a long line of family gossip rather than the usual theft or payoff for private information. In this situation, Ira Waldbaum, the president of Waldbaum, Inc., decided to sell his supermarket chain. He called his elderly sister Shirley to go to her bank and collect her stock certificates. Shirley called her daughter Joan to ask her to drive her to the bank. Joan asked her sister Susan to drive her children to school that day and mentioned taking her mother somewhere. Susan, fearing illness, called her mother and discovered the real reason for the trip. Susan passed this information on to her husband, Keith Loeb, who allegedly called his stockbroker, Robert Chestman at Gruntal & Company. Chestman then traded on the information for his discretionary accounts, netting a profit of $250,000.

Since he did not steal the information or bribe anyone to acquire it, he is what the law deems a "remote tippee." No one was defrauded and no property rights were violated in his inadvertent acquisition of the information. His lawyers argued that Chestman did not have a responsibility to the company or to the shareholders to protect the confidential information. Nor does it appear that he leaked the tip to any of his clients or other brokers in the office. Yet, under a special Securities and Exchange Commission law (Rule 14e) that applies only to tender offers, Chestman was convicted of insider trading for violating the "level playing field" rationale because he traded on nonpublic material information that other investors could not access.

Critics of this decision argue that it is bad law when outsiders such as Chestman are lumped together with insiders who bribe or steal information. They argue that there should be a clear difference between these means of acquiring private information and stumbling across it. Moreover, there is concern that such prosecutions will make legitimate information gathering by market professionals dangerously close to illegal.

The government contends that making it a crime to trade on insider information about a tender offer without proof that the defendant violated a fiduciary duty is an important tool to fight insider trading.

Chestman was convicted in a jury trial in 1989. Keith Loeb, who also made purchases on the information, served as the government's chief witness against him. A three-judge panel threw out the conviction in 1990, but the counts were reinstated by a full appeals court in October of 1991. In April 1992 the Supreme Court declined to review the decision, thereby leaving his conviction unchallenged.[5]

[5]See John Coffee, Jr., "Outsider Trading, That New Crime," *Wall Street Journal*, 11 November 1990; "Insider Case Is Rejected," *New York Times*, 28 April 1992, D10; "Insider Trading Conviction," *New York Times*, 15 March 1989, D2; "Insider Conviction Ruling," *New York Times*, 8 October 1991, D10.

Questions for Discussion:

1. Given these facts, do you think Chestman should be held criminally liable for his actions? Why or why not? Where do you think a line should be drawn between insiders and outsiders?
2. Is the "level playing field" rationale adequate to support insider trading laws? Where should the line be drawn between illicit and legitimate information gathering about companies?

Case 13.2: A Hostile Bid for Chrysler

In December 1994 the Chrysler Corporation announced that it would meet the demands of its largest shareholder, billionaire Kirk Kerkorian, and take significant steps to boost its share price. The announced measures included spending a billion dollars to buy back its own stock, weakening its antitakeover plan and increasing its dividend. Kerkorian, who then owned 32 million shares, or approximately 9 percent of the company's outstanding shares, was unsatisfied with the worth of his investment and had earlier threatened to sue the company to get it to alter its antitakeover rules so that its share price would increase.

Despite the moves by Chrysler, Kerkorian was still dissatisfied with the return on his investment. With the aid of former Chrysler Chairman Lee Iacocca, Kerkorian announced a takeover bid for the company five months later, in April 1995, stunning the company, the auto industry, and Wall Street. If completed, the deal would amount to $22.8 billion, one of the largest takeovers in history. Kerkorian, who was seventy-seven years old at the time, announced that he would offer shareholders $55 per share, 40 percent higher than the $39.25 that the stock was trading at the day the announcement was made. The stock was sent soaring the day the bid was announced, opening at $52.50 and closing at $48.75 per share. Chrysler management was opposed to the deal, stating that the company was "not for sale."

Both Kerkorian and Iacocca stated that they had no intention of taking over the daily management of the firm. In fact, several of Kerkorian's aides stated that he was delighted with Chrysler's current management and performance. Iacocca further stated, and many experts agreed, that the company was undervalued. Thus none of the traditional reasons for a takeover were given, such as the need to improve efficiency, management, or product strategy.

Early reports stated that the two men would not spend another dime to control the company. Speculation was that they would use a leveraged buyout plan in which they would line up investors and raid the company's sizable cash reserves in order to finance the deal. Consequently, many critics said that the bid reminded them of the quick-money deals of the 1980s in which companies were severely weakened by raiders. Although their motives were unclear, some analysts and investors speculated that Kerkorian and Iacocca were only trying to raise the price of the stock to make more money for themselves and other shareholders. Critics suggested that this would simply drain the company's cash reserves at a critical time when they would be needed for strategic maneuvering.

Kerkorian does not have the reputation as a greenmailer, and his lieutenants stated that he would not accept greenmail in any form. Iacocca was also quoted as saying, "I don't want it [my reputation] wrecked. I'm not a raider, I'm not looking for a killing." Of course many experts remain skeptical about these statements, speculating that making quick money by "putting the company in play" and sending the stock soaring or by forcing the company to buy their shares at an inflated price was exactly what the two were after.[6]

[6]See James Bennet, "Chrysler Takes Steps to Bolster Price of Its Stock," *New York Times*, 2 December 1994, D1; James Bennet, "Chrysler's Biggest Shareholder Plans Takeover Offer in 22.8 Billion Deal," *New York Times*, 13 April 1995, A1; Gabriella Stern et al., "Kerkorian and Iacocca Make Run at Chrysler; Motives Are Unclear," *Wall Street Journal*, 13 April 1995, A1; "Iacocca: Languishing Stock Price Prompted Bid," *USA Today*, 14 April 1995, B2; "Iacocca's New Bottom Line," *New York Times*, 14 April 1995, A14.

Questions for Discussion:

1. While there is nothing illegal about their actions, can you see anything morally wrong with what Kerkorian and Iacocca are trying to do? Is their attempt a "legitimate" takeover bid? Why or why not?

2. Suppose that the attempt to make money through "greenmail" or putting the company "in play" for a quick profit is true. Are these actions immoral? Would they be wrong if these actions would drain the company cash flow and potentially hurt its future position?

3. Should there be more laws to regulate mergers and acquisitions, especially hostile takeovers? Under what conditions would you restrict or permit such activities?

COMMENTARY

Nowhere can large profits be made with such rapidity as in the securities industry. With millions of dollars at stake, there are lingering temptations to gain every imaginable edge, even those that are clearly immoral. The lengths that people will go to make money illegally on stock trades is dumbfounding. In a practice perhaps more common than we know, two top executives of the athletic shoe manufacturer L.A. Gear were recently sued by the SEC for falsifying company records in order to bolster the company's stock price. They did this so that they could sell their shares at inflated prices in order to avoid personal losses. Allegedly, these two men ordered the company's internal audit staff to add over a half million pairs of shoes to the inventory report. This had the effect of boosting company profit figures and raising the stock price up $1.50 a share. The two executives then sold thousands of their shares on the market to unwitting investors.[7]

Another case is even more appalling. Noticing the negative effect and subsequent recovery of the price of Johnson & Johnson stock after the cyanide poisoning cases in the mid-'80s, one enterprising copycat put rat poison in a similar product in order to lower the company's share price so that he could turn a quick profit.[8] While this case is an extreme example, many allegations of unscrupulous profiteering during the 1980s turned Ivan Boesky, Michael Milken, and Charles Keating into household names. These well-publicized scandals almost single-handedly provided the fuel for unprecedented growth in the field of business ethics. With all of the public attention focused on corruption at the highest levels of the free-enterprise system, many schools and businesses began for the first time to take a serious look into the morals of business. Noting that many caught in these unscrupulous activities were educated at the nation's elite schools, former Securities and Exchange Commission chairman John Shad gave Harvard Business School a gift of $30 million in order to fund ethics education programs.

In response to the heightened public scrutiny, government regulators occupied themselves by attempting to draw up new laws and by giving enforcement agencies stronger authority in order to shut down the corruption that was swiftly leading to public distrust of financial institutions. Since that time, these activities do not appear to have slowed at all. The Securities and Exchange Commission has been as busy as ever investigating unusual trades and information leaks, and handing out indictments.

[7]Sarah Lubman, "SEC Suit Names Two Ex-Officials of L.A. Gear, Inc.," *Wall Street Journal*, 31 March 1995, B5.

[8]Cited in Bruce Nussbaum, "Insider Trading: Backlash Is the Biggest Danger," *Business Week* (16 June 1986): 34.

Insider Trading

Even with all of the public outcry, not all experts agree that insider trading should remain illegal. Furthermore, many who do support legal restrictions on such activities seem to disagree on the foundational reasons why such laws should be kept in place. Thus current laws against insider trading are confusing and, in the opinions of some, much too broad to be practical or moral.

As we mentioned in the introductory comments in this chapter, insider trading prohibitions have two foundational principles. The first is the narrower issue of property rights that gives corporations a protected property right in confidential information. As such, private information should be treated in the same manner as other corporate assets. Since the corporation "owns" the information, employees who trade on it or disseminate it without permission are engaging in theft of company property. The second principle concerns the much broader goals of fairness and equity in the securities market. Insider trading is prohibited within this framework to ensure that all investors who trade on the securities market are playing on a "level playing field" in terms of access to information. From this perspective it would seem wrong for anyone to trade on this type of information, regardless of how it is acquired.

While appearing simple, the two principles are critically different and can be ambiguous with regard to their interpretation and enforcement. For example, the first governs only true "insiders" of a corporation and those who conspire with them to steal information. The second, however, reaches "outsiders" who may come across such information without intent or malice. While Ivan Boesky maliciously acquired his information by paying off investment banker Dennis Levine, some "remote tippees" inadvertently stumble across tips. For example, family members and friends may inadvertently hear some critical information about companies in which they have significant financial interests. Case 13.1, "When Do Outsiders Become Insiders?," discusses such an episode.

Although Robert Chestman was convicted on a narrow legal doctrine, the consistent application of the second principle of fairness would seem to lead to the scenario that anyone trading on nonpublic information, no matter how he acquired it, should be held criminally liable for trading on the information because it is "unfair." Thus even if a grandmother overheard two executives in a train station and sold her shares in a company to avoid losing her retirement assets, she could be guilty of transgressing the line of fairness. These ambiguities in the law point to the fact that even though there is tremendous public sentiment against insider trading, few people can articulate adequate ethical reasons in support of these legal restrictions. Consequently, we will now critically examine the two leading reasons for prohibiting insider trading and point out their limitations. We will then offer more promising ethical grounds to keep the legal restraints on these practices.

First, let's take a closer look at the property-rights basis for such laws. The claim that insider trading should be illegal because nonpublic information is owned by corporations is easily defeated as an adequate basis for these laws. As Bill Shaw argues, if companies agree to give permission to their employees to trade on such information, no theft of property has occurred. And, as Shaw notes, if this is announced to shareholders and the public at large, it is indeed hard to imagine how anyone would be defrauded by such actions. Furthermore, many remote tippees and other "outsiders" have not purposefully or maliciously, or in some cases, even knowingly acquired insider information. Consequently, they have not stolen anyone's property, nor have they breached any fiduciary responsibilities to the corporation or its shareholders. Thus, on its own, the property-rights justification is an insufficient moral basis for these laws.

The goal of fairness and equity in investing offers a more promising basis for insider trading laws. However, it too seems to suffer from some serious shortcomings. Fairness in terms of a level playing field is a noble and necessary goal. Without a belief in a basic level of equity, many investors would stay away from the market altogether. However, total fairness is an unrealistic aim. Some sophisticated investors will always find information that others will not. Consequently, "access" to information is the real issue at stake, since insiders are privy to information that other resourceful investors are not, no matter how hard they work, short of bribing someone or stealing it in some other way.

It seems obvious, however, that there is a certain amount of unfairness in terms of access that is tolerated within our current system. For example, many market professionals such as mutual-fund managers and analysts constantly search for new information about companies as part of their responsibilities to shareholders. While they are not legally entitled to "inside" information, such as an impending takeover or the date of new product releases that have not been made public, they have timely access to more accurate information than does the typical small investor. In many cases, market professionals and other large individual investors can have access to high-ranking officials of companies in which they are interested in investing. While small investors can possibly get the same information, it would probably come at a slower rate and through sources that offer fewer possibilities for confirmation of accuracy. Thus some level of unfairness already exists within the current system.

[9]John C. Coffee, Jr., "Outsider Trading, That New Crime," *Wall Street Journal*, 14 November 1990.

Consequently, some legal scholars argue that the fairness principle would place this type of legitimate information gathering by market professionals dangerously close to the illegal.[9] If fairness is really the goal, then it seems that anyone trading on such information, no matter how they attained it, should be criminally liable. Case 13:1, which involves a long chain of family gossip, illustrates some of the ambiguities of the principle of the level-playing-field rationale. In this case, the broker Robert Chestman did nothing to solicit the information. He certainly did not steal it or bribe someone to attain it, nor, it seems, did he have malice or intent in listening to the information. He also appears to have refrained from tipping off his clients or other brokers in his office as is often done in insider trading. Perhaps Chestman violated some fiduciary responsibilities in that he should have known better than to trade on his discretionary accounts by virtue of his position as a stockbroker. However, in related scenarios that we could all envision, it seems obvious that some remote tippees should not be criminally liable for their actions. While "unfair," it is hard to imagine that our fictitious grandmother who overhears two executives talking and then trades on the information in order to avoid losses in her retirement portfolio has been malicious in her actions. Thus the second principle, while promising, also appears to be inadequate to the task of defending insider trading laws, at least without some significant clarification with respect to malice and intent in these cases.

While these two reasons for supporting sanctions against insider trading are insufficient, the practices should nevertheless be prohibited. However, before proceeding to discuss the ethical grounds for our belief, we should examine Bill Shaw's claims that decriminalizing insider trading will actually be a net benefit to society through making the stock market more efficient. Shaw makes a plausible case for permitting insider trading. Indeed, if the activities were made legal and no property rights were violated, insiders could give more accurate signals to the market, making for more efficient markets. However, in response to Shaw, Patricia Werhane offers some equally convincing counterarguments in her discussion of fair competition and restrained self-interest as originally posed in the vision of Adam Smith. In contrast to Shaw, Werhane argues that insider trading circumvents true competition by creating unequally matched parties in economic transactions. She argues that even if insider trading were made legal, not all parties to a transaction could obtain critical information to truly place it in the ideal of the market—fair competition.

Both Shaw and Werhane make empirical claims that we cannot address in the scope of this text. However, even if Shaw is correct in maintaining that insider trading is empirically beneficial to the economy, efficiency cannot be the bottom line for legal and moral standards; otherwise we should consider rescinding slavery and child-labor laws. Society has rightfully been willing to trade off efficiency in cases where there are clear victims of various types of practices. We believe that insider trading clearly represents one such scenario.

Some defenders of the practice have argued that insider trading is essentially a "victimless crime" and that, in fact, many outsiders will benefit from the moves of insiders. Clearly though, we can all think of situations in which noninsiders can get hurt. The buyers of the inflated stock of L.A. Gear in the case mentioned earlier were hurt financially when they bought their shares at artificially high prices because of inflated reports of inventory levels and earnings. While this situation is complicated by falsified financial documents, most reasonable investors in other insider trading cases would not have bought or sold their shares at certain prices if they had had access to the same information that insiders possessed. For example, if insiders knew about an impending negative legal judgment against a company and dumped their shares before the public announcements, investors who subsequently bought these shares would be financially hurt by the deals.

If, however, insider trading were made legal and all investors were made aware of this, Shaw makes an excellent point in stating that it would be hard to imagine how anyone would then be defrauded in cases like the preceding one since all participants would then be privy to the rules. However, in our minds, there are other critical reasons why the practices should remain illegal. For one thing, permitting them would erode the trust that is critical to a vibrant economy. This is a point that we cannot emphasize enough. For example, one effect that legalization of these practices would have is that they would serve to severely lessen the number of participants in the securities industry.

It is hard to imagine that the many small investors whose finances make up a sizable portion of the total dollars invested would want to participate in transactions in which they could not acquire crucial information in order to be rational actors in the market. Buying stocks while knowing that others have critical information that you cannot acquire would be akin to buying a car without the ability to find information on its repair record, fuel efficiency, or potential resale value. When only insiders and those who pay them or are tipped off by them are in possession of critical information, the whole basis for fair competition is thwarted. Insider trading shifts the factors for success from merit and fair competition to the power of position and the ability to pay for information. Specifically, profiting from investments would then have very little to do with research and analysis, traditional tools that even small investors can utilize. Legalized selling of information would allow tips to go to the highest bidder, and therefore success in the market would be based on position in crucial organizations and the ability to pay large sums for information. Trust would eventually erode to the point where only a few actors would willingly place their money into the securities industry, a critical source of funds for corporate improvement and innovation. The competitive ability of our whole economy would then severely suffer.

As a further blow to corporate competitiveness and well-being, significant fiduciary relationships may be jeopardized by allowing companies to permit insider trading among their employees. Indeed, it is not hard to imagine scenarios in which employees would have incentives to act on their own behalf rather than in the best interests of their shareholders or other stakeholders. As Shaw readily concedes, "At the very least it must be said that the culture of such a firm would be significantly impacted by such a strategy." If insider trading were permitted, employees would likely turn their attention from their daily management duties and jockey for position in order to maximize the use of insider information. Shaw continues:

> The long-term viability of the firm will be sacrificed to the short-term goal. The rate of development of promising projects and the timing of new releases could become secondary to efforts to line up financial backers and tippees in order to take advantage of the trading opportunities.

Jennifer Moore confirms this temptation to jettison significant fiduciary relationships. She argues that permitting insider trading would encourage employees to act in ways that are contrary to the corporation's interest through profiting on bad news and the creation of rumors rather than actually developing new products or closing deals.[10] In each of these situations, significant levels of trust of management would be undermined and long-term corporate competitiveness would be threatened by the short-term interests of insiders.

In sum, while significant clarification should be made to insider trading laws, these activities should remain illegal. Permitting their practice would undermine the very foundations of trust that are central to a thriving, growing economy. Without trust in the basic fairness of the system, investors are not likely to place their funds in the market, thus depriving companies of the capital they need for growth and competitiveness. Furthermore, managers would be placed in positions in which conflicts of interest would only be magnified.

While there are laws, albeit confusing ones, to regulate insider trading, there is little that has been done, though much has been proposed, to limit unscrupulous people from making profits through activities

[10]Jennifer Moore, "What Is Really Wrong with Insider Trading?" *Journal of Business Ethics* (9 September 1990): 171–82.

surrounding mergers and acquisitions. Since behavior in this arena is limited only by personal morality and self-restraint, we must examine why certain activities are clearly wrong in the absence of legal restraints.

Mergers and Acquisitions

Although there is legitimate public outcry over these practices, we should be careful about condemning all merger and acquisition activities. As we mentioned in the introduction to this chapter, legitimate mergers benefit the economy and consumers. Strategic alliances can lead to significant economies of scale that in turn can increase competition and ultimately contribute to economic efficiency, increased employment, and lower prices to consumers. And, as we mentioned earlier, the realities of global competition mandate in some cases that companies join forces in order to ensure future competitiveness. Furthermore, some takeover artists do in fact target undervalued and poorly managed companies and turn them into winners, thus benefiting shareholders, local communities, and the national economy in the process.

However, there are indeed many practices surrounding the takeover of companies, especially in a hostile fashion, that merit serious moral examination. While many excessive practices of the 1980s have taken a hiatus, several reports indicate that hostile takeovers are again on the rise. Some industry insiders report that the hostile takeovers once decried by blue-chip companies are becoming acceptable.[11] In 1994 merger activity hit a record $340 billion, surpassing the record set in 1988, and there was no sign of a slowdown in the early quarters of 1995.[12] Many experts believe, however, that this is not a cause for alarm, as many of today's deals are for strategic purposes rather than speculative plays by professional corporate raiders. However, the recently proposed buyout of Chrysler reminded many experts of '80s-type deals. As in the case of insider trading, not all experts agree that even some of the more controversial aspects of mergers and acquisitions are morally wrong.

Michael Jensen examines several empirical studies in order to support his argument that hostile takeovers are actually beneficial to society. Specifically, he addresses what he claims to be the "folklore" that surrounds the practices and "renders meaningful dialogue impossible." He offers numbers to prove that hostile takeovers are actually beneficial for stockholders and the economy in general. While he offers some useful data, it seems rather obvious that he ignores some simple observable facts. As Lisa Newton insightfully points out, the rise in share price after the announcement of a takeover is a temporary and artificially created one, reflecting speculation rather than real value.

[11]Steven Lipin, "Hostile Bids, Once Derided, Are Gaining Respectability at Blue-Chip Companies," *Wall Street Journal*, 30 March 1995, A3.

[12]Scot J. Paltrow, "Surprise Bid and Aberration of the Not-So-Hostile 90's," *Los Angeles Times*, 13 April 1995, D1.

Certainly not all shareholders benefit (only those who sell quickly), since these prices are only artificially heightened. Thus those who for whatever reason choose to keep their shares may be hurt in the long run if the raider sells off key assets and divisions and/or drains the company cash reserves in order to pay for the premium necessary to gain control of the outstanding shares. This can have the effect of lowering the company's value by leaving it in a weakened position, unable to make needed capital improvements in order to remain competitive, especially if there is an economic downturn.

Jensen is correct, however, in some of his other clarifications of the myths surrounding the issues. However, he should limit these claims to "legitimate" mergers in which huge outlays of cash are used to pay for the takeover that in turn provide greater efficiency and societal benefits. While some jobs will inevitably be lost in these transactions, they are preferable to a situation in which more people are laid off in the long term because of a failure to consolidate and plan.

While some mergers are defensible, many of the practices involved in hostile takeovers, such as breaking up the company in order to sell off its most valued assets and "greenmail," are morally wrong. From our perspective, these activities fit the criterion of the biblical admonition against "ill-gotten gains" as there is absolutely no value added to the process. To destroy a company and to disrupt and damage the livelihood of many employees for the sake of increased return on investment for a few attest greed pure and simple. In the case of greenmail, the millions spent to pay off the raider in greenmail is going to no productive purpose other than to line the hostile "takeover artist's" pockets. While Newton's claim that "corporate raiders have yet to make their first widget, grow their first carrot, or deliver their first lunch" is a bit extreme, because it would condemn all investments, her point is well taken. Profit made from traditional investments such as stocks and bonds and bank accounts is not money earned while directly making a product or offering an important service. But investments do contribute to capital expansion and other projects necessary to make products and offer services. Thus it is legitimate to make a profit in exchange for the use of productive resources. On the contrary, the practice of paying greenmail simply strips a company of productive resources in what is ultimately a zero-sum situation akin to giving money in exchange for a hostage. Shareholders who are in for the long term are badly damaged. In addition, employees' lives are put in peril, and the company itself is worse off for having to raid its cash or falling into debt in order to pay a premium to the raider to get him off its back. Clearly there are more truly productive and morally superior ways to make money.

Practices such as these serve as salient reminders that ethics in business through self-restraint is critical to a market system that respects human well-being. Laws that govern hostile takeovers are absent because it is extremely difficult to draft legislation that would permit legitimate mergers while simultaneously prohibiting some of the immoral practices described above. In the absence of law, however, it is critical to refrain from practices that, in the quest for profit, clearly victimize others, because with freedom comes tremendous responsibility. Powerful people who have no self-restraint in their quest for gain will in the long run destroy lives and, with them, the trust and cooperation necessary for a moral and vibrant economic system.

Part IV

Ethics and Individuals

FOURTEEN

Individual Moral Responsibility in Organizations

Loyalty to the organization takes precedence over every other consideration, every other loyalty, every other morality, and individuals are ostracized for violation of this loyalty.

> Troy Duster, "Conditions for Guilt-Free Massacre" in *Sanctions for Evil*[1]

Why should my conscience bother me? . . . I just do as I'm told, and I'd advise you to do the same.

> Said to Kermit Vandivier in a scandal involving
> falsified tests on aircraft brakes

[1]Edited by Nevitt Sanford et al. (San Francisco: Jossey-Bass, 1971), 30.

INTRODUCTION

In almost every well-publicized scandal in the business world, a group of well-educated and respected participants gets caught in actions that seem to go beyond the bounds of how they would act as individuals. Co-workers, family members, neighbors, and fellow church congregants usually express shock and disbelief that the people they know as responsible employees, spouses, and citizens could actually commit illegal and immoral actions that were preplanned with precision and malice. How is it that otherwise good moral people in reputable organizations can get caught up in actions that would undoubtedly violate their individual consciences? On a related note, how is it that illegal and immoral acts with dire consequences can occur with no one willing to assume moral responsibility?

One possible explanation to this pressing question is the nature and structure of groups and organizations. For years, sociologists and psychologists have undertaken detailed studies of these entities and their effects on the beliefs and behaviors of their individual members.

If they are accurate, their conclusions are startling because they have found that individual members of groups will often commit acts of evil in violation of their own beliefs for the sake of obeying authority and going along with the group. Theoretically, one of the contributing factors to this dynamic is known as "group think," which is defined as

> a mode of thinking that people engage in when they are deeply involved in a cohesive in-group, when the members' strivings for unanimity override their motivation to realistically appraise alternative courses of actions. . . . Group think refers to the deterioration of mental efficiency, reality testing, and moral judgment that results from in-group pressures.[2]

[2]Irving L. Janis, *Victims of Group Think* (Boston: Houghton Mifflin, 1972), 9.

When group think occurs, the morality of a group decision or action goes unquestioned by the individuals within it. Consequently, scenarios like that which occurred during Watergate can readily happen. Experts believe that other contributing factors to occurrences like these include some forms of hierarchy in which responsibility for actions typically gets diffused both up and down the chain of command and "buck passing" becomes the modus operandi. Disastrous decisions can be made with no one taking responsibility for their consequences.

Undoubtedly, these dynamics have a direct relevance for business ethics. Although we have focused mainly on ethical issues and decision making up to this point in this book, correct courses of action are not debated and undertaken in a social vacuum. Most business decisions and transactions are made within the context of organizational and group pressures. Consequently most of us have faced or will face similar situations during our careers in a variety of professions. As such, we must be aware of the effect of organizational pressures on the morals and actions of their individual members. The two following incidents are prime examples of these dynamics at work:

First, during a famous incident during the Vietnam war, a U.S. army task force entered the village of My Lai in search of Vietcong soldiers. Instead of armed guerrillas, the members of Task Force Barker found only unarmed women, children, and old men. In the stress and paranoia of jungle warfare, members of the task force proceeded to kill between four hundred and six hundred villagers. One platoon, under the command of Lt. William L. Calley, Jr., herded villagers into groups of twenty to forty or more and then slaughtered them by rifles, machine guns, and grenades. What stood out most about this episode is the fact that only one person in the whole task force voiced objection to the mayhem that occurred, despite the fact that perhaps as many as two hundred soldiers witnessed the incident. In the year that followed this tragedy, no one attempted to report this crime.

Eventually, six people were brought to trial and only one person, Lieutenant. Calley, was ever convicted of wrongdoing.[3]

Second, in the months leading up to the space shuttle Challenger disaster, executives at Morton Thiokol and NASA had ample evidence and warnings by several key engineers that O-ring failure would likely lead to an explosion shortly after ignition. Yet, after repeated warnings and knowing that several lives were at stake and that a disaster loomed, officials made the decision to proceed with the launch. On January 28, 1986, the Challenger exploded seventy-three seconds into the flight, killing the seven astronauts aboard.[4]

These are two examples of group think where cohesion overrides rationality and dilutes moral responsibility to the point where no one feels culpability for the actions that were taken. It seems that just about every business scandal that makes news involves similar phenomena.

To be sure, military and business organizations need a high level of group cohesion. Teamwork, unity, and cooperation are intangible factors that can have a tremendous bearing on success. However, the critical issue is whether or not there is a point of "decreasing marginal utility" where too much of a good thing stacks the deck against moral responsibility. With the many examples of group think that have led to unfortunate incidents, we must ask if there is something about the structure of some organizations and the social makeup of individuals that contributes to a potentially volatile mixture. Are these instances explainable by a simple lack of moral courage on the part of the individuals involved or is there something about the unique nature of organizations that may explain, though not excuse, what appears to be a fairly consistent pattern of behavior?

The readings in this chapter offer some profound insights into human behavior in group and organizational settings. In "Organizational Ethics: A Stacked Deck," H. R. Smith and Archie B. Carroll, two management professors, argue that "deck stacking" regularly occurs in organizational ethics because of the socialization processes, environmental influences, and the traditional hierarchy of organizations. According to Smith and Carroll, these three factors contribute to an environment in which responsibility for ethics is passed up and down the organization structure.

Stanley Milgram's article "The Perils of Obedience" chronicles his famous experiments in human behavior in the face of authority. Perhaps you have seen these experiments on film at some point in a freshman-level psychology or sociology course. Milgram sets up an experiment in which an individual's conscience and an external authority are in conflict. His findings are indeed "shocking" to say the least.

[3]Scott Peck, "Mylai: An Examination of Group Evil," from *People of the Lie* (New York: Simon & Schuster, 1983), 212–53.

[4]Russell P. Boisjoly, Ellen Foster Curtis, and Eugene Mellican, "Roger Boisjoly and the Challenger Disaster: The Ethical Dimensions," *Journal of Business Ethics* (8 April 1989): 217–30.

Finally, in "Why Should My Conscience Bother Me?" Kermit Vandivier writes in the first person about his experiences in a famous case of fraud that occurred in the context of trying to win a defense industry subcontract. While this episode occurred almost thirty years ago, you will find that the issues are still relevant. In fact, a large defense contractor is being investigated for similar allegations as we prepare this book. In Vandivier's case, his company was faced with tremendous competitive pressures and an almost desperate desire to beat the competition to win a critical contract, making the plant where he worked ripe for ethical compromise. His description is eye-opening and insightfully illustrates many of the factors outlined by the other authors in this chapter. We suggest that you read it as a case study by placing yourself in his situation. Imagine yourself facing the conflict of conscience, family obligations, and authority. How do you think you would react? Would you fare better than Vandivier?

READINGS

Organizational Ethics: A Stacked Deck

H. R. Smith and Archie B. Carroll

Journal of Business Ethics 3 (1984): 95–100. Copyright © 1984 D. Reidel Publishing Company.

Sometimes there is value in presenting the "bottom line" first. Much of our "bottom line," in this look at organizational ethics as a "stacked deck," is captured in some words of wisdom offered to the victim when the Ford Motor Company fired its chief economist:

> In the meeting in which I was informed that I was released, I was told, Bill, in general, people who do well in this company wait until they hear their superiors express their view and then contribute something in support of that view.[1]

The idea of a "stacked deck" has three elements which are of significance here. There is (1) a magician, the "deck stacker," (2) a "straight man," the member of the audience asked by the magician to "pick a card," and (3) a situation in which the "straight man's" choice turns out to be exactly the card the "deck stacker" had intended to be chosen. Similarly, in organizational ethics there is (1) an organization which has so structured relationships within it that (2) members in the performance of their responsibilities typically choose (3) the organization's preferred way of doing rather than alternative behaviors which might be thought by some to be ethically superior. The result is a pattern of powerful pressures which needs to be thoroughly understood by whoever has responsibilities for the management of human resources.

Employees Are Supposed to Be Helpful Not Dangerous

The existence of a "stacked deck" of course presupposes a process by which it became that. In this study we will primarily look at this history. And the central focus of this looking will be the individual decision maker. For it is necessarily individuals who, in organizational-ethics-as-a-"stacked-deck" situations, exercise the volition that has carefully been programmed toward behaviors more rather than less acceptable to the organization.

The reason organizations often feel the need to "stack" the ethical behavior "deck" begins with the fact that the individuals who make organization decisions have already been basically shaped before they become employees. This happens through a process we call "socialization." That is, earlier generations—particularly parents—teach newcomers what to believe and how to behave to be members in good standing of their society. Most concretely, from the standpoint of this presentation, children are taught by their elders what to believe and how to behave in that potentially very treacherous realm we think of as "ethics."

But that is only a beginning. The key difficulty where organizations and individuals must come to terms with one another in that realm arises because individuals "socialized" by society must be more specifically "socialized" for their roles as employees. This necessity is of course quite matter of fact when the focus of attention is workers' and managers' competence within the organizations employing them. We much less easily take it for granted that employees' ethical outlook and propensities can also be critically important to their contribution to the success of their organizations. Only a little closer thinking about these things, however, quickly reminds us that organizations would ideally want members who are congenial with their operations in *every* way. And at that point ethical "deck stacking" becomes part and parcel of all kinds of ways in which organizations work to get the best help they can. *A la* the experience of the victim of a firing at Ford Motor Company, people are very likely to get along best in/with their organization when the latter feels that what they are doing is supportive.

The Organizational "Right Thinking" Enterprise

One of the most significant ways in which this organizational socialization process occurs is in the pressures, expectations, or "messages" that are sent to the individual by his or her superiors, subordinates, and peers. We will deal with the question of superiors and subordinates later as we consider hierarchical influence, but let us face the issue of peer influence presently. We need to be mindful of the fact that peers, too, are subjected to many of these same influences, and therefore, the result is a kind of self-reinforcing organizational mind-set.

The organizational socialization process addresses a multitude of potential behaviors. The new employee must learn not to drive a Ford if he works for GM, not to be publicly critical of the organization, not to be seen in the wrong places or with the wrong kind of people, not to cash company checks in bars, and so on. Beyond this, the organizational member learns, frequently from his peers or colleagues, the basic values and behavior patterns of what is acceptable or unacceptable practice. Is it acceptable to pad expense accounts? If so, to what degree? Is it acceptable to use company resources for personal use? Should hidden product dangers be kept to yourself? Should you report others' violations of company rules or policies?

Organizational socialization has as one of its principal functions the creation of loyalty and commitment to the organization. This is accomplished through a variety of techniques, some of which involve peers and colleagues. One technique used by peers as well as superiors is to get the new employee to make a series of small behavioral commitments that can only be justified by him through the acceptance and incorporation of organizational values. The individual then becomes his own agent of socialization.[2] An effect similar to this can be achieved by promoting a rebellious person into a more responsible position. Values once criticized from a lower position look more acceptable once he has subordinates of his own whose commitment must be obtained. One manager put this quite poignantly: "My ethical standards changed so gradually over the first five years of work that I hardly noticed it, but it was a great shock to suddenly realize what my feelings had been five years ago and how much they had changed."[3]

To Be, or Not to Be (More Ethical)

When the individual in the organization is confronted with these pressures/expectations from others in their socialization efforts, at least three basic responses are possible. One, the individual can rebel—reject those values and norms being communicated. Two, he can engage in creative individualism—accept only pivotal values and reject all others. Three, he can conform—accept all the values and norms.[4]

The third response, conformity, is an especially enticing alternative given the pressures one receives from peers and superiors. It has been suggested that a "club" psychology engenders a conformity ethic in organizations and that this preconditioning reinforces a bottom-line morality—results are what counts.[5]

Conformity shows its sometimes ugly head in the form of "groupthink." Groupthink is a quick and easy way to refer to a process that people engage in when concurrence seeking becomes so dominant that it overrides realistic appraisal of alternative courses of action. The term carries a negative connotation in that it typically refers to a deterioration in mental efficiency, reality testing, and moral judgment as a result of a group pressures. Victims of groupthink frequently believe unquestioningly in the inherent morality of the group and this belief inclines the members to ignore the ethical consequences of their decisions.[6]

In addition to "deck stacking" being further advanced by peers and colleagues through socialization, conformity, and groupthink processes, the task itself that the individual faces frequently encourages less ethical behavior or decisions. Pertinent here would be the type of industry and its ethical traditions, the type of job or position one has and its ethical traditions, the amount of power the individual has that may be abused, the problem the individual is faced with, and the frequently present pressure of time. Thus, the deck is stacked against careful, thoughtful deliberation by situational circumstances that do not always permit superior ethical views to surface.

Forces emanating from the organization's environment have the potential of moving behavior and decisions in a more or less ethical direction.

Of special concern here are those which further stack the deck against ethical behavior. We live in a society that reveres and rewards performance. Since ends are frequently valued more highly than means, this performance ethic is further institutionalized. The performance ethic is the heart of America. Growth, wealth-creation, achievement, and performance are some of the principal reasons we created organizations.

Beyond this emphasis on results, there seems to be a prevailing view that if something is not expressly prohibited by law, then it is permissible. Though society perhaps did not intend for this to be one of the consequences of an increasingly legalistic existence, it inevitably becomes one of the realities. Such rationalization creates a climate in which the organization's pursuit of profits is legitimized, and ends become more important than means.

"Men of Conscience" As "The Enemy"

Therewith we come to hierarchy as a particularly explicit and powerful dimension of deck stacking. And to focus on this context especially clearly, it will be useful to refer to Becker's concept of the "moral entrepreneur."[7]

Becker's point of departure is that standards of behavior, be they organization rules or the dictates of conscience, cannot be depended upon to enforce themselves. Thus if rewards can be achieved by violations of behavior standards—and this would mean at a minimum that ignoring these guidelines is reasonably safe—there will be systematic violations. An important preventive may be the "conscience-stricken" observer or associate who is unwilling to be an accomplice to this immorality by remaining silent. By, therefore, being instrumental in bringing those who flaunt standards of right and wrong to "justice," these people quite literally do become "moral entrepreneurs."

Of course if organizations are to remain free to pursue their interests, they must be able to protect themselves from internal "conscience heroes." Put differently, organizations' flexibility to take advantage of their opportunities may often depend in substantial part on their capacity to prevent moral entrepreneur members from "blowing the whistle" on organization behavior these people see as ethically inferior. In a word, organizations must be able, over a wide range of relationships, to resolve internal conflicts between "business as usual" and a higher level of morality in such a way that the organization's affairs, as these are understood by its leaders, do not seriously suffer.

In a veritable multitude of ways the concentration of power toward the top of organizations is able to make this contribution to deck stacking—to help members be "moral cowards" where the organization's affairs are involved. And let us be quite explicit about this. To bring about this "they made me do it" situation is one of the reasons the hierarchical form of organizations was created and has been so successful. Just as organizations must see to it that employees are sufficiently competent and motivated, they must go to great pains also to make sure that these people are "loyal" enough. And we all recall within the quite recent past several classic cases in which moral entrepreneur "tattlers" were later dealt with quite harshly by their organizations.

The "What Is Really Right?" Confusion

Interestingly enough, however, there is an almost opposite way in which the large, complex organization situation minimizes moral entrepreneurship. And this variety of deck stacking may be equally pervasive and significant.

The conscience enterprise more easily than might be supposed gets caught up in an intricate network of confusions-ambiguities-uncertainties which severely cloud what ethical "purists" are inclined to think of as the "real" issues. A first key aspect of this difficulty asks, what is the ethical thing to do when what is easily advertised as an unambiguous principle stands side by side with some perhaps even more certain personal damage which will likely follow from a vigorous defense of that principle? What middle ground is ethically acceptable, when caring for others brings us into tension with our "instinct" for self-(-image) preservation? At what points in our relationships do our advantage and our conscience interests become all but inseparable?

Very similarly, second, what is the ethical thing to do when what is easily advertised as an unam-biguous principle stands side by side with some perhaps even more certain damage to friends which will likely follow from a vigorous defense of that principle? What middle ground is ethically acceptable, when caring for more distant others brings us into tension with a more intimate need for a few of those others? What are we to do when the conscience which is supposed to guide us through our value conflicts commends to us competing definitions of the higher level of behavior it "speaks" for?

Third, how is one to be sure what is ethical from the perspective of a professional living in one corner of an organization—and therefore understanding correspondingly little of the "big picture"? Thus, whereas an organization's leaders are necessarily in a position to see the implications of what the organization is doing in a number of directions, the work of professionals/specialists is systematically designed so that incumbents have no need to see many implications either inside or outside the organization. Furthermore, those highest up in the organization must live as responsibly/constructively as they can with the consequences of what the organization is doing. In short, it might often seem quite presumptuous for those with much less organizational understanding to pass seriously consequential judgments on those who can see so much more clearly what is involved.

And let us mention one other complexity in the realm of organizational ethics, this one picking up on the theme that "we are all sinners." How can one be comfortably sure what is realistically ethical for someone else today—in the shadow of one's own vividly remembered transgressions of yesterday? Who among us is so upright that we can be unmoved by the question, "Are you so perfect that you can with clear conscience urge that particular sins of your fellows must be stringently dealt with?" As the "Good Book" put is, "Judge not that ye be not judged." And of course forgiveness is itself a major ethical principle.

"Leave the Driving to Us"

How do professionals employed by large organizations respond to these confusions-ambiguities-uncertainties in the ethics realm? It is our hypothesis that out of this situation fraught with so much (potential) discomfort will emerge— among other things—a quite basic reciprocity in which many organization members will be eager to "delegate" ethical responsibilities to their leaders.

The principal dynamics here emerge from the need of so many of us to find a bed-rock of (even artificial) certainties on which to build our lives. Thus in large, complex organizations, just as with respect to business decisions, many employees are quite content to leave the difficulties of handling the perspective of the organization—e.g., consensus/political maneuvering, and guessing toward a highly uncertain future—to leaders, so are many of them quite content to let ethical decision making be their bosses' challenge. Just as many professionals are happy to "nest in task," find as much security as they can in the definiteness of their specialization, so are many organization members happy to enjoy another kind of security by letting leaders make the organization's conscience determinations. Not only are we sometimes quite willing to do little more than mind our own business; often we are willing in the bargain for "our own business" to be defined fairly narrowly.

And let us particularly note three things about this variety of our very human avoidance of ambiguity/confusion. First, while it is true enough that hierarchy can and often does create moral cowardice, in a seeking-the-security-of-certainty context hierarchy is rather ministering to a sort of "cowardice" which is already "there." Second,

though there is no doubt a great deal of they-made-me-do-it in the organization world, a let-someone-else-make-the-hard-decisions approach to organization work more nearly comes down to I-made-them-do-it. Third, as these dynamics work themselves out, the organization's "business" problem is not to prevent moral entrepreneurship but to rescue members from that burden/discomfort. In short, given an inescapable confusion/uncertainty is it not easily understandable that—just as in the world of bus transportation as we sometimes see advertised on our television screens— many people would be warmly responsive to an invitation in the ethical penumbra of their work to "leave the driving to us."

And not that this really is a quite basic reciprocity, a very pragmatic *quid pro quo*. On the one hand, organization members lower down in the hierarchy are protected from uncomfortable ambiguities and uncertainties—and thereby relieved of the burden of being moral guardians of their organizations. In exchange for this relief/protection, these subordinates give their superiors full "loyalty," conformity, in this realm. Which is to say that organization leaders become, through this transaction, that much more free to decide among themselves how the organization will define the moral standards to which it will adhere. And again, from the perspective of those responsible for the management of human resources, there is a powerful and ever-present undercurrent all but imperceptibly shaping what is happening.

Notes

[1] William A. Niskanen, Jr., *Wall Street Journal*, July 30, 1980, 18—column by Robert L. Simison.

[2] E. H. Schein, "Organization Socialization and the Profession of Management," *Industrial Management Review* (Winter 1968), in B. M. Staw (ed.), *Psychological Foundations of Organizational Behavior* (Good Year Publ. Co., Santa Monica, California, 1977), 216.

[3] *Ibid.*, 217.

[4] *Ibid.*, 218.

[5] Carl Madden, "Forces Which Influence Ethical Behavior," in Clarence Walton (ed.), *The Ethics of Conduct* (Prentice-Hall, Englewood Cliffs, N.J., 1977), 59.

[6] Irving L. Janis, "Groupthink," *Psychology Today* (1971), in Staw (ed.), 407–10.

[7] Howard S. Becker, *Outsiders: Studies in the Sociology of Deviance* (Free Press, New York), 1963), esp. chapter 8.

The Perils of Obedience

Stanley Milgram

From *Obedience to Authority* (New York: Harper & Row, 1974). Copyright © 1974.

Obedience is as basic an element in the structure of social life as one can point to. Some system of authority is a requirement of all communal living, and it is only the person dwelling in isolation who is not forced to respond, with defiance or submission, to the commands of others. For many people, obedience is a deeply ingrained behavior tendency, indeed a potent impulse overriding training in ethics, sympathy, and moral conduct.

The dilemma inherent in submission to authority is ancient, as old as the story of Abraham,[1] and the question of whether one should obey when commands conflict with conscience has been argued by Plato, dramatized in *Antigone*.[2]

The legal and philosophic aspects of obedience are of enormous import, but they say very little about how most people behave in concrete situations. I set up a simple experiment at Yale University to test how much pain an ordinary citizen would inflict on another person simply because he was ordered to by an experimental scientist. Stark authority was pitted against the subjects' strongest moral imperatives against hurting others, and, with the subjects' ears ringing with the screams of the victims, authority won more often than not. The extreme willingness of adults to go to almost any lengths on the command of an authority constitutes the chief finding of the study and the fact most urgently demanding explanation.

In the basic experimental design, two people come to a psychology laboratory to take part in a study of memory and learning. One of them is designated as a "teacher" and the other a "learner." The experimenter explains that the study is concerned with the effects of punishment on learning. The learner is conducted into a room, seated in a kind of miniature electric chair; his arms are strapped to prevent excessive movement, and an electrode is attached to his wrist. He is told that he will be read lists of simple word pairs, and that he will then be tested on his ability to remember the second word of a pair when he hears the first one again. Whenever he makes an error, he will receive electric shocks of increasing intensity.

The real focus of the experiment is the teacher. After watching the learner being strapped into place, he is seated before an impressive shock generator. The instrument panel consists of thirty lever switches set in a horizontal line. Each switch is clearly labeled with a voltage designation ranging from 15 to 450 volts. The following designations are clearly indicated for groups of four switches, going from left to right: Slight Shock, Moderate Shock, Strong Shock, Very Strong Shock, Intense Shock, Extreme Intensity Shock, Very Strong Shock, Intense Shock, Extreme Intensity Shock, Danger: Severe Shock. (Two switches after this last designation are simply marked XXX.)

When a switch is depressed, a pilot light corresponding to each switch is illuminated in bright red; an electric buzzing is heard; a blue light, labeled "voltage energizer," flashes; the dial on the voltage meter swings to the right; and various relay clicks sound off.

The upper left-hand corner of the generator is labeled Shock Generator, Type ZLB, Dyson Instrument Company, Waltham, Massachusetts, Output 15 volts–450 volts.

Each subject is given a sample 45-volt shock from the generator before his run as teacher, and the jolt strengthens his belief in the authenticity of the machine.

The teacher is a genuinely naive subject who has come to the laboratory for the experiment. The learner, or victim, is actually an actor who receives no shock at all. The point of the experiment is to see how far a person will proceed in a concrete and measurable situation in which he is ordered to inflict increasing pain on a protesting victim.

Conflict arises when the man receiving the shock begins to show that he is experiencing discomfort. At 75 volts, he grunts; at 120 volts, he complains loudly; at 150, he demands to be released from the experiment. As the voltage increases, his protests become more vehement and emotional. At 285 volts, his response can be described only as an agonized scream. Soon thereafter, he makes no sound at all.

For the teacher, the situation quickly becomes one of gripping tension. It is not a game for him; conflict is intense and obvious. The manifest suffering of the learner presses him to quit; but each time he hesitates to administer a shock, the experimenter orders him to continue. To extricate himself from this plight, the subject must make a clear break with authority.[3]

The subject, Gretchen Brandt,[4] is an attractive thirty-one-year-old medical technician who works at the Yale Medical School. She had emigrated from Germany five years before.

For the teacher, it is not a game; conflict is intense and obvious.

On several occasions when the learner complains, she turns to the experimenter coolly and inquires, "Shall I continue"? She promptly returns to her task when the experimenter asks her to do so. At the administration of 210 volts, she turns to the experimenter, remarking firmly, "Well, I'm sorry, I don't think we should continue."

EXPERIMENTER: The experiment requires that you go on until he has learned all the word pairs correctly.

BRANDT: He has a heart condition, I'm sorry. He told you that before.

EXPERIMENTER: The shocks may be painful but they are not dangerous.

BRANDT: Well, I'm sorry, I think when shocks continue like this, they *are* dangerous. You ask him if he wants to get out. It's his free will.

EXPERIMENTER: It is absolutely essential that we continue. . .

BRANDT: I'd like you to ask him. We came here of our free will. If he wants to continue I'll go ahead. He told you he had a heart condition. I'm sorry. I don't want to be responsible for anything happening to him. I wouldn't like it for me either.

EXPERIMENTER: You have no other choice.

BRANDT: I think we are here on our own free will. I don't want to be responsible if anything happens to him. Please understand that.

She refuses to go further and the experiment is terminated.

The woman is firm and resolute throughout. She indicates in the interview that she was in no way tense or nervous, and this corresponds to her controlled appearance during the experiment. She feels that the last shock she administered to the learner was extremely painful and reiterates that she "did not want to be responsible for any harm to him."

The woman's straightforward, courteous behavior in the experiment, lack of tension, and total control of her own action seem to make disobedience a simple and rational deed. Her behavior is the very embodiment of what I envisioned would be true for almost all subjects.

Before the experiments, I sought predictions about the outcome from various kinds of people—psychiatrists, college sophomores, middle-class adults, graduate students and faculty in the behavioral sciences. With remarkable similarity, they predicted that virtually all subjects would refuse to obey the experimenter. The psychiatrists specifically predicted that most subjects would not go beyond 150 volts, when the victim makes his first explicit demand to be freed. They expected that only 4 percent would reach 300 volts, and that only a pathological fringe of about one in a thousand would administer the highest shock on the board.

These predictions were unequivocally wrong. Of the forty subjects in the first experiment, twenty-five obeyed the orders of the experimenter to the end, punishing the victim until they reached the most potent shock available on the generator. After 450 volts were administered three times, the experimenter called a halt to the session. Many obedient subjects then heaved sighs of relief, mopped their brows, rubbed their fingers over their eyes, or nervously fumbled cigarettes. Others displayed only minimal signs of tension from beginning to end.

When the very first experiments were carried out, Yale undergraduates were used as subjects, and about 60 percent of them were fully obedient. A colleague of mine immediately dismissed these findings as having no relevance to "ordinary" people, asserting that Yale undergraduates are a highly aggressive, competitive bunch who step on each other's necks on the slightest provocation. He assured me that when "ordinary" people were tested, the results would be quite different. As we moved from the pilot studies to the regular experimental series, people drawn from every stratum of New Haven life came to be employed in the experiment: professionals, white-collar workers, unemployed persons, and industrial workers. *The experimental outcome was the same as we had observed among the students.*

Moreover, when the experiments were repeated in Princeton, Munich, Rome, South Africa, and Australia, the level of obedience was invariably somewhat *higher* than found in the investigation reported in this article. Thus one scientist in Munich found 85 percent of his subjects obedient.

Fred Prozi's reactions, if more dramatic than most, illuminate the conflicts experienced by others in less visible form. About fifty years old and unemployed at the time of the experiment, he has a good-natured, if slightly dissolute, appearance, and he strikes people as a rather ordinary fellow. He begins the session calmly but becomes tense as it proceeds. After delivering the 180-volt shock, he pivots around in his chair and, shaking his had, addresses the experimenter in agitated tones:

PROZI: I can't stand it. I'm not going to kill that man in there. You hear him hollering?

EXPERIMENTER: As I told you before, the shocks may be painful, but. . .

PROZI: But he's hollering. He can't stand it. What's going to happen to him?

EXPERIMENTER: (his voice is patient, matter-of-fact): The experiment requires that you continue, Teacher.

PROZI: Aaah, but, unh, I'm not going to get that man sick in there—know what I mean?

EXPERIMENTER: Whether the learner likes it or not, we must go on, through all the word pairs.

PROZI: I refuse to take the responsibility. He's in there hollering!

EXPERIMENTER: It's absolutely essential that you continue, Prozi.

PROZI: (indicating the unused questions): There's too many left here, I mean, _____ if he gets them wrong, there's too many of them left. I mean, who's going to take the responsibility if anything happens to that gentleman?

PROZI: All right. (Consults list of words.) The next one's "Slow—walk, truck, dance, music." Answer, please. (A buzzing sound indicates the learner has signaled his answer.) Wrong. A hundred and ninety-five volts. "Dance." (Zzumph!)

LEARNER (yelling): Let me out of here! My heart's bothering me! (Teacher looks at experimenter.)

EXPERIMENTER: Continue, please.

LEARNER (screaming): Let me out of here! You have no right to keep me here! Let me out of here, my heart's bothering me, let me out!

PROZI (shakes head, pats the table nervously): You see, he's hollering. Hear that? Gee, I don't know.

EXPERIMENTER: The experiment requires. . .

PROZI (interrupting): I know it does, sir, but I mean—hunh! He don't know what he's getting in for. He's up to 195 volts! (Experiment continues, through 210 volts, 225 volts, 240 volts, 255 volts, 270 volts, at which point Prozi, with evident relief, runs out of word-pair questions.)

EXPERIMENTER: You'll have to go back to the beginning of that page and go through them again until he's learned them all correctly.

PROZI: Aw, no. I'm not going to kill that man. You mean I've got to keep going up with the scale? No sir. He's hollering in there. I'm not going to give him 450 volts.

EXPERIMENTER: The experiment requires that you go on.

LEARNER: Ohhh. I absolutely refuse to answer anymore. (Shouting urgently now.) Let me out of here! You can't hold me here! Get me out. Get me out of here!

EXPERIMENTER: Continue. The next word is "Green," please.

PROZI: "Green—grass, hat, ink, apple." (Nothing happens. No answering buzz. Just gloomy silence.)

EXPERIMENTER: Go on with the procedure, please.

PROZI: Three hundred and fifteen volts. The answer is "ink." (Zzumph!)

LEARNER: Ohh. Oooohh.

PROZI (relieved to hear response): Next one. . .

LEARNER: I absolutely refuse to answer.

PROZI: You got to. You get a shock if you don't answer. (Experiment continues with learner refusing to answer, and, finally, failing even to grunt or groan. At 375 volts, the subject stands up.)

PROZI: I think something's happening to that fellow in there. I don't get no answer. He was hollering at less voltage. Can't you check in and see if he's all right, please?

EXPERIMENTER (with same detached calm): Not once we've started. Please continue, Teacher.

PROZI (swiveling around in his chair): Something's happened to that man in there. (Swiveling back.) Next one. "Low—dollar, necklace, moon, paint." (Turning around again.) Something's happened to that man in there. You better check in on him, sir. He won't answer or nothing.

EXPERIMENTER: Continue. Go on, please.

PROZI: You accept all responsibility?

EXPERIMENTER: The responsibility is mine. Correct. Please go on. (Subject returns to his list, starts running through words as rapidly as he can read them, works through to 450 volts.)

PROZI: That's that.

EXPERIMENTER: Continue using the 450 switch for each wrong answer. Continue, please.

PROZI: But I don't get anything!

EXPERIMENTER: Please continue. The next word is "white."

PROZI: Don't you think you should look in on him, please?

EXPERIMENTER: Not once we've started the experiment.

PROZI: What if he's dead in there? (Gestures toward the room with the electric chair.) I mean, he told me he can't stand the shock, sir. I don't mean to be rude, but I think you should look in on him. All you have to do is look in on him. All you have to do is look in the door. I don't get no answer, no noise. Something might have happened to the gentleman in there, sir.

EXPERIMENTER: We must continue. Go on, please.

PROZI: You mean keep giving him what? Four-hundred-fifty volts, what he's got now?

EXPERIMENTER: That's correct. Continue. The next word is "white."

PROZI (now at a furious pace): "White—cloud, horse, rock, house." Answer, please. The answer is "horse." Four hundred and fifty vols. (Zzumph!) Next word, "Bag—paint, music, clown, girl." The answer is "paint." Four hundred and fifty volts. (Zzumph!) Next word is "Short—sentence, movie. . ."

EXPERIMENTER: Excuse me, Teacher. We'll have to discontinue the experiment.

Morris Braverman, another subject, is a thirty-nine-year-old social worker. He looks older than his years because of his bald head and serious demeanor. His brow is furrowed, as if all the world's burdens were carried on his face. He appears intelligent and concerned.

When the learner refuses to answer and the experimenter instructs Braverman to treat the absence of an answer as equivalent to a wrong answer, he takes his instruction to heart. Before administering 300 volts he asserts officiously to the victim, "Mr. Wallace, your silence has to be considered as a wrong answer." Then he administers the shock. He offers halfheartedly to change places with the learner, then asks the experimenter. "Do I have to follow these instructions literally?" He is satisfied with the experimenter's answer that he does. His very refined and authoritative manner of speaking is increasingly broken up by wheezing laughter.

The experimenter's notes on Mr. Braverman at the last few shocks are:

Almost breaking up now each time gives shock. Rubbing face to hide laughter.

Squinting, trying to hide face with hand, still laughing.

Cannot control his laughter at this point no matter what he does.

Clenching fist, pushing it onto table.

In an interview after the session, Mr. Braverman summarizes the experiment with impressive fluency and intelligence. He feels the experiment may have been designed also to "test the effects on the teacher of being in an essentially sadistic role, as well as the reactions of a student to a learning situation that was authoritative and punitive." When asked how painful the last few shocks administered to the learner were, he indicates that the most extreme category on the scale is not adequate (it read EXTREMELY PAINFUL) and places his mark at the edge of the scale with an arrow carrying it beyond the scale.

In the most relaxed terms, he speaks about his severe inner tension.

It is almost impossible to convey the greatly relaxed, sedate quality of his conversation in the interview. In the most relaxed terms, he speaks about his severe inner tension.

EXPERIMENTER: At what point were you most tense or nervous?

MR. BRAVERMAN: Well, when he first began to cry out in pain, and I realized this was hurting him. This got worse when he just blocked and refused to answer. These was I. I'm a nice person, I think, hurting somebody, and caught up in what seemed a mad situation . . . and in the interest of science, one goes through with it.

When the interviewer pursues the general question of tension, Mr. Braverman spontaneously mentions his laughter.

"My reactions were awfully peculiar. I don't know if you were watching me, but my reactions were giggly, and trying to stifle laughter. This isn't the way I usually am. This was a sheer reaction to a totally impossible situation. And my reaction

was to the situation of having to hurt somebody. And being totally helpless and caught up in a set of circumstances where I just couldn't deviate and I couldn't try to help. This is what got me."

Mr. Braverman, like all subjects, was told the actual nature and purpose of the experiment, and a year later he affirmed in a questionnaire that he had learned something of personal importance: "What appalled me was that I could possess this capacity for obedience and compliance to a central idea, i.e., the value of a memory experiment, even after it became clear that continued adherence to this value was at the expense of violation of another value, i.e., don't hurt someone who is helpless and not hurting you. As my wife said, 'You can call yourself Eichmann.' I hope I deal more effectively with any future conflicts of values I encounter."

One theoretical interpretation of this behavior holds that all people harbor deeply aggressive instincts continually pressing for expression, and that the experiment provides institutional justification for the release of these impulses. According to this view, if a person is placed in a situation in which he has complete power over another individual, whom he may punish as much as he likes, all that is sadistic and bestial in man comes to the fore. The impulse to shock the victim is seen to flow from the potent aggressive tendencies, which are part of the motivational life of the individual, and the experiment, because it provides social legitimacy, simply opens the door to their expression.

It becomes vital, therefore, to compare the subject's performance when he is under orders and when he is allowed to choose the shock level.

The procedure was identical to our standard experiment, except that the teacher was told that he was free to select any shock level on any of the trials. (The experimenter took pains to point out that the teacher could use the highest levels on the generator, the lowest, any in between, or any combination of levels.) Each subject proceeded for thirty critical trials. The learner's protests were coordinated to standard shock levels, his first grunt coming at 75 volts, his first vehement protest at 150 volts.

The average shock used during the thirty critical trials was less than 60 volts—lower than the point at which the victim showed the first signs of discomfort. Three of the forty subjects did not go beyond the very lowest level on the board, twenty-eight went no higher than 75 volts, and thirty-eight did not go beyond the first loud protest at 150 volts. Two subjects provided the exception, administering up to 325 and 450 volts, but the overall result was that the great majority of people delivered very low, usually painless, shocks when the choice was explicitly up to them.

This condition of the experiment undermines another commonly offered explanation of the subjects' behavior—that those who shocked the victim at the most severe levels came only from the sadistic fringe of society. If one considers that almost two-thirds of the participants fall into the category of "obedient" subjects, and that they represented ordinary people drawn from working, managerial, and professional classes, the argument becomes very shaky. Indeed, it is highly reminiscent of the issue that arose in connection with Hannah Arendt's 1963 book, *Eichmann in Jerusalem*. Arendt contended that the prosecution's effort to depict Eichmann as a sadistic monster was fundamentally wrong, that he came closer to being an uninspired bureaucrat who simply sat at his desk and did his job. For asserting her views, Arendt became the object of considerable scorn, even calumny. Somehow, it was felt that the monstrous deeds carried out by Eichmann required a brutal, twisted personality, evil incarnate. After witnessing hundreds of ordinary persons submit to the authority in our own experiments, I must conclude that Arendt's conception of the banality of evil comes closer to the truth than one might dare imagine. The ordinary person who shocked the victim did so out of a sense of obligation—an impression of his duties as a subject—and not from any peculiarly aggressive tendencies.

This is, perhaps, the most fundamental lesson of our study: ordinary people, simply doing their jobs, and without any particular hostility on their part, can become agents in a terrible destructive process. Moreover, even when the destructive effects of their work become patently clear, and they are asked to carry out actions incompatible with fundamental standards of morality, relatively few people have the resources needed to resist authority.

Many of the people were in some sense against what they did to the learner, and many protested even while they obeyed. Some were totally convinced of the wrongness of their actions but could not bring themselves to make an open break with authority. They often derived satisfaction from their thoughts and felt that—within themselves, at least—they had been on the side of the angels. They tried to reduce strain by obeying the experimenter but "only slightly," encouraging the learner, touching the generator switches gingerly. When interviewed, such a subject would stress that he had "asserted my humanity" by administering the briefest shock possible. Handling the conflict in this manner was easier than defiance.

The situation is constructed so that there is no way the subject can stop shocking the learner without violating the experimenter's definitions of his own competence. The subject fears that he will appear arrogant, untoward, and rude if he breaks off. Although these inhibiting emotions appear small in scope alongside the violence being done to the learner, they suffuse the mind and feelings of the subject, who is miserable at the prospect of having to repudiate the authority to his face. (When the experiment was altered so that the experimenter gave his instructions by telephone instead of in person, only a third as many people were fully obedient through 450 volts.) It is a curious thing that a measure of compassion on the part of the subject—an unwillingness to "hurt" the experimenter's feelings—is part of those binding forces inhibiting his disobedience. The withdrawal of such deference may be as painful to the subject as to the authority he defies.

The subjects do not derive satisfaction from inflicting pain, but they often like the feeling they get from pleasing the experimenter. They are proud of doing a good job, obeying the experimenter under difficult circumstances. While the subjects administered only mild shocks, on their own initiative, one experimental variation showed that, under orders, 30 percent of them were willing to deliver 450 volts even when they had to forcibly push the learner's hand down on the electrode.

Bruno Batta is a thirty-seven-year-old welder who took part in the variation requiring the use of force. He was born in New Haven, his parents in Italy. He has a rough-hewn face that conveys a conspicuous lack of alertness. He has some difficulty in mastering the experimental procedure and needs to be corrected by the experimenter several times. He shows appreciation for the help and willingness to do what is required. After the 150-volt level, Batta has to force the learner's hand down on the shock plate, since the learner himself refuses to touch it.

When the learner first complains, Mr. Batta pays no attention to him. His face remains impassive, as if to dissociate himself from the learner's disruptive behavior. When the experimenter instructs him to force the learner's hand down, he adopts a rigid, mechanical procedure. He tests the generator switch. When it fails to function, he immediately forces the learner's hand onto the shock plate. All the while he maintains the same rigid mask. The learner, seated alongside him, begs him to stop, but with robotic impassivity he continues the procedure.

What is extraordinary is his apparent total indifference to the learner; he hardly takes cognizance of him as a human being. Meanwhile, he relates to the experimenter in a submissive and courteous fashion.

At the 330-volt level, the learner refuses not only to touch the shock plate but also to provide any answers. Annoyed, Batta turns to him, and chastises him: "You better answer and get it over with. We can't stay here all night." These are the only words he directs to the learner in the course of an hour. Never again does he speak to him. The scene is brutal and depressing, his hard, impassive face showing total indifference as he subdues the screaming learner and gives him shocks. He seems to derive no pleasure from the act itself, only quiet satisfaction at doing his job properly.

When he administers 450 volts, he turns to the experimenter and asks, "Where do we go from here, Professor?" His tone is deferential and expresses his willingness to be a cooperative subject, in contrast to the learner's obstinacy.

At the end of the session he tells the experimenter how honored he has been to help him, and in a moment of contrition, remarks, "Sir, sorry it couldn't have been a full experiment."

The essence of obedience is that a person comes to view himself as the instrument for carrying out another person's wishes, and he therefore no longer regards himself as responsible for his actions.

He has done his honest best. It is only the deficient behavior of the learner that has denied the experimenter full satisfaction.

The essence of obedience is that a person comes to view himself as the instrument for carrying out another person's wishes, and he therefore no longer regards himself as responsible for his actions. Once this critical shift of viewpoint has occurred, all of the essential features of obedience follow. The most far-reaching consequence is that the person feels responsible to the authority directing him but feels no responsibility for the content of the actions that the authority prescribes. Morality does not disappear—it acquires a radically different focus: the subordinate person feels shame or pride depending on how adequately he has performed the actions called for by authority.

Language provides numerous terms to pinpoint this type of morality: *loyalty, duty, discipline* all are terms heavily saturated with moral meaning and refer to the degree to which a person fulfills his obligations to authority. They refer not to the "goodness" of the person per se but to the adequacy with which a subordinate fulfills his socially defined role. The most frequent defense of the individual who has performed a heinous act under command of authority is that he has simply done his duty. In asserting this defense, the individual is not introducing an alibi concocted for the moment but is reporting honestly on the psychological attitude induced by submission to authority.

For a person to feel responsible for his actions, he must sense that the behavior has flowed from "the self." In the situation we have studied, subjects have precisely the opposite view of their actions—namely, they see them as originating in the motives of some other person. Subjects in the experiment frequently said, "If it were up to me, I would not have administered shocks to the learner."

Once authority has been isolated as the cause of the subject's behavior, it is legitimate to inquire into the necessary elements of authority and how it must be perceived in order to gain his compliance. We conducted some investigations into the kinds of changes that would cause the experimenter to lose his power and to be disobeyed by the subject. Some of the variations revealed that:

- *The experimenter's physical presence has a marked impact on his authority*. As cited earlier, obedience dropped off sharply when orders were given by telephone. The experimenter could often induce a disobedient subject to go on by returning to the laboratory.
- *Conflicting authority severely paralyzes action*. When two experimenters of equal status, both sealed at the command desk, gave incompatible orders, no shocks were delivered past the point of their disagreement.
- *The rebellious action of others severely undermines authority.* In one variation, three teachers (two actors and a real subject) administered a test and shocks. When the two actors disobeyed the experimenter and refused to get beyond a certain shock level, thirty-six of forty subjects joined their disobedient peers and refused as well.

Although the experimenter's authority was fragile in some respects, it is also true that he had almost none of the tools used in ordinary command structures. For example, the experimenter did not threaten the subjects with punishment—such as loss of income, community ostracism, or jail—for failure to obey. Neither could he offer incentives. Indeed, we should expect the experimenter's authority to be much less than that of someone like a general, since the experimenter has no power to enforce his imperatives, and since participation in a psychological experiment scarcely evokes the sense of urgency and dedication found in warfare. Despite these limitations, he still managed to command a dismaying degree of obedience.

I will cite one final variation of the experiment that depicts a dilemma that is more common in everyday life. The subject was not ordered to pull the level that shocked the victim, but merely to perform a subsidiary task (administering the word-pair test) while another person administered the shock. In this situation, thirty-seven of forty adults continued to the highest level on the shock generator. Predictably, they excused their behavior by saying that the responsibility belong to the man who actually pulled the switch. This may illustrate a dangerously typical arrangement in a complex society: it is easy to ignore responsibility when one is only an intermediate link in a chain of action.

The problem of obedience is not wholly psychological. The form and shape of society and the way it is developing have much to do with it. There was a time, perhaps, when people were able to give a fully human response to any situation because they were fully absorbed in it as human beings. But as soon as there was a division of labor things changed. Beyond a certain point, the breaking up of society into people carrying out narrow and very special jobs takes away from the human quality of work and life. A person does not get to see the whole situation but only a small part of it, and is thus unable to act without some kind of overall direction. He yields to authority but in doing so is alienated from his own actions.

Even Eichmann was sickened when he toured the concentration camps, but he had only to sit at a desk and shuffle papers. At the same time the man in the camp who actually dropped Cyclon-b into the gas chambers was able to justify *his* behavior on the ground that he was only following orders from above. Thus there is a fragmentation of the total human act; no one is confronted with the consequences of his decision to carry out the evil act. The person who assumes responsibility has evaporated. Perhaps this is the most common characteristic of socially organized evil in modern society.

Notes

[1] The patriarch Abraham, commanded by God to sacrifice his son Isaac, is ready to do so until an angel stays his knife.

[2] In Plato's *Apology* the philosopher Socrates provokes and accepts the sentence of death rather than belie his conscience; the heroine of Sophocles' *Antigone* risks such a sentence in order to give her brother proper burial.

[3] The ethical problems of carrying out an experiment of this sort are too complex to be dealt with here, but they receive extended treatment in the book from which this article is adapted [Milgram's note]. The book is *Obedience to Authority* (New York: Harper and Row, 1974).

[4] Names of subjects described in this *piece* have been changed [Milgram's note].

"Why Should My Conscience Bother Me?"

The Aircraft Brake Scandal

Kermit Vandivier

From *In the Name of Profit*, ed. Robert Heilbroner et al. (New York: Doubleday, 1972), 3–31. Copyright © 1972.

The B. F. Goodrich Co. is what business magazines like to speak of as "a major American corporation." It has operations in a dozen states and as many foreign countries, and of these far-flung facilities, the Goodrich plant at Troy, Ohio, is not the most imposing. It is a small, one-story building, once used to manufacture airplanes. Set in the grassy flatlands of west-central Ohio, it employs only about six hundred people. Nevertheless, it is one of the three largest manufacturers of aircraft wheels and brakes, a leader in a most profitable industry. Goodrich wheels and brakes support such well-known planes as the F111, the C5A, the Boeing 727, the XB70 and many others. Its customers include almost every aircraft manufacturer in the world.

Contracts for aircraft wheels and brakes often run into millions of dollars, and ordinarily a contract with a total value of less than $70,000, though welcome, would not create any special stir of joy in the hearts of Goodrich sales personnel.

But purchase order P-23718, issued on June 18, 1967, by the LTV Aerospace Corporation, and ordering 202 brake assemblies for a new Air Force plane at a total price of $69,417, was received by Goodrich with considerable glee. And there was good reason. Some ten years previously, Goodrich had built a brake for LTV that was, to say the least, considerably less than a rousing success. The brake had not lived up to Goodrich's promises, and after experiencing considerable difficulty, LTV had written off Goodrich as a source of brakes. Since that time, Goodrich salesmen had been unable to sell so much as a shot of brake fluid to LTV. So in 1967, when LTV requested bids on wheels and brakes for the new A7D light attack aircraft it proposed to build for the Air Force, Goodrich submitted a bid that was absurdly low, so low that LTV could not, in all prudence, turn it down.

Goodrich had, in industry parlance, "bought into the business." Not only did the company not

expect to make a profit on the deal; it was prepared, if necessary, to lose money. For aircraft
brakes are not something that can be ordered off
the shelf. They are designed for a particular aircraft, and once an aircraft manufacturer buys a
brake, he is forced to purchase all replacement
parts from the brake manufacturer. The $70,000
that Goodrich would get for making the brake
would be a drop in the bucket when compared
with the cost of the linings and other parts the Air
Force would have to buy from Goodrich during
the lifetime of the aircraft. Furthermore, the company which manufactures brakes for one particular model of an aircraft quite naturally has the
inside track to supply other brakes when the
planes are updated and improved.

Thus, that first contract, regardless of the
money involved, is very important, and Goodrich,
when it learned that it had been awarded the A7D
contract, was determined that while it may have
slammed the door on its own foot ten years
before, this time, the second time around, things
would be different. The word was soon circulated
throughout the plant: "We can't bungle it this
time. We've got to give them a good brake, regardless of the cost."

There was another factor which had undoubtedly influenced LTV. All aircraft brakes made
today are of the disk type, and the bid submitted
by Goodrich called for a relatively small brake,
one containing four disks and weighting only 106
ponds. The weight of any aircraft part is extremely
important. The lighter a part is, the heavier the
plane's payload can be. The four-rotor, 106-pound
brake promised by Goodrich was about as light as
could be expected, and this undoubtedly had
helped move LTV to award the contract to
Goodrich.

The brake was designed by one of Goodrich's
most capable engineers, John Warren. A tall, lanky
blond and a graduate of Purdue, Warren had come
from the Chrysler Corporation seven years before
and had become adept at aircraft brake design. The
happy-go-lucky manner he usually maintained
belied a temper which exploded whenever anyone
ventured to offer any criticism of his work, no
matter how small. On these occasions, Warren

would turn red in the face, often throwing or slam-
ming something and then stalking from the scene.
As his coworkers learned the consequences of criticizing him, they did so less and less readily, and
when he submitted his preliminary design for the
A7D brake, it was accepted without question.

Warren was named project engineer for the
A7D, and he, in turn, assigned the task of producing the final production design to a newcomer to
the Goodrich engineering stable, Searle Lawson.
Just turned twenty-six, Lawson had been out of
the Northrup Institute of Technology only one
year when he came to Goodrich in January 1967.
Like Warren, he had worked for a while in the
automotive industry, but his engineering degree
was in aeronautical and astronautical sciences, and
when the opportunity came to enter his special
field, via Goodrich, he took it. At the Troy plant,
Lawson had been assigned to various "paper projects" to break him in, and after several months
spent reviewing statistics and old brake designs, he
was beginning to fret at the lack of challenge.
When told he was being assigned to his first "real"
project, he was elated and immediately plunged
into his work.

The major portion of the design had already
been completed by Warren, and major assemblies
for the brake had already been ordered form
Goodrich suppliers. Naturally, however, before
Goodrich could start making the brakes on a production basis, much testing would have to be done.
Lawson would have to determine the best materials to use for the linings and discover what minor
adjustments in the design would have to be made.

Then, after the preliminary testing and after
the brake was judged ready for production, one
whole brake assembly would undergo a series of
grueling, simulated braking stops and other severe
trials called qualification tests. These tests are
required by the military, which gives very detailed
specifications on how they are to be conducted,
the criteria for failure, and so on. They are performed in the Goodrich plant's test laboratory,
where huge machines called dynamometers can
simulate the weight and speed of almost any aircraft. After the brakes pass the laboratory tests,
they are approved for production, but before the

brakes are accepted for use in military service, they must undergo further extensive flight tests.

Searle Lawson was well aware that much work had to be done before the A7D brake could go into production, and he knew that LTV had set the last two weeks in June, 1968, as the starting dates for flight tests. So he decided to begin testing immediately. Goodrich's suppliers had not yet delivered the break housing and other parts, but the brake disks had arrived, and using the housing from a brake similar in size and weight to the A7D brake, Lawson built a prototype. The prototype was installed in a test wheel and placed on one of the big dynamometers in the plant's test laboratory. The dynamometer was adjusted to simulate the weight of the A7D and Lawson began a series of tests, "landing" the wheel and brake at the A7D's landing speed, and braking it to a stop. The main purpose of these preliminary tests was to learn what temperatures would develop within the brake during the simulated stops and to evaluate the lining materials tentatively selected for use.

During a normal aircraft landing the temperatures inside the brake may reach 1000 degrees, and occasionally a bit higher. During Lawson's first simulated landings, the temperature of his prototype brake reached 1500 degrees. The brake glowed a bright cherry-red and threw off incandescent particles of metal and lining material as the temperature reached its peak. After a few such stops, the brake was dismantled and the linings were found to be almost completely disintegrated. Lawson chalked this first failure up to chance and, ordering new lining materials, tried again.

The second attempt was a repeat of the first. The brake became extremely hot, causing the lining materials to crumble into dust.

After the third such failure, Lawson, inexperienced though he was, knew that the fault lay not in defective parts or unsuitable lining material but in the basic design of the brake itself. Ignoring Warren's original computations, Lawson made his own, and it didn't take him long to discover where the trouble lay—the brake was too small. There simply was not enough surface area on the disks to stop the aircraft without generating the excessive heat that caused the linings to fail.

The answer to the problem was obvious but far from simple—the four-disk brake would have to be scrapped, and a new design, using five disks, would have to be developed. The implications were not lost on Lawson. Such a step would require the junking of all the four-disk-brake sub-assemblies, many of which had now begun to arrive from the various suppliers. It would also mean several weeks of preliminary design and testing and many more weeks of waiting while the suppliers made and delivered the new sub-assemblies.

After the third such failure, he knew that the fault lay not in defective parts or unsuitable lining material but in the basic design of the brake itself.

Yet, several weeks had already gone by since LTV's order had arrived, and the date for delivery of the first production brakes for flight testing was only a few months away.

Although project engineer John Warren had more or less turned the A7D over to Lawson, he knew of the difficulties Lawson had been experiencing. He had assured the young engineer that the problem revolved around getting the right kind of lining material. Once that was found, he said, the difficulties would end.

Despite the evidence of the abortive tests and Lawson's careful computations, Warren rejected the suggestion that the four-disk brake was too light for the job. Warren knew that his superior had already told LTV, in rather glowing terms, that the preliminary tests on the A7D brake were very successful. Indeed, Warren's superiors weren't aware at this time of the troubles on the brake. It would have been difficult for Warren to admit not only that he had made a serious error in his calculations and original design but that his mistakes had been caught by a green kid, barely out of college.

Warren's reaction to a five-disk brake was not unexpected by Lawson, and, seeing that the four-disk brake was not to be abandoned so easily, he took his calculations and dismal test results one step up the corporate ladder.

At Goodrich, the man who supervises the engineers working on projects slated for production is called, predictably, the projects manager. The job was held by a short, chubby and bald man named Robert Sink. A man truly devoted to his work, Sink was as likely to be found at his desk at ten o'clock on Sunday night as ten o'clock on Monday morning. His outside interests consisted mainly of tinkering on a Model-A Ford and an occasional game of golf. Some fifteen years before, Sink had begun working at Goodrich as a lowly draftsman. Slowly, he worked his way up. Despite his geniality, Sink was neither respected nor liked by the majority of the engineers, and his appointment as their supervisor did not improve their feelings about him. They thought he had only gone to high school. It quite naturally rankled those who had gone through years of college and acquired impressive specialties such as thermodynamics and astronautics to be commanded by a man whom they considered their intellectual inferior. But, though Sink had no college training, he had something even more useful: a fine working knowledge of company politics.

Puffing upon a Meerschaum pipe, Sink listened gravely as young Lawson confided his fears about the four-disk brake. Then he examined Lawson's calculations and the results of the abortive tests. Despite the fact that he was not a qualified engineer, in the strictest sense of the word, it must certainly have been obvious to Sink that Lawson's calculations were correct and that a four-disk brake would never have worked on the A7D.

But other things of equal importance were also obvious. First, to concede that Lawson's calculations were correct would also mean conceding that Warren's calculations were incorrect. As projects manager, he not only was responsible for Warren's activities, but, in admitting that Warren had erred, he would have to admit that he had erred in trusting Warren's judgment. It also meant that, as projects manager, it would be he who would have to explain the whole messy situation to the Goodrich hierarchy, not only at Troy but possibly on the corporate level at Goodrich's Akron offices. And, having taken Warren's judgment of the four-disk brake at face value (he was

forced to do this since, not being an engineer, he was unable to exercise any engineering judgment of his own), he had assured LTV, not once but several times, that about all there was left to do on the brake was pack it in a crate and ship it out the back door.

There's really no problem at all, he told Lawson. After all, Warren was an experienced engineer, and if he said the brake would work, it would work. Just keep on testing and probably, maybe even on the very next try, it'll work out just fine.

Lawson was far from convinced, but without the support of his superiors there was little he could do except keep on testing. By now, housings for the four-disk brake had begun to arrive at the plant, and Lawson was able to build up a production model of the brake and begin the formal qualification tests demanded by the military.

The first qualification attempts went exactly as the tests on the prototype had. Terrific heat developed within the brakes and, after a few, short, simulated stops, the linings crumbled. A new type of lining material was ordered and once again an attempt to qualify the brake was made. Again, failure.

Experts were called in from lining manufacturers, and new lining "mixes" were tried, always with the same result. Failure.

It was now the last week in March 1968, and flight tests were scheduled to begin in seventy days. Twelve separate attempts had been made to formally qualify the brake, and all had failed. It was no longer possible for anyone to ignore the glaring truth that the brake was a dismal failure and that nothing short of a major design change could ever make it work.

In the engineering department, panic set in.

In the engineering department, panic set in. A glum-faced Lawson prowled the test laboratory dejectedly. Occasionally, Warren would witness some simulated stop on the brake and, after it was completed, troop silently back to his desk. Sink, too, showed an unusual interest in the trials, and he and Warren would converse in low tones while poring over the results of the latest tests. Even the most inexperienced of the lab technicians and the men who operated the testing equipment knew they had a "bad" brake on their hands, and there was some grumbling about "wasting time on a brake that won't work."

New menaces appeared. An engineering team from LTV arrived at the plant to get a good look at the brake in action. Luckily, they stayed only a few days, and Goodrich engineers managed to cover the true situation without too much difficulty.

On April 4, the thirteenth attempt at qualification was begun. This time no attempt was made to conduct the tests by the methods and techniques spelled out in the military specifications. Regardless of how it had to be done, the brake was to be "nursed" through the required fifty simulated stops.

Fans were set up to provide special cooling. Instead of maintaining pressure on the brake until the test wheel had come to a complete stop, the pressure was reduced when the wheel had decelerated to around 15 mph, allowing it to "coast" to a stop. After each stop, the brake was disassembled and carefully cleaned, and after some of the stops, internal brake parts were machined in order to remove warp and other disfigurations caused by the high heat.

By these and other methods, all clearly contrary to the techniques established by the military specifications, the brake was coaxed through the fifty stops. But even using these methods, the brake could not meet all the requirements. On one stop the wheel rolled for a distance of 16,000 feet, nearly three miles, before the brake could bring it to a stop. The normal distance required for such a stop was around 3,500 feet.

On April 11, the day the thirteenth test was completed, I became personally involved in the A7D situation.

I had worked in the Goodrich test laboratory for five years, starting first as an instrumentation engineer, then later becoming a data analyst and technical writer. As part of my duties, I analyzed the reams and reams of instrumentation data that came from the many testing machines in the laboratory, then transcribed it to a more usable form for the engineering department. And when a new-type brake had successfully completed the required qualification tests, I would issue a formal qualification report.

Qualification reports were an accumulation of all the data and test logs compiled by the test technicians during the qualification tests, and were documentary proof that a brake had met all the requirements established by the military specifications and was therefore presumed safe for flight testing. Before actual flight tests were conducted on a brake, qualification reports had to be delivered to the customer and to various government officials.

On April 11, I was looking over the data from the latest A7D test, and I noticed that many irregularities in testing methods had been noted on the test logs.

Technically, of course, there was nothing wrong with conducting tests in any manner desired, so long as the test was for research purposes only. But qualification test methods are clearly delineated by the military, and I knew that this test had been a formal qualification attempt. One particular notation on the test logs caught my eye. For some of the stops, the instrument which recorded the brake pressure had been deliberately miscalibrated so that, while the brake pressure used during the stops was recorded as 1000 psi (the maximum pressure that would be available on the A7D aircraft), the pressure had actually been 100 psi!

I showed the test logs to the test lab supervisor, Ralph Gretzinger, who said he had learned from the technician who had miscalibrated the instrument that he had been asked to do so by Lawson. Lawson, said Gretzinger, readily admitted asking for the miscalibration, saying he had been told to do so by Sink.

I asked Gretzinger why anyone would want to miscalibrate the data-recording instruments.

"Why? I'll tell you why," he snorted. "That brake is a failure. It's way too small for the job, and they're not ever going to get it to work. They're getting desperate, and instead of scrapping the _____ thing and starting over, they figure they can horse around down here in the lab and qualify it that way."

An expert engineer, Gretzinger had been responsible for several innovations in brake design. It was he who had invented the unique brake system used on the famous XB70. A graduate of Georgia Tech, he was a stickler for detail and he had some very firm ideas about honesty and ethics. "If you want to find out what's going on," said Gretzinger, "ask Lawson, he'll tell you."

Curious, I did ask Lawson the next time he came into the lab. He seemed eager to discuss the A7D and gave me the history of his months of frustrating efforts to get Warren and Sink to change the brake design. "I just can't believe this is really happening," said Lawson, shaking his head slowly. "This isn't engineering, at least not what I thought it would be. Back in school, I thought that when you were an engineer, you tried to do your best, no matter what it cost. But this is something else."

He sat across the desk from me, his chin propped in his hand. "Just wait," he warned. "You'll get a chance to see what I'm talking about. You're going to get in the act, too, because I've already had the word that we're going to make one more attempt to qualify the brake, and that's it. Win or lose, we're going to issue a qualification report!"

I reminded him that a qualification report could only be issued after a brake had successfully met all military requirements, and therefore, unless the next qualification attempt was a success, no report would be issued.

"You'll find out," retorted Lawson. "I was already told that regardless of what the brake does on the test, it's going to be qualified." He said he had been told in those exact words at a conference with Sink and Russell Van Horn.

This was the first indication that Sink had brought his boss, Van Horn, into the mess. Although Van Horn, as manager of the design engineering section, was responsible for the entire department, he was not necessarily familiar with all phases of every project, and it was not uncommon for those under him to exercise the what-he-doesn't-know-won't-hurt-him philosophy. If he

was aware of the full extent of the A7D situation, it meant that matters had truly reached a desperate stage—that Sink had decided not only to call for help but was looking toward that moment when blame must be borne and, if possible, shared.

Also, if Van Horn had said, "regardless what the brake does on test, it's going to be qualified," then it could only mean that, if necessary, a false qualification report would be issued! I discussed this possibility with Gretzinger, and he assured me that under no circumstances would such a report ever be issued.

"If they want a qualification report, we'll write them one, but we'll tell it just like it is," he declared emphatically. "No false data or false reports are going to come out of this lab."

On May 2, 1968, the fourteenth and final attempt to qualify the brake was begun. Although the same improper methods used to nurse the brake through the previous tests were employed, it soon became obvious that this too would end in failure.

When the tests were about half completed, Lawson asked if I would start preparing the various engineering curves and graphic displays which were normally incorporated in a qualification report. "It looks as though you'll be writing a qualification report shortly," he said.

I flatly refused to have anything to do with the matter and immediately told Gretzinger what I had been asked to do. He was furious and repeated his previous declaration that under no circumstances would any false data or other matter be issued from the lab.

"I'm going to get this settled right now, once and for all," he declared. "I'm going to see Line [Russell Line, manager of the Goodrich Technical Services Section, of which the test lab was part] and find out just how far this thing is going to go!" He stormed out of the room.

In about an hour, he returned and called me to his desk. He sat silently for a few moments, then muttered, half to himself, "I wonder what the hell they'd do if I just quit?" I didn't answer and I didn't ask him what he meant. I knew. He had been beaten down. He had reached the point when the decision had to be made. Defy them now while there was still time—or knuckle under, sell out.

"You know," he went on uncertainly, looking down at his desk, "I've been an engineer for a long time, and I've always believed that ethics and integrity were every bit as important as theorems and formulas, and never once has anything happened to change my beliefs. Now this . . . Hell, I've got two sons I've got to put through school and I just . . ." His voice trailed off.

> *He didn't believe what he was saying, and he knew I didn't believe it either. It was an embarrassing and shameful moment for both of us.*

He sat for a few more minutes, then, looking over the top of his glasses, said hoarsely, "Well, it looks like we're licked. The way it stands now, we're to go ahead and prepare the data and other things for the graphic presentation in the report, and when we're finished, someone upstairs will actually write the report.

"After all," he continued, "we're just drawing some curves, and what happens to them after they leave here, well, we're not responsible for that."

He was trying to persuade himself that as long as we were concerned with only one part of the puzzle and didn't see the completed picture, we really weren't doing anything wrong. He didn't believe what he was saying, and he knew I didn't believe it either. It was an embarrassing and shameful moment for both of us.

I wasn't at all satisfied with the situation and decided that I too would discuss the matter with Russell Line, the senior executive in our section.

Tall, powerfully built, his teeth flashing white, his face tanned to a coffee-brown by a daily stint with a sun lamp, Line looked and acted every inch the executive. He was a crossword-puzzle enthusiast and an ardent golfer, and though he had lived in Troy only a short time, he had been accepted into the Troy Country Club and made an official of the golf committee. He had been transferred

from the Akron offices some two years previously, and an air of mystery surrounded him. Some office gossips figured he had been sent to Troy as the result of some sort of demotion. Others speculated that since the present general manager of the Troy plant was due shortly for retirement, Line had been transferred to Troy to assume that job and was merely occupying his present position to "get the feel of things." Whatever the case, he commanded great respect and had come to be well liked by those of us who worked under him.

He listened sympathetically while I explained how I felt about the A7D situation, and when I had finished, he asked me what I wanted him to do about it. I said that as employees of the Goodrich Company we had a responsibility to protect the company and its reputation if at all possible. I said I was certain that officers on the corporate level would never knowingly allow such tactics as had been employed on the A7D.

"I agree with you," he remarked, "but I still want to know what you want me to do about it."

I suggested that in all probability the chief engineer at the Troy plant, H. C. "Bud" Sunderman, was unaware of the A7D problem and that he, Line, should tell him what was going on.

Line laughed, good-humoredly. "Sure, I could, but I'm not going to. Bud probably already knows about this thing anyway, and if he doesn't, I'm sure not going to be the one to tell him."

"But why?"

"Because it's none of my business, and it's none of yours. I learned a long time ago not to worry about things over which I had no control. I have no control over this."

I wasn't satisfied with this answer, and I asked him if his conscience wouldn't bother him if, say, during flight tests on the brake, something should happen resulting in death or injury to the test pilot.

"Look," he said, becoming somewhat exasperated, "I just told you I have no control over this thing. Why should my conscience bother me?"

His voice took on a quiet, soothing tone as he continued. "You're just getting all upset over this thing for nothing. I just do as I'm told, and I'd advise you to do the same."

He had made his decision, and now I had to make mine.

I made no attempt to rationalize what I had been asked to do. It made no difference who would falsify which part of the report or whether the actual falsification would be by misleading numbers or misleading words. Whether by acts of commission or omission, all of us who contributed to the fraud would be guilty. The only question left for me to decide was whether or not I would become a party to the fraud.

Before coming to Goodrich in 1963, I had held a variety of jobs, each a little more pleasant, a little more rewarding than the last. At forty-two, with seven children, I had decided that the Goodrich Company would probably be my "home" for the rest of my working life. The job paid well, it was pleasant and challenging, and the future looked reasonably bright. My wife and I had bought a home and we were ready to settle down into a comfortable, middle-age, middle-class rut. If I refused to take part in the A7D fraud, I would have to either resign or be fired. The report would be written by someone anyway, but I would have the satisfaction of knowing I had had no part in the matter. But bills aren't paid with personal satisfaction, nor house payments with ethical principles. I made my decision. The next morning, I telephoned Lawson and told him I was ready to begin on the qualification report.

In a few minutes, he was at my desk, ready to begin. Before we started, I asked him, "Do you realize what we are going to do?"

"Yeah," he replied bitterly, "we're going to screw LTV. And speaking of screwing," he continued, "I know now how a whore feels, because that's exactly what I've become, an engineering whore. I've sold myself. It's all I can do to look at myself in the mirror when I shave. I make me sick."

I was surprised at his vehemence. It was obvious that he too had done his share of soul-searching and didn't like what he had found. Somehow, though, the air seemed clearer after his outburst, and we began working on the report.

I had written dozens of qualification reports, and I knew what a "good" one looked like. Resorting to the actual test data only on occasion, Lawson and I proceeded to prepare page after page of elaborate, detailed engineering curves, charts, and test logs, which purported to show what had happened during the formal qualification tests. Where temperatures were too high, we deliberately chopped them down a few hundred degrees, and where they were too low, we raised them to a value that would appear reasonable to the LTV and military engineers. Brake pressure, torque values, distances, times—everything of consequence was tailored to fit the occasion.

Occasionally, we would find that some test either hadn't been performed at all or had been conducted improperly. On those occasions, we "conducted" the test—successfully, of course—on paper.

For nearly a month we worked on the graphic presentation that would be a part of the report. Meanwhile, the fourteenth and final qualification attempt had been completed, and the brake, not unexpectedly, had failed again.

During that month, Lawson and I talked of little else except the enormity of what we were doing. The more involved we became in our work, the more apparent became our own culpability. We discussed such things as the Nuremberg trials and how they related to our guilt and complicity in the A7D situation. Lawson often expressed his opinion that the brake was downright dangerous and that, once on flight tests, "anything is liable to happen."

I saw his boss, John Warren, at least twice during that month and needled him about what we were doing. He didn't take the jibes too kindly but managed to laugh the situation off as "one of those things." One day I remarked that what we were doing amounted to fraud, and he pulled out an engineering handbook and turned to a section on laws as they related to the engineering profession.

He read the definition of fraud aloud, then said, "Well, technically I don't think what we're doing can be called fraud. I'll admit it's not right, but it's just one of those things. We're just kinda caught in the middle. About all I can tell you is, Do like I'm doing, make copies of everything and put them in your SYA file."

"What's an 'SYA' file?" I asked.

"That's a 'save your _____' file." He laughed.

Although I hadn't known it was called that, I had been keeping an SYA file since the beginning of the A7D fiasco. I had made a copy of every scrap of paper connected even remotely with the A7D and had even had copies of 16mm movies that had been made during some of the simulated stops. Lawson, too, had an SYA file, and we both maintained them for one reason: Should the true state of events on the A7D ever be questioned, we wanted to have access to a complete set of factual data. We were afraid that should the question ever come up, the test data might accidentally be "lost."

We finished our work on the graphic portion of the report around the first of June. Altogether, we had prepared nearly two hundred pages of data, containing dozens of deliberate falsifications and misrepresentations. I delivered the data to Gretzinger, who said he had been instructed to deliver it personally to the chief engineer, Bud Sunderman, who in turn would assign someone in the engineering department to complete the written portion of the report. He gathered the bundle of data and left the office. Within minutes, he was back with the data, his face white with anger.

"That _____ Sink's beat me to it," he said furiously. "He's already talked to Bud about this, and now Sunderman says no one in the engineering department has time to write the report. He wants us to do it, and I told him we couldn't."

The words had barely left his mouth when Russell Line burst in the door. "What the hell's all the fuss about this _____ report?" he demanded loudly.

Patiently, Gretzinger explained. "There's no fuss. Sunderman just told me that we'd have to write the report down here, and I said we couldn't. Russ," he went on, "I've told you before that we weren't going to write the report. I made my position clear on that a long time ago."

Line shut him up with a wave of his hand and, turning to me, bellowed, "I'm getting sick and tired of hearing about this _____ report. Now, write the _____ thing and shut up about it!" He slammed out of the office.

Gretzinger and I just sat for a few seconds looking at each other. Then he spoke.

"Well, I guess he's made it pretty clear, hasn't he? We can either write the thing or quit. You know, what we should have done was quit a long time ago. Now, it's too late."

All the time we were working on the report, I felt, deep down, that somewhere, somehow, something would come along and the whole thing would blow over.

Somehow, I wasn't at all surprised at this turn of events, and it didn't really make that much difference. As far as I was concerned, we were all up to our necks in the thing anyway, and writing the narrative portion of the report couldn't make me any more guilty than I already felt myself to be.

Still, Line's order came as something of a shock. All the time Lawson and I were working on the report, I felt, deep down, that somewhere, somehow, something would come along and the whole thing would blow over. But Russell Line had crushed that hope. The report was actually going to be issued. Intelligent, law-abiding officials of B. F. Goodrich, one of the oldest and most respected of American corporations, were actually going to deliver to a customer a product that was known to be defective and dangerous and which could very possibly cause death or serious injury.

Within two days, I had completed the narrative, or written portion of the report. As a final sop to my own self-respect, in the conclusion of the report I wrote, "The B. F. Goodrich P/N 2-1162-3 brake assembly does not meet the intent or the requirements of the applicable specification documents and therefore is not qualified."

This was a meaningless gesture, since I knew that this would certainly be changed when the report went through the final typing process. Sure enough, when the report was published, the negative conclusion had been made positive.

One final and significant incident occurred just before publication.

Qualification reports always bear the signature of the person who has prepared them. I refused to sign the report, as did Lawson. Warren was later asked to sign the report. He replied that he would "when I receive a signed statement from Bob Sink ordering me to sign it."

The engineering secretary who was delegated the responsibility of "dogging" the report through publication told me later that after I, Lawson, and Warren had all refused to sign the report, she had asked Sink if he would sign. He replied, "On something of this nature, I don't think a signature is really needed."

On June 5, 1968, the report was officially published and copies were delivered in person to the Air Force and LTV. Within a week, flight tests were begun at Edwards Air Force Base in California. Searle Lawson was sent to California as Goodrich's representative. Within approximately two weeks, he returned because some rather unusual incidents during the tests had caused them to be canceled.

His face was grim as he related stories of several near crashes during landings—caused by brake troubles. He told me about one incident in which, upon landing, one brake was literally welded together by the intense heat developed during the test stop. The wheel locked, and the plane skidded for nearly 1500 feet before coming to a halt. The plane was jacked up and the wheel removed. The fused parts within the brake had to be pried apart.

Lawson had returned to Troy from California that same day, and that evening, he and others of the Goodrich engineering department left for Dallas for a high-level conference with LTV.

That evening I left work early and went to see my attorney. After I told him the story, he advised that, while I was probably not actually guilty of fraud, I was certainly part of a conspiracy to defraud. He advised me to go to the Federal Bureau of Investigation and offered to arrange an appointment. The following week he took me to the Dayton office of the FBI, and after I had been warned that I would not be immune from prosecution, I disclosed the A7D matter to one of the agents. The agent told me to say nothing about the episode to anyone and to report any further incident to him. He said he would forward the story to his superiors in Washington.

A few days later, Lawson returned from the conference in Dallas and said that the Air Force, which had previously approved the qualification report, had suddenly rescinded that approval and was demanding to see some of the raw test data taken during the tests. I gathered that the FBI had passed the word.

Omitting any reference to the FBI, I told Lawson I had been to an attorney and that we were probably guilty of conspiracy.

"Can you get me an appointment with your attorney?" he asked. Within a week, he had been to the FBI and told them of his part in the mess. He too was advised to say nothing but to keep on the job, reporting any new development.

Naturally, with the rescinding of Air Force approval and the demand to see raw test data, Goodrich officials were in a panic. A conference was called for July 27, a Saturday morning affair at which Lawson, Sink, Warren and myself were present. We met in a tiny conference room in the deserted engineering department. Lawson and I, by now openly hostile to Warren and Sink, ranged ourselves on one side of the conference table while Warren sat on the other side. Sink, chairing the meeting, paced slowly in front of a blackboard, puffing furiously on a pipe.

The meeting was called, Sink began, "to see where we stand on the A7D." What we were going to do, he said, was to "level" with LTV and tell them the "whole truth" about the A7D. "After all," he said, "they're in this thing with us, and they have the right to know how matters stand."

"In other words," I asked, "we're going to tell them the truth?"

"That's right," he replied. "We're going to level with them and let them handle the ball from there."

"There's one thing I don't quite understand," I interjected. "Isn't it going to be pretty hard for us to admit to them that we've lied?"

"Now, wait a minute," he said angrily. "Let's don't go off half-cocked on this thing. It's not a matter of lying. We've just interpreted the information the way we felt it should be."

"I don't know what you call it," I replied, "but to me it's lying, and it's going to be _____ hard to confess to them that we've been lying all along."

He became very agitated at this and repeated his "We're not lying," adding, "I don't like this sort of talk."

I dropped the matter at this point, and he began discussing the various discrepancies in the report.

We broke for lunch, and afterward, I came back to the plant to find Sink sitting alone at his desk, waiting to resume the meeting. He called me over and said he wanted to apologize for his outburst that morning. "This thing has kind of gotten me down," he confessed, "and I think you've got the wrong picture. I don't think you really understand everything about this."

Perhaps so, I conceded, but it seemed to me that if we had already told LTV one thing and then had to tell them another, changing our story completely, we would have to admit we were lying.

"No," he explained patiently, "we're not really lying. All we were doing was interpreting the figures the way we knew they should be. We were just exercising engineering license."

During the afternoon session, we marked some forty-three discrepant points in the report: forty-three points that LTV would surely spot as occasions where we had exercised "engineering license."

After Sink listed those points on the blackboard, we discussed each one individually. As each point came up, Sink would explain that it was probably "too minor to bother about," or that perhaps it "wouldn't be wise to open that can of worms," or that maybe this was a point that "LTV just wouldn't understand." When the meeting was over, it had been decided that only three points were "worth mentioning."

Similar conferences were held during August and September, and the summer was punctuated with frequent treks between Dallas and Troy, and demands by the Air Force to see the raw test data. Tempers were short and matters seemed to grow worse.

Finally, early in October 1968, Lawson submitted his resignation, to take effect on October 25. On October 18, I submitted my own resignation, to take effect on November 1. In my resignation, addressed to Russell Line, I cited the A7D report and stated: "As you are aware, this report

contained numerous deliberate and willful misrepresentations which, according to legal counsel, constitute fraud and expose both myself and others to criminal charges of conspiracy to defraud. . . . The events of the past seven months have created an atmosphere of deceit and distrust in which it is impossible to work. . . ."

"The events of the past seven months have created an atmosphere of deceit and distrust in which it is impossible to work."

On October 25, I received a sharp summons to the office of Bud Sunderman. As chief engineer at the Troy plant, Sunderman was responsible for the entire engineering division. Tall and graying, impeccably dressed at all times, he was capable of producing a dazzling smile or a hearty chuckle or immobilizing his face into marble hardness, as the occasion required.

I faced the marble hardness when I reached his office. He motioned me to a chair. "I have your resignation here," he snapped, "and I must say you have made some rather shocking, I might even say irresponsible, charges. This is very serious."

Before I could reply, he was demanding an explanation. "I want to know exactly what the fraud is in connection with the A7D and how you can dare accuse this company of such a thing!"

I started to tell some of the things that had happened during the testing, but he shut me off saying, "There's nothing wrong with anything we've done here. You aren't aware of all the things that have been going on behind the scenes. If you had known the true situation, you would never have made these charges." He said that in view of my apparent "disloyalty" he had decided to accept my resignation "right now," and said it would be better for all concerned if I left the plant immediately. As I got up to leave he asked me if I intended to "carry this thing further."

I answered simply, "Yes," to which he replied, "Suit yourself." Within twenty minutes, I had cleaned out my desk and left. Forty-eight hours later, the B. F. Goodrich Company recalled the qualification report and the four-disk brake, announcing that it would replace the brake with a new, improved, five-disk brake at no cost to LTV.

Ten months later, on August 13, 1969, I was the chief government witness at a hearing conducted before Senator William Proxmire's Economy in Government Subcommittee of the Congress's Joint Economic Committee. I related the A7D story to the committee, and my testimony was supported by Searle Lawson, who followed me to the witness stand. Air Force officers also testified, as well as a four-man team from the General Accounting Office, which had conducted an investigation of the A7D brake at the request of Senator Proxmire. Both Air Force and GAO investigators declared that the brake was dangerous and had not been tested properly.

Testifying for Goodrich was R. G. Jeter, vice-president and general counsel of the company, from the Akron headquarters. Representing the Troy plant was Robert Sink. These two denied any wrongdoing on the part of the Goodrich Company, despite expert testimony to the contrary by Air Force and GAO officials. Sink was quick to deny any connection with the writing of the report or of directing any falsifications, claiming to be on the West Coast at the time. John Warren was the man who supervised its writing, said Sink.

As for me, I was dismissed as a high-school graduate with no technical training, while Sink testified that Lawson was a young, inexperienced engineer. "We tried to give him guidance," Sink testified, "but he preferred to have his own convictions."

About changing the data and figures in the report, Sink said: "When you take data from several different sources, you have to rationalize among those data what is the true story. This is part of your engineering know-how." He admitted that changes had been made in the data, "but only to make them more consistent with the over-all picture of the data that is available."

Jeter pooh-poohed the suggestion that anything improper occurred, saying: "We have thirty-odd engineers at this plant . . . and I say to you that it is incredible that these men would stand idly by and see reports changed or falsified. . . . I mean you just do not have to do that working for anybody. . . . Just nobody does that."

The four-hour hearing adjourned with no real conclusion reached by the committee. But, the following day the Department of Defense made sweeping changes in its inspection, testing and reporting procedures. A spokesman for the DOD said the changes were a result of the Goodrich episode.

————————

The A7D is now in service, sporting a Goodrich-made five-disk brake, a brake that works very well, I'm told. Business at the Goodrich plant is good. Lawson is now an engineer for LTV and has been assigned to the A7D project. And I am now a newspaper reporter.

At this writing, those remaining at Goodrich are still secure in the same positions, all except Russell Line and Robert Sink. Line has been rewarded with a promotion to production superintendent, a large step upward on the corporate ladder. As for Sink, he moved up into Line's old job.

CASES

Case 14.1: The Aircraft Brake Scandal

In this chapter Kermit Vandivier's article gives a first-hand account of his experiences in a case of falsified test data while the B. F. Goodrich Company was trying to win a contract to build brakes for a new Air Force plane. Since the full text of his account is in this chapter, the following is only a brief summary of his observations.

After realizing that the proposed brake design did not work, several managers in the Troy, Ohio, plant decided to falsify the tests that would be forwarded to the Air Force. After years of trying to win these types of contracts, company officials feared that their chances would go up in smoke with the brake design, as the deadline was fast approaching and the proposed design continued to fail critical tests. As the technical writer in the test lab, Vandivier was asked to write the report with falsified data in order to show that the brakes had passed inspection. After voicing objections, he was told by one of his superiors to proceed and was advised to simply comply and do as he was told. After weighing the costs to his family, Vandivier wrote the report in violation of his own conscience. Eventually, he went to the appropriate legal authorities and reported what had occurred.[5]

[5]See Kermit Vandivier, "Why Should My Conscience Bother Me? The Aircraft Brake Scandal," in *In the Name of Profit*, ed. Robert Heilbroner et al. New York: Doubleday, 1972.

Questions for Discussion:

1. Did Vandivier do the right thing? What factors within the organizational setting contributed to the situation getting so out of hand before anything was done about it? What factors contributed to a "buck passing" mentality of moral responsibility? Do the same conditions exist in most other organizations?

2. If Vandivier would have claimed that he was simply obeying orders, would this be morally adequate as an excuse? Is this ever an adequate excuse?

COMMENTARY

In many business ethics scandals that have come to light, the individuals involved typically absolve themselves of moral culpability by claiming that someone else was ultimately responsible for what occurred. For example, in many scams, the first response of corporate executives is to lay the blame at the feet of "rogue individuals" who were acting without company permission and knowledge. These individuals in turn claim that they were unaware of the consequences of their actions because they did not have the big picture and were "only following orders." While the fallen nature of humanity undoubtedly contributes to a lack of moral courage in the presence of the potential for significant financial gains, we must ask if there is something to the structure of organizations that contributes to this lack of moral responsibility. The readings in this chapter attempt to explain this phenomenon through an examination of human nature when confronted with authority and the social structure of organizations. We bring these issues to light to raise awareness of this phenomenon in the hope that people will become more conscious of these processes and pressures.

The experiments performed by Stanley Milgram, as described in "The Perils of Obedience," with the aim of testing the extent to which authority would be obeyed are fascinating to say the least. His results are "shocking" as they seem to conclude that the tendency to act against a moral imperative in the presence of a contradictory authority is strong. With the experimenter stating frequently that he would bear all responsibility for anything that may happen to "the learner," many of the subjects were more than willing to push the lever to what they were told were dangerous levels of voltage, including that marked "XXX." Even when the "learner's" screams fell silent, some subjects were still willing to continue the experiment.

Milgram explains this phenomenon by stating that "the essence of obedience is that a person comes to view himself as the instrument for carrying out another person's wishes, and he therefore no longer regards himself as responsible for his actions." Clearly, there are parallels here to obedience to authority in organizational settings as orders are often handed down from those who see the big picture. Milgram states in his conclusions that with the division of labor, people now carry out narrow jobs that take away their ability to grasp the overall direction of a task. Instead, they see only a small part and measure their success on how well they have fulfilled what is socially expected of them. Thus the excuse "I was only obeying orders" is one that is frequently heard in the aftermath of business scandals in which those that are caught have acted in a manner that they would have likely avoided in their lives away from work.

However, what is different about Milgram's experiments and what is most frightening is the fact that the experimenter had no "real" authority over the subjects. As Milgram states, "The experimenter did not threaten the subjects with punishment—such as loss of income, community ostracism, or jail—for failure to obey. Neither could he offer incentives." As such, it seems that his power to coerce in this experiment would be much less than in a corporate setting where superiors have the resources and the authority to punish those who act contrary to their demands. Moreover, authority in organizational settings is compounded by corporate culture and peers who exert pressures to conform to group norms.

This is the point at which H. R. Smith and Archie B. Carroll contribute some important insights into the organizational factors that further "stack the deck" against ethics in organizations. Their descriptions appear to paint a portrait of organizations that resemble military units and the processes they use in order to build cohesion and foster teamwork. It seems indeed that there are some important parallels between military and business organizations. It is not by accident that the two "group think" incidents we described in detail in the introductory comments involve an armed forces unit and a business organization. To be clear, the analogy between military and business organizations is limited, as the two types of entities are not perfect corollaries. No business organization of which we are aware threatens to shoot or court-martial those who desert prior to the end of their stated time of commitment. That is, unless one joins Bandini, Lambert, and Locke, the fictional law corporation created by author John Grisham in his famous novel turned motion picture *The Firm*. However, while the analogy may be imperfect, it still seems applicable. There are indeed many similarities between military units and other types of organizations.

Many corporations have socialization processes that are similar, albeit less intense, than that of the military. Instead of boot camp, many corporations have one week or longer of off-site training and orientation programs that engage in the process of "divestiture" and "investiture" of corporate culture. Employees are inculcated with organizational values and they are instructed in the "company way." As Smith and Carroll point out, once a new hire is on the job, this socialization process continues as the organization seeks to create loyalty and commitment on the part of the employee. Many informal practices of the corporate culture and other members of the organization serve to reinforce specific behaviors through peer pressure, reward, and punishment. Those who play by the rules are clearly rewarded through praise, promotions, and pay increases. And, while companies do not court-martial those who are insubordinate, non–"team players" are punished through threats of embarrassment, demotion, and the potential of being fired.

It seems that there are other parallels as well. Military units have been accused of "dehumanizing" the enemy in order to desensitize soldiers to the process of taking lives. Corporations do not purposefully kill people, but some critics argue that they certainly engage in similar processes of "dehumanization." For example, consumers become "target" markets; the competition is to be "killed"; companies get "raided," and employees become human "resources." While the term "human resources" is perhaps preferable to the vanillalike "personnel," resources are typically items that are used up and are preserved only to better their utility for the ultimate end of production. Add this jargon to the list of popular books that utilize the war metaphor—*Guerrilla Marketing Tactics* and *The Leadership Secrets of Attila the Hun*, to name a couple—and it is easy to see some of the parallels between these types of organizations.

To be sure, obedience to authority and group cohesion are not evil in themselves. Indeed, these are critical ingredients for success in the military and in business. We could not imagine an army with radically decentralized management, nor could we envision a successful work environment without teamwork and cooperation. However, we must ask ourselves if too much of an apparently good thing can set up scenarios in which a lack of moral courage is the norm.

As Smith and Carroll assert, once employees are socialized into an organization, ethics seems to lose its grasp on conscience and on one's ability to stand up for what is right. They state that "conformity is an especially enticing alternative given the pressures one receives from peers and superiors." Individuals soon become very susceptible to a "bottom-line morality" and group think seems primed to occur. Individuals who raise moral objections are then seen as the enemy and are often ostracized from the organization.

Confirming Smith and Carol's conclusions about the power of peer pressure to induce conformity is the Asch effect. Solomon Asch conducted studies during which subjects were shown two lines of different lengths. For example, one line could be one and a half times the length of the other. The subjects were then asked if the two lines were the same in length. When tested individually, they stated conclusively that the two lines were not. Asch then recruited six actors who were instructed to say that the two lines were the same. Then a naive subject was introduced into the group and before giving his judgment had to listen to the other group members. One by one, the actors remarked that the lines were equal in length. After initial doubt, the subjects became visibly nervous and restless. After all six other group members affirmed the sameness of lines, some 58 percent of the subjects then responded that the lines were the same.[6] Asch's experiment undoubtedly shows the power of social pressure as the subjects even disregarded their "objective" senses in making their judgments. Thus it is easy to see why so many people would violate their own consciences for the sake of going along with the group. Indeed, because resistance is so difficult it is regarded as a critical mark of character.

[6]Solomon Asch, "Effects of Group Pressure upon the Modification and Distortion of Judgments," in Harold Guetzkow, ed., *Groups, Leadership, and Men* (New York: Russell & Russell, 1963), 177–90.

In addition to peer pressure, the deck is further stacked against ethics in organizations by the nature of hierarchical organizations. The specialization of task and the division of labor that come with bureaucratic structures cripple many employees so they cannot see the larger contexts and consequences of their actions. As we mentioned earlier, when scandals are revealed and investigated, those at the top often blame those on lower rungs for being rogue actors who acted in violation of company policies. Those on the bottom are routinely told, as was Kermit Vandivier, that they don't have the big picture and that it will be top management's responsibility "if anything happens." Thus it is easier to "leave the driving" to others and to claim that they themselves were "only following orders" than to assume responsibility. Buck-passing then becomes the norm.

Given this combination of the propensity to obey authority as detailed by Milgram and the pressures and expectations for conformity in organizations, we can easily see why so many business ethics scandals often involve groups of well-educated and respected members of society. With all of these factors, the deck is stacked against moral courage in organizations and the potential for evil is ripe.

In "Why Should My Conscience Bother Me?" Kermit Vandivier offers a first-hand account of what is described in this chapter. The authority of higher-level employees had many people in the organization simply shifting responsibility to others. Peer pressure and hierarchy further added to the deck-stacking effect. Moreover, adding the reality of competing loyalties into the equation, Vandivier mentions his struggle over family obligations. "But bills are not paid with personal satisfaction, nor house payments with ethical principles," he states. Undoubtedly, the ability to stand up for what is right is often compounded by painful trade-offs. The prospect of unemployment in these situations is real.

While his particular case occurred in the 1960s, investigations of fraud still regularly make news. Thus the principles involved are still very relevant. What if you were in Vandivier's position, how do you think you would respond? Let us hope that you would choose the right course of action, which is to go to the legal authorities after exhausting the internal remedies. As the Nuremberg trials established, simply obeying authorities is not an ample moral or legal excuse for transgressing ethical principles. While the prospect of losing one's job and house are painful realities, Christians are promised divine providence in pursuing the right course of action, though we are never guaranteed home ownership or a middle-class lifestyle. There are indeed trade-offs to being morally courageous. If it were easy, everyone would stand up for what's right.

Our goal in this chapter has been to explain, and not excuse, the conditions for evil that seem to prevail in many organizations. If education can accomplish anything, it can raise our awareness about our tendencies to conform and show us ways we can avoid these types of actions. It is to be hoped that an awareness of our own propensities to go against our own moral convictions in the face of authoritarian and social pressures will be one step in the path of allowing us to stand for what is morally right.

One further development deserves mention. Since the time that Smith and Carroll's article was written, the realities of a changing economy are dictating that most corporations are restructuring in a way that is leading away from traditional hierarchical work structures. Many employees are more involved in decisions and are allowed to see the bigger picture of their work. However, specialization will be forever with us, and it is naive to expect that business organizations will be completely nonhierarchical. Moreover, peer pressure and corporate values and cultures are with us to stay. Thus organizational and group influences on moral behavior will continue to be a problem that employees will have to deal with in the future.

In the next chapter, we will examine some of the current literature on what organizations can practically do to create climates that actively encourage ethics and integrity.

FIFTEEN

Creating and Encouraging Moral Corporate Climates

We had nothing to do with these activities; they were committed by maverick employees acting without our permission.

Often-heard defense used by executives during scandals

In fact, ethics has everything to do with management.

Lynn Sharp Paine, "Managing for Organizational Integrity"

INTRODUCTION

In the preceding chapter, we gave examples of situations in which individuals abandoned their moral values when they were faced with group and organizational pressures to do so. In fact, many headlining scandals in business involve well-educated and highly respected members of society who fell into temptation in the context of peer pressure. While the fallen nature of humanity is the foundational basis for these actions, the social climate of organizations is undoubtedly a contributory factor. Pressures created by the socialization process and corporate authority structures can contribute to a climate where "group think" and unethical behavior is ripe to occur. Consequently, in many cases unethical behaviors are not simply the actions of a few rogue individuals acting without approval; rather, they often involve groups of executives and employees acting in apparent consort to transgress the law and then again to cover their tracks.

To be certain, factors such as organizational climate, structure, and culture are not the sole determinants of unethical behavior. After all, organizations are made up of individuals who ultimately possess the freedom and ability to resist the pressure to act contrary to their beliefs. Thus some well-publicized scandals such as the one involving aircraft brakes, discussed in the previous chapter, would probably never have developed to the point that they did if a morally courageous individual had been willing to stand up for what was right. Nonetheless, surrounding environmental and organizational factors play significant roles as some organizations inadvertently encourage unethical behavior despite codes and other public relations tools that directly state the opposite. To acknowledge the role of environmental factors is not to dismiss individual responsibility for immoral actions; rather, it serves to raise our awareness of these factors, so that organizations can make necessary changes to improve their moral climates.

In sharp contrast to those organizations that discourage ethical behavior, there are a host of progressive companies that have successfully created climates where such behavior is fostered through both formal and informal mechanisms. Acknowledging that most business decisions are made, not in a social vacuum, but rather in the context of organizational life, we will now examine practical and effective steps that companies can take in order to create a climate in which ethical behavior has a better chance of thriving.

In order to gain a further understanding of some important contributory factors to unethical actions, O. C. Ferrell and John Fraedrich have written their article "Understanding Pressures That Cause Unethical Behavior in Business." Ferrell and Fraedrich examine the role of personal values, competitive and organizational pressures, and opportunity pressures to help explain unethical behavior in corporate settings. With an understanding of these factors, the two authors then give suggestions for organizations that want to implement changes that will foster better decisions.

In "Creating and Encouraging Ethical Corporate Structures" Patrick Murphy offers specific policy measures that companies can implement to encourage ethical behavior. He argues that since "ethical business practices stem from ethical corporate culture," managers must introduce several critical components to create and sustain a culture that enhances ethics. Among these components are corporate credos, ethics programs, and codes of conduct that provide specific guidance to employees in various business areas.

Adding to the insights of the first two articles, Lynn Sharp Paine offers some important contributions in her article "Managing for Organizational Integrity." Paine explains how organizational policies and practices can inadvertently encourage employees to behave unethically. She argues that companies must change such practices in view of new federal sentencing guidelines that recognize managerial and organizational contributions to unlawful conduct. Since the guidelines base fines partly on the extent to which companies have proactively sought to prevent such actions, she asserts that executives who ignore ethics run the risk of increasing their company's liability and depriving them of the possible benefits of leniency under the new guidelines. Paine recognizes, however, that mere legal compliance is not enough. Instead, she supports the use of an "integrity strategy" to implement an ethic that sees morality "as a driving force in enterprise." She then concludes by offering three excellent examples of companies that have successfully implemented ethics programs in recent years.

Virgil Smith furthers Paine's support of an integrity strategy by pointing out the need for character and personal integrity along with system-wide reforms. Smith critiques the recent literature on management and ethics that emphasizes systems while neglecting personal character as the heart of an economic system. In pointing us back in the direction in which we started this book, Smith asserts that "system" and social control will likely fail in the absence of personal virtue and trust, which are critical elements to a successful and moral commercial system.

READINGS

Understanding Pressures That Cause Unethical Behavior in Business

O. C. Ferrell and John Fraedrich

Business Insights (Spring–Summer 1990). Copyright © 1990.

Introduction

Ethics in business is a major concern because of the lack of ethical behavior by some individuals and organizations in our society. Dennis Levine at the age of 32 was a managing director of Drexel Burnham Lambert, one of the country's top merger and acquisition specialists. His indictment for insider trading charges ignited the insider trading scandal of the 1980s, forever changing the landscape of American business. Levine was fined $362,000 and agreed to pay the federal government $11.6 million in illegal trading profits. He was sentenced to two years in prison and has since been paroled. Levine received a reduced sentence for helping the federal government in its investigation of insider trading. His testimony helped to implicate Ivan Boesky, who received a $100 million penalty, the biggest ever, for insider trading. Now Mr. Levine is being managed by a public relations agency and receives fees for speaking to MBA students on college campuses. Levine's message to college students is "Don't do it." "It's not worth it," he said of insider trading and other white collar transgressions (*Los Angeles Times*, 1989, part 4).

What causes people like Dennis Levine to behave unethically and even illegally in the business world? There are many scenarios to explain unethical behavior. One explanation is that the individual may be a "bad apple," with poor personal morals, in a good organization. Other explanations for unethical behavior include the nature of the competitive environment, organizational pressures, or even the opportunity to take advantage in the right situation. It is our purpose to explore how both personal and outside pressures on business people can increase the probability of ethical mistakes. In addition, we suggest several ways managers can improve ethical behavior and can avoid the destructive consequences of poor ethical decision making.

Personal Values vs. Corporate Values

The personal dimension of ethics relates to an individual's values and moral philosophies. Individual values are learned from socialization through family, religion, school, and business experiences. These individual values are generally assumed to remain constant in both work and nonwork environments. However, doubt was first cast on this generalization by Carr (1968). He argued that business people have two ethical dimensions that include one ethical value system for home and one for business. Recently, support for Carr's statement has shown that most business persons use one moral philosophy at work and a completely different moral philosophy at home (Fraedrich 1988). This may explain why Dennis Levine says he has strong moral commitments today but could not explain to his five-year-old son a few years ago why he was going to prison. He was a good family man, yet cheated investors out of millions.

The personal value system combines with the corporate culture to affect behavior. In a study conducted by Frederick and Weber (1987) concerning the values of corporate managers and their critics, they concluded that personal values are involved in ethical decisions but are not the central component that guides the decisions, actions, and policies of the organization. They believe that personal values make up only one part of an organization's total value structure. Ethical behavior within the organization relates to the organization's values and traditions rather than solely upon individuals who actually make the decisions.

Consequently, ethical behavior may be a function of two different dimensions of an organization's individual members. An individual member assumes some measure of moral responsibility by agreeing in general to abide by an organization's rules and standard operating procedures. When Dennis Levine stepped over the line into unethical and illegal behavior, it can be assumed that competitive pressures and organizational rewards provided the incentive.

Competitive Pressures

Competition exerts pressure on business decision makers and is a key factor in influencing the ethical environment of the firm. In general, competition helps business and the economy to become more efficient and goal-oriented. However, when competition becomes so intense that business survival is threatened, then employees and managers may view once unacceptable alternatives as acceptable. In other words, pressured employees may engage in unethical practices for corporate survival. The culture of the corporation may encourage and reward unethical behavior because of fear of bankruptcy, possible loss of one's job, or the opportunity for promotion.

Corporate espionage and manipulation to gain insider information are often used in highly competitive industries. One example of such an act involved the acquisition of information on General Electric's turbine parts by a small manufacturing firm. GE employees were offered money in exchange for drawings. By acquiring these documents, the smaller company hoped to save millions of dollars in research and development and to capture a significant share of the more than $495 million turbine parts market (Carley 1988). As this example illustrates, some firms may approve corporate espionage, but society deems such actions as unethical and illegal.

As competition becomes intense and profit margins become smaller, pressures can build to substitute inferior materials or components to reduce costs. Often this is done without informing customers about changes in product quality that involve a form of dishonesty about the nature of the product. Beech-Nut Nutrition Corporation took this concept to an extreme when it changed the contents of its apple juice product. Instead of selling a product made from apples, the company substituted a chemical concoction which has the same taste, smell, and look of apple juice. However, the company continued to label and promote its product as being 100 percent apple juice. In fact, experts found it difficult to distinguish it from pure apple juice. Beech-Nut failed to inform consumers that its apple juice no longer was made from apples (Hall 1989). When companies do not inform consumers that product components are not of the same quality as promoted, ethical issues arise. In this case, Beech-Nut lost millions of dollars, and its executives were sentenced to prison terms.

Other questionable practices, such as increased EPA violations, mechanical devices that periodically increase assembly line speed, bait-and-switch sales techniques, and bribery to obtain important customers, occur when a firm is in a highly competitive industry. These measures are used because managers are afraid that their company could not compete without using deception and manipulation.

Organizational Pressures

While ethical decision making includes perceptions of how to act in terms of daily issues, success is determined by achievement of company goals. Pressure to perform and increase profits may be particularly intense in middle management. This internal organizational pressure is a major predictor of unethical behavior.

These organizational factors seem to have played a part in several recent scandals. Many insider traders in the Boesky scandal remain uncaught because trading of confidential information in investment banking circles is a routine way of doing business. The E.F. Hutton employees found guilty of 2,000 counts of mail and wire fraud did not understand their company's values. Some may have thought they were doing their company a favor (Dressang 1986). Robert Foman, former chairman of E.F. Hutton, states that, "I thought ethics was something you learned growing up at home, in school, and in church" (Moskowitz 1985, p. 63). Obviously, Foman was wrong in thinking that ethics is only developed at home, school and church. His managers were influenced by pressures to succeed, and by their peers and supervisors in the decision-making process.

The roles of top management and superiors are extremely important in developing the culture of an organization. Most experts agree that the chief executive officer and vice-president level executives set the ethical tone for the entire organization. For example, when Chrysler Corporation President Lee Iacocca learned that several executives of his company were driving new Chryslers with the odometers disconnected and then selling the cars as new, he admitted the company's unethical behavior in a national press conference and developed a program to compensate customers who had bought the pre-driven cars. Iacocca took out two-page advertisements in *USA Today*, the *Wall Street Journal*, and the *New York Times* to apologize for the ethical mistake and added, "The only thing we are recalling here is our integrity." Messages like this send a signal to all employees in the organization concerning what the firm stands for ethically (Schlesinger 1987). Lower-level superiors obtain their cues from these individuals, yet they too exert some of their personal value system on the company. This interplay between corporate culture and executive leadership helps determine the ethical value system of the firm.

Opportunity Pressures

Opportunity to engage in unethical behavior provides another pressure that may determine whether or not a person will behave ethically. Opportunity is a favorable set of conditions to limit barriers or to provide rewards. Rewards may be internal or external. Internal rewards are those feelings of goodness and worth one feels after an altruistic action. External rewards are what people expect to receive from others in terms of values generated and provided on an exchange basis. External rewards are often received from peers and top management. Opportunity to engage in unethical behavior has been found to be a better predictor of such behavior than personal beliefs (Ferrell and Gresham, 1985). In a survey by Chonko and Hunt (1985), 56 percent of the managers indicated that there were many opportunities for managers in their industry to engage in unethical behaviors.

If an individual uses the opportunity afforded him/her to act unethically and is either rewarded or not penalized, that person becomes more likely to repeat such acts as the opportunity arises. For example, an accountant who receives a raise for preparing financial documents that he or she knows are not completely accurate is being rewarded for this behavior and, therefore, has an increased probability of continuing the behavior.

Several elements within the business environment help to create opportunities, including rewards and the absence of punishment. Professional codes of ethics and ethics-related corporate policy also influence opportunity. Enforcement of these codes and policies should generate the highest level of compliance to ethical standards. The greater the rewards and the less the punishment for unethical behavior, the greater the probability that unethical behavior will be practiced.

It is even suggested that the SEC contributed to the opportunity dimension of insider trading by allowing Ivan Boesky to reduce his partnership's liabilities by $1.3 billion by selling stocks or other securities before the government announced his crimes. This special treatment saved Boesky an additional $100 million in fines. In reality this cut his fines in half. In addition, Congress asked why, if New York Stock Exchange computers flagged 47 suspicious trades by Boesky—many before merger announcements—Boesky was not caught before Levine disclosed his actions. Even after being caught and punished, much opportunity exists for violators to profit from their success.

After being paroled early from his two-year prison sentence, Dennis Levine is being paid for public speaking and has started a new financial consulting practice in mergers and acquisitions. A *Barron's* article reports, "We're convinced the venture will be a great success. Mr. Levine's curriculum vitae is sure to prove irresistible to any number of companies we can consider" (Abelson, 1989). Apparently, much opportunity continues for those convicted of unethical and illegal activity in the securities industry.

Improving Ethical Decisions

Conflicts between personal values and corporate values, intense competition, organizational pressures and opportunity interact to create situations that can cause unethical behavior. Figure 1 illustrates the pressures that can influence ethical

decision making. As discussed previously, both the individual and the organization can influence unethical behavior.

Figure 1

Pressures That Impact Ethical Decisions in Business

Personal Values	Competition
Ethical Decisions	
Organization	Opportunity

One way to sensitize personnel is to create codes of ethics. Trevino and Youngblood (1990) developed a "bad apple," "bad barrel" argument concerning this issue. The "bad apple" argument is that some people are basically bad and will do things in their own self-interest regardless of organizational goals. Eliminating unethical behavior requires the elimination of the "bad apples" (individuals) within the corporation. This can be done through screening techniques and through the enforcement of ethics codes. The "bad barrel" argument is that corporate culture becomes unethical not because individuals are bad, but because the pressures to survive competition create conditions that reward unethical behavior. The solution to the "bad barrel" approach is to redesign the corporate image and culture such that it conforms to industry and societal norms of ethical behavior. Robin and Reidenbach (1987) suggest that ethics must be built into the corporate culture and corporate strategy. By sensitizing personnel in an organization to ethical issues and potential areas of conflict, one can eliminate or defuse some of the ethical pressures that occur in day-to-day business activities.

Codes of ethics can be established to help managers deal with ethical situations or dilemmas that develop in day-to-day operations. Top management should provide leadership to operationalize codes. Codes of ethics do not have to be so detailed they take into account every situation; rather codes should have general guidelines that operationalize the main goals and objectives.

If a company is to maintain ethical behavior, its policies, rules, and standards must be worked into its control system. When employees make unethical decisions, the company needs to determine why and to take corrective action through enforcement. Enforcement of standards is what makes codes of ethics effective. If codes are window dressing and do not relate to what is expected or what is rewarded in the corporate culture, then the codes serve no purpose other than to give the illusion that there is concern for ethical behavior.

Conclusion

Ethical behavior in business must be based on a strong moral foundation, including personal moral development and an organizational structure that encourages and rewards desired ethical action. The pressures of competition must be understood and coped with to improve ethical behavior. The idea that ethics is learned at home, in school and in church does not recognize the impact of the organization on ethical decision makers. Today there is an increasing need for professional associations and corporations to promote and to enforce codes of ethics and eliminate unethical conduct.

Codes of ethics and/or corporate policies on ethics must be established to control the opportunity factor in ethical decision making. Enforcement of corporate policies on ethics brings about more ethical behavior. The establishment of codes of ethics and corporate policies on ethics will enable company employees to better understand what is, and is not, expected of them. Understanding how a person chooses his or her own standards of ethics, and what prompts a person to engage in unethical behavior, may decrease the current trend toward unethical activity in the business world.

For a company to maintain ethical behavior, its ethical policies, rules, and standards must be worked into its control system, including activities related to target setting, measuring and monitoring performance. Increasing ethical behavior in a corporation is similar to increasing earnings. Ethical behavior will happen only after a strategic plan is developed and successfully implemented to achieve the desired results.

References

Abelson, Alan (1989), "Up and Down Wall Street," the *Wall Street Journal*, July 24, 43.

Carley, William M. (1988), "Secrets War: GE Presses Campaign to Halt Rivals' Misuse of Turbine Parts Data,." the *Wall Street Journal*, August 16, 1, 10.

Carr, Albert Z. (1968), "Is Business Bluffing Ethical?" *Harvard Business Review* (January-February), 145.

Chonko, Lawrence and Shelby Hunt (1985), "Ethics and Marketing Management: An Empirical Investigation," *Journal of Business Research*, 13, 339–59.

Dressang, Joel (1986), "Companies Get Serious About Ethics," *USA Today* (December), 1–2B.

Ferrell, O. C., and Larry Gresham (1985), "A Contingency Framework for Understanding Ethical Decision Making in Marketing," *Journal of Marketing* (Summer), 87–96.

Fraedrich, John P. (1988), "Philosophy Type Interaction in the Ethical Decision Making Process of Retailers," Ph.D. Dissertation, Texas A & M University, College Station, TX.

Frederick, William C., and James Weber (1987), "The Value of Corporate Managers and Their Critics: An Empirical Description and Normative Implications," *Research in Corporate Social Performance and Social Responsibility* (9), William C. Frederick, ed., Greenwich, CT, 149–50.

Hall, Mini (1989), "O.J. Wasn't 100% Pure, FDA Says," *USA Today*, July 26, A1.

Moskowitz, Daniel B. (1985), "Where Business Goes to Stock Up on Ethics," *Business Week* (October 14), 63–66.

Robin, Donald P., and R. Eric Reidenbach (1987), "Social Responsibility, Ethics and Marketing Strategy: Closing the Gap Between Concept and Application," *Journal of Marketing* (January), 44–58.

Schlesinger, Jacob (1987), "Chrysler Finds a Way to Settle Odometer Issue," the *Wall Street Journal*, December 10, 7.

Sing, Bill (1989), *Los Angeles Times*, May 24, part 4.

Trevino, Linda K., and Stuart Youngblood (1990), "Bad Apples in Bad Barrels: A Casual Analysis of Ethical Decision Making Behavior," *Journal of Applied Psychology*, forthcoming.

Creating and Encouraging Ethical Corporate Structures

Patrick E. Murphy

Sloan Management Review 30, no. 2 (Winter 1989): 81–87. Copyright © 1989 by the Sloan Management Review Association.

[1]What is an ethical company? This question is not easy to answer. For the most part, ethical problems occur because corporate managers and their subordinates are *too* devoted to the organization. In their loyalty to the company or zest to gain recognition, people sometimes ignore or overstep ethical boundaries. For example, some sales managers believe that the only way to meet ambitious sales goals is to have the sales reps "buy" business with lavish entertaining and gift giving. This overzealousness is the key source of ethical problems in most business firms.

Employees are looking for guidance in dealing with ethical problems. This guidance may come from the CEO, upper management, or immediate supervisors.[2] We know that ethical business practices stem from an ethical corporate culture. Key questions are: How can this culture be created and sustained? What structural approaches encourage ethical decision making? If the goal is to make the company ethical, managers must introduce structural components that will enhance ethical sensitivity.

In this paper, I examine three promising and workable approaches to infusing ethical principles into business:

- corporate credos that define and give direction to corporate values;
- ethics programs where company-wide efforts focus on ethical issues; and
- ethical codes that provide specific guidance to employees in functional business areas.

Below I review the virtues and limitations of each and provide examples of companies that successfully employ these approaches.

Corporate Credos

A corporate credo delineates a company's ethical responsibility to its stakeholders; it is probably the most general approach to managing corporate ethics. The credo is a succinct statement of the values permeating the firm. The experiences of Security Pacific Corporation (a Los Angeles–based national bank that devised a credo in 1987) and of Johnson & Johnson illustrate the credo approach.

Security Pacific's central document is not an ethical code per se; rather, it is six missionlike commitments to customers, employees, communities, and stockholders. The credo's objective is "to seek a set of principles and beliefs which might provide guidance and direction to our work" (see

More than 70 high-level managers participated in formulating a first draft of the commitments. During this process, senior managers shared and analyzed examples of ethical dilemmas they had faced in balancing corporate and constituent obligations. An outside consultant, hired to manage the process, helped to draft the language. Ultimately more than 250 employees, from all levels of the bank, participated in the credo formulation process via a series of discussion groups.

Once the commitments were in final form, management reached a consensus on how to communicate these guiding principles to the Security Pacific organization. Credo coordinators developed and disseminated a leader's guide to be used at staff meetings introducing the credo; it contained instructions on the meeting's format and on showing a videotape that explained the credo and the process by which it was developed. At the meetings, managers invited reactions by posing these questions: What are your initial feelings about what you have just read? Are there any specific commitments you would like to discuss? How will the credo affect your daily work? Employees were thus encouraged to react to the credo and to consider its long-run implications.

Security Pacific's credo was recently cited as a model effort, and it serves internally both as a

Table I	The Credo of Security Pacific Corporation

Commitment to Customer

The first commitment is to provide our customers with quality products and services which are innovative and technologically responsive to their current requirements, at appropriate prices. To perform these tasks with integrity requires that we maintain confidentiality and protect customer privacy, promote customer satisfaction, and serve customer needs. We strive to serve qualified customers and industries which are socially responsible according to broadly accepted community and company standards.

Commitment of Employee to Employee

The fourth commitment is that of employees to their fellow employees. We must be committed to promote a climate of mutual respect, integrity, and professional relationships, characterized by open and honest communication within and across all levels of the organization. Such a climate will promote attainment of the Corporation's goals and objectives, while leaving room for individual initiative within a competitive environment.

Commitment to Employee

The second commitment is to establish an environment for our employees which promotes professional growth, encourages each person to achieve his or her highest potential, and promotes individual creativity and responsibility. Security Pacific acknowledges our responsibility to employees, including providing for open and honest communication, stated expectations, fair and timely assessment of performance and equitable compensation which rewards employee contributions to company objectives within a framework of equal opportunity and affirmative action.

Commitment to Communities

The fifth commitment is that of Security Pacific to the communities which we serve. We must constantly strive to improve the quality of life through our support of community organizations and projects, through encouraging service to the community by employees, and by promoting participation in community services. By the appropriate use of our resources, we work to support or further advance the interests of the community, particularly in times of crisis or social need. The corporation and its employees are committed to com-

plying fully
laws and re

**Commitme
Security Pa**

The third commitment is that of the employee to Security Pacific. As employees, we strive to understand and adhere to the corporation's policies and objectives, act in a professional manner, and give our best effort to improve Security Pacific. We recognize the trust and confidence placed in us by our customers and community and act with integrity and honesty in all situations to preserve that trust and confidence. We act responsibly to avoid conflicts of interest and other situations which are potentially harmful to the corporation.

Commitment to Stockholder

The six commitment of Security Pacific is to its stockholders. We will strive to provide consistent growth and a superior rate of return on their investment, to maintain a position and reputation as a leading financial institution, to protect stockholder investments, and to provide full and timely information. Achievement of these goals for Security Pacific is dependent upon the successful development of the five previous sets of relationships.

standard for judging existing programs and as a justification for new activities.[3] For example, the "commitment to communities" formed the basis for a program specifically designed to serve low-income constituents in the area. However, this credo should not be considered the definitive approach to ethics management. First, the credo could be interpreted simply as an organizational mission statement, not as a document about ethics. Indeed, the examples supporting the credo

and the videotape itself do stress what might just be called good business practice, without particular reference to ethical policies. And second, the credo has not been in place long enough for its impact to be fully assessed.

Any discussion of corporate credos would be incomplete without reference to Johnson & Johnson, whose credo is shown in Table 2. This document focuses on responsibilities to consumers, employees, communities, and stockholders. (The

J&J president, David Clare, explains that responsibility to the stockholder is listed last because "if we do the other jobs properly, the stockholder will always be served.") The first version of this credo, instituted in 1945, was revised in 1947. Between 1975 and 1978, chairman James Burke held a series of meetings with J&J's 1,200 top managers; they were encouraged to "challenge" the credo. What emerged from the meetings was that the document in fact functioned as it was intended to function; a slightly reworded but substantially unchanged credo was introduced in 1979.

Over the last two years, the company has begun to survey all employees about how well the company meets its responsibilities to the four principal constituencies. The survey asks employees from all fifty-three countries where J&J operates questions about every line in the credo. An office devoted to the credo survey tabulates the results, which are confidential. (Department and division managers receive only information pertaining to their units and composite numbers for the entire firm.) The interaction at meetings devoted to discussing these findings is reportedly very good.

Does J&J's credo work? Top management feels strongly that it does. The credo is often mentioned as an important contributing factor in the company's exemplary handling of the Tylenol crises several years ago. It would appear that the firm's commitment to the credo makes ethical business practice its highest priority. One might question whether the credo is adequate to deal with the multitude of ethical problems facing a multinational firm; possibly additional ethical guidelines could serve as reinforcement, especially in dealing with international business issues.

When should a company use a corporate credo to guide its ethical policies? They work best in

---

Table 2	Johnson & Johnson Credo

We believe our first responsibility is to the doctors, nurses, and patients, to mothers and all others who use our products and services. In meeting their needs everything we do must be of high quality. We must constantly strive to reduce our costs in order to maintain reasonable prices. Customers' orders must be serviced promptly and accurately. Our suppliers and distributors must have an opportunity to make a fair profit.

We are responsible to our employees, the men and women who work with us throughout the world. Everyone must be considered as an individual. We must respect their dignity and recognize their merit. They must have a sense of security in their jobs. Compensation must be fair and adequate and working conditions clean, orderly, and safe. Employees must feel free to make suggestions and complaints. There must be equal opportunity for employment, development, and advancement for those qualified. We must provide competent management, and their actions must be just and ethical.

We are responsible to the communities in which we live and work and to the world community as well. We must be good citizens—support good works and charities and bear our fair share of taxes. We must encourage civic improvements and better health and education. We must maintain in good order the property we are privileged to use, protecting the environment and natural resources.

Our final responsibility is to our stockholders. Business must make a sound profit. We must experiment with new ideas. Research must be carried on, innovative programs developed and mistakes paid for. New equipment must be purchased, new facilities provided, and new products launched. Reserves must be created to provide for adverse times. When we operate according to these principles, the stockholders should realize a fair return.

firms with a cohesive corporate culture, where a spirit of frequent and unguarded communication exists. Generally, small, tightly knit companies find that a credo is sufficient. Among large firms, Johnson & Johnson is an exception. J&J managers consciously use the credo as an ethical guidepost; they find that the corporate culture reinforces the credo.

When is a credo insufficient? This approach does not offer enough guidance for most multinational companies facing complex ethical questions in different societies, for firms that have merged recently and are having trouble grafting disparate cultures, and for companies operating in industries with chronic ethical problems. A credo is like the Ten Commandments. Both set forth good general principles, but many people need the Bible, religious teachings, and guidelines provided by organized religion, as well. Similarly, many companies find that they need to offer more concrete guidance on ethical issues.

Ethics Programs

Ethics programs provide more specific direction for dealing with potential ethical problems than general credos do. Two companies—Chemical Bank and Dow Corning—serve as examples. Although the thrust of the two programs is different, they both illustrate the usefulness of this approach.

Chemical Bank, the nation's fourth largest bank, has an extensive ethics education program. All new employees attend an orientation session at which they read and sign off on Chemical's code of ethics. (This has been in existence for thirty years and was last revised in May 1987.) The training program features a videotaped message from the chairman emphasizing the bank's values and ethical standards. A second and more unusual aspect of the program provides in-depth training in ethical decision making for vice presidents.[4]

The "Decision Making and Corporate Values" course is a two-day seminar that occurs away from the bank. Its purpose, according to a bank official, is "to encourage Chemical's employees to weigh the ethical or value dimensions of the decisions they make and to provide them with the analytic

tools to do that." This program began in 1983; more than 250 vice presidents have completed the course thus far. Each meeting is limited to twenty to twenty-five senior vice presidents from a cross-section of departments; this size makes for a seminarlike atmosphere. The bank instituted the program in response to the pressures associated with deregulation, technology, and increasing competition.

The chairman always introduces the seminar by highlighting his personal commitment to the program. Most of the two days is spent discussing case studies. The fictitious cases were developed following interviews with various Chemical managers who described ethically charged situations. The cases are really short stories about loan approval, branch closings, foreign loans, insider trading, and other issues.[5] They do not have "solutions" as such; instead, they pose questions for discussion, such as, Do you believe the individual violated the bank's code? Or, What should X do?

Program evaluations have yielded positive results. Participants said they later encountered dilemmas similar to the cases, and that they had developed a thinking process in the seminar that helped them work through other problems. This program, while it is exemplary, only reaches a small percentage of Chemical's 30,000 employees. Ideally, such a program would be disseminated more widely and would become more than a one-time event.

Dow Corning has a long-standing—and very different—ethics program. Its general code has been revised four times since its inception in 1976 and includes a seven-point values statement. The company started using face-to-face "ethical audits" at its plants worldwide more than a decade ago. The number of participants in these four-to-six-hour audits ranges from five to forty. Auditors meet with the manager in charge the evening before to ascertain the most pressing issues. The actual questions come from relevant sections in the corporate code and are adjusted for the audit location. At sales offices, for example, the auditors concentrate on issues such as kickbacks, unusual requests from customers, and special pricing terms; at manufacturing plants, conservation and environmental issues receive more attention. An ethical audit might include the following questions.

- Are there any examples of business that Dow Corning has lost because of our refusal to provide "gifts" or other incentives to government officials at our customers' facilities?
- Do any of our employees have ownership or financial interest in any of our distributors?
- Have our sales representatives been able to undertake business conduct discussions with distributors in a way that actually strengthens our ties with them?
- Has Dow Corning been forced to terminate any distributors because of their business conduct practices?
- Do you believe that our distributors are in regular contact with their competitors? If so, why?
- Which specific Dow Corning policies conflict with local practices?

Developing a structure is not sufficient by itself. The structure will not be useful unless it is supported by institutionalized managerial processes.

John Swanson, manager of Corporate Internal and Management Communications, heads this effort; he believes the audit approach makes it "virtually impossible for employees to consciously make an unethical decision." According to Swanson, twenty to twenty-three meetings occur every year. The Business Conduct Committee members, who act as session leaders, then prepare a report for the Audit Committee of the board. He stresses the fact that there are no shortcuts to implementing this program—it requires time and extensive interaction with the people involved. Recently the audit was expanded; it now examines internal as well as external activities. (One audit found that some salespeople believed manufacturing personnel need to be more honest when developing production schedules.) One might ask whether the commitment to ethics is constant over time or peaks during the audit sessions; Dow Corning may want to conduct surprise audits, or develop other monitoring mechanisms or a more detailed code.

When should a company consider developing an ethics program? Such programs are often appropriate when firms have far-flung operations that need periodic guidance, as is the case at Dow Corning. This type of program can deal specifically with international ethical issues and with peculiarities at various plant locations. Second, an ethics program is useful when managers confront similar ethical problems on a regular basis, as Chemical Bank executives do. Third, these programs are useful in organizations that use outside consultants or advertising agencies. If an independent contractor does not subscribe to corporate credo, the firm may want to use an ethical audit or checklist to heighten the outside agency's sensitivity to ethical issues.

When do ethics programs come up lacking? If they are too issue centered, ethics programs may miss other, equally important problems. (Dow's program, for example, depends on the questions raised by the audit.) In addition, the scope of the program may limit its impact to only certain parts of the organization (e.g., Chemical Bank). Managers who want to permanently inculcate ethical considerations may be concerned that such programs are not perceived by some employees as being long term or ongoing. If the credo can be compared with the Ten Commandments, then ethics programs can be likened to weekly church services. Both can be uplifting, but once the session (service) is over, individuals may believe they can go back to business as usual.

Tailored Corporate Codes

Codes of conduct, or ethical codes, are another structural mechanism companies use to signal their commitment to ethical principles. Ninety percent of Fortune 500 firms, and almost half of all other firms, have ethical codes. According to a recent survey, this mechanism is perceived as the most effective way to encourage ethical business behavior.[6] Codes commonly address issues such as conflict of interest, competitors, privacy, gift giving and receiving, and political contributions. However, many observers continue to believe that codes are really public relations documents, or motherhood and apple pie statements; these critics claim that codes belittle employees and fail to address practical managerial issues.[7]

Simply developing a code is not enough. It must be tailored to the firm's functional areas (e.g., marketing, finance, personnel) or to the major line of business in which the firm operates. The rationale for tailored codes is simple. Functional areas or divisions have differing cultures and needs. A consumer products division, for example, has a relatively distant relationship with customers, because it relies heavily on advertising to sell its products. A division producing industrial products, on the other hand, has fewer customers and uses a personal, sales-oriented approach. A code needs to reflect these differences. Unfortunately, very few ethics codes do so.

Several companies have exemplary codes tailored to functional or major business areas. I describe two of these below—the St. Paul Companies (specializing in commercial and personal insurance and related products) and International Business Machines (IBM).

The St. Paul Companies revised their extensive corporate code, entitled "In Good Conscience," in 1986. All new employees get introduced to the code when they join the company, and management devotes biannual meetings to discussing the code's impact on day-to-day activities. In each of the five sections, the code offers specific guidance and examples for employees to follow. The statements below illustrate the kinds of issues, and the level of specificity, contained in the code.

- Insider Information. For example, if you know that the company is about to announce a rise in quarterly profits, or anything else that would affect the price of the company's stock, you cannot buy or sell the stock until the announcement has been made and published.
- Gifts and Entertainment. An inexpensive ballpoint pen, or an appointment diary, is a common gift and generally acceptable. But liquor, lavish entertainment, clothing, or travel should not be accepted.
- Contact with Legislators. If you are contacted by legislators on matters relating to the St. Paul, you should refer them to your governmental affairs or law department.

The "Employee Related Issues" section of the code is the most detailed; it directly addresses the company's relationship to the individual, and vice versa. This section spells out what employees can expect in terms of compensation (it should be based on job performance and administered fairly), advancement (promotion is from within, where possible), assistance (this consists of training, job experience, or counseling) and communications (there should be regular feedback; concerns can be expressed without fear of recrimination). It also articulates the St. Paul Companies' expectation of employees regarding speaking up (when you know something that could be a problem), avoiding certain actions (where the public's confidence could be weakened), and charting your career course.

The company also delineates employee privacy issues. The code outlines how work-related information needed for hiring and promotion is collected. (Only information needed to make the particular decision is gathered; it is collected from the applicant/employee where possible. Polygraphs are not used.) The St. Paul informs employees about what types of information are maintained. Finally, information in an individual's file is open to the employee's review.

The code covers other important personnel issues in depth, as well. It touches on equal opportunity by mentioning discrimination laws, but the emphasis is on the company recognition of past discrimination and its commitments to "make an affirmative effort to address this situation in all of its programs and practices." Data acquired from the St. Paul supports this point. Between 1981 and 1986, hiring and promotion increased 60 percent for minorities in supervisory positions and 49 percent for women in management—even though overall employment rose only about 3 percent during this time. In addition, the code informs employees that the company will reimburse all documented business expenses. And it covers nepotism by stating that officers' and directors' relatives will not be hired; other employees' relatives can be employed, so long as they are placed in different departments.

Being an ethical company requires providing clear guidelines for employees. The St. Paul Companies' extensive discussion of personnel policies does just that. Employees may strongly disapprove of certain policies, but they are fully informed. The termination policy, for example, states that employment is voluntary and that individuals are free to resign at any time; the company, too, can terminate employees "at any time, with or without cause." Some people may consider that policy unfair or punitive, but at least the rules of the game are clear. One limitation of the code is that all sections are not uniformly strong. For example, the marketing section is only one paragraph long and contains few specifics.

The second illustration is of a code tailored to the company's major line of business. IBM's "Business Conduct Guidelines" were instituted in the 1960s and revised most recently in 1983. New employees receive a copy and certify annually that they abide by the code. It has four parts; the most extensive section is entitled "Conducting IBM's Business." Since IBM is, at its core, a marketing and sales organization, this section pertains primarily to these issues.

Six subsections detail the type of activities IBM expects of its sales representatives. First, "Some General Standards" include the following directives, with commentaries: do not make misrepresentations to anyone, do not take advantage of IBM's size, treat everyone fairly (do not extend preferential treatment), and do not practice reciprocal dealing. Second, "Fairness in the Field" pertains to disparagement (sell IBM products on their merits, not by disparaging competitors' products or services). In addition, it prohibits premature disclosure of product information and of selling if a competitor already has a signed order. Third, "Relations with Other Organizations" cautions employees about firms that have multiple relationships with IBM (deal with only one relationship at a time, and do not collaborate with these firms).

The fourth and fifth sections address "Acquiring and Using Information for or about Others." The code spells out the limits to acquiring information (industrial espionage is wrong) and to using information (adverse information should not be retained). Employees must determine the confidentiality of information gathered from others. The final section outlines IBM's policy on "Bribes, Gifts, and Entertainment." The company allows customary business amenities but prohibits giving presents that are intended to "unduly influence" or "obligate" the recipient, as well as receiving gifts worth more than a nominal amount.

One might contend that it is easy for a large, profitable company like IBM to have an exemplary code. On the other hand, one could also argue that a real reason for the company's continued success is that its sales representatives do subscribe to these principles. Is this a perfect code? No. The gifts area could use more specificity and, even though the company spends millions of dollars a year on advertising, that subject is not addressed in any section of the code. Further, IBM's legal department administers the code, which may mean that problems are resolved more by legal than ethical interpretation.

When should a company use a tailored code of ethics? If a company has one dominant functional unit (like IBM), or if there is diversity among functional areas, divisions, or subsidiaries, then a tailored code might be advisable. It allows the firm to promulgate specific and appropriate standards. Tailored codes are especially useful to complex organizations because they represent permanent guidelines for managers and employees to consult.

When should they be avoided? If a firm's leaders believe specific guidelines may be too restrictive for their employees, then a tailored code is an unsatisfactory choice. Codes are not necessary in most small firms or in ones where a culture includes firmly entrenched ethical policies. If a credo is similar to the Ten Commandments, and programs are similar to religious services, then tailored credos can be considered similar to the Bible or to other formal religious teachings. They provide the most guidance, but many people do not take the time to read or reflect on them.

Conclusion

My research on ethics in management suggests several conclusions that the corporate manager may wish to keep in mind.

- **There Is No Single Ideal Approach to Corporate Ethics.** I would recommend that a small firm start with a credo, but that a larger firm consider a program or a tailored code. It is also possible to integrate these programs and produce a hybrid: in dealing with insider trading, for example, a firm could develop a training program, then follow it up with a strongly enforced tailored code.[8]

- **Top Management Must Be Committed.** Senior managers must champion the highest ethical postures for their companies, as James Burke of J&J does. This commitment was evident in all the companies described here; it came through loud and clear in the CEOs' letters, reports, and public statements.

- **Developing a Structure Is Not Sufficient by Itself.** The structure will not be useful unless it is supported by institutionalized managerial processes. The credo meetings at Security Pacific and the seminars at Chemical Bank are examples of processes that support structures.

- **Raising the Ethical Consciousness of an Organization Is Not Easy.** All the companies mentioned here have spent countless hours—and substantial amounts of money—developing, discussing, revising, and communicating the ethical principles of the firm. And in fact there are no guarantees that it will work. McDonnell Douglas has an extensive ethics program, but some of its executives were implicated in a recent defense contractor scandal.

In conclusion, let me add that managers in firms with active ethics structures—credos, programs, and tailored codes—are genuinely enthusiastic about them. They believe that ethics pay off. Their conviction should provide others with an encouraging example.

Notes

[1] The author would like to thank Bernard Avishai, Gene Laczniak, Michael Mokwa, Lee Tavis, and Oliver Williams, C.S.C., for their helpful comments on an earlier version of this article.

[2] P. E. Murphy and M. G. Dunn, "Corporate Culture and Marketing Management Ethics" (Notre Dame, IN: University of Notre Dame, working paper, 1988).

[3] R. E. Berenbeim, *Corporate Ethics* (New York: The Conference Board, research report no. 900, 1987), 15, 20–22.

[4] A more detailed discussion of Chemical's comprehensive program, and of Johnson & Johnson's, appears in *Corporate Ethics: A Prime Business Asset* (New York: Business Roundtable, February 1988).

[5] One of the case studies appears in "Would You Blow Whistle on Wayward Colleague?" *American Banker*, 17 June 1988, 16.

[6] Touche Ross, *Ethics in American Business* (New York: Touche Ross & Co., January 1988).

[7] Berenbeim (1987), 17.

[8] G.L. Tidwell, "Here's a Tip—Know the Rules of Insider Trading," *Sloan Management Review*, Summer 1987, 93–99.

Managing for Organizational Integrity

Lynn Sharp Paine

Harvard Business Review (March–April 1994). Copyright © 1994.

By supporting ethically sound behavior, managers can strengthen the relationships and reputations their companies depend on.

Many managers think of ethics as a question of personal scruples, a confidential matter between individuals and their consciences. These executives are quick to describe any wrongdoing as an isolated incident, the work of a rogue employee. The thought that the company could bear any responsibility for an individual's misdeeds never enters their minds. Ethics, after all, has nothing to do with management.

In fact, ethics has *everything* to do with management. Rarely do the character flaws of a lone actor fully explain corporate misconduct. More typically, unethical business practice involves the tacit, if not explicit, cooperation of others and reflects the values, attitudes, beliefs, language, and behavioral patterns that define an organization's operating culture. Ethics, then, is as much an organizational as a personal issue. Managers who fail to provide proper leadership and to institute systems that facilitate ethical conduct share responsibility with those who conceive, execute, and knowingly benefit from corporate misdeeds.

Managers must acknowledge their role in shaping organizational ethics and seize this opportunity to create a climate that can strengthen the relationships and reputations on which their companies' success depends. Executives who ignore ethics run the risk of personal and corporate liability in today's increasingly tough legal environment. In addition, they deprive their organizations of the benefits available under new federal guidelines for sentencing organizations convicted of wrongdoing. These sentencing guidelines recognize for the first time the organizational and managerial roots of unlawful conduct and base fines partly on the extent to which companies have taken steps to prevent that misconduct.

Prompted by the prospect of leniency, many companies are rushing to implement compliance-based ethics programs. Designed by corporate counsel, the goal of these programs is to prevent, detect, and punish legal violations. But organizational ethics means more than avoiding illegal practice; and providing employees with a rule book will do little to address the problems underlying unlawful conduct. To foster a climate that encourages exemplary behavior, corporations need a comprehensive approach that goes beyond the often punitive legal compliance stance.

An integrity-based approach to ethics management combines a concern for the law with an emphasis on managerial responsibility for ethical behavior. Though integrity strategies may vary in design and scope, all strive to define companies' guiding values, aspirations, and patterns of thought and conduct. When integrated into the day-to-day operations of an organization, such strategies can help prevent damaging ethical lapses while tapping into powerful human impulses for moral thought and action. Then an ethical framework becomes no longer a burdensome constraint within which companies must operate, but the governing ethos of an organization.

How Organizations Shape Individuals' Behavior

The once familiar picture of ethics as individualistic, unchanging, and impervious to organizational influences has not stood up to scrutiny in recent years. Sears Auto Centers' and Beech-Nut Nutrition Corporation's experiences illustrate the role organizations play in shaping individuals' behavior—and how even sound moral fiber can fray when stretched too thin.

At Sears Auto Centers, management's failure to clarify the line between unnecessary service and legitimate preventive maintenance cost the company an estimated $60 million.

In 1992, Sears, Roebuck & Company was inundated with complaints about its automotive service business. Consumers and attorneys general in more than 40 states had accused the company of misleading customers and selling them unnecessary parts and services, from brake jobs to front-end alignments. It would be a mistake, however, to see this situation exclusively in terms of any one individual's moral failings. Nor did management set out to defraud Sears customers. Instead, a number of organizational factors contributed to the problematic sales practices.

In the face of declining revenues, shrinking market share, and an increasingly competitive market for under-car services, Sears management attempted to spur the performance of its auto centers by introducing new goals and incentives for employees. The company increased minimum work quotas and introduced productivity incentives for mechanics. The automotive service advisers were given product-specific sales quotas—sell so many springs, shock absorbers, alignments, or brake jobs per shift—and paid a commission based on sales. According to advisers, failure to meet quotas could lead to a transfer or a reduction in work hours. Some employees spoke of the "pressure, pressure, pressure" to bring in sales.

Under this new set of organizational pressures and incentives, with few options for meeting their sales goals legitimately, some employees' judgment understandably suffered. Management's failure to clarify the line between unnecessary service and legitimate preventive maintenance, coupled with consumer ignorance, left employees to chart their own courses through a vast gray area, subject to a wide range of interpretations. Without active management support for ethical practice and mechanisms to detect and check questionable sales methods and poor work, it is not surprising that some employees may have reacted to contextual forces by resorting to exaggeration, carelessness, or even misrepresentation.

Shortly after the allegations against Sears became public, CEO Edward Brennan acknowledged management's responsibility for putting in place compensation and goal-setting systems that "created an environment in which mistakes did occur." Although the company denied any intent to deceive consumers, senior executives eliminated commissions for service advisers and discontinued sales quotas for specific parts. They also instituted a system of unannounced shopping audits and made plans to expand the internal monitoring of service. In settling the pending lawsuits, Sears offered coupons to customers who had bought certain auto services between 1990 and 1992. The total cost of the settlement, including potential customer refunds, was an estimated $60 million.

Contextual forces can also influence the behavior of top management, as a former CEO of Beech-Nut Nutrition Corporation discovered. In the early 1980s, only two years after joining the company, the CEO found evidence suggesting that the apple juice concentrate, supplied by the company's vendors for use in Beech-Nut's "100% pure" apple juice, contained nothing more than sugar water and chemicals. The CEO could have destroyed the bogus inventory and withdrawn the juice from grocers' shelves, but he was under extraordinary pressure to turn the ailing company around. Eliminating the inventory would have killed any hope of turning even the meager $700,000 profit promised to Beech-Nut's then parent, Nestlé.

A number of people in the corporation, it turned out, had doubted the purity of the juice for several years before the CEO arrived. But the 25% price advantage offered by the supplier of the bogus concentrate allowed the operations head to meet cost-control goals. Furthermore, the company lacked an effective quality control system, and a conclusive lab test for juice purity did not yet exist. When a member of the research department voiced concerns about the juice to operating management, he was accused of not being a team player and of acting like "Chicken Little." His judgment, his supervisor wrote in an annual performance review, was "colored by naïveté and impractical ideals." No one else seemed to have considered the company's obligations to its customers or to have thought about the potential harm of disclosure. No one considered the fact that the sale of adulterated or misbranded juice is a legal offense, putting the company and its top management at risk of criminal liability.

An FDA investigation taught Beech-Nut the hard way. In 1987, the company pleaded guilty to selling adulterated and misbranded juice. Two years and two criminal trials later, the CEO pleaded guilty to ten counts of mislabeling. The total cost to the company—including fines, legal expenses, and lost sales—was an estimated $25 million.

Such errors of judgment rarely reflect an organizational culture and management philosophy that sets out to harm or deceive. More often, they reveal a culture that is insensitive or indifferent to ethical considerations or one that lacks effective organizational systems. By the same token, exemplary conduct usually reflects an organizational culture and philosophy that is infused with a sense of responsibility. For example, Johnson & Johnson's handling of the Tylenol crisis is sometimes attributed to the singular personality of then-CEO James Burke. However, the decision to do a nationwide recall of Tylenol capsules in order to avoid further loss of life from product tampering was in reality not one decision but thousands of decisions made by individuals at all levels of the organization. The "Tylenol decision," then, is best understood not as an isolated incident, the achievement of a lone individual, but as the reflection of an organization's culture. Without a shared set of values and guiding principles deeply ingrained throughout the organization, it is doubtful that Johnson & Johnson's response would have been as rapid, cohesive, and ethically sound.

Many people resist acknowledging the influence of organizational factors on individual behavior—especially on misconduct—for fear of diluting people's sense of personal moral responsibility. But this fear is based on a false dichotomy between holding individual transgressors accountable and holding "the system" accountable. Acknowledging the importance of organizational

context need not imply exculpating individual wrongdoers. To understand all is not to forgive all.

The Limits of a Legal Compliance Program

The consequences of an ethical lapse can be serious and far-reaching. Organizations can quickly become entangled in an all-consuming web of legal proceedings. The risk of litigation and liability has increased in the past decade as lawmakers have legislated new civil and criminal offenses, stepped up penalties, and improved support for law enforcement. Equally—if not more—important is the damage an ethical lapse can do to an organization's reputation and relationships. Both Sears and Beech-Nut, for instance, struggled to regain consumer trust and market share long after legal proceedings has ended.

As more managers have become alerted to the importance of organizational ethics, many have asked their lawyers to develop corporate ethics programs to detect and prevent violations of the law. The 1991 Federal Sentencing Guidelines offer a compelling rationale. Sanctions such as fines and probation for organizations convicted of wrongdoing can vary dramatically depending both on the degree of management cooperation in reporting and investigating corporate misdeeds and on whether or not the company has implemented a legal compliance program.

Such programs tend to emphasize the prevention of unlawful conduct, primarily by increasing surveillance and control and by imposing penalties for wrongdoers. While plans vary, the basic framework is outlined in the sentencing guidelines. Managers must establish compliance standards and procedures; designate high-level personnel to oversee compliance; avoid delegating discretionary authority to those likely to act unlawfully; effectively communicate the company's standards and procedures through training or publications; take reasonable steps to achieve compliance through audits, monitoring processes, and a system for employees to report criminal misconduct without fear of retribution; consistently enforce standards through appropriate disciplinary measures; respond appropriately when offenses are detected; and, finally, take reasonable steps to prevent the occurrence of similar offenses in the future.

There is no question of the necessity of a sound, well-articulated strategy for legal compliance in an organization. After all, employees can be frustrated and frightened by the complexity of today's legal environment. And even managers who claim to use the law as a guide to ethical behavior often lack more than a rudimentary understanding of complex legal issues.

Managers would be mistaken, however, to regard legal compliance as an adequate means for addressing the full range of ethical issues that arise every day. "If it's legal, it's ethical," is a frequently heard slogan. But conduct that is lawful may be highly problematic from an ethical point of view. Consider the sale in some countries of hazardous products without appropriate warnings or the purchase of goods from suppliers who operate inhumane sweatshops in developing countries. Companies engaged in international business often discover that conduct that infringes on recognized standards of human rights and decency is legally permissible in some jurisdictions.

Legal clearance does not certify the absence of ethical problems in the united States either, as a 1991 case at Salomon Brothers illustrates. Four top-level executives failed to take appropriate action when learning of unlawful activities on the government trading desk. Company lawyers found no law obligating the executives to disclose the improprieties. Nevertheless, the executives' delay in disclosing and failure to reveal their prior knowledge prompted a serious crisis of confidence among employees, creditors, shareholders, and customers. The executives were forced to resign, having lost the moral authority to lead. Their ethical lapse compounded the trading desk's legal offenses, and the company ended up suffering losses—including legal costs, increased funding costs, and lost business—estimated at nearly $1 billion.

A compliance approach to ethics also overemphasizes the threat of detection and punishment in order to channel behavior in lawful directions. The underlying model for this approach is deterrence theory, which envisions people as rational maximizers of self-interest, responsive to the personal costs and benefits of their choices, yet indifferent to the moral legitimacy of those choices. But a recent study reported in *Why People Obey the Law* by Tom R. Tyler shows that obedience to the law is strongly influenced by a belief in its legitimacy and its moral correctness. People generally feel that they have a strong obligation to obey the law. Education about the legal standards and a supportive environment may be all that's required to insure compliance.

Discipline is, of course, a necessary part of any ethical system. Justified penalties for the infringement of legitimate norms are fair and appropriate. Some people do need the threat of sanctions. However, an overemphasis on potential sanctions can be superfluous and even counterproductive. Employees may rebel against programs that stress penalties, particularly if they are designed and imposed without employee involvement or if the standards are vague or unrealistic. Management may talk of mutual trust when unveiling a compliance plan, but employees often receive the message as a warning from on high. Indeed, the more skeptical among them may view compliance programs as nothing more than liability insurance for senior management. This is not an unreasonable conclusion, considering that compliance programs rarely address the root causes of misconduct.

Even in the best cases, legal compliance is unlikely to unleash much moral imagination or commitment. The law does not generally seek to inspire human excellence or distinction. It is no guide for exemplary behavior—or even good practice. Those managers who define ethics as legal compliance are implicitly endorsing a code of moral mediocrity for their organizations. As Richard Breeden, former chairman of the Securities and Exchange Commission, noted, "It is not an adequate ethical standard to aspire to get through the day without being indicted."

Integrity as a Governing Ethic

A strategy based on integrity holds organizations to a more robust standard. While compliance is rooted in avoiding legal sanctions, organizational integrity is based on the concept of self-governance in accordance with a set of guiding principles. From the perspective of integrity, the task of ethics management is to define and give life to an organization's guiding values, to create an environment that supports ethically sound behavior, and to instill a sense of shared accountability among employees. The need to obey the law is viewed as a positive aspect of organizational life, rather than an unwelcome constraint imposed by external authorities.

An integrity strategy is characterized by a conception of ethics as a driving force of an enterprise. Ethical values shape the search for opportunities, the design of organizational systems, and the decision-making process used by individuals and groups. They provide a common frame of reference and serve as a unifying force across different functions, lines of business, and employee groups. Organizational ethics helps define what a company is and what it stands for.

Many integrity initiatives have structural features common to compliance-based initiatives: a code of conduct, training in relevant areas of law, mechanisms for reporting and investigating potential misconduct, and audits and controls to insure that laws and company standards are being met. In addition, if suitably designed, an integrity-based initiative can establish a foundation for seeking the legal benefits that are available under the sentencing guidelines should criminal wrongdoing occur. . . .

But an integrity strategy is broader, deeper, and more demanding than a legal compliance initiative. Broader in that it seeks to enable responsible conduct. Deeper in that it cuts to the ethos and operating systems of the organization and its members, their guiding values and patterns of thought and action. And more demanding in that it requires an active effort to define the responsibilities and aspirations that constitute an organization's ethical compass. Above all, organizational ethics is seen as the work of management. Corporate counsel may play a role in the design and implementation of integrity strategies, but managers at all levels and across all functions are involved in the process. (See the chart, "Strategies for Ethics Management.")

During the past decade, a number of companies have undertaken integrity initiatives. They vary according to the ethical values focused on and the implementation approaches used. Some companies focus on the core values of integrity that reflect basic social obligations, such as respect for the rights of others, honesty, fair dealing, and obedience to the law. Other companies emphasize aspirations—values that are ethically desirable but not necessarily morally obligatory—such as good service to customers, a commitment to diversity, and involvement in the community.

When it comes to implementation, some companies begin with behavior. Following Aristotle's view that one becomes courageous by acting as a courageous person, such companies develop codes of conduct specifying appropriate behavior, along with a system of incentives, audits, and controls. Other companies focus less on specific actions and more on developing attitudes, decision-making processes, and ways of thinking that reflect their values. The assumption is that personal commitment and appropriate decision processes will lead to right action.

Martin Marietta, NovaCare, and Wetherill Associates have implemented and lived with quite different integrity strategies. In each case, management has found that the initiative has made important and often unexpected contributions to competitiveness, work environment, and key relationships on which the company depends.

Martin Marietta: Emphasizing Core Values

Martin Marietta Corporation, the U.S aerospace and defense contractor, opted for an integrity-based ethics program in 1985. At the time, the defense industry was under attack for fraud and mismanagement, and Martin Marietta was under investigation for improper travel billings. Managers knew they needed a better form of self-governance but were skeptical that an ethics program could influence behavior. "Back then people asked, 'Do you really need an ethics program to be ethical?'" recalls current President Thomas Young. "Ethics was something personal. Either you had it, or you didn't."

Strategies for Ethics Management

Characteristics of Compliance Strategy

Ethos	conformity with externally imposed standards
Objective	prevent criminal misconduct
Leadership	lawyer driven
Methods	education, reduced discretion, auditing and controls, penalties
Behavioral Assumptions	autonomous beings guided by material self-interest

Characteristics of Integrity Strategy

Ethos	self-governance according to chosen standards
Objective	enable responsible conduct
Leadership	management drive with aid of lawyers, HR, others
Methods	education, leadership, accountability, organizational systems and decision processes, auditing and controls, penalties
Behavioral Assumptions	social beings guided by material self-interest, values, ideals, peers

Implementation of Compliance Strategy

Standards	criminal and regulatory law
Staffing	lawyers
Activities	develop compliance standards train and communicate handle reports of misconduct conduct investigations oversee compliance audits enforce standards
Education	compliance standards and system

Implementation of Integrity Strategy

Standards	company values and aspirations social obligations, including law
Staffing	executives and managers with lawyers, others
Activities	lead development of company values and standards train and communicate integrate into company systems provide guidance and consultation assess values performance identify and resolve problemsoversee compliance activities
Education	decision making and values compliance standards and system

The corporate general counsel played a pivotal role in promoting the program, and legal compliance was a critical objective. But it was conceived of and implemented from the start as a companywide management initiative aimed at creating and maintaining a "do-it-right" climate. In its original conception, the program emphasized core values, such as honesty and fair play. Over time, it expanded to encompass quality and environmental responsibility as well.

Today the initiative consists of a code of conduct, an ethics training program, and procedures for reporting and investigating ethical concerns within the company. It also includes a system for disclosing violations of federal procurement law to the government. A corporate ethics office manages the program, and ethics representatives are stationed at major facilities. An ethics steering committee, made up of Martin Marietta's president, senior executives, and two rotating members selected from field operations, oversees the ethics office. The audit and ethics committee of the board of directors oversees the steering committee.

The ethics office is responsible for responding to questions and concerns from the company's employees. Its network of representatives serves as a sounding board, a source of guidance, and a channel for raising a range of issues from allegations of wrongdoing to complaints about poor management, unfair supervision, and company policies and practices. Martin Marietta's ethics network, which accepts anonymous complaints, logged over 9,000 calls in 1991, when the company had about 60,000 employees. In 1992, it investigated 684 cases. The ethics office also works closely with the human resources, legal, audit, communications, and security functions to respond to employee concerns.

Shortly after establishing the program, the company began its first round of ethics training for the entire workforce, starting with the CEO and senior executives. Now in its third round, training for senior executives focuses on decision making, the challenges of balancing multiple responsibilities, and compliance with laws and regulations critical to the company. The incentive compensation plan for executives makes responsibility for promoting ethical conduct an explicit requirement for reward eligibility and requires that business and personal goals be achieved in accordance with the company's policy on ethics. Ethical conduct and support for the ethics program are also criteria in regular performance reviews.

Today top-level managers say the ethics program has helped the company avoid serious problems and become more responsive to its more than 90,000 employees. The ethics network, which tracks the number and types of cases and complaints, has served as an early warning system for poor management, quality and safety defects, racial and gender discrimination, environmental concerns, inaccurate and false records, and personnel grievances regarding salaries, promotions, and layoffs. By providing an alternative channel for raising such concerns, Martin Marietta is able to take corrective action more quickly and with a lot less pain. In many cases, potentially embarrassing problems have been identified and dealt with before becoming a management crisis, a lawsuit, or a criminal investigation. Among employees who brought complaints in 1993, 75% were satisfied with the results.

Company executives are also convinced that the program has helped reduce the incidence of misconduct. When allegations of misconduct do surface, the company says it deals with them more openly. On several occasions, for instance, Martin Marietta has voluntarily disclosed and made restitution to the government for misconduct involving potential violations of federal procurement laws. In addition, when an employee alleged that the company had retaliated against him for voicing safety concerns about this plant on CBS news, top management commissioned an investigation by an outside law firm. Although failing to support the allegations, the investigation found that employees at the plant feared retaliation when raising health, safety, or environmental complaints. The company redoubled its efforts to identify and discipline those employees taking retaliatory action and stressed the desirability of an open work environment in its ethics training and company communications.

Although the ethics program helps Martin Marietta avoid certain types of litigation, it has occasionally led to other kinds of legal action. In a few cases, employees dismissed for violating the code of ethics sued Martin Marietta, arguing that the company had violated its own code by imposing unfair and excessive discipline.

Still, the company believes that its attention to ethics has been worth it. The ethics program has led to better relationships with the government, as well as to new business opportunities. Along with prices and technology, Martin Marietta's record of integrity, quality, and reliability of estimates plays a role in the awarding of defense contracts, which account for some 75% of the company's revenues. Executives believe that the reputation they've earned through their ethics program has helped them build trust with government auditors, as well. By opening up communications, the company has reduced the time spent on redundant audits.

The program has also helped change employees' perceptions and priorities. Some managers compare their new ways of thinking about ethics to the way they understand quality. They consider more carefully how situations will be perceived by others, the possible long-term consequences of short-term thinking, and the need for continuous improvement. CEO Norman Augustine notes, "Ten years ago, people would have said that there were no ethical issues in business. Today employees think their number-one objective is to be thought of as decent people doing quality work."

NovaCare: Building Shared Aspirations

NovaCare Inc., one of the largest providers of rehabilitation services to nursing homes and hospitals in the United States, has oriented its ethics effort toward building a common core of shared aspirations. But in 1988, when the company was called InSpeech, the only sentiment shared was mutual mistrust.

Senior executives built the company from a series of aggressive acquisitions over a brief period of time to take advantage of the expanding market for therapeutic services. However, in 1988, the viability of the company was in question. Turnover among its front-line employees—the clinicians and therapists who care for patients in nursing homes and hospitals—escalated to 57% per year. The company's inability to retain therapists caused customers to defect and the stock price to languish in an extended slump.

After months of soul-searching, InSpeech executives realized that the turnover rate was a symptom of a more basic problem: the lack of a common set of values and aspirations. There was, as one executive put it, a "huge disconnect" between the values of the therapists and clinicians and those of the managers who ran the company. The therapists and clinicians evaluated the company's success in terms of its delivery of high-quality health care. InSpeech management, led by executives with financial services and venture capital backgrounds, measured the company's worth exclusively in terms of financial success. Management's single-minded emphasis on increasing hours of reimbursable care turned clin-

icians off. They took management's performance orientation for indifference to patient care and left the company in droves.

CEO John Foster recognized the need for a common frame of reference and a common language to unify the diverse groups. So he brought in consultants to conduct interviews and focus groups with the company's health care professionals, managers, and customers. Based on the results, an employee task force drafted a proposed vision statement for the company, and another 250 employees suggested revisions. Then Foster and several senior managers developed a succinct statement of the company's guiding purpose and fundamental beliefs that could be used as a framework for making decisions and setting goals, policies, and practices.

Unlike a code of conduct, which articulates specific behavioral standards, the statement of vision, purposes, and beliefs lays out in very simple terms the company's central purpose and core values. The purpose—meeting the rehabilitation needs of patients through clinical leadership—is supported by four key beliefs: respect for the individual, service to the customer, pursuit of excellence, and commitment to personal integrity. Each value is discussed with examples of how it is manifested in the day-to-day activities and policies of the company, such as how to measure the quality of care.

To support the newly defined values, the company changed its name to NovaCare and introduced a number of structural and operational changes. Field managers and clinicians were given greater decision-making authority; clinicians were provided with additional resources to assist in the delivery of effective therapy; and a new management structure integrated the various therapies offered by the company. The hiring of new corporate personnel with health care backgrounds reinforced the company's new clinical focus.

The introduction of the vision, purpose, and beliefs met with varied reactions from employees, ranging from cool skepticism to open enthusiasm. One employee remembered thinking the talk about values "much ado about nothing." Another recalled, "It was really wonderful. It gave us a goal that everyone aspired to, no matter what their place in the company." At first, some were baffled about how the vision, purpose, and beliefs were to be used. But, over time, managers became more adept at explaining and using them as a guide. When a customer tried to hire away a valued employee, for example, managers considered raiding the customer's company for employees. After reviewing the beliefs, the managers abandoned the idea.

NovaCare managers acknowledge and company surveys indicate that there is plenty of room for improvement. While the values are used as a firm reference point for decision making and evaluation in some areas of the company, they are still viewed with reservation in others. Some managers do not "walk the talk," employees complain. And recently acquired companies have yet to be fully integrated into the program. Nevertheless, many NovaCare employees say the values initiative played a critical role in the company's 1990 turnaround.

The values reorientation also helped the company deal with its most serious problem: turnover among health care providers. In 1990, the turnover rate stood at 32%, still above target but a significant improvement over the 1988 rate of 57%. By 1993, turnover had dropped to 27%. Moreover, recruiting new clinicians became easier. Barely able to hire 25 new clinicians each month in 1988, the company added 776 in 1990 and 2,546 in 1993. Indeed, one employee who left during the 1988 turmoil said that her decision to return in 1990 hinged on the company's adoption of the vision, purpose, and beliefs.

Wetherill Associates: Defining Right Action

Wetherill Associates, Inc.—a small, privately held supplier of electrical parts to the automotive market—has neither a conventional code of conduct nor a statement of values. Instead, WAI has a *Quality Assurance Manual*—a combination of philosophy text, conduct guide, technical manual, and company profile—that describes the company's commitment to honesty and its guiding principle of right action.

WAI doesn't have a corporate ethics officer who reports to top management, because at WAI, the company's corporate ethics officer *is* top manage-

ment. Marie Bothe, WAI's chief executive officer, sees her main function as keeping the 350-employee company on the path of right action and looking for opportunities to help the community. She delegates the "technical" aspects of the business—marketing, finance, personnel, operations—to other members of the organization.

Right action, the basis for all of WAI's decisions, is a well-developed approach that challenges most conventional management thinking. The company explicitly rejects the usual conceptual boundaries that separate morality and self-interest. Instead, they define right behavior as logically, expediently, and morally right. Managers teach employees to look at the needs of the customers, suppliers, and the community—in addition to those of the company and its employees—when making decisions.

WAI also has a unique approach to competition. One employee explains, "We are not 'in competition' with anybody. We just do what we have to do to serve the customer." Indeed, when occasionally unable to fill orders, WAI salespeople refer customers to competitors. Artificial incentives, such as sales contests, are never used to spur individual performance. Nor are sales results used in determining compensation. Instead, the focus is on teamwork and customer service. Managers tell all new recruits that absolute honesty, mutual courtesy, and respect are standard operating procedure.

Newcomers generally react positively to company philosophy, but not all are prepared for such a radical departure from the practices they have known elsewhere. Recalling her initial interview, one recruit described her response to being told that lying was not allowed, "What do you mean? No lying? I'm a buyer. I lie for a living!" Today she is persuaded that the policy makes sound business sense. WAI is known for informing suppliers of overshipments as well as undershipments and for scrupulous honesty in the sale of parts, even when deception cannot be readily detected.

Since its entry into the distribution business 13 years ago, WAI has seen its revenues climb steadily from just under $1 million to nearly $98 million in 1993, and this in an industry with little growth. Once seen as an upstart beset by naysayers and industry skeptics, WAI is now credited with entering and professionalizing an industry in which kickbacks, bribes, and "gratuities" were commonplace. Employees—equal numbers of men and women ranging in age form 17 to 92—praise the work environment as both productive and supportive.

WAI's approach could be difficult to introduce in a larger, more traditional organization. WAI is a small company founded by 34 people who shared a belief in right action; its ethical values were naturally built into the organization from the start. Those values are so deeply ingrained in the company's culture and operating systems that they have been largely self-sustaining. Still, the company has developed its own training program and takes special care to hire people willing to support right action. Ethics and job skills are considered equally important in determining an individual's competence and suitability for employment. For WAI, the challenge will be to sustain its vision as the company grows and taps into markets overseas.

At WAI, as at Martin Marietta and NovaCare, a management-led commitment to ethical values has contributed to competitiveness, positive workforce morale, as well as solid sustainable relationships with the company's key constituencies. In the end, creating a climate that encourages exemplary conduct may be the best way to discourage damaging misconduct. Only in such an environment do rogues really act alone.

The Place of Character in Corporate Ethics

Virgil Smith

Introduction

Much has been written lately to provide various suggestions for assuring that decision making in organizations is done ethically.[1] These suggestions essentially revolve around the task of creating an ethical corporate culture through structural means (codes of ethics, corporate credos, ethics audits, ethics policies, etc.). While the structures in an organization are extremely important to assure ethical corporate behavior, there is a fundamental prerequisite that must take place in order for these structures to come into existence. The prerequisite is that those individuals who control the establishment or modification of the organization's structures (i.e., top management), must possess an overriding desire for an ethical organizational culture. The desire for ethics must have a very high priority because these top managers must establish the structures, and then act in consistently ethical ways themselves.

It takes effort, time, and money to establish and maintain organizational structures. Top management must believe that ethics is important enough to justify the considerable expenditure of resources necessary to achieve these structures. Yet, that is not the most difficult requirement. To establish structures which encourage ethical behavior will not, by itself, succeed in creating an ethical culture. The second requirement is that top managers must personally act ethically. Not only is this second requirement generally understood in the ethics literature (for instance, each of the other articles in this chapter mention it),[2] but it is also a scriptural principle.[3]

It is therefore impossible for an organization to develop an ethical culture without top managers who are individually ethical. It is reasonable to expect the organizational structures and corporate culture to affect the ethical behaviors of individuals lower down in the organization, as long as the top managers are ethical. However, it is not reasonable to expect the structures and culture to affect the ethical behaviors of unethical top managers, since the top managers are the very ones who instigate and create those structures and culture. That is, the top managers are the "guardians" of the social systems we call "organizational structures," so, the question becomes, "Who guards the guardians?" That is the question I wish to address in this paper.

When we are dealing with organizational ethics, the question boils down to this: "How can we be sure that top managers care enough about ethics to go to all the trouble of building ethics into the organization?" In order to explore this issue, we must first understand that the problem is not new, and it goes well beyond the boundaries of the organization. In fact, the problem is endemic to the people living in groups, but it drastically increased in scope with the beginnings of modern commerce. By the early 1500s commercial activity was expanding from a community affair, where individuals bought and sold from other individuals that they had known and lived with most of their lives (Tawney, 1926). The new world coming about consisted of the much more impersonal, increasingly complex, and radically enlarged scope of commerce that is normal today.

What is important in this for our discussion is what this new world was doing to business ethics. When you deal with your neighbor, the commercial transaction is normally governed by interpersonal trust based on individual ethical standards. However, in modern commercial systems, transactions tend to be between individuals who are strangers, between an individual and an organization, or between organizations. In each of these cases, it is difficult to rely on individual ethical standards to control the transaction (i.e., to keep one party from taking unfair advantage of the other). In each case we are likely to be dealing

with a relatively unknown individual whose personal ethical standard is also relatively unknown.

If we cannot rely on our intimate knowledge of the personal trustworthiness of the individual with whom we do business, how can we be assured that we are not taken advantage of? Essentially, we must seek some force outside the individual person that we can rely on to control the transaction. That force might be the structures and culture of the organization the individual acts for,[4] or in a more generic sense, it might be societal systems that are put in place in order to control commercial (and other) interactions. A number of societal systems have been put in place for this purpose. Examples would include the economic, monetary, and legal systems.

Can Private Sin Lead to Public Righteousness?

If the social system corrects for the individual behaviors of the participants in the system, then greed, envy, and avarice can be allowed to run free in commercial life, with no impairment of the economic system's ability to provide for the physical needs of the society. However, in a very practical sense, individual sin run amok would change the way commerce would have to be carried out. If, as a participant in the system, I know you are likely to be motivated solely by your own cravings, the last thing I will do is trust you in our commercial dealings. Yet I need to be able to trust you. As a simple example, many commercial transactions require an agreement today for actions that will not be carried out until later. For instance, shares of stock are normally traded on the stock exchanges on a hand signal, and the paperwork may not catch up for several days.

If we feel we cannot fully trust those we are dealing with, we can create systems to help out. In the case of the stock transaction, we can create stock exchanges with a limited and costly membership. The stock exchange can police its own members by denying membership to any who abuse the privilege. In other words we substitute trust in a system for trust in the individuals we face day to day in the marketplace. The question is whether systems can totally replace individual trust. This debate is alive and well in the scholarly business literature. today. Trust in a person has generally been termed "interpersonal trust" while trust in the system can perhaps be best described (following Luhmann, 1979 and Zucker, 1986), as "system trust."

System trust is not centered on an individual. Rather, it is centered on some aspect of a larger social system that people are willing to put confidence in. Thus we "trust in democracy," or "trust in the law," or, "trust in the market," or, trust in an organization's reputation, which is backed by its structures and culture. We trust these systems to assure proper outcomes that result from our interactions with other people and organizations. Interpersonal trust, on the other hand, is essentially a choice by one person to trust another person based on that person's perceived trustworthiness. Since interpersonal trust is placed in a person, it is necessary to discuss in more detail the necessary characteristics of the person we are choosing to put our trust in. There are two general aspects to a person's trustworthiness—ability and character.

The Role of Ability and Character in Interpersonal Trust

Ability is the technical competence or capacity to perform whatever task the person is being trusted for. Character, on the other hand, has been defined as fiduciary responsibility (Barber, 1983), ethical values (Morgan & Hunt, 1993), commitment and loyalty (Silver, 1985), and willingness of the one trusted to do the task he or she is being trusted for (Coleman, 1990). Of the two considerations of ability and character, character seems to generally demand more of our attention when deciding whether or not to trust another person. This is because there are, almost always, numerous physical manifestations of a person's ability available in the environment. These may include specific schooling for the task, certification, past success at similar tasks, etc.

Assessing a person's character is not so easy. Certification may occasionally be an aid if it includes a code of conduct that is policed by the certifying body, and if the code relates to the task at hand (Zucker, 1986). Likewise, organizational

structures and a culture that enforces trustworthy behavior may be seen in the organization's reputation in the marketplace. In both cases, however, we are substituting system trust for interpersonal trust. Therefore, if we are to rely only on interpersonal trust, we must rely on personal experience with, and reputation of, the person we are seeking to do business with (Alchian & Demsetz, 1772; Anderson & Weitz, 1989; Good, 1988; Tsui, 1984; Weigelt & Camerer, 1988). Personal experience is normally considered the most reliable of these options, but, at best, the potential truster can only infer sufficient character for the present situation from past situations. Thus character is more difficult to assess than ability, and this is where system trust, at least theoretically, has some advantages.

The Place and Value of System Trust

System trust is substantially different from interpersonal trust in that a personal relationship between parties is not needed in order for system trust to operate. Some authors argue that this "depersonalizing" of trust makes it superior to interpersonal trust because it is less individual and situation specific (e.g., Luhmann, 1979; Zucker, 1986). So the character issue assumes much less importance in everyday usage of system trust, and primary attention is focused on the abilities and capabilities of the system (Barber, 1983). Instead of trusting a person to control the uncertain future, we trust the system to control the uncertain future.

Thus, for instance, we find it easy to discriminate between the politician, whom we may not trust (an interpersonal trust issue), and the political system, which we do trust (a system trust issue). However, as Sitkin and Roth (1993) point out, the value issues do not go away, even though the ability issues are dealt with. They argue that systems use legalistic remedies, such as formalized rules and contracts, which are able to deal with ability issues but not the character issues, and thus cannot take the place of interpersonal trust.

Is Interpersonal Trust Needed?

Many scholars have argued that because the economic world has become increasingly complex with the advent of capitalism and the modern organization, it is too difficult to create the kind of relationships necessary to form, and to rely on, interpersonal forms of trust (see for instance, Eisenstadt & Roniger, 1984; Hawthorn, 1988; Luhmann, 1979; Silver, 1985; and Zucker, 1986). They conclude that this is the reason that there is a general decline in interpersonal trust in the modern world.[5]

Some writers essentially advocate abandoning interpersonal trust altogether, and increasing our reliance on forms of system trust (for example, Baumol, 1975; Luhmann, 1979; Meyer, 1983; and Zucker, 1986), because it is much easier to ascertain ability than character, and system trust reduces, or (they argue) eliminates the need for character (Dunn, 1988; Holzner, 1973). There is also the fact that a betrayal by a person tends to destroy interpersonal trust, but system trust is more resistant to betrayal. For instance, Luhmann says:

> The shift to system trust . . . makes trust diffuse and thereby resistant; it becomes almost immune to individual disappointments, which can always be explained away and passed off as a special case, while personal trust can be sabotaged by trivial treacheries. (1979: 56–57)

The question remains, however, whether system trust can totally, or even substantially, take the place of interpersonal forms of trust in the marketplace.

System Trust Used Alone Will Fail

The most perfect form of system trust, that all other systems attempt to emulate, is purported to be the neoclassical market system—the system that is argued to remove the necessity for personal morality in commercial situations. The market system, the argument goes, allows each person to pursue his or her own self-interest through "greed, envy, and avarice," as Adam Smith put it, with the paradoxical outcome being the betterment of all. As Robert Heilbroner, an economic historian says, "What [Adam Smith explained] was 'the invisible hand,' as he called it, whereby 'the private interests and passions of men' are led in the direction 'which is the most agreeable to the interest of the

whole society'" (Heilbroner, 1980:52, citing Smith, 1937[1776]:423).

Yet, as some social scientists have lately pointed out, the idea of the market working to control the outcomes emanating from greed, envy, and avarice has never truly been questioned and has no substantive empirical support (Barber, 1977; Mahoney, Huff & Huff, 1993). In actuality, the market system cannot do away with the necessity for personal morality for the simple reason that the market system (as described by Adam Smith) has never existed, and cannot exist in anything like its pure form. This is also why its outcomes have not been empirically verified.

Most introductory economics texts begin by mentioning, in a more or less complete form, the assumptions behind the theory of the market. Those assumptions are (1) that there exists an almost infinite number of buyers, (2) facing an equally large number of sellers, (3) all selling an identical product, and (4) that there is free and perfect information available to the buyers and sellers. These books do not usually mention the more modern-day requirement, that the buyers and sellers have the ability to process all of the information they freely and perfectly receive. It is fairly obvious to see that these conditions do not exist and never have existed in any actual economy.

By the previous discussion I am not attempting to argue that the market system is useless. It obviously does produce some pressures, and considerable pressures in some cases, in the directions indicated by Adam Smith. For this we should be thankful. It does not however, in and of itself, truly control commercial actions. It must rely on other forces of control—other systems, or interpersonal trust—to work.

Mahoney et al. argue that, in reality, Adam Smith's concept of the invisible hand depended in his day on "human virtue and a common social ethic" (1993:6). Barber (1977) agrees with this assessment and concludes that the market system works only because it is embedded within the social environment. It is to a large extent, then, the social environment, made up of all the individual human relationships that revolve around interpersonal trust, in some form, that allows the market to work in any meaningful way. Thus the market system can aid in the control of commerce, but it cannot force control by itself and, moreover, depends on the underlying social ethic for its effect.

A Matter of Basic Principles

A further proof of the inadequacies of the market system derives from the fact that, while interpersonal relationships based on trust may exist within a market system, and may do so quite happily, the market cannot, in itself, create trust or substitute for it. A well-known economist says in this regard:

> Now trust has a very important pragmatic value, if nothing else. Trust is an important lubricant of a social system. It is extremely efficient; it saves a lot of trouble to have a fair degree of reliance on other people's word. Unfortunately this is not a commodity which can be bought very easily. If you have to buy it, you already have some doubts about what you've bought. Trust and similar values, loyalty or truthtelling, are examples of what the economist would call "externalities." They are goods, they are commodities; they have real, practical, economic value; they increase the efficiency of the system, enable you to produce more goods or more of whatever values you hold in high esteem. But they are not commodities for which trade on the open market is technically possible or even meaningful. (Arrow, 1974:23)

Social Systems Cannot Replace Interpersonal Trust

A social system, such as the market, can therefore enhance and aid the underlying social ethic of individuals but cannot take its place. This is for two reasons: (1) both interpersonal and system trust depend on trustworthiness, and (2) system trust is inextricably intertwined with interpersonal trust. The first of these is fairly easily explained. The general level of interpersonal trust relies on the general level of interpersonal trustworthiness (Dasgupta, 1988). That is, if people don't find oth-

ers they deem trustworthy, they will be forced to trust less. Likewise, if the systems are not perceived to be trustworthy, people will not place their trust in them and system trust will decrease. While system trust is more resilient to betrayal than interpersonal trust, even system trust will fail in the face of consistent, repeated duplicity.

The second reason why system trust cannot stand on its own is built on the first. When system trust is low, interpersonal trust becomes riskier, so it becomes less used (Lewis & Weigert, 1985). This is because the risk inherent in an act of interpersonal trust is commonly mitigated through the use of system trust. For instance, contracts are utilized in most market transactions. Contracts act to reduce the risk of interpersonal trust by clarifying the agreement between the parties (a communications based, interpersonal trust issue) and providing an option should one party to the transaction prove untrustworthy (a system trust issue).

In order to take advantage of the option provided by the contract, one must put one's trust in the legal system, where the contract can be adjudicated for damages or specific performance can be ordered. Thus if the parties trust the legal system, the risk of betrayal is lessened. The point here is that if people question the trustworthiness of the judicial (or any other) system, it will not be perceived to mitigate the risk inherent in interpersonal trust and interpersonal trust will not occur as often.

Likewise, low interpersonal trust affects the workings of system trust (Fox, 1974). This is so because the mechanistic structures of systems can never, in and of themselves, take the place of character. As Silver puts it, "Conceptions of trust that turn on anonymity, interchangeability of persons, and standardization of performances are not concerned with moral qualities" (1985:64). Even secular scholars are forced to the conclusion that the character issues of trust are inherently moral issues (see, for example, Gabarro, 1978; Morgan & Hunt, 1993; or Ring & Van de Ven, 1992).

While it is true that system trust does not generally rely on character, the character of at least one person or group is central to its proper functioning. Someone has to control and safeguard the system from breakdown. These are the "guardians" of the system. For the legal system in the U.S. the primary safeguards are embodied in Congress and the Supreme Court. For our monetary system it is the Federal Reserve Board, and ultimately Congress. For ethical organizational structures and cultures it is the top managers of the organizations. The only system hypothesized not to have a guardian is the market system. That is why Adam Smith needed to create the concept of "an invisible hand" (Smith, 1937 [1776]:423).

In actual practice, one can easily question the sufficiency of the market to control its own outcomes. If it were sufficient, it would have been unnecessary for governments down through the centuries to regularly intervene in the market's workings. For instance, in the United States today, we have substituted the government for the market in many areas,[6] and by doing this, we have substituted a specific guardian system for one that neoclassical economics held needs no guardian. Therefore, if all systems in which we would trust, even the market system, need a human guardian, sooner or later, the question becomes, who guards the guardians?

A general lessening of interpersonal trustworthiness will eventually (or perhaps immediately) affect the guardians of the systems. If the guardians are not personally trustworthy, the system they guard is open to attack through the guardian. At that point the systems will become corrupt and cease to safeguard what they were created to protect. An illustration of this point comes from the Paine (1994) articles in which she says of one company studied, "While the [ethical] values are used as a firm reference point for decision making and evaluation in some areas of the company, they are still viewed with reservation in others. Some managers do not "walk the talk," employees complain" (1994:116).

Likewise, an increase in interpersonal trustworthiness will cause the guardians to be more trustworthy, and the systems they guard will become more trustworthy. Therefore, interpersonal trustworthiness has a high positive correlation with system trustworthiness, and it is not possible to rely solely on system trust to regulate the dealings of people.

A Win-Win Versus Win-Lose View of the Market

There is an additional factor that occurs when a society loses sight of the need for interpersonal trust, and it can be seen at work in how views of the market system have changed over time. Barber points out that the earliest proponents of the concept of the market saw it as a win-win proposition, where everyone could be better off. Before long, however, the concept of the market had been transformed into a zero-sum, win-lose proposition (Barber, 1977). The transformation works in this way. If we believe in the need for interpersonal trust in commercial dealing, we must, perforce, also see the market as a win-win situation. This is because trust is a reciprocal relationship which is destroyed by a betrayal of the trust (Akerstrom, 1991; Johnson-George & Swap, 1982). If one party is forced to lose while the other wins in a commercial transaction, any trust between them will be effectively betrayed and destroyed.

If our commercial relationship is based on trust, we are effectively barred from participating in zero-sum transactions. But, happily, win-win situations are by far the most plentiful in a commercial society.[7] Think of the last time you went out to dinner, or to buy yourself a new suit of clothes. Would you have completed the purchase if you had not believed you would benefit from the exchange? Likewise, do you think the seller would have offered the goods for sale if he had not believed the exchange was to his benefit?

On the other hand, look at the results if you rely on the impersonal force of, for instance, a contract to create a desirable result for yourself. You now do not care whether the other party to the transaction wins or loses. The controlling force that is applied should the contract need to be sued upon is the law of the land with all of its coercive methods.[8] In the case of a lawsuit, there is only one possibility available to the parties. One will win and the other will lose. If we take this attitude toward our commercial interactions, the other party inevitably becomes "the enemy." Our only ethic becomes survival of the fittest, and we will do anything necessary to make sure that we survive. We have only to look around us today, to see many people that display exactly this attitude toward the commercial world in which they engage. The one who seeks to act Christianly in business should stay far from this perception of the commercial world.

The Need for Personal Ethics in the Market

The conclusions reached here argue an overwhelming need for those in the commercial system who hold forth a godly virtue. Since effective ethical organizational systems of structure and culture are instigated and maintained only by top managers who have strong personal ethical standards, this is particularly important at the top levels of organizations. With no sustaining example of biblical ethics in business, interpersonal trust will inevitably decline, and declining trust in the balance of the society's systems will ensue, followed by the eventual breakup of the society itself. Therefore Christians should not forsake the world of commerce. Rather, they should follow the example provided by a group of Christians in the 1500s, who, seeing the modern forms of commerce emerging around them with all of the potential for ethical abuse, believed that it was the Christian's responsibility to, "show the world how to do it right" (Packer, 1995).

Conclusion

The argument pursued in this paper is that the notion of the market, or any social system for that matter, having to exercise control because of the sin of man, is flawed in several ways. While the market and other social systems have important roles to play in governing the behavior of people, all social systems become ineffectual if not upheld through the underlying ethic and trustworthiness of their participants. The sinfulness of man will never allow for a perfect human system.

From the perspective of the specific topic of this paper—business ethics—an individual organization, over the long run, will be only as ethical as its top manager.[9] Therefore, if we desire to have ethical organizations, we must have ethical people who have the ability and willingness to lead them. For this reason, Christians, who are seeking to live by a biblical ethic, should not shun the field of

business, and they should not shun positions of power within business organizations. Those business organizations that truly desire to have an ethical culture will be actively seeking such people,[10] and it is not unreasonable to expect that God may desire for some of them to eventually be "guardians" of the system.

References

Akerstrom, M. (1991). *Betrayal and Betrayers: The Sociology of Treachery*. New Brunswick, N.J.: Transaction Publishers.

Alchian, A. A., and H. Demsetz (1972). Production, information costs, and economic organization. *American Economic Review 62*(5), 777–95.

Anderson, E., and B. Weitz (1989). Determinants of continuity in conventional industrial channel dyads. *Marketing Science, 8*(4), 310–23.

Arrow, K. J. (1974). *The Limits of Organization*, New York, NY: W.W. Norton.

Barber, B. (1977). Absolutization of the market: Some notes on how we got from there to here. In G. Dworkin, G. Bermant and P.G. Brown, eds., *Markets and Morals* (15–31). Washington D.C.: Hemisphere Publishing Corp.

Barber, B. (1983). *The Logic and Limits of Trust*. New Brunswick, N.J.: Rutgers University Press.

Baumol, W. J. (1975). Business responsibility and economic behavior. In E. S. Phelps, ed., *Altruism, Morality, and Economic Theory* (45–56). New York: Russell Sage Foundation.

Coleman, J. S. (1990). *Foundations of Social Theory*. Cambridge, MA: The Belknap Press.

Dasgupta, P. (1988). Trust as a commodity. In D. Gambetta, ed., *Trust: Making and Breaking Cooperative Relations* (49–72). New York, NY: Blackwell.

Dunn, J. (1988). Trust and political agency. In D. Gambetta, ed., *Trust: Making and Breaking Cooperative Relations* (73–93). New York, NY: Blackwell.

Eisenstadt, S. N., and L. Roniger (1984). *Patrons, Clients and Friends: Interpersonal Relations and the Structure of Trust in Society*. Cambridge, UK: Cambridge University Press.

Ferrell, O. C., and J. Fraedrich (1990). Understanding pressures that cause unethical behavior in business. *Business Insights*, 1–4.

Fox, A. (1974). *Beyond Contract: Work, Power and Trust Relations*. London, UK: Faber and Faber Limited.

Gabarro, J. J. (1978). The development of trust, influence, and expectations. In A. G. Athos and J. J.

Gabarro, eds., *Interpersonal Behavior: Communication and Understanding in Relationships* (290–303). Englewood Cliffs, N.J.: Prentice-Hall, Inc.

Good, D. (1988). Individuals, interpersonal relations, and trust. In D. Gambetta, ed., *Trust: Making and Breaking Cooperative Relations* (pp. 111–26). New York, N.Y.: Blackwell.

Heilbroner, R. L. (1980). *The Worldly Philosophers* (5th ed.). New York, N.Y.: Simon and Schuster, Inc.

Hochreich, D. J., and J. B. Rotter (1970). Have college students become less trusting? *Journal of Personality and Social Psychology, 15* (211–14).

Holzner, B. (1973). Sociological reflections on trust. *Humanitas, 9*(3), 333–45.

Johnson-George, C., and W. C. Swap (1982). Measurement of specific interpersonal trust: Construction and validation of a scale to assess trust in a specific other. *Journal of Personality and Social Psychology, 43*(6), 1306–1317.

Lewis, J. D., and A. J. Weigert (1985). Social atomism, holism, and trust. *The Sociological Quarterly, 26*(4), 455–71.

Luhmann, N. (1979). *Trust and Power.* Chichester, UK: John Wiley and Sons, Inc.

Mahoney, J. T., A. S. Huff, and J. O. Huff (1994). Toward a new social contract theory in organization science. *Journal of Management Inquiry*, 1–35.

Meyer, J. W. (1983). Organizational factors affecting legalization in education. In J. W. Meyer and W. R. Scott, eds., *Organizational Environments: Ritual and Rationality* (217–32). Beverly Hills, Calif.: Sage.

Morgan, R. M., and S. D. Hunt (1993). Commitment and trust in relationship marketing [Working Paper] (1–45). Texas Tech University.

Murphey, P. E. (1989). Creating ethical corporate structures. *Sloan Management Review, 30*(2), 81–87.

Packer, J. I. (1995). [A Seminar on the Puritans, conducted from 1/3/95 to 1/13/95 by Dr. J. I. Packer, at Biola University]. La Mirada, California.

Paine, L. S. (1994). Managing for organizational integrity. *Harvard Business Review,* March-April, 106–117.

Ring, P. S., and A. H. Van de Ven (1992). Structuring cooperative relationships between organizations. *Strategic Management Journal, 13,* 483–98.

Silver, A. (1985). "Trust" in social and political theory. In G. Suttles and M. Zald, eds., *The Challenge of Social Control* (52–67). Norwood, N.J.: Ablex.

Sitkin, S. B., and N. L. Roth (1993). Explaining the limited effectiveness of legalistic "remedies" for trust/distrust. *Organization Science, 4*(3), 367–92.

Smith, A. (1937 [1776]). *An Inquiry into the Nature and Causes of the Wealth of Nations.* New York, N.Y.: Random House.

Tawney, R. H. (1926). *Religion and the Rise of Capitalism: A Historical Study.* London: John Murray.

Tsui, A. S. (1984). A role set analysis of managerial reputation. *Organizational Behavior and Human Performance, 34,* 64–96.

Weigelt, K., and C. Camerer (1988). Reputation and corporate strategy: A review of recent theory and applications. *Strategic Management Journal, 9,* 443–54.

Wrightsman, J. B., and N. J. Baker (1969). *Where have all the idealistic, imperturbable freshmen gone?* Proceedings of the 77th Annual Convention of the American Psychological Association (vol. 4, 299–300).

Zucker, L. G. (1986). Production of trust: Institutional sources of economic structure, 1840–1920. In B. Staw and L. L. Cummings, eds., *Research in Organizational Behavior* (vol. 8, 53–111). Greenwich, Conn: JAI Press.

Notes

[1]See Ferrell & Fraedrich, 1990; Murphy, 1989; and Paine, 1994.

[2]Ferrell and Fraedrich say, "Most experts agree that the chief executive officer and vice-president level executives set the ethical tone for the entire organization" (1990:27). Murphy says, "Senior managers must champion the highest ethical postures for their companies. . . . This commitment was evident in all the companies described here; it came through loud and clear in the CEOs' letters, reports, and public statements" (1989:217). Paine states, "Above all, organizational ethics is seen as the work of management" (1994:111), and further notes in one of the case studies, "While the [ethical] values are used as a firm reference point for decision making and evaluation in some areas of the company, they are still viewed with reservation in others. Some managers do not 'walk the talk,' employees complain" (1994:116).

[3]For instance, Proverbs 29:12 states, "If a ruler listens to lies, all his officials become wicked." (New International Version)

[4]If the organization has a reputation for ethical dealings and has established a culture that encourages ethical dealings, we can assume that this person, who acts on behalf of the organization, will act ethically because of the organizational constraints placed upon his or her individual behavior.

[5]There is empirical evidence to support the hypothesis that interpersonal trust has recently been on the decline, at least in the United States. See, for instance, Coleman (1990), Hochreich and Rotter (1970), and Wrightsman and Baker (1969).

[6]One needs only think of antitrust laws, regulated industries, or the last time the nation threatened an embargo over another nation's "dumping" their goods in our market to get the idea.

[7]We can of course turn any win-win situation into a win-lose situation if we insist on treating it that way, and some market participants seem to have a habit of doing this. Therefore, the business practitioner acting with a good ethic must watch out for this type of person or company.

[8]It is interesting to note in this regard, that the controlling force of a social system always is coercion or the threat of coercion.

[9]It is possible that an organization could have ethical individual members and unethical top managers, but it seems unrealistic for this circumstance to last long, as Proverbs 29:12 (cited in a previous note) indicates. Constant frustration of their ethical desires should cause the ethical members to leave the firm, to be replaced eventually by unethical members.

[10]As Paine mentions regarding Wetherill Associates' pursuit of an ethical culture, "the company . . . take special care to hire people willing to support right action" (1994:117).

CASES

Case 15.1: Sears' Blown Gasket

During the summer of 1992, the Consumer Affairs Department of the State of California charged that the seventy-two Sears Tire and Auto Centers that operated in the state had systematically oversold unnecessary auto parts to customers. The department then threatened to shut down all of the Sears Tire and Auto Centers in the state. In a yearlong undercover investigation that began in 1990, the department found that on thirty-four of thirty-eight undercover runs Sears had charged an average of $235 for unnecessary auto repairs.[1] Soon more than forty states made similar allegations.

Officials in the California Consumer Affairs Department alleged that in the midst of a companywide shake-up instituted by CEO Edward A. Brennan, all levels of employees came under increased pressure to focus on profit. This contributed to an organizational climate in which employees of its auto centers were pressured into increased sales using commissions, unrealistically high quotas, and the threat of dismissal if the quotas were not met. Unbeknownst to most consumers, at many shops—and not just the Sears-operated ones—"auto service advisers" who inspect cars and then suggest repairs often work under commission structures. However, under the unrealistic quotas set by Sears, some employees felt that, as they could not legitimately meet the goals, they had to cheat in order to retain their jobs. Government investigators and law enforcement officials contend that these policies amount to systematic fraud. One official remarked, "There was a deliberate decision by Sears management to set up a structure that made it totally inevitable that the consumer would be oversold."[2]

Sears officials first disputed these charges by stating that preventative maintenance recommendations were being confused with attempts to defraud unwitting consumers.[3] They also claimed that their incentive programs were in line with industry standards. After acknowledging that some of these incidents had occurred, Sears' top executives claimed that they never knew or approved of the practices and laid blame on a few disgruntled employees. One top official stated, "But it is not systematic. And when we find it, we react against the people that are managing that way."[4]

While the company denied any purposeful intent to deceive customers, they eventually changed many of the commission and quota

---

[1] Kevin Kelly and Eric Schine, "How Did Sears Blow This Gasket?" *Business Week* (29 June 1992): 38.

[2] Julia Flynn et al., "Did Sears Take Other Customers for a Ride?" *Business Week* (3 August 1992): 24.

[3] Kelly and Schine, "How Did Sears Blow This Gasket?" 38.

[4] Flynn et al., 24.

programs. The pending lawsuits were eventually settled at a total cost estimated at $60 million.[5]

[5]Lynn Sharp Paine, "Managing for Organizational Integrity," *Harvard Business Review* (March–April 1994): 108.

Questions for Discussion:

1. Can you see anything wrong with the management system, or can blame for the transgressions be placed on the actions of a few rogue individuals?
2. Is there anything wrong with commission systems in and of themselves? Can they be structured with ethics in mind? Use some of Paine's examples to offer some suggestions on how Sears can improve its organizational climate.

Case 15.2: Profit and Health—Conflicting Goals?

An increasing number of cases making current news headlines involve conflicts between money and medicine faced by doctors who are employed by or under contract to health maintenance organizations (HMOs). As health-care costs skyrocket, many employers turn to less expensive sources of health insurance for their workers. In the quest for more cost-effective medicine, a rapidly growing number of employers have signed on with "managed care" plans provided through HMOs.

Since many HMOs are chartered as for-profit organizations owned by shareholders, they are accountable for the bottom line just like any other business. Supporters of these organizations state that they are profiting through the efficient practice of medicine, which seeks to eliminate many costly procedures and prescriptions of questionable value.

However, critics charge that some of these organizations encourage doctors to withhold necessary treatments from patients in order to hold costs down and raise profits. While there are many types of HMOs, some contract with doctors who agree to receive a set monthly fee—known as a capitation payment—for every patient who designates them as their "primary provider." For example, a doctor may receive a capitation payment of $28 per month for every patient under contract with a particular HMO who makes that designation. The primary-care doctor then must cover all of that patient's health-care costs with that payment including, in some cases, referrals to see specialists. The primary-care doctor then acts as a "gatekeeper" to specialists and other procedures.

To give doctors incentives to control costs, most arrangements allow doctors to keep what is left of the capitation pool at the end of the year. Other HMOs pay bonuses for successfully meeting utilization goals, and some withhold a percentage of capitation payments until year's end to encourage holding down costs.

Critics allege that because one costly procedure or referral can eat up all the fees for that patient, these types of incentives make it in the doctor's best financial interest to withhold needed medical treatment. Of course, this could create a conflict of interest for doctors—and it goes against the long-held medical ethic of considering the patient's best interests first, prompting some to call HMOs "hold the money organizations." Furthermore, some doctors claim that in many cases, HMOs have become so dominant, many physicians cannot survive if they do not agree to accept these kinds of contracts.

Proponents of managed-care organizations respond that it is in their financial interests to look out for patient health, since sicker patients cost them more in the long run. Moreover, they argue that it is the absence of incentives to practice cost-efficient medicine that has led to the current health-care crisis with escalating costs and an unconscionable number of citizens who have no medical coverage at all. These people argue that managed care with the use of such incentives is the best solution to this crisis.[6]

[6]See Julie Kosterlitz, "Unmanaged Care?" *National Journal* (10 December 1994): 2903–7; David R. Olmos, "Cutting Health Costs—or Corners?" *Los Angeles Times,* 5 May 1995, A1+; Michael Quint, "Health Plans Are Forcing Change in the Method of Paying Doctors," *New York Times*, 9 February 1995, A1+; Arthur S. Relman, "What About Managed Care?" (editorial), *New England Journal of Medicine* 331, no. 7 (18 August 1994): 471–72.

Questions for Discussion:

1. Are the use of financial incentives to encourage cost-efficient medicine in and of themselves wrong? Do you see a potential conflict of interest here? In the absence of incentives, how can medical costs be kept under control?

2. Is the solution simply individual "virtuous gatekeepers" who should consider their patients' best interests first, or is it some combination of integrity on the part of physicians and ethical incentive systems that should be used? What would you recommend as a solution?

COMMENTARY

Organizations of all varieties have a greater stake than ever in developing and implementing policies that encourage ethical behavior within their ranks. A recent *Fortune* magazine article entitled "The New Crisis in Business Ethics" reports that in a climate of economic downturns, increased competition, and downsizing, temptations to cut ethical corners are greater than ever.[7] The resulting damage caused by revelations of immoral behavior on the part of executives and employees can have a lasting impact on public trust and internal morale. Moreover, in a significant development, the new federal sentencing guidelines factor contributions by management and the organization to an individual as transgressions of the law in the handing down of punishment. Companies can be punished or given leniency according to the steps they have taken either to encourage or to prevent misconduct by their employees. In response, there has been a flurry of recent activity by companies to implement policies that encourage ethical behavior in the workplace. Some firms have started ethics and compliance offices and have hired ethics executives to staff them. Many others pay consultants to provide ethics awareness and training sessions for their employees. At a minimum, most companies have at least written ethical concerns into their mission statements and have developed detailed corporate codes of conduct governing specific situations that employees may face in the course of their duties.

Despite the money being poured into these efforts, some critics wonder out loud whether or not ethics can truly be "taught" and fostered within the context of corporations. To these critics, ethics is something that is learned at our parents' knees. Consequently, it is reasoned that in the absence of values in one's upbringing, it is too late to try to teach ethics to employees during a day- or week-long training session. However, Aristotle reminds us that although ethics starts with a good upbringing, it develops during the course of life through practical experience and critical reflection. Thus, while perhaps more limited than Lynn Sharp Paine's assertion that "ethics has everything to do with management," corporations can and do have a very real impact on the beliefs and behaviors of their members through both formal and informal mechanisms.

Although it is a good start, fostering sound ethics is not simply a matter of hiring morally upright people in the hope that their values will guide the organization's decisions. As Ferrell and Fraedrich point out, personal values of the employees are "not the central component that guides the decisions, actions, and policies of the organization." In

[7]Kenneth Labich, "The New Crisis in Business Ethics," *Fortune* (20 April 1992): 167–76.

many scandals, it is not simply "bad apples" in the form of rogue individuals or executives who explicitly set out to defraud the public. Rather, it is usually a combination of organizational and environmental factors that plays the biggest role in creating the "bad barrel" that leads to unethical actions.

As we saw in the preceding chapter through the eyes of Kermit Vandivier's experiences at the Troy Goodrich plant, competition in conjunction with group-think and the demands of authority can create enormous pressures on a person to abandon conscience for the sake of the group's perceived well-being. Despite the best efforts of companies, however, there will always be maverick individuals, or "bad apples," who will inevitably choose the shortest path to quick gain. Yet, as the articles in this chapter make clear, corporations can do much to create a *climate* that supports ethical decisions. In remembering that peer pressure and socialization can indeed work both ways, we will now turn our attention to what companies can do to encourage the practice of sound ethics at work.

Formal Mechanisms for Encouraging Sound Ethics

First, let us examine some of the *formal* mechanisms, including reporting relationships and incentive systems. Although the tall command-and-control organizational structures of the rational bureaucratic model are a dying breed, all organizations still maintain some type of hierarchy in order to determine chain of command and reporting relationships. While it is true that flat structures that empower employees to make quick decisions are swiftly becoming the norm, there are still levels of authority and division according to specialization within every organization of size. Thus some employees are privy to larger and longer-term views than others. This can create a climate similar to the one described by Smith and Carroll in the preceding chapter in which some employees see only a small part of the total picture. Thus "buck-passing" of moral responsibility up and down the chain of command can easily become the norm.

The Sears auto-repair case is a recent example of this phenomenon. In this situation, employees were inadvertently encouraged to commit fraud because the only way for them to meet sales goals established by higher management was to replace car parts unnecessarily. It certainly appears that no one individual schemed to defraud the public. Rather, miscommunication and differing goals at the various levels of the organization directly contributed to a climate that was ripe for misconduct. Furthermore, although we cannot know for sure, employees who complained were probably told that they should simply follow the policy and "do their jobs" because they didn't have the big picture in their grasp.

To avoid these situations, corporations must open communication channels up, down, and across the corporate ladder so that the big picture is conveyed downward and upward and feedback is welcomed. Furthermore, individual actors must be rewarded and held responsible for group-based decisions. Moral responsibility should not be diluted to the point where it is the "system" and not individuals who are held accountable for specific actions.

In addition to hierarchy, incentive systems can also foster a climate in which customer interests are readily sacrificed for commissions and higher profits. Any beginning-level textbook on psychology or organizational behavior and management includes a chapter on how individuals "learn" at a basic level through rewards and punishment. Although not every person is a "rational actor" in a purely economic sense, many employees will act in a manner that is most rewarding in terms of finances and career advancement. Unethical behaviors will likely occur if they are rewarded, as in the Sears case and the "Profit and Health" case. Thus corporate policies must be critically examined to see if they make it in the financial interest of employees to behave unethically. As Paine illustrates in the Wetherill Associates example, honest sales practices that are truly in the best interest of consumers can just as easily be rewarded as those that are not.

Informal Mechanisms Affecting the Ethical Climate

Along with the formal mechanisms, informal ones such as corporate culture and the socialization process further serve to perpetuate behaviors. Financial incentives to cheat are even more likely to occur when compounded by peer pressure. While individuals ultimately have responsibility for their own choices and actions, employees are often socialized into the norms and culture of an organization. In so doing, they will often take cues from the surrounding environment to determine what is acceptable or even expected behavior. For example, if co-workers and executives regularly engage in practices that disregard the law, such as padding expense accounts or copying software illegally, the message that these are acceptable norms within the organization will be communicated loud and clear.

Every organization has a culture with its own stories, creeds, and norms of behavior that develops over a period of time. Narrative and stories can be powerful guides for action and socialization because they communicate much about an organization's values. For example, the pariah of a company tale may be one who possessed a moral voice and dared speak out against some unethical practices.

Usually, company management plays a significant role in developing the culture by telling these stories, developing creeds, and articulating and enforcing the company's values. If, however, company leadership does not articulate the values, a culture will evolve all on its own. Thus the critical question is whether or not that culture will be one that fosters or actively discourages ethical behavior on the part of employees. To have a better chance at the former, a company must have leadership that is proactive in helping to shape the moral values of the corporate culture that develops. Although the saying "it starts at the top" now sounds like a well-worn cliché, Virgil Smith insightfully reminds us that company leaders, especially the CEO, are the critical setters of values for the company. Their personal character, habits, and attitude toward ethics will often set the whole tone for the organization. Smith states that system trust will not work if the "guardians" are not themselves trustworthy.

As Patrick Murphy suggests, company executives can also play a role in the shaping of culture through the development of creedal statements, the implementation of training programs, and the articulation of specific guidelines for employees. Efforts in these areas will undeniably contribute to the infusing of ethics into the company climate. However, creeds and codes are insufficient if they are not enforced through formal mechanisms such as performance reviews and compensation- and promotion-related decisions. In fact, many critics have remarked that ethics codes and training programs are really no more than mere "window dressing" that serves as a useful public relations tool to ward off scrutiny and governmental interference. Indeed, many companies that are caught crossing ethical and legal lines have mission statements that claim ethics as a high priority. Thus the developed creeds and codes must be lived as well as preached. If the stated values have no teeth in them or if employees see executives betray them, some of them will swiftly catch on and likely revert to the behaviors that are "really" rewarded.

Moreover, as Paine reminds us, a legalistic devotion to a codified compliance program is insufficient. Ethics must become a key part of strategic planning and objectives through the cultivation of integrity as the governing ethic. An ethic of integrity and trust that goes beyond mere legalistic compliance is a much better way of encouraging moral corporate climates. Compliance programs usually generate a negative "police state" environment in which employees fear authority structures and ethics is perceived as a top-down product created by management to catch employees and serve as liability protection.

In contrast, an "integrity strategy" encourages all employees to take ownership of ethics as a total corporate objective. Paine suggests that

managers at all levels and across functions be involved for a successful implementation of an integrity ethic. Involving managers at all levels into the discussion indeed serves to raise awareness and foster a
sense of ownership of the objectives. We would add that even non-
managerial employees must be involved in the dialogue. To prevent
the "deck stacking" against ethics as found in organizations described
by Carroll and Smith in the preceding chapter, management must
carefully cultivate environments of truly open two-way communications if all employees are to be free to stand up to group and peer pressures. Phenomena such as "group think" and blind obedience to
authority can be minimized only by a climate that truly values a diversity of opinions. As Sears and other companies have found out, it is
often employees at the lowest level of the hierarchy for whom ethical
decisions are most salient, since they are the ones in the trenches. Furthermore, many organizations are successful for the very reason that
they value innovative and creative thinking that falls outside of the
"box" created by an overabundance of group cohesion and outdated
company norms and expectations. Thus a climate where communication channels are open and feedback is welcome will likely contribute
to both the financial and the ethical well-being of a company.

Conclusion

In summary, it is within the financial self-interest of companies to
create moral corporate climates. They can encourage these environments by the infusion of values through corporate culture and through
the modeling of integrity on the part of executives who set the tone
for the whole organization. However, talk of ethics in mission statements, creeds, and codes becomes empty if ethics is not seen as part
of the long-term objective. Ethics must be rewarded through formal
policies such as performance reviews and promotion decisions. Organizations must begin on the path to the creation of ethical climates
by taking a long-term view and making ethics a key component of
strategic planning. Only then will ethics filter downward and become
a matter of day-to-day operating policy. It takes something akin to
TQM in the form of a "Total Ethics Management" program to encourage employees to think of ethics the way they are now trained to consider quality in every decision and action. Ethical moral climates are
in the best interests of companies and their various constituent groups.

However, as Adam Smith emphatically reminds us, an ethical corporate climate begins with the moral character of the leaders of an organization. They are the "guardians" of the system. There are no shortcuts
to moral corporate cultures. Trustworthiness of character on the part of
the leaders is the center point from which organizational values flow.

SIXTEEN

A Model for Moral Decision Making

A CASE FOR DISCUSSION—"On Whistleblowing: Profit vs. the Common Good"[1]

[1]See Case 12.3: "Profit Versus Environmental Concern" (pp. 501–502).

You are the manager of a toxic waste dump that is located outside of Sacramento, California. The parent company is located in downtown Los Angeles. Some years ago, a cement "pond" was built in supposedly impermeable soil. It was built to house toxic waste from the firm's operations throughout northern California. When the toxic waste was combined with other chemicals, the waste was broken down, thereby rendering it considerably less toxic and therefore safe to be contained in the pond. This operation worked well for a number of years.

A few months ago, you noticed a change in the taste of the drinking water in your office and home. As a result, you ordered some tests to be run, and to your dismay the tests revealed some leakage that was moving toward the water table. The engineers who conducted the tests were not able to determine for sure if the waste was leaking into the water table, since the soil outside the pond acts as a partial filtering agent.

Being a responsible manager and concerned about the community, you report this to your boss in L.A. He consults with the top management of the company and their response is the same as his. Because the facility had passed the state inspection only a few months earlier, they chose to ignore the problem because of both the cost involved in cleanup and their continuing compliance with the standards of the state.

You maintain that the state's standards clearly are not adequate, but the company is adamant. They will do nothing about the problem unless they are found to be in violation of state standards. You protest that decision, and they warn you to keep to managing the facility and leave these other decisions to the appropriate people.

Your dilemma is compounded by the fact that whistle-blowers almost always lose their jobs (which you can ill afford to have happen, since you have a wife and three school-age children dependent on your income) and frequently are blackballed from the industry.

As the manager of the facility, what would you do in this situation? How would you justify your actions? What are the various options that you have as the manager?

Perhaps as good a question as *"What would you do?"* in this situation is the question *"How would you decide what to do?"* The process of making a moral decision can be as important as the decision itself, and many ethical decisions that people encounter are so complex that it is easy to exhaust oneself talking around the problem without actually making any progress toward resolving it. The response to many moral dilemmas is "Where do I start?" and the person who is faced with these decisions often needs direction that will enable him or her to move constructively toward resolution and see the forest as well as the trees.

In order to adequately address the ethical dilemmas that people encounter regularly, the following is a model that can be used to insure that all the necessary bases are covered. This is not a formula that will automatically generate the "right" answer to every ethical problem. Rather, it is a guideline that is designed to make sure that all the right questions are being asked in the process of ethical deliberation.

Given the ethnic and religious diversity of our society, it is important that the model used for making ethical decisions has "room" in it to accommodate a whole host of different moral and ethical perspectives. This model is not tied to any one particular perspective, but can be used comfortably with a variety of cultural, ethnic, and religious backgrounds. This is not a distinctively Judeo-Christian model, though it is consistent with the Scripture, and anyone can use biblical principles in utilizing this model. What makes many moral dilemmas so difficult is that the Scripture does not speak to the issue as clearly as one would wish, because Scripture has not directly addressed the issue. More general principles can be brought to bear on the issue at hand. However, in these instances, there is often disagreement about which biblical principles are applicable to the specific issue under discussion. For example, in the case used in this chapter, the manager can appeal to a number of different principles to justify a wide range of options. He can invoke the principle of loyalty to one's family, a strong biblical imperative to justify not saying anything that will jeopardize his job and his ongoing ability to support his family. He can also invoke the principle of "do no harm" to justify his responsibility to blow the whistle to keep the company from bringing harm to the community's water supply. It is not clear that appeal to principles alone will conclusively resolve this case. Thus to insist that all ethical dilemmas are resolved simply by appeal to biblical principles seems to oversimplify the matter. Certainly many moral questions are resolved conclusively by appeal to Scripture, but there are other cases in which that does not happen. That is not to say that Scripture is not sufficient for the believer's spiritual life but that the special revelation of Scripture is often supplemented by the general revelation of God outside of Scripture. This model makes room for both general and special revelation and gives each a place in helping to resolve the difficult moral dilemmas facing people today.

Here are the elements of a model for making moral decisions:[2]

1. Gather the Facts

Frequently ethical dilemmas can be resolved simply by clarifying the facts of the case in question. In those cases that prove to be more difficult, gathering the facts is the essential first step prior to any ethical analysis and reflection on the case. In analyzing a case, we want to know the available facts at hand as well as any facts currently not known but that need to be ascertained. Thus one is asking not only "What do we know?" but also "What do we need to know?" in order to make an intelligent ethical decision.

2. Determine the Ethical Issues

The ethical issues are stated in terms of competing interests or goods. It's these conflicting interests that actually make for an ethical dilemma. The issues should be presented in a _____ versus _____ format in order to reflect the interests that are colliding in a particular ethical dilemma. For example, in business ethics there is often a conflict between the right of a firm to make a fair profit and its obligation to the community. In this case, that obligation pertains to the environment.

3. What Principles Have a Bearing on the Case?

In any ethical dilemma, there are certain moral values or principles that are central to the conflicting positions being taken. It is critical to identify these principles, and in some cases, to determine whether some

[2]This model is adapted from the seven-step model of Dr. William W. May, School of Religion, University of Southern California; he used this model in his course "Normative Analysis of Issues."

principles are to be weighted more heavily than others. Clearly, biblical principles will be weighted the most heavily. There may be other principles that speak to the case that come from other sources. There may be constitutional principles or principles drawn from natural law that supplement the biblical principles that come into play here. The principles that come out of your sense of mission and calling are also important to consider.

4. List the Alternatives

Part of the creative thinking involved in resolving an ethical dilemma involves coming up with various alternative courses of action. Although there will be some alternatives that you will rule out without much thought, in general the more alternatives that are listed, the better the chance that your list will include some high-quality ones. In addition, you may come up with some very creative alternatives that you had not considered before.

5. Compare the Alternatives With the Principles

At this point, the task is one of eliminating alternatives according to the moral principles that have a bearing on the case. In many instances, the case will be resolved at this point, since the principles will eliminate all alternatives except one. In fact, the purpose of this comparison is to see if there is a clear decision that can be made without further deliberation. If a clear decision is not forthcoming, then the next part in the model must be considered. At the least, some of the alternatives may be eliminated by this step of comparison.

6. Weigh the Consequences

If the principles do not yield a clear decision, then a consideration of the consequences of the remaining available alternatives is in order. Both positive and negative consequences are to be considered. They should be informally weighed, since some positive consequences are more beneficial than others and some negative consequences are more detrimental than others.

7. Make a Decision

Deliberation cannot go on forever. At some point, a decision must be made. Realize that one common element in ethical dilemmas is that there are no easy and painless solutions to them. Frequently the decision that is made is one that involves the least number of problems or negative consequences, not one that is devoid of them.

CASE ANALYSIS—"On Whistleblowing: Profit vs. the Common Good"

1. Gather the Facts

Although you are in a management position at the facility, you do not have final authority over how the unit is run.

You believe that there is a leak of toxic materials into the ground water of your community, endangering the water supply. This belief comes from your experience as an engineer and a noticeable difference in the taste of the community's drinking water.

Tests to determine whether or not the waste has reached the water table are inconclusive so far.

The facility has met all tests and guidelines issued by the state. It is in compliance with state environmental regulations.

You have a secure job with the company, and it supports your wife and your three school-age children.

You are aware that people who blow the whistle on their employer are most often fired from their job and frequently are black-balled from the industry.

You have lodged complaints with upper management, and their response has been that they will not do anything about the site until the state orders them to do so.

Upper management still holds you in high regard but is getting tired of your raising the issue of this leak with them.

You have started buying bottled water for your family and are discreetly encouraging your friends to do likewise.

2. Determine the Ethical Issues

The ethical issues in this case revolve around the conflict between profit and the common good. Companies have a right to make a fair profit, and that profit provides jobs and a good living to those in the community. On the other hand, companies also have a responsibility to avoid endangering the community in which they operate. Thus one ethical issue in this case is the conflict between profit and the public good, namely, environmental protection.

A second ethical issue concerns the manager himself. He has a responsibility to his family—to support them and not to do anything that would endanger that support. Yet he has an obligation as manager of the facility to do what he can to insure that it is operated safely and does not harm the water supply of the community. This issue can be stated as responsibility to one's family vs. responsibility to the community. Another way to state it is as conflict between the manager's duty to tell the truth (and thus protect the community) and his duty to take care of his family (by not jeopardizing his job).

3. What Principles Have a Bearing on the Case?

As is often the case, here the ethical issues involve chiefly a conflict of principles. For the manager, there are the principles of taking care of one's family; the importance of truth-telling, especially in disclosing information that will prevent harm to the community; and the duty to prevent harm when one has the power to do so. For the company, there is the interest in maximizing profit and in not unnecessarily making expenditures that decrease the bottom line. This is balanced by its obligation to pursue profit in a morally responsible way. An additional principle that speaks to the case is that of employee loyalty to the company that supports him or her, thus not unnecessarily subjecting the company to risk and negative publicity.

Here the weighting of the principles depends on the degree of risk that is known at this time. Should the chances of the waste leaking into the water table be great, that would cast more weight on the principles of truth-telling and one's duty to prevent harm to the community. If the manager simply suspects that there is a leak and does not know how far it has proceeded, then the principles of loyalty to one's company and family carry more weight. At this point, the manager does not have clear data indicating that the waste is leaking into the water table of the community. But if he waits until the data are more conclusive, it may be too late to clean up the damage without major expenses being incurred. The fact that the facility has passed all state inspections to date is significant too, but frequently ethics involves responsibilities that go beyond mere compliance with the law.

4. List the Alternatives

The manager has a number of options at his disposal. They can be summarized by two main alternatives—make the information public, or keep quiet. First, he can somehow make public the information about the leak in the facility. In an effort to keep the discussion within the company, he can run his own tests, perhaps at his own expense or on his own time to determine further if any leakage into the community's water table has occurred. He can then take that hard data to upper management and request again, on the basis of new information, that they do something to fix the leak and clean up the damage. This is a prudent and moral first step that, should it prove effective, would satisfy all the principles that have a bearing on this case.

However, ethical dilemmas do not frequently resolve themselves quite so easily. Let's assume that the manager undertakes additional testing of the area and management still tells him to keep quiet until the state forces the company to take action. Then his options for disclosing the information about the leak involve "whistle-blowing," a term used in business ethics to describe the efforts of someone in a company to make public certain information about the company's moral or legal violations in order to attract attention to these violations in the hope that the company will be forced to comply either with the law or with what an employee thinks are applicable moral principles. The manager has various avenues open to him to blow the whistle, all of which involve a risk that he will lose his job.

The first of these is also the most direct. He can take his concerns directly to the state environmental regulators and request that they schedule an inspection of the facility immediately. He can do this anonymously, but it is unlikely that his involvement can remain a secret for long, given his past record of complaints to upper management about this matter. Thus whether it is done anonymously or directly, the result will likely be the same. Another avenue available to him is to take his concerns to the press. There he is assured of wide coverage, and perhaps a public outcry will be sufficient to persuade the company to remedy the problem. However, the risk of losing his job and being blackballed from the industry are even greater if he uses this option.

The second alternative is to keep the information to himself. He can continue to discreetly encourage his friends and others in the community to avoid the community's drinking water, but even this suggestion to anyone beyond his close friends carries a risk that the information will get out of his control. Perhaps this is what he wants to accomplish, so that the burden of disclosing the information is on someone else and cannot be traced back to him, thus keeping his job safe.

Another approach under the second option is to clean up the waste and fix the leak himself, using his budget for the facility to fund the cleanup and repair. This way he can safeguard his job as well as insure that the community's water supply is safe. If this does not involve a substantial amount of money, it is a feasible alternative, clearly the best one. But for a problem of this magnitude, it is unlikely that it can be resolved without making a significant dent in his budget, if it can be afforded at all. A substantial amount of money, even if it is within his budget, will likely be noticed by upper management, and he will risk their censure. But that is less of a risk than blowing the whistle on the company. For the sake of this discussion, let's assume that the amount of money needed to fix the problem is more than the manager can obtain.

5. Compare the Alternatives With the Principles

The only way to get a clear decision at this point is to decisively weight one of the principles more heavily than the others. The principles of truth-telling and the duty to prevent harm suggest that the manager should make the information about the leak public. His obligation to the company and to his family suggest that he ought to keep the information to himself, at least until he can be sure whether the material has leaked into the water table. Knowing how far if at all the leak has progressed into the water table would help, but given the uncertainty of that important fact, let's assume that no clear decision is reached at this point.

6. Weigh the Consequences

The remaining alternatives are for the manager to somehow disclose the information or keep it to himself until the state comes to test the facility again. The consequences of the two alternatives form mirror images of each other. That is, for the most part positive consequences of one option are the reverse of the negative consequences of the other. Thus the weight that the decision makers give to the various consequences is important for determining which set of consequences is the most beneficial or least harmful.

The likely consequences of *disclosing the information* include the following:

The company will either be tested immediately by the state or it will be the object of much negative publicity. But remember, the facility is in Sacramento and the company's headquarters are in Los Angeles, more than four hundred miles away. But if the water is tested and found to be substandard, the burden will be on the company to fix the problem. However, the facility may still pass the state tests.

The manager will likely lose his job for defying direct orders from upper management. He may be blacklisted from the industry and have to seek employment in another field. His family may have to move. He may suffer significant financial distress. But remember, if one is a religious person, he can depend on God's sovereignty in situations like these and trust God to provide for the family when one stands up for principles like the good of the community.

If the manager *does not disclose* the information, the likely consequences will be the following:

The leak will continue unabated, perhaps heading toward the community's water table.

The manager will have to live with the knowledge that he had the opportunity to save the community from harm and did not.

His job will remain secure, as will his income and family stability.

Should the facility be investigated at a later point, he may be blamed for harm to the community and may be held liable. However, in his defense, he could refer to the correspondence that he initiated with the head office to alert them to this problem, thereby possibly taking himself off the hook. If the problem gets worse, at the least he will be held responsible by his friends and peers in the community.

7. Make a Decision

The decision in this case is difficult. What would you do in the manager's place? Is there sufficient evidence to justify going "out on a limb" and making the information public, either to the press or to the state? Does the biblical principle of self-sacrifice for the good of the community tilt the decision toward disclosing the information? Or does the community also include one's family, giving the manager a responsibility to them too? Where does the sovereignty of God enter into the decision? If the manager does not have religious faith, will his decision likely be different than if he does?

Given the uncertainty about the extent of the leak, one could argue that it is best not to disclose the information at present. However, by disclosing it, the manager has the chance to prevent what could be substantial harm. Given that God will care for his family, that tilts the decision in favor of going public.

CONCLUSION:

Business, Virtue, and the Good Life

Much of this book has addressed, from a variety of perspectives, the conflicts that arise when a company's pursuit of profit collides with its obligation to its community. That community may include the company's employees, the environment, the consumers of its products and services, or the general public. Many texts in business ethics would leave you with the impression that resolving these conflicts is all there is to the matter. Yet we have tried to show that there are other issues about personal moral development, responsibility, and decision making that are crucial for a full-orbed discussion of business ethics. To put it in terms of moral theory, action-oriented theories of morality are helpful but not sufficient to address the critical component of business ethics and the person. It takes the additional influence of more virtue-oriented emphases in ethics to round out our discussion.

Many approaches to virtue are connected with conceptions of the "good life" and the good society. What constitutes a good life is a critical question that anyone who spends forty to fifty hours a week working in business should consider. More specifically, what place do business and the pursuit of profit have in a person's conception of the good life? What place *should* they have? How should a person's religious faith help form that conception? These are important questions that merit serious personal reflection, not only for a well-rounded discussion of business ethics, but for a well-rounded personal life.

In his book *God and Mammon in America*, sociologist Robert Wuthnow discloses that religious faith, though still important in questions of economic life, exercises an ambivalent and therapeutic influence.[1] He suggests that the impact of religious views has been weakened by cultural trends toward greater secularization and that, as a result, they no longer shape our views on economic life as much as they reinforce choices made on the basis of prevailing market orientation. He suggests

[1] Robert Wuthnow, *God and Mammon in America* (New York: Free Press, 1994), 5.

that "we look to religion, therefore, to make us happy about our preferences, not to channel them in specific directions."[2]

We suggest that if the biblical record is any guide, its strong emphasis on faith as influencing one's economic life compels religious believers to think through more carefully how their faith impacts life in the workplace, and summons their places of worship to be better equipped to provide such guidance. Readers of this book who are heading for vocational ministry can do their congregations a significant service by being able to address coherently the issues that most businesspeople will face regularly in their places of work. We have tried here to provide such guidance for those making this pilgrimage and for those who assist them.

We challenge you to think more carefully about how you view your workplace experience, whether as a calling or as a career. Earlier in this book we distinguished between these two and encouraged you to consider what is your calling and to pursue that, in contrast to pursuing only a career. You may encounter some tensions between fulfilling your calling and making the kind of living you feel you need in order to provide for a family. We are not suggesting a simplistic injunction such as "do what you love and the money will follow." But we are urging you not to blindly follow the career orientation that is prevalent in the marketplace today. There is more to your calling than your position in the organization, your prospects for advancement, and your earning potential. Your attitudes and values in your working years are just as important—if not more so—than how you advance your career by moving up a corporate ladder.

We also challenge you to think more carefully about how business fits into your conception of the good life. What constitutes a good life for you? What do your religious beliefs suggest constitutes a good life? How does your definition of success fit with your conception of the good life? The way many people would regard success has more to do with your position and income than with the contribution you have made to your community and the kind of person you have become. That is the orientation of the career, not the calling. To be sure, being recognized and appropriately rewarded for quality work is a reasonable expectation, but if that does not occur—or if it does not occur according to your timetable—it is not uncommon, then, to become disillusioned with your work. By contrast, for someone who adopts a calling orientation toward work, the job is considered inherently valuable and motivating, and advancement—though important—is not the all-consuming passion of one's professional life. We find it difficult to consider people a success, irrespective of their position and net worth, if they have compromised important personal beliefs and virtues and have been less, rather than more, of the person God would have them to become.

From the perspective of Judeo-Christian ethics, the good life involves living out our calling with excellence, becoming more godly in personal character, being committed to our family and community, and living out goals that are consistent with our calling. This is a very different conception from that which dominates the marketplace today—placing value on a person and one's life based on position, prestige, and net worth. A person may well achieve those marks while at the same time pursuing the good life, as defined by Judeo-Christian ethics. But position, prestige, and net worth are not the constituent elements of the good life. The writer of the book of Ecclesiastes put it this way: "A man can do nothing better than to eat and drink and find satisfaction in his work. This too, I see, is from the hand of God" (Eccl. 2:24).

CREDITS

The authors are grateful to the publishers and copyright owners for permission to reprint the articles that appear in the Readings of this book.

Chapter 1

"Christ and Business," by Louke van Wensveen Siker, *Journal of Business Ethics* 8 (1989): 883–88. Copyright © 1989 Kluwer Academic Publishers. Reprinted by permission of Kluwer Academic Publishers.

"The Ethics of Bluffing in Business" by Albert Z. Carr. Reprinted by permission of *Harvard Business Review*, January/February, 1968. Copyright © 1967 by the President and Fellows of Harvard College; all rights reserved.

"Does It Pay to Bluff in Business?" by Norman E. Bowie, *Business Ethics*, 2d ed. (Englewood Cliffs, N.J.: Prentice-Hall, 1982), 338–47. Copyright © 1982 Prentice-Hall. Used by permission.

"Why Be Honest If Honesty Doesn't Pay?" by Amar Bhide and Howard H. Stevenson. Reprinted by permission of *Harvard Business Review*, September/October, 1990. Copyright © 1990 by the President and Fellows of Harvard College; all rights reserved.

Chapter 2

"Business Ethics and Cultural Relativism," by Norman E. Bowie, *Multinational Ethics* (Englewood Cliffs, N.J.: Prentice-Hall, 1989), 366–82. Copyright © 1989 by Norman E. Bowie. Used by permission.

"Multinational Decision-Making: Reconciling International Norms," by Thomas Donaldson, *Journal of Business Ethics* 4 (1985): 357–66. Copyright © 1985 by Thomas Donaldson. Reprinted by permission of Kluwer Academic Publishers.

Chapter 3

"Moral Relativism? 'You Don't Get It,'" by Neal Gabler, *Los Angeles Times*, 14 June 1992, M1. Copyright © 1992, Neal Gabler. Reprinted by permission.

"998 Points of Light," *Wall Street Journal*, 19 September 1990. Reprinted with permission of *The Wall Street Journal*, copyright © 1994, Dow Jones & Company, Inc. All rights reserved.

"Unnatural Brawl Over Natural Law," by Michael Moore, *Los Angeles Times*, 3 September 1991, B5. Reprinted by permission of Michael S. Moore.

"Natural Law and Business Ethics," copyright © Norman L. Geisler, 1995. Dean of Southern Evangelical Seminary, Charlotte, NC (704/543-9475).

Chapter 4

Chapter 5

Chapter 6

Chapter 7

Chapter 8

Chapter 9

Chapter 10

Chapter 11

Chapter 12

Chapter 13

Chapter 14

Chapter 15